Guide to Reference Materials for Canadian Libraries

EIGHTH EDITION

Editor
Kirsti Nilsen
with the assistance of Alanna Kalnay

Consulting Editor
Claire England

Published for the Faculty of Library and Information Science
by University of Toronto Press
1992

© Faculty of Library and Information Science
University of Toronto
1992
Printed in Canada
ISBN 0-8020-6004-8

No part of this book may be reproduced
without written permission of the
Faculty of Library and Information Science
University of Toronto

Canadian Cataloguing in Publication Data
Main entry under title:

Guide to reference materials for Canadian libraries. — Toronto : University of Toronto Press, 1991.

    Title of editions 1-7: *Guide to basic reference materials for Canadian libraries*.
    First 4 eds. edited by: Edith T. Jarvi; 5th and 6th eds. edited by: Diane Henderson. 7th ed. edited by: Claire England. 8th ed. edited by: Kirsti Nilsen, with the assistance of Alanna Kalnay, consulting editor: Claire England.
    Includes indexes.
    ISBN 0-8020-6004-8.

1. Reference books - Bibliography. 2. Bibliography - Bibliography. I. Nilsen, Kirsti. II. England, Claire. III. Kalnay, Alanna. IV. University of Toronto. Faculty of Library and Information Science.

Z1035.1.G91 1991   011'.02

INTRODUCTION

With this eighth edition, the title has been changed from *Guide to Basic Reference Materials for Canadian Libraries* to *Guide to Reference Materials for Canadian Libraries* to reflect the increased coverage of this major revision and expansion. As with previous editions, this selection of reference works is designed primarily as a guide for students in the Faculty of Library and Information Science. Intended for use with courses in the reference, collections, and literature streams at the Faculty, the *Guide* is an introduction to basic and representative reference works in all major fields. General reference materials are studied more intensively than works in the subject fields, and Part (A) *General Reference Materials* is more extensive than Parts (B) *Humanities*, (C) *Social Sciences* and (D) *Science and Technology*. Part A continues to cover library and information science, the book trade and information industries, and national bibliography more widely than would be representative of most libraries, but not beyond the needs of students and many practitioners. All other sections have been expanded, in particular, the *History* section, which now includes subsections for General World History and Area Studies; the *Environment and Energy* section, which has greater coverage of environmental topics; and the *Biology* section, which is now subdivided into botany and zoology. Sections for *Geography* and *Sports and Games* have also been added to this edition.

Since the *Guide* has been widely used by other educational programs, and by librarians in many libraries, we have attempted to provide important historical and current materials in all areas. The *Guide* is not intended as a buying guide for any library, and items included are not necessarily in print. It is not intended to be comprehensive, but is a representative selection from the vast amount of reference material available. Each successive edition of the *Guide* has increased in size, and this is immediately apparent with this completely redesigned eighth edition, which cites almost 4,000 reference titles within 3,000 annotated entries.

This edition, as with earlier editions, reflects the advice and help of librarians and students who suggested and verified entries and who contributed to the content. The advice of previous editors, Claire England and Diane Henderson, was most welcome. Without the unflagging and inspired assistance of Alanna Kalnay, the project could not have been finished as quickly as it was.

Special thanks are extended to the following contributors, whose input into the sections noted is gratefully acknowledged:

Ray Banks (Librarian, Michener Institute of Applied Health Sciences) - *Health Sciences*, (DI);

Claire England (Associate Professor, FLIS) - *Biography* (AL), *Language Dictionaries* (AJ), *General Reference in Science and Technology* (DA), and *Selection Aids* (AC) (with suggestions for children's materials from **Eva Martin**, Librarian, Anglican Book Centre);

Karen Evans (Librarian, Anglican Church of Canada, National Office) - *Religion* (BC);

Patricia Fleming (Professor, FLIS) - *Directories to Periodicals and Newspapers* (AE), and *Indexes to Periodicals and Other Materials* (AF);

Elaine Granatstein (Head, Engineering Library, University of Toronto) - *Engineering and Technology*)DL) and *Environmental Sciences and Energy Resources (DK)*, with contributions on environment from **Cathy Lindsey-King** (Librarian and Information Officer, Concord Environmental Corp.);

Peter Hajnal (Government Publications Specialist, University of Toronto Library) - *Intergovernmental Information* (AN);

Helen Katz (Coordinator, Library Services, Ontario Ministry of Treasury and Economics) - *Economics* (CB), and *Business (CC)*;

Margaret A. Keefe (Coordinator of Government Documents Collection, Business and Social Sciences Collection, Metropolitan Toronto Reference Library) - the Canadian and United States sections of *Government Information* (AM), with thanks to Karen Wierucki (Assistant Director of Information and References Services, Ontario Legislative Library) for access to the collection;

Andrew Lofft (Librarian Supervisor, Science and Technology Department, North York Public Library) -*Mathematics* (DB) and *Computer Science* (DC);

Joanne Marshall (Assistant Professor, FLIS) - *Health Sciences* (DI), with suggestions from her students;

Kathleen McMorrow (Librarian of Faculty of Music, University of Toronto) - *Music* (BF);

Ann Morrison (Head, Information Services, Bora Laskin Law Library, University of Toronto) - *Law and Legal Materials* (CE);

Susan Murray (Director, Cinemateque Ontario Film Reference Library) - *Audiovisual Materials* (AG) and the Cinema and Film sections of *Performing Arts* (BG);

Marian Press and **Carolyn Bosley** (Reference Librarians and Reference Library Associate respectively, R.W.B. Jackson Library, Ontario Institute for Studies in Education) - *Education* (CI);

Rhonda Roth (Head, Public Services, Newnham Campus Library, Seneca College) - *Sociology* (CG);

Sherry Smugler (Reference Librarian, Robarts Library) - *Maps and Atlases* (AK), and atlas contributions to other sections;

Carl Spadoni (Research Collection Librarian, Mills Memorial Library, McMaster University) - *Philosophy* (BB);

Sharon Virtue (Manager, Health Sciences Library, The Doctors Hospital) - *Health Sciences* (DI);

Jiabin Wang (Doctoral Candidate, FLIS) - *Astronomy* (DD), *Physics* (DE), *Chemistry* (DF), *Earth Sciences* (DG), and *Agricultural Sciences* (DJ);

Mary F. Williamson (Fine Arts Bibliographer, York University Library) - *Fine and Applied Arts* (BF).

Special thanks are also due to recent graduates Linda Anne Sturgeon, Dierdre Chrichton, and doctoral candidate Mary Bissell, who verified many entries, and to Marcia Chen and Julie Tong of the FLIS office staff.

Those sections not mentioned above were prepared in full by the editor and the editorial assistant. The resources of Toronto area libraries and published reviews were used to verify entries. While every attempt was made to examine each item, this was not always possible.

The editor assumes final responsibility for the overall work, continuing the principles of utility for students in library and information sciences, and value to practising librarians and researchers. Suggestions that would improve future editions are welcome.

ORGANIZATION

The *Guide* is organized in a way that the compilers hope is useful to students in understanding the organization of a literature. Entries are usually arranged alphabetically within subsections by type of reference tool. However, some sections are first arranged geographically, and others, chronologically.

Items are arranged by author or by title if there is no author given. *The Chicago Manual of Style* (13th ed., University of Chicago Press, 1982), with some variation, is the basis for bibliographical style. Style follows the humanities for Parts A, B and C; style follows the sciences for Part D. Titles appear in bold, titles within notes are in italics. Subtitles are included; series titles are not normally provided.

Annotations accompany most entries, and describe the scope, arrangement, and other features of a title. The length of an annotation does not necessarily reflect the importance of the work. In many cases, annotations also refer users to other similar works.

Call numbers follow the notes. FLIS numbers, if available, are provided for part A, if the FLIS holding is not the most recent edition, the date is included. Guides to the literature and bibliographies in all disciplines show FLIS numbers if available. Call numbers for University of Toronto Libraries are provided if there is no FLIS holding; in many cases both numbers are provided. Unless otherwise indicated, the University of Toronto number is that for John P. Robarts Research Library reference collection (GENR). If the item is not held by Robarts reference collection, a location code for other University of Toronto Libraries is included. (See Table of Abbreviations). In those cases where an item is not held by University of Toronto libraries, Metropolitan Toronto Reference Library locations are provided, if available.

Authors and titles are indexed. Only editors of Canadian works are indexed, although some exceptions have been made.

Each entry has a unique number; indexes and cross references refer to these numbers. Titles in the annotations are indexed to the unique number of the entry in which they appear. Cross references in annotations which refer to titles in other annotations are so noted, (e.g. BD7n).

SAMPLE ENTRIES

This entry is an example of a monograph entry:

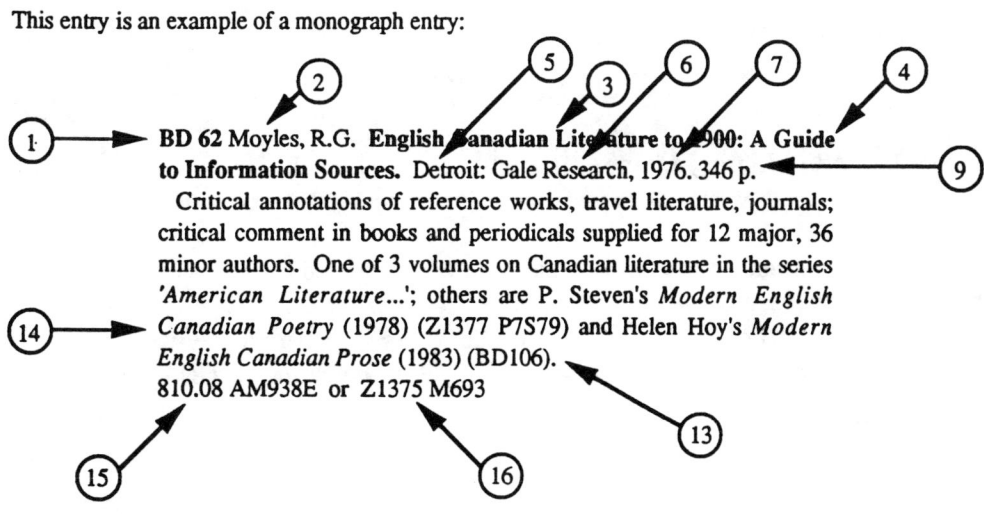

This entry is an example of an entry in Part A: *Sciences:*

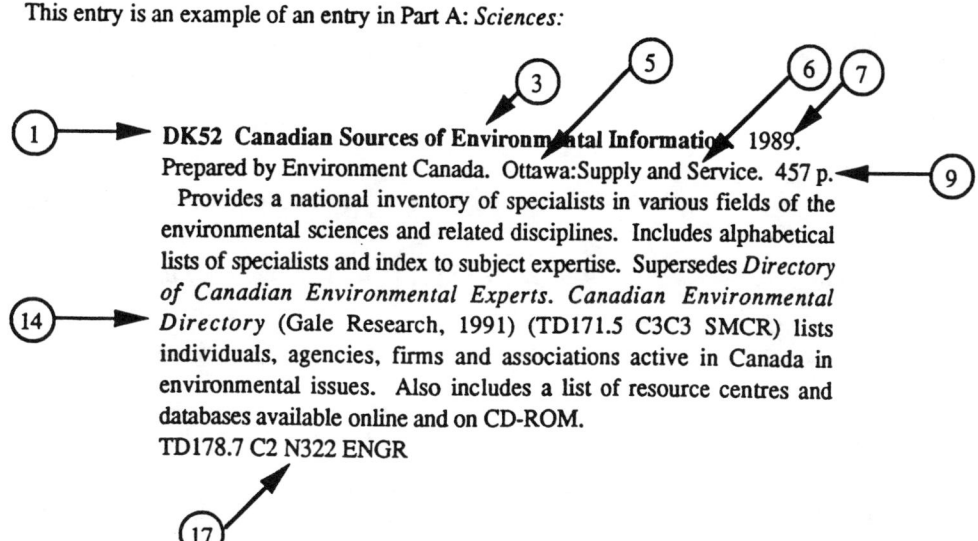

SAMPLE ENTRIES

This entry is an example of a serials entry:

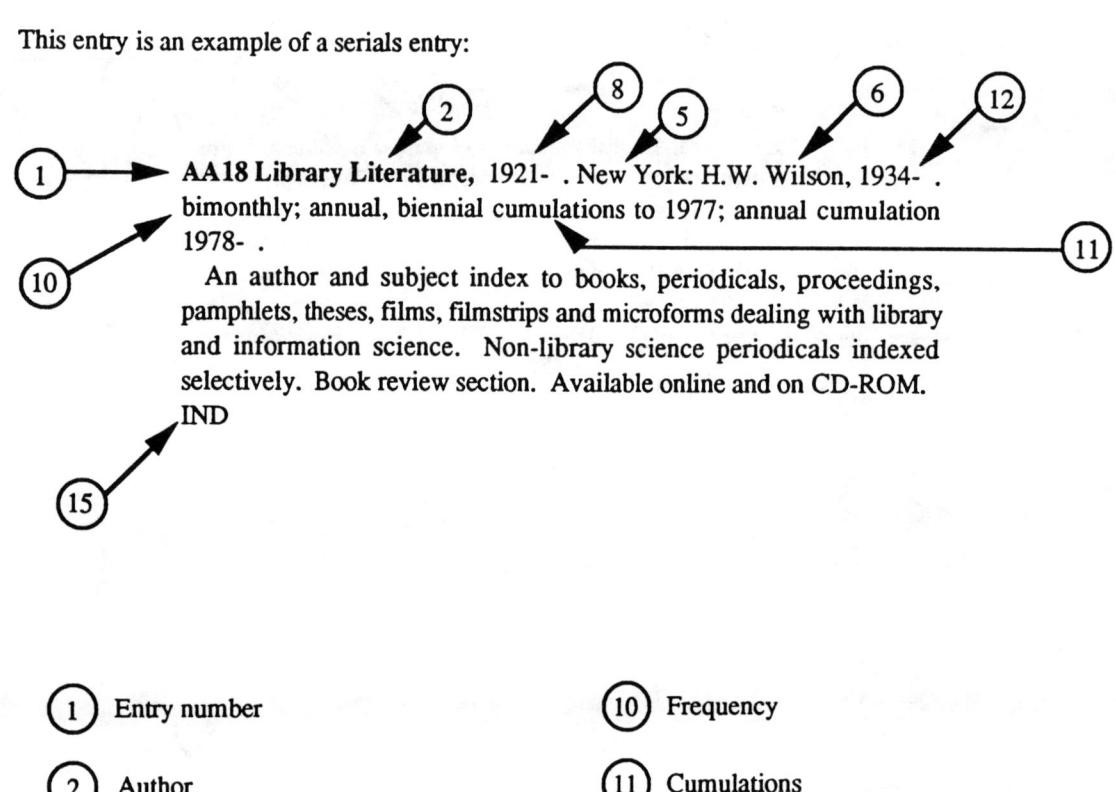

1. Entry number
2. Author
3. Title
4. Subtitle
5. Place of publication
6. Publisher
7. Date of publication
8. Commencement of serial publication
9. Paging
10. Frequency
11. Cumulations
12. Date of publication by this publisher
13. Cross reference to another entry in *Guide*
14. Reference to another title, call number
15. FLIS call number, location
16. Robarts (GENR) call number
17. Call number, location (not FLIS or Robarts)

TABLE OF ABBREVIATIONS

FORM OF ABBREVIATION   **FULL NAME**

The following abbreviations refer to library locations within the University of Toronto Library System:

AERO	Aerospace Studies Library
ARCH	Architecture
AVL	Audio-Visual
BMED	Science and Medicine - Monographs
BMER	Science and Medicine - Reference
BOTA	Earth Sciences
BUSI	Management Studies
CHEM	Chemistry
CSCI	Computer Science
DUNO	Astronomy
EAST	East Asian
EDUC	Education
ENGI	Engineering - Monographs
ENGR	Engineering - Reference
ENVI	Environmental Studies
ERIN	Erindale College
ESCI	Earth Sciences
FORE	Earth Sciences
GENR	Robarts Reference
GEOL	Earth Sciences
GOVT	Government Publications
KNOX	Knox College
LAW	Bora Laskin law library
MAPL	Map Library
MATH	Mathematics
MUSI	Music
OISE	Ontario Institute for Studies in Education

PASC	Science and Medicine - Monographs
PASR	Science and Medicine - Reference
PHYS	Physics
PRRH	Periodicals Reading Room
PRRS	Periodicals Reading Room - Science
ROBA	Robarts, Main Collection
ROMU	Royal Ontario Museum
SCAR	Scarborough College
SIGS	Sigmund Samuel - Main Collection
SIGR	Sigmund Samuel - Reference
SMC	St. Michael's College
TRIN	Trinity College
ZOOL	Zoology

The following abbreviations refer to libraries within Metropolitan Toronto:

MTRL*	Metropolitan Toronto Reference Library
TPL	Toronto Public Library System

* Department within MTRL is also noted: e.g. MTRL LANG/LIT

Other Abbreviations:

ALA	American Library Association
CGPC	Canadian Government Publishing Centre
CLA	Canadian Library Association
ERIC	Education Resource Information Center
GPO	Government Printing Office (U.S.)
HMSO	Her Majesty's Stationery Office (U.K.)
IFLA	International Federation of Library Associations
IGO	Intergovernmental Organizations
ISBN	International Standard Book Number
ISSN	International Standard Serial Number
NAC	National Archives of Canada
NLC	National Library of Canada
PAC	Public Archives of Canada

TABLE OF CONTENTS

AA - **Library and Information Science**   3
     Guides to the Literature, Bibliographies, Abstracts and Indexes, Reviews and Annuals, Encyclopedias and Handbooks, Dictionaries and Glossaries, Directories

AB - **Book Trade and Information Industries**   14
     Book Trade Directories, Book Trade News, Book Trade Dictionaries, Information Industry Directories and Catalogues, Database Directories, Database Searching (Bibliographies, Manuals)

AC - **Selection Aids**   21
     Guides to Reference Books, Current Selection, Book Reviewing Periodicals for the General Public, Indexes to Book Reviews, Children and Young Adults

AD - **National Bibliography**   33
     Bibliography of Bibliographies, National Library Catalogues, National and Trade Bibliographies, Buying Guides - Rare and Out of Print Materials, (Microforms), Archives, Manuscript Collections

AE - **Directories to Periodicals and Newspapers**   57
     Bibliographies and Directories, Union Lists

AF - **Indexes to Periodicals, Newspapers and Other Materials**   62
     Databases, Periodical Indexes, Newspaper Indexes, News Services, Indexes to Other Materials, Research or Dissertations Abstracts and Indexes, Translation Indexes

x *Guide to Reference Materials for Canadian Libraries*

AG - Audio Visual Materials 71
    Catalogues and Directories, Selection Aids, Dictionaries, Encyclopedias, Annuals

AH - Annuals, Directories, and Handbooks 77
    Directories of Organizations, Directories, Handbooks (Annuals, Almanacs, Awards and Prizes, Consumer Information, Emblems and Heraldry, Etiquette and Forms of Address, Holidays and Events, Parliamentary Procedure, Speeches, Quotations and Mottoes, Record Books)

AI - Encyclopedias 90
    Indexes, Bibliographies and Buying Guides, Comprehensive General Encyclopedias (For Adults, Desk Encyclopedias, For Young Adults, Children's to Young Adults), Comprehensive Foreign Encyclopedias

AJ - Dictionaries 96
    Bibliographies and Guides, English Language Dictionaries on Historical Principles, American English Dictionaries, British English Dictionaries, Canadian English Dictionaries, Children's and Students Dictionaries, Abbreviations, Eponyms, Etymology, Foreign Words and Phrases, Pronunciation, Sign Language, Slang, Allusions and Expressions, Symbols, Synonyms, Usage, Grammars and Style Manuals, Visual Dictionaries, Word Elements, French Dictionaries, Canadian French Dictionaries, Other Language Dictionaries

AK - Maps and Atlases 117
    Guides, Bibliographies and Library Catalogues, Directories to Collections, International Atlases, Atlases with National Emphasis (Canada and the United States), Gazetteers, Place Names

AL - Biography 126
    Bibliographies, Abstracts and Indexes (Obituaries), National Biographical Dictionaries, Genealogy and Heraldry, International Authors, Wilson Series, Children's Authors

AM - Government Publications 140
    Multinational Bibliographies and Guides to the Literature, Canada (Organization, Procedures of Government, Bibliographies, Catalogues and Indexes, Pre-Confederation Government Publications, Provincial Government Publications, Parliamentary Publications, Legislative Publications),

Great Britain (Organization of Government, Guides to the Literature, Bibliographies and Indexes, Catalogues), United States (Organization of Government, Bibliographies and Guides, Abstracts and Indexes, Catalogues, State Government Publications

AN - Intergovernmental Publications 161
Multi-organizational, United Nations System, European Communities, Organisation for Economical Co-operation and Development

BA - General Reference in the Humanities 169
Guides to the Literature, Bibliographies and Indexes, Encyclopedias, Dictionaries, Directories

BB - Philosophy 172
Guides to the Literature, Bibliographies, Indexes and Abstracts, Encyclopedias and Dictionaries, Directories, Histories of Philosophy

BC - Religion 176
General Religion (Bibliographies and Guides, Abstracts and Indexes, Encyclopedias, Dictionaries, Handbooks and Directories, Quotations), Buddhism, Hinduism, Islam, Judaism, Alternative Movements, Christianity (Bibliographies and Indexes, Dictionaries, Encyclopedias, Biographical Sources and Directories), The Bible (Concordances, Encyclopedias and Dictionaries, Handbooks, Atlases), Mythology and Folklore

BD - Literature and Language 191
General Literature (Bibliographies and Guides to the Literature, Abstracts and Indexes, Reviews and Annuals, Dictionaries, Encyclopedias and Handbooks, Literary Criticism, Biographies, and Directories, Pseudonyms, Characters, Writers Guides), National Literatures (Canadian, American, British), Literary Genres (Fiction: Mystery and Westerns, Science Fiction, Fantasy and Horror, Short Stories, Poetry, Drama, Play Indexes), Classical Literature, Children's Literature, Language

BE - Art and Architecture 221
Bibliographies and Guides, Abstracts and Indexes, Encyclopedias and Dictionaries, Biographical Dictionaries, Directories, Canadian Museums and Galleries, General Histories of Art, Reproductions, Auction Records, Architecture, Coins and Stamps, Costume, Decorative Arts and Design, Graphic Arts, Photography

xii Guide to Reference Materials for Canadian Libraries

BF - Music   238
Bibliographies and Guides to the Literature, Bibliographies and Indexes of Music, Library Catalogues, Abstracts and Indexes, Encyclopedias and Dictionaries (Biographical Dictionaries, Popular Music, Opera, Hymnology), Directories, Histories of Music, Discographies

BG - Performing Arts   248
Performing Arts, Dance, Theatre, Cinema and Film, Radio and Television

CA - General Reference in the Social Sciences   265
Bibliographies and Guides to the Literature, Abstracts and Indexes, Periodical Directories and Union Lists, Encyclopedias and Dictionaries, Directories, Statistical Information (International, Compendia, Canada, Great Britain, United States), Urban Materials and Information

CB - Economics   279
Bibliographies and Guides to the Literature, Abstracts and Indexes, Encyclopedias and Dictionaries, Statistical Handbooks, Atlases

CC - Business   283
Bibliographies and Guides to the Literature, Abstracts, Indexes and Databases, Statistical Handbooks, Handbooks, Encyclopedias and Dictionaries, Directories (Canada, United States, International), Biographical Sources, Business Service Publications, Consumer Information

CD - Political Science   296
Bibliographies and Guides, Abstracts and Indexes, Encyclopedias and Dictionaries, Annuals, Directories, Handbooks and Atlases, Peace and Disarmament, Human Rights

CE - Law   308
Guides to Legal Research, Bibliographies and Union Lists, Abstracts and Indexes, Encyclopedias and Handbooks, Dictionaries and Glossaries, Directories, Legal Systems, Statutory Materials

Table of Contents xiii

CF - Anthropology and Ethnology 316
Bibliographies, Guides and Catalogues, Abstracts, Indexes and Reviews, Encyclopedias and Dictionaries, Atlases, Biographical and Directory Sources, Ethnic Studies, Native Peoples, Archaeology

CG - Sociology 327
Bibliographies and Guides to the Literature, Abstracts and Indexes and Reviews, Encyclopedias and Dictionaries, Aging, Animal Rights, Child Abuse, Death, Drugs and Alcoholism, Marriage and the Family, Sex and Sex Roles, Social Work, Women's Studies

CH - Psychology 337
Bibliographies and Guides to the Literature, Abstracts and Indexes, Reviews and Annuals, Encyclopedias and Dictionaries, Manuals, Handbooks, Tests and Measurement, Directories

CI - Education 343
Bibliographies and Guides to the Literature, Abstracts and Indexes, Encyclopedias, Dictionaries, Handbooks and Annuals, Directories, Education Statistics

CJ - History and Area Studies 351
General World History: *Bibliographies and Guides, Abstracts and Indexes, Encyclopedias, Dictionaries and Handbooks, Chronologies, Outlines, Tables, Atlases, Ancient History, Medieval History, Modern History,* ***Area Studies:*** *Multinational, North America, Canada, United States, Latin America and the Caribbean, Western Europe, Great Britain, France, Eastern Europe, Middle East / Near East / North Africa, Africa, Far East and Australasia, Asia, Australia and New Zealand, Arctic*

CK - Geography 379
Bibliographies and Guides, Abstracts and Indexes and Databases, Encyclopedias and Dictionaries, Directories and Biographical Sources, Travel Guides

CL - Sports and Games 384
Bibliographies, Abstracts, Indexes and Databases, Encyclopedias, Dictionaries and Handbooks, Directories, Baseball, Football, and Hockey Handbooks and Directories

DA - General Reference in Science and Technology 391
Bibliographies and Guides to the Literature, Periodicals and Union Lists, Abstracts, Indexes and Databases, Conference Papers and Proceedings, Translations, Theses, Research and Technical Reports, Patents and Trademarks, Standards, Handbooks, Encyclopedias and Yearbooks, Encyclopedias (Children and Young Adult), Dictionaries, Histories and Chronologies, Biographical Sources, Directories

DB - Mathematics 404
Bibliographies and Guides to the Literature, Abstracts, Indexes and Databases, Handbooks, Encyclopedias and Dictionaries, Histories, Biographies and Directories

DC - Computer Science 409
Bibliographies and Guides to the Literature, Abstracts, Indexes and Databases, Annuals and Handbooks, Encyclopedias and Dictionaries, Directories and Buying Guides

DD - Astronomy 414
Guides to the Literature, Abstracts and Indexes, Reviews and Annuals, Encyclopedias and Dictionaries, Guides for Amateur Astronomers, Handbooks, Atlases, Directories

DE - Physics 421
Bibliographies and Guides to the Literature, Abstracts, Indexes and Databases, Reviews and Annuals, Encyclopedias and Dictionaries, Handbooks, Directories and Biographical Sources

DF - Chemistry 426
Bibliographies and Guides to the Literature, Abstracts, Indexes and Databases, Reviews and Annuals, Encyclopedias and Dictionaries, Handbooks, Directories and Biographical Sources

DG - Earth Sciences 435
Bibliographies and Guides to the Literature, Abstracts, Indexes and Databases, Reviews and Annuals, Encyclopedias and Dictionaries, Handbooks and Almanacs, Directories

Table of Contents xv

DH - Biology   445

Biology (Bibliographies and Guides to the Literature, Abstracts and Indexes, Reviews and Annuals, Dictionaries, Encyclopedias, Handbooks and Directories) Botany and Horticulture (Bibliographies and Guides, Abstracts, Indexes and Reviews, Encyclopedias, Dictionaries and Handbooks, Directories), *Zoology* (Bibliographies, Abstracts and Indexes, Encyclopedias, Dictionaries, Handbooks and Directories, General, Invertebrates, Reptiles and Amphibians, Mammals, Birds, Domestic Animals, Fish and Marine Mammals, Endangered Species)

DI - Health Sciences   464

Guides to the Literature, Bibliographies and Catalogues, Abstracts, Indexes and Databases, Reviews and Annuals, Encyclopedias and Dictionaries, Handbooks, Meetings, Statistics, Directories, Consumer Health Information, Drug Information, Occupational Safety and Health

DJ - Agriculture   480

Agriculture (Bibliographies and Guides, Abstracts, Indexes and Databases, Reviews, Annuals and Statistical Sources, Dictionaries, Handbooks and Manuals, Directories, Atlases), Food and Food Production, Wine, Veterinary Science, Forestry

DK - Environment and Energy   492

Environment (Bibliographies and Guides to the Literature, Abstracts, Indexes and Databases, Reviews and Annuals, Encyclopedias and Dictionaries, Handbooks, Atlases, Directories), *Energy* (Bibliographies and Guides to the Literature, Abstracts, Indexes and Databases, Reviews and Annuals, Handbooks and Dictionaries, Directories

DL - Engineering   505

Bibliographies and Guides to the Literature, Abstracts, Indexes and Databases, Reviews and Annuals, General Encyclopedias and Dictionaries, General Handbooks, Specialized Encyclopedias, Dictionaries and Handbooks

Indexes   524

Part A
GENERAL REFERENCE

AA LIBRARY AND INFORMATION SCIENCE

Guides to the Literature

AA1 Prytherch, Roy. **Sources of Information in Librarianship and Information Science.** 2d ed. Aldershot, U.K.: Gower, 1987. 153 p.

This "brief and practical" introduction to the literature covers the principal services and provides information on the nature and pattern of publishing in this area.
R020 P973 S2

AA2 Purcell, Gary with Gail A. Schlachter. **Reference Sources in Library and Information Services: A Guide to the Literature.** Santa Barbara: ABC-Clio Information Services, 1984. 359 p.

An annotated guide in two parts. Part 1, arranged by type of publication, covers nearly 700 works. Part 2, arranged by subject, lists more than 450 works on library-related issues, developments, institutions or techniques. Title, author and geographic indexes.
R020 AP985R

Bibliographies

AA3 **ABHB: Annual Bibliography of the History of the Printed Book and Libraries,** 1970- . Dordrecht, Netherlands: Kluwer Academic, 1973- . annual.

"Aims at recording all books and articles of scholarly value which relate to the history of the printed book, to history of arts, crafts, techniques, equipment and of the economic, social and cultural environment" of the book. International coverage with topical arrangement. Author, anonym, geographical and personal name indexes; an extensive list of periodicals. Volume 17A is *Cumulated Subject Index 1970–1986* (1989).
R070.5 A615A

AA4 **ARBA Guide to Library Science Literature, 1970–83.** Ed. by Donald G. Davis Jr. and Charles D. Patterson. Littleton, CO: Libraries Unlimited, 1987. 682 p.

Compilation of reviews published in *ARBA*

American Reference Books Annual (AC1) volumes from 1970 to 1984 with some exclusions. In addition to reference works, *ARBA* evaluated all books in library science, both reference and non-reference, until 1985. From 1985 to 1989, library science works are reviewed in *Library and Information Science Annual* (AA26).
R020 A111A

AA5 Cannons, Harry G.T. **Bibliography of Library Economy.** Chicago: American Library Association, 1927. 680 p. Reprint/ New York: Burt Franklin, 1970.

Classified index to library literature in professional journals, 1876–1920. Author access provided by *An Author Index with Citations* (Scarecrow Press, 1976) (R020 AC22A).
R020 AC22

AA6 Columbia University. School of Library Service. **Dictionary Catalog.** 7 vols. Boston: G.K. Hall, 1962. Supplement 4 vols. (1976).

This collection, begun by Melvil Dewey, dates back to 1876. Includes a large reference collection, historical collection of children's books, in addition to the largest librarianship collection in the United States, for the period covered.
R020 AC726

AA7 **Information Reports and Bibliographies,** 1972- . New York: Science Associates International. 6 issues per year.

Title varies. In addition to one or more articles on a topic useful to librarians in their work, most issues contain "In the Literature" (selected contents from leading library and information science journals) and a bibliography of recent ERIC documents (see AA19). The "JAL Guide to the Professional Literature", which appears in each issue of the *Journal of Academic Librarianship*, (PER) provides article abstracts, annotations of new titles and summaries of reviews from selected library, higher education and administration journals.
PER

AA8 **Library and Information Science Journals and Serials: An Analytical Guide.** Comp. by Mary Ann Bowman. Westport, CT: Greenwood Press, 1985. 140 p.

Annotated bibliography of over 300 English language journals and serials. Provides descriptive publishing and indexing information.
R020.5 AB787L

AA9 **Library Hi Tech Bibliography,** 1986- . Ed. by C. Edward Wall. Ann Arbor, MI: Pierian Press. irregular.

Annotated bibliographies on important and timely topics in library automation and information technology. Bibliographies list articles and some monographs.
R020.285 AL697L

AA10 Schlachter, Gail A., and Dennis Thomison. **Library Science Dissertations 1925-1972: An Annotated Bibliography.** Littleton, CO: Libraries Unlimited, 1974. 293 p. Research Studies in Library Science, No. 12.

Supplemented by *Library Science Dissertations 1973–1981* (1983). Set covers more than 1,600 doctoral dissertations in library science and related fields accepted by academic institutions in the U.S. and Canada. Entries are chronological by date of acceptance. Abstracts of dissertations produced between 1983 and 1987 can be found in *Library and Information Science Annual* (AA26), and *Dissertation Abstracts International* (1938-) (AF42), which contains dissertations on all subjects.
R020.7 AS338

Abstracts and Indexes

AA11 Current Index to Journals in Education, 1969- . Phoenix, AZ: Oryx Press (for ERIC). monthly; semi-annual cumulation. (CIJE Main Entry Cumulation 1969–1980, annual updates, microfiche).

Part of the ERIC family of publications, (AA19). Indexes about 760 journals in education and related fields such as library science. Available online and on CD-ROM.
IND

AA12 Current Research in Library and Information Science, 1983- . London: Library Association. quarterly.

Continues *Radials Bulletin* (Research and Development Information and Library Science), (1974–83), which was published twice yearly as a cumulative listing of research projects in the U.K. or done by U.K. nationals abroad. The title change marks expanded international coverage and increase in frequency of issue. The scope includes archives, documentation, library and information. Research citations, with abstracts, are in a classed order; name, subject indexes. National Library of Canada's Library Development Centre contributes information on Canadian research projects   Available online.

Before 1983, international coverage of research projects was provided by *R & D Projects in Documentation and Librarianship*, (IND) which was published by the International Federation for Documentation in the Hague from 1971-1987.
PER

AA13 Danton, J. Periam. **Index to Festschriften in Librarianship.** New York: R.R. Bowker, 1970. 461 p. Covers period of 1864–1966. Supplemental volume covers 1967-75 (Saur, 1979) (R020.8 AD194A). Together these indexes list some 4,800 articles written to honour an individual. International coverage with an author/subject listing
R020.8 AD194

AA14 Informatics Abstracts, 1977- . Moscow: VINITI. monthly, with annual index.

The English language version of *Referativnyj Zhurnal* (DA20), Section 59 "Informatika"; supersedes *Abstract Journal Informatics 1963-1976*. Covers much material not included elsewhere in English language sources.
IND

AA15 Information Science Abstracts, 1966- . New York: Plenum. bimonthly with annual cumulated index.

Supersedes *Documentation Abstracts*. Founded by American Society for Information Science, the Special Libraries Association, and a division of the American Chemical Society, the abstracts are still edited by Documentation Abstracts. Covers approximately 450 journals, some selectively, plus books, conference proceedings, reports, patents. International coverage with over 800 abstracts per issue. Intended for information scientists, special librarians, educators, equipment developers, systems analysts and for persons in related fields of publishing, translation, technical writing. Abstracts are classified by subject, then listed alphabetically by author. Author and subject indexes. Available online.
IND

AA16 Library and Information Science Abstracts, 1969- . London: Library Association. monthly. Cumulative Index 1969–73 (1975), and 1976-80 (1982).

Beginning in 1991, published by Bowker/Saur. *LISA* was bimonthly until 1982. Continues *Library Science Abstracts (1950–1968)*. A classified listing of abstracts of journal articles, books and reports in library, information science and related fields, e.g. printing, electronic publishing and databases, media. Name and subject indexes. Available online and on CD-ROM.
IND

AA17 Library and Information Sciences: An Abstract Newsletter, 1973- . Springfield VA: National Technical Information Service. weekly, with annual index.

Lists technical reports in the areas of information systems, marketing and user services, operations and planning, personnel, and reference materials. Abstracted reports are available from NTIS in microfiche or paper copy.
IND

AA18 Library Literature, 1921- . New York: H.W. Wilson, 1934- . bimonthly; annual, biennial cumulations to 1977; annual cumulation 1978- .

An author and subject index to books, periodicals, proceedings, pamphlets, theses, films, filmstrips and microforms dealing with library and information science. Non-library science periodicals indexed selectively. Book review section. Available online and on CD-ROM.
IND

AA19 Resources in Education, 1975- . Washington: GPO (for ERIC, National Institute of Education, U.S. Dept. of Education). monthly with annual cumulation in 3 vols.

Continues *Research in Education, 1966–1974*. The Educational Resources Information Center (ERIC), established in 1964, is composed of 16 clearinghouses, (e.g. IR: Information Resources), and covers all significant facets of education and cognate fields. ERIC is sponsored by the National Institute of Education, U.S. Dept. of Health and Welfare. *RIE* complements *CIJE* (AA11) by providing abstracts of report literature (research findings, technical reports, speeches, books) in education and related fields. Includes indexes for subject, name, publication type, and institution. Various cumulations of *CIJE* and *RIE* are available through Oryx Press, for example: *RIE Main Entry Cumulation 1966–1980*; *Complete RIE/CIJE Cumulation 1966-1980;* *Combined RIE/CIJE Subject and Fiche Index 1966-1980* (with annual supplements for 1981-1983), and *RIE/CIJE Annual Updates* on microfiche, and can be searched using the *Thesaurus of ERIC Descriptors* (AA43). Available online and on CD-ROM.
IND

Reviews and Annuals

AA20 Advances in Librarianship, 1970- . New York: Academic Press. annual.

Articles and bibliographic essays critically reviewing published literature of library and information science in broad areas. A publishing lag results in a delay of several years between publications.

Annual reviews on specific topics in library science are also available from JAI Press, including, *Advances in Library Administration and Organization,* (1982-) (025.1 A244A); *Advances in Serials Management,* (1986-) (025.1732 A244A); and *Advances in Library Automation and Networking,* (1987-) (025.00285 A244A).
R020 A244

AA21 ALA Yearbook of Library and Information Services: A Review of Library

Events, 1976- . Chicago: American Library Association. annual.

A review of library events with an American emphasis, but with international coverage. Includes short and feature articles and obituaries. Volume 13 (1988) includes a cumulative index to "Features" section from 1976-1988. Volume 14 (1989) has a cumulative index to biographies and obituaries from 1976-1989.
R020.62273 A512Y

AA22   Alternative Library Literature: A Biennial Anthology, 1982/83- . Ed. by Sanford Berman and James P. Danky. Jefferson, NC: McFarland. biennial.

Eclectic collection of articles from a wide range of journals (traditional and alternative) discussing current library and information issues "from a critical, non-traditional, socially responsible perspective."
R020 A466A

AA23   Annual Review of Information Science and Technology, 1966- . Washington: American Society for Information Science. annual. *Cumulative Index 1966–75* (1976).

Provides bibliographic essays reviewing the literature and recent developments in information science and related areas. Keyword and Author Index to volumes 1–23 (Volume 23, 1988).
R020 A615A

AA24   British Librarianship and Information Work 1981–1985. 2 vols. Ed. by David Bromley. London: Library Association, 1988. Series published every five years.

Begun in 1928 as the annual *Year's Work in Librarianship*, and became *Five Year's Work in Librarianship* in 1951. In 1966–70 the publication took on its present title. Describes major events and publications in various areas of library and information science, with an emphasis on current trends and issues of interest to all types of libraries. The Library Association issues the *Library Association Year Book* (1932-annual) (PER) which includes the LA's charter, bylaws, and membership list.
R020.941 B862BB

AA25   Library and Book Trade Almanac, 1956- . New York: R.R. Bowker. annual.

Formerly titled *Bowker Annual of Library and Book Trade Information*. Almanac of statistics, legislation, grants, literary commendations, directory information, bibliographies and short articles on topics of current interest to library and publishing fields. Available on CD-ROM on *Library Reference Plus*.
R027.07 B786L

AA26   Library and Information Science Annual, 1985-1989. Littleton, CO: Libraries Unlimited. annual.

Originally titled *Library Science Annual*. Organized in two parts: Part 1 provided informative essays on current issues; Part 2 contained comprehensive book reviews of monographs, journal literature, series, and databases in the discipline, complete with descriptive and critical evaluations. From 1987, Canadian, British and Irish materials were included. Also contained abstracts of recent library science dissertations. See *ARBA* (AA4) for earlier book reviews.
R020 AL697LA

AA27   Library Lit. - the Best of, 1970- . Metuchen, NJ: Scarecrow Press. annual.

Reproduces outstanding articles selected from the library literature each year. Arranged in broad subject areas.
020.5 L697L

Encyclopedias and Handbooks

AA28 **ALA World Encyclopedia of Library and Information Services.** 2d ed. Ed. by R. Wedgeworth. Chicago: American Library Association, 1986. 896 p.

Includes short articles, statistics, biographies with a North American emphasis.
R020.3 A111A2

AA29 **Encyclopedia of Library and Information Science.** 35 vols. New York: M. Dekker, 1968–1983. Supplement 3 vols. Vol. 36- (1983-).

Includes articles of varying length in a topical arrangement. Volumes 46 and 47 are the author and subject indexes to Volumes 1-45. (Volumes 34 and 35 index the first 33 volumes). Volumes 36-38 (1983-1985) provide a three volume supplement which updates the material in volumes 1–35. The set is now supplemented at least annually beginning with Volume 39 (1985). Supplements update articles in main set and add new articles on topics currently important in the field, recently deceased individuals, etc. Volume 36 has the updated article, "Libraries in Canada 1970-1979" which supplements information in the main set.
R020.3 E56

AA30 **Library Technology Reports,** 1965- . Chicago: American Library Association. bimonthly; with cumulated index.

Evaluations, descriptions of systems, equipment, supplies, etc. for libraries. *The Sourcebook of Library Technology* cumulates reports from 1965–79 in microfiche with hardcopy table of contents and index.
R025.078 A512

AA31 Wertsman, Vladimir F. **The Librarian's Companion. A Handbook of Thousands of Facts and Figures on Libraries / Librarians, Books / Newspapers, Publishers / Booksellers.** New York: Greenwood Press, 1987. 166 p.

Reference work for librarians, about librarians, libraries and the publishing industry. Part One provides library and publishing information for over 200 countries. Part Two includes chapters of special interest to librarians and the profession, such as noted librarians, quotes, and librarians in novels and plays.
R020.2 W499L

Dictionaries and Glossaries

AA32 **The ALA Glossary of Library and Information Science.** Ed. by Heartsill Young. Chicago: American Library Association, 1983. 245 p.

"Terms and definitions are utilitarian, reflecting current practices of libraries and related information agencies in the U.S." Includes terms drawn from library and information science, printing and publishing, graphic arts, reprography, and archives administration. Excludes names of persons, corporate bodies, and commercial products. Contains brief definitions, with cross references.
R020.3 A512AA

AA33 **Dictionary of Library and Educational Technology.** 3d ed. Ed. by Kenyon C. Rosenberg and John J. Elsbree. Englewood, CO: Libraries Unlimited, 1989. 196 p.

Provides definitions to over 1,000 technical terms relating to computers, telecommunications and recording material. Part two includes guidelines for selection criteria for the purchase

of AV projectors, sound systems, videotape systems, reprographics, microform equipment, computer hardware and software, and optional equipment, found in libraries and educational institutions.
R371.33 R813M3

AA34 Elsevier's Dictionary of Library Science, Information and Documentation in Six Languages. Comp. by W.E. Clason. New York: Elsevier Scientific Publishing, 1976. 708 p.

Includes terms used in library and information science in 6 languages, including English/American, French, Spanish, Italian, Dutch, and German, arranged in an English alphabet. Includes an Arabic supplement.
R020.3 E49E

AA35 Glossary of Basic Archival & Library Conservation Terms. Munich: K.G. Saur, 1988. 151 p. ICA Handbooks Series Volume 4.

Provides definitions in English to over 400 terms used by archivists, librarians and conservators with term equivalents in Spanish, German, Italian, French and Russian. Each language has its own alphabetical index. A slightly different work is *Dictionary of Archival Terminology / Dictionnaire de terminologie archivistique* (2d ed, K.G. Saur, 1988) (R025.171 E92D2) which defines archival terms in English and French and lists term equivalents in Dutch, German, Italian, Russian and Spanish.
R025.8403 G563G

AA36 Harrod's Librarians' Glossary of Terms Used in Librarianship, Documentation and the Book Crafts, and Reference Book. 7th ed. Comp. by Ray Prytherch. Brookfield, VT: Gower, 1990. 673 p.

Formerly *Librarians' Glossary of Terms Used in Librarianship, Documentation and the Book Crafts, and Reference Book.* Strong on British terms and book terms.
R020.3 H323L7

AA37 Macmillan Dictionary of Information Technology. 2d ed. Ed. by Dennis Longley and Michael Shain. London: Macmillan Press, 1985. 382 p.

Includes over 6,000 entries of varying length providing definitions of terms used in information technology, written for the professional or layperson. Includes cross references.
R020.3 L856D2

AA38 Montgomery, A.C. **Acronyms and Abbreviations in Library and Information Work: A Reference Handbook of British Usage.** 3rd ed. London: Library Association, 1986. 220 p.

Lists over 6,000 English language acronyms and abbreviations used in librarianship and information work.
R020.148 M787A2

AA39 New International Dictionary of Acronyms in Library and Information Science and Related Fields. Ed. by Henryk Sawoniak and Maria Witt. New York: K.G. Saur, 1988. 449 p.

Useful guide to over 28,500 acronyms used in library science literature around the world. Includes institutions, systems, methods, programming languages, and titles of publications.
R020.148 S271N

AA40 Pipics, Z. **The Librarian's Practical Dictionary in 22 Languages.** 7th ed. Munich: Verlag Dokumentation, 1977. 385 p.

Provides equivalents to almost 4,000 terms used in library cataloguing and classification. Part 1 is arranged in tabular form in alphabetical order by the English term; part 2 gives the word lists in individual languages.
R020.3 P665D7

AA41 Soper, Mary Ellen. **The Librarian's Thesaurus: A Concise Guide to Library and Information Terms.** Chicago: American Library Association, 1990. 165 p.
Arrangement by important concepts, with terms defined and explained and inter-relationships among concepts shown.
R020.3 S712L

AA42 Tayyeb, R. and K. Chandna. **A Dictionary of Acronyms and Abbreviations in Library and Information Science.** 2d ed. Ottawa: Canadian Library Association, 1985. 279 p.
International guide to acronyms used in library and information science as well as related terms for computers and automation. Both English and French acronyms are included.
R020.148 T247 DA2

AA43 **Thesaurus of ERIC Descriptors.** 12th ed. Phoenix, AZ: Oryx Press, 1990. 627 p.
Controlled vocabulary useful for searching ERIC (AA19). Each "descriptor" explained in scope notes; with posting (number of items in database) and terms defined as broader, narrower, related or invalid.
SAS 025.33 37T413T

* * * *

Directories

Directories of Libraries and Library Schools

AA44 **American Library Directory,** 1980- . 2 vols. New York: R.R. Bowker. annual.
Frequency varies; biennial to the 1979 edition, and in one volume before 1983. *ALD* covers all types of libraries in the U.S. and Canada, including networks, consortia, public and school library agencies, library schools. Geographical arrangement. Available online and on CD-ROM.
R027.07 A51

AA45 **Canadian Library Yearbook / Annuaire des bibliothèques canadiennes.** 5th ed. Toronto: Micromedia Limited. 1990. 614 p.
Formerly titled *Canadian Library Handbook / Guide des bibliothèques canadiennes*, which was published in three editions between 1979/80 and 1983. Alphabetical list of over 7,000 libraries in Canada, indexed by subject and location. Also lists archives, library schools and library technician programs, associations, and library science periodicals. A library services directory which lists book wholesalers and magazine subscription agents is also provided. Includes library statistics, a library salary overview, and an annual review of library trends both nationally and by region. See also *Directory of Canadian Archives* (AD93).
R027.071 C212CC

AA46 **Directories of Canadian Libraries / Répertoires des bibliothèques canadiennes.** Rev. ed. Ed. by Pauline Stace. Ottawa: Library Documentation Centre, National Library of Canada, 1989. 17 p.

A bibliography of directories of Canadian libraries. Other bibliographies prepared by LDC include: *Guide to Legislative Libraries and Public and School Agencies in Canada* (4th ed., 1980) (R027.071 C212G4); *Guide to Provincial Library Agencies in Canada* (1985) (R354.7100852 R649G).
R027.071 AD598D

AA47   Directory of Information Sources in the United Kingdom. 6th ed. 2 vols. Ed. by Ellen M. Codlin. London: Aslib, 1990.

Prepared by the Association for Information Management (formerly ASLIB, the Association of Special Libraries and Information Bureaux), and known as the *ASLIB Directory*. Provides access to over 6,500 British and Irish libraries and other organizations "able to make information available". Includes research services, professional, voluntary, academic, scientific organizations, experts, and producers of data, statistics and abstracts.

A shorter version, *The Shorter Aslib Directory of Information Sources in the U.K.*, (R026 A835S) published in 1985 in a single volume with similar format to earlier editions, updates the fifth edition.

A similar work is *Libraries in the United Kingdom and the Republic of Ireland 1990* (16th ed, Library Association, 1990) (R021.002542 L697L), which lists all public and academic libraries, selected government, national and special libraries and all faculties of librarianship and information science.
R026 A835D4 (4th ed.)

AA48   Directory of Special Libraries and Information Centers, 1963- . 2 vols. Detroit: Gale Research. irregular.

(14th ed, 1991). Describes holdings, personnel, services of over 18,000 special libraries and information centres in the U.S. and Canada. Volume 1, in 2 parts, is arranged alphabetically by name of library with subject index. Volume 2 contains geographic and personnel indexes. Volume 3, *New Special Libraries*, is a semi-annual supplement.
R026 D598D or D14

AA49   International Guide to Library and Information Science Education. Ed. by Josephine R. Fang and Paul Nauta. New York: K.G. Saur, 1985. 537 p. IFLA Publication 32.

Provides data for comparing educational qualifications for librarians and information specialists throughout the world.
R020.711 I613I

AA50   Special Libraries in Canada / Bibliothèques specialisées au Canada. Ed. by Diane Gallagher. Toronto: Micromedia Ltd, 1985. 176 p.

Directory of over 2,000 special libraries in Canada in all subject areas. The "Main Directory" section is alphabetical by library, with subject, geographical and personal name indexes. Regional lists of special libraries, such as *Toronto Chapter's Directory of Special Libraries*, (12th ed, 1990) (R026 S74T12), provide current information.
R026.00971 S741S

AA51   World Guide to Libraries. 9th ed. Ed. by Helga Lengenfelder. New York: K.G. Saur, 1989. 1001p.

Directory and brief collection information on almost 40,000 libraries (government, national, federal, regional, academic, school, public school, special) in over 160 countries. Arranged by country, then by type of library and city, with name index.
R027 I61I9

AA52 World Guide to Special Libraries. 2d ed. 2 vols. New York: K.G. Saur, 1990.

Included in this directory are over 32,000 libraries in 160 countries arranged by subject, subarranged by English form of country name. Indexed.
R026.00025 W927W2

Directories of Library Collections

AA53 Ash, Lee. **Subject Collections: A Guide to Special Book Collections and Emphases as Reported by University, College, Public and Special Libraries and Museums in the United States and Canada.** 2 vols. 6th ed. rev. and enl. New York: R.R. Bowker, 1985.

Provides a subject listing of specialized collections of over 11,000 libraries, and museums in Canada and the U.S. Subject headings used are LCSH. A similar work for European libraries is Richard Lewanski's *Subject Collections in European Libraries: A Directory and Bibliographic Guide* (2d ed, R.R. Bowker, 1978) (R026.000254 L669S2) which arranges libraries by country within broad subject classes based on DDC.
R026 A819S5 (5th, 1978) or Z688 A2A8

AA54 Special Collections in College and University Libraries. Comp. by MODOC Press. New York: Macmillan Pub. Co., 1989. 639 p.

Directory of special collections held in U.S. college and university libraries. Includes information about the institution and description of the special collection. Main entry by institution within state, with a general index and institution index.
R026 S741T

Directories of Librarians and Library Associations

AA55 ALA Handbook of Organization and Membership Directory. 1980/81- . Chicago: American Library Association. annual.

Title varies. An *ALA Membership Directory* (R020.622 A51) has appeared since 1948, and a handbook has also separately appeared at various times. The present *Handbook* combines an outline of the structure of ALA, its officials, committees, and key publications together with a membership roster.
R020.62273 A512H

AA56 Biographical Directory of National Librarians. Ed. by Frances L. Carroll and Philip Schwartz. New York: Mansell Publishing, 1989. 134 p.

Biographical information on the current executive directors in national libraries around the world.
R020.922 C319B

AA57 Canadian Library-Related Expertise: A Directory and Guide to Who Knows What? 2d ed. Ed. by Helen Rogers. Ottawa: Canadian Library Association. Forthcoming, Fall, 1991.

The new edition carries over 200 entries of

Canadian individuals and companies specializing in expertise sought by the library profession. A guide for all library consultive needs.
R020.25 K64WA (1984)

AA58 CLA Directory of Members, 1983/84- . Ottawa: Canadian Library Association. irregular.
(1987 ed.) Title varies (1983/84 to 1985 *CLA Directory & Members' Handbook*.) Supersedes *CLA Directory* 1978/79, with Supplement 1979-/80. Includes information on CLA, such as organization, executives, committees and groups, and a list of personal and institutional members, with addresses and divisional affiliation.
R020.6 C21AC

AA59 Dictionary of American Library Biography. Ed. by B.J. Wynar. Littleton, CO: Libraries Unlimited, 1978. 596 p.
Sketches of 302 deceased prominent librarians in the U.S., including some Canadians. Continued by *Supplement to the Dictionary of American Library Biography* (Libraries Unlimited, 1990), which includes a further 51 library leaders. Supplementary sketches in *Libraries and Culture*, formerly *Journal of Library History* (PER).
R020.922 D554D

AA60 Directory of Library and Information Professionals. 2 vols. Woodbridge, CT: Research Publications in collaboration with American Library Association and other organizations, 1988.
Comprehensive biographical reference to 43,000 individuals. Volume 1: alphabetical listings. Volume 2: indexes by name, specialty, employer, consulting expertise, geographic area. Replaces *Who's Who in Library and Information Services*. Available on CD-ROM.
R020.922 D598D

AA61 Who's Who in Special Libraries, 1981- . Washington: Special Libraries Association. annual.
Includes information about the Special Library Association, and a list of SLA members, with address, specialty, and Division and Chapter indexes.
R026 S74DA

AA62 Who's Who in the U.K. Information World 1990. 2d ed. Comp. and ed. by Mary Ann Colyer. London: TFPL Publishing, 1990. 343 p.
Directory of experienced librarians, faculty, consultants and information brokers, information industry personnel in the U.K.
R020.92241 W628 W2

AA63 World Guide to Library, Archive, and Information Science Associations. Ed. by Josephine R. Fang and Alice H. Songe. New York: K.G. Saur, 1990. 516 p. IFLA Publication 52/53.
Guide offers access to nonprofit organizations and associations related to librarianship, archives and information science. Part 1, international associations; Part 2, national associations. Alphabetical list by country.
R020.6 F211I2

AB BOOK TRADE AND INFORMATION INDUSTRIES

Book Trade Directories

AB1 **American Book Trade Directory,** 1915- . New York: R.R. Bowker. annual.

(36th ed. 1990/91). Lists U.S. and Canadian retail and antiquarian bookstores, wholesalers, auctioneers of literary properties, appraisers of literary collections and dealers in foreign language books. Arranged alphabetically by state/province, city. Available on CD-ROM on *Library Reference Plus.* Companion volume is *International Book Trade Directory* (2d ed, 1989) (Z282 I632) which lists booksellers in 134 countries.
R655.473 A512

AB2 **The Book Trade in Canada: With Who's Where,** 1975- . Ed. by E. Thorne and E. Matheson. Ottawa: Ampersand. annual.

Supersedes *Book Publishers in Canada.* A directory of publishers and distributors, alphabetical by name; and booksellers by province. Includes notices of awards, book deposit regulations, suppliers, special services, and associations.
R070.50971 B724B

AB3 **Canadian ISBN Publishers Directory,** 1981- . Ottawa: National Library of Canada. annual.

(8th ed., 1990). Includes an alphabetical list of publishers with addresses, telephone, telex, fax, and ISBN numbers; followed by a list of ISBN numbers with names of corresponding publishers. Because all Canadian organizations which have been assigned an ISBN are included, this is the most complete directory available.
R070.50971 C212CI

AB4 International ISBN Agency. **Publishers' International ISBN Directory,** 1974- . 3 vols. Münich: Saur. annual.

(17th ed., 1990). Combines *International ISBN Directory* and *Publishers International Directory.* Provides access to some 232,000 trade and non-trade, active publishers. Volume 1 lists publishers by country. Volume 2 is a numerical ISBN directory. Volume 3 contains the alphabetical index.
R070.5 P976P

AB5 **International Literary Market Place,** 1965- . New York: R.R. Bowker, annual.

Directory of publishers, arranged by country, with general information about each country and other information of interest to the book trade, including book clubs, major booksellers, major libraries, associations. "Yellow Pages" index arranged by name of publisher.
R070.52 I616I

AB6 **Library Reference Plus.** New York: R.R. Bowker. CD-ROM.

Updated annually. Merges 5 Bowker databases: *American Book Trade Directory*, *American Library Directory*, *Library and Book Trade Almanac* (Bowker Annual), *Literary Market Place*, and *Publishers, Distributors, and Wholesalers of the U.S.*

AB7 **Literary Market Place,** 1972/73- . New York: R.R. Bowker. annual.

LMP is published in the Fall; its "Yellow Pages" section is the telephone book for publishers, including print and micropublishers, agents, photographers, columnists, wholesalers, packagers, translators, and public relations people. Directory information includes ISBN prefix, product or service descriptions of firms, individuals in over 2,000 major U.S. and Canadian publishing houses. Available on CD-ROM.
R070.52 L776L

AB8 **Microform Market Place: An International Directory of Micropublishing,** 1974/75- . Westport, CT: Meckler. biennial.

1990/91 edition published by K.G. Saur. Directory of micropublishers, with a subject index. Meckler also publishes *Guide to Microforms in Print* (Z1033 M5G803). See AD92.
R070.57 M626D (1986/87)

AB9 **Publishers' Directory,** 1977- . 2 vols. Detroit: Gale Research. annual.

(10th ed., 1990). Guide to over 20,000 U.S. and Canadian publishers of all types (commercial, non-profit, private, alternative) and publishing programs of institutions, associations and corporations. Lists distributors, wholesalers and jobbers. Includes publishers of books and classroom materials, databases, prints and reports. Excludes only vanity presses. Available online.
R070.50257 P976P

AB10 **Publishers, Distributors, and Wholesalers of the United States,** 1981- . New York: R.R. Bowker. annual.

Directory of over 50,000 publishers, wholesalers, distributors, software firms, museum and association imprints, and other trade organizations. Lists editorial offices, ordering addresses, ISBN prefixes, etc. Available online and on CD-ROM.
R070.502573 P976P

AB11 Waller, Adrian. **Canadian Writer's Market.** 9th rev. ed. Toronto: McClelland & Stewart, 1990. 230 p.

Directory of Canadian magazines, trade journals, farm publications (arranged by subject), daily newspapers (by location), book publishers, literary agents, prizes, awards, writers' organizations, and creative writing and journalism courses.
R070.52 W198C9

Book Trade News

AB12 Library and Book Trade Almanac, 1955- . New York: R.R. Bowker. annual.
Formerly *Bowker Annual of Library and Book Trade Information*. Contains directory information for the book industry, including organizations, individuals, conference dates, and book trade news and statistics. Available on CD-ROM. See AA25 for additional information.
R027.07 B786L

AB13 Publishers Weekly: The International News Magazine of Book Publishing, 1872- . New York: Bowker Magazine Group. weekly.
Major newspaper of the trade, contains brief announcements, interviews, articles on every aspect of the publishing industry. Includes annual summary statistics and regular seasonal features and supplements.
PER

AB14 Quill & Quire, 1935- . Toronto: Key Publishers. monthly.
Paper of the Canadian book trade with library and publishing news, reviews, recent trade and educational books. Regular special issue on education. Each issue contains an insert, *Forthcoming Books*, provided by the National Library of Canada, which lists CIP entries. Subscription includes *Canadian Publishers Directory* listing publishers and agents. Available on microfilm, with index 1935-75.
PER

* * * *

Book Trade Dictionaries

AB15 Bodian, Nat G. **Bodian's Publishing Desk Reference: A Comprehensive Dictionary of Practices and Techniques for Book and Journal Marketing and Bookselling.** Phoenix, AZ: Oryx, 1988. 439 p.
Contains almost 4,000 entries for "terms, jargon, tools and techniques". Includes eighteen appendices of techniques, ideas and information for publishers. Indexed.
R070.5 B667B

AB16 Bookman's Glossary. 6th ed. Ed. by Jean Peters. New York: Bowker, 1983. 223 p.
Defines 1,800 terms used in book publishing, selling and manufacturing, the antiquarian trade and librarianship. Includes biographical sketches of men and women of historic importance in bibliography, the graphic arts and book publishing.
R655.03 H72B6

AB17 The Language of the Foreign Book Trade: Abbreviations, Terms, Phrases. 3d ed. Ed. by Jerrold Orne. Chicago: American Library Association, 1976. 333 p.
Multilingual dictionary of European languages. Arrangement by language. Terms listed alphabetically with English definitions.
R010.3 O74L3

AB18 The Publisher's Practical Dictionary in 20 Languages. Ed. by Imre Móra. Budapest: Akadémiai Kiadò, jointly with K.G. Saur, 1984. 417 p.
Lists technical terms used by publishers in twenty languages, in all phases of publishing

trade from manuscript to bookseller. Table arrangement with English headwords.
R070.5 M827W (1974)   or   Z1006 M58

Information Industry Directories and Catalogues

AB19 **CD-ROM Directory 1990.** 4th ed. Ed. by Joanne Mitchell and Julie Harrison. London: TFPL Publishing, 1989. 450 p.

International guide to the CD-ROM industry. Includes CD-ROM products, organization information, CD-ROM drives, relevant books, journals and conferences/exhibitions. Software, subject, organization type indexes are provided.
R004.56 C386D

AB20 **CD-ROM Yearbook,** 1986- . Redmond, WA: Microsoft Press, 1989- . annual.

Includes articles on all aspects of CD-ROM technology and application. Provides a directory of CD-ROM titles, arranged by title and subject, with description, audience, publisher, technical specifications, frequency, and price.
R004.56 M626M.

AB21 **CD-ROMS In Print [Year]: An International Guide,** 1987- . Westport, CT: Meckler. annual.

Alphabetical listing of almost 1,400 commercially available CD-ROMs. Notes discontinued and out-of-print titles. Entries include titles, providers, drives, hardware/software, subscription and descriptions. Indexed.
R004.56 C386C

AB22 **Children's Media Market Place,** 1978- . New York: Neal-Schuman. irregular.

(3d ed., 1988). Directory of sources for locating periodicals and books, software, audiovisuals, and television and radio programs designed for children and those who work with children, preschool to Grade 12.
R028.5 C536 CA3

AB23 **Computer Publishers and Publications: An International Directory and Yearbook,** 1984- . Larchmont, NY: Communications Trends. irregular annual, incl. supplements.

(3d ed., 1988/89). Comprehensive source of information for "everybody in computer publishing". Provides directory information on over 300 book publishers, individual publishers, journals, magazines, newspapers, newsletters, looseleafs, and personnel in the industry. Reviews trends and developments, and provides statistics and tables, ceased titles, bibliography, "master index", plus additional specialized indexes.
016.00164 C7382 OISE REF

AB24 **Directory of Library and Information Retrieval Software for Microcomputers.** 4th ed. Comp. by Hilary Dyer. Brookfield, VT: Gower, 1990. 134 p.

Provides information on microcomputer software for libraries arranged alphabetically by name of program. Index by hardware, supplier, and function.
R025.002854   or   G259 D3

AB25 **Information Industry Directory,** 1991- . 2 vols. Detroit: Gale Research. annual.

Formerly *Encyclopedia of Information Systems and Services* (1979-1990). "Comprehensive international descriptive guide to more than 4,500 organizations, systems and services involved in the production and distribution of information in electronic form." Multiple access

through subject, name, geographic, and analytic indexes to computerized information or data management services, vendors, networks, associations, etc. Supplemented by *Information Industry Supplement.*
R025.04025 E56E11

AB26 Information Industry Factbook, 1987- . Stamford, CT: Digital Information Group. annual.

"The information industry's annual report." Provides facts and statistics on revenues, profits, growth, markets of U.S. and Canadian information industry. Includes overviews, trends, public policy issues.
R025.04025 I43I

AB27 Optical Publishing Directory. 3d ed. Ed. by Richard A. Bowers. Medford NJ: Learned Information, 1988. 319 p.

International coverage of CD-ROM products, described in "product profiles", and optical service vendors. Indexed by product type and applications. Includes a glossary and bibliography.
R004.56 O62R

AB28 Software Catalog: Microcomputers, 1983- semi-annual.

Information on over 25,000 software programs available for microcomputers. See DC30 for full entry information.

AB29 Truett, Carol. **Microcomputer Software Sources: A Guide for Buyers, Libraries, Programmers, Businesspeople and Educators.** Englewood, CO: Libraries Unlimited, 1990. 176 p.

Lists and describes guides to the software industry including guides to information, journals and newsletters, microcomputer market and industry guides.
R005.3 AT866M

Database Directories

AB30 Books and Periodicals Online: A Guide to Publication Contents of Business and Legal Databases, 1987- . Oxford: Learned Information. semi-annual.

International directory of journals and books, arranged by title. Provides name of database vendor and indicates which parts of each journal are indexed or abstracted. Publishers, producers, vendors addresses provided. List by database included.
R025.04025 AB724B (1987)   or
HF5351 B66 LAWR (1990-)

AB31 Canadian Machine-Readable Databases: A Directory and Guide / Bases de données canadiennes lisibles par machine. Comp. by Helen Rogers. Ottawa: National Library of Canada, 1987. 140 p.

Databases created and produced in Canada arranged by database name. Indexed by subject, database producers, and vendors; master list of database names, former names, abbreviations and acronyms also included.
R025.0402571 R726C

AB32 Computer Readable Data Bases: A Directory and Data Sourcebook, 1979- . Detroit: Gale Research. biennial.

(7th ed. 1991). Alphabetical list of more than 5,000 commercial online and offline bibliographic and numeric databases. Also indicates availability on CD-ROM, diskette, magnetic tape and batch mode. International coverage.

Details include producer, processor, name, subject index. Available online as *Database of Databases*.
R025.04025 C738CA

AB33 Directory of Online Databases, 1979-. Detroit: Gale Research, 1991- . 2 issues a year.

Formerly published by Cuadra/Elsevier, and known as the *Cuadra Directory*. Authoritative directory of more than 4,800 databases, including descriptions, addresses of producers and services, indexes by subject, producer, online service, names. Issues are cumulative. Available online.
R025.04025 D598D

AB34 Directory of Periodicals Online, 1985- irregular. See AE5 for full entry information.

AB35 Directory of Portable Databases, 1990- . Detroit: Gale, 1991- . 2 issues per year.

Formerly published by Cuadra/Elsevier (1990). Describes databases on CD-ROM, diskette, and magnetic tape. Includes information on provider, vendor, format, system requirements, software, price, type, subject, content. International coverage.
R025.04025 D598E

AB36 Directory of United Nations Databases and Information Services. 4th ed, 1990.

Lists 872 databases of the U.N. system. See AN8 for full entry information.
R025.04025 D598U

AB37 The ESPIAL Canadian Database Directory. Prepared by H.C. Campbell. Toronto: Espial Productions, 1990. 109 p.

Subtitled: *A Guide to Current Canadian Information Contained in National and International Databases and Data Banks, 1989/90*. Includes contents, type, language, producer, vendor and print equivalents of databases listed. Addresses of vendors provided. Available online, with monthly updates, in either French or English.
R025.0402571 E77EC

Database Searching

Bibliographies

AB38 Byerly, Greg. **On-line Searching: A Dictionary and Bibliographic Guide.** Littleton, CO: Libraries Unlimited, 1983. 288 p.

The selective annotated bibliography covering the period up to June 1982 is dated, but dictionary is still useful, with concise definitions of more than 1,200 terms related to searching.
R025.524 AB994P

AB39 Hawkins, Donald T. **Online Information Retrieval: Bibliography 1964–1982.** Medford, NJ: Learned Information, 1983. 311 p.

Supplemented by volumes covering 1983–1986, 1987–1989. Updated annually in August supplement to *Online Review*. Covers bibliographic, numeric and non-bibliographic retrieval systems. Entries arranged alphabetically within broad sections, with an author and KWIC title indexes
R025.524 AH393HA2/3

* * * *

Manuals

AB40 **BRS/ Search System Users' Manual,** 1986- . Latham, NY: BRS Informaiton Technologies. irregular loose-leaf.

Introduces the basic searching procedures and commands which are applicable to all BRS databases. Supplemented by *Basics/BRS Information Technology*, which consists of Aid Pages for BRS/ Search Services, and by *Database Guides*. Vendor's name changed from Bibliographic Retrieval Systems, Inc.
R025.524 B111E

AB41 Canada Institute for Scientific and Technical Information. **CAN/OLE II System Guide,** 1989- . Ottawa: CISTI. irregular loose-leaf.

Describes the new command language of the CAN/OLE II system. Supplemented by *CAN/OLE, CAN/SDI Database Catalogue* (1990), and *CAN/OLE Selected Database User Guide* (1990).
R025.524 C111C

AB42 **QL/SEARCH: User's Manual and Database Description Manual.** Kingston, ON: QL Systems, [1986]. loose-leaf.

Manual for searching full text databases for government documents, Canadian law, tax, news and scientific data on the QL system.
R025.524 Q1Q

AB43 **Searching DIALOG: The Complete Guide.** 4 vols. Palo Alto, CA: DIALOG Information Services, 1987. loose-leaf.

Basic reference manual, includes *Bluesheets* and *Yellowsheets*. Also available is *DIALOG-Basics: A Brief Introductory Guide to Searching* (15 p.); *Searching DIALOG: The Tutorial Guide* (1 vol.); *DIALOG Lab Workbook and Reference Manual* (1 vol.); and *DIALOG On Disc: User's Guide* (1 vol.), and other guides.
R025.524 D536S

AC   SELECTION AIDS

Guides to Reference Books

AC1   American Reference Books Annual, 1970- . Englewood, CO: Libraries Unlimited. annual with quinquennial cumulative indexes, 1970-74; 1975-79; 1980-84; 1985-89.

ARBA covers all types of reference books published or distributed in the U.S. and Canada. Signed reviews are short, descriptive and evaluative. Reviews are arranged by broad subject and indexed by author, title and subject. The annual *Recommended Reference Books for Small and Medium-Sized Libraries and Media Centers* (Libraries Unlimited, 1981-) (R011.02 R311R) edited by Bohdan Wynar provides a selected subset of titles from *ARBA*.
R025.5 AA512

AC2   Canadian Reference Sources: A Selective Guide. 2d ed. Ed. by Dorothy E. Ryder. Ottawa: Canadian Library Association, 1981. 311 p.

Approximately 2,000 works, published to the end of 1980, are annotated and grouped under general reference, history and allied subjects, humanities, science, social sciences. The second edition added works on women's studies, labour movement, archives, ethnic groups and children's literature.

A new bilingual publication, the *Guide to Canadian Reference Sources*, is being compiled at the National Library of Canada. In a concept and format similar to Dorothy Ryder's work, this publication will include some 6,000 works to reflect an increased number of reference publications and an enlarged subject coverage for science and technology, computer science, medicine, bioethics and public health, ethnic and folk materials, etc. Canadian content or interest in a work, rather than Canadian authorship or publication, is a criterion for inclusion. Two volume publication is anticipated, with volume 1 (forthcoming 1992) for general reference works, humanities and history, and volume 2 (forthcoming 1994/95) for social sciences and sciences.
R025.5 AR992C

AC3   General Reference Books for Adults: Authoritative Evaluations of Encyclopedias, Atlases and Dictionaries. Ed. by Marion Sader. Bowker Buying Guide. New York: R.R. Bowker, 1988. 615 p.

Reviews covers about 215 titles readily

available and in-print (as of mid 1988) in the United States. For ease of use in comparing reviews or answering questions from the public, the author provides comparative charts, "facts at a glance" and some facsimile pages of the books reviewed. Other Bowker buying guides include *Reference Books for Young Readers* (1988) (see AC45), a consideration of encyclopedias, atlases and dictionaries for juveniles, and *Topical Reference Books*, (1991), an annotated list of basic and noteworthy books for adults arranged by subject for academic and public libraries.
R025.5 AG326G

AC4 **Guide to Reference Books.** 10th ed. Ed. by Eugene P. Sheehy with other contributors. Chicago: American Library Association, 1986. 1588 p.

An annotated, comprehensive, international guide, but with emphasis on American sources and materials distributed in the U.S.
R025.5 AM94G10

AC5 **Guide to Reference Material.** 5th ed. 3 vols. General editor: A.J. Walford. London: Library Association, 1989- in progress.

Volume 1 *Science and Technology* (1989); Volume 2, *Social and Historical Sciences, Philosophy and Religion* (1990); Volume 3, *Generalia, Language and Literature, The Arts* (4th ed. 1987).

Complements *Sheehy* (AC4). The volumes are individually edited by different specialists and emphasize British and European titles including non-Western titles. *Walford's Concise Guide to Reference Material* (1981) (R025.5 AW174C) contains some 2,500 entries selected from Volume 1 of the fourth edition, 1979, and Volumes 2-3 of the third edition, 1975-79, and other additional material.
R025.5 AW174G3

AC6 **Guide to Reference Materials for Canadian Libraries.** 8th ed., rev. and enl. Ed. by Kirsti Nilsen. With the assistance of Alanna Kalnay. Consulting editor: Claire England. Toronto: University of Toronto Press, for the Faculty of Library and Information Science, 1991. 596 p.

Primarily intended as an instructional guide for library personnel and researchers who work with reference materials, the *Guide* surveys the basic and most familiar or typical resources for general reference work, and for work with the disciplines of the humanities, social sciences, and pure and applied sciences.
R025.5 AG976J

AC7 **Science and Technology Annual Reference Review,** 1989- . Phoenix, AZ: Oryx Press. annual.

Provides detailed reviews for over 700 science and technology reference books each year.
Z7401 S337 PASR

AC8 **Books for College Libraries: A Core Collection of 50,000 Titles.** 3d ed. 6 vols. Chicago: American Library Association, 1988.

Vol. 1, *Humanities*; Vol. 2, *Language and Literature*; Vol. 3, *History*; Vol. 4, *Social Sciences*; Vol. 5, *Psychology, Science, Technology, Bibliography*; Vol. 6, *Index*.

Identified on the spine as *BCL 3*, this project of ALA's Association of College and Research Libraries recommends a basic collection for

undergraduate libraries. Without neglecting such subjects as business, computers, engineering and health, the focus of *BCL* is on the traditional book-enriched disciplines that commonly constitute a liberal arts and sciences education.
R011 AB724B3

AC9 Canadian Book Review Annual, 1975- . Toronto: Simon & Pierre. annual.

Evaluative short original reviews of English language trade books with Canadian imprint arranged by broad subject classes with indexes for author, subject, and title. Books are primarily current publishing. Some appropriate federal government publications, educational titles with trade appeal, and translations (French to English) are included.
R819.08 C212B

AC10 Canadian Selection: Books and Periodicals for Libraries. 2d ed. Comp. by Mavis Cariou, Sandra J. Cox, Alvan Bregman. Toronto: University of Toronto Press, 1985. 501 p.

Designed as a selective guide to Canadian books and periodicals for adults using public and other libraries, inclusion of a title implies suitability for consideration as a library acquisition. With an author, title, and subject index, and list of Canadian award winners.
R015.71 J38CC2

AC11 Fiction Catalog. 12th ed. Ed. by Juliette Yaakov and John Greenfield. New York: H.W. Wilson, 1991. 943 p. Four annual paper supplements between editions.

The *Wilson Standard Catalogs* (see AC13, AC39, AC42, AC46) are in three parts - a main section with cataloguing and classification information and annotation; an index section, and a publisher's directory.

In the *Fiction Catalog* the main section is an author list citing over 5,000 of the "best" English language in-print and out-of-print titles. The entries have full bibliographic citations, and bookreview excerpts, tables of contents from anthologies, or brief plot summaries. Includes a title and subject index. *Fiction Catalog* is a companion to *Public Library Catalog* (AC13) and to the more specialized choices in *Senior High School Library Catalog* (AC46).
R823 AF448C12   or   Z5916 F5

AC12 Magazines for Libraries, 1969- . New York: R.R. Bowker. triennial since 5th ed.

(7th ed. forthcoming 1992). Subtitled: *For the General Reader and School, Junior College, College, University and Public Libraries*. Lists more than 6,500 magazines selected as the best or most useful titles for the libraries noted in the subtitle. Entries have full bibliographic information and a description of the magazine together with notes on indexing, microform editions, audience level and availability of samples. Canada appears as a section in the general subject arrangement. Title and subject index.
R050 AM189 (6th ed. 1989)

AC13 Public Library Catalog. 9th ed. Ed. by Paula B. Entin and Juliette Yaakov. New York: H.W. Wilson, 1989. 1338 p. Four annual paper supplements between editions.

Complements *Fiction Catalog* (AC11), and designed for use in public, college, university libraries. The main section of the *PLC* is a Dewey classified list of nonfiction titles with author, title, subject and analytic indexes and directory of publishers.
R011 AP976C9

AC14 **The Reader's Adviser: A Layman's Guide to Literature.** 13th ed. 6 vols. General eds. Barbara A. Chernow and George A. Vallasi. New York: R.R. Bowker, 1986–88.

At head of title, *"The Best In."* Volume 1: *...American and British Literature, Bibliography and Reference.* Volume 2: *...American and British Drama and World Literature.* Volume 3: *...Reference, The Social Sciences, History and the Arts.* Volume 4: *...Philosophy and World Religions.* Volume 5: *...Science, Technology and Medicine.* Volume 6: *Indexes.*

Begun in 1921 as *The Bookman's Annual*, *RA* has expanded in size and coverage over its various editions to this survey of "the best" (or best-known and basic) readings in various subjects. Generally American in orientation, the volumes, each with its own index, are available separately and individually edited. Volume 6 is a name, title, and subject index to the entire set.
R011 R286

Current Selection

AC15 **The Booklist,** 1905- . Chicago: American Library Association. semimonthly, 22 issues/yr (monthly July, August).

Title varies. Purpose is "to provide a guide to current print and nonprint materials worthy of consideration for purchase by small and medium-sized public libraries and school media centers" (editorial statement). Covers the current trade production with "Upfront" prepublication reviews, features such as occasional special lists, best books, plus regular coverage of children's material, and a separate section, *Reference Books Bulletin* (see AC23) which operates under its own policies and procedures. With the exception of *RBB* coverage, a review in *Booklist* constitutes a recommendation for library purchase.
PER

AC16 **British Book News,** 1940- . London: British Council. monthly.

Self-styled as The British Council's "monthly survey for bookbuyers throughout the world," the magazine has brief, descriptive articles about books and the book trade, and standard short reviews and notices.
PER

AC17 **Canadian Literature / Littérature canadienne: A Quarterly of Criticism and Review,** 1959- . Vancouver: University of British Columbia. quarterly.

In addition to the articles on literature, the books reviewed emphasize English Canada's production, but are not limited to Canadian books.
PER

AC18 **Choice: Current Reviews for College Libraries,** 1964- . Chicago: Association of College and Research Libraries. 11 issues/yr with annual index, 1980-.

Choice reviews print and nonprint materials of potential value for undergraduate libraries. It is also useful to public libraries. Annually contains section "Outstanding Academic Books and Nonprint Materials" which lists titles without annotation but with reference to the signed review in the monthly periodical. "Reviews on Cards" service available.
PER

AC19 **Kirkus Reviews,** 1933- . New York: Kirkus Service. semimonthly.

Head of title: *Jim Kobak's Kirkus Reviews.* Title, publisher varies. This looseleaf publication is oriented to public libraries serving the general reader with fiction and nonfiction choices. Both adult and juvenile material is included, and

reviews are typically prepublication. Author indexes cumulate quarterly and semiannually.
R011 K59K

AC20 Letters in Canada, 1936- . Toronto: University of Toronto Press. annual.

Enlarged Fall issues of the *University of Toronto Quarterly*, 1931- (AP5 U55 ROBA) with single issue availability. A critical survey of both French and English fiction, poetry, drama, translations and related works in the humanities.
Z1375 L47O2 ROBA

AC21 Library Journal, 1876- . New York: R.R. Bowker. semimonthly, 21 issues/yr.

Provides librarians reviews of a substantial number of trade books (4,000–5,000 titles). Special features such as "best" lists or other selection lists appear regularly on various topics (e.g., religion, science). The books covered are of broad interest to public and academic libraries. "Reviews on Cards" service is also available.
PER

AC22 New Technical Books: A Selective List with Descriptive Annotations, 1915- . New York: Research Libraries of the New York Public Library. 6 issues/yr.

Provides short notes to works classed in the 500 and 600 Dewey Decimal System, (i.e. coverage is of pure and applied physical sciences, mathematics, engineering and industrial technology plus architecture). The level of books described is technical, from selected college texts to specialized research monographs and conference proceedings. Includes an author index.
PER

AC23 Reference Books Bulletin, 1983/84- . Chicago: American Library Association, 1930-. annual.

Title and frequency varies. *RBB* is an annual reprinting of reviews of reference materials from the *RBB* section inside *Booklist* (22 issues/yr, see AC15). Initially these reviews appeared separately as *Subscription Books Bulletin*, (1930-56); *Subscription Books Bulletin Reviews* (1956--1968); and *Reference and Subscription Book Reviews* (1968/70 to 1983/84).

Reviews are by committee, and the reviewing of a title does not constitute a recommendation by virtue of selection for scrutiny.

Microform publishing, and the microfilming of major reference sets not readily available in other formats are described at length in *Microform Review*, (1972-, K.G. Saur, 1991- , quarterly) (Z265 M59 MICR).

Reprints of older materials generally of interest only to large academic libraries are reviewed in *Reprint Bulletin Book Review*, (1955-, Glanville Pub., quarterly) (PER).
R016 S941AA

AC24 Reference Services Review, 1973- . Ann Arbor, MI: Pierian Press. quarterly.

At head of title: *RSR Reference Services Review*. Contains reviews, bibliographies and review articles on a wide variety of subjects. Other library-related periodicals specifically review reference works, e.g. *RQ (Reference Quarterly)*, (1960-, American Library Association) (PER) which includes sections on databases, reference and professional materials. Most library periodicals have reviewing sections for particular formats, publishing areas, or audiences, e.g., *Wilson Library Bulletin* (1914-, H.W. Wilson) (PER), with its public library orientation, and *College & Research Libraries* (1939-, American Library Association) (PER), with its mid-range university orientation.
PER

AC25   Science Books & Films, 1965- .
Washington: American Association for the Advancement of Science. 5 issues/yr. Annual cumulative index.

Formerly *Science Books*. Evaluates trade, text, and reference books for all age groups. The AAAS aim in this publication is "to promote quality science education and foster greater public understanding" of science and its applications. Books are also substantively reviewed in the AAAS members' journal *Science*. *Science Book List* which began as an occasional paper in 1964, grew into the *AAAS Science Book List* (1970) and *Supplements* (1978; 1978-1986). These books contain reviews culled from the journal and are recommended books for high school, junior undergraduates, teachers and general audiences. The 1978-1986 supplement (R500 AD285A3) lists 2,100 books.
PER

Book Reviewing Periodicals for the General Public

AC26   Books in Canada, 1971- . Toronto: Canadian Review of Books. 9 issues/yr.

A national review of about 400 books a year, emphasizing trade books with articles on the book trade, authors, etc. Available on microfiche, 1971–78 (McLaren Micropublishing) with microfiche *Author Title Reviewer Index 1971–76*. Regional reviews can be found in such sources as the newspaper format *Atlantic Provinces Book Review*, (1974-, St. Mary's University, quarterly) (PER) or publications from provincial library associations which stress regional imprint coverage, e.g. *BCLA Reporter*, (1957-, British Columbia Library Assoc., 6 issues/yr) (PER).
R011 B724B

AC27   London Review of Books, 1979- .
London: London Review of Books Ltd. bimonthly.

A newspaper format review with an approach similar to that of the *New York Review of Books* with lengthy reviews of approximately 15–20 books. Books are usually British and the magazine complements, but does not substitute for, *Times Literary Supplement*.
PRRH Desk

AC28   The New York Review of Books, 1963- . New York: New York Review Inc. 22 issues/yr.

Mixes longer essays, opinion pieces about books and ideas, with shorter reviews. Tends to emphasize recent fiction.
PER

AC29   The New York Times Book Review, 1896- . New York: New York Times. weekly with annual index. *Cumulated Index 1896–1970*, 5 vols.

Published with the Sunday *NY Times*, this major review of books has critical pieces, lengthy essays and brief descriptions ranging in every literature from children's books, through bestsellers to scholarly materials.
PRRH Desk; AP2 N6582 (Index)

AC30   The Times Literary Supplement, 1902- . London: Times Newspapers. weekly (Friday edition). *TLS Index*: 1902–1939, 2 vols. (1978); 1940–80, 3 vols. (1982).

Titled *T.L.S.* from 1969. Widely known for its well-written reviewing and criticism, this tabloid newspaper supplement covers fiction and nonfiction from all disciplines including

children's books. There is emphasis on literary reviewing in the humanities and social sciences.
PRRH Desk; AP4 T553 (Index)

Indexes to Book Reviews

AC31 **Book Review Digest,** 1905- . New York: H.W. Wilson. monthly (except Feb., July); quarterly, with annual cumulations.

BRD surveys periodicals in the U.S., U.K., and Canada and indexes and excerpts reviews for those books which receive a minimum number of reviews. *BRD* covers about 6,000 books a year. Previous restrictions to books published or distributed in the U.S. was relaxed in 1983 to include Canada. *BRD* normally excludes government publications, texts, technical books, and children's literature. Available online and on CD-ROM. The cumulated editions: *BRD Author Title Index* 1905–74 and 1975–84, provide access to some 360,000 titles in the digest.

The *Technical Book Review Index,* 1935–88 (Special Libraries Association, 10 issues/yr, mfm) cited reviews of technical books taken from some 2,500 journals with extracts from the published reviews.
R016 B72

AC32 **Book Review Index,** 1965- . Detroit: Gale Research. 6 bimonthly issues/yr; with quarterly and annual cumulation, title index.

BRI Master Cumulation, 1965–1984 (10 vols) places approximately 1.6 million citations to reviews in alphabetical sequence by author with title index. The annual *Children's Book Review Index*, (1976-) (PER) cites reviews of juvenalia taken from *BRI*. Other related titles include *Book Review Index: Reference Books 1965–1984* citing 87,000 reviews and *Book Review Index: Periodical Reviews 1976–84* (Z1035 A1B56 SCAR) citing 15,000 reviews. Available online.
R028.1 AB724B

AC33 **Canadian Magazine Index,** 1985- monthly.

Provides book, movie and drama reviews listed alphabetically by title under form headings, e.g., "Book reviews, Fiction - Canadian". Includes author and subject entries. See AF7 for full entry information.

AC34 **Canadian Periodical Index,** 1964- monthly.

Provides book, movie and drama reviews listed alphabetically by title under form headings, e.g., "Book reviews, Fiction - Canadian". Includes author and subject entries. See AF8 for full entry information.

AC35 **Combined Retrospective Index to Book Reviews In Scholarly Journals, 1886-1974.** 15 vols. Comp. by E.I. Farber, and others. Arlington, VA: Carrollton Press, 1979–82.

Offers author and title access to reviews in 458 journals in history, political science, sociology. There are companion titles such as *Combined Retrospective Index to Book Reviews In Humanities Journals, 1802–1974* (BA10n); and *Combined Retrospective Index to Book Reviews in History 1838–1974* (11 volumes).
Z1035 A1C64

Children and Young Adults

The following list is a guide to selection aids for children's literature. Additional information can also be found in the Children's Literature section, in *Languages and Literature*, BD161 to BD177.

Retrospective Selection

AC36   Best Books for Children: Preschool Through Grade Six. 4th ed. Ed. by John T. Gillespie and Corinne J. Naden. New York: R.R. Bowker, 1990. 1002 p.

Provides a list of 12,382 recommended fiction and nonfiction books for children from preschool to grade 6. Arranged by subject. Companion volume is *Best Books for Junior High Readers* (1991), which provides similar information for grades 7 to 9. *Books for Children to Read Alone: A Guide for Parents and Librarians* (Bowker, 1988) (R028.5 AW748B) is a guide to books specifically geared for independent reading for the beginning reader to Grade 3. Also for the child beginning to read is *Beyond Picture Books: A Guide to First Readers*, edited by Barbara Barstow (1989) (R028.5 AB282B), an annotated bibliography of over 1,600 books for Grade 1 and 2 readers, with a list of the "200 Outstanding First Readers" in the bibliography.
028.5 AB561 A4

AC37   Canadian Books for Young People / Livres canadiens pour la jeunesse. 4th ed. Edited by André Gagnon and Ann Gagnon. Toronto: University of Toronto Press, 1988. 186 p.

First published as *Canadian Books for Children/ Livres canadiens pour enfants* (1976), by Irma McDonough, the work had annotated titles, some adult titles, series, fiction and nonfiction, for preschool to age 14, grade nine. Originally, many of the choices were also in the journal *In Review: Canadian Books for Young People, 1967–1982* (Ontario Ministry of Culture and Recreation). This 4th edition enlarges the work to contain a representative sample of an increased Canadian production of English and French titles, and extends the upper age to 18. Suggested reading levels are given for each title.
R028.52 C212L4

AC38   Canadian Picture Books / Livres d'images canadiens. Ed. by Jane McQuarrie and Diane Dubois. Toronto: Reference Press, 1986. 217 p.

Similar in format to *A to Zoo: Subject Access to Children's Picture Books* (BD172), provides a list of Canadian illustrated fiction and nonfiction books written for preschool and primary school-aged children. Organized by title, subject and author. Short annotations are written in English or French, depending on the language of the book.
R028.5 AM173C

AC39   Children's Catalog. 15th ed. Ed. by E. Dill. Standard Catalog Series. New York: H.W. Wilson, 1986. 1298 p. Four annual paper supplements between editions.

Claims a balanced survey of nearly 6,000 titles representing the best books suitable for preschool, grades K to 6. Each annual supplement adds about 550 titles. The classified section organizes the titles into nonfiction (including biography), fiction, story collections and easy books. Index has author, title, subject, and analytic entries. Also includes a directory of publishers and distributors.
R028.5 AW74C15

AC40 Children's Choices of Canadian Books, 1979- . Ottawa: Citizen's Committee on Children. 2 issues per year.

Provides reviews of Canadian children's books written by parents and children, ranking books for popularity, age group, type of story, and setting. Reviews include candid comments from children.
028.5 AC536CB

AC41 The Elementary School Library Collection: A Guide to Books and Other Media. 17th ed., Phases 1-2-3. Edited by L. Winkel and others. Williamsport, PA: Brodart Co., 1990. 1149 p.

The ESL Collection, published by a library supply company for schools, continually revises its content, and is issued every few years. In three sections (phases), the main classified section is a very briefly annotated list of in-print resources to meet the curricula needs and personal interests of children from preschool to grade 6. There are professional and reference works, nonfiction, fiction, easy books, periodicals and audiovisual items. Section 2 supplies author, subject and title indexes. Section 3 has various appendices of particular value to teachers and others when using books and media with children.
R028.5 AE38E17

AC42 Junior High School Library Catalog. 6th ed. Standard Catalog Series. New York: H.W. Wilson, 1990. 850 p. Four annual paper supplements between editions.

Includes slightly more than 3,000 titles in the base volume, grades 7-9, and extends the coverage in the *Children's Catalog* (AC39). *JHSL Catalog* is a classified list with author, title, subject, and analytic index, with a directory of publishers and distributors.
R027.8 AJ95H (4th edition)

AC43 Notable Canadian Children's Books / Un choix de livres canadiens pour la jeunesse, 1973- . Prepared by Irene Aubrey. Ottawa: National Library of Canada. irregular annual.

(1987 Supplement, 1991). *NCCB* represents a range, from historic to contemporary, of notable Canadian children's books. The first edition of this work was an annotated catalogue, prepared by Sheila Egoff and Alvine Bélisle, for a 1973 exhibition at NLC. It was revised in 1976 to include books published to December, 1974. Cumulative editions cover 1975-1979 (1985) and 1980-1984 (1989).

A committee, directed by I. Aubrey at the Children's Literature Service, NLC, compiles the irregularly published annual supplements to update the work.

The Children's Literature Service / Service de littérature de jeunesse at NLC provides reference service, promotional programs (see AC44n), various publications, and lists, often free on request, related to Canadian children's literature. Lists normally accompany or follow exhibits of displays, e.g. *Pictures to Share: Illustration in Canadian Children's Books* (1982), or are compiled as an aid for librarians, e.g. *Animal World in Canadian Books for Children and Young People* (1983).
028.52 N899N2B

AC44 Our Choice / Your Choice: Canadian Children's Books, Authors and Illustrators, 1986/87- . Toronto: Canadian Children's Book Centre. annual.

Title varies. From slim beginnings almost when the Centre opened in 1977, this publication has grown to a booklet of some 30 pages and is revised each September. A committee chooses the 300 Canadian titles, "deserving special attention" from the previous three years. If of continuing value, book titles within the time period may be repeated. Arranged by subject, the books have reading and interest level indications, and are for babies through mid-teen years.

Like the Children's Book Centre, Communication-Jeunesse in Montreal provides information on Quebec's French-language publishing for children and young adults. C-J's annual choices are noted, with recommended age range from 4 to approximately 14 years, in a pamphlet *Abracadabra: Sélection de livres québécois pour enfants*.

Both the Children's Book Centre's *Our Choice / Your Choice*, and Communication-Jeunesse, *Abracadabra*, are used by the National Library for its annual program, *Read Up on It / Lisez sur le sujet*, which promotes Canadian books and reading.
010 093 CR OISE

AC45   Reference Books for Young Readers. Ed. by Marion Sader. New York: R.R. Bowker, 1988. 615 p.

Provides 200 descriptive evaluations of American encyclopedias (online and print), world atlases, dictionaries and word books, and appropriate large print books for preschool to high school. Includes facsimiles of actual pages from many of the books, a glossary, and "what to look for in..." sections for encyclopedias and dictionaries.
R011.02 R325R

AC46   Senior High School Library Catalog. 13th ed. Standard Catalog Series. New York: H.W. Wilson, 1987. 1324 p. Four annual paper supplements between editions.

Covers grades 9–12, including some 5,000 titles in the base volume with some adult titles suitable to high school curricula. *SHSL Catalog* is a classified list with author, title, subject, and analytic index, and a directory of publishers and distributors.
R027.8 AS785SA (11th ed.)

Current Selection

The titles below are exclusively devoted to materials for young people; but please note that children's and young adults' materials may also be covered in the book trade newspapers, library periodicals and regular review sources previously listed, e.g. *Quill & Quire* (AB14), *Wilson Library Bulletin* (AC24n), *Kirkus Reviews* (AC19), *Booklist* (AC15).

AC47   Appraisal: Science Books for Young People, 1967– . Boston: Boston University School of Education and the New England Round Table of Children's Librarians. quarterly. index cumulates in each vol/yr.

Books are listed alphabetically by author, with two reviews per book. One of the two reviews is by a children's librarian, the other by a subject specialist. Each reviewer rates the title with a comment from unacceptable to excellent.
PER

AC48   Bulletin of the Center for Children's Books, 1947– . Chicago: University of Chicago, Graduate Library School. monthly (except August).

Several symbols (special interest, curricular or developmental value, marginal, recommended etc.) are used to extend the information in the short reviews. The *Bulletin* only carries reviews, approximately 50 or so per issue. Zena Sutherland edited an offspring publication *The Best in Children's Books*, 1966–72 (University of Chicago, 1973) (028.5 AS966B), followed by a subsequent issue for 1973–78 (1980), and 1979–84 (1986).
PER

*   *   *   *

AC49 CM: A Reviewing Journal of Canadian Materials for Young People, 1971– . Ottawa: Canadian Library Association. 6 issues a year.

Formerly *CM: Canadian Materials for Schools and Libraries* (1980-86); and *Canadian Materials: An Annotated Critical Bibliography for Schools and Libraries* (1971-79). Evaluates 800 or more items annually, in all media including games and kits produced in Canada or about Canada, for young people from pre-kindergarten to age 15. Subject arrangement.
R015.71 AC212CB

AC50 Canadian Children's Literature / Littérature canadienne pour la jeunesse, 1975– . Guelph, ON: Canadian Children's Press. quarterly.

In addition to reviews, there are often long review articles.
PER

AC51 Emergency Librarian, 1973– . Vancouver, BC: Dyad Services. 5 issues a year (bimonthly, except July, August).

Head of title: *EL Emergency Librarian*. With some emphasis on schools, and an audience in Washington state, as well as across Canada, *EL* has regular review columns and notices for books, audiovisual items, and professional reading. Notes bookstore reports of bestsellers, K to 12, for U.S. and Canada.
PER

AC52 The Horn Book Guide, 1990– . Boston: Horn Book. semi–annual (available, Feb., Sept.).

This journal of short reviews attempts to cover all U.S. hardcover trade books for children and young adults published in the previous season. Has brief, evaluative reviews with a rating from outstanding (1) to unacceptable (6); there is grade, genre and subject information and indexes for authors, titles, subjects, series etc. In the first issue of the year, a "Fanfare" page lists best books for the previous year. Since the *Guide* can cover approximately 1,500 or more books in an issue, it reviews significantly more books (of any quality) than its parent publication, *Horn Book Magazine* (below).

AC53 The Horn Book Magazine, 1924– . Boston: Horn Book. bimonthly.

The *Horn Book Index 1924–1989* (Oryx Press, 1990) (PER) is a brief subject index giving limited access to past reviews. The magazine is "about books for children and young adults" and, in its Booklist section, there are fairly long reviews for some 50 or more books. There is a "brief recommendation" section; outstanding books are starred, and the selected coverage is from picture books through the older reader.
PER

AC54 The Reviewing Librarian, 1974– . Toronto: Ontario School Library Association. quarterly, with annual cumulative index.

Arranged in Dewey classes for professional, reference and nonfiction, with fiction listed separately. Reviews all media. Emphasizes Ontario curriculum, noting Ontario government publications useful to school librarians. Other provincial school library associations also provide reviews either in their journals or separately, e.g. *BCSLA Reviews*.
PER

AC55 School Library Journal, 1954– . New York: R.R. Bowker. monthly (September to May), with annual cumulative index.

Head of title: *SLJ*. Reviews cumulated annually, 1968–70 (028.5 S372). Librarians and

teachers write generally descriptive reviews for more than 2,500 books available through the U.S. publishing trade in a year. Titles with stars are excellent in relation to others on the same subject or in the same genre.
PER

AD NATIONAL BIBLIOGRAPHIES

This section begins with Bibliographies of Bibliographies, and then continues in the following order: National Library Catalogues (France, Great Britain, United States); National and Trade Bibliographies (Canada, Canadian Regions and Provinces, Great Britain, United States, International, France, Germany); Rare and Out-of Print Materials; Microforms; Archives and Manuscript Collections.

Bibliographies

Bibliographies of Bibliographies

AD1 Besterman, Theodore. **A World Bibliography of Bibliographies and of Bibliographical Catalogues, Calendars, Abstracts, Digests, Indexes and the Like.** 4th ed. 5 vols. Lausanne: Societas Bibliographica, 1965–66.

Of interest for retrospective searching. Includes only separately published bibliographies (stating number of items in bibliography) arranged under broad subjects, personal and place names, with author index. Also published as subject volumes, e.g. *A World Bibliography of Oriental Bibliographies* (1975). *A World Bibliographiy of Bibliographies 1964–74*, compiled by Alice F. Toomey (2 volumes, Rowman and Littlefield, 1977) (Z1002 T67) is a decennial supplement based on Library of Congress holdings.
R011 AB56W4

AD2 **Bibliographic Index: A Cumulative Bibliography of Bibliographies,** 1937- . New York: H.W. Wilson, 1938- . 3 issues per year; annual cumulation.

A subject index to bibliographies of fifty or more citations, published separately or included in books, pamphlets or periodical articles; includes Romance or Germanic languages. Available online and on CD-ROM.
IND

AD3 **Bibliographical Services Throughout the World,** 1951/52- . Paris: Unesco, 1953- . annual; decennial, then quinquennial cumulations. *1950–59* (1961); *1960–64* (1969); *1970–74* (1977); *1975–79* (1984); *1980, 1981–82* (1985); *1983–84* (1987).

Annual reviews by/for Unesco, of the bibliographic activity of member states. Cumulations are prepared by different authors, most recently Marcelle Beaudiquez of Bibliothèque Nationale in Paris. Useful for familiarization with worldwide bibliographic publications.
R010 B582BA or Z1001 B5148 ROBA

AD4 Lochhead, Douglas. **Bibliography of Canadian Bibliographies / Bibliographie des bibliographies canadiennes.** 2d ed, rev. and enl. Toronto: Published in association with the Bibliographical Society of Canada by the University of Toronto Press, 1972. 312 p.

First edition by Tanghe (1960) may still be of some interest. Main approach is by broad subject. Includes bibliographies with "some Canadian connection either by subject, compiler, geographical location." Most bibliographies listed were separately issued, but a few formed parts of books or periodical articles. Arranged alphabetically by main entry, with subject, compiler and editor indexes. New edition in progress.
R015.71 AL812B2

National Library Catalogues

This section is arranged in chronological order.

France

AD5 Bibliothèque nationale. **Catalogue général des livres imprimés de la Bibliothèque nationale: auteurs.** 231 vols. Paris: Imprimerie nationale, 1897–1981. Reprint 1974.

Volumes 1 to 186 contain complete cataloguing information for all works of an author held at the BN to the date of volume's publication. From volume 187, only works published before 1960 entered. The complete set contains more than 5 million works. Separate purchase is available for *Actes royaux* (6 volumes); *Incunables* (1 volume); *Auteurs: D'Aristotle à Zola 1895–1981* (57 volumes), etc.
R018.1 B582   or   Z927 P2

AD6 Bibliothèque nationale. **Catalogue général des livres imprimés: auteurs, collectivités / auteurs, anonymes,** Paris: Imprimerie nationale, 1960-67; 1972-78; 1983-85.

Updates *Catalogue général* (AD5). A 12 volume set *1960-64* was published in 1965-67 (R108.1 B582).   Superseded by the series *1960–69, Série 1: Caractères latins* (23 vols); and *Série 2: Caractères non latins* (4 vols) published in 1972-78; and the *1970–79, Série 2: Caractères non latins*, (10 vols), published between 1983-1985.

A microfiche edition of the *BN* catalogues, including *Auteurs 1897–1959* (1500 fiche); *Auteurs, collectivités - anonymes; Supplément*, with additional entries from the unpublished "Card Catalogue 1897–1959", became available in 1986.
Z927 P22 (1972-78; 1983-85)

Great Britain

AD7 British Museum. Dept. of Printed Books. **British Museum General Catalogue of Printed Books to 1955.** Photolithographic edition. 263 vols. London: Trustees of the British Museum, 1959–66. *Ten Year Supplement 1956–65*, (50 volumes); *Five Year Supplement*[s] 1966–70, (26 volumes); 1971–75, (13 volumes); 1976-80 (microfiche). Supplements since 1970 published by British Library. Microfiche version available.

Editions of the *General Catalogue of Printed Books* have been used in libraries since the end of the 19th century. This edition, the so-called *Third Generation Catalogue (GK3)*, was completed in 1966 and is found in many libraries. *GK3* contains all entries in earlier catalogues, plus additions, corrections, etc. An author catalogue, with some title and subject entries, of the holdings of the British Museum Department of Printed Books (now the British Library), except Oriental collections, it includes books from the end of 15th century to 1955. Several separately published sections for specific collections or subjects or languages are available, e.g., *BLC of Printed Maps, Charts and Plans*; *Catalogue of Books Printed in the 15th Century*; *Catalogue of Printed Music* and catalogues for oriental languages, manuscript collections.

Superseded by Bingley-Saur edition, (AD9).
R017 B86   or   Z921 B86G4

AD8 British Museum. Dept. of Printed Books. **Subject Index of Modern Books.** 1881-1975. London: Trustees of the British Museum, 1920- . quinquennial to 1960; 1961–70, (12 vols, 1982); 1971–75 (4 vols, 1986).

These indexes provided an alphabetical subject guide to "modern" British and foreign works added to the Library since 1881. Beginning 1975, name changed to *General Subject Catalogue*, see AD11.
R017 B86   or   Z921 B87/to B8722

AD9 British Library. **The British Library General Catalogue of Printed Books to 1975.** 360 vols. London: Bingley / Munich: K.G. Saur, 1980–1987.

Cumulates in one alphabetical sequence the *BM Catalogue*, (AD7) and *Supplements*, plus additions and corrections. Includes holdings of printed books, except those in Oriental languages. The sequence for *England* (8 volumes 1982) is available for separate purchase with independent title and subheading indexes (2 volumes, 1982). Other separate sequences are the *Bible* (4 volumes, 1981), and the *Liturgies* (2 volumes, 1984).

This edition is available on three CD-ROM discs as *British Library Catalogue on CD-ROM* (Chadwyck-Healey).
Z921 B86G4

AD10 British Library. **British Library General Catalogue of Printed Books, 1976–1982.** 50 vols. Ed. by the British Library. Munich: K.G. Saur, 1983.   microfiche ed. 1976–82. *Supplement* 1982–1985, (26 vols., 1986); 1986–87, (22 vols., 1988); 1988–1989, (28 vols., 1991).

Supplement to Bingley-Saur edition, (above); records British and overseas acquisitions.
Z921 B86G4

AD11 British Library. **The British Library General Subject Catalogue 1975–1985.** 75 vols. Munich/New York: K.G. Saur, 1986–87.

Lists items catalogued during the decade. Available on microfiche as *Subject Catalogue of Printed Books, 1975-1985*.
Z921 B8723

United States

AD12 Library of Congress. The main catalogue of the Library of Congress closed in January 1981; it contains over 24 million cards. No complete printed reproduction (author, title, subject) of this catalogue exists although information in the catalogue is available through various published catalogues and services. K.G. Saur has reproduced the complete main catalogue; 1898–1980 on COM fiche (see AD13).

LC cataloguing data is now available on

magnetic tape through its MARC distribution service, online as *LCMARC: Books All* (1969-), and in microfiche. *LCMARC: Books Canada* includes monographs bearing Canadian imprints or imprints relating to Canada, catalogued by LC. A number of other subsets of LCMARC exist, covering, for example, maps; manuscript collections; Chinese, Japanese, and Korean monographs, etc.

National Union Catalog covers currently issued cataloguing for monographs, pamphlets, maps, atlases and serials regardless of publication date or place. Includes Roman and non-Roman alphabet materials catalogued by LC, and monographic publications reported by more than 1,000 North American libraries. The arrangement is alphabetical by author or title with cross references.

The *NUC Register of Additional Locations (NUC/RAL)* (1968-) (Microfiche only, 1978-) is a supplement to *NUC*, listing added locations for monographs which appear in the catalogues.

Listed below are printed and microfiche Author Catalogues (AD13-AD15); Subject Catalogues (AD16-AD17) and Author/Subject Catalogues (AD18-AD19)

For more complete information and a brief history of Library of Congress catalogues see *Sheehy* (AC4)

AD13 Library of Congress. **The Main Catalog of the Library of Congress 1898–1980.** New York: K.G. Saur, 1984- 1989. microfiche.

The world's most comprehensive library catalogue, it includes items catalogued or re-catalogued between 1898 and 1980 at Library of Congress. Once filmed for this project, no further changes are made in the card catalog.
ZL533 mfe

*   *   *   *

AD14 Library of Congress. **The National Union Catalog Pre-1956 Imprints: A Cumulative Author List Representing Library of Congress Printed Cards and Titles Reported by Other American Libraries.** 754 vols. London: Mansell, 1968–82. Includes *Supplement* 70 vols., 1980–81.

Supplement (vols. 686–754), includes material accumulated since editorial work began.

Known as "Mansell", this catalogue has a reputation as the last of the monumental printed catalogues, with some 12 million items (books, pamphlets, periodicals, maps, atlases, music and ephemera) in many languages and for all disciplines. *Pre-1956* is the largest, most comprehensive, single record, in print form, of the world's historic literature.

Supersedes the basic LC set, the *Catalog of Books Represented by Library of Congress Printed Cards Issued to July 31, 1942*, (167 vols., Edwards, 1942–1946) (R018.1 N275 or Z881 A1C3); and *Author Catalogues* covering *1942–1947* (42 vols., Edwards, 1948); *1948–1952*, (24 vols., Edwards, 1953); *1952–1955* (30 vols., Edwards, 1961).
Z881 A1U372

AD15 Library of Congress. **The National Union Catalog: 1956 Through 1967.** 125 vols. New York: Rowman and Littlefield, 1970–72.

A continuation of *Pre–1956*, (AD14). Cumulates two earlier series of *NUC*: *1958–1962* (54 vols, Rowman and Littlefield, 1963) (FLIS); *1963–1967* (72 vols. Edwards, 1969) (FLIS).

Continued by sets covering *1968–1972* (128 volumes, Edwards, 1973) (FLIS); *1973–1977* (135 volumes, Rowman and Littlefield, 1978) (FLIS). Continued in a monthly format from *1978–1982*, with a multi-volume annual cumulation (FLIS). Annual cumulations of *NUC* in print format ceased with the 1982 set, and

from January, 1983, Library of Congress began publication of *NUC* in microfiche only, (see AD18).
R018.1 N277   or   Z881 A1U352

AD16   Library of Congress. **Subject Catalog,** 1950- . Washington: Library of Congress. monthly; quarterly, annual, quinquennial cumulative 1950 through 1974; [1975–1980, to be announced]. Annual cumulations: *1975* (18 vols); *1976* (17 vols); *1977* (15 vols); *1978* (19 vols); 1979, (21 vols); *1988* (no cumulation); *1981* (15 vols); *1982* (17 vols).

Quinquennial cumulations noted below, AD17. Ceased, incorporated in *NUC Books* (AD18), 1983-. Catalogues from 1950–82 available on microfiche.
R017 U58

AD17   Library of Congress. **Library of Congress Catalog - Books: Subject: A Cumulative List of Works Represented by Library of Congress Printed Cards.** Ann Arbor, MI: J.W. Edwards, 1955.

Originally published monthly by Library of Congress, (see *Subject Catalog* above), a series of quinquennial cumulations was published commercially, by Edwards, (unless otherwise noted) *1950–1954* (20 vols, 1955); *1955–1959* (22 vols, Pageant, 1960); *1960–1964* (25 vols., 1965); *1965–1969* (42 vols, 1970); *1970–1974* (100 vols, Rowman and Littlefield, 1976).

Includes entries for books, pamphlets, serials, maps and atlases arranged by subject. Entries are primarily current publications.
R017 U58   or   Z881 A1U376

AD18   Library of Congress. **National Union Catalog. Books,** 1983- . Washington: Library of Congress. monthly; cumulative index. microfiche publication.

Cumulations in the twelve monthly issues are complete within one year, and do not carry forward into the next year. *NUC Books* consolidates information formerly included in the printed paper editions, *National Union Catalog*: *Cumulative Author List,   Subject Catalog, Monographic Series,* and *Chinese Cooperative Catalog.*

Arranged in two registers. One register with the full record and one register with four cumulative indexes (name, title, LC subject, LC series). The scope is somewhat altered from *NUC* (AD15); *NUC Books* contains records for monographs, pamphlets, printed sheets and some microforms in Roman alphabets and with Romanized records for various scripts catalogued by LC or by the contributing institutions. Available online on LCMARC. and on CD-ROM as *Current Cataloging Database.*
R018.1 N277B mfe

AD19   Library of Congress. **National Union Catalog. U.S. Books,** 1983- . Washington: Library of Congress. monthly; cumulative index. microfiche publication.

Cumulations in the twelve monthly issues are complete within one year, and do not carry forward into the next year. *NUC U.S. Books* is the first U.S. national bibliography to be published by LC. It is similar to *NUC Books*, (above), but, its scope is restricted to items bearing U.S. imprints in all languages; including monographs, pamphlets, printed sheets as well as some microforms and atlases in book form. LC provides this catalogue as being "of particular interest to small and medium-sized libraries." Available online as *LCMARC: Books U.S.*

*   *   *   *

National and Trade Bibliographies

Canada

LIBRARY CATALOGUES

See also the National Library Catalogues for Great Britain, and United States (AD7 - AD19) which contain Canadian materials, and Government Publications AM6 - AM80. See also Regional Bibliographies, AD38 to AD57.

AD20 Gagnon, Philéas. **Essai de bibliographie canadienne: inventaire d'une bibliothèque comprenant imprimés, manuscrits, estampes, etc., relatifs à l'histoire du Canada et des pays adjacents avec des notes bibliographiques.** 2 vols. Québec: L'Auteur, 1895. *Ajoutes à la collection* (La Patrie, 1913). Reprint/ Brown, 1962.

Includes books, pamphlets, periodicals, autographs, manuscripts, prints. This private collection served as nucleus of the Montreal Public Library.
015.71 G13 (SC)   or   Z1365 G2

AD21 **The Lawrence Lande Collection of Canadiana in the Redpath Library of McGill University.** Montreal: Lawrence Lande Foundation for Canadian Historical Research, 1965. 301 p. *Rare and Unusual Canadiana: First Supplement to the Lande Bibliography*, (1971, 779 p.).

The collection, "a valuable, unique and historically significant accumulation" of manuscripts, maps, pictures, prints, published or unpublished items relating to Canadian political, cultural, economic development, is now in the National Archives of Canada. *The Edgar and Dorothy Davidson Collection of Canadiana at Mount Allison University* (Centre for Canadian Studies, Mount Allison University, 1991) is an illustrated bibliography describing 600 early imprints from the 17th to 19th centuries. The items are in five sections covering the French and English context, Arctic exploration, the western frontier, and early Canadian imprints.
R015.71 M145   or   Z1365 M35

AD22 Toronto Public Library. **A Bibliography of Canadiana: Being Items in the Public Library ... Relating to the Early History and Development of Canada.** Ed. by Frances M. Staton and Marie Tremaine. Toronto: Toronto Public Library, 1934. 828 p. *First Supplement* by G.M. Boyle and M. Colbeck, 1959. *Second Supplement* ed. by Sandra Alston, assisted by Karen Evans, 4 vols, 1984–1989.

Items are arranged by date of subject matter to form a chronological record of the history and development of Canada to 1867. Included are T.P.L. holdings of pre-Confederation Canadian imprints (books, pamphlets, broadsides, government publications) to 1841 held in the library and material on Canadian subjects from 1534 to 1867 wherever printed. The entry describes Toronto Public Library's copy. Author index, with some title and subject entries.

Second Supplement describes some 3,500 titles acquired by the library since 1959, arranged by imprint date. In 4 volumes, 1: *1511–1800*; 2: *1801–1849*; 3: 1850–1867. Volume 4 contains eight computer generated indexes to the *Second Supplement* for names (including illustrators), titles, subjects, illustrations, maps and plans, place of publication, printers and publishers.
R015.71 T68B incl. supplements

RETROSPECTIVE BIBLIOGRAPHIES

Retrospective Materials are arranged chronologically by date of coverage. Current Materials which follow are arranged alphabetically.

AD23 **Canada's Printed Record: A Bibliographic Register with Indexes / Catalogue d'imprimés canadiens: répertoire bibliographique avec index.** [Ottawa]: Canadian Institute for Historical Microreproductions, 1982. microfiche publication.

A catalogue of the items microfilmed by CIHM, established 1978 by the Canada Council.

Working with NLC, it is developing a collection of pre-1900 Canadiana in microform. Includes monographs, pamphlets, annuals and serials and printed ephemera. Excludes newspapers and government publications.

The catalogue is modelled on the *Canadiana* (AD35) format of register and indexes. CIHM records available online.
015.71 C212C Microfiche area.

AD24 Amtmann, Bernard. **Contributions to a Short-title Catalogue of Canadiana.** 4 vols. Montreal: Bernard Amtmann Inc., 1971-73.

Lists about 45,000 books and pamphlets, relating to Canada, compiled from listings in the Amtmann catalogues since 1950.
R015.71 AB522

AD25 Waldon, Freda Farrell. **Bibliography of Canadiana Published in Great Britain, 1519–1763.** Rev. and enl. ed. by William F.E. Morley. Toronto: ECW Press, in association with the National Library of Canada, 1990. 535 p.

"Includes books, pamphlets, maps, broadsides, and broadsheets which concern in some way any part of the present area of Canada." About 865 titles are listed in chronological arrangement. Canadian locations provided when available.
R015.71 W165B   or   Z1365 W27

AD26 Tremaine, Marie. **A Bibliography of Canadian Imprints, 1751–1800.** Toronto: University of Toronto Press, 1952. 705 p.

The compiler's aim was to include every item printed in Canada from 1751 to 1800, including those no longer extant. A detailed bibliographical description of a perfect copy is given, indicating line endings on the title page and the number of leaves in each signature. Entries are arranged chronologically by imprint date, with author, subject and distinctive title index. Locations are given. All titles still available were microfilmed by NLC and all newspapers were microfilmed by CLA. A new edition is in progress.
R015.71 T71   or   Z1365 T7

AD27 Morgan, Henry J. **Bibliotheca Canadensis: Or, A Manual of Canadian Literature.** Ottawa: G.E. Desbarats, 1867. 411 p. Reprint / Gale Research, 1968.

Materials published from 1760 to 1867 in Canada, about Canada or written by Canadians in English or French. Includes books, periodical articles, pamphlets with short description and note on the authors.
015.71 M84

AD28 Amtmann, Bernard **Early Canadian Children's Books, 1763–1840 / Livres de l'enfance et livres de la jeunesse au Canada.** Montreal: B. Amtmann Inc. 1976. 151 p.

Supplemented by *A Bibliography of Canadian*

Children's Books and Books for Young People 1841–1867/ Livres de l'enfance et livres de la jeunesse au Canada (Amtmann, 1977). Arranged to note, first, items published in Canada and writings of Canadians published abroad, and, secondly, writings of non-Canadians relating to Canada or the Canadian Arctic published abroad.
R809.89282 AA528E/EA

AD29 Haight, Willet Ricketson. **Canadian Catalogue of Books, 1791–1895.** Toronto: Author, 1896. 130 p. *Supplement 1896* (1898); *1897* (1904). Reprint / London: H. Pordes, 1958.

The main volume is a retrospective list with the annual supplements planned as a tool for the publishing trade. Arranged by author with title and chronological indexes.
R015.71 H14

AD30   Canadiana, 1867–1900, Monographs. 1980– . Ottawa: National Library of Canada. irregular. cumulated indexes. microfiche.

Each new issue cumulates all records listed in earlier editions, with additions, revisions, and corrections.

Includes books, pamphlets, leaflets, offprints, broadsides; excludes official publications, serials (with some exceptions), newspapers and maps. Also lists foreign monographs from the period which are of special interest to Canadian studies. Locations in Canadian libraries noted. Format is a register for full bibliographic record with five indexes,   A: Author/Title/Series; B: Chronological; C: Publishers, Printers; D: Places of Publication, Printing; E: Subjects.
R015.71C21BA mfe   or   ZC453 mfe

AD31   A Check List of Canadian Imprints, 1900–1925. Comp. by Dorothea D. Tod and Audrey Cordingley. Ottawa: Canadian Bibliographic Centre, 1950. 370 p.

Intended as a preliminary checklist, to fill a gap in Canadian bibliography, with entries arranged alphabetically by author. Excludes pamphlets, government publications, serials, and has no index or annotations.
R015.71 T63

AD32   The Canadian Catalogue of Books: Published in Canada, About Canada, as well as Those Written by Canadians, with Imprint 1921–1949. 2 vols. Toronto: Toronto Public Libraries, 1959. Reissued as a consolidated English language reprint with cumulated author index. 1 vol., 1967.

Volume 1, 1929–1939. Volume 2, 1940–1949. Author indexes in each volume.
Canadian Catalogue of Books was prepared annually by the TPL, and included books, pamphlets and selected government publications. The cumulation retains the arrangement by year and broad class, but does not include French language books which appeared irregularly in the original edition. *Notices en langue française du Canadian Catalogue of Books 1921–1949*, (Reprint / Bibliothèque nationale du Québec, 1975) (R015.71 T68CD) consolidates the French listings in one volume. Superseded by *Canadiana*, AD35.
R015.71 T68CC

*   *   *   *

CURRENT BIBLIOGRAPHIES

AD33 Canadian Books In Print: Author and Title Index, 1967- . Toronto: University of Toronto Press, 1968- . annual; quarterly supplement, 1980- (in microfiche only).

Contains English language books published in Canada and currently in print, bearing a Canadian publisher's imprint or works originated by Canadian subsidiaries of international publishers. From 1967–1973, title was bilingual to demonstrate inclusions, i.e. *CBIP / Catalogue des livres canadiens en librairie.* French language titles now in *Liste des livres disponibles...* (AD36).

CBIP includes imprints, available as of August, from Canadian publishers or subsidiaries; with a directory of publishers. Microfiche supplements are completely revised and updated.

Non-English language material is included if items are published by an English language Canadian publisher. General interest items published by the government and available through (trade) book stores are included; maps, sheet music, newspapers, periodicals, catalogues, annuals or materials not of general interest are excluded. Available online.
R014.71 C212A   or   Z1365 C22

AD34 Canadian Books in Print: Subject Index, 1975- . Toronto: University of Toronto Press, 1974- . annual.

In three sections, 1) list of subject headings with cross references; 2) the subject index, with headings based on *Library of Congress Subject Headings* and the supplementary *Canadian List* published by CLA; and 3) the publisher index (a directory). Biographies are included by placing them under a subject (e..g. Biography - Science); also includes literary works (and children's literature) entered under form headings (drama, poetry, fiction).
R015.71 C212A   or   Z1365 C221A

AD35 Canadiana: Canada's National Bibliography / La bibliographie nationale du Canada, 1950- . Ottawa: Supply and Services [for NLC], 1953- . monthly (July/August issue merged). annual cumulations. Available in print and on microfiche as *Canadiana (Microfiche).* Cumulations available on microfiche: *Canadiana 1973–1980; 1981–1985; 1986–1989.*

To 1979, subtitled "Publications of Canadian Interest Received by the National Library". Created at NLC, *Canadiana* includes material received under book deposit regulations as well as material published in other countries but written by Canadians or about Canada. Format varies. Before 1981, arranged by DDC and divided into eight parts, with Part V, (*Sound Recordings*), separately published, and with indexes for author, title, series and English or French subject headings.

From 1981, the print version adopts the format of the microfiche edition, i.e. in two parts with five indexes. Part 1: *Canadian Imprints* ; Part 2: *Foreign Imprints*, each with a register in one numerical sequence, of complete bibliographic entries, including all notes and tracing and locations. Indexes are A: *Author/Title/Series*; B: *English Subject Headings*; C: *French Subject Headings*; D: *ISBN*;; E: *ISSN*.

A ten volume index covers 1968–1976 (NLC, 1978).

Canadian material is also found in *LCMARC: Books Canada* which includes Canadian imprints or imprints relating to Canada catalogued by Library of Congress, (see AD12n).
R015.71 C21 print and mfe

AD36 La Liste des livres disponibles de langue française: Canadian French Books in Print. 1981- . Outremont, PQ: Bibliodata. quarterly; (microfiche ed. also available; 10 issues a year).

Published in 3 parts: Auteurs, Sujets, Titres. Includes imprints (books or periodicals) from Quebec province and any French language publishing from other provinces.

Catalogue de l'édition au Canada français, published from 1965 to 1970 (Z1377 F8R4), was superseded by an irregular annual *Répertoire de l'édition au Québec* (Edi-Québec) (Z1377 F8R4) published to cover the years 1972 to 1976. Publications of 1967–73 also listed in *CBIP* (AD33).
Z1365 L582

AD37 New and Forthcoming Canadian Books, 1973- . Toronto; Quill & Quire. semi-annual.

Published in June and December, and supplemented each month in *Quill & Quire* insert, *Forthcoming Books* (see AB14n). Includes Canadian trade titles published during the current six month period. Arranged by subject area. Provides bibliographic citation and ordering information, a brief abstract, age level, and month of publication.
R015.71 N532N

REGIONAL BIBLIOGRAPHIES - ATLANTIC PROVINCES

See also Government Publications AM39-AM44.

AD38 Atlantic Provinces Checklist, 1958-1966; 1972. Halifax: Atlantic Provinces Library Associaton in cooperation with the Atlantic Provinces Economic Council. annual.

Subtitled: *A Guide to Current Information in Books, Pamphlets, Government Publications and Magazine Articles Relating to the Four Atlantic Provinces.* Arrangement is by province, then by general subjects with an author index. Published annually from 1958 to Volume 9, 1966, revived with 1972 issue (1974) and then ceased.
R015.715 AA881

AD39 Fleming, Patricia. **Atlantic Canadian Imprints, 1801–1820: A Bibliography.** Toronto: University of Toronto Press, 1991. 188 p.

Descriptive bibliography with full collation and historical notes, in chronological arrangement. Includes books, pamphlets, broadsides, serials, and government publications. Continues *Tremaine* (AD26).
Z1392 A8F54

AD40 O'Dea, Agnes C. **A Bibliography of Newfoundland, 1611–1975.** 2 vols. Ed. by Anne Alexander. Toronto: University of Toronto Press in association with Memorial University, 1986. 1450 p.

A record covering five centuries for Newfoundland and Labrador.
R971.8 AO23B

REGIONAL BIBLIOGRAPHIES - QUEBEC

See also Government Publications
AM45 - AM50.

AD41 La Bibliographie de bibliographies québécoises. 2 vols. Compilé sous la direction d'Henri-Bernard Boivin. Montréal: Bibliothèque nationale du Québec, 1979. *Supplément*(s) vol. 1, 1980; vol. 2, 1981.

Set records nearly 4,000 bibliographies (books, pamphlets, theses, government publications) arranged by subject with author, title, subject index. Items are Quebec imprints or works about Quebec or by Quebec authors.
R015.714 AB582BA

AD42 **Bibliographie du Québec 1821–1967: notices établies par le Bureau de la bibliographie rétrospective, BNQ,** 25 vols. Québec: l'Éditeur officiel du Québec. Montréal: Bibliothèque nationale, 1980– in progress.

Completed to Volume 23 (Tome XXIII, 1991). Covers all monographs published in Quebec by non-government sources, held by the BNQ (about 50,000 titles). Each volume (except volume 22) in two parts; Part 1, notices; Part 2, an index with six approaches (author, editor, printer, name, place, chronology). Volumes 1-20 each contain 1,000 notices; Volumes 21-22 have 3,000 notices, Volume 23 has 5,000 notices. Volume 24 is projected to have 5,000 notices plus index, and Volume 25 will have 6,500 notices plus index. A cumulated index for volumes 1-25 is projected as well.
R015.714 B582B to Volume 10 or
Z1392 Q3B54

AD43 **Bibliographie du Québec: une mensuelle des publications québécoises,** 1968– . Montréal: Bibliothèque nationale du Québec, 1970– . monthly; annual cum. *Index* 1968–73; 1974–76; annual index, 1976–.

One volume publication for 1968; then 3 issues / year, 1969- April, 1972; then monthly. Lists items received on legal deposit at the BNQ. In two parts, books or pamphlets arranged by broad LC class and Quebec government publications. Author / title and subject index to both parts.

Catalogue de la Bibliothèque nationale du Québec is an annual microfiche publication with author/title and subject access.
R015.714 AB582B

AD44 Dionne, Narcisse-Eutrope. **Inventaire chronologique.** 4 vols. + supplement. Québec: Royal Society of Canada, 1905–12. Reprint / B. Franklin, 1969; New York: AMS Press, 1974 (5 parts in 1).

Records French-Canadian publishing from 1764 and books about Quebec published elsewhere to the publication date. Arranged chronologically by imprint.
R015.71 C59A

AD45 Hamelin, Jean, André Beaulieu, and Gilles Gallichan. **Brochures québécoises, 1764–1972.** Québec: Ministère des communications, Direction générale des publications gouvernementales, 1981. 598 p.

A checklist of some 10,000 brochures alphabetically ordered in a chronology; author, subject indexes. Entries are in language of publication. Items were compiled using libraries "particulièrement riches en brochures" and locations are given for these Quebec libraries, the Library of Parliament and the National Archives of Canada. Compilers used LC definition of a pamphlet (less than 49 pages; excluding periodicals, offprints, circulars, government publications, calendars and manuals) as a basis for inclusion but exercised their discretion to enlarge the definition and include certain monographs and documents.
R015.714 H213B

AD46 **Laurentiana parus avant 1821.** M. Vlach avec la collaboration de Y. Buono. Montreal: Bibliothèque nationale du Québec, 1976. 416 p. + 120 p. index.

Descriptive bibliography of Quebec imprints and titles about Quebec to 1820, held in BNQ. Title, name, subject, illustrator, maps and plans, place of publication, printed and imprint date indexes. *Les imprimés dans le bas-Canada*, volume 1, 1801–1810, by J. Hare and J.P. Wallot, (Presses de l'Université de Montréal, 1967) (Z1365 H37) covers books, pamphlets, broadsides and nine newspapers for the first decade of the 19th century.
R015.714 B582C

AD47 Liste des livres disponible de langue française For full entry see AD36.

AD48 Vlach, Milada, and Yolande Buono. **Catalogue collectif des impressions québécoises, 1764–1820.** Québec: Bibliothèque nationale du Québec, 1984. 195 p.
Lists Quebec imprints from the beginning of printing in Quebec (1764) to 1820, with locations in 11 Quebec libraries. Includes all typographically produced publications, excluding only serials and forms. This work, with *Bibliographie du Québec 1821–1967* (AD42) and *Bibliographie du Québec* (AD43), form a trilogy of publications covering all Quebec imprints.
R015.714 V865C   or   Z1392 Q3V5

REGIONAL BIBLIOGRAPHIES - ONTARIO

See also Government Publications
AM51 - AM55 and AM75 to AM80.

AD49 **The Bibliography of Ontario History, 1867–1976: Cultural, Economic, Political, Social,** (1980), and *Bibliography of Ontario History, 1976-1986* (1989). See CJ64 for full entry information.

AD50 Fleming, Patricia. **Upper Canadian Imprints, 1801–1841: A Bibliography.** Toronto: University of Toronto Press in cooperation with the National Library of Canada and the Canadian Government Publishing Centre, 1988. 555 p.
A descriptive bibliography with full collations and historical notes, in chronological arrangement. Indexes for name, title, place of publication, language, trades (illustrators, editors, bookbinders, publishers), genre, and subject, give access to the books, government publications, serials, pamphlets and other ephemeral items included. Continues *Tremaine* (AD26).
R015.71 F598U

REGIONAL BIBLIOGRAPHIES - WESTERN CANADA

See also Government Publications for the individual provinces and territories, AM56 - AM62.

AD51 **Alberta Bibliography 1954–1979: A Provincial Bibliography.** Comp. by Gloria M. Strathern. Edmonton: University of Alberta, 1982. 745 p.
Lists popular, scholarly works (books, theses, pamphlets, etc.) excluding serials, scientific, technical materials (some exception for agriculture) and government publications. (Complements *Peel* AD56)
Z1392 A4A45

AD52 Arora, Ved P. **The Saskatchewan Bibliography.** Regina: Saskatchewan Provincial Library, 1980. 787 p.
Nearly 6,400 entries for all forms of material, including government publications, fiction, theses, published in or about Saskatchewan from

1905 to cut-off date of 1979. Author, title, subject indexes.
R015.7124 A769S   or   Z1392 A76

AD53 Artibise, Alan F. **Western Canada Since 1870: A Select Bibliography and Guide.** Vancouver, BC: University of British Columbia, 1978. 312 p.

Arranged by subject, then by province with author, name, series indexes. Includes books, articles, and theses to 1977 in the social sciences and humanities.
Z1365 A7

AD54   A Bibliography of British Columbia. 3 vols. Victoria, BC: University of Victoria, 1968–75.

The three volumes are separately titled. *Navigations, Traffiques & Discoveries, 1774–1848* by Gloria M. Strathern; *Laying the Foundations, 1849–1899* by Barbara Lowther; *A Bibliography of British Columbia: Years of Growth, 1900–1950* by Margaret H. Edwards and John C. Lort.
R015.711 B582

AD55 Morley, Marjorie. **A Bibliography of Manitoba from Holdings in the Legislative Library of Manitoba.** Winnipeg: Legislative Library of Manitoba, 1970. 267 p.

Over 2,000 items arranged alphabetically by author; includes listing of some 300 newspapers and periodicals as well as books.
R015.712 AM864B   or   Z1392 M35M6

AD56   Peel, Bruce B. **A Bibliography of the Prairie Provinces to 1953: With Biographical Index.** 2d ed. Toronto: University of Toronto Press, 1973. 780 p.

Books and pamphlets relating to the Prairie Provinces arranged chronologically by date of publication with some exceptions, such as accounts of early travels published later but listed by date of event. Subject, title, author indexes.
R015.712 P374B2

AD57   Yukon Bibliography: 1897–1963. Ottawa: Department of Northern Affairs and National Resources, 1964. 151 p. *Yukon Bibliography Update*(s) 1964–1984.

The *Update*(s) were issued as *Boreal Institute Publications*, no. 8:1-13, compiled at the Canadian Circumpolar Institute, University of Alberta. The bibliography has a *Yukon Bibliography: Cumulated Subject Index to 1980* (1984) and *Yukon Bibliography: Cumulated Author Index to 1980* (1984). Contains descriptions of items received at the Circumpolar Institute (formerly Boreal Institute) or selected from Yukon Archives. Includes books, government and consultant reports, theses, periodical articles, and any unpublished items to which the owner provides access. Maps and nonprint items not included. Available online as *Yukon Bibliography*.
Z1392 Y816

Great Britain - Retrospective Bibliographies

See also the British Library / British Museum Catalogues (AD7-AD11) and Government Publications (AM81 - AM97).

Retrospective materials listed below are arranged chronologically by date of coverage. Current materials which follow are arranged alphabetically.

AD58 Lowndes, William Thomas. **The Bibliographer's Manual of English Literature: Containing an Account of Rare, Curious, and Useful Books, Published in or Relating to Great Britain and Ireland, from the Invention of Printing.** London: H.G. Bohn, 1858–64. Reprint / 8 vols. Detroit: Gale Research, 1967.

About 50,000 works are alphabetically arranged by author, with some titles or catchwords.
R015.42 L919

AD59 Watt, Robert. **Bibliotheca Britannica: Or, A General Index to British and Foreign Literature.** 4 vols. Edinburgh: Constable, 1824. Reprint / New York: Burt Franklin, [1965].

Volumes 1-2: author list with biographical and book information; volumes 3-4: subject list. Includes 40,000 authors from early British printers to about 1800. Watt's work was used and corrected by Samuel Allibone in his *A Critical Dictionary of English Literature and British and American Authors: Living and Deceased from the Earliest Accounts to the Latter Half of the Nineteenth Century*, (5 vols, 1863–91, reprint, Gale Research, 1965) (R820.9 A43A). Allibone's biographical dictionary is primarily of historical interest for its many minor authors, together with notes on their works.
R011 W346

AD60 Pollard, A.W., and G.R. Redgrave. **A Short-Title Catalogue of Books Printed in England, Scotland & Ireland and of English Books Printed Abroad, 1475–1640.** London: Bibliographical Society, 1926. 609 p.

2d revised, enlarged, and corrected edition compiled by W.A. Jackson, F.S. Ferguson and K.F. Pantzer: Vol. 1, *A-H* (1986); Vol. 2, *I-Z* (1976); supplementary volume forthcoming (Bibliographical Society, 1976-)(R015.42 P77S2).

Catalogue of extant titles, in brief form, arranged by author according to the British Museum rules; no indexing. Gives a limited number of locations, mostly British. Related material includes *A Checklist of American Copies ...* of STC locations in North American libraries by W.W. Bishop (Greenwood Press, 1968 c.1950) (015.42 B62); and *An Index of Printers, Publishers and Booksellers...* by Paul G. Morrison (University of Virginia Library, 1950).
R015.42 P77

AD61 Wing, Donald. **Short-title Catalogue of Books Printed in England, Scotland, Ireland, Wales and British America and of English Books Printed in Other Countries, 1641–1700.** 3 vols. New York: Columbia University Press, 1945–51.

Second revised and enlarged edition includes new titles, locations, and corrections to the first edition (edited by Timothy Crist, 3 vols. Modern Language Association, 1972-1982) (R015.42 W769S2).

Continues Pollard and Redgrave's *STC* (AD60), listing publications with locations. An *Index of Printers, Publishers and Booksellers* compiled by Paul G. Morrison, (1955). Wing compiled *A Gallery of Ghosts* (Modern Language Assocation, 1967) (R015.42 W769A) adding about 5,000 entries.
R015.42 W769S

AD62 **The Eighteenth Century Short Title Catalogue.** Ed. by Robin C. Alston. London: British Library, 1977–1983. 175 microfiche. new file forthcoming.

ESTC includes every notable item printed in any language in Great Britain and its colonies, or printed in English anywhere in the world from 1701–1800. Excludes some ephemera, newspapers, serials, maps, or music. It is an author/title file (with added entries) and with indexes by date and place of publication, and by selected genres. Available online and on CD-ROM.

The 1983 file included only holdings of the British Library. Forthcoming file includes also the holdings of over 1,000 libraries worldwide. Since 1983, Research Publications has produced a microfilm collection of the titles listed in *ESTC*. Arranged in units of 35 microfilm reels, by broad subject (religion, philosophy, fine arts, science and technology, etc.) (DA485 E54 1982 MICR mfm). *Factotum*, (PER), the ESTC newsletter outlines history and progress of the *ESTC* project.
ZB7576

AD63 The Nineteenth Century Short Title Catalogue. Newcastle upon Tyne, U.K.: Avero Publications, 1984- in progress.

The *NSTC* is planned to cover 1801 through 1918 in three series (I: *1801–15*; II: *1816–1870*; III: *1871–1918*) with multiple volumes in each series. Series I, now complete with 6 volumes, is a union catalogue of all books in English wherever published, held by the Bodleian Library; British Library; University Library Cambridge; Library of Trinity College, Dublin; National Library of Scotland; University Library, Newcastle. Series II, currently completed to Volume 23 (Kieg-Lecom), and Series III will also include the holdings of Library of Congress and Harvard University Library.

NSTC lists works published in the U.K., its colonies, the U.S., books published in English or translations from English published anywhere in the world. Author entry in each volume; a final volume has general sections on directories, periodicals, ephemera, with headings for England, Ireland, Scotland, London, plus a subject/imprint index and fiche addenda for titles in alphabetical order. Books published in Great Britain during the 19th century and the first half of the 20th century were listed in the standard trade list, *The English Catalogue of Books, 1801-1968* (015.42 E58), which is still useful for retrospective searching.
Z2001 N652

Great Britain - Current Bibliographies

AD64 The British National Bibliography, 1950- . London: British Library, Bibliographic Services Division. weekly; interim, annual cumulation, 1964- . (in 2 vols); microfiche ed. available, 1981- .

Cumulates into Volume 1: *Subject Catalogue*; Volume 2: *Indexes*. Includes books, newspapers, periodicals, government publications, pamphlets, maps, and printed music, received on legal deposit at the British Library. From 1977 has CIP entries for forthcoming titles. Entries in *BNB* are in full cataloguing form, arranged by modified DDC, with author/title series index in each weekly issue. Last issue for each month contains cumulated author, title, and *PRECIS* subject index. Cumulated subject catalogues (1951–54; 1955–59; 1960–64; 1965–67; 1968–70) and cumulated index catalogues (1950–54; 1955–57; 1960–64; 1965–67; 1968–70; 1971–73) are available. *BNB* is available online on *BNBMARC Online* (formerly *UKMARC*; and on CD-ROM (as *BNB CD-ROM*) with all records for the years 1950–85 on an archival file, and with a current file (1986-) updated quarterly. *Books in English 1970–86*, (continued semi-monthly) is microfiche, with annual cumulations.
R015.42 B862R

AD65 Whitaker's Book List, 1924- . London: J. Whitaker & Sons. annual.

Continues *Whitaker's Cumulative Book List*. Until 1984, issued quarterly with annual

cumulation. Published in April, *WBL* is an alphabetical author/ title list with some subject access supplied by an abbreviation or by subject as part of a title. Whitaker series is based on the author-title lists in the weekly trade periodical, *The Bookseller* (PER), which lists publications of the past week, and on the monthly periodical, *Whitaker's Books of the Month & Books to Come* (PER) which lists new titles of the past month plus forthcoming titles for two months ahead. Available on CD-ROM on Whitaker's *BOOKBANK*.
R015.42 W57

AD66 **Whitaker's Books in Print,** 1965- . 4 vols. London: J. Whitaker & Sons. annual. microfiche ed. available, 1983- . monthly.

Supersedes *British Books in Print*, and earlier titles, (1874–). Author, title, keyword subject in one alphabetical sequence listing more than 475,000 titles from over 15,500 publishers with directory information and ISBN prefixes. Includes "books published in the United Kingdom as well as books published worldwide which are printed in the English language and which are available in Western Europe from an exclusive stockholding agent." Appears in the Fall recording books available at the end of March of the same year. A monthly cumulative edition, (1978-, microfiche) also includes forthcoming books. Updated weekly in *The Bookseller* and *Whitaker's Weekly List on Microfiche*. Available on CD-ROM on *BOOKBANK*.

Specialist titles such as *Whitaker's Religious Books in Print* (1991-) provide author, title, keyword arrangement with a classified index. *Children's Books in Print*, (title formerly *Whitaker's Children's Books in Print*, 1969-), lists children's books available in the U.K. by title and classification.
R015.42 B862P

AD67 **Whitaker's Classified Monthly Book List,** 1983- . London: J. Whitaker & Sons. monthly.

Books published in the U.K. during the month plus books forthcoming within ensuing two months. Books are entered under 53 subject headings including divisions within fiction (e.g. historical, war, short stories). Main entry, with full order information, is alphabetical by author, editor, (or first significant word in title) within each classification. Whitaker's, the major U.K. book trade publisher, also prepares trade directories, e.g. *Whitaker's Publishers in the United Kingdom and Their Addresses* (R070.5042541 W578W).
R015.42 W57

United States - Retrospective Bibliographies

See also Library of Congress and Nation Union Catalogues (AD12-AD19) and Government Publications (AM98 - AM125).

Retrospective materials are listed chronologically by date of coverage, followed by current materials arranged alphabetically.

AD68 Sabin, Joseph. **A Dictionary of Books Relating to America, From Its Discovery to the Present Time.** New York: Sabin, 1868–92; 29 vols. Bibliographical Society of America, 1928–36. Reprint / 15 vols. Amsterdam: N. Israel, 1961–62.

Also known as *Bibliotheca Americana*. It includes books, pamphlets, periodicals, some government publications printed in North America, works about North America printed elsewhere from 1493–1892. Indexing provided by John E. Molnar's *Author Title Index to Joseph Sabin's Dictionary...* (3 vols, Scarecrow,

1974) (R015.73 S116A). Titles listed in Sabin are available on microfiche, (Lost Cause Press). R015.73 S116

AD69 Thompson, Lawrence S. **The New Sabin: Books Described by Joseph Sabin and his Successors, Now Described Again on the Basis of Examination of Originals, and Fully Indexed by Title, Subject, Joint Authors, and Institutions and Agencies.** Troy, NY: Whitston Pub. Co., 1974- In progress. *Cumulative Index*, volumes 1-10. 1986.

Completed to Volume 10, 1984; each volume with separate index. Lists works from the same period as Sabin, although not all are in Sabin. R917.303 A7473N (vols 1-6) or Z1201 S3

AD70 Evans, Charles. **American Bibliography: A Chronological Dictionary of all Books, Pamphlets and Periodicals Printed in the United States of America from the Genesis of Printing in 1639 Down to and Including the Year 1820, with Bibliographical and Biographical Notes.** Chicago: Privately Printed for the Author, 1903-34. Vols. 1-12. Worcester, MA: American Antiquarian Society, 1955-59. Vols. 13-14. Reprint / Gloucester, MA: P. Smith, 1967. *Supplement* (University Press of Virginia, 1970).

Evans' intention was to take entries to 1820, but he only reached 1799. In 1955 the bibliography was completed through 1800. Entries are arranged by year, subarranged by author or other main entry; author/title indexes in each volume. Volume 14 is a cumulated index to authors and titles. The supplement, by Roger P. Bristol, adds 11,000 items.

The *National Index of American Imprints Through 1800: the Short-Title Evans,* prepared by Clifford K. Shipton and James E. Mooney (American Antiquarian Society, 1969), includes items from *Evans*, with additions and corrections in one alphabetical order with locations (R015.71 E92A).

Early American Imprints 1639–1800 (Readex Film Products, 1981-82) (AC E274 MICR) is a microform set of the items in Evans, arranged according to Evans numbers. It corrects Evans which "while still embodying a work of considerable achievement ... lost considerable eminence," and adds 12,000 overlooked works. R015.73 E92

AD71 **American Bibliography: A Preliminary Checklist for 1801–1819.** 22 vols. Comp. by Ralph R. Shaw and Richard H. Shoemaker. New York: Scarecrow Press, 1958–66.

A continuation of Evans (above). Associated aids include a *Title Index* (1965); *Corrections and Author Index* (1966); and *American Bibliography ... Printers, Publishers and Booksellers Index, Geographical Index,* (1983) compiled by Frances P. Newton. This latter work in 3 sections: 1) Printer/ Publisher/ Bookseller Names; 2) Geographical Place Names; and 3) Omissions, which lists ghosts and other erroneous entries, (Z1215 N58).
R015.73 S535

AD72 **A Checklist of American Imprints,** 1820- . Metuchen, NJ: Scarecrow Press, 1964- In progress .

Continues *American Bibliography* (Shaw and Shoemaker, AD71); *Checklist... 1820–1829*, compiled by Richard H. Shoemaker; Supplemented by *Title Index, 1820–29* (1972), *Author Index, Corrections And Sources, 1820–1829* (1973). *Checklist... 1830-1839* (various compilers), 1975–1988). Supplemented by *Title Index* (1989).

Will replace various individual bibliographies, e.g. Roorbach's *Bibliotheca Americana, 1852–61* (R015.73 R779) and Kelly's *The American Catalogue of Books ... Published in the United States From January 1861 to January 1871* (R015.73 K29) in an attempt to bring the sequence into the 1870s.
R015.73 S559

AD73 American Catalogue of Books, 1876–1910. New York: Publishers Weekly, 1876–1910. Reprint / New York: P. Smith, 1941.

Cumulates *Annual American Catalog*. Comprehensive list based on publishers' reports. The "Books-in-Print" of the period.
Z1215 A5

AD74 Books in Series: Original, Reprinted, Inprint, and Out-of-print Books, Published or Distributed in the U.S. in Popular, Scholarly and Professional Series. New York: R.R. Bowker, 1982-1989.

Title changed from *Books in Series in the United States*. Published in three sets: *1876–1949* (3 vols, 1982); *1950–1984* (6 vols, 1985); and *1985–1989* (2 vols, 1989). Foreign titles appear if available from a U.S. distributor. Includes a directory of publishers and distributors. Most recent volume available online and on CD-ROM.
Z1215 B63/ B63/5

United States - Current Bibliographies

AD75 American Book Publishing Record, 1960- . New York: R.R. Bowker. monthly; annual. *ABPR Cumulative 1876–1949*, (14 vols. 1980); *1950–1977*, (15 vols., 1979); *1975–1979*, (5 vols., 1981, microfiche available).

Annual volumes called *American BPR Annual*. *ABPR* cumulates *Weekly Record* (AD81). A classified listing by Dewey Decimal System, with separate sections for adult and juvenile fiction. Author/title/subject indexes. Microfiche cumulations available covering 1876–1981; 1970–1974; 1975–1979. Index covering 1876–1981 available on microfiche.
R015.73 A51   or   Z1219 A54

AD76 Books in Print, 1948- . 8 vols. New York: R.R. Bowker. annual. mid-year *Supplement*.

"The record of U.S. publishing activity." Lists well over 860,000 books from approximately 32,000 publishers. Books published and distributed in the U.S. are listed in separate author and title volumes. *BIP* covers primarily current and trade books in any binding (e.g. paperback, spiral) with publishers' directory. Published in the Fall for books available to July; the *Supplement* published in the Spring lists books published after July and forthcoming titles, revisions, address changes, etc. Separate volumes include *Publishers Index* and *OP/OSI* (Out-of-Print and Out-of-Stock-Indefinitely) volumes. Older out-of-print titles are listed in *Books-Out-of-Print* (1980–1983; 1984–1988) and are now listed on CD-ROM on *Books-Out-of-Print Plus*.

Subject Guide to Books in Print (5 volumes, 1957- annual) (R015.73 P97AB) is published simultaneously with *Books in Print*, and indexes nearly 700,000 non-fiction titles under Library of Congress subject headings with cross-references. Includes separate *Subject Thesaurus* useful for CD-ROM and online searching.

Both *BIP* and *SGBIP* are available on microfiche, online and on CD-ROM as *Books in Print Plus* with quarterly updates.

Separate volumes are also available for

children's books (see BD162); elementary/high school books; medical; scientific and technical books (see DA8); large type books, etc. These usually list serials as well. Serials in print are also listed in Ulrich's (AE13).
R015.73 P97A

AD77 Cumulative Book Index: A World List of Books in the English Language, 1898- . New York: H.W. Wilson. monthly, annual.

CBI records current publishing (excluding government publications, periodicals, maps, music, pamphlets) in one list by author, title, subject, series, editor and translator. English language books from countries other than the U.S., U.K. and Canada are listed by country at the beginning of each monthly issue. Directory of publishers and distributors in the back of annual volumes. Available online and on CD-ROM on *Wilson Line/Disc*, which also notes out-of-print items.

CBI was cumulated in four editions (covering 1898–1928) of *The United States Catalog: Books in Print*. The most useful of these is the 4th (1928) edition, (R011 C971 or Z1215 U6).
R011 C971A

AD78 Forthcoming Books: Now Including Subject Guide to Forthcoming Books, 1966- . New York: R.R. Bowker. bimonthly.

Each issue has author and title listings of books to be published for the next five months, as well as books published since the previous summer. From January 1989 publishers provide annotated entries for many titles which they designate important. Available on microfiche, online and on CD-ROM on *Books in Print Plus*.
R015.73 F739B

AD79 Paperbound Books in Print, 1955- . 3 vols. New York: R.R. Bowker. biennial.

Title, author and subject listings of more than 376,000 titles. Available online and on CD-ROM on *Books in Print Plus*.
R015.73 P214   or   Z1033 P3P32

AD80 The Publishers' Trade List Annual, 1873- . 44 vols. New York: R.R. Bowker. annual.

PTLA is a compilation of U.S. and Canadian publishers' catalogues and booklists in alphabetical order by publisher. Includes overseas publishers with U.S. agents plus a special large section of small or specialty press firms. All titles in catalogues are indexed, and catalogues themselves are indexed by subject. *The Publishers' Trade List Annual 1903–1980* (1983) is a microfiche publication giving year-by-year coverage; cloth and fiche indexes.
R015.73 P97   or   Z1215 P97

AD81 Weekly Record, 1974- . New York: R.R. Bowker.

Formerly included in *Publishers Weekly* (AB13). Current American book listings, with cataloguing entries, for about 800 new titles each week. Excludes government publications, subscription books, dissertations, pamphlets, periodicals, most school texts, specialized works. Mass market paperbacks, reprints, annuals and yearbooks listed only if item sent to R.R. Bowker for inclusion. Arranged by main entry with LC/CIP cataloguing. Cumulates into *ABPR* (AD75) which provides subject approach.
R015.73 A51B

*   *   *   *

International

International Books in Print, listed below, provides international coverage to English language publishing. See National Library Catalogues (AD5-AD19) for materials published anywhere in the world. National bibliography for France and Germany is listed below. For additional information or information on other national or trade bibliographies, see listings of various bibliographies in *Sheehy*, (AC4).

AD82   International Books in Print, 1980- . 4 vols. Munich: K.G. Saur, 1979- . biennial. *Subject Guide* 1984- (2 vols). Available on microfiche.

Subtitled: *English Language Titles Published in Africa, Asia, Australia, Canada, Continental Europe, Latin America, New Zealand, Oceania, and the Republic of Ireland*. Part 1: *Author Title List* in one alphabetical sequence for authors, or main entries, and titles; Part 2: *Subject Guide* arranged in modified Dewey classes plus a separate country arrangement.

Lists 185,000 in-print English language fiction, nonfiction, books, microforms, pamphlets, trade and non-trade items from 113 countries. Excludes only publications of U.S. and U.K. Includes directory information on publishers, including U.S. and U.K. distributors of foreign publications.

A number of "in-print" sources (many distributed by R.R. Bowker or Gale Research) are available for various countries, e.g. *Libros en Venta* for Latin American and Spanish books; *Italian Books in Print*; *Australian Books in Print*, etc.
Z1011 I5

FRANCE

AD83   Bibliographie de la France: Bibliographie officielle, 1972- . Paris: Cercle de la librairie.   weekly; quarterly, with annual cumulation.

Title varies. Continues numbering of *Bibliographie de la France* (1811–1971) which merged with *Biblio, Catalogue des ouvrages parus en langues française dans le monde entier*, (1934–1970) .

Includes publications, maps, music received on legal deposit at the Bibliothèque nationale.

Weekly classed lists, now titled *Livres-hebdo*, cumulate into *Les livres du mois*. These are further cumulated into quarterly and semi-annual publications (*Trois mois de nouveautés, Six mois de nouveautés*), and annually into *Un an de nouveautés*, (Z2165 L573). Supplemented by *Publications officielles*.

Available on CD-ROM as *La bibliographie nationale française (BNF) depuis 1975 sur CD-ROM*, (Paris: Chadwyck-Healey France, quarterly).
R015.44 AB582B   or   Z2165 B58/ L55

AD84   Les Livres disponibles/French Books in Print, 1977- . 6 vols. Paris: Cercle de la Librairie. annual. available on microfiche.

Supersedes *Catalogue de l'édition française* (1970–1976) and *Répertoire des livres disponibles* (1972–77). Author, title, subject volumes provide worldwide coverage of French language publishing; inclusion is to July 1st of the year previous to publication. Also available is *La liste exhaustive des ouvrages publiés en langue française dans le monde*; *La liste des éditeurs et la liste des collections de langue française*; and *Les livres au format de poche, répertoire* (annual, 1981-).
Z2161 L82

GERMANY

AD85 Gesamtverzeichnis des Deutschsprachigen Schriftums, 1700–1910; 1911–1965. 160 vols; 150 vols. Munich: K.G. Saur, 1976–86. Available on microfiche.

These (*GV*) bibliographies of German language publications cumulate three national and several quasi-national bibliographies and university library retrospective catalogues including Austria and Switzerland. Does not replace current national bibliographies since subject indexes are not integrated and some sources are only partly represented. *GV 1911–1965* however does combine in one alphabet some 3 million main title and subsidiary entries; it includes books, maps, journals and non-trade publications (e.g. theses).

K.G. Saur is also publishing *Bayerisches Staatsbibliothek Alphabetischer Katalog, 1501–1840*, which has valuable collections of early printed works. A 60 volume *Preliminary Edition* published 1987–90, (Z929 B39). Final edition (1993–) will be 80 volumes.
Z2231 G4

AD86 Deutsche Bibliographie: Wochentliches Verzeichnis. 1947– . Frankfurt a.M.: Buchhandler-Vereinigung GmbH. weekly; semi-annual, quinquennial cumulations.

Includes publications for all of Germany, as well as German language publications issued elsewhere. Issued in series at different frequencies, A: trade (weekly); B: non-trade (monthly); and C: maps (bimonthly); H: theses; N: new publications. Available on CD-ROM covering 1986– (updated yearly).
Z2221 D4632

AD87 Deutsche Nationalbibliographie und Bibliographie der im Ausland Erschienenen Deutschsprachigen Shriftums. 1931– . Leipzig: Verlag für Buch und bibliothekswesen. weekly; quarterly, annual, quadrenniel/quinquennial cumulations.

Quinquennial titles *Deutsches Bücher Verzeichnis*. Similar in coverage to *DB* (AD86). In three parts, issued at different frequencies: trade (weekly), non-trade (semi-monthly), dissertations (monthly).
Z2221 D4532 02

AD88 Verzeichnis Lieferbarer Bücher / German Books in Print, 1971/72– . 6 vols. Frankfurt a.M.: Verlag der Buchhandler-Vereinigung, GmbH. annual, semi-annual (Spring) supplements.

Items in *VLB* are from publishers in Germany, Austria, Switzerland and other countries, with author, title, keyword approaches. Set includes separate indexes of series and of publishers. To complete the *VLB* set, there are four additional publications, *ISBN Index*, 1978– ; *Subject Guide*, 1978– ; *Spring Supplement*; and *ISBN Index to Spring Supplement*.
R015.43 V574   or   Z2221 V4

Buying Guides

Rare, Out-of-Print Materials

AD89 American Book-Prices Current, 1894/95– . Washington, CT: Bancroft, Parkman Inc. annual; quadrennial/quinquennial cumulation.

Subtitled: *A Record of Literary Properties Sold at Auction in the United States and in London, England*. In two parts; Part 1: Books, Broadsides, Maps and Charts; Part 2: Autographs and Manuscripts. Gives details and prices of items sold. Most recent index covers

1983–1987 (2 volumes). Indexes also available on microfiche. Available online as *ABPC*.
018.3 A512 or Z1000 A5 ROBA

AD90 **Books on Demand 1980.** 3 vols. Ann Arbor, MI: University Microfilms International, 1979. *Supplement 1980* (1981).

Author/ title/ subject guide to some 93,000 out-of-print books available from UMI as xerographic reprints.
Z1033 E3B65

AD91 **Guide to Reprints,** 1967- . Kent, CT: Guide to Reprints. annual.

Subtitled *International Bibliography of Scholarly Reprints,* provides international coverage of reprints from more than 400 publishers. Includes books, journals, government publications, collections, and other materials that are available in reprint (by virtue of photo-offset process). Author/title list, with list of publishers.

Reprints of older materials generally of interest only to large academic libraries are reviewed in *Reprint Bulletin Book Review*, (1955- Glanville Pub., quarterly) (PER).
R011 G946 or Z1033 E3G7

Microforms

AD92 **Guide to Microforms in Print,** 1961-. 2 vols. Westport, CT: Meckler, 1983- . annual.

From 1977, has subtitle: *Incorporating International Microforms in Print*. Books, journals and other materials excluding theses, offered for sale in microform, by publishers worldwide. Directory of publishers included. *Guide to Microforms in Print Author / Title Guide, 1961–1977,* (17 vols); *Guide to Microforms in Print Subjects, 1961–77,* (Meckler, 1983-) available separately.

Microform publishing, and the microfilming of major reference sets not readily available in other formats are described at length in *Microform Review*, (1972- K.G. Saur, 1991-, quarterly) (Z265 M59 MICR).
R001.5523 AG946 or Z1033 M5G8

AD93 Library of Congress. **National Register of Microform Masters,** 1965- . Washington: Library of Congress. annual, 1965–83. *Cumulation 1965–75*, (6 vols., 1979–83).

A listing of microfilmed library materials and locations at which the master negatives are held. Annual cumulations in 1 or 2 volumes. Includes U.S. and non-U.S. books, pamphlets, serials, technical reports, manuscripts and foreign dissertations. Copies of microforms are entered in the *National Union Catalog*(s). Available online.
R018.1 N277AA or Z1033 M5N3

Archives, Manuscript Collections

Canada

AD94 **Directory of Canadian Archives / Annuaire des dépôts d'archives canadiens.** 1981- . Ottawa: Bureau of Canadian Archives, irregular.

Continues *Directory of Canadian Records and Manuscripts Repositories* (1977). Information on 540 archival repositories, providing name and address, contact person, hours of operation, and summary of holdings. Indexed by institution name and by broad subject. For the U.S. consult *Directory of Archives and Manuscript Repositories in the United States* (Oryx Press, 2d ed, 1988) (R025.1714 U585D2).
R025.171 A849DB

AD95 **Ontario's Heritage: A Guide to Archival Resources.** 13 vols. Cheltenham, ON: Boston Mills Press, 1978-1986.

A project of the Toronto Area Archivists to survey systematically local records in Ontario and to publish regional guides to resources.
CD3645 O6O5

AD96 Public Archives of Canada. **Catalogue of the Public Archives Library of Canada / Catalogue de la bibliothèque des archives publiques. Ottawa: A Collection of Published Material with a Chronological List of Pamphlets.** 12 vols. Boston: G.K. Hall, 1979.

PAC, now National Archives of Canada (NAC), is responsible for government records of historical value and other historical material, contains primary, secondary material received as manuscripts, federal records (particularly early government material). NAC collects in the traditional areas of Canadiana, e.g. cartography, exploration, travellers' narratives, etc.

The catalogue is in three parts (1) an author/title index with about 40,000 items; (2) bilingual subject; (3) chronological catalogue of pamphlets extending from 1495- .

Records in the manuscript division of the Public Archives of Canada are listed in *General Inventory: Manuscripts/ Inventaire général: manuscrits* (8 vols, 1971–1977) (R971 C212G), edited by E. Grace Maurice, which covers documents in the public "Records Group" (RG) and "Manuscript Group" (MG) in the Manuscript Division of the PAC.
Z1365 A35

AD97 Public Archives of Canada. **Union List of Manuscripts in Canadian Repositories / Catalogue collectif des manuscrits conservés dans les dépôts d'archives canadiens.** 2 vols. Ed. by E. Grace Maurice. Ottawa: Public Archives of Canada, 1975. Supplement(s) 1976 (1976); 1977/78 (1979); 1979/80 (1982); 1981/82 (1985).

Supplements published 1982, 1985 edited by Peter Yurkiw. "Comprehensive list of significant manuscripts and records in Canadian archival institutions." Arranged by title of unit (name of individual, corporate body, or government agency which received, created or accumulated the papers). Provides description and extent of papers. Indexed by repository, names, subject, with cross-references.
R091 AC212A   or   Z6620 C3A4

Great Britain

AD98 British Library. Dept. of Manuscripts. **Index of Manuscripts in the British Library.** 10 vols. Cambridge: Chadwyck-Healey, 1984-86.

Represents all major collections with items, in one alphabetical sequence, indexed by personal or place name giving name of collection for item and its number with the collection. Consolidates, with corrections, the indexes to over 30 separate (unpublished, printed or out-of-print) catalogues describing the collections. Also available is *The British Library Guide to the Catalogues and Indexes of the Department of Manuscripts*, (2d rev. ed., 1982) (Z6621 B837B73).
Z6621 B837B75

AD99 **National Inventory of Documentary Sources of the United Kingdom and Ireland.** Cambridge: Chadwyck-Healey, 1984- . microfiche

Brings together finding aids, registers, indexes, guides, and lists in repositories throughout the U.K. Accessible name and subject indexes. Includes county, city, and borough record offices and archives; national and central government libraries (including, for example, British Library India Office records); university and polytechnic

archives, etc. Another directory for British archives is *British Archives: A Guide to Archive Resources in the U.K.*, (2d ed, Stockton Press, 1989) (R025.171 F754B 1984).
ZN268 mfe

United States

AD100 Library of Congress. Manuscripts Section. **National Union Catalog of Manuscript Collections,** 1959- . annual.

Some volumes have index and some are biennial. Collections reporting are in American repositories. Complete bibliographic descriptions for collections of manuscripts of historical and research importance that are catalogued by Library of Congress. Manuscripts include letters, transcripts or oral recordings and other items of research value. Descriptions are to the "folder" level in boxes, not necessarily to individual items. Available online on LCMARC (1989-).
Z6620 U5N3

AD101 **National Inventory of Documentary Sources in the United States.** Teaneck, NJ: Chadwyck-Healey, [1985-]. microfiche.

Finding aids, registers, indexes, and collection guides, prepared in repositories throughout the U.S are included. Part 1: Federal Records, including Presidential libraries, National Archives, Smithsonian Institution; Part 2: Manuscript Division, Library of Congress; Part 3: State Archives, Libraries and Historical Societies; Part 4: Academic libraries and other repositories. These finding aids are described to the item level. Name and subject indexes on microfiche (1983, 1988).
Z N272 mfe

AE DIRECTORIES TO PERIODICALS AND NEWSPAPERS

Bibliographies and Directories

AE1 **Canadian Newspapers on Microfilm / Catalogue de journaux canadiens sur microfilm.** Ottawa: Canadian Library Association, 1959-1973. looseleaf with irregular supplements.

Part I lists newspapers microfilmed by CLA, arranged by province with a title index. Part II, revised in 1969, includes more than 1,500 Canadian newspapers, some not microfilmed by CLA. This part is also arranged by province, then place of publication, with title index. Both parts list holdings. Superseded in part by national and provincial union lists, this catalogue is consulted for its fine historical notes about the newspapers.
R070 AC212

AE2 **Canadian Serials Directory / Répertoire des publications seriées canadiennes,** 1987- . Toronto: Reference Press. irregular annual.

Revived after a ten year lapse (published by University of Toronto Press, 1972–77) but more recent edition delayed. Listing is alphabetical by title with indexes by subject and publisher or sponsor. *Canadian Writer's Market* (AB11) lists Canadian magazines, trade journals, farm publications, newspapers, book publishers, literary agents, and other information.
R050 AC212CA

AE3 **CARD: Canadian Advertising: Rates & Data, The Media Authority,** 1928- . Toronto: Maclean Hunter. monthly.

Canadian periodicals and other media that accept advertising are listed by type, such as business, ethnic publications, weekend newspapers. Also lists radio and television stations, outdoor advertising. Includes fees, sizes of advertising, and contact people.
R659.1 S785C   or   HF801 C272

AE4 **CONSER (Cooperative ONline SERials).** Ottawa: National Library of Canada. annual. database.

CONSER is a machine-readable serials database built and maintained since 1975 as a cooperative effort among 22 American and Canadian libraries using OCLC. More than 467,000 records have been added, 50,000 for Canadian titles. Available in microform as *CONSER microfiche* with a base file listing all records (1975–1978) and annual supplements. Arranged by register number with indexes by author, title and series, ISSN, and control numbers for *Canadiana*, LC, and OCLC.

AE5 **Directory of Periodicals Online,** 1985- . Toronto: Infoglobe, 1990- . irregular.

Published separately in two parts, subtitled *News, Law and Business*; and *Science and Technology*. Each provides an alphabetical list of periodicals available online in North America on English language commercial databases. Includes information about each periodical (publisher, ISSN, frequency, subjects covered) and lists all databases on which they appear. For each database, lists producer, coverage, dates, updates, time lag, vendors. Periodicals also listed by database, and by subject. *Books and Periodicals Online: A Guide to Publication Contents of Business and Legal Databases* (AB30) is an international directory listing the database vendors of business and legal journals and books available online, and indicating which parts of the journal/book are indexed or abstracted.
FLIS   or   Z6941 D572 (Part 1)
Z7403 D56 PASR; ENGR   (Part 2)

AE6 **Gale Directory of Publications and Broadcast Media.** 1869- . Detroit: Gale Research. annual.

Title varies. Formerly *Gale Directory of Publications*, *Ayer Directory of Publications*, and *IMS Directory of Publication*. Directed to the advertising industry, and beginning 1991, radio and television stations and cable companies in Canada, U.S. and Puerto Rico. Information on periodicals includes advertising rates, circulation frequency, etc. Information on broadcast media includes station call letters, network affiliations, advertising rates. Contact names and addresses, telephone and fax number provided. Available online and on diskette.
R070 AA971

AE7 **Magazines for Libraries.** 1969- . New York: R.R. Bowker, 1989. triennial since the 5th ed.

Subtitled: *For the General Reader and School, Junior College, College, University and Public Libraries*. An annotated selection, arranged by subject, of more than 6,500 of the "best and most useful" current titles. Focus is American, but Canadian and European titles are included. Title and subject indexes. Bowker has also published *Magazines for Young People* (2d ed, 1991).
R050 AM189

AE8 Library of Congress. **Newspapers in Microform, 1948–1983.** 3 vols. Washington: Library of Congress, Catalog Publication Division, 1984.

Volumes 1 and 2 cover American cities, arranged by place, with title index. Volume 3 is *Foreign Countries*. The United States Newspaper Program *National Union List* (3d ed. Dublin, Ohio: OCLC, 1989) continues coverage of American papers (mfe Z6945 U6115). Supplemented in *Newspapers in Microform* (1973- annual).
Z6945 U5N44

AE9 **Newsletters in Print.** 4th ed. Detroit: Gale, 1990. 1397 p.

Title varies: *Newsletters Directory* (3d. ed., 1987), and *National Directory of Newsletters and Reporting Services* (1st ed, 1966; 2d ed, 4 vols, 1978–81). Lists more than 10,000 subscription, membership, and free newsletters,

digests, and bulletins published in the United States and Canada. Subject arrangement with title, publisher, and subject indexes. Available online and on diskette.
Z6944 N4G32

AE10 Periodical Title Abbreviations. 2 vols. Ed. by Leland G. Alkire Jr. Detroit: Gale Research.

Lists more than 117,000 entries in all disciplines. Volume 1 *By Abbreviation* (7th ed, 1989) provides access to serial titles by abbreviation; Volume 2 *By Title* (6th ed, 1988) is a reverse directory of Volume 1, with access by title. Access also available by publisher. *New Periodical Title Abbreviations* supplements the 2 volumes in two alphabetic tabulations, one by abbreviation and one by title.
Z6945 A2W342

AE11 The Serials Directory: An International Reference Book, 1986- . 3 vols. Birmingham, AL: EBSCO. annual.

Competition for *Ulrich's* (AE13) from a major subscription service, turned publisher. Detailed entries for more than 130,000 serials, including annual and irregular series and newspapers, from over 200 countries. Indexes by titles, ceased titles, and ISSN. Available on CD-ROM.
R050 AS485S

AE12 The Standard Periodical Directory, 1964/65- . New York: Oxbridge Communications. annual.

Subject arrangement for more than 70,000 international magazines, newsletters, house organs, government publications, directories, yearbooks, and, society transactions and publications, issued more often than once every two years. Title index. Available online.
R050 AS785

AE13 Ulrich's International Periodicals Directory: Now Including Irregular Serials and Annuals, 1932- . 3 vols. New York: R.R. Bowker. annual.

Standard guide to some 120,000 regular and irregular serials currently published worldwide. Now incorporates *Irregular Serials and Annuals* (1965/66–) (R050 AU45A). Excludes newspapers. Classified arrangement by subject with index by titles and ISSN. Features added to recent editions include identification of refereed serials, availability of serials online and on CD-ROM, notations for new titles, and titles ceased within last 3 years. Includes addresses of nearly 64,000 publishers worldwide. ISSN index for all serials in the Bowker international serials database, including ceased titles. *Ulrich's* available online, on CD-ROM, and on microfiche. Updated by *Ulrich's Update: A Quarterly Supplement to Ulrich's International Periodical Directory*, formerly *Bowker International Serials Database Update.*
R050 AU45

AE14 Willing's Press Guide: A Guide to the Press of the United Kingdom and to the Principal Publications of Europe and the U.S.A., 1871- . London: T. Skinner Directories. annual.

An alphabetical directory of more than 11,500 U.K. newspapers, periodicals, and annuals with separate lists of new and ceased titled. The U.K. section ends with a publisher index and geographical listing of newspapers. The overseas section includes newspapers and magazines worldwide. Classified index to both sections.
Z6956 E5W5

Union Lists

AE15 CUSS List. Cooperative Union Serials System List. 17th ed. Downsview, ON: York University Libraries, 1990. 88 microfiche.

Supersedes earlier printed versions (3d ed, 1975). An unedited COM list created from the merged serial files of 15 Ontario university libraries. The Quebec equivalent is *CACTUS* (mfe Z6945 C13).
mfe ZC665

AE16 Guide to Periodicals and Newspapers in the Public Libraries of Metropolitan Toronto, 1970- . Toronto: Metropolitan Toronto Library Board. annual.

Holdings for approximately 9,800 current periodicals and newspapers, and 7,100 retrospective records, in the library systems in Metropolitan Toronto. Arrangement is alphabetical by title. Indexes provide geographical access to newspapers and access by languages other than English.
R050 AM594A

AE17 National Library of Canada. Union List of Canadian Newspapers / Liste collective des journaux canadiens. Ottawa: National Library of Canada, 1989. 33 microfiche.

Microform edition with *Register* and two indexes: *A* for name/title and *B* for geographic access. Expanded from the 1977 *Union List of Canadian Newspapers* (R071.1 AC212U) by the addition of entries from provincial lists compiled as part of NLC's Decentralized Program for Canadian Newspapers. An example of these more detailed lists and directories is Brian Gilchrist's *Inventory of Ontario Newspapers, 1703–1986*, (Micromedia, 1987) (R071.13 A14671). Other provincial lists can be found at Z6954 C2.
R071.1 AC212UA

AE18 New Serial Titles: A Union List of Serials Held by Libraries in the United States and Canada. 1950- . Washington: Library of Congress. 8 monthly and 3 quarterly issues, with annual cumulation.

Twenty year cumulation, 1950–70; quinquennial cumulations thereafter to 1986–89. Continues *Union List of Serials* (AE22). Entries, arranged by title of serial, provide detailed holdings of more than 500 libraries in the U.S. and Canada. Until 1980, limited to new serials. A product of *CONSER* (AE4) since 1981, *NST* now covers serials reported by contributing libraries regardless of date of publication.
R050 AN532

AE19 Serials in the British Library, 1981- . London: British Library. microfiche and paper in 3 quarterly issues and annual.

Titles newly acquired by the British Library and a selected number of other libraries. Continues *British Union Catalogue of Periodicals* (1964-1980) with fewer library locations.
Z6945 B8723

AE20 Union List of Scientific Serials in Canadian Libraries. 12th ed. 3 vols. Ottawa: CISTI, 1988.

Holdings for more than 88,000 titles in 300 Canadian libraries. Available online. Microfiche edition is 1986.
R505 AU58U (1986) mfe or Z7403 U34

AE21 Union List of Serials in the Social Sciences and Humanities: CANUC:S, 1990- .

Ottawa: National Library of Canada. annual updates. microfiche.

Titles contained in the union catalogue of serials with locations in libraries across Canada. Continues *ULSSSHCL* (held by Canadian libraries). Available online.
mfe Z U5462

AE22 Union List of Serials in the Libraries of the United States and Canada. 3d ed. 5 vols. New York: H.W. Wilson, 1965.

Holdings of 956 libraries for 156,000 serials which began publication anywhere in the world before 1950. Alphabetical by name of journal, with no subject access. Continued by *New Serial Titles* (AE18).
R050 AU58G3

AF INDEXES TO PERIODICALS AND OTHER MATERIALS

This section includes indexes and databases to periodicals (current and retrospective) and newspapers, news services, and indexes to other materials, such as books, bibliographies and ephemera material, research, dissertations, and translations. Indexes to conference papers and proceedings can be found in *General Reference in Science and Technology* DA. Indexes and abstracts for subject disciplines can be found within the subject section.

Databases

Databases listed here are included as examples. Many hundreds of databases which provide indexing are listed in various directories. See AB30 to AB37 for database directories.

AF1   ABI/INFORM: Business Periodicals Ondisc. database. 1971- .
Provides indexing to over 800 business periodicals. See CC15 for full entry information.

AF2   Canadian Business and Current Affairs / CBCA OnDisc. Toronto: Micromedia.
Online and CD-ROM access to *Canadian Business Index* (CC18); *Canadian Foreign Relations* (CD6n); *Canadian Magazine Index* (AF7); and *Canadian News Index* (AF26).
ROBA

Periodical Indexes

Current

AF3   Alternative Press Index, 1969- . College Park, MD: Alternative Press Center. quarterly.
Indexes about 200 English language periodicals which may not be indexed elsewhere. Covers journals of "leftist to radical opinion" including those covering environmental issues, animal rights, senior citizens, gay/lesbian issues, and area studies. Indexes articles, editorials, interviews, fiction, etc. which are five paragraphs or longer.
Z6514 U5A4

AF4   Applied Science and Technology Index, 1913- monthly. See DA13 for full entry information.

AF - Indexes to Periodicals and Other Materials 63

AF5 **Arts & Humanities Citation Index,** 1915- monthly. See BA3 for full entry information.

AF6 **British Humanities Index,** 1962- . London: Library Association. quarterly, with annual cumulation.

Subject index to articles in about 300 primarily British journals and newspapers covering the arts, economics, history, philosophy, politics, and society. Fiction, poetry, and book reviews are not included. Author index in annual volumes.
AI13 B7

AF7 **Canadian Magazine Index,** 1985- . Toronto: Micromedia. monthly with annual cumulation.

Covers more than 400 English language popular and special interest titles, including 15 popular U.S. periodicals and 9 "key" business titles. Contents divided into personal name and subject, with form entries for reviews, etc. Also indexes new nonfiction trade monographs which have been listed in *Quill & Quire*, and published in Canada. Available online and on CD-ROM on *Canadian Business and Current Affairs (CBCA)*, AF2.
C255 (IND)

AF8 **Canadian Periodical Index,** 1938- . Toronto: InfoGlobe, 1986- . monthly. annual cumulation.

Formerly published by the Canadian Library Association. Indexes more than 370 Canadian periodicals in all subject areas. The majority of periodicals are English Canadian, with core French Canadian titles and, since 1987, a selection of popular American titles, (17 titles as of 1991), dealing with North America and international issues. Indexed by author and subject, with form entries by genre for reviews, poems, short stories and obituaries. Available online.

Canadian Periodical Index 1920–1937: An Author and Subject Index by Grace Heggie and others, (Canadian Library Association, 1988) (IND), is a retrospective addition to *CPI* providing access to popular and scholarly titles. Excludes *Saturday Night* which is available through *An Index to Saturday Night: The First Fifty Years, 1887–1937*, (Micromedia, 1987) (AP5 S982). A companion supplement to *CPI*, also by Gordon Adshead, is *Index to the Financial Post* (Micromedia, 1990) (HG3 F57 IND) covering the years before the *Financial Post* was added to *CPI*.
IND

AF9 **Current Contents,** 1958- weekly. See DA15 for full entry information.

AF10 **French Periodical Index,** 1973/74- . Morgantown, WV: Department of Foreign Relations, West Virginia University. annual.

A subject index to 50 French language journals from Europe, Africa, and Canada.
AI7 F7

AF11 **General Periodical Index,** 1987- . Belmont, CA: Information Access. database. monthly updates.

Formerly titled *InfoTrac*, this is now the name of the system on which this and other indexes are marketed. Available in two versions: *Academic Library Version* which indexes approximately 1,100 general interest business and scholarly publications; and *Public Library Version* which covers about the same number of popular magazines and journals. Both include a few Canadian titles. Available only online and on CD-ROM, as are other products of the publisher, such as *The Magazine Index*, covering approximately 400 popular American (and some Canadian) magazines plus the *New York Times*; *National Newspaper Index* (AF28); and subject specific indexes such as *Business Index* and *Health Index* (DI21n). The publisher provides full text microfilm service, which is accessed using the indexes.

AF12   General Science Index, 1978- monthly. See DA18 for full entry information.

AF13   Humanities Index, 1974- monthly. See BA9 for full entry information.

AF14   Internationale Bibliographie der Zeitschriftenliteratur aus allen Gebieten des Wissens, 1963/64- . Osnabruck: Dietrich, 1965- . semi-annual, (in two parts).

English title: *International Bibliography of Periodical Literature Covering All Fields of Knowledge.* Known as *IBZ* or *Dietrich.* Subject index to about 8,000 periodicals from many countries. Cross references in English and French to German subject headings. Author index.
AI9 I6

AF15   PAIS International in Print, 1991- . New York: PAIS.   monthly with annual cumulation.

Merger of *Public Affairs Information Service Bulletin* (1915-1990) and *PAIS Foreign Language Bulletin* (1968/71-1990). *PAIS Bulletin* (weekly, with annual cumulations) provided subject indexing to periodicals, books, government publications, pamphlets and reports, selected for material in public administration, international affairs, social and economic conditions and concentrating on factual, statistical, and policy oriented literature. Cumulations include: *Cumulative Subject Index 1915–74* (Carrollton Press, 1976) and *Author Index 1965–69* (Pierian Press, 1973). *PAIS Foreign Language Index,* (quarterly) included subject indexing to French, German, Italian, Portuguese, and Spanish periodicals on the same topics. Available online and on CD-ROM.
Z7163 P9

AF16   Point de repère: Index analytique d'articles de périodiques de lange française, 1972- . Québec: Bibliothèque nationale. 10 issues a year; annual cumulation.

Continues *RADAR: Répertoire analytique d'articles de revues du Québec* (1972–1983). From 1984-1988 subtitled *Index analytique d'articles périodiques québécois et étrangers.* Author and subject access to 275 French language periodicals, the majority from Quebec with 12 from the rest of Canada, and 70 European. Book reviews listed separately. Supersedes *Index Analytique* 1966–72 which covered Quebec periodicals, and *Periodex* 1972–83 which covered other French language periodicals. Available online as *REPÈRE.*
AI7 P4

AF17   Readers' Guide to Periodical Literature, 1900- . New York: H.W. Wilson, 1905- . semi-monthly; monthly; quarterly and annual cumulation.

Author and subject index to 186 popular U.S. periodicals in all fields. Book reviews in a section at the back; other reviews by genre in the main index. *Abridged Readers' Guide...,* (9 issues per year), indexes 65 of the most popular magazines covered in *RGPL. Readers' Guide Abstracts* (1984- microfiche) provides indicative and informative abstracts of 60,000 articles indexed in *RGPL,* and *Readers' Guide Abstracts:*

Print Edition (1988-) contains abstracts of 25,000 articles. All versions are available online and on CD-ROM.
AI3 R48 (IND)5

AF18   Science Citation Index, 1945-. See DA22 for full entry information.

AF19   Social Sciences Citation Index, 1956-. See CA13 for full entry information.

AF20   Social Sciences Index, 1974/75- . See CA14 for full entry information.

Retrospective

AF21   Cumulated Magazine Subject Index, 1907–1949: A Cumulation of the F.W. Faxon Company's Annual Magazine Subject Index. 2 vols. Boston: G.K. Hall, 1964.

The annual volumes are consolidated into one alphabetical sequence indexing 175 American, Canadian, and British journals not included in the Wilson indexes. Subjects emphasize state and local history, art, architecture, geography, education, and political science.
R050 AC971

AF22   Nineteenth Century Readers' Guide to Periodical Literature, 1890–1899, With Supplementary Indexing 1900–1922. 2 vols. New York: H.W. Wilson, 1944.

Author, subject, and illustrator index to 51 periodicals, 7 not listed in *Poole's* (see below). Supplementary indexing adds years missing from other Wilson indexes.
R050 AN71

AF23   Poole's Index to Periodical Literature, 1802–1906. Vol. 1, Boston: Osgood, 1882; Supplementary vols. 2–6, Boston: Houghton, 1888–1908.

A catchword subject index to the contents of 479 British and American journals. Entries do not provide inclusive paging and year of cited volume. *Date and Volume Key* (1957) (R050 AP822A) and *Cumulative Author Index for Poole's Index* (Pierian, 1971) (050 AP822C) broaden access.
R050 AP822

AF24   Wellesley Index to Victorian Periodicals, 1824–1900. 5 vols. Ed. by Walter E. Houghton, and others. Toronto: University of Toronto Press, 1966–1989.

Each volume is organized in 3 sections: Part A provides tables of contents and identification of 11,500 contributors to 43 British nineteenth-century monthlies and quarterlies writing between 1824-1900, with some earlier coverage between 1802-1832; Part B contains bibliographies of contributors, and Part C is an Index of Pseudonyms. Volume 5 includes indexes, additions, and emendations to Volumes 1-4, and a compilation of Part B and Part C from the 4 volumes. Includes introductory essays to the periodicals.
Z2005 H6

Newspaper Indexes

AF25 Burrows, Sandra, and Franceen Gaudet. **Checklist of Indexes to Canadian Newspapers.** Ottawa: National Library of Canada, 1987. 148 p.

Comprehensive list of published and unpublished indexes and clipping files to Canadian newspapers.   Arranged by province, with

institutions indexing newspaper(s) listed alphabetically by place. Includes address, contact person, titles of newspapers indexed, frequency, place of publication, dates and types of information indexed, and availability of unpublished indexes. Indexed geographically and by name of newspaper. The National Library of Canada also publishes *Checklist of Indexed Canadian Newspapers: A Checklist Based on the Holdings of the Newspaper Division*, (Z6954 C2N37 ROBA 1982) updated approximately every two years. See *Canadian Newspapers on Microfilm* (AE1) for information on availability of individual titles.
R070.72 AB972C

AF26 Canadian News Index, Vol. 4, 1980- . Toronto: Micromedia. monthly with annual cumulation.

Continues *Canadian Newspaper Index*, Vol. 1-3, 1977–79. Selectively indexes 7 daily newspapers: *Calgary Herald; Globe and Mail; Halifax Chronicle-Herald; Montreal Gazette; Toronto Star; Vancouver Sun; Winnipeg Free Press*. Available online and on CD-ROM on *CBCA* (AF2). Full text companion to *CNI* is *CNI Clips*, formerly *Canadian Press Newsfile*, (Micromedia 1984- monthly), which offers all Canadian Press news and other features on microfiche. Arrangement is by date with access through CNI. Canadian Press *NEWSTEX* wire service is also available online. Full text access to *The Globe and Mail* is available online through InfoGlobe. *La Presse* is planning distribution of complete editorial content on CD-ROM, updated monthly.
IND (to 1989)   or   AI3 C261

AF27 Index de l'actualité, 1988- . Montreal: Inform II-Microfor. monthly with annual cumulation.

Originally an index only to *Le Devoir*, now covers also *La Presse*, and *Le Soleil ou Le Journal de Montréal*. Includes abstracts. Available online on *QUÉBAC*. Continues *Index de l'actualité vue à travers la presse écrite* (1972–1987) and formerly called *Index du journal Le Devoir* (1966-1971).
AI21 D422

AF28 National Newspaper Index, 1979- . Belmont, CA: Information Access. monthly. microfiche, CD-ROM.

Subject index to five major American newspapers: *New York Times*, *The Wall Street Journal*, *Christian Science Monitor*, *Washington Post*, and *Los Angeles Times*. More up-to-date than printed indexes, indexing is current to the last four weeks. Available online as *NEWSEARCH*. Full text of news is available online on *NEXIS*. Translations of newspaper articles from worldwide sources are available on *Transdex* (AF48).

AF29 New York Times Index, 1851- . New York: New York Times, 1913- . semimonthly, quarterly, with annual cumulations.

Summarizes in chronological order, under subject headings and names, important items from the late city edition. Includes full text of major speeches and documents. Provides comprehensive subject access to all articles, including reviews and obituaries. Less current than *National Newspaper Index* (AF28), which also indexes *NYT*, it appears about three months after date of coverage. Because of its chronological organization and provision of abstracts, *New York Times Index* can be used as a daily record of events. Available online.
AI21 N442

AF30 The Times Index, 1785- . Reading, U.K: Research Publications. monthly with annual cumulation.

Indexes issued by various publishers from 1785 to the present. Available from 1990 on CD-ROM as *British News Index*, along with the *Times* supplements, the *Financial Times*, and the *Independent*.
AI21 T4 to T462

News Services

AF31 Canadian News Facts: The Indexed Digest of Canadian Current Events, 1967- . Toronto: Marpep Publishing Co. semi-monthly; cumulative index. looseleaf.

A topical summary of news in Canada, from the major newspapers. Similar to the U.S. *Facts on File* (see below).
F5000 C283

AF32 Facts on File: A Weekly World News Digest, 1940- . New York: Facts on File. weekly; cumulative index; quinquennial index. looseleaf.

Reports from more than fifty foreign, U.S. newspapers, magazines. Editors write concise news summaries highlighting factual content. Available online and on CD-ROM with full text of articles from 1980-, and updated annually. Cumulated Index 1946–85.
D410 F32

AF33 Kaleidoscope: Current World Data, 1956- . Greenwich, CT: DMS. weekly. card service.

Formerly called *Deadline Data on World Affairs*. Contains current information on all countries and major international organizations. Arranged by country; subject index.
D843 D4

AF34 Keesing's Record of World Events, 1931- . London: Keesings Publications, 1931–1986. Harlow, U.K.: Longman, 1987- . monthly; annual cumulative index. looseleaf.

Title changed from *Keesing's Contemporary Archives: Record of World Events* with volume 33, 1987. In older editions, subtitle varies; formerly "Record of International Current Affairs with Continually Updated Indexes". Available in four languages (French, German, English, Dutch). Weekly until 1983; then monthly. Arranged by geographic area. Covers developments in economics, sciences, and other fields with verbatim accounts, excerpts of international treaties, charters, conferences. Includes texts of speeches and documents, obituaries, statistics, etc. and cites source of report. Detailed name and subject indexes.
D410 K4

AF35 The Third World Guide 89/90: The World as Seen by the Third World: Facts-Figures-Opinions. Montevideo, Uruguay: Editora Tercer Mundo, 1988. 625 p.

Provides information about the Third World, written by people (primarily journalists) from the Third World.
JF60 G845

Indexes to Other Material

AF36 Bibliographic Index: A Cumulative Bibliography of Bibliographies, 1937-, 3 issues per year with annual cumulation.

Subject index to bibliographies of fifty or more citations published in books, pamphlets or periodical articles. See AD2 for complete entry information.

AF37   Essay and General Literature Index, 1900- . New York: H.W. Wilson, 1934- . semi-annual with annual cumulation, five year cumulations.

An index to essays and articles in English language essay collections and anthologies, with a particular emphasis on the humanities and social sciences. Author and subject indexes. Supplemented by monthly buying guides, previewing works to be indexed. Available online and on CD-ROM.
AI3 E752

AF38   Vertical File Index, 1932- . New York: H.W. Wilson. monthly with annual cumulation.

"A subject and title index to selected pamphlet material". Arranged by subject, provides citations to pamphlets, articles, brochures, reports, government documents, and other ephemera which can be used for vertical file collections. Addresses are included. Available online.
MTRL GIS

Research or Dissertations Abstracts and Indexes

AF39   American Doctoral Dissertations, 1955/56- Compiled for the Association of Research Libraries. Ann Arbor, MI: University Microfilms.

Continues *Doctoral Dissertations Accepted by American Universities, 1934-1955.* Consolidates information on dissertations for which doctoral degrees were granted in U.S. and Canada, including those not listed in *DAI* (AF42). Cumulates into *Comprehensive Dissertation Index*, (AF42n).
R378.73 AD637A   or   Z5053 D52

AF40   Current Research in Britain, 1985- . 4 vols. Boston Spa, U.K.: British Library Lending Division. annual.

Continues in part *Research in British Universities, Polytechnics and Colleges* (1983–84), which in turn superseded *Scientific Research in British Universities and Colleges.* A register of research in four volumes: *Biological Sciences, Humanities, Physical Sciences, Social Sciences.* Available online.
AZ188 G7C8

AF41   Directory of Federally Supported Research in Universities, 1972/73. See DA69 for full entry information.

AF42   Dissertation Abstracts International, 1938- . Ann Arbor, MI: University Microfilms. monthly.

The major North American source for access to doctoral dissertations from 550 institutions worldwide. Published in 3 sections, A: *The Humanities and Social Sciences*; B: *The Sciences and Engineering*; and C: *Worldwide* (published quarterly, formerly *European Abstracts*, expanded coverage beginning 1989). Contains abstracts of dissertations submitted to UMI by participating institutions. Abstracts, which describe research projects in detail, are arranged by subject with keyword and author indexes. Available online and on CD-ROM. All dissertations in sections A and B are available on microform or paper from UMI. Section C items which are available from UMI are also listed in Sections A or B.

Cumulates into *Comprehensive Dissertation Index, 1861-1972* (37 vols); *CDI Ten Year Cumulation, 1973-1982* (38 vols); *CDI Five Year Cumulation, 1983-1987* (22 vols); and continued by annual cumulatiions. Also available are *Masters Abstracts International* (quarterly), and published with it, *Research Abstracts,* which contains summaries of post-doctoral and non-degree published research in special subjects.
Z5053 D5   and   Z5055 U49C6

AF43   Dossick, Jesse J. **Doctoral Research on Canada and Canadians, 1889-1983.** Ottawa: National Library of Canada, 1986. 559 p.

Information (author, title, university, date) for each dissertation is arranged within specific subject categories. Includes name index.
R971 AD724D   or   Z1365 D68

AF44   Index to Theses with Abstracts Accepted for Higher Degrees by the Universities of Great Britain and Ireland and the Council for National Academic Awards, 1986- London: Aslib. annual.

Continues *Aslib Index to Theses Accepted...* (1950/51–1985). Arranged by subject with author index. For earlier theses see *Retrospective Index to Theses of Great Britain and Ireland, 1716–1950* (ABC–Clio, 1975–76) (Z5055 G9R47).
Z5055 G69A82

AF45   National Library of Canada **Canadian Theses (Microfiche),** 1981- . Ottawa: Supply and Services. semi-annual.

Continues *Canadian Theses/ thèses canadiennes*, a printed annual bibliography covering the period 1947–1980. Microfiche lists all masters and doctoral theses microfilmed, published and catalogued since 1981, all theses of universities not participating in microfilming program, and foreign theses of Canadian authorship or association catalogued by NLC. Microfiche consists of two registers, one listing Canadian university theses; the other, non-Canadian university theses. Each register has 4 indexes: A: Author/title; B: KWOC; C: DDC; and D: ISBN. Cumulations: 1980/81–1984/85, 1985/86-. Filmed theses can be obtained in Canada from Micromedia, and outside of Canada from University Microfilms.
R378.71 C21TA (paper only)   or   ZC447 mfe

Translation Indexes

AF46   Canadian Translations / Traductions canadiennes, 1984/85- . Ottawa: National Library of Canada, 1987- . annual.

Published annually, but appears two to three-years after date of coverage. A compilation of monographs translated and published in Canada in any language, and catalogued by the NLC. Includes pamphlets and brochures; excludes government publications. Subject classified arrangement by UDC classification, with author/title index. See also *Canadian Index of Scientific Translations* (DA27).
Z1365 N4

AF47   Index Translationum: Répertoire international des traductions / International Bibliography of Translations, 1948- . Paris: Unesco. annual.

The 1984 volume, published in 1990, includes more than 52,000 translated works published in 53 member states. Arranged by country then divided by subject. Author index. The *World Translations Index* (1987-) (DA29) is an index to translations in science and technology.
Z6514 T71

*   *   *   *

AF48 Transdex, 1970/71- . Ann Arbor, MI: University Microfilms. monthly. annual cumulations on microfiche.

Indexes U.S. Joint Publications Research Service (JPRS) translations of newspaper and periodical articles, speeches and broadcasts published worldwide. Covering a wide range of subject areas, indexed by personal name, keywords in title, country, tables of contents. Provides access via JPRS report numbers to reports which are available from University Microfilms, and in many libraries.

AG   AUDIO VISUAL MATERIALS

This section includes catalogues and directories of sources for multimedia, film, video and audio cassettes, and records. Also included are dictionaries, encyclopedias, guides specific to audiovisual topics and educational media. Reference sources on cinema and film, including reviews, can be found in BG *Performing Arts*; sources on music, including discographies, can be found in BE *Music*; and sources on photography can be found in BF *Fine and Applied Arts*.

Catalogues and Directories

AG1   The American Film Institute Catalog of Motion Pictures Produced in the United States. New York: R.R. Bowker, 1971- in progress.

This planned 19 volume set will cover features, shorts and newsreels from 1893-1970. Volumes now available inlcude: *Feature Films 1911-1920* (2 vols, 1989); *Feature Films, 1921-30* (2 vols, 1971); and *Feature Films, 1960-69* (2 vols, 1976). Alphabetical title entries include detailed description, physical format, bibliographic details, cast, genre, synopsis. Exhaustive index of credits, subjects.
791.438 A512A OISE   or   PN1998 A57

AG2   AV Market Place: A Multimedia Guide. 1989- . New York: R.R. Bowker. annual.

Continues *AVMP: Audio Visual Market Place* (1984–88). Subtitle varies. Lists "more than 5,900 companies that create, supply or distribute AV equipment and services for business, education, science and government." Includes periodicals and resource books.
R371.33 A111A

AG3   Bowker's Complete Video Directory, 1990- . 2 vols. New York: R.R. Bowker. annual.

Formerly *Variety's Complete Home Video Directory* (1988-). Volume 1: *Entertainment and Education*; Volume 2: *Special Interest*. Designed as an in-print source, listing over 62,000 videos in all formats. Includes citations to reviews, comprehensive indexing, and ordering information. Also available on CD-ROM.
016.79143 V299 (1988) OISE

AG4   British Film Catalogue, 1895-1985: A Guide to Entertainment Film. Ed. by Dennis Gifford. New York: Facts on File, 1986.

Chronological list of British entertainment films, with brief synopses. Title index.
PN1998 G55

AG5 The British National Film & Video Catalogue, Vol. 22-, 1984- . London: British Film Institute. quarterly, with annual cumulation.

Volumes 1-21 (1963–1983) titled *British National Film Catalogue*. A record of British and foreign films and videos released for non-theatrical loan in the U.K. Classified by subject, with production, subject and title indexes, listing of distributors, production companies, sponsors, technicians. Includes television programmes, feature filsm, educational and training films, documentaries and independent productions.
Z5784 M9B752

AG6 Canadian Feature Film Index, 1913-1985 / Index des films canadiens de long métrage. Ed. by D.J. Turner and Micheline Morisset. Ottawa: Public Archives, National Film, Television, and Sound Archives, 1987. 816 p.

Annotated list of films with plot summaries and production notes. Chronologically listed in two sections, made in Canada; and set in Canada. Title indexes in each volume.
791.43 M877C   or   PN1998 M67

AG8 Canadian Film Institute. **Guide to the Collection of the Film Library of the Canadian Film Institute.** Comp. by Debbie Green. Ottawa: Canadian Film Institute, 1984. 108 p.

The CFI library, the largest film library in Canada, has "over 10,000 education, scientific, cultural films... from the most outstanding productions around the world." This guide lists over 6,000 films and videos, arranged by title with subject and name indexes.
R791.43 C212G   or   PN1998 C343

AG9 Canadiana, 1950- . See AD35 for full entry information on Part V *Sound Recordings* (1950-1983), when it changed format and films and sound recordings were incorporated into the main body of the work. For Part VI *Film and Filmstrips*, see *Film-Video Canadiana* (AG12).

AG10 Educational Film & Video Locator. 4th ed. 2 vols. New York: R.R. Bowker, 1990.

Union list of films and videos available for rental from members of the Consortium of College and University Media Centres. Evaluative annotated entries provide curriculum guidance, and note running time, rental source, producers, price, etc. Indexed by subject, audience, title.
R371.335 C755 E2 (2d ed.)   or
791.43016 E24   OISE

AG11 Feature Films: A Directory of Feature Films on 16mm and Videotape Available for Rental, Sale, and Lease. 8th ed. New York: Bowker, 1985. 734 p.

An "in-print" index of about 25,000 feature films, with essential order information. Arranged alphabetically by title, with index of directors.
791.438 F288   OISE

AG12 Film/Video Canadiana, 1985/86- . Montreal: National Film Board of Canada, 1988- . biennial.

Publisher, frequency varies. From 1948–64, films produced in Canada were listed in *Canadian Periodical Index* (see AF8); from 1964–76 as Part VI *Films and Filmstrips* in *Canadiana* (AD35); from 1976, Part 6 no longer published with *Canadiana*, but published instead with *Film*

Canadiana (Canadian Film Institute, 1969-, quarterly, then annual). Previously covering Canadian and some foreign films, this publication became solely dedicated to Canadian films since the 1972/73 edition. NLC, from 1973, provided data sheets to CFI on all Canadian feature, short, or made for TV films. *Canadiana* and *Film Canadiana* duplicated coverage until 1976, when *Film Canadiana* became "the national bibliography" of film. To reflect the expanded filmography to include video, the 1985/86 edition was titled *Film/Video Canadiana* (most recent edition to date is *1987/88* (1990). Available online.
R791.438 F487F   or   Z5784 M9F42

AG13 Library of Congress. **National Union Catalog. Audiovisual Materials,** 1983- . Washington: Library of Congress. microfiche. quarterly with annual cumulation.

Available on microfiche. Supersedes earlier print versions, *Audiovisual Materials*, (1979–82), *Films and Other Materials for Projection*, (1972-1978), and *Library of Congress Catalog: Motion Pictures and Filmstrips*, (1953-1973). The scope includes all motion pictures, video recordings, filmstrips, slide sets, transparencies released in the U.S. or Canada. Restricted to films which have instructional or educational value and are catalogued by LC. See AD12 for information on *National Union Catalog*.
R018.1 N277FA   or   R018.1 N277FB MRR

AG14 Library of Congress. **National Union Catalog. Library of Congress Catalogs: Music, Books on Music and Sound Recordings,** 1973-   semi-annual with annual cumulation. See BF23 for full entry information.

AG15 National Film Board of Canada. **Film and Video Catalogue,** 1984- . Montreal: National Film Board. annual.

The catalogue, once restricted to NFB films, now lists films and videos by "Canadian production companies or independent producers, as well as co-productions with foreign companies, short films and TV productions released for general distribution". Subject, series, directors index. Available online.
R791.438 C212A (1988)   or
PN1995.9 D6C294

AG16 National Film Board of Canada. **The NFB Film Guide: The Productions of the National Film Board of Canada from 1939 to 1989 / Le répertoire des films de l'ONF: la production de l'Office National du Film du Canada de 1939 à 1989.** 2 vols. Montreal: National Film Board, 1991.

"Authoritative reference source on over 7,800 English and French-language films produced by the National Film Board during its first 50 years." Indexed by filmmaker, producer, subject, series and year of production. Provides a bibliography of books, theses and journal articles on the NFB. Includes complete information on ordering videos, films, stock shorts and excerpts.

AG17 National Information Center for Educational Media. **Film & Video Finder,** 1987- . 3 vols. Albuquerque, NM: Access Innovations.

Combines and supersedes *NICEM Index to 16 mm Educational Films* and *NICEM Index to Educational Videotapes*. Lists some 90,000 films and videos, noting title, date, producer, format, distributor, suggested audience, and running time for each title, with brief,

non-evaluative annotations. Prices are not provided. Includes subject indexing and a directory of distributors and producers. A companion publication is *Audiocassette Finder* (1986-) (011 A912 OISE). Other indexes include: *Audiovisual Review Digest: A Guide to Reviews of Audio and Video Materials Appearing in Specialized Periodicals* (Gale, 1989–); and *Index to AV Producers and Distributors* (7th ed., Plexus, 1989). Each index has a subject guide, lists titles with full bibliographic citations with a directory of producers and distributors. NICEM indexes are available in microfiche and print formats, on CD-ROM, and online on *A–V Online*.
371.330216 I38 OISE

AG18 On Cassette: A Comprehensive Bibliography of Spoken Word Audio-Cassettes, 1985- . New York: R.R. Bowker. annual.

Formerly titled *Words on Cassette*. Comprehensive listing of spoken-word audiocassettes, with annotations to over 38,500 tapes in over 100 subject areas. Indexed by title, subject, author, producer-distributor, and reader.
011.38 O58 AV (1985)

AG19 Schwann-1 Record and Tape Guide, 1949- . Boston: Schwann. monthly; semi-annual called *Schwann-2*.

Standard guide to recordings. There is also a *Schwann Compact Disc Catalog*, (1985-) (ML156.2 S3845 MUSI). See also *OPUS* (BF60).
ML156.2 S3862 MUSI

AG20 16MM Films Available From the Public Libraries of Metropolitan Toronto, 1969- . 2 vols. Toronto: Metropolitan Toronto Library Board. irregular.

(1986 ed.) A local guide produced for patrons' use, as a guide to public library holdings. Because of the size of the collection, it is also useful as a selection guide for other libraries. Subject index; main entry by title.
R791.438 T686   or   TN1998 M48 ROBA

AG21 Le Tessier 86: répertoire 83-86 des documents audiovisual canadiens / Directory of Canadian French-language Audiovisual Materials. Montreal: La Centrale des Bibliothèques, 1986. 1309 p.

Named for Quebec motion picture pioneer, Albert Tessier, this French language catalogue lists Canadian 16mm films, video recordings, filmstrips and other AV in the French language. Entries arranged by DDC with title, subject, author, and series indexes and a directory of Canadian producers, distributors. Available online and on CD-ROM as part of *DAVID* (Services Documentaires Multimedia (DSM), Montreal, 1960-), a database which provides bibliographic descriptions of French-language audiovisuals available in Canada.
LB1043 Z9 T48 AVL

AG22 Video Source Book, 1979- . 2 vols. Detroit: Gale Research. annual.

Comprehensive listing of currently available videos in business, education, medicine, and entertainment, Indexed by subject, credits, format. Includes information on acquistion and distributors. (1990 lists 125,000 titles). Notes award winning programs.
016.79143 V652 OISE   or
PN1922.95 V52 AVL

AG23 Words on Tape: An International Guide to the Audio Cassette Market, 1984- . Westport, CT: Meckler Publishing. biennial.

Lists commercially available "books on cassette", including novels, children's fiction, plays,

short stories, self-help, inspirational, business, poetry, arts magazines, literary and political interviews, and radio and television broadcasts. Brief information includes number of cassettes, playing time, publisher and order information. Indexed by title, author, with extensive cross-referencing.
Z5347 W67 AVL

Selection Aids

AG24 Canadian Selection: Filmstrips. Comp. by Helene Rothwell. Toronto: University of Toronto Press, 1980. 537 p.

Buying guide for schools, public libraries. Lists about 1,900 filmstrips, produced in Canada, for grades K-13. Arranged by DDC with subject, title, series indexes and directory of distributors.

AG25 Media Review Digest, 1973- annual.

Index and digest of reviews for all forms of non-book material. See BG77 for full entry information.

AG26 Selected Videos and Films for Young Adults 1975-1985. Comp. by Patsy H. Perritt and Jean T. Kreamer. Chicago: ALA, 1986. 101 p.

Lists 200 outstanding films/videos by title, with evaluative annotations, subject index. Other useful lists for children and young adults include *Canadian Films for Children and Young Adults* (CLA, 1987) (R791.43 AC212C), which provides bibliographic information and brief annotations for each entry; and *Exploring the Arts: Film and Video Programs for Young Viewers* by Paula Rohrlick (Bowker, 1982) (700.345 R739E), which, although dated, still provides useful suggestions.
791.43 AP458S

AG27 Sive, Mary R. Selecting Instructional Media: A Guide to Audiovisual and Other Instructional Media Lists. 3d ed. Littleton, CO: Libraries Unlimited, 1983. 171 p.

Guide to audiovisual aids, particularly for elementary and high schools. Dated, but evaluates some items which are still published. Includes purpose, criteria, level, special features, scope of aids, with indexes by subject, media, instructional level, author, title.
371.33 AS5624M

AG28 Video Movies: A Core Collection for Libraries. Ed. by Randy Pitman and Elliott Swanson. Santa Barbara, CA: ABC-Clio, 1990. 266 p.

Provides essential details and evaluative annotations of 505 films noted for their quality and/or as important examples of film genre.

AG29 Video Rating Guide for Libraries, 1990- . Santa Barbara, CA: ABC-Clio. quarterly.

Video buying guide for all types of libraries. Does not include feature films, popular music-videos, highly technical or promotional materials. Intended to be quarterly. Premiere issue Winter, 1990.
R791.45 V652V

* * * *

Dictionaries, Encyclopedias, Annuals

AG30 **Dictionary of Library and Educational Technology**, 3d ed, 1989.
Includes terms relating to audiovisual equipment. See AA33 for full entry information.

AG31 **Educational Media and Technology Yearbook**, 1985- .
Includes articles on major trends and status of research, and directories of associations and educational opportunities. See CI14 for full entry information.

AG32 Longman, Larry. **The New Video Encyclopedia.** New York: Garland Publishing, 1990. 312 p.
Defines and discusses over 1,100 terms used with video hardware and software, video literature, satellite television, projection TV, video art, cable TV, and pay TV. Alphabetical arrangement.
TK6634 L36

AH   ANNUALS, DIRECTORIES AND HANDBOOKS

Directories of Organizations

Bibliographies of Directories

AH1   Access Canada: Micromedia's Directory of Canadian Information Resources. Ed. by Donna Yawching. Toronto: Micromedia, 1990. 310 p.

Comprehensive list of sources for current information about Canada and things Canadian; essentially a directory of directories. Excludes statistical publications because they are well covered in *Canadian Statistics Index* (CA48). Excludes French language publications. Includes buyers guides, directories, handbooks, lists, market surveys, membership lists, and product guides. Also includes periodicals and books published between January 1987 and March 1990. Excludes bibliographies, catalogues, indexes, travel guides and policy manuals. Arrangement includes: Title/Abstract section which provides abstracts, publishing information, price, ISBN/ISSN; Subject Section; Publishers Section; Telephone Directories Section.
R971 AA169A

AH2   Canadian Directories, 1790–1987: A Bibliography and Place-Name Index / Annuaires canadiens 1790–1987: une bibliographie et un index des noms de lieux. 3 vols. Comp. by Mary E. Bond. Ottawa: National Library of Canada, 1989.

A bibliography of holdings of the Canadian Directory Collection in the National Library and the National Archives of Canada. Includes 1,210 print and non-print (microfilm) directories of Canadian cities and towns, counties, regions, provinces, etc. Holdings and location are noted in entries.
R971.0025 AC212C

AH3   Directories in Print, 1980- . Detroit: Gale Research. annual with supplements.

(7th ed, 1990). Formerly *Directory of Directories* (1980-1988). Provides a listing of about 14,000 directories, including more than 4,000

international items formerly listed in *International Directories in Print*. Arranged according to broad subject area. Each entry indicates the coverage of the directory, arrangement, frequency and price. Detailed indexes are included. Gale also publishes a *Directory of Directories Publishers* (1990-).
R011 D598D   or   Z5771 D572

Directories

AH4   Annual Register of Grant Support, 1969- . New York: Macmillan. annual.

Contains 2,800 listings of public, private and corporate sources. Arranged by subject, with multiple indexes.
R001.44 A615   or   LB2336 A55

AH5   Associations Canada 1991: An Encyclopedic Directory. Toronto: Canadian Almanac & Directory Publishing Co., 1991. var. pg.

Extensive directory for Canadian associations, organizations, conferences, trade shows, and conventions. The main section lists over 20,000 Canadian and international organizations represented in Canada, arranged under 33 broad categories, and including both English and French language organizations. Entries list professional staff, elected officials, membership profiles, services provided, libraries and resource centres, publications, and information on meetings and conventions. Other sections include: *Canadian Conferences and Meetings*, which lists, by date, location, and group, meetings to be held across Canada and internationally, including major exhibitions, shows and events, such as Agricultural and Fall Fairs, Film and Video Festivals, and Consumer and Trade Shows; *Convention Planning*, which includes directory information on organizations associated with meetings and tourism; a *Publications* section which lists publications produced by Canada's organizations, arranged by broad subject. Includes an executive name index and a category index for the main section.
R061.1 A849A

AH6   Directory of Associations in Canada / Répertoire des associations du Canada, 1973- . Ed. by Brian Land. Toronto: Micromedia. annual.

(11th ed., 1990). Lists voluntary, non-government associations in an alphabetical arrangement with a subject index. Includes local, regional, provincial and national associations; international, foreign associations with branches in Canada. Available online and on CD-ROM as of 1991-92.
R061.1 D598C   or   AS40 A7D57

AH7   Encyclopedia of Associations, 1956- . Detroit: Gale Research. annual.

(1991, 25th ed). A guide to over 25,000 national and international nonprofit trade and professional associations, social welfare and public affairs organizations, religious, sports and hobby groups, and other types of organizations. Brief entries provide address, number of members, programs, publications and convention/meetings. Volume 1: *National Organizations of the U.S.*; Volume 2: *Geographic & Executive Indexes*; Volume 3: *Supplement*. Available on CD-ROM on *Gale Global Access*.
R061 G151E12   or   HS17 G32

AH8   Foundation Directory, 1960- . New York: The Foundation. biennial.

Provides information on over 25,000 American

private grant-making foundations, community foundations and corporations who provide grants, including name, address, purpose and activities, grants given, geographical limitations, etc. Available online.
R061 F771F5 (5th ed, 1975)   or
AS911 A2F65

AH9   The International Foundation Directory. 4th ed. rev. and enl. Ed. by H.V. Hodson. Detroit: Gale Research. 1986. 434 p.

Guide to 770 international charitable, permanent and independent foundations. Brief entries describe interests, origins, publications, address, governing board.   Shares   many entries with *The Grants Register* (1970-, St. James Press) (LB2338 G73). Arranged by country; indexed by name of foundation and by activity.
HV7 157 ROBA

AH10   Research Centers Directory, 1960- . Detroit: Gale Research. irregular. Inter-editions supplement.

(16th ed., 1991, 2 vols.). Over 12,300 university and non-profit organizations in the U.S. and Canada listed under 5 broad categories: Life sciences, Physical sciences and engineering, Private and public policy, Social and cultural studies, Multidisciplnary and coordinating centers. Includes detailed subject, sponsoring institution, and research unit indexes. Supplement entitled *New Research Centers*. Related publications from Gale Research are (primarily U.S.) *Government Research Directory* (6th ed, 1991), which is a guide to American federal research facilities; *Medical Research Centres* (9th ed,

1990); *European Research Centres* (8th ed, 1990); and *International Research Centers Directory*, (1988-89, 2 volumes),   covering independent, university-related and government centres. *RCD* is available online.
R007 R432R4   or   AS25R47

AH11   Sources: The Directory of Contacts for Editors, Reporters and Researchers, 1977- .   Ed. by Barrie Zwicker.   Toronto: Sources. biennial.

Lists organizations, individuals, and businesses representing a wide range of subject interests. Alternative source of information primarily intended for use by journalists.
Z674.3 S78

AH12   Yearbook of International Organizations: The Encyclopedic Dictionary of International Organizations, Their Officers, Their Abbreviations, 1948- . Ed. by the Union of International Associations [Brussels]. Munich: K.G. Saur, 1983- . irregular.

(27th ed., 1990). Nearly 26,700 organizations and administrators, embassies, government agencies concerned with international affairs. Includes a geographic and subject index. As of 1983, issued in three volumes. Volume 1: *Organization Descriptions and Index*, with varying amounts of information given (i.e. address, history, structure, aims, etc.). Volume 2: Geographic volume *International Organization Participation Country Directory of Secretariats and Membershi*p; and Volume 3: *Global Action Networks* with a subject and region directory.
R060 Y39   or   JX1904 Y4

Handbooks

Annuals, Almanacs - Canada

AH13 **Annuaire du Québec,** 1914- .
Quebec: Bureau de la statistique du Québec. irregular.

Separate French, English editions, 1914-34; bilingual; unilingual French from 53rd ed. (1973).
HA747 Q2A32

AH14 **Canada: A Portrait: The Official Handbook of Present Conditions and Recent Progress,** 1989- . Ottawa: Statistics Canada. biennial.

Formerly *Canada Handbook* (1930–1988). Arranged in a popular format and style, with colour photographs, providing general information on country, environment, culture, government. Beginning with 1990 edition bibliographical references lists are included in each chapter.
R317.1 C212C

AH15 **Canada Year Book: Review of Economic, Social and Political Developments in Canada,** 1905- . Ottawa: CGPC, Supply and Services [for Statistics Canada], 1972- . biennial, 1978/79- .

Frequency varies. French edition: *Annuaire du Canada.* Includes statistics and brief descriptions of the work of federal government. Discusses topics in essay format such as constitution, physical geography, population and other topics. Appendices feature special articles, books about Canada, synopses of legislation, a chronology, honours, etc.
R317.1 C212   or   HA471 C32

AH16 **Canadian Almanac and Directory,** 1847- . Toronto: Canadian Almanac & Directory Publishing Co., 1991– . annual.

Canada's oldest almanac (1848 ed.). A variety of useful information, arranged in four sections: directory; almanac; information and statistics; law firms and lawyers. Almost 90% directory information.
R317.1 C212A   or   AY414 C2

AH17 **Canadian Annual Review of Politics and Public Affairs,** 1960- irregular.

(1986 ed, 1990). Reviews the year's events and developments in a series of essays by specialists. Comprehensive index provides access to the information. For additional information see CD42.

AH18 **Canadian World Almanac and Book of Facts,** 1986– . Toronto: Global Press. annual.

Published each November. Records Canadian and international news events relating to politics, history, business, arts, sports, etc. Many statistical charts are derived from Statistics Canada information.
R317.1 C212W   or   AY414 C25

AH19 **The Corpus Almanac and Canadian Sourcebook,** 1966- . Don Mills, ON: Corpus Information and Communications Group. annual.

Title varies: *McGraw-Hill Directory and Almanac of Canada,* (1966-71); *Corpus Directory and Almanac of Canada,* (1971-72); *The Corpus Almanac of Canada,* (1973-82). Covers aspects of Canadian life, highlighting current events, public and national affairs, statistical

information taken from census information, and detailed government information from federal to municipal levels and intergovernmental agencies. Election results and government plans and programs are included. Keyword Index provided. More detailed than *Canadian Almanac and Directory*.
R317.1 C822   or   F5003 M3

AH20 Quick Canadian Facts: The Canadian Pocket Encyclopedia, 1945- . Toronto: Quick Canada Facts. annual.

Published in January, contains concise information, facts, statistics, and a chronology of Canada's history to the present.
R317.1 Q6   or   F5003 M3

Annuals, Almanacs - National and World

AH21 The Annual Register: A Record of World Events, 1965- . London: Longmans. irregular.

Title, publisher vary. A brief summary of the year's events. Arranged by political unit (the U.N., Commonwealth), or regions (Middle East); then by subject (law, religion, science and technology, arts, economics). Obituaries, statistics, text of documents, abstracts of important speeches are included in the last chapter.
R905.8 A615   or   D2 A72

AH22 Britain: An Official Handbook, 1950- . London: Central Office of Information. annual.

Like *Canada Year Book* (AH15), it covers the work of government, but extends to non-government features such as sports, list of newspapers, British books, and other general information. *The Annual Abstract of Statistics* (CA63) provides more detailed British statistics.
R914.1 B862B   or   DA630.A17

AH23 The Europa World Year Book, 1926- . 2 vols. London: Europa. annual.

Formerly *The Europa Year Book: A World Survey*, until 1989. Volume 1 covers international organizations; and Afghanistan to Jordan; Volume 2 Kenya to Zimbabwe. Information includes an overview, economic and demographic statistics, government and directory addresses in religion, tourism, publishing, universities. Europa also issues annual regional surveys, *The Far East and Australasia; The Middle East and North Africa; South America, Central America and the Caribbean; The USA and Canada; Western Europe;* and *Africa South of the Sahara*. See CJ "Area Studies" section for full entry information for these items.
R320.5 E89   or   JN1 E852

AH24 Information Please Almanac: The New Universe of Information, 1947- . New York: Information Please. annual.

Some overlap with *World Almanac* (AH28). One or two topical articles; mainly concise facts, statistics of general interest.
R317 I43   or   AY64 I55

AH25 The Statesman's Year-Book: Statistical and Historical Annual of the States of the World, 1864- . London: Macmillan. annual.

Similar, but more concise, information to that found in AH23. Arranged alphabetically by country. Information on history, government, geography, defense, economy, resources, communications, law, education is provided.

Includes a bibliography. In celebration of the 125th annual edition in 1988, Macmillan published the *Statesman's Year Book Historical Companion* (D358 S7 VUPR), which records important constitutional and political events for the past 125 years.
R320.5 S797   or   JA 51.57

AH26   Statistical Abstract of the United States, 1878- annual. See CA65 for full entry information.

AH27   Whitaker, Joseph. **Whitaker's Almanack**, 1869- . London: Whitaker. annual.

Contains a wealth of information on government, public affairs, industry, commerce, the arts. Thorough coverage of current events and political, economic and social events in Great Britain and the world.
R310 W577   or   AY754 W5

AH28   The World Almanac and Book of Facts, 1868- . New York: Newspaper Enterprise Association. annual.

This is the oldest of the American handbooks of miscellaneous information. Some overlap with *Information Please Almanac* (AH24).
Detailed index to the records, lists, dates and statistics for countries, personalities, sports, churches, historical events and disasters, etc.
R317 W927   or   AY67.N5W7

AH29   World Fact File, 1990- .   Ed. by Roger East and the staff of CIRCA Reference. New York: Facts on File. irregular.

Intended as a complement to *Stateman's Yearbook* (AH25), this work provides information on the "world's political and major geographical divisions." The areas of history, social history, and physical geography are well covered.
D843 W636 Ref ERIN

AH30 U.S. Central Intelligence Agency. **The World FactBook.** 1981- . Washington: GPO. annual.

Up-to-date government and economic data on almost 250 nations. This item is frequently republished by private publishers under another title, e.g. *Handbook of the Nations* (10th ed, Gale Research, 1990).   Also available on CD-ROM.
G123 W67 MAPL

Awards and Prizes

AH31   Awards, Honors and Prizes: An International Directory of Awards and Their Donors. 9th ed. 2 vols. Detroit: Gale Research, 1989.

Provides brief descriptions of more than 19,000 awards, honors and prizes offered by private and public organizations, foundations and government agencies. Scholarships and academic grants are not included. Volume 1 covers the United States and Canada. Volume 2 covers awards offered by organizations in 95 additional countries. Arrangement is alphabetical by administering organizations and by country. Organization, award and subject indexes are included in both volumes. Supplements published between editions for new awards.
R001.44 A964A

AH32   The Register of Canadian Honours / Registre des distinctions honorifiques canadiennes. Mississauga, ON: Canadian Almanac & Directory Publishing Co., 1990. 388 p.

Register of Canada's honours system including

a lists of all members of The Order of Canada; The Order of Military Merit; Decorations for Bravery with record of deeds; Exemplary Service and other medals; Canadian Heraldic Arms; Order of Precedence, etc. Includes colour illustrations of all medals, ribbons and insignia. Coats of arms and armorial bearings for Canada are also included.
CR6257 R43 Ref ERIN

AH33 World Dictionary of Awards and Prizes. London: Europa, 1979. 580 p.

Provides information on "2,000 international and national awards from 62 countries." Selection is based on intellectual nature and national/international standing. Prizes for heroism, voluntary service and sports are not included. Includes alphabetical, geographic, and subject indexes.
AS 911 A2W58

AH34 World of Winners. 2d ed. Detroit: Gale Research, 1991. 977 p.

Contains lists of award winners of over 2,400 awards presented in Canada, the U.S., and internationally, in all fields, including sports, entertainment, politics, literature, business, the arts, etc. Entries list name of award, winners' names, name of administering organization, and general information about the award itself.
AS8 W76

Consumer Information

AH35 Canadian Consumer, 1971- . Ottawa: Consumer's Association. monthly.

Provides consumer product information and consumer related information of interest to Canadians. French edition called *Le consommateur canadien.*
MTRL BU/SS

AH36 Consumer Reports, 1936- . Mount Vernon, NY: Consumers Union. monthly.

Provides results of product tests, investigations of consumer services from automobiles and appliances to food and cleaning products. December issue is an annual buying guide. Available online and on CD-ROM from 1985.
TX335 A1C602

Emblems and Heraldry

AH37 The Arms, Flags and Emblems of Canada. 3d ed. Ottawa: Deneau, in cooperation with Secretary of State, 1984. 113 p.

French ed: *Les armoiries drapeaux et emblemes floraux du Canada.* An illustrated description of the heraldic symbols and emblems for each province and territory. With glossary and section on flag etiquette.
CR212 A85 ROBA

AH38 Beddoe's Canadian Heraldry. Rev. ed. by Strome Galloway. Belleville, ON: Mika Publishing Company, 1981. 224 p.

Covers federal, municipal, academic, ecclesiastical, commercial and personal heraldry in Canada. Well illustrated with black and white and colour. Selective glossary.
CR212 B4

AH39 Boutell's Heraldry. Rev. by J.P. Brooke-Little. London/New York: F. Warne, 1983. 368 p. + col. plates.

First published in 1950, and based on a 1863 work, the *Manual of Heraldry*, by Charles Boutell. Boutell's work is a traditional text on the history and practice of heraldry, with particular attention to the U.K.
CR21 B7

AH40 Briggs, Geoffrey. **National Heraldry of the World.** London: Dent, 1973. 147 p.

Coloured drawings illustrate the arms and emblems over 140 sovereign and independent states (as of 1971). The heraldic symbols, as distinct from flags, are very briefly described in non-technical terms.
CR191 B74

AH41 **Flags of All Nations.** 2d ed. London: H.M.S.O., 1989. looseleaf, 6 sections, var. pg.

At head of title: *BR20*. Prepared by the British Ministry of Defence; contains British royal standards, British military flags, the national flags, ensigns and merchant flags of other nations. Flags are pictured and described in short phrases. Sections cover Commonwealth, European communities, NATO and the rest of the world. A lead section has some information on flag terminology. An easier source to use, with additional brief information on emblems and crests, is William Crampton's *The Complete Guide to Flags: Identifying and Understanding the Flags of the World* (London: Kingfisher Books / Grisewood & Dempsey, 1989) (CR109 C73). The page spreads for a country include photographs and concise information, for example Canada has its national flag with a paragraph on its history, coats of arms and flags of the provinces.
CR109 F53

AH42 Fox-Davies, Arthur Charles. **A Complete Guide to Heraldry.** Rev. and annotated by J.P. Brokke-Little. London: Thos. Nelson & Sons, 1969. 513 p.

First published in 1909 as a revision of *The Art of Heraldry* (1904), and many times reissued and edited. Fox-Davies' several books on heraldry and armory, including this title, are an older, standard generation of well annotated guides. The *Complete Guide* covers the wide area of heraldry, which includes ceremonial matters, as well as armory, which is the meaning, use and display of symbols and emblems for shields, helmets, banners. A more modern and much more general summary of heraldic topics is in the *Oxford Guide to Heraldry* (Oxford University Press, 1988) (CR492 W66 ROBA). The information, with illustrations, concentrates on Great Britain with appendixes of royal arms, but there is a general history and chapters on Europe and America.
CR21 F73 (1969)

AH43 **A New Dictionary of Heraldry.** Ed. by Stephen Friar. London: A.C. Black, 1987. 384 p.

A dictionary with some illustrations, and short entries on heraldry, armorial matters and symbols. Includes technical terms and many very general terms like chivalry and knighthood. Another illustrated standard dictionary is James Parker's *A Glossary of Terms Used in Heraldry* (Charles E. Tuttle, 1970) (CR1618 P3).
CR13 N49

AH44 Swan, Conrad. **Canada: Symbols of Sovereignty: An Investigation of the Arms and Seals Borne and Used from the Earliest Times to the Present in Connection with Public Authority in and over Canada, along with Consideration of Some Connected Flags.** Toronto: University of Toronto Press, 1977. 272 p.

Well illustrated with drawings and photographs. First chapter describes federal arms, seals and flags. Remainder of book outlines symbols of authority.
R929.60971 S972C

Etiquette and Forms of Address

AH45   The Amy Vanderbilt Complete Book of Etiquette. Rev. by Letitia Baldridge. New York: Doubleday, 1978. 879 p.

A North American view on deportment. A paper edition, with subtitle, *A Guide to Contemporary Living* (Bantam, 1981) is also available.
BJ1853 V27 SIGR

AH46   Debrett's Correct Form. Comp. and ed. by Patrick Montague-Smith. Exeter: Webb & Bower in association with Debrett's, 1990. 421 p.

A reissue of the 1970 edition. A standard guide to the etiquette of correspondence. Covers formal, written and informal, social forms of address for royalty, peerage, and officials in church, military, academic, diplomatic, professional walks of life. Commonwealth forms plus chapters on American and foreign use are included. There is information on precedence, some rules for flags, and information on etiquette for official and social occasions, public functions involving government and other dignitaries.
CR3891 M65

AH47   Debrett's Etiquette and Modern Manners. Ed. by Elsie B. Donald. London: Debrett's Peerage, 1981. 400 p.

A British view on everyday conventions and manners.
BJ1873 D34

AH48   Emily Post's Etiquette. 14th ed. Ed. by Elizabeth L. Post. New York: Harper & Row, 1984. 1018 p.

The standard general-purpose etiquette book covering both business and social manners.
BJ1853 P6

AH49   Letitia Baldrige's Complete Guide to the New Manners for the 90's. New York: Rawson Associates, 1990. 646 p.

Instruction on everyday manners, from rites of passage, entertaining, gift giving, and difficult times. Telephone etiquette for answering machines has been added. *Letitia Baldrige's Complete Guide to Executive Manners* (1985) provides tips on business etiquette (correspondence, gift-giving, wardrobe, social activities, etc.) (BJ2193 B33).
TPL

AH50 Newman, Dorothy and Jean Norman. **Forms of Address.** Toronto: McGraw-Hill Ryerson, 1980. 124 p.

Covers forms in Canada, U.K. and U.S.A. for honours, orders, decorations, government, religious orders, academic degrees, and various professions. Text is a chapter from the *Canadian Business Handbook*, (3d ed, 1979) (R650.0202 N552C3) by the same authors. Business information in the *Handbook* is outdated, but the chapters on forms of address, preparation for meetings and of minutes and reports, and secretarial responsibilities are still useful.
CR3515 N39

AH51   Titles and Forms of Address: A Guide to Correct Use. 18th ed. London: A&C Black, 1985. 212 p.

Covers the correct use of title and other distinguishing marks of honour and office for royalty,

peerage, military and navy, ecclesiastical and academic institutions, British government, and holders of orders, decorations. With lists of abbreviations and Commonwealth designations. Forms and rules of etiquette are excluded.
CR3515 T57

Holidays and Events

AH52 Days to Remember: Observances of Significance in Our Multicultural Society. Toronto: Ministry of Culture and Recreation, 1980. 159 p.

Part One describes 31 public holidays and general observances in Ontario. Part Two outlines observances by 84 cultural groups in the province. Dated, but only comprehensive source available.
R394.269713 A425D

AH53 Gregory, Ruth W. **Anniversaries and Holidays.** 4th ed. Chicago: American Library Association, 1983. 262 p.

A useful guide which includes calendars of fixed days, and calendars of moveable days (including sections for Christian, Islamic, Jewish and other religious events). An annotated list of books is also provided.
R394.26 G823 A3 (1975)   or   GT 3939 H38

AH54 **Newnes Dictionary of Dates.** 2d rev. ed. Comp. by Robert Collison. London: Newnes, 1966. 428 p.

An older standard in two sections. The first section gives dates and a few brief words about persons, places, events in an alphabetical sequence. The other section lists people and events in a calendar. Dates covered include world history from B.C. to 1960.
R902 C713N2

AH55 Parry, Caroline. **Let's Celebrate.** Toronto: Kids Can Press, 1987. 256 p.

Description of Canadian holidays and festivals celebrated by various cultural groups. Arranged by season, then by date. Includes drawings and suggestions for children's activities. Good for elementary school-age children and up.
GT 4813 A2P37

AH56 The People's Chronology: A Year by Year Record of Human Events from Prehistory to the Present. Ed. by J. Trager. New York: Holt, Rinehart and Winston, 1979. 1206 p.

Organized by the year; brief entries are arranged in groups using easily understood graphics (e.g. $ for economics). Any trivia entries appear strongly to favour U.S. Includes a name/subject index.
D11 T83

AH57 The World Almanac Dictionary of Dates. Ed. by Lawrence Urdang. New York: Longman in cooperation with World Almanac, 1982. 318 p.

More than 10,000 events from B.C. to the present in a subject/proper name arrangement. Events chosen reflect popular interest.
D9 W73

Parliamentary Procedure

AH58   **Bourinot's Rules of Order.** 3d ed. Ed. by Geoffrey H. Stanford. Toronto: McClelland and Stewart, 1977. 112 p.

The standard source for Canadian parliamentary procedure and procedures at public assemblies.
R328 B77R2 (1963)   or   JL164 B7

AH59 **Robert's Rules of Order.** Rev. ed. Ed. by Henry M. Robert. Glenview, IL: Scott, Foresman. 594 p.

"Robert's Rules" are a North American standard for the conduct of deliberative assemblies.
JF515 R692 1981

Speeches, Quotations and Mottoes

Additional reference sources for foreign words and phrases are listed in *Dictionaries*, Section AJ, AJ42 - AJ45.

AH60 Bartlett, John. **Familiar Quotations: A Collection of Passages, Phrases and Proverbs Traced to their Sources in Ancient and Modern Literature.** 15th ed. Ed. by Emily Morison Beck. Boston: Little, Brown, 1980. 1540 p.

A standard collection of quotations arranged chronologically by author with sections of Biblical and anonymous quotations. Author and extensive keyword index.
R808.8 B28F14 (1968)   or   PN6081 B27

AH61 Columbo, John Robert. **New Canadian Quotations.** Edmonton: Hurtig, 1987. 480 p.

"Remarkable remarks or quotable quotes" by Canadians or about Canada. Includes 4,000 new quotations in this volume together with 600 "touchstone quotations" carried over from his 1974 *Columbo's Canadian Quotations*. Arranged by subject, including persons and places, with a personal name index.
R808.8 C718CA   or   PN6081 C566

AH62 Hamilton, R.M. and D. Shields. **The Dictionary of Canadian Quotations and Phrases.** Rev. and enl. Toronto: McClelland and Stewart, 1979. 1063 p.

More than 10,000 quotes or phrases about Canada or Canadians, the majority from Canadian sources. Subject arrangement.
R808.8 H21   or   PN6081 D5

AH63 **The Macmillan Dictionary of Quotations.** New York: Macmillan, 1989. 790 p.

Selected for "interest, relevance, or wit", the 20,000 quotations are arranged by subject with biographical and keyword indexes.
PN6081 M27

AH64 **Mottoes.** Ed. by L. Urdang, C.D. Robbins, and F.R. Abate. Detroit: Gale Research, 1986. 1162 p.

More than 9,000 mottoes (or quotations and sayings as mottoes) of individuals, institutions and families arranged under themes with alphabetic indexes. There is a table of thematic categories, and the foreign language mottoes (primarily Latin and French) are identified as to language of origin and given their English meaning. L.G. Pine's compilation *A Dictionary of Mottoes* (Routledge & Kegan Paul, 1983) (PN6309 D5) list mottoes alphabetically without regard to language of origin. Most mottoes are Latin or French, but there is a short appendix of classical Greek mottoes. Mottoes are translated into English and identified as to their association with individuals or institutions, etc.
PN6309 M68

AH65 **The Oxford Dictionary of Quotations.** 3d ed. corr. London: Oxford University Press, 1987. 907 p.

Contains almost 14,000 quotations from biblical times to 1979, drawn from writers, public figures, Christian sacred writings, ballads, classical and European literature, and famous historical utterances. It excludes proverbs, nursery rhymes, slogans, homely wisdom and

moralizing reflections. Arranged by author, with a detailed keyword index. Available online as *Quotations Database*.
R808.8 O98

AH66 Partnow, Elaine. **The Quotable Woman, 1800–1981.** New York: Facts on File, 1982. 602 p.

Balancing the neglect of women in standard quotation sources, this collection is arranged chronologically by birthdate of contributor. Biographical and subject indexes. A companion volume is *The Quotable Woman From Eve to 1799* (1985) (PN6081.5 Q58).
PN6081.5 Q6

AH67 **Quotation Location: A Quotation Seeker's Source Guide.** Ottawa: Canadian Library Association, 1990. 73 p.

Lists 500 quotation books under topics such as notable books of quotations, proverbs, aphorisms, fables, etc.
PN6081 B365 ROBA

AH68 Stevenson, Burton. **The Macmillan Book of Proverbs, Maxims and Famous Phrases.** New York: Macmillan, 1987. 2976 p.

Traces sayings from their original source to current English and American use. Entries in other languages are given in English followed by original language. Subject arrangement with keyword index.
R808.8 S847M (1948) or
PN6405 S8 UNIV (1976)

AH69 Sutton, Roberta Briggs. **Speech Index.** 4th ed, rev. and enl. New York: Scarecrow Press, 1966. 947 p. *Supplement 1966-1980* (1982).

The 4th edition, subtitled *An Index to 259 Collections of World Famous Orations and Speeches for Various Occasions*, incorporates the three earlier editions. Speeches, orations and miscellaneous works on public speaking, etc. are identified in English-language books published from 1900 on. The 4th edition *Supplement 1966-1980*, by C. Mitchell, replaces two interim supplements 1966-70 and 1971-75, adding 115 titles published between 1966 and 1980. Arrangement is by subject with the occasional name entry; speeches are then listed alphabetically by speaker's name under the topic; the supplement has a title index. Only books (single speeches, anthologies, etc.) are indexed; speeches published in periodicals are excluded. *Vital Speeches of the Day*, (1934-, biweekly) (Mt. Pleasant, SC: City News Publ.) (PN6121 V52 O2 ROBA; recent issue in PRRH) reprints the text of speeches, addresses made by recognized leaders of public opinion.
R808.85 S96S4 (1966)   or   AI3 S85

Record Books

AH70 Cuddon, J.A. **The International Dictionary of Sports and Games.** New York: Schocken, 1980. 870 p.

Brief definition, history, etymology, rules and other pertinent information on major sports and games. Includes a chronology of events from 5200 B.C. to A.D. 1979. Official and slang terminology are also included.
GV567 C8

AH71 **The Guinness Book of Records,** 1955- . London: Guinness. annual.

American edition: *The Guinness Book of World Records*. Records and achievements that are "measurable and comparable to other

performances in the same category". Unique occurences, interesting peculiarities are not necessarily a category for record.
R031 G964   or   AG243 G85

AH72   The Guinness Sports Record Book. 1972- . Ed. by David Boehm. New York: Sterling Publishing. annual.

Formerly titled *Guinness Book of Sports Records: Winners and Champions*. Contains records and statistics for all sporting events, professional and non-professional, from earliest times to present. Organized alphabetically by sport. Each entry gives brief history of the sport, followed by records, winners, record holders. Includes useful charts, tables, and some photographs. Subject, but no name, index.
MTRL SCI/TECH

AH73   The Information Please Sports Almanac, 1989- . Boston: Houghton Mifflin. annual.

Provides statistical updates and information on sporting events, primarily American events, but does include international sports as well.
MTRL SCI/TECH

AH74   Wallechinsky, David. **The Complete Book of the Olympics.** New York: Viking Press, 1984. 628 p.

Information about the Olympics from the start of the modern games up to 1980. Organized by summer or winter events, then by type of sport and event. Includes photographs of famous athletes and stories about their achievements.
GV721.5 W25

AI   ENCYCLOPEDIAS

This section contains comprehensive general and desk encyclopedias for adults, young adults, and children. Regional encyclopedias are found in *Area Studies*, see CJ52 - CJ164. Subject encyclopedias are found in each subject section.

Indexes

AI1   **First Stop: The Master Index to Subject Encyclopedias.** Ed. by Joe Ryan. Phoenix, AZ: Oryx Press, 1989. 1582 p.

An index to over 400 subject encyclopedias, dictionaries, handbooks, yearbooks and other standard reference sources, published in English, and which are readily available in North America. Organized by subject, with a citation to relevant articles from the selected reference works. Includes a list of reference works arranged by broad subject area. Does not include biographical dictionaries, general encyclopedias, and subject encyclopedias covering an individual, an era, or single foreign countries.
Z5848 F57

*   *   *   *

Bibliographies and Buying Guides

AI2   **ARBA Guide to Subject Encyclopedias and Dictionaries.** Ed. by Bohdan S. Wynar. Englewood, CO: Libraries Unlimited, 1986. 570 p.

A representative list of about 1,300 items evaluated in lengthy reviews, and arranged under 43 subject headings. Most entries drawn from *ARBA* (AC1) and updated.
Z5848 A72

AI3   **Encyclopedias and Dictionaries of the World.** New York: Pergamon, [1985]. 154 p.

Covers 22 countries, with information on encyclopedias and dictionaries available through Pergamon.
R030 AE56E

AI4   Kister, Kenneth F. **Best Encyclopedias: A Guide to General and Specialized Encyclopedias.** Phoenix, AZ: Oryx Press, 1986. 356 p.

Updated, expanded version of *Encyclopedia Buying Guide* (3d ed., Bowker, 1981) (R032 AE56B). Includes reviews of 52 popular general English language encyclopedias and an annotated list of 482 general foreign language and specialized encyclopedias. Provides comparative analysis. Bibliography of works about encyclopedias included, along with lists of publishers/distributors.

Kister's *Concise Guide to Best Encyclopedias*, (Oryx, 1988) (R030 AK61K) is a condensed version with profiles of 33 general encyclopedias for adults and juveniles "presently on the North American market". Also includes annotated list of 187 specialized subject encyclopedias.
R030 AK61B

Comprehensive General Encyclopedias

For Adults

AI5 **Collier's Encyclopedia.** 24 vols. New York: Macmillan. issued annually.

A standard, general article encyclopedia with article space allocated according to studies on the information needs of the general reading public (adult and young adult). Style, vocabulary at the junior college level. Bibliographies are grouped under broad subjects in the index volume. Supplemented by *Collier's Year Book* (1939-).
R031 C69(1979)   or   AE5 C682 (1990)

AI6 **The Encyclopedia Americana.** 30 vols. Danbury, CT: Grolier. issued annually.

Well balanced authoritative encyclopedia with good illustrations and separate index in Volume 30. Most articles are short and on specific topics, with some extensive articles on broader topics. Particularly useful for coverage of U.S. and Canadian material, places, topics in business, industry, science and technology. Intended for adults, college and advanced high school students. Supplemented by The Americana Annual (1923-) which has events, survey articles and a necrology.
R031 E56(1990)   or   AE5 E333

AI7 **Funk & Wagnalls New Encyclopedia.** 29 vols. New York: Funk & Wagnalls. issued annually.

A compact, family encyclopedia intended for home and high school readers in U.S. and Canada, with little background in the material. Many articles written by authorities. Most articles are short; long articles present the general and simple information first. The set underwent a major revision in 1983 to increase the number of illustrations, update the Hammond maps, revise the bibliographies (in Volume 28) and content.
R031 F982E (1971)

AI8 **New Encyclopaedia Britannica.** 15th ed. 32 vols. Chicago: Encyclopaedia Britannica. issued annually.

Formerly titled *Encyclopaedia Britannica*. The 15th ed (1974) called *Britannica 3*, marked a major revision of content and a new format in three parts. This arrangement was further revised beginning 1985, with addition of 2 volume *Index*. The *Propaedia* (1 vol.) is a detailed outline of the structure of human knowledge; the *Macropaedia* (17 vols.) contains in-depth articles on over 4,000 topics; the *Micropaedia* (12 vols.) has concise, 'ready reference' material, with some longer articles. The format provides information at varying levels of interest and readability. Supplemented by the *Britannica Book of the Year*, (1938-) which contained feature articles, short entries on the year's events, and which has now been superseded by *Britannica World Data Annual* (1991-). The latter also contains demographic and economic statistics and annual current affairs data which will no longer appear in main volumes.

See also the *Yearbook of Science and the Future* (DA46); and the *Medical and Health Annual*. The *New EB* is available online, 1981-.
R032 E56BN(1970)   or   AE5 E363

Desk Encyclopedias

AI9   The Cambridge Encyclopedia. Ed. by David Crystal. Cambridge: Cambridge University Press, 1990. 1494 p., various paging.

British desk encyclopedia with 25,000 alphabetically arranged entries, a *Ready Reference* section and 16 colour plates, in addition to numerous illustrations, etc. Wide coverage of biographical, geographical material. Extensive cross-references.

Another British desk encyclopedia, *The Hutchinson Encyclopedia,* is widely used in the U.K, with focus on Britain and Western Europe, and noted for strength in science and technology. The forthcoming ninth edition is also available on CD-ROM.
AG5 C26

AI10   Concise Columbia Encyclopedia. 2d ed. New York: Columbia University Press, 1989. 944 p.

Based on, and abridged from, *New Columbia Encyclopedia* (1975) (R031C72E4). *Concise Columbia* is designed for adults and older students.
AG5 C722 LAWR

AI11   The Random House Encyclopedia. 3d ed. New York: Random House, 1990. 212 p.

Family desk encyclopedia in two sections, the *Colorpedia* has articles arranged under broad topics (e.g. Earth; History and Culture) with many illustrations; the *Alphapedia* has 25,000 concise, factual entries on specific topics. Includes atlas, bibliography, fold-out time chart.
AG5 R25

For Young Adults

AI12   Academic American Encyclopedia. 21 vols. Danbury, CT: Grolier. issued annually.

A good standard "ready reference" encyclopedia suitable for the high school and undergraduate user and the "inquisitive adult". Known for its currency, it has brief factual articles, many illustrations, coverage of a wide range of topics, and international scope. Emphasizes North American curriculum for secondary to college students doing initial research. Separate index volume. Designed from inception with an online edition, 1980- ; it is online and on CD-ROM as *The Electronic Encyclopedia* with bibliographies, 30,000 brief articles (300 words) or "factboxes" on contemporary, curriculum topics. *Academic American* is also published as *Lexicon Universal Encyclopedia*, *Grolier Academic Encyclopedia*, and *Macmillan Family Encyclopedia*.
R031 A168A (1990)

AI13   Compton's Encyclopedia and Fact Index. 26 vols. Chicago: Compton/Encyclopaedia Britannica. issued annually.

Keyed to curriculum needs, and interests of students aged 9 to 18, it also provides practical information for adults. Articles written for age level at which subjects are first encountered in school; simple concepts are provided first.

Bibliographies have materials for various age levels. "Master Fact-Index" in final volume contains more than 26,000 very brief articles or fact entries and defines many terms not in the main text, with references to the main text. Supplemented by *The Compton's Yearbook*. Available on CD-ROM as *Compton's Multi-Media Encyclopedia*.
R031 C738

AI14 **Merit Students Encyclopedia.** 20 vols. New York: Macmillan. issued annually.

Intended for students from 5th grade through secondary school, and adults. Clearly written, extensively illustrated. Longer articles have bibliographies. Supplemented by *Merit Students Yearbook*.
R031 M562 (1975)

AI15 **The World Book Encyclopedia.** 22 vols. Chicago: World Book. issued annually.

A well-designed and balanced family encyclopedia, but intended especially for the reference needs of elementary to secondary school students. Tied closely to U.S. and Canadian curriculum, but with definite American emphasis. Most articles are short and factual, with long articles on broad subjects. Articles and vocabulary are designed to be understood at the level at which the subject is likely to be studied. A research guide and index added with the 1972 edition. Extensively illustrated. Supplemented by the *World Book Year Book*; *Science Year: The World Book Science Annual* (DA44) and *World Book Dictionary* (AJ31). Available online.
R031 W927W (1989)   or   AE5 W55

*   *   *   *

Children's to Young Adults

AI16 **Children's Britannica.** 4th ed. 20 vols. Chicago: Encyclopaedia Britannica, 1988.

Supersedes *Britannica Junior Encyclopedia*, which it closely resembles. Designed for grades 4 to 8 (ages 7 to 14), with many long articles; and 6,000 short capsule entries, instant facts and index in volume 20. Emphasis is geographic and scientific.

AI17 **Compton's Precyclopedia.** 16 vols. Chicago: Encyclopedia Britannica. issued annually.

With aids for separate purchase, e.g. *Teaching Guide* and reproduceable worksheets. This set has material for children in the pre-school to early school years. Each volume includes a "Thing to Do" section with activities geared to topic.

AI18 **The Junior Encyclopedia of Canada.** 5 vols. Ed in Chief James Marsh. Edmonton: Hurtig, 1990.

Contains over 4,100 articles written at a basic language level, on topics which students are likely to encounter in schoolwork. Includes 3,000 illustrations, maps, aerial photographs. Articles cover all topics from a Canadian perspective.
R971.003 J95J

AI19 **The New Book of Knowledge.** 21 vols. Danbury, CT: Grolier. issued annually.

Designed specifically for elementary school children and based on analysis of school curricula. Dictionary index, on blue pages, is included in each volume, along with separate index in volume 21.
R031 N532N (1990)

Comprehensive Foreign Encyclopedias

French

AI20 **Encyclopaedia Universalis.** 2d ed. 30 vols. Paris: Encyclopaedia Universalis France, 1985.

Consists of *Thesaurus Index* (4 vols) with 16,000 short entries *Corpus* (23 vols) with 6,000 long articles; and *Symposium* (3 vols). Designed for advanced secondary school and college students, and faculty, for research and independent study. Includes an annual supplement: *Universalia*.
AE25 E463 (1985)

AI21 **La Grande encyclopédie.** 21 vols. Paris: Librairie Larousse, 1972–78.

Revises 19th century edition with same title (31 vols, 1886–1902). Emphasizes 20th century developments. Extensively illustrated. Volume 21 contains the index.

The *Grande Larousse encylopédique en dix volumes* (10 vols + 2 supplements, 1960–64, 1968, 1975) combines concise encyclopedic entries with a dictionary of 450,000 French words. (R034 G751).
AE25 G69

German

AI22 **Der Grosse Brockhaus.** 18th ed. 12 vols. Wiesbaden: F.A. Brockhaus, 1977-82.

Previous edition of this standard German multi-volume set was titled *Brockhaus Enzyklopadie* (20 vols, 1966-75 and 5 supplements) (R033.1 B864).

Articles are usually short, authoritative but unsigned. *DGB* is a comprehensive family edition with an atlas (vol.13) and a dictionary (vol.14).
R033.2 B864   or   AE27G67

Italian

AI23 **Enciclopedia Italiana de Scienze, Lettere ed Arti.** 41 vols. Rome: Istituto della Enciclopedia Italiana, 1928–1937. Four appendices in 8 parts, 1938–78.

Emphasis is on arts and humanities in lengthy scholarly articles, accompanied by lavish illustrations. A more recent work, *Enciclopedia Europea Garzanti*, (12 vols, Milan: Garzanti, 1976–1984) has many international contributors (AE35 E48).
AE35 E5

Spanish

AI24 **Enciclopedia Universal Illustrada Europeo-Americana.** 72 vols. Madrid: Espasa Calpe, 1905–1933. *Supplement* 10 vols., plus annual supplements, 1934- .

Espasa is the monumental standard multi-volume historical encyclopedia for Spanish speaking peoples, with illustrations, long bibliographies, and maps. Emphasis is biography, geography. A middle range standard with long articles and many illustrations, is *Gran Enciclopedia Rialp*, (20 vols., Madrid: Ediciones Rialp, 1971–76). An encyclopedia written for Spanish language students in North America is *Encyclopedia Barsa*, (rev. ed. 16 vols., Encyclopedia Britannica, 1985). *Barsa* is Latin American in orientation and North American in its format, general revision program.
AE61 E6

Russian

AI25 The Great Soviet Encyclopedia. 32 vols. New York: Macmillan, 1973–83.
 An approved English translation of the official encyclopedia *Sovetskaia Entsiklopediia* (3rd edition, 30 vols., Moscow, 1970–78) (AE55 B6). Contains many illustrations and colour plates, with long scholarly articles, with an emphasis on arts and humanities. Volume 32 is index.
AE55 B613

AJ DICTIONARIES

Bibliographies and Guides

AJ1   ARBA Guide to Subject Encyclopedias and Dictionaries, 1986. See AI2 for full entry information.

AJ2   Dictionaries, Encyclopedias and Other Word-Related Books. 4th ed. 2 vols. Ed. by Annie M. Brewer. Detroit: Gale Research, 1988.

Arranged by LC Class numbers: volume 1, *AC-PM*; volume 2, *PN-Z*, with subject indexes. (Earlier editions arranged with English and foreign languages in separate alphabets). A guide to all types of word-related books including those for terms and phrases, acronyms, Americanisms, colloquialisms, etymologies, glossaries, idioms, expressions, orthography, provincialisms, slang, vocabularies in English and other languages.
Z7004 D5B65

AJ3   Encyclopedias and Dictionaries of the World, [1985]. See AI3 for full entry information.

AJ4   Kister, Kenneth F. Dictionary Buying Guide: A Consumer Guide to General English Language Wordbooks in Print. New York: R. R. Bowker, 1977. 358 p.

Dated, but provides evaluations of titles which are to be found in libraries, or are in-print. Evaluates 58 adult, 50 school or children's dictionaries and 225 special wordbooks on etymology, use, slang, abbreviations etc.
R423 AK61D

English Language Dictionaries on Historical Principles

English Language Dictionaries on Historical Principles - Dictionaries in which the meanings of words are entered chronologically tracing the history of a word from early use forward to present time. Contemporary meanings appear last in entry. Dictionaries intended for current and everyday reference use are often organized on current principles. Here recent and common meanings are given first in the entry. Many older and obsolete meanings are unlikely to be included.

AJ5   A Dictionary of American English on Historical Principles. 4 vols. Comp. by Sir William A. Craigie, and James R. Hulbert. Chicago: University of Chicago Press, 1938–44.

Abridged edition published 1966.   A com-

panion set to the *OED* (AJ8); its purpose is to distinguish American English from English spoken elsewhere. Included are words and phrases clearly of American origin, connected with the history of the U.S. or having greater currency in the U.S. Quotations trace the history of a word from its earliest use in the colonies to 1900. A supplementary publication with the same title brings the record to 1950 (ed. M. M. Matthews, University of Chicago Press, 1951) (R427.973 D554). It also lists words for which new meanings have evolved.
R427.973 C886

AJ6 **A Dictionary of Canadianisms on Historical Principles: Dictionary of Canadian English.** Toronto: Gage, 1967. 926 p.

Provides "a historical record of words and expressions characteristic of the various spheres of Canadian life," with illustrations, explanation, meaning, etymology. *A Concise Dictionary of Canadianisms* (1973) (R427.971 C44C) omits bibliographies and adds no new words. The *Australian National Dictionary: A Dictionary of Australianisms on Historical Principles* (Oxford University Press, 1988) (PE3601 Z5A97) is another example of dictionaries based on historical principles, covering words that originated in Australia, have a special meaning there, or are more prevalent there than elsewhere.
R427.971 D554   or   PE3243 D5

AJ7 **Dictionary of Newfoundland English.** 2d ed. with *Supplement*. Ed. by G.M. Story, W.J. Kirwin, and J.D.A. Widdowson. Toronto: University of Toronto Press, 1990. 770 p.

First published in 1982 (625 p.) and based on the structure of the *OED* (AJ8). Words and phrases unique to Newfoundland are documented with citations to sources dating back to 1610. Includes introduction to English in Newfoundland, and discussion of sources. The *Dictionary of Prince Edward Island English* edited by T.K. Pratt, (University of Toronto Press, 1988) (PE3245 P75D53) is a similar undertaking. Dictionaries of regional speech and local colloquialisms are often popular in format and ephemeral in appeal. The *DNE* represents a scholarly approach to documenting regional speech in Canada.
PE245 N4D5

AJ8 **Oxford English Dictionary.** 2d ed. 20 vols. Prep. by J.A. Simpson and E.S.C. Weiner. Oxford: Clarendon Press, 1989.

Amalgamates text of first edition (12 vols, 1933), *Supplements* (4 vols) (1972–1986), and about 5,000 new words, or new senses of existing words, which have gained currency since relevant supplements were published. Includes 400,000 quotations.

OED is the great scholarly dictionary of the English language. "The aim of the dictionary is to present an alphabetical series of words that have formed the English vocabulary from the time of earliest records down to the present day." In volume 20 a 143 page bibliography is included with titles most commonly quoted in the dictionary. The bibliography cites first editions, without publishers' imprints. The *Shorter Oxford Dictionary...* (AJ18) is a related title.

The 1933 edition was a corrected reissue of *A New English Dictionary on Historical Principles* (10 vols, 1888–1928) (423 M98N), "founded mainly on the materials collected by the Philological Society" and edited by Sir James A. H. Murray.

The second edition is computer accessible and available on CD-ROM.
R423 O89P2

*   *   *   *

American English Dictionaries

Unabridged

AJ9 American Heritage Dictionary of the English Language. Ed. by William Morris. Boston: American Heritage, 1969. 1550 p.

A standard, with later printings, from which the college editions and *The Concise American Heritage Dictionary* (Houghton-Mifflin, 1987) derive. Indicates informal, nonstandard, slang forms. *The American Heritage Dictionary: Second College Edition* (Houghton-Mifflin, 1985) is an encyclopedic, illustrated dictionary with place and proper names, a style manual, articles on language, biographical list and list of American colleges. The *American Heritage Dictionary of the English Language; New College Edition* (2d ed., 1983), is intended to serve users from grade 9 up and is available with ease-of-use features. There is also an *American Heritage Illustrated Encyclopedic Dictionary* (1987).

Available on CD-ROM as *American Heritage Electronic Dictionary* in a somewhat condensed version.
R423 A512H   or   PE1625 A54 (2nd college edition)

AJ10 Funk & Wagnalls New Comprehensive International Dictionary of the English Language. 12 vols. Newark, NJ: Publishers International, 1982. 1928 p.

A revision of *Funk & Wagnalls New (International) Standard... (1964) (R453 F98N192)* with addition of copious encyclopedic material. An unabridged illustrated dictionary arranged according to current principles. Explanations for each word are brief. Includes atlas, quotations list, articles on U.S. political history, world's population and religions, and business letter writing.
PE1625 F77

AJ11 The Random House Dictionary of the English Language. 2d ed. New York: Random House, 1987. 2478 p. + atlas, 32 p.

Comprehensive unabridged, illustrated dictionary with 300,000 entries. Reflects current usage, with a goal of including very current terms. The date of each term's entry into the language is noted. Includes several useful addenda (an atlas, manual of style, historical and pronunciation essays, list of words commonly confused or misspelled), and four concise bilingual dictionaries for English with French, German, Italian, and Spanish. *The Random House College Dictionary* (rev. ed., 1988) is a large desk dictionary, with about 150,000 entries.
R423 R192R2   or   PE1625 R3

AJ12 Webster's Third New International Dictionary, Unabridged: The Great Library of the English Language. Springfield, MA: Merriam Webster, [1961]. 2766 p.

Title varies. Noah Webster's *An American Dictionary of the English Language* (1828) was the early progenitor of *Webster's Third*. The second edition (1934) (R423 W38N2) was reprinted many times. It included words in use from 1500, with obsolete and seldom used words at the bottom of the page. It had several appendices, and was more encyclopedic and helpful for usage and pronunciation than *Webster's Third*. The *Third* features new words but with fewer entries than the second edition, partly because it excludes words obsolete before 1775; it also has long definitions with many shades of meaning and variant pronunciations. Labels are used less frequently to indicate usage. Includes more than 470,000 entries, 200,000 usage examples, 3,000 illustrations.

New words that have become firmly established since its publication appear in *12,000 Words: A Supplement to Webster's Third New International*, (1986) (PE1625 W3 SCAR).

Among the Webster's college editions, *Webster's Ninth New Collegiate Dictionary* (1990) (PE1628 W4M4, 1983) has almost 160,000 entries, with "a clear authoritative guide to good usage" for words often misused or confused. Dates indicate first use of words.
R423 W38N3   or   PE1625 W36

Abridged

AJ13 **Facts on File Dictionary of New Words.** Ed. by Harold Lemay and others. New York: Facts on File, 1988. 163 p.

First edition published as *The New New Words Dictionary* (1985). Contains 500 new words and phrases.
PE1630 L4

AJ14 **Oxford American Dictionary.** Comp. by E. Ehrlich and others. New York: Oxford University Press, 1980. 816 p.

Not intended to be comprehensive. Includes short definitions, simplified pronunciation with some help for correct American usage. Includes slang, informal, technical words, phrases, geographical place names for U.S. and Canada.
PE2835 O9

AJ15 **The Third Barnhart Dictionary of New English.** Ed. by Robert K. Barnhart, and others. New York: H.W. Wilson, 1990. 565 p.

Updates entries from *First* and *Second Barnhart....* . Lists 12,000 new terms not yet found in general purpose dictionaries, with at least one quotation for each term. Includes new scientific and techncial terms, initialisms, slang, borrowings. *The Barnhart Dictionary Companion* (1982- quarterly), with *Index: Vols I–IV, 1982–85* (Lexic House, 1987) (PE1625 B38) updates general dictionaries. It records terms, expressions, words and meanings, which have recently entered the language. Other information frequently included is a commentary on words and their use, word formations, and retrospective consideration of the extent to which new words and meanings have become part of the language.
R423 B262D (1974)   or   PE1630 B3

AJ16 **Webster's New World Dictionary of American English.** 3d ed. Ed. By Victoria Neufeldt. New York: Webster's New World, 1988. 1574 p.

Emphasis on current American English, with wide coverage of colloquial, slang and idiomatic vocabulary. Desk dictionary of 170,000 entries, occupying the middle ground between *Webster's Ninth* and *American Heritage.*
PE1625 N55

AJ17 **Chambers English Dictionary.** 7th ed. Edinburgh: Chambers; New York: Cambridge University Press, 1988. 1792 p.

Earlier editions called *Chambers Twentieth Century Dictionary.* Includes 265,000 definitions and 195,000 references. Definitions are arranged in "etymological nesting system" which traces history of meanings from first use of word to modern usage. British slant. Many cross-references.
PE1628 C43 (older edition)   or   PE1625 C43 LAWR

British English Dictionaries

Unabridged

AJ18 **The Shorter Oxford Dictionary on Historical Principles.** 3d ed., reset with rev. etymologies and rev. addenda. Prep. by William

Little and others. Ed. by C.T. Onions. Addenda ed. by R. W. Burchfield and others. 2 vols. Oxford: Clarendon Press, 1973.

Abridgement of the *OED* (1933 edition) (AJ8n), with approximately two thirds of the vocabulary, shortened definitions and fewer quotations. The vocabulary is of literary and colloquial English and technical words from the arts and sciences with a considerable proportion of older, less common words and their uses. First published in 1933, the *Shorter OED* has often been reprinted. The third edition has substantial revision to the etymologies. The addenda, based on the 1972 supplement to the *OED*, has further information on words already treated and previously unrecorded words.
R423 M98S3

Abridged

AJ19 The Concise Oxford Dictionary of Current English. 8th ed. Ed. by R. E. Allen. New York/Oxford: Clarendon Press, 1990. 1454 p.

Based on the second edition of the *OED* (AJ8). Emphasizes current English as spoken in the U.K. *The Pocket Oxford* (1984), with simplified entries is based on the *Concise* and has approximately half the number of entries.
PE1628 F6

AJ20 The Longman Dictionary of Contemporary English. Ed. by Paul Proctor. London: Longman, 1987. 1311 p.

Describes spoken English, using phonetic alphabet, controlled vocabulary, examples, and illustrations, for over 55,000 entries. For people who use English as a second or foreign language. Complemented by the *Longman Dictionary of English Idioms* (1979) (PE1460 L65) which explains some 1,000 idioms amd clichés in use in the U.K. Available also is a *Longman Dictionary of the English Language* (1988) (PE1625 L66).
PE1628 L64 (1978) ROBA

AJ21 Longman Guardian New Words. Ed. by Simon Mort. London: Longman Group, 1986. 219 p.

Records new words from newspapers which reflect the fashion and pattern of new word formations dictated in the mid-1980s. The idea behind this dictionary continued by *The Longman Register of New Words*, (1989- annual) (Vol. 2, 1990) (PE1630 A97), edited by John Ayto. The *Register* lists a range of new words and acronyms or new meanings of old words culled from broadcast media and some 200 English-language newspapers and journals worldwide.
PE1630 L68

Canadian English Dictionaries

AJ22 Funk & Wagnalls Canadian College Dictionary. Rev. ed. Ed. by Walter S. Avis, and others. Markham, ON: Fitzhenry and Whiteside, 1981. 1590 p.

Editions prior to a 1986 revision were titled the *Funk & Wagnalls Standard College Dictionary: Canadian Edition* (1976). The post-1986 college dictionary is the same text as the *Funk & Wagnalls Canadian School Dictionary* (rev.ed., 1989). Described as a "superficial reissue of *Funk & Wagnalls American College Dictionary*," the *Canadian College* is a large desk dictionary with 158,000 entries of standard, informal, and some slang terms. Includes more Canadian words than other desk dictionaries; these have been inserted into the overall American work. Appendices provide useful Canadian material,

lists of Canadian universities and community colleges, Canadian Charter of Rights and Freedoms, lists of Fathers of Confederation, Governors General, Prime Ministers.
PE1628 S586

AJ23   The Gage Canadian Dictionary. Ed. by Walter S. Avis, and others. Toronto: Gage, 1983. 1313 p.

Gage produces a set of graded dictionaries based on a U.S. Thorndike-Barnhart education-related series with the inclusion of Canadian words. There is a *Beginning* (1982) (PE3225 B42, ROBA, 1962 ed), *Junior* (1977), *Intermediate* (1979), and *Senior* (1973) (originally based on *Thorndike-Barnhart High School Dictionary*, corresponds also to *College Revised* in the U.S.). The *Gage Canadian* was issued as a paperbound edition of the *Senior*. Earlier editions of this dictionary were titled *Dictionary of Canadian English*, now the series title. *Gage Canadian* states that it is a comprehensive, authoritative dictionary for general use in homes, offices, schools, and universities. Entries have substrantial information and there is an introductory essay on Canadian English.
R423 D554CA   or   PE3235 S45

AJ24   Houghton Mifflin Canadian Dictionary. Markham, ON: Houghton Mifflin Canada, 1980   1550 p.

Minimal Canadianization of a typically American college dictionary. Attention is given to making text readable, with simplified abbreviations in entries, and illustrations in wide margin space. The front matter has essays on the origin of English and on use, grammar, pronunciation and spelling. *The Canadian Word Book: Based on the Houghton Mifflin Canadian Dictionary* (1986) (R428.1 C212C) is a small-sized spelling list of 40,000 commonly used words.
423 H838 Ref OISE

AJ25   Penguin Canadian Dictionary Ed. by Thomas M. Paikeday. Markham, ON: Penguin Books Canada and Copp Clark, 1990. 852 p.

Viewed by the compiler as a "Canadian alternative to midsize Webster's." This dictionary, with simplified pronunciations, has some 75,000 entries for words, idioms, collocations, slang and other current English.
PE3235 P46

AJ26   The Winston Dictionary of Canadian English. Intermediate Ed. Toronto: Holt, Rinehart and Winston, 1969. 844 p.

Designed for secondary grades; includes slang, idioms. Later Winston editions include a paperbound *The Compact Dictionary of Canadian English* (1970, reprinted 1976); *The Winston Dictionary of Canadian English: Intermediate Edition* (1970) for upper elementary to high school; *The Winston Dictionary of Canadian English: Elementary Edition* (1975) for children in grades 4 to 6; and *The Winston Canadian Dictionary for Schools* (1976) to span the elementary, junior high school range.
R423 W783

Children's and Students' Dictionaries

Childrens/Student Dictionaries - See also the entries for *Gage Canadian Dictionary* (AJ23) and notes on *Winston Dictionary of Canadian English* (AJ26), and notes on thesauri for young people under *Roget* (AJ61) For French language dictionaries, see note under *Collins Robert French Dictionary* (AJ77)

AJ27   American Heritage Children's Dictionary. Boston: Houghton Mifflin, 1986. 848 p.

A comprehensive, but accessible, dictionary for elementary school children, grades 3-6, with 1,500 illustrations, photographs. The appendix includes a children's thesaurus. Somewhat less comprehensive is *Webster's New World Children's Dictionary* (Webster's New World, 1991), intended for ages 8 to 11, with many colourful illustrations, word history paragraphs and spelling tips. American Heritage also publishes an *American Heritage First Dictionary* and a *...Student's Dictionary* (both 1986).

AJ28 The Facts on File Junior Visual Dictionary. Ed. by Jean-Claude Corbeil and Ariane Archambault. New York: Facts on File, 1989. 159 p.

Similar in concept to *The Stoddart Visual Dictionary* (AJ74). Includes coloured illustrations of everyday objects, with all parts named.

AJ29 Macmillan Dictionary for Children. Rev. ed. Ed. by W. D. Halsey. New York Macmillan, 1989. 896 p.

For approximate ages 6 to 12, grades 3 to 7, this dictionary is in large type with many colour illustrations. It pays particular attention to common words (conjunctions, prepositions) that are difficult to define for children. Variant titles, *A Magic World of Words* (J423 M167MA) and *Macmillan First Dictionary* were assigned to an edition for younger readers based on the 1977 edition. The *Macmillan First Dictionary* (rev. ed., 1990) is intended for grades K to 3, and the *Macmillan Very First Dictionary* (1983) covers preschool to grade 2.

The *Canadian Dictionary for Children* (Collier Macmillan, 1984) (C14 J20. C212 OISE) is closely based on the *Macmillan Dictionary for Children.*

AJ30 The Oxford Senior Dictionary. London: Oxford, 1982. 768 p.

Generally, the dictionaries in the Oxford juvenile series are intended for British school children; there are several in-print with a choice of reading levels and learning aids. The *Senior* is for students over 14 years old; it is attuned to the British school curriculum with a wide selection of general vocabulary. The entries have notes on confusing words, use, and grammar. *The Oxford School Dictionary* (4th ed., 1981) has fewer words and is for the 11 to 14 year age range. One step down, *The Oxford Intermediate Dictionary* (1981) reduces the entries by about a third, and reduces the coverage given each word. It is intended for children in primary and middle elementary grades; it spells many inflected forms in full and has examples of use. *The Oxford Junior Dictionary* (2d ed., 1988) is for children ages 7 to 9, with two colour printing and various lists of weekdays, months, numbers, shapes. *The Oxford Illustrated Junior Dictionary* (1989) is for children 6 years and older, and corresponds to the American *Macmillan Dictionary* (AJ29). *The Oxford Students Dictionary* (2d ed., 1988) contains 40,000 words and phrases, with notes on lexical and grammatical problems. However, it is intended for foreign learners of the English language who have an intermediate or slightly better level of language facility and need.

AJ31 Thorndike, E.L. and Clarence L. Barnhart. **Scott Foresman Advanced Dictionary.** Glenview, IL: Scott Foresman, 1988. 1302 p.

Identical to *The Thorndike-Barnhart Student Dictionary* (Harper Collins, 1988). Also available are *Scott Foresman Beginning Dictionary* and *...Intermediate Dictionary* (both 1988), corresponding to other *Thorndike-Barnhart* dictionaries. The *Gage Canadian Dictionary* (AJ23) is based on this series.

AJ32 **The Winston Canadian Dictionary for Schools,** see AJ26 for full entry information.

AJ33 **The World Book Dictionary, 1990.** 2 vols. Ed. by C. L. Barnhart and R. K. Barnhart. Chicago: World Book/Doubleday, 1989.

Formerly *The World Book Encyclopedia Dictionary* and compatible with *World Book Encyclopedia* (AI31) which carries supplementary words annually in *World Book Year Book.* This frequently updated dictionary follows Thorndike Barnhart principles of graded dictionaries. It is comprehensive and suitable for grades 4-12, defines words for the age level at which they are encounterd. No biographical or geographical information included. For grades 3-6, there is a *World Book Student Dictionary* (1989) and for younger children, World Book publishes *Childcraft Dictionary* (1989) which includes word histories and games.
R423 W927W   or   PE1625 W65

Abbreviations

AJ34 **Acronyms, Initialisms and Abbreviations Dictionary,** 1960- . 3 vols in 7 parts. Detroit: Gale Research. irregular.

(15th ed., 1990; 16th ed forthcoming 1991). Volume 1, (3 parts), *Acronyms, Initialisms and Abbreviations Dictionary* lists some 500,000 short forms in alphabetical sequence; Volume 2, *New Acronyms, Initialisms and Abbreviations,* is an inter-edition supplement; Volume 3, (3 parts), *Reverse Acronyms, Initialisms and Abbreviations Dictionary* provides arrangement by meaning. Coverage is international. Gale also publishes *World Guide to Abbreviations of Organizations* (9th ed., 1990) (PE1693 G3), which lists initials and abbreviations "currently used to identify companies, institutions, international agencies and government departments throughout the world," and *International Acronyms, Initialisms and Abbreviations Dictionary* (2d ed., 1987, 3d ed. forthcoming 1993) (PE1693 I5) as a subset of the larger dictionary.
R421.8 R452R   or   PE1693 G3

AJ35 De Sola, Ralph. **Abbreviations Dictionary.** 7th ed. New York: Elsevier, 1986. 1240 p.

Subtitled *Augmented International Seventh Edition*, the title page notes extent of coverage: e.g. "Abbreviations, Acronyms, Airlines, Anonyms, Appellations, Astronomical Terminology, Bafflegab Divulged (euphemisms explained), Birthstones, British and Irish Country abbreviations, Canadian Provinces, Chemical Elements, Citizen Band Cell Jargon, Chemical Elements, Computer Jargon, Contractions, Criminalistic Terms ... Ports of the World, Prisons of the World, Racetracks, Roman Numerals ... Short Forms, Shortcuts, Sign and Symbols, Slang, Superlatives, Wedding Anniversaries, Winds of the World, Zip Codes, Zodiac."
R421.8 D4465A4   or   PE1693 D4

AJ36 **Everyman's Dictionary of Abbreviations.** 2d ed. Ed. by John Paxton. London: Dent & Sons, 1986. 384 p.

This compact dictionary of 27,000 entries is a "representative selection of old and new (but not the potentially ephemeral)" short forms and contractions. It includes the conventional signs of everyday business and technology.
P365 P38

Eponyms

AJ37 Beeching, Cyril L. **A Dictionary of Eponyms.** 3d ed. London: Library Association, 1989. 218 p.
Brief histories of 511 eponyms and the persons behind them. Subject index. A very similar work is M. Manser's *Dictionary of Eponyms* (London: Sphere/Penguin, 1988) (PE1-596 M36).
PE1596 B43

AJ38 **Eponyms Dictionaries Index: A Reference Guide to Persons both Real and Imaginary and to Terms Derived from Their Names.** Ed. by James Ruffner, and others. Detroit: Gale Research, 1977. 730 p. *Eponyms Index Supplement 1*, 1984.
Lists about 20,000 words and the 13,000 persons upon which the word is based with citations to biographies and dictionaries.
PE1596 E6

Etymology

AJ39 **The Barnhart Dictionary of Etymology.** Ed. by Robert K. Barnhart. New York: H.W. Wilson, 1988. 1284 p.
Prepared in collaboration with American linguists, this title "pays particular attention to American aspect of semantic development of English words." Origins of basic vocabulary of modern English traced in 30,000 detailed entries. Includes a glossary of language names and linguistic items.
R422 B262B   or   PE1580 B35

AJ40 Klein, Ernest. **A Comprehensive Etymological Dictionary of the English Language: Dealing with the Origin of Words and Their Sense Development Thus Illustrating the History of Civilization and Culture..** 2 vols. Amsterdam: Elsevier, 1966–67. (Reissued 1 vol., 1971).
Has scientific, technical terms, personal and mythological names. English words are compared with as many correspondences as possible in other Indo-European, including Semitic languages.
R422 K64   or   PE1580 K54

AJ41 **The Oxford Dictionary of English Etymology.** Oxford: Clarendon Press, 1966. 1025 p.
A standard reference and useful for older terms. With some emphasis on the humanities, it includes words more likely to be found in works published in the U.K. *The Concise Oxford Dictionary of English Etymology* (1986) (PE1580 C66), is an abridged version of this 1966 edition.
R422 O98   or   PE1580 O5

Foreign Words and Phrases

AJ42 Bliss, Alan J. **Dictionary of Foreign Words and Phrases in Current English.** London: Routledge & Kegan Paul, 1983. 389 p.
Originally published 1966. A lengthy introduction describes foreign words and phrases in context of full or partial anglicization, history and origins, currency, use and abuse. Dictionary contains some abbreviations and titles (e.g. from ecclesiastical Latin) as well as technical and commonly used words and phrases.
R422.4 B649 (1966)   or   PE1670 B55   SIGR

AJ43 Guinagh, Kevin. **Dictionary of Foreign Phrases and Abbreviations.** 3d ed. New York: H.W. Wilson, 1982. 288 p.

Includes a list of phrases arranged by language; Latin is the most represented language, followed by French, some Spanish and other languages. No Canadian and only a few widely known British mottoes of societies, royalty are included. Items are identified as to language of origin, given a simplified pronunciation and translated.
R418 G964   or   P361 G8

AJ44 The Harper Dictionary of Foreign Terms. 3d ed. Ed. by Eugene Ehrlich. New York: Harper and Row, 1987. 423 p.

A revision of Mawson's *Dictionary of Foreign Terms Found in English and American Writings Yesterday and Today* (1934). Contains 50,000 foreign expressions; excludes fully anglicized terms, but does cover military and naval terms, food and menu items, and archaic terms that might be encountered when reading older literature. Has an English index to terms.
R422.4 M462D2 (2d ed., 1975)   or
PE1670 M3

AJ45 **Loanwords Dictionary.** Ed. by Laurence Urdang and F.R. Abate. Detroit: Gale Research, 1988. 324 p.

Defines 6,500 words and phrases from foreign languages that retain elements of their foreign flavour (spelling, pronunciation, phrasing) but are frequently used in English-language context. Laurence Urdang also edited the *Loanwords Index* (Gale Research, 1983) (PE1670 L6), which indexed 19 dictionaries for about 14,000 words assimilated into English from 80 languages; there is a list of words by language, but no definitions are given in the *Index*.
PE1670 L58

Pronunciation

AJ46 **BBC Pronouncing Dictionary of British Names.** 2d rev. ed. By G. E. Pointon. London: Oxford University Press, 1990. 274 p.

Contains some 20,000 proper (personal and place) names that present pronunciation problems in English, Welsh or Scots orthography. To indicate pronunciation, the dictionary uses both the International Phonetic Association system and a modified English spelling system for persons unfamiliar with *IPA*.
PE1660 B3

AJ47 Lass, A. and B. Lass. **Dictionary of Pronunciation.** New York: Quadrangle, 1976. 334 p.

Some 6,000 problem words with no information given other than pronunciation, which is keyed in the same manner as *Webster's New World Dictionary* (AJ16). The pronunciations rely on the standard American dictionaries. *A Pronouncing Dictionary of American English* by J.S. Kenyon and T.A. Knott (Merriam-Webster, 1944) (PE1137 K45 ROBA) is still in-print.
PE1137 L38

AJ48 **Longman Pronunciation Dictionary.** Comp. by John C. Wells. London: Longman Group, 1990. 802 p.

Although British in orientation, this work claims to cover both British and American English with a readable authoritative explication of some 75,000 words, including common technical words, proper names. Uses International Phonetic Association system, and gives a recommended, contemporary pronunciation with alternatives indicated.
PE1137 W45

Sign Language

AJ49 Sternberg, Martin L.A. **American Sign Language: A Comprehensive Dictionary.** New York: Harper and Row, 1981. 132 p.

Exhaustive coverage of American Sign Language. English words are listed alphabetically, with line drawings and explanations of each equivalent sign. Foreign language indexes refer readers from French, German, Italian, Japanese Portuguese, Russian, and Spanish to the English terms used in the text. Extensive bibliography with its own subject index. *The Perigree Visual Dictionary of Signing* by Rod R. Butterworth and Mickey Flodin (Putnam, 1983) (HV2475 B87 ROBA) is subtitled *An A-Z Guide to Over 1,200 Signs of American Sign Language.* Also by the same authors and publisher is *The Pocket Dictionary of Signing* (1987), which is less comprehensive than *Sternberg* but provides good explanations of usage and a useful synonyms index.
HV2475 S77

Slang, Allusions, and Expressions

AJ50 **Allusions: Cultural, Literary, Biblical and Historical: A Thematic Dictionary.** 2d ed. General ed. L. Urdang, with others. Detroit: Gale Research, 1986. 634 p.

Contains 8,700 entries organized under themes, with a table of categories, and cross references in the text. Many references come from the bible, mythology, very well-known authors of fiction and popular culture. Real persons are generally excluded unless their names epitomize a thematic category.
PN3 A4

* * * *

AJ51 Green, Jonathon. **A Dictionary of Jargon.** London: Routledge Kegan Paul, 1987. 615 p.

Covers specialist occupational slang, including euphemisms. With about 21,000 entries this work updates his *Newspeak: A Dictionary of Jargon* (1983). He has also published *A Dictionary of Contemporary Slang* (Stein and Day, 1985) (PE3721 G68 SIGR), which is a comprehensive survey of current usage, with worldwide scope, including slang of U.K, U.S., Canada, Australia, New Zealand, South Africa and the West Indies. No historical notes provided.
PE1689 G73

AJ52 **Kind Words: A Thesaurus of Euphemisms.** New ed. exp. & rev. Ed. by Judith S. Neaman. New York: Facts on File, 1990. 373 p.

Euphemisms defined. American emphasis. *Faber Dictionary of Euphemisms* (Faber & Faber, 1989) offers more British terms.
PE1449 N34

AJ53 Lewin, Esther and Albert Lewin. **Thesaurus of Slang.** New York: Facts on File, 1988. 435p.

Arrangement by 12,000 standard English terms, with slang terms listed underneath. Includes 150,000 "uncensored contemporary slang terms, common idioms and colloquialisms."
PE3721 L45

AJ54 Makkai, Adam **Dictionary of American Idioms.** 2d ed. New York: Barron's, 1987. 398 p.

Indicates if phrase is slang, vulgar, or cliché. Numerous cross references.
PE2839 D5 SCAR

AJ55 Partridge, Eric H. **A Dictionary of Slang and Unconventional English: Colloquialisms and Catachreses, Solecisms and Catchphrases, Nicknames, Vulgarisms and Such Americanisms as Have Been Naturalized.** 8th ed. 2 vols. Ed. by Paul Beale. London: Routledge Kegan Paul, 1984. 1400 p.

Historical dictionary of slang designed as a companion to *OED* (AJ8). Eighth edition includes all addenda in a single alphabetical sequence. Partridge also compiled several special dictionaries, e.g. *A Dictionary of the Underworld, British and American*, (1963); *A Dictionary of Catch Phrases* (1977); *A Dictionary of Clichés* (1978).
R427.09 P275   or   PE3721 P3

AJ56   **Similes Dictionary.** Ed. by E. Sommer. Detroit: Gale Research, 1988. 950 p.

Arranges over 16,000 similes, from past and present language, and taken from a variety of sources (folklore, theatre, books, newspapers, etc.), into 500 thematic categories. Includes a table of themes and an alphabetical index. A similar work is *Picturesque Expressions: A Thematic Dictionary*, edited by Laurence Urdang (2d ed, Gale Research, 1985) (PE1689 P5), which includes over 7,000 expressions, grouped under themes, describing origin, usage, and a sample quotation. Another work by Urdang, *Idioms and Phrases Index*, (Gale Research, 1983, 3 vols) (PE1689 I3), contains over 400,000 entries of significant words and phrases, with reference to the sources defining the phrase.
PN6084 S5S56

AJ57   Wentworth, Harold and Stuart B. Flexner. **Dictionary of American Slang.** 2d ed. New York: Crowell, 1975. 766 p.

Comprehensive alphabetical list with classified lists appended. In two parts: a basic (earlier) volume; with supplements for added terms. *A New Dictionary of American Slang,* edited by Robert L. Chapman, (Harper & Row, 1986) (PE3729 U5W4) includes words from Wentworth and Flexner and focuses on non-standard, unconventional terms usually not found in dictionaries, with many cross references.
R427.0973   or   PE3729 U5W4 ROBA

Symbols

AJ58   Arnstein, Joel. **The International Dictionary of Graphic Symbols.** London: Kogan Page, 1983. 239 p.

Arranged by broad fields. Excludes pottery, silvermarks and trademarks, but includes other symbols frequently encountered in everyday and technical fields. Includes national and international symbols.
AZ108 A75

AJ59 Dreyfuss, Henry. **Symbol Sourcebook: An Authoritative Guide to International Graphic Symbols.** New York: Van Nostrand Reinhold, 1984. 292 p.

Tables of symbols arranged by subject. Contents page in 18 languages; subject index.
symbols

Synonyms

AJ60   **Chambers Thesaurus: A Comprehensive Word Finder.** New York: Cambridge University Press, 1988. 750 p.

Based on *Chambers English Dictionary*, 7th ed (AJ17). Earlier editions called *Chambers 20th Century Thesaurus*. Dictionary arrangement

of 18,000 entries, including 350,000 synonyms and antonyms.
PE1591 C53 (1986)

AJ61 Roget, Peter M. **Thesaurus of English Words and Phrases.** New ed. London: Longman, 1987. 1254 p.

Words arranged in a classified list of ideas, under broad headings, such as time and space, with subdivisions. Alphabetic word index. There are many editions of *Roget*, which was first published in 1852. Some of these use a dictionary arrangement. Harper Row has a series for young people: *Roget's Beginning Thesaurus*, pre-school to grade 3 (1990); *Roget's Beginning Thesaurus* (from the Harper Row Scott, Foresman Division), grades 3-7 (1990) and a *Roget's Junior Thesaurus* (Scott Foresman, forthcoming 1992) for grades 5-9. *The Oxford Children's Thesaurus* (1987) (423.1 S764, OISE), corresponds to the Oxford children's dictionaries (see AJ30) and covers 10,000 words with sample sentences to show use. *Roget's* is available on CD-ROM.
PE1591 R7

AJ62 **Webster's New Dictionary of Synonyms.** Springfield: MA: Merriam-Webster, 1984. 909 p.

"Synonyms are defined, discriminated, illustrated" with quotations. Includes lists of antonyms, analogous words, and contrasted words. *Webster's Compact Dictionary of Synonyms* (1987) is a pocket dictionary with 700 brief essays.
R424 W38D1 (1968)   or   PE1591 W4

Usage, Grammars, and Style Manuals

AJ63 **The Canadian Style: A Guide to Writing and Editing.** Toronto: Dundurn Press in cooperation with the Dept. of the Secretary of State and CGPC, 1985. 256 p.

Replaces the *Government of Canada Style Manual for Writers and Editors* (1966), and is intended primarily but not exclusively, for public servants who prepare English-language materials from memoranda to reports and technical publications. The chapters answer a wide variety of questions about forms of address, abbreviations, hyphenation, capitalization, numbers, and citation in specifically Canadian context. Spelling advice is based on the *Gage Canadian Dictionary* (1983 edition) (AJ23). There is information on the format of presentation of material and language use, including advice on the elimination of stereotypical writing (sexual, racial, or ethnic). Danielle Thibault compiled NLC's *Bibliographic Style Manual* (Ottawa: National Library of Canada, 1990; French edition *Guide de rédaction bibliographie*) (R010.44 T425B or Z694 T5513) to reflect conventions for bibliographic entries according to standards of the International Organization for Standardization. The manual covers the forms, fields and elements of an entry including special types of citations (legal, theses, patents, standards, bilingual documents). Although the declared audience is bibliographers, librarians, researchers and writers, librarians who are accustomed to professional technical rules for description will find this work more immediately accessible than will many other persons with bibliographical style problems.
R808.02 C212C   or   PN147 C3

AJ64 The Canadian Writer's Handbook. 2d ed. Ed. by William E Messenger, and J. de Bruyn. Scarborough, ON: Prentice-Hall, 1986. 621 p.

Covers sentence structure, grammar, pronunciation, spelling and the conventions and mechanics of writing well. Discusses creating and presenting a paper for college level work, and presents a sample essay showing grading comments.
PE1408 M47

AJ65 The Chicago Manual of Style. 13th ed. rev. and expanded. Chicago: University of Chicago Press, 1982. 738 p.

Subtitled *For Authors, Editors and Copywriters*, this manual is a standard for North American scholarly publishing, and is widely used as the authority for general scholarly writing, including dissertations. Two parts of the text (bookmaking; production and printing) are addressed to the publishing industry, but the main body of the text is concerned with style and the correct presentation of written work. Offers no grammatical or other help in effective or correct writing. This style manual answers a greater variety of documentation and format questions than most other general style and composition handbooks, and is recognized in disciplines where no preferred presentation style is recommended. *The Webster's Standard American Style Manual* (Merriam Webster, 1985) (PN147 W35) covers much the same material (format, presentation, documentation, and without grammar, style instruction) for authors, publishers and others making editorial decisions about a manuscript.
R808.02 U5558 M13   or   Z253 C45

AJ66 A Comprehensive Grammar of the English Language. Ed. by R. Quirk, and others. London/New York: Longman, 1985. 1779 p.

Compiled in Britain, but with regard to American use. Some discussion is labelled American or British English. Authoritative information is in topical chapters such as parts of speech, syntax, understanding grammar, and writing problems. Index helps user to find particular problems.
PE1106 C65

AJ67 Follett, Wilson. **Modern American Usage: A Guide.** New York: Hill & Wang, 1966. 436 p.

American counterpart of Fowler (see below).
R425 F667

AJ68 Fowler, H.W. **A Dictionary of Modern English Usage.** 2d rev. ed. Ed. by Ernest Gowers. Oxford: Clarendon Press, 1987. 750p.

Title varies. Earlier editions titled *Fowler's Modern English Usage* (2d ed., 1965) and *Modern English Usage*. *Fowler*, first published in 1926 and reissued many times (sometimes with corrections), is the recognized progenitor, and "name" in British English usage dictionaries. Opinion on the use, spelling, pronunciation, meaning and abuse of common words; although British in orientation, there are many comparisons of English and American use.
R428 F78D3 (2d ed rev., 1965)

AJ69 Harbrace College Workbook for Canadian Writers. Ed. by John C. Hodges and others. Toronto: Harcourt, Brace, Jovanovich Canada, 1990. 586 p.

First published as the *Harbrace College Handbook: Canadian Edition*. This manual is the American *Harbrace College Handbook* (10th ed., 1986) (PE1411 H6, ROBA) with minimal Canadianization of examples, and some spelling based on the *Gage Canadian Dictionary* (AJ23). In textbook format, the handbook clarifies problems of grammar, punctuation, spelling, diction and writing. There are sections on business writing and preparing college essays including the handling of documentation according to the Modern Language Association and the American Psychological Association. From the 9th edition, a section on MLA documentation appears in the handbook.

There is an *MLA Handbook for Writers of Research Papers, Theses and Dissertations* (3d ed., Modern Language Association, 1988) (PE1-478 M57, 1985), prepared by J. Gibaldi, which also covers the "how-to" of effective writing and the mechanics of preparing materials for publication or university departments. *The New Oxford Guide to Writing* (New York: Oxford, 1988) (PE1408 K2728), by T.S Kane and *The Random House Handbook* (4th ed., Random House, 1984) (PE1408 C715), by Frederick Crews, are similar titles giving guidance to university students and others on the art of writing well.
PE1411 H62

AJ70 Morris, William, and Mary Morris. **Harper Dictionary of Contemporary Usage.** 2d. ed. New York: Harper & Row, 1985. 641 p.

Comprehensive up-to-date dictionary of American usage. Tackles problems of current usage.
PE1680 M59

AJ71 **The Oxford Guide to the English Language.** London: Oxford University Press, 1984. 577 p.

Combines the *Oxford Guide to English Usage* compiled by E.S.C. Weiner (1983), with the *Oxford Minidictionary* compiled by J.M. Hawkins (1981 ed.). Includes short essays on language and covers word formation, pronunciation, grammar, vocabulary. Appendices discuss punctuation, diction, and English overseas.
PE1628 O87

AJ72 Todd, Loreto and Ian Hancock. **International English Usage.** New York: New York University Press, 1987. 520 p.

Discusses usage in all countries where English is primary or important second language. Well indexed and cross referenced.
PE1460 T64

AJ73 **Webster's Dictionary of English Usage.** Springfield, MA: Merriam-Webster, 1989. 1978 p.

In 2,300 entries, covers words that "pose special problems of confused or disputed usage." Quotations illustrate the history of usage problems.
PE1460 W425 TRIF

Visual Dictionaries

AJ74 **The Stoddart Visual Dictionary.** Ed. by Jean-Claude Corbeil. Toronto: Stoddart, 1986. 797 p.

English translation of *Dictionnaire thématique visuel* (AJ78n). Also published as *Facts on File Visual Dictionary* (AG250 C673 SIGR). Includes 3,000 black and white line drawings illustrating 25,000 English words. The parts of each illustrated item are labelled. A children's version is available (AJ28) as well as a French/English visual dictionary, (AJ78). The *Oxford-Duden Pictorial Dictionary* (Oxford, 1990); is similar in concept and based on the *Concise Oxford* (AJ19). The Oxford-Duden pictorial dictionaries are also available in paperback volumes for separate subjects, the *O-DPD: Business and Technical; ...Leisure and Art;... Science and Medicine*, and for some foreign languages.
AG250 G673

Word Elements

AJ75 Prefixes and Other Word-Initial Elements of English. General ed. L. Urdang, with others. Detroit: Gale Research, 1986. 634 p.

Nearly 300 words (e.g. check–), or syllables (e.g. ab–) that are initial forms either frequently encountered in combination with other words or always occurring with other words.
PE1175 P68

AJ76 Suffixes and Other Word-Final Elements of English. General ed. L. Urdang, with others. Detroit: Gale Research, 1982. 363 p.

Includes 1,500 common and technical free or bound words and roots that are frequently encountered at the end of words. Gives examples, origins, meaning, use and variants for each word ending. Another title, by the same authors, focusing on word-final elements of English is *-Ologies and Isms: A Thematic Dictionary* (3d ed, 1986) (PE1680 O4) in which 15,000 words omitted or not easily accessible in standard dictionaries are arranged under themes covering ideas, actions, attributes; with an alphabetic word index.
PE1175 S9

French

AJ77 Collins-Robert French-English / English-French Dictionary. 2d ed. Ed. by B. Atkins, and others. London/Paris: Collins/Robert, 1987. 930 p.

(2d rev. ed. forthcoming 1993). French equivalent is *Robert-Collins Dictionnaire français-anglais / anglais-français*. Created by lexicographers in each country, and conceptually a dictionary for the native speaker of either language. Includes entries for over 100,000 terms of contemporary French and English, "not confined to British English or metropolitan French; American English and Canadian French are given due attention." Includes vocabulary abbreviations and areas of modern interest such as travel, social sciences, sciences and common technology. Sections on verbs and an essay on communicating in the languages concludes the dictionary. Also available is a *Collins-Robert Concise French-English/English-French Dictionary* (1990); the standard *Collins French-English/English-French Dictionary* (1987); and a *Collins-Robert School French-English/English-French Dictionary* (1983) for intermediate and higher grades. The *Dictionnaire actif Nathan: 1000 mots illustrés en couleurs*, edited by F. Marchand and M. Barnoud-Maisden (Paris: Nathan, 1976) (C14 P21 OISE) is an accessible dictionary for French-speaking and French immersion children in the primary and junior grades.

AJ78 Corbeil, Jean-Claude and Ariane Archambault. **The Dictionnaire thématique visuel français-anglais/ French-English Visual Dictionary.** Montreal: Éditions Québec/Amérique, 1987. 924 p.

Republished as *Facts on File English/French Visual Dictionary* (Facts on File, 1987). Illustrations are line drawings in black and white with the parts of each object labelled using British and American English, French from France, and North American French. Colour printing and typefaces distinguish language and use differences. The drawings are grouped thematically, with separate general and thematic indexes. The dictionary is intended for people in modern industrial society who require knowledge of many everyday technical terms. The specialized terminology of experts is excluded, but the

specialized vocabulary widely disseminated in every field is presented. Corbeil has also prepared a monolingual visual dictionary, *Dictionnaire thématique visuel*, (1986) (PC2625 D53), which was translated into English and published as *The Stoddart Visual Dictionary*, (see AJ74). Also available is an *Oxford-Duden Pictorial French-English Dictionary* (Oxford, 1989) (PC2680 093 1983).
PC3640 C67

AJ79 Dupré, Paul. **Encyclopédie du bon français dans l'usage contemporain: difficultés, subtilités, complexités, singularités.** 3 vols. Paris: Editions de Trévise, 1972.

Some 10,000 words which pose problems of genre, use, spelling, documented by opinions as found in major dictionaries, quotations.
PC2640 D88

AJ80 **Grand larousse de la langue français.** 7 vols. Ed. by Louis Guilbert, Rene Lagane, and Georges Niobey. Paris: Larousse, 1971-78.

Larousse is a major publisher of dictionaries and encyclopedias in France and elsewhere; there are numerous works entitled *Larousse*. This title is not to be confused with the encyclopedia, *Grande dictionnaire encyclopédique larousse en dix volumes*, (AI21n).
PC2625 G7

AJ81 **Harrap's New Standard French-English Dictionary.** 4 vols. Ed. by J.E. Mansion, and others. London: Harrap, 1980.

Complemented by *Harrap's English French Dictionary of Slang and Colloquialisms* (1975).
PC640 H3

AJ82 Robert, Paul. **Le grand Robert de la langue française: dictionnaire alphabétique et analogique de la langue française.** 2d ed. 9 vols. Dirigée par Alain Ray. Paris: Dictionnaires Robert, 1986.

First published 1951–1966 by Paul Robert. Sponsored by the Académie Française; organized on historical principles with etymology and quotations. Also available *Le Petit Robert* (2 vols, 1989) (PC2625 R553).
R443 R642 (1st ed.)   or   PC2625 R55

AJ83 **Trésor de la langue française XIXe - XXe siècle (1789-1960).** Vols 1-7 under the direction of Paul Imbs; Vol. 8- under the direction of Bernard Quemada. Paris: Gallimard, 1983- . In progress.

Volume 14, 1990 (*ptère - salaud*). Dictionary is produced at the Centre National de la Recherche Scientifique, Nancy Institut National de la Langue Française, and volumes 1-10, 1971–83, were published by the CNRS.
PC2625 T74

Canadian French

AJ84 Bélisle, Louis-Alexandre. **Dictionnaire nord-américain de la langue française au Canada.** Montreal: Beauchemin, 1979. 1196 p.

Earlier editions titled *Dictionnaire général de la langue française au Canada*. An illustrated general French dictionary with some 8,000 Canadianisms.
R447.971 B431 (1975)   or   PC3637 B4

AJ85 Bergeron, Léandre. **Dictionnaire de la langue québécoise.** Montreal: VLB Éditeur, 1980. 574 p. *Supplément* (1981).

General dictionary featuring words commonly found in a *Larousse* or *Robert* but adding, with supplement, over 18,000 entries, including slang

phrases, that are distinctively Canadian French. Based on usage in Quebec. *The Québécois Dictionary* (Lorimer, 1982) (PC3635 B4713) is an abridged translation.
PC3635 B47

AJ86 DesRuisseaux, Pierre. **Dictionnaire des expressions québécoises.** Nouvelle éd. révisée et augmentée. Montreal: Bibliothèque québécoise, 1990. 446 p.
Monolingual. Includes phrases that have gained currency in the Quebec community since an earlier edition (1979) of this book.
PC3628 D474

AJ87 **Dictionnaire canadien: français-anglais, anglais-français / The Canadian Dictionary: French English, English French.** Ed. by J-P Vinay Toronto: McClelland & Stewart, 1962. 862 p.
About 40,000 words, intended as a general dictionary of English/French with added Canadianisms. An authoritative source, with an introduction on phonology, spelling. Few scientific or technical terms.
R443.2 D554   or   PC2640 D53

AJ88 **Dictionnaire du français plus: À l'usage francophone amérique.** Montreal: CEC Centre Educatif et Culturel, 1988. 1856 p.
A standard dictionary with useful appendices.
PC3635 D473

AJ89 Dulong, Gaston. **Larousse dictionnaire des canadianismes.** Montreal: Larousse, 1989. 461 p.
Based on the author's work for *Atlas linguistique de l'Est du Canada* (Ministère des Communications, Québec, 1980), this text has normalized French words, regionalisms and many local ironical expressions.
PC3643 D85

Other Languages

Other Language Dictionaries - Only some selected languages can be included here from the range of languages and the variety of dictionaries available to meet the needs of library patrons. More extensive choices of dictionaries are found in various selection aids and general reference guides; see *Selection Aids*, Section AC.

Arabic

AJ90 Wehr, Hans. **A Dictionary of Modern Written Arabic.** 4th ed. enl & amended. Ed. by J. Milton Cowan. Wiesbaden: Otto Harrassowitz, 1980. 1300 p.
Translated from German edition. Also available is the *Concise Oxford English Arabic Dictionary* edited by N.S. Doniach (Oxford, 1982) (PJ6640 C662).
PJ6640 W43

Chinese

AJ91 Corbeil, Jean-Claude and Mein-Ven Lee. **The Stoddart English / Chinese Visual Dictionary.** Toronto: Stoddart, 1988. 823 p.
Similar in concept to other visual dictionaries, provides line drawings with parts of objects and items labelled in both Chinese and English.

Includes a table of contents and an alphabetical index. Reprinted as *Facts on File English/Chinese Visual Dictionary*. Also available is an *Oxford-Duden Pictorial English-Chinese Dictionary: Simplified Character Edition* (1989) (PL1455 O94).
PL1455 C77

AJ92 **Hsin han ying tz'u tien / A New Chinese English Dictionary.** Ed. by Ding Guang-Xun. Seattle, WA: University of Washington Press, 1985. 1401 p.

Includes 4,600 commonly used Chinese characters in simplified form, and 36,000 entries. Includes words and expressions in general use and English equivalents of characters, proverbs, idioms. Arrangement alphabetical by Pinyin Romanization. Includes a conversion table of characters. *Han ying tz'u tien/Pinyin Chinese English Dictionary*, (Hong Kong, Commercial Press, 1979) (PL1455 H34), was prepared by the Beijing Foreign Language Institute. It gives all lexical units in characters and official romanization.
PL1455 H7847 EAST

Classical

AJ93 **A Greek English Lexicon.** Comp. by H.G. Liddell and R. Scott. New ed. [9th] rev. by H. Jones. 2 vols. Oxford: Clarendon Press, 1940. *Supplement* 1968.

Also published in an abridged edition (1986) (PA445 E5L8 VUPR). *English-Greek Dictionary with a Supplement of Proper Names Including Greek Equivalents for Famous Names in History* (London: Routledge Kegan Paul, 1972) by S.C. Woodhouse, was originally published 1932, with subtitle: *A Vocabulary of the Attic Language*.
PA2365 E5O88

AJ94 **Oxford Latin Dictionary.** Ed. By P.G. W. Glare. New York: Oxford University Press, 1982. 2126 p.

A one volume edition of *Oxford Latin Dictionary* (8 fascicles, in 2 volumes, 1968–1982), which replaces the older standard *Latin Dictionary* (1879) (R473.2 L673) compiled by C.T. Lewis and C. Short. It followed the format of the *OED*, and examined classical Latin from its beginnings to second century A.D., excluding Christian Latin. *Cassell's Latin-English, English-Latin Dictionary* by D.P. Simpson (3d ed., Cassell, 1979) is a modern standard. (PC2365 E5C3).
PA2365 E5O88

German

AJ95 **Duden Das grosse Wörterbuch der deutschen Sprache.** 6 vols. Under drection of G. Drosdowski and others. Mannheim: Bibliographisches Institute, 1966–1981.
Monolingual.
PF3625 G75

AJ96 **Langenscheidt's Encyclopedic Dictionary of the English and German Languages.** 2 parts in 4 vols. Berlin: Langenscheidt, 1962-75.

In Roman type. Emphasizes definitions over equivalent meanings. *Langenscheidt's Condensed Muret Sanders German Dictionary* (1982) covers everyday current language, specialized terminology from all major fields, translating from German to American/British English. *Collins-Klett German-English/German-French Dictionary* (2d ed., London/Stuttgart: Collins/Klett, 1984) (PE3640 C6), edited by P. Terrell, and others, has contemporary language with a range of older and technical words. Includes regionalisms; represents American English, Swiss, Austrian German and East German before reunification. Also available in separate volumes. The German equivalent is the Klett *Pons Grosswörterbuch Deutsch-Englisch/Englisch-Deutsch*. Collins produces other comprehensive dictionaries in this two-publisher format, (see AJ77 and AJ98n).

Oxford-Duden German Dictionary: German-English/English-German (Oxford, 1990) (PE3640 O94 ERIN) is comprehensive and up-to-date; it provides both literal and figurative meanings of words with many usage examples. The *Oxford Duden Pictorial German English Dictionary* (1988) (PF3629 O9, SIGR 1980), is a visual dictionary emphasizing technical terms.
PF3640 L3

Hebrew

AJ97 Zilkha, A **Modern Hebrew-English Dictionary.** New Haven CT: Yale University Press, 1989. 305 p.

A more comprehensive work in 4 volumes, prepared by Reuben Alclay, is *The Complete Hebrew English Dictionary* (Tel Aviv, Massadah Publishing, 1959-61) (PJ4833 A45).
PJ4833 Z57

* * * *

Italian

AJ98 The Cambridge Italian Dictionary. 2 vols. Under the direction of B. Reynolds. Cambridge: University Press, 1962–81.

Volume 1, Italian English (1962); volume 2, English Italian (1981) Extensive dictionary of words, terms, phrases, to help English speakers in Italian expression. Follows principle of translational equivalents, but lacks pronunciation, labelling or irregular verbs, and other common aids. A one volume edition of this work has been published as *Cambridge Signorelli Dizionario Italiano-Inglese, Inglese-Italiano* (ed. by Barbara Reynolds, 1985). Designed for those familiar with Italian.

There is a *Collins-Sansoni Italian-English/English/Italian Dictionary* (3d rev. ed., London/Florence: Collins/Sansoni, 1989) (PC1640 D58; SCAR 1988) edited by V. Macchi, and other lexicographers in each country to achieve a contemporary vocabulary and contemporary look. Also available in separate volumes, the Italian equivalent is the Sansoni *Dizionario delle lingue - italiana e inglese* (PC1625 D533, 1978). *Il dizionario della lengua italiana* (Florence: Le Monnier, 1990) (PC1625 D47) is an illustrated monolingual comprehensive dictionary. Other bilingual dictionaries include a standard, desk-sized *Collins Italian-English/English-Italian Dictionary* (1983). The comprehensive *Oxford English-Italian/Italian-English Dictionary* (1981) is also available in an abridgement as *The Oxford Italian Minidictionary* (1986).
R453.2 C178   or   PC1640 R4

* * * *

Japanese

AJ99 **The Japan Foundation Basic Japanese English Dictionary.** New York: Oxford University Press, 1989. 958 p.

Originally published in Tokyo (Bonjinsha, 1986). Designed for non-Japanese students. Uses Japanese script and romanization with English equivalents. Also available is a visual dictionary, the *Oxford-Duden Pictorial English Japanese Dictionary* (1983) (PL679 P29 ERIN Ref).
PL679 B37 EAST

Russian

AJ100 **Elsevier's Russian-English Dictionary.** 4 vols. Comp. by Paul Macura. Amsterdam: Elsevier, 1990.

Includes 240,000 entries covering terms in the humanities, social sciences, arts, and scientific terms in anthropology, botany, chemistry, engineering, geography, geology, mathematics, medicine, physics, zoology. Includes extensive grammatical information. For Russian speakers, but useful to English students of Russian is *Bolshoi Anglo Russkii Slovar/ New English Russian Dictionary* (2 vols Sovetskaia entsikopediia, 1987) (PG2640 G3). Kenneth Katzner's *English-Russian/Russian-English Dictionary* (Wiley, 1984) (PG2640 K34) is based on American English, with all explanations in English, information on verbs, declensions, and a glossary of proper names.
PG2640 M32

Spanish

AJ101 **The American Heritage Larousse Spanish Dictionary: Spanish/English, English/Spanish.** Boston: Houghton Mifflin, 1986. 1152 p.

Emphasizes Latin American usage, but with continental meanings as well. Includes verb tables, synonyms. A concise edition published 1989. The *University of Chicago Spanish Dictionary: A New Concise Spanish-English and English-Spanish Dictionary* (4th ed., University of Chicago Press, 1987) (PC4640 U5) is designed for Americans learning Spanish-American, and Spanish speakers learning American English. The *Oxford-Duden Pictorial Spanish-English Dictionary* (ClarendonPress/Oxford, 1986) (PC4629 O94) is a visual dictionary with illustration, with parts of objects, items, labelled with Spanish names and British English equivalents. Real Academia Española prepared *Diccionario de la Lengua Española* (20th ed., Madrid: Espasa Calpe, 1984)(PC4625 A35), a standard monolingual Spanish dictionary, with etymologies.
PC4640 A54

AK   MAPS AND ATLASES

For additional coverage of cartography and geography, please consult the following sections: *Geography*, CK; *Earth Sciences*, DG, and *Astronomy*, DD. Atlases on biblical lands are under the Bible subsection in *Religion*, BC; atlases of a historical nature are listed in *History*, Section, CJ.

Guides to the Literature

AK1   Farrell, Barbara and Aileen Desbarats. **Guide for a Small Map Collection.** 2d ed. Ottawa: Association of Canadian Map Libraries, 1984. 101 p.
  Covers collection assessment and planning. Reviews materials, sources, technical services and reference work.
025.176 F245G   or   Z692 M3F3 MAPL

AK2   Hodgkiss, A.G. and Tatham, A.F. **Keyguide to Information Sources in Cartography.** London: Mansell, 1986. 253 p.
  A useful reference aid for anyone involved in cartographic work or research. Includes a thorough discussion of cartography and its literature, annotated bibliographies of historical and contemporary cartography and a directory of organizations. International orientation.
Z6021 H6 MAPL

AK3   **Information Sources in Cartography.** Ed. by C.R. Perkins, and E.R. Perry. New York: K.G. Saur, 1990. 384 p.
  Covers the literature of cartography and mapping. Also covers map librarianship, types of mapping, and mape use, production, and promotion, written in bibliographic essays.
Z6021 I53 MAPL

AK4   Kister, Kenneth F. **Kister's Atlas Buying Guide: General English–Language World Atlases Available in North America.** Phoenix, AZ: Oryx, 1984. 236 p.
  Provides concise descriptive and evaluative information for 105 English–language world atlases. Includes atlas evaluation guidelines and references to reviews.
Z6021 K5 MAPL

AK5   Nicholson, N.L. and L.M. Sebert. **The Maps of Canada: A Guide to Official Canadian Maps, Charts, Atlases and Gazetteers.** Hamden, CT: Archon/ Shoe String Press, 1981. 251 p.
  A comprehensive survey and historical guide to official Canadian map and chart series. Arranged by series with a section on important provincial map series.
R912.71 N627M   or   GA473.7 A1N53 MAPL

AK6 Parry, R.B. and C.R. Perkins. **World Mapping Today.** London: Butterworths, 1987. 583 p.

Valuable information about the acquisition of modern topographic and thematic maps in print in the mid–1980s. Includes hard–to–find map indexes as well as geographical and publishers' indexes. Arranged by region and country. Also offers an overview of the state of world mapping in the 1980s.
Z692 M3W67 MAPL

Bibliographies and Catalogues

AK7 **Bibliographia Cartographica: International Documentation of Cartographical Literature,** 1974– . Munich: K.G. Saur. irregular annual.

(Volume 15, 1988 [1989]). Title, publisher varies. An earlier set of 30 volumes, titled *Bibliotheca Cartographia*, covers a span from 1936–1972. Essential for large map libraries (over 100,000 maps) or libraries supporting cartography courses. A bibliography covering applications, history and theory of cartography. Includes recent periodical article citations. Arranged by general subject area. Items primarily from English, German and French sources.
Z6021 B48 MAPL

AK8 **Bibliographic Guide to Maps and Atlases,** 1979- . Boston: G.K. Hall. annual.

This subject bibliography lists selective publications catalogued by the Research Libraries of the New York Public Library and the Library of Congress. Included in this guide are maps, atlases, globes, books about cartography and journal articles. Serves as a selective index to cartographic literature.
Z6028 N482

AK9 Hale, Elizabeth. **The Discovery of the World: Maps of the Earth and the Cosmos from the David M. Stewart Collection.** Montreal: David M. Stewart Museum, 1985. 87 p.

A catalog of map reproductions from an exhibition of maps held at the David M. Stewart Museum in Montreal, dating from the invention of the printing press to the end of the French regime and including maps of the Old and New Worlds. Useful source for history of Canada in maps.
GA300 D5 MAPL

AK10 Library of Congress. **A List of Geographical Atlases in the Library of Congress.** 8 vols. Washington: Library of Congress, 1909–74.

Volume 1 lists atlases held at Library of Congress to 1909. Volume 2 is an author and analytical index to volume 1. Volume 3 is a supplement, covering 1909–1914. Volume 4 covers 1914–1920. Volume 5 describes world atlases received at LC 1920–1955. Volume 6 covers atlases of Europe, Asia, Africa, Australia, Oceania and the polar regions and oceans, 1920–1960. Volume 7 covers North, Central and South America, 1920–1969. Volume 8 is the index to volume 7. Entries give full information and include contents notes.
Z6028 U54 MAPL

AK11 Library of Congress. **National Union Catalog. Cartographic Materials,** 1983– . Washington: Library of Congress. quarterly. annual cumulation (microfiche).

A register of full bibliographic records with five indexes (name, title, subject, series, geographic classification codes). The indexes are cumulative (i.e. the 1990 indexes provide access to 1983 to 1990 materials). Records all single and multi–sheet thematic map sets, atlases and

maps treated as serials by LC. For information on the *National Union Catalog* see AD12.
ZN2795 mfe MAPL

AK12 The Map Catalog: Every Kind of Map and Chart on Earth and Even Some above It. Ed. by Joel Makower. New York: Vintage Books/Random House, 1986. 252 p.

Guide to the various types of maps (land maps, sky maps, water maps), and map products. Thematic maps of all types, many for the U.S. but also internationally, are included. Includes information such as address, price, and illustrated samples of each type of map, for those seeking map sources.
Z6028 M23 MAPL

AK13 Numeric Map Catalogue / Catalogue numérique des cartes, 1978- . Ottawa: Survey and Mapping Branch, Dept. of Energy, Mines and Resources. microfiche, monthly.

A listing of maps from the Canada Map Office, providing stock numbers and sheet names for editions available. Supersedes the paper *Catalogue of Published Maps/ Catalogue des cartes publiées* (1967–1978).

AK14 Public Archives of Canada. **Catalogue of National Map Collection / Catalogue de la collection nationale de cartes et plans.** 16 vols. Boston: G.K. Hall, 1976.

Represents less than 15% of the National Map Collection in 1976. Almost 98,000 catalogue cards reproduced in area, author and subject sections. The Archives have also published numerous subject catalogues of their holdings of Canadian and international maps and atlases, (e.g. *County Atlases of Canada: A Descriptive Catalogue*; 1970).
Z6028 N348 MAPL

AK15 Union List of Foreign Topographic Map Series Available in Canadian Map Collections. Ottawa: Public Archives Canada, 1986. 148 p.

A listing of foreign topographic map holdings in Canadian map collections.
Z6028 N3847

AK16 Winearls, Joan. **Mapping Upper Canada, 1780-1867: An Annotated Bibliography of Manuscript and Printed Maps.** Toronto: University of Toronto Press, 1991. 986 p.

A comprehensive bibliography to manuscripts and printed maps of Upper Canada and Canada West, from the beginning of British settlement to Confederation. Each entry includes a physical description of the map as well as its location. Appendices group more than 2,000 township surveys. Includes name, subject and title indexes.

Directories to Collection

AK17 Directory of Canadian Map Collections. 5th ed. Compiled by Lorraine Dubreuil. Ottawa: Association of Canadian Map Libraries, 1986. 163 p.

122 Canadian map collections are listed alphabetically by province and city. Notes basic directory information, specialization and use of computer systems.
026.912 D598M (1980) or
GA193 C3D5 MAPL

AK18 Map Collections in the United States and Canada: A Directory. 4th ed. New York: Special Libraries Association, 1985. 178 p.

A classic work containing 804 entries arranged alphabetically by city within a state or province. Includes contact information, size, area specialization and lending policies.
026.912 S74M3 (1978 3d ed)   or
GA193 U5S7 MAPL

AK19 **World Directory of Map Collections.** 2d ed. IFLA Publication, no. 31. New York: K.G. Saur, 1986. 405 p.

Lists 707 collections in 65 countries. In addition to directory information, it notes subject and chronological range of collections, lending policies, classification schemes, publications, etc.
GA192 W67 MAPL

International Atlases

AK20 Chaliand, Gerard and Jean-Pierre Rageau. **A Strategic Atlas: Comparative Geopolitics of the World's Powers.** Rev. ed. New York: Harper & Row, 1990. 224 p.

An atlas based on the Napoleonic principle that the policy of a state lies in its geography. Using colour maps, statistics and unusual cartographic principles, the authors graphically display global political, military and economic issues from a variety of national perspectives.
G1046 F1 C43413 MAPL

AK21 **Concise Earth Book World Atlas.** Denver, CO: Earthbooks, 1990. 184 p.

Compact atlas providing maps and statistical information for each country in the world. Colour maps for each country include data such as population, national and state capitals, national boundaries, disputed national boundaries, waterfalls, major roads, railway systems, and sea levels. World maps show environment, religions, languages, time zones and endangered species.

A larger edition of this atlas is the *Earth Book World Atlas* (Graphic Learning International, 1987), which includes an encyclopedia of the earth, the world in maps, and a glossary and index. Many of the maps are environmental maps depicting vegetation, mountains, croplands, etc.
G1021 E85 MAPL (1987)

AK22 **Goode's World Atlas.** 18th ed. Ed. by E.B. Espenshade, and J. Morrison. Chicago: Rand McNally, 1991. 368 p.

A small desk-sized general reference atlas noted for accuracy and legibility. Includes maps of large urban areas, thematic maps and a discussion of mapping and projections.
R912 G647W2   or   G1019.G67 MAPL

AK23 Goss, John. **The Mapping of North America: Three Centuries of Map-Making, 1500-1860.** Secaucus, NJ: Welfleet Press, 1990. 184 p.

Illustrates changing perspectives of the world by tracing the mapping of the continent of North America. Each facsimile map reproduction is accompanied by a brief description.

AK24 Grant, Neil and Nick Middleton. **Atlas of the World Today.** New York: Harper & Row, 1987. 159 p.

The authors of this work have sought to "put into focus the state of human society and its physical environment in the 1980s". Simple colour maps illustrate comparative economic, physical and social conditions around the world.
G1021 G675 MAPL

AK25 **The Great World Atlas.** New York: American Map Corporation, 1986. 351 p.

Topographic maps constitute the major part of this new world atlas. Also includes thematic maps arranged by single topic and thematic groups and a selection of satellite photos.
G1021 A524 MAPL

AK26 **Hammond Large Type World Atlas.** Maplewood NJ: Hammond, 1989. 144 p.

Intended for elementary school, but useful for the visually-impaired. Major administrative boundaries, cities, towns, lakes and rivers (but not roads) are indicated in this large type atlas and gazetteer.
G1021 H2727 MAPL

AK27 **National Geographic Atlas of the World.** 6th ed. Washington: National Geographic Society, 1990. 405 p.

Covers all areas and countries of the world with emphasis on United States and Canada. Includes maps of the solar system, oceans, natural resources, over 200 urban inset maps and a 150,000 entry index. Also available is the *National Geographic Atlas of North America: Space Age Portrait of a Continent* (1985) (G1106 N3 MAPL fo), which includes remote sensing images, satellite images, and thematic maps of sections covering Canada, United States and Middle America at different times of the day and year.
R912 N277 (1966)   or   G1019 N28 MAPL

AK28 Nebenzahl, Kenneth. **Atlas of Columbus and the Great Discoveries.** Chicago: Rand McNally, 1990. 168 p.

Useful source for those studying the history of cartography, particularly after the discovery of the New World and of a sea route to Asia. Contains over 50 colour and black-and-white maps from the 15th and 16th centuries, many drawn by famous explorers and early cartographers. Text and references complement the maps.

AK29 **The New International Atlas.** Chicago: Rand McNally, 1980, c1986. 320, 232 p.

Earlier editions called *The International Atlas*. A multilingual, visually attractive reference atlas with balanced map coverage of the world, both topographic and thematic. Includes a comprehensive, 160,000 entry gazetteer-index.
R912 R187I (1969)   or   G1091 R43 MAPL

AK30 **New Oxford Atlas.** 3d rev. ed. London: Oxford University Press, 1978. 202 p.

A British metric atlas with physical, political and thematic maps. Emphasis on the United Kingdom and Western Europe. Concludes with a 50,000 entry gazetteer-index.
G1019 N493 MAPL

AK31 **Peters Atlas of the World.** New York: Harper Collins, 1990. 188 p.

A new world view based on concepts of equal scale and area projection developed by Arno Peters. It promises and delivers "a new geographical picture of the world based on equal status of all the peoples of the earth." Includes 43 physical maps and 246 thematic maps.
G1021 P38 MAPL

AK32 **The Times Atlas and Encyclopaedia of the Sea.** 2d ed. Ed. by Alastair Couper. New York: Harper & Row, 1990. 272 p.

Includes over 600 full colour maps, photographs and illustrations covering a wide range of topics such as the ocean environment, resources, trade, naval warfare and sea life. Previously

published as *The Times Atlas of the Oceans* (1983).
G2800 T55 MAPL

AK33 **The Times Atlas of the World.** 8th ed. New York: Time Books, 1990. 225 p.

The (London) *Times Atlas* was prepared in its "comprehensive" format by John Bartholomew & Sons of Edinburgh in 1977. This edition revises the "7th comprehensive" (1985). Consists of 3 parts: an introduction to the earth and universe, an extensive map section and an index–gazetteer. The condensed version is *The Times Concise Atlas of the World* (1987) (G1019 T535 MAPL fo). A new form of this *Atlas*, geared to the younger user, is *The Times Atlas of the World: Family Edition* (1990).
G1021 T55 MAPL

AK34 **Atlas de la Nouvelle-France**, 1968.

Contains maps of New France. See CJ93 for full entry information.

Atlases with a National Emphasis - Canada and the United States

AK35 **Canada Gazetteer Atlas.** Toronto: Macmillan of Canada in cooperation with Energy, Mines and Resources and Supply and Services, 1980. 164 p.

French edition: *Canada atlas toponymique* (Guerin, 1980). A companion volume to the *National Atlas of Canada* (AK41). Concise informative introduction; 48 maps, mainly political and demographic. Gazetteer–index of 30,000 names in two sections, populated places and physical features. Geographical names presented in language approved by provincial/territorial name authorities.
G1115 C36 MAPL; GENR

AK36 Cloutier, André, Erik Graf and Michel Villeneuve. **Atlas thématique du Canada et du monde.** Montreal: Éditions du Renouveau Pédagogique, 1987. 185 p.

A French language atlas exploring Canada's geography, with an emphasis on Quebec, in a global context. Arranged thematically, this work covers such topics as climate, population, natural resources, transportation and communications.
G1115 M36

AK37 Gentilcore, R. Louis and C. Grant Head. **Ontario's History in Maps.** Toronto: University of Toronto Press, 1984. 284 p.

Text and maps explore the development of the province as recorded in early manuscript and printed maps. The concerns and values of a developing Ontario are reflected through the 300 watercolour maps of the Simcoe era to 19th and 20th century Canadian mapping. With a cartobibliography by Joan Winearls.
G1146 S1G46 MAPL

AK38 Matthews, Geoffrey J. and Robert Morrow Jr. **Canada and the World: An Atlas Resource.** Scarborough, ON: Prentice–Hall Canada, 1985. 201 p.

Provides a detailed view of Canada in its world setting. Uses maps, flow diagrams, graphs, tables, satellite images and colour photographs in a thematic and regional approach to this country's geography and history.
G1115 M36

AK39 **Historical Atlas of Canada**, 1987-1990.

A multi-volume, award-winning atlas set. Provides a visual record of Canada's history and geography through text, maps, charts and graphs. See CJ87 for full entry information.

AK40 Matthews, Geoffrey J. **Nelson Canadian Atlas.** Scarborough, ON: Nelson Canada, 1988. 96 p.

Designed for school use, this basic atlas contains information and maps specifically for Canada. Includes thematic maps depicting major physical, economic, historical and cultural aspects of Canada, with complementary colour photographs around the maps.

AK41 **The National Atlas of Canada.** 5th ed. Ottawa: Dept. of Energy, Mines and Resources, Surveys & Mapping Branch. 1985–

Title varies. French edition: *L'Atlas national du Canada*. Continues a tradition established in 1906 with the first *National Atlas of Canada*. This edition issued as a continuing serial publication of separate maps in portfolio. A comprehensive thematic atlas organized within 44 subject areas with an expected completion at about 200 maps. Revision of these maps will also be undertaken.
G1115 C21 MAPL

AK42 **National Atlas of the United States of America.** Washington: Geological Survey, 1970. 417 p.

"The 765 maps ... constitute a scientific presentation in cartographic format, of the principal characteristics of the country, including its physical features, historical evolution, economic activities, socio–cultural conditions, administrative subdivisions, and place in world affairs."
G1200 U57 MAPL

Gazetteers

AK43 **Chambers World Gazetteer: An A–Z of Geographical Information.** 5th ed. Ed. by Dr. David Munro. Edinburgh: Chambers, 1988. 733 p.

Worldwide in scope, this directory of places contains over 200,000 entries, 150 line maps, political maps of each country, and a 120 page colour atlas. Includes detailed information on location, population, topography, history, and political and economic activity. Pronunciations are also provided. This is a standard pocket-sized reference work, similar to, but about half the size of, *Webster's New Geographical Dictionary* (AK51).
G103.5 C43

AK44 **The Columbia Lippincott Gazetteer of the World.** With 1961 Supplement. New York: Columbia University Press, 1962. 2148 p.

A descriptive standard gazetteer, now dated, but useful for older names. Supplement describes major geographical changes since date of original edition, 1952.
R910.3 C72   or   G103 L7 MAPL

AK45 **Foreign Gazetteers of the U.S. Board on Geographic Names.** Bethesda, MD: Congressional Information Service, 1987. 1505 microfiche.

A comprehensive microfiche file consisting of the most current Defense Mapping Agency (DMA) gazetteers of most countries in the world, (except the U.S.), plus Antarctica and underseas areas. A four page printed bibliography accompanying the microfiche lists the countries included in the file and provides cross references to previous names or to several countries in one gazetteer.

AK46 **Gazetteer of Canada / Répertoire géographique du Canada,** 1952– . Ottawa: Permanent Committee on Geographical Names, Surveys and Mapping Branch, Dept. of Energy, Mines and Resources. irregular. *Additions and Corrections*, 195[?]– irregular.

Published in parts with a separate volume for each province and territory except Quebec (see AK48). This comprehensive Canadian series lists co–ordinates and provides references to National Topographic Series (NTS) sheet numbers for both physical features and administrative place–names. Latest editions: *New Brunswick* (1972), *Prince Edward Island* (1990), *Alberta* (1988), *Nova Scotia* (1977), *Northwest Territories* (1980, reprinted 1984), *Manitoba* (1981), *Yukon* (1988), *Newfoundland* (1983), *British Columbia* (1985), *Saskatchewan* (1985), *Ontario* (1988). Some volumes also available on microfiche.
R917.1 C21   or   F5008 G3

AK47 **Guide to Places of the World.** New York: Reader's Digest Association, 1987. 735 p.

A geographical dictionary of over 7,000 entries of places, natural and man-made, in the world. Includes colour photographs and diagrams, and relief maps. Arranged by country, with a section on international geographical terms in several languages with short definitions.
G63 G85 MAPL

AK48 **Répertoire toponymique du Québec.** 1987. [Prepared by] La Commission de la toponymie. Québec: Éditeur officiel du Québec, 1987. 1900 p.

This French–language gazetteer, produced by the Quebec government, includes physical features, administrative regions and municipalities; listing their coordinates and NTS numbers. Some 93,000 approved names are listed.
F5451 R48 GENR; MAPL

AK49 **The Statesman's Year-Book World Gazetteer.** 3d ed. Ed. by John Paxton. New York: St. Martin's Press, 1986. 665 p.

Brief entries listing location, population, and other relevant information on over 8,000 places. Complements *Statesman's Year-Book* (AH25).
G103.5 S8O2

AK50 **The Times Index–Gazetteer of the World.** London: The Times, 1965. 964 p.

A comprehensive guide to 345,000 geographical locations with coordinates. Includes map–references to places included in the mid–century edition of *The Times Atlas of the World*.
R910.3 T583   or   G103.T5 GENR; MAPL

AK51 **Webster's New Geographical Dictionary.** Rev. ed. Springfield, MA: Merriam–Webster, 1988. 1376 p.

Consists of more than 47,000 entries of geographical international place names and terms, and 218 small maps. Provides brief essential information on spelling, pronunciation and, depending on the nature of the entry's location, population, size, economy and history. Emphasis on United States and Canada.
G103 W45

Place Names

AK52 Hamilton, William B. **The Macmillan Book of Canadian Place Names.** 2d ed. Toronto: Macmillan of Canada, 1983. 287 p.

The origin of about 1,800 Canadian place

names arranged alphabetically by province. Largely replaces *The Origin and Meaning of Place Names in Canada* by G.H. Armstrong (Macmillan, 1930) (R917.1 A735).
R917.1003 H222M   or   F5008 H3

AK53 Harder, Kelsie B. **Illustrated Dictionary of Place Names: United States and Canada.** New York: Van Nostrand Reinhold, 1976. 631 p.

Describes the origin of place names in the United States and Canada.
E155 H37 GENR; MAPL

AK54 Sealock, R.B., M.M. Sealock, and M. Powell. **Bibliography of Place-Name Literature: United States and Canada.** 3d ed. Chicago: American Library Association, 1982. 435 p.

A comprehensive bibliography of place-name literature available in books, periodicals and selected manuscripts. Arranged geographically, and containing an author and personal name index and a subject index.
R929.4 AS43B3   or   Z6824 S4

AK55 The **United States Dictionary of Places.** New York: Somerset Publishers, 1988. 644 p.

A "national place-name directory" of the United States limited mainly to incorporated places. Includes population, zip codes, co-ordinates and place-name origins.
E155 U55

AL   BIOGRAPHY

Bibliographies

AL1   ARBA Guide to Biographical Dictionaries. Ed. by Bohdan S. Wynar. Littleton, CO: Libraries Unlimited, 1986. 444 p.

A representative selection of annotated titles (serial and monograph) from *ARBA* (AC1), in print in the mid-80s and created since the mid-60s. Coverage is universal, national and by specific subjects, e.g. science and technology.
Z5301 A82

AL2   Biographical Books, 1876–1949. New York: R.R. Bowker, 1983. 1768 p. Updated with *Biographical Books, 1950–1980*, Bowker, 1982. 1557 p.

"Virtually every biography published or distributed in the U.S." for the years stated. Autobiographies, letters, diaries, journals, collective biographies, etc. are alphabetically arranged in a name/subject index containing some 16,500 names and 3,500 LC subjects. Nearly comprehensive for U.S. trade publications.
R920 AB582B (1876–1940)   or   Z5301 B47 (1950–1980)

AL3   Biographical Dictionaries and Related Works: An International Bibliography.... 2d ed. 2 vols. Ed. by Robert B. Slocum. Detroit: Gale Research, 1986.

A lengthy subtitle explains that this work is compiled from collective biographies, bio-bibliographies, genealogical works, dictionaries of acronyms and pseudonyms, historical and specialized dictionaries, government manuals with biographical material, bibliographies of biographies, biographical indexes and portrait catalogues. Volume 1: Universal, National, Area Biography; Volume 2: Biography by Vocation. With author, title, and subject indexes.
Z5301 S55

AL4   International Bibliography of Biography 1970–1987. 12 vols. London/New York: K.G. Saur, 1988.

A list of biographical works published throughout the world between 1970–87, compiled from U.S./U.K. MARC records of British Library holdings. Includes a subject sequence (alphabetical list of individuals covered) and an Author/Title Index.
Z5301 I57

Abstracts and Indexes

AL5   Almanac of Famous People. 4th ed. 3 vols. Ed. by Susan L. Stetler. Detroit: Gale Research, 1989.

Formerly *Biography Almanac*. Covers some 25,000 famous and infamous individuals and groups labelled "newsmakers" from Biblical times to the present. In Volumes 1 & 2, under

the popular name, there is a brief identification, description and citation to other biographical sources. Volume 3 lists the biographees in chronologies, occupations and geographic regions.
Z5301 B488 ROBA (1987)

AL6 Biography and Genealogy Master Index. 2d ed. 8 vols. Ed. by Miranda C. Herbert and Barbara McNeil. Detroit: Gale Research, 1980. *Annual Supplements* 1981-82 (in various vols), or as *Cumulation* 1981-85 (5 vols); 1986-90 (3 vols); continued by annual update (1991-single vol).

First edition called *Biographical Dictionaries Master Index* (1975-76) with *Supplement* (1980). In the base set (2d ed) and updates through the 1980s, *BGMI* claims well over 7 million citations gathered from several hundred contemporary who's whos and other works of collective biography. *Abridged BGMI* (1988, 3 volumes), taken from the base set through the 1987 supplement, has over 1.6 million citations. With the 1991 supplement, there are now nearly 5 million citations.

Other continuing titles in the Biographical Index Series are *Author Biography Master Index* (see AL52); and *Writers for Young Adults* (AL72).

BIO-BASE (1990 Master Cumulation, with annual updates, 1991-) is a microfiche version of *BGMI*. The fiche index has a printed list of sources indexed. *BIO-BASE* cumulates every five years from inception (the 1980 *BGMI*) to current edition, and is updated annually. Also available online and on CD-ROM.
Z5305 U5

AL7 Biography Index: A Cumulative Index to Biographical Material in Books and Magazines, 1946- . New York: H.W. Wilson. quarterly; annual; biennial cumulations.

An index to biographical material in over 2,700 current popular and scholarly journals and over 1,800 books primarily in the English language. Includes an index by name, profession and occupation. Available online and on CD-ROM.
IND

Obituaries

AL8 The Annual Obituary, 1980- . London/Chicago: St. James Press, 1983- . annual.

Essays of varying length combine a who's who with a newspaper report approach for prominent persons who died during the year. Entry has photograph and bibliographic references, and is chronological under month. Alphabetical and profession indexes.
CT120 A55

AL9 The New York Times Obituaries Index, 1858–1968. New York: New York Times, 1969. 1136 p.

Names from the newspaper which were entered under deaths of newsworthy persons, not paid obituary notices. Continued by *New York Times Obituaries II, 1969–1978* (1980, 2 vols) (E176 N4) and by the *New York Times Obituary Index*, 1988- (annual, Meckler Pub. Co.). More recent obituaries can be found using *New York Times Index* (see AF31). *Current Biography* (AL12) also contains obituaries.
R920.3 N532 (1858–1968) or E176 N4

AL10 Obituaries on File. 2 vols. Comp. by Felice Levy. New York: Facts on File, 1979.

Short notices culled from *Facts on File*, (AF32), 1940 through 1978, arranged in one alphabetical sequence with chronological and

subject (including vocational and geographical reference) indexes.
CT120 L43

International Biographical Dictionaries

AL11 Chambers Biographical Dictionary. Ed. by Magnus Magnusson. London: Chambers, 1990. 1604 p.

A comprehensive source for brief entries. While editors try to be comprehensive for the U.K., this much revised and enlarged edition is also intended to broaden the international coverage considerably and extend the coverage of popular figures from sports and media.
CT103 C4

AL12 Current Biography, 1940- . New York: H.W. Wilson. 11 monthly issues with annual cumulation in *Current Biography Yearbook*; *Index 1940–1985*.

Although international in scope and with all fields (arts, politics, science etc.) represented, coverage is heavily American. Each issue includes 16-18 profiles between 2,500-3,000 words in length, of people "who make today's headlines and tomorrow's history." Includes portraits and bibliographies. Articles are verified by biographees before inclusion in the annual *Current Biography Yearbook*. Each *Yearbook* contains a cumulated index to all previous issues of the decade. *CB* has obituaries, which are generally short, with citation to earlier coverage.
R920.3 C976

AL13 Dictionary of National Biography from Earliest Times to 1900. 63 vols. London: Smith, Elder, 1895–1901. Edited by Leslie Stephen and Sidney Lee. With 3 vols. Supplement, 1903. Last reissue, 22 vols. Oxford, 1963–64. Twentieth century supplements: 8 decennial 1901–80 with cumulative indexes; quinquennial 1980–85.

The *DNB* has been issued by Oxford since 1917, and is commonly seen in the 22 volume set (main set is Volumes 1-21; supplement is Volume 22). It is the major British national biographical dictionary, commemorating persons in Great Britian, Ireland and the Commonwealth. Excludes living persons. A concise version called *Dictionary of National Biography: The Concise Dictionary* was published in 1948-61 in 2 volumes: Volume 1: "From the Beginnings to 1900"; and Volume 2: 1901–1950 (DA28 D45). A revision to volume 2 was published in 1982, called *Concise Dictionary of National Biography* and covers the years 1901-1970 (DA28 D45).
R920.3 D55B2
(Volume 1-22, and supplements)

AL14 The International Dictionary of Women's Biography. New York: Continuum, 1982. 534 p.

Short biographies of some 1,500 women throughout history. Other biographical reference sources about women include: *The World Who's Who of Women* (CG56), which provides illustrated biographical information of leading women in the world; *Who's Who of American Women* (1958/59-, Chicago: Marquis Who's Who) (E747 W55), which includes more than 21,000 women in all areas of achievement; formerly called *Who's Who of American Women and Women of Canada*. For Canadian women, there is the *Who's Who of Canadian Women* (1983-, Toronto: Trans-Canada Press, irregular annual) (F5009 W64).
CT3202 I57 SIGR

AL15 **The International Who's Who,** 1935- . London: Europa. annual.

Brief information on over 20,000 prominent people in all fields. Europa also publishes or copublishes / distributes, in irregular editions, national or regional titles e.g. *Who's Who in International Affairs* (1990). Titles are often those in the International Red Series (AL23).
R920.3 I61   or   CT120 I5

AL16 **Longman Dictionary of 20th Century Biography.** Ed. by A. Isaacs and E. Martin. Harlow, Essex: Longman, 1985. 548 p.

Brief entries for a wide variety of people whose names were culled from widely available and accessible sources.
CT120 L64

AL17 **Macmillan Dictionary of Biography.** 2d rev. ed. Ed. by Barry Jones and M.V. Dixon. Melbourne: Macmillan, 1986. 917 p.

Short entries on some 7,500 persons, living and dead.
CT103 J6

AL18 **The New York Times Biographical Service,** 1970- . Ann Arbor, MI: University Microfilms International, 1984- . monthly; monthly index with semiannual, annual cumulation.

Began as the *New York Times Biographical Edition*. A looseleaf "compilation of current biographical information of general interest" with more than 1,400 profiles annually, with full text and photos from the *New York Times* and *New York Times Magazine*.
CT120 N45

AL19 Newsmakers, 1991- . Detroit: Gale Research, 1986- . quarterly with annual cumulation.

Formerly *Contemporary Newsmakers* (1985-90). A similar publication and competitor with the longer running *Current Biography* (AL12), although intentional duplication is avoided by *Newsmakers* which has about 200 profiles a year, with an obituary section. Covers all fields (business, arts, literature, sports).
MTRL GIS

AL20 **Pseudonyms and Nicknames Dictionary.** 3d ed. 2 vols. Ed. by Jennifer Mossman. Detroit: Gale Research, 1987.

Includes figures from all walks of life. Entries furnish original and assumed names, birth and/or death dates, nationality and occupation with reference to some sources of additional information.
CT120 P8

AL21 **Webster's Biographical Dictionary.** Springfield, MA: Merriam, 1980. 1679 p.

Brief information on alphabetically listed figures throughout history to the present. Upwards of 40,000 names with pronunciation. Universal but intended for English speakers with a fuller treatment of British and American names. "Only in certain classes ... some inadequacies," i.e. for sports, media, entertainment world, where names are numerous and fame possibly fleeting. *Webster's* also has useful lists of historical rulers, etc.
R920.3 W38 (1972)   or   CT103 W4

AL22 Who's Who, 1849- . London: Black. annual.

Concise authoritative biographies of distinguished living Britons and international figures.
R920.3 W62   or   DA28 W6

AL23 Who's Who. International Red Series. Worthsee, Germany: Who's Who Verlag.

Approximately 18 titles are published in series. Some titles are available under the Europa imprint (AL15). Published in English with entries, in alphabetical order by name, for life and career history of prominent persons. Appendices in volumes give lists of diplomatic representatives, government officials, some chambers of commerce, municipal offices, or the like, and associations and publishers. Most editions have a subject index. The "National Editions," e.g. *Who's Who in Germany* (2 vols, 1991), ... *In Italy* (2 vols, 1991) are annual or biennial; the "Special Editions" (e.g. AL24) are often triennial.

AL24 Who's Who in European Institutions, Organizations, and Enterprises, 1982- . Worthsee, Germany: Who's Who Verlag. irregular annual.

An International Red Book Who's Who (see AL23), includes over 3,000 personalities in organizations, associations, European parliament etc. German publishers Saur/SVK also produce or copublish/distribute similar English language irregular annuals of occupational and area who's who, e.g. *Who's Who in International Organizations* (3 vols, 1991); ... *In the Socialist Countries of Europe* (1989); ... *In the Arab World 1990–91* (1990); ... *In Japan 1987–88* (1987).
AS98 W52

AL25 Who's Who in the World, 1971/72- . Chicago: Marquis Who's Who. biennial.

Represents all fields of endeavour, listing more than 24,000 biographees in brief sketches covering education, career, politics and special achievement.
R920.3 W622   or   CT120 W47

AL26 Who Was Who, 1897-1980. 7 vols. London: St. Martin's, 1961–81.

Vol. 1: 1897–1915; Vol. 2: 1916–28; Vol. 3: 1929–40; Vol. 4: 1941–50; Vol. 5: 1951–60; Vol. 6: 1961–70; Vol. 7: 1971–80;

These companion volumes to *Who's Who* (AL22) include entries for deceased people, as they appeared in the original volumes with death dates and sometimes added or corrected information. There is a separate *Index to Who Was Who* (1981) cumulated 1897 to 1980.
R920.3 W62AW   or   DA28

AL27 Who Was Who in the Greek World, 776 B.C. - 30 B.C., 1982. See CJ34 for full entry information.

AL28 Who Was Who in the Roman World, 753 B.C. - A.D. 476, 1980. See CJ34n for information.

National Biographical Dictionaries

Canada

AL29 Biographies canadiennes - françaises / Who's Who in Quebec, 1920- . Montreal: J.A. Fortin. irregular.

(31st ed, 1984-85). Entries in French and English provide biographical information such as position, education, career, office address. Includes portraits.
R920.3 B615B   or   F5452 B58

AL30   The Canadian Men and Women of the Time: A Handbook of Canadian Biography of Living Characters. 2d ed. Ed. by Henry J. Morgan.   Toronto: William Briggs, 1912. 1281 p.

This and first edition (1898) are important for coverage of noteworthy persons of the late 1800's. Portraits are often included. Morgan's *Sketches of Celebrated Canadians* (1862) contains some 460 biographies of pre-Confederation Canadians in Upper Canada (Ontario) and Lower Canada (Quebec).
R920.3 M84C2

AL31   The Canadian Who's Who, 1910- . Toronto: University of Toronto Press, 1978- . annual.

CWW Index 1898–1984; CWW 1979–1988 (microfiche); *CWW: A Complete Index 1-898–1988* (microfiche).

Title, publisher and frequency varied before the *CWW*'s acquisition by the University of Toronto Press and the establishment of the annual with the 14th (1979) edition. With the second edition in 1936, it incorporated *Canadian Men and Women of the Time A Biographical Dictionary of Notable Living Men and Women. CWW* provides descriptions, with addresses, about the life, honours, profession, leisure interests of approximately 11,000 notable living Canadians each year, selected for inclusion on the basis of merit and position. Entries are alphabetically by name. The *Canadian Who's Who Index 1898–1984* (1986) compiled by E. McMann is an index of both *CWW* and *Canadian Men and Women of the Time*, listing over 33,000 names.
R920.3 C211   or
F5009 C3; Index F5009 C32

AL32   Dictionary of Canadian Biography. 12 vols. Ed. by Francess Halpenny. Toronto: University of Toronto Press, 1965–90. With separate *Cumulative Index.*

Vol. 1: 1000–1700; Vol. 2: 1701–40; Vol. 3: 1741–70; Vol. 4: 1771–1800; Vol. 5: 1801–20; Vol. 6: 1821–35; Vol. 7: 1836–50; Vol. 8: 1851–60; Vol. 9: 1861–70; Vol. 10: 1871–80; Vol. 11: 1881–90; Vol. 12: 1891–1900.

French ed: *Dictionnaire biographique du Canada* (Presses de l'Université Laval) (R920.3 D554A) edited by Jean Hamelin. This significant biographical dictionary documents the lives of noteworthy Canadians. Based on the concept of a national dictionary like *DNB* (AL13) but departing from alphabetical arrangement, the *DCB*'s volumes are organized to demonstrate social as well as biographical history from the year 1000 to the cut-off for biographees who died in/ before 1900. Volumes cover a time span with entries alphabetically arranged within volume. There was an interim *Index to Volumes 1-4: 1000–1800* (1981), now superseded. Each volume has its own index, and the separately published index to the 12 volume set cumulates names with geographical, professional or other designation.
R920.3 D554

AL33   The Macmillan Dictionary of Canadian Biography. 4th ed. Ed. by W.A. McKay. Toronto: Macmillan, 1978. 914 p.

Contains sketches (30 to 600 words) on more than 5,000 noteworthy Canadians deceased before 1976. First edition (1926) and subsequent editions, edited by W. Stewart Wallace. Fourth

edition adds dimension of business, science, arts to the emphasis on authors, politicians, government people in the third edition. In the fourth edition, politics and government still account for about a third of the entries; with corrections to earlier entries and updated bibliographical references.
R920.3 M167

AL34   Standard Dictionary of Canadian Biography. 2 vols.   Ed. by Charles G.D. Roberts, and Arthur L. Tunnell. Toronto: Trans-Canada Press, 1934–38.

Biographies, with bibliographies, of Canadians who died 1875–1937.
R920.3 S785

AL35   Who's Who in Canada, 1910- . Toronto: Global Press, 1984- . biennial.

Title, subtitle and publisher varies. Scope is primarily of financial and government figures. Covers over 2,000 biographees in each edition, with portraits usually accompanying the short entries. Previously a random arrangement with name index, the 75th anniversary edition of 1984/85 established the alphabetical listing and added a corporate index, which lists companies, principal officers and their titles.
R920.3 W62C   or   F5009 W62

United States

AL36   Dictionary of American Biography. 17 vols. Sponsored by the American Council of Learned Societies.   New York: Charles Scribner's Sons. 1985. First published in 20 vols, New York: Scribner, 1928–77. Reissued 20 vols. in 10. With 8 supplements, entries cover to 1970. *Comprehensive Index* (complete through 8 supplements, 1990).

Includes biographies of 14,870 deceased Americans who made a significant contribution to American life from earliest times to December 1940. The index volume includes a list of contributors with citations to their articles and an occupation index.   A single volume *Concise Dictionary of American Biography* (3d ed, 1980) (E176 D564) summarizes every biography in the major work and five supplements, and adds an additional 100 biographies for notable Americans who died between 1951-61. A successor series, the *American National Biography* to be published by Oxford in both print and electronic form, is due in the mid-1990s.
R920.3 D553   or   E176 D56

AL37   National Cyclopedia of American Biography, 1888-1984. 75 vols. Clifton, NJ: James T. White, 1892–1984. *Index Volume* 1984.

A comprehensive illustrated dictionary which covers from earliest days of American history but with emphasis after 1850. Published as two series, the *Permanent Series*, (volumes are numbered, 1–62) for deceased people, and the *Current Series*, (volumes are lettered A–M) for living persons. The final volume is lettered and numbered as N–63 (1984) to show that it completes the set, and contains both living and dead persons. The final *Index* (1984) covers the set. Biographies include an illustration, vital statistics and other personal information, public career and accomplishments in essays of varying length. A companion publication, *Notable Names in American History* (1973) (E176 N2816) is a cross reference for individuals and institutions.
E176 N2814

AL38   Who's Who in America: A Biographical Dictionary of Notable Living Men and Women, 1899- . 2 vols.   Chicago: Marquis Who's Who. biennial.

Includes a wide range of Americans and some international figures. Four regional volumes (... *In the East; ... West; ... Midwest; ... South and Southwest*) are also indexed in the main set. Volumes by profession (... *In Government; ... In Finance and Industry; ... In Entertainment*) or by designation (... *Of American Women*) also published.
R920.3 W62AM

AL39   Who was Who in America, 1942- . Chicago: Marquis Who's Who. irregular, index cumulates.

Historical Volume 1607–1896; Vol. 1: 1897–1942; Vol. 2: 1943–50; Vol. 3: 1951–60; Vol. 4: 1961–68; Vol. 5: 1969–73; Vol. 6: 1974–76; Vol. 7: 1977–81; Vol. 8: 1982–85; Vol. 9: 1986–89. *Index*: 1607–1989 (1989).

Companion volumes to *Who's Who in America* (AL38).
R920.3 W62AH   or   E663 W54

Genealogy and Heraldry

AL40 Baxter, Angus. **In Search of Your Canadian Roots: Tracing Your Family Tree in Canada.** Toronto: Macmillan, 1989. 350 p.

First ed. (1980) called *In Search of Your Roots: A Guide for Canadians Seeking Their Ancestors*. An elementary introduction to producing family history, beginning with Canadian sources and branching primarily to U.K. sources, with some information on U.S., Europe. Baxter has similar related titles, e.g. *In Search of Your British and Irish Roots* (1982, CS414 B38); ... *Your European Roots* (1985, CS402 B38).
CS16 B39 (1980)

AL41   Burke's Peerage and Baronetage. 105th ed. Ed. by P. Townend. London: Burke's Peerage, 1970. 3260 p.

Burkes's is recognized as a standard "peerage" publisher since 1826.   This large volume includes lineage of British royalty and nobility, tables of precedence, and regulations about the wearing of decorations. There was an interim abridged edition in 1975, but generally *Burke's* appears in new editions every generation (i.e. 20 years).

Other Burke's Peerage biographical publications, include *Burke's Landed Gentry* (R929.72 B959), *Burke's Presidential Families of the United States* (2d ed, 1981) (E176.1 B86 ROBA) and *Burke's Royal Families of the World (1977-80)* (D352.1 B87 ROBA)   in 2   volumes: Volume 1: *Europe and Latin America*; Volume 2: *Africa & Middle East*, and with a proposed third volume for Asia and Oceania. Families covered are from the mid-19th century forward.
R929.7 B959 (1967, 104th)   or
CS420 B85

AL42   Debrett's Peerage and Baronetage 1990. Ed. by C. Kidd and D. Williams. London: Debrett's, 1990. var. pg.

Founded in 1769, title and publisher vary; now Debrett's, Macmillan, St. Martin's. *Peerage* contains information on the royal family, the peerage, Privy Counsellors, Scottish Lords of Session, baronets, Scottish chieftains - a who's who of the United Kingdom and Northern Ireland.   More concise listings than *Burke's* (AL41), and with precedence, forms of address, orders including foreign and Commonwealth. Other related titles include *Debrett's Kings and Queens of Europe* (1988, CS404 W5) and

Debrett's Presidents of the U.S.A. (1989, E176.1 W7233). *Debrett's Guide to Tracing your Ancestry* (1990, CS415 C8) also provides a general introduction to U.K. sources.
CS420 D322

AL43 Filby, P. William. **American and British Genealogy and Heraldry: A Selected List of Books.** 3d ed. Boston, MA: New England Historic Genealogical Society, 1983. 736 p. *Supplement* 1982-85 (1987).

Authoritative reference source for U.S. and British books on genealogy, heraldry and local history. This edition includes 4,000 entries published between 1975 and 1981, and the three editions (1st ed, 1970, 2d ed, 1976) now contain close to 11,000 entries. Emphasis is on U.S., Latin America, Canada, Great Britain, British island areas and former dominions and selected other countries. Arranged alphabetically by country, then further divided. Sections for Canada include: General Information, Loyalists, and Provinces.
Z5305 G7F55

AL44 Mennie-de Varennes, Kathleen. **Bibliographie annotée d'ouvrages généalogiques au Canada / Annotated Bibliography of Genealogical Works in Canada.** 6 vols. Markham, ON: Fitzhenry & Whiteside in association with the National Library of Canada and the Canadian Government Publishing Centre, 1986.

A bilingual set consisting of four indexes (author/title; parishes for vital records; subject; family names) and two lists (periodicals; genealogical societies in Canada). In all there are 6,000 author/title references and over 22,000 family names represented; the entries under an item cover the range of genealogical materials from monographs, manuscripts, pamphlets, microforms, journal articles.
R929.10971 AM547B

AL45 Tracing Your Ancestors in Canada. Rev. 9th ed. Comp. at the Reference Division, National Archives of Canada. Ottawa: Supply and Services, 1988. 47 p.

French ed.: *Guide des sources généalogiques au Canada.* A free pamphlet listing and describing, in general terms, the various federal and provincial archives, and other records (census, births, military, immigration) that are a basis for a genealogical search.
R929.10971 T759T9

AL46 Weir, Alison. **Britain's Royal Families: The Complete Genealogy.** London: Bodley Head, 1989. 386 p.

Quick and easy identification of persons from the Saxon and Danish kings to the present Windsor family.
CS418 W45

Authors

The following entries list reference sources for authors writing in all fields, and is arranged as follows: Canadian Authors, International Authors, Wilson Author Series, and Children's Authors. Additional sources for literary authors can be found in *Literature*, Section BD.

Canadian Authors

AL47 Canadian Writers / Écrivains Canadiens. 2d ed. Ed. by Guy Sylvestre, Brandon Conron and Carl Klinck. Montreal: Editions HMH, 1966. 186 p.

Has information about 300 authors from 1608 to 1966, with chronological table of important works and index of titles. Biographies (50 to 1,000 words) are in English or French according to the language of the biographee.
R920.3 S985C

AL48   Canadian Writers Series.
Canadian Writers Series is a part of the *Dictionary of Literary Biography* (AL55). Individual volumes refer to volume numbers in *DLB*. The *CWS* series covers four time periods, and more than one volume may be published for each time period. These are described as "First Series", "Second Series", etc. in *DLB*.

Published to date are:
Canadian Writers Before 1890
   (*DLB* Vol. 99, 1990);
Canadian Writers 1890–1920
   (*DLB* Vol. 92, 1990);
Canadian Writers 1920–1959
   (*DLB* Vol. 68 in first series, 1988; and Vol. 88 in second series, 1989);
Canadian Writers Since 1960
   (*DLB*, Vol. 53, first series, 1986; and Vol. 60 in second series, 1987).

Although there may be some correction or supplementary information in the second or later series, no duplication is intended in the volumes covering the same time period.

AL49   Dictionnaire pratique des auteurs québécois. Ed. by Reginald Hamel, John Hare and Paul Wyczynski. Montreal: Fides, 1976. 725 p.
Alphabetical arrangement bio-bibliographies of French language authors in Quebec, and other provinces, with photographs.
PS9081 H34

AL50 Thomas, Clara. **Canadian Novelists, 1920–1945.** Toronto: Longmans, 1946. 129 p.
Short biographical and bibliographical essays about Canadian authors, or established writers living in Canada, who published fiction between 1920 and 1945.
R920.3 T45S

AL51   Who's Who in Canadian Literature, 1983/84- . Ed. by Gordon Ripley and Anne Mercer. Toronto: Reference Press. biennial.
(4th ed. 1989/90). Brief biographical information, including dates, addresses, publications, etc., of living Canadian authors, playwrights, critics, translators active in the literature field. Written in English or French according to the entrant's preference.
R819 W628W   or   PS8081 W56

International Authors

AL52   Author Biographies Master Index. 2 vols. 3d ed. Ed. by Barbara McNeil. Detroit: Gale Research, 1989.
Subtitle reads: *A consolidated guide to biographical information concerning authors living and dead as it appears in a selection of principal biographical dictionaries devoted to authors, poets, journalists and other literary figures.* Includes over 845,000 entries from over 290 biographical dictionaries, encyclopedias, directories, criticisms and bio-bibliographies published between 1816 and 1988. International in scope and covers all time periods, with emphasis on modern U.S. and British writers. Similar information also appears in *BGMI* (AL6), the *Children's Authors and Illustrators* (4th ed, 1987) (Z1037 A1S2 1981 ROBA), and *Twentieth Century Author Biographies Master Index* (1984) (Z5304 A8T83).
Z5304 A8A87

AL53 Contemporary Authors, 1962- . Detroit: Gale Research. annual; cumulated index alternate years.

Volumes 1-100, with periodic cumulated indexes, are issued in sets of 4, to cover the volume year; Volume 101 (1984-) began a new numbering system. A subtitle explains that *CA* is a bio-bibliographical guide to current writers in fiction, general nonfiction, poetry, journalism, drama, motion pictures, television and other fields. Entries, in the form of short biographical notes and interviews, highlight new and established authors and media personalities. Personal facts, career, and full bibliography of works and comments on work in progress are provided. Volumes 1-44 have been revised and cumulated into 11 volumes in the *1st Revision* (1967–79). A *"New Revision Series"* (1980- irregular), updates information on authors due to death, activity or popularity. The latest *Contemporary Authors* cumulative index also serves as an index to the *New Revision Series*. Finally, the *"Permanent Series"*, published irregularly since 1975, consists of updated and revised biographical sketches which were formerly in *Contemporary Authors*. Entries are chosen for inclusion either due to the death of the author, or the retirement of the author from their writing career. The *"Permanent Series"* is also indexed in the latest *Contemporary Authors* index.
R920.3 C761C2   or   Z1224 C62

AL54 Cyclopedia of World Authors II. 4 vols. Ed. by Frank N. Magill. Englewood Cliffs, NJ: Salem Press, 1989.

Short (200 - 1,000 word) entries discuss the life and work of 711 authors, providing birth/death dates, list of works, and bio-bibliographical references. Combined with the first edition, there are approximately 1,500 authors included.
R803 M194W   or   PN41 M26

AL55 Dictionary of Literary Biography, 1978- . Detroit: Gale Research. irregular.

Contains essays by noted scholars on American, British, and world literatures and authors. Each volume runs between 400 and 500 pages, and covers a specific literary movement, genre or period, e.g. Volume 1: *The American Renaissance in New England* (1978); Volume 8, *Twentieth-Century American Science Fiction Writers* (1981); Volume 101 *British Prose Writers 1660–1800* (1990). The alphabetically arranged essays have descriptions of an author's life and work, with a chronology and references. Some volumes are issued in series, e.g. the Canadian materials, (see AL48).

DLB Yearbook (1980-) (PS129 D53) revises entries in the *DLB*, adds new writers and reports on literary news of the year. A *DLB: Documentary Series* (1982-) (PS129 D48) reproduces samples of texts, literary documents pertaining to authors, genres and movements.

The *Concise Dictionary of American Literary Biography*, a 6 volume set published 1988-89 contains 200 updated author entries selected from the 2,300 American author entries in the *DLB* series covering the period of 1640 to 1988. A similar work for British writers, the *Concise Dictionary of British Literary Biography*, an 8 volume set, covers major literary figures of all eras, from Middle English and Renaissance era (pre 1660) to contemporary times, 1960-1990.
PS129 D53

AL56 European Writers. 14 vols. New York: Scribners, 1983-1991.

Forms part of Scribner's "World Literature Series". Includes lengthy signed articles on authors from the Middle Ages and Renaissance to the 20th century, describing works, biographical information, and their historical importance, with a list of references. Other works in this series are: *American Writers*, *British Writers* (8 vols, 1979-84) (PR85 B688 ROBA), and

Ancient Writers: Greece and Rome (2 vols, 1982) (PA3002 A5).
PN501 E9

AL57 **Great Foreign Language Writers.** Ed. by James Vinson and Daniel Kirkpatrick. New York: St. Martin's, 1984. 714 p.

Over 400 writers (dramatists, novelists, poets) typically chosen for study, from languages other than English. Includes a brief biographical sketch, a short critical comment, and a list of works by and about each author. The work also treats epics, legends, etc. of a country. A companion volume in this *Great Writers Series* is *Contemporary Foreign Language Writers* (1984) (PN41 C68).
PN41 G7

AL58 **Major Twentieth Century Writers.** 4 vols. Ed. by Bryan Ryan. Detroit: Gale: Research, 1991.

More than 1,000 authors, particularly fiction authors, that are "most often studied in high school and college." With genre, national and ethnic group indexes. The entries are taken from *Contemporary Authors* (AL53) with correction where necessary.

Wilson Series

AL59 **An Index to the Wilson Author Series.** Rev. ed. New York: H.W. Wilson, 1986. 104 p.

Provides name access to the 8,600 biographical sketches in the 10 volumes published to 1985. See description of series below.
PN451 I44

AL60 **American Authors, 1600–1900.** Ed. by Stanley J. Kunitz and Howard Haycraft. New York: H.W. Wilson, 1938. 584 p.

Nearly 1,300 authors who contributed to the development of American literature from Colonial days to the end of the 19th century.
R920.3 K96AM

AL61 **British Authors Before 1800.** Ed. by Stanley J. Kunitz and Howard Haycraft. New York: H.W. Wilson, 1952. 584 p.

Some 650 major and minor authors from the beginning of English literature to the time of Cowper and Burns.
R920.3 K96B

AL62 **British Authors of the Nineteenth Century.** Ed. by Stanley J. Kunitz and Howard Haycraft. New York: H.W. Wilson, 1936. 677 p.

Over 1,000 of the eminent figures in all fields associated with literary and scholarly endeavour.
R920.3 K96B2

AL63 **European Authors, 1000–1900.** Ed. by Stanley J. Kunitz and Vineta Colby. New York: H.W. Wilson, 1967. 1016 p.

Over 950 of the poets, philosophers, humanists and others from different literatures with principal works available in English.
R920.3 K96E

AL64 Grant, Michael. **Greek and Latin Authors 800 B.C. - A.D. 1000.** New York: H.W. Wilson, 1980. 492 p.

This is the earliest times span covered in the *"Wilson Author Series"*. Portraits, biographical and critical information, and bibliographies are

provided for familiar Classical writers and their works.
PA31 G7

AL65   Twentieth Century Authors. Ed. by Stanley J. Kunitz and Howard Haycraft. New York: H.W. Wilson, 1942. 1577 p. *Supplement* 1955.

Coverage of some 1,850 authors whose work is available in English, and who were active between 1900 and 1942. The supplement updated information on persons in the main volume and added 700 more sketches bringing the title to mid-century currency.
R920.3 K96T

AL66   World Authors, 1950–1970. Ed. by John Wakeman. New York: H.W. Wilson, 1975. 1593 p.

Supplies information on 959 authors who came into prominence between 1950 and 1970. This volume has been updated by 5 year segments, beginning with *World Authors 1970–1975; 1975–1980; 1980–1985*. Coverage has broadened to include well-known as well as lesser-known authors and to more effectively represent the literatures of Eastern Europe, Latin America, Asia and Africa, available in English.
R920.3 K96TA

Children's Authors

AL67 Stott, J.C. and R.E. Jones. **Canadian Books for Children: A Guide to Authors and Illustrators.** Toronto: Harcourt, Brace Jovanovich Canada, 1988. 246 p.

Brief biographical and critical entries for 105 Canadian writers, with a chapter on Canadian stories in the language arts curriculum. *Profiles 2: Authors and Illustrators* (CLA, 1982) (921 M136P2), edited by I. McDonough, contained sketches of Canadian writers who were interviewed for the journal, *In Review*. This journal carried biographical sketches in every issue, and *Profiles* cumulates those sketches. Between the two editions of *Profile* (1971, rev. 1975, and 1982) there are 89 Canadian author/illustrators profiled.

American authors and illustrators are profiled in *Children's Authors and Illustrators* (Gale Research, 4th ed, 1987) (Z1037 A1S2 1981 ROBA).
809.89282 S888B

AL68   The Junior Book of Authors. 2d ed. Ed. by Stanley J. Kunitz and Howard Haycraft. New York: H.W. Wilson, 1951. 309 p.

This is the first book in the Wilson set of children's authors, called the *"Junior Authors and Illustrators"* series. Each book has information on some 250 or more authors, and follows the pattern of other *Wilson Author* series books (AL59). The editors vary in the series. Most titles in the children's series have articles that are written in a simple style for possible use with younger readers. Together the six books in the series contain over 1,500 biographies with photographs, career and personal information. The volumes, as
published, also cumulate a complete index to all previous volumes. The continuing titles are: *More Junior Authors* (1963) (R920.3 F967); *Third Book of Junior Authors* (1972) (R920.3 K96J3); *Fourth Book of Junior Authors & Illustrators* (1978) (R920.3 K96J4), with cumulative index for earlier titles; *Fifth Book of Junior Authors & Illustrators* (1983); and *Sixth Book of Junior Authors & Illustrators* (1989).
R920.3 K96J2

AL69   Something About the Author: Facts and Pictures about Authors and Illustrators of

Books for Young People, 1971- . Detroit: Gale Research. annual; cumulative index.

Taken from *Contemporary Authors* (AL53). Contains portraits, photographs, and book illustrations. Author / illustrator index. A separate *Something About the Authors: Autobiography Series* (1985- semiannual) contains first person essays by authors and illustrators of children's and young adult books. Each volume has approximately 20 essays with photographs of writers and their work. *Authors and Artists for Young Adults* (1988- semi-annual) also selects authors from *CA* who appeal to a particular age of readership.
R920.3 C734S

AL70 Twentieth Century Children's Writers. 3d ed. Ed. by Tracy Chevalier. Chicago: St. James Press, 1989. 1288 p.

Includes entries for selected English language authors of fiction, poetry and drama for children and young people. Notable 19th century writers are included in the appendix. Entries consist of a biography, a complete list of published works (U.S. or British editions listed if original edition) and a critical essay. Comments from some authors are included.
R028.5 T971T or PN4511 T8

AL71 Yesterday's Authors of Books for Children. 2 vols. Ed. by Anne Commire. Detroit: Gale Research, 1977–78.

Some 80 authors or illustrators from early times to 1960 are described in well-illustrated essays.
R920.3 Y47

AL72 Writers for Young Adults: Biographies Master Index: An Index to Sources of Biographical Information... 3d ed. Ed. by Joyce Nakamura. Detroit: Gale, 1989. 183 p.

Provides brief biographical information and a list of references to over 16,000 writers for young adults, including popular teen-age fiction, adult fiction and nonfiction whose works are used by young adults, and writers of nonbook media. Over 145,000 reference items are included.

AM GOVERNMENT PUBLICATIONS

This section is arranged as follows: Multinational guides to government publications are listed first, followed by publications of Canada, Great Britain, and United States. For Intergovernmental publications (United Nations, etc.) see *International Government Documents*, Section AN. See also *Political Science*, Section CD.

Multinational Bibliographies and Guides to the Literature

AM1 Cherns, J.J. **Official Publishing: An Overview. An International Survey and Review of the Role, Organization and Principles of Official Publishing.** Oxford: Pergamon, 1979. 527 p.

Part 1 is an introduction on scope and importance of government publishing. Part 2 provides background information on government publishing in twenty countries, in considerable detail.
070.595 C521C or Z286 G69C47 GOVT

AM2 **Guide to Official Publications of Foreign Countries.** Ed. by Gloria Westfall. Bethesda, MD: Government Documents Round Table, 1990. 350. p. Distr. by Congressional Information Service.

Known as *ALA/GODORT Guide...* Lists most important publications for 157 countries, often with abstracts. English translations provided when necessary. Covers 17 categories of publications including, guides, bibliographies, directories, manuals, statistical yearbooks, laws and regulations, legislative proceedings, and publications in various subject areas. Arranged by country, titles listed alphabetically.
Z7164 G7G85 GOVT

AM3 New York Public Library. The Research Libraries. **Catalog of Government Publications in the Research Libraries.** 40 vols. New York: G.K. Hall, 1972. *Supplement* 2 vols. 1974.

Catalogue of NYPL holdings of documents of all national and colonial governments. Supplemented annually by *Bibliographic Guide to Government Publications: U.S.* and *Bibliographic Guide to Government Publications: Foreign* (Z7164 G7N63).
Z7164 G7B5

AM4 **Official Publications of the Soviet Union and Eastern Europe, 1945–1980: A Select Bibliography.** Ed. by Gregory Walker. London: Mansell, 1982. 620 p.

AM - Government Publications **141**

Covers the "most important sources of officially issued documents from the end of German occupation in 1944-5 up to 1980." Includes general bibliographies and reference works, constitutional documents, law codes, legislative documents, party documents, general statistical publications. Other publications arranged by subject, and also includes leaders' works. Translations noted.
Z2483 O34 GOVT

AM5 **Official Publications of Western Europe.** 2 vols. Ed. by Eve Johansson. London: Mansell, 1983, 1988.
General guide designed to "help the non-specialist by giving an overview of the main publications, their indexing and bibliographic control, the language in which they appear, and their availability." Volume 1 (1983) covers Denmark, Finland, France, Ireland, Italy, Luxembourg, Netherlands, Spain, Turkey. Volume 2 (1988) covers Austria, Belgium, Federal Republic of Germany, Greece, Norway, Portugal, Sweden, Switzerland, United Kingdom.
025.1734O32P or Z291 O38 GOVT

Canada

Organization, Procedures of Government - Canada

AM6 Canada. House of Commons. **Standing Orders of the House of Commons.** Ottawa: Supply and Services, 1990. 95 p.
Formerly titled *Permanent and Provisional Standing...* Official guide to procedure in the House. Indexed. Also available is the *Annotated Standing Orders of the House of Commons, 1989 / Règlement annoté de la Chambre des communes, 1989,* (Queen's Printer, 1989) (JL164 C85).
R328.71C212S or CA1 X7 S75 GOVT

AM7 **Canada Year Book,** 1905- . Ottawa: Statistics Canada. biennial.
Published annually until 1978. In addition to acting as a statistical compendium, *Canada Year Book* includes information on the Constitution, government organizations, related agencies, Royal Commissions and Commission of Inquiry, federal legislation, and a political update.
R317.1 C212 or HA74C32

AM8 **Canadian Almanac and Directory,** 1848- annual.
Includes sections on the federal, provincial and municipal levels of government in Canada, including addresses of government departments. (See AH5 for full entry).
R317.1 C212A or AY414 C2 GOVT

AM9 **Canadian Government Programmes and Services,** 1971- . Don Mills, ON: CCH Canadian Ltd. loose-leaf.
Comprehensive listing of federal government executive, legislative and judicial departments, agencies, etc. Especially useful for detailed descriptions of their activities. Includes a section entitled "Canadian Parliamentary Papers: An Outline and Summary" by Brian Land (revised irregularly).
JL5 C26 GOVT

AM10 **Canadian Legislatures: The [year] Comparative Study,** 1979- . Toronto: Ontario. Legislative Assembly. annual.
Administrative arrangements and structures

"presently in place" for Canadian federal and provincial legislatures are described in essays. Also includes information on U.S. national and state legislatures. Statistical tables.
328.71 C212C (1986)   or
CA2 ON X20 C14 GOV

AM11   The Canadian Parliamentary Guide, 1962- . Toronto: Infoglobe. annual.

Edited and published until 1989 by Pierre Normandin (Ottawa). Includes biographies of current members of Parliament and the provincial legislatures, a record of election results, and other information on Canada's government. Similar material, for federal level only, is found in *Canadian Parliamentary Handbook* (Ed. by John Bejermi, Borealis Press, 1982-). Available online.
R328.71 C21   or   JL5 A3

AM12   Current Inquiries of the Government of Canada (Other Than Committees of the House of Commons and Senate). Ottawa: Library of Parliament. irregular.

Includes Committee title; citation of establishing legislation; name of chairperson; with address and telephone number of the Commission/ Committee.

AM13 Forsey, Eugene. **How Canadians Govern Themselves.** 2d ed. Ottawa: Supply and Services, 1988. 66 p.

Elementary guide to Canadian government, available free of charge.
354.71 F732H2   or   CA1 IF71 H51 GOVT

AM14   Government of Canada Telephone Directory/ Gouvernement du Canada annuaire téléphonique. Ottawa: Supply and Services. semi-annual.

Prepared by Government Telecommunications Agency. Issued in regional volumes: *National Capital*; *Atlantic*; *Ontario*; *Quebec*; *Pacific* (includes Yukon); *Prairie (*includes NWT). Each volume lists federal department offices by municipality.
R354.71 C721G (Ontario)   or
CA1 IF G52 GOVT

AM15   Government Relations Handbook, 1989/90- . Don Mills, ON: Corpus Information and Communications Group. annual.

Includes chapters on: influencing government policy; federal law making process; federal departments, agencies; associations contacts; government relations consultants. Provides a list of federal statutes indicating which federal departments administer them. The same publisher publishes *Corpus Alamanac and Canadian Sourcebook* (AH19) which includes sections on the federal, provincial and municipal governments, and the Constitution; and *Corpus Administrative Index* (JL5 C67 GOVT), which is a quarterly directory of provincial and federal administrations, with telephone contact numbers.
JL148.5 C684 GOVT

AM16   Guide to Federal Programs and Services, 1979- . Ottawa: Supply and Services. annual

Title changed with 1990 issue from *Index to Federal Programs and Services*. Lists and describes programs and services available from federal departments, agencies and Crown corporations. Directory information, subject index.
R354.71 C212G10

AM17 InfoSource: Sources of Federal Government Information, 1990/91- . Prepared by Treasury Board Canada Secretariat. Ottawa: Supply and Services. annual.

Updated by bulletin issued twice yearly. Combines and replaces *Access Register* and *Index to Personal Information* (1983-1989/90). Lists all federal departments, agencies (with some exceptions) and provides information on background, responsibilities, organizations, legislation administered, program records, personal information banks, and access procedures for the information banks. Prepared in response to requirements of *Access to Information Act* and *Privacy Act* for an inventory of government information holdings.
R354.7100819 I43J   or   GOVT

AM18   Organization of the Government of Canada, 1958-1980; 1990- . Ottawa: Supply and Services. irregular annual.

Publication suspended 1981-1989. 1990 volume published in cooperation with Canadian Chamber of Commerce. Official guide to federal government, includes historical background, overall responsibilities, officers and organization charts for each government institution. General inquiry telephone numbers. Large fold-out organization chart of government organization bound in.
R354.71 O658P   or   CA1 IF O63 GOVT

AM19   Ottawa's Senior Executives Guide, 1985- . Ottawa and Toronto: Infoglobe. annual.

Identifies and provides information on senior ranking officials in federal departments, agencies, etc. including ministers and key officials.
JL95 O8 GOVT

*   *   *   *

Organization, Procedures of Government - Ontario

Information on structure, organization, and procedures of government of Ontario follow. Similar publications exist for most provinces.

AM20   Bell, George G. **Ontario Government: Structure and Functions.** Toronto: Wall and Thompson, 1988. 413 p.

Useful compilation of information on the various ministries, including roles and functions, background history, organization, programs, expenditures, estimates, agencies, boards and commission, legislation administered. Also available from the same author and publisher is *The System of Government in Ontario* (1988) (JL270 B45 GOVT).
320.4713 B433N   or   JL270 B44 GOVT

AM21   Government of Ontario Telephone Directory, 1973- . Toronto: Ministry of Government Services. semi-annual.

Arranged by department, with an index of personal names. Government telephone directories are published by most provincial governments.
R354.713 G712G

AM22 Ontario. Management Board of Cabinet. Secretariat. **Directory of Records, Provincial Ministries and Agencies,** 1990- . Toronto: Publications Ontario. annual.

Prepared by the Freedom of Information and Privacy Branch of the Management Board Secretariat. Continues both the *Directory of General Records* (1988) (342.7130853 O59G) and *Directory of Personal Information Banks* (1989) (342.1730853 O59H). Describes the organization, mandate, types of records maintained by

provincial ministries, agencies, etc. Includes telephone number and address of information access coordinators in each government body.
R342.7130853 O59G

AM23 Ontario. Ministry of Government Services. **KWIC Index to Services,** 1975- . Toronto: Ministry of Government Services. annual.

Title varies, formerly *KWIC Index to Your Ontario Government Services*. Directory of all government programs and services, with brief descriptions of agency activites. Available online as *Ontario Government Information*. Also published annually in several languages is *Newcomer's Guide to Services in Ontario* (Ministry of Citizenship, 1978-) (CA2ON CI N27 GOVT)
R354.713 O59N

AM24 Ontario Public Sector: The Periodical of Official Personnel in Federal, Provincial, and Municipal Governments in the Province of Ontario, 1988- . Willowdale, ON: Ontario Public Sector. annual.

Provides "detailed information of the functions" of provincial, municipal, and federal govrrnments in Ontario. Includes directory information by provincial ministry and by towns.
JL272 O67 GOVT

Canadian Government Publications

Canadian government publications are arranged as follows: Federal; Pre-Confederation; Provincial; followed by Parliamentary publications and Legislative publications.

Bibliographies, Catalogues and Indexes

AM25 Bishop, Olga. **Canadian Official Publications.** Oxford: Pergamon Press, 1981. 297 p.

A useful overview, with emphasis on historical documents. Up-to-date information can be found in "A Description and Guide to the Use of Canadian Government Publications" by Brian Land (in *Politics Canada* by Paul Fox and Graham White (McGraw Hill Ryerson, 1991, pp 527-551). It also contains information on provincial government publications.
015.71 B622C

AM26 Canadian Statistics Index, 1985- . Toronto: Micromedia. annual.

Indexes statistical publications of federal, provincial, and municipal governments. Arranged by issuing agency, with subject index. See CA48 for full information.
HA741 C43 GOVT

AM27 Canadiana, 1950- See AD35 for full entry information.

Includes full cataloguing entries for most federal and provincial government publications, in Part 1: *Canadian Imprints*. Before 1981 these were listed in separate sections (Parts 7 and 8).
R015.71 C21

AM28 Federal Royal Commissions, 1867-1966: A Checklist. Comp. by George Fletcher Henderson. Toronto: University of Toronto Press [1967]. 212 p.

Arranged by name of commission, with names of commissioners, dates of appointment, names of reports. Indexed. Updated by *Commissions*

of Inquiry Under the Inquiries Act, prepared by Denise Ledoux and C. Laferriere (Library of Parliament, 1986 Z1373 H44 Supp).
354.71 H496F   or   JL78 1967 H46 GOVT

AM29   Government of Canada Publications, 1953- . Ottawa: Supply and Services. quarterly.

Prepared by Canada Communication Group - Publishing (formerly Canadian Government Publishing Centre) the official government publisher. Supersedes *Canadian Government Publications Catalogue*, (monthly). Cumulates *Weekly Checklist of...* (formerly *Daily Checklist*), which lists items available to depository libraries. Also includes publications listed in *Special List of Canadian Government Publications* (irregular) which lists publications not available on deposit. CCG-P also publishes *Publishing News* (irregular, annotated listing for bookstores of new publications) and *Subject List* (irregular annotated lists covering single topics).

Some individual departments and agencies publish their own catalogues and checklists, see, for example, Statistics Canada (CA61) Some of these are available online (e.g. National Research Council's *NRCPUBS* (DA4n)).

Full text of government announcements, press releases, announcements of pending legislation, statutory legislation, motions, appointments and speeches are available online on *Key Government Documents Database*.
R015.71 C21G   or   CA1 PS C13 GOVT

AM30 Higgins, Marion V. **Canadian Government Publications: A Manual For Librarians.** Chicago: American Library Association, 1935. 582 p.

A large proportion of federal publications from 1867 to 1931 are recorded; the period from 1841 to 1867 is covered less adequately. For each issuing office there is an outline organization, history, function, with a list of documents. Sets such as sessional papers are not analyzed.
R025.173 H63   or   Z1373 H5 GOVT

AM31   Microlog: Canadian Research Index, 1979- . Toronto: Micromedia. monthly with annual cumulation.

Title varies.   Supersedes *Publicat Index* (1977-78) and *Profile Index* (1973-78). Includes citations to Canadian research and report literature issued by all levels of government in Canada, and by research institutions, universities, libraries and professional associations; in all subject fields. Available online and on CD-ROM.
R015.71 M626MA   or   Z1373 M532 GOVT

AM32   Statistics Canada Catalogue. See CA51 - CA61 for this and other Statistics Canada publications bibliographies and catalogues.

The *Guide to Managing Statistics Canada Publications in Libraries* (Supply and Services, 1991, looseleaf) provides notes on history of series/publications, name changes, retention guidelines, frequency, etc.

AM33   White Papers / Livres blancs, 1939-1987. Ottawa: Library of Parliament, 1987. 73 p.

Compiled by Michele Robichaud and Audrey Dubé. Lists all *White Papers* published by the federal government between 1939 and 1987. Gives title, issuing department, and a brief summary of contents. Indexed. Also available is *Green Papers / Livres verts, 1971-1986*, (1986, J103 R63 LAWR)

Pre-Confederation Government Publications

AM34 Bishop, Olga B. **Publications of the Governments of Nova Scotia, Prince Edward Island, New Brunswick, 1758-1952.** Ottawa: National Library of Canada, 1957. 237 p.
 Arranged by department, with useful historical notes. For the Pre-Confederation period see also Patricia Fleming's *Atlantic Canadian Imprints, 1801-1820* (AD39).
R015.716 B622   or   Z1373.5 A1B5 GOVT

AM35 Bishop, Olga B. **Publications of the Government of the Province of Canada, 1841-1867.** Ottawa: National Library of Canada, 1963. 351 p.
 The Province of Canada consisted of Canada East (Quebec) and Canada West (Ontario). Over 4,000 titles are arranged by department with list of printers and a chronology of parliamentary sessions.
R015.71 B622

AM36 Bishop, Olga B. **Publications of the Province of Upper Canada and of Great Britain Relating to Upper Canada, 1791-1840.** Toronto: Ministry of Citizenship and Culture, 1984. 288 p.
 Publications listed chronologically by issuing body, with at least one location given for each document. Also useful for extensive historical notes. Appendices include dates of parliamentary sessions, lists of printers, etc. Indexed. See also Patricia Fleming's *Bibliography of Upper Canadian Imprints* (AD50).
R015.713 B622N

Provincial Government Publications

Bibliographies and guides covering all provinces are listed first, followed by provincial publications arranged from east to west: Atlantic Provinces (alphabetical), Quebec, Ontario, Western Provinces, arranged from east to west: Manitoba, Saskatchewan, Alberta, British Columbia; then Territorial publications: Northwest Territories, Yukon.

BIBLIOGRAPHIES AND GUIDES - ALL PROVINCES

AM37 Pross, Catherine. **A Guide to Identification and Acquisitions of Canadian Government Publications: Provinces and Territories.** 2d ed. Occasional Paper No. 16. Halifax: Dalhousie University Libraries and Dalhousie University School of Library Service, 1983. 103 p.
 A discussion of provincial government publishing, with background information and bibliographical sources.
R025.173 P966G2   or   Z1373.3 P76 GOVT

AM38 **Provincial Royal Commissions and Commissions of Inquiry, 1867-1982: A Selective Bibliography.** Comp. by Lise Maillet. Ottawa: National Library of Canada, 1986. 254 p.
 Includes Royal Commissions and Commissions of Inquiry, provided that a *Public Inquiries Act* was the authorizing statute. Only relevant reports such as interim and final reports are

listed, unless other documents are bound to the reports. Indexed by subject and chairperson. Locations given for each report. Supersedes a number of lists prepared by provincial libraries.
R354.7109 AM221P   or
CA1 LC86 A66 GOVT

ATLANTIC PROVINCES

AM39   Atlantic Provinces Checklist.
Includes provincial government publications for the period 1957-1965. See AD38 for full entry information. For earlier publications see *Bishop* (AM34).
R015.715 AA881

AM40 Guilbeault, Claude. **Guide to Official Publications of New Brunswick 1952-1970.** Ottawa: University of Ottawa Library School, 1974. 382 p. M.L.S. Thesis.
See *Bishop* (AM34) for earlier publications.
MFILM 1039

AM41   New Brunswick Government Documents: A Checklist. 1956- . Fredericton, NB: Legislative Library. annual.
Supplemental *Quarterly List* published beginning Jan/Mar, 1986. Includes all items received at the Legislative Library.
R015.715 N53   or   CA2NB XL N21 GOVT

AM42   List of Publications of the Government of Newfoundland and Labrador, 1974-1979. St. John's, NF: Information Services. irregular.
Ceased publication.
R015.718 N547L

AM43   Publications of the Province of Nova Scotia. 1967- . Prepared by the Legislative Library. Halifax: Queen's Printer. annual.
Supplemented by the *Monthly Checklist* (formerly *Quarterly Checklist* June, 1980-). Also available is a *Publications Catalogue: Nova Scotia Government Bookstore*, (irregular, quarterly supplements). See *Bishop* (AM34) for earlier publications.
R015.716 N935   or   CA2NV YL P72 GOVT

AM44   Prince Edward Island Provincial Government Publications Checklist, 1976- . Charlottetown: Island Information Service. monthly.
See *Bishop* (AM34) for earlier publications.
R015.717 P954P

QUEBEC

AM45 Beaulieu, André, Jean-Charles Bonenfant and Jean Hamelin **Répertoire des publications gouvernementales du Québec de 1867 à 1964.** Québec: Imprimeur de la Reine, 1968.
Supplément 1965-1968 by A. Beaulieu, J. Hamelin, and G. Bernier. (Éditeur officiel, 1970). Arranged by departments, with chronological lists of publications with bibliographic information.
R015.714 B377

AM46   Bibliographie du Québec, 1821-1967; 1968- .   For full information see AD42-43.
National bibliography of Quebec; contains government publications.
R015.714 AB582B

AM47 Catalogue de l'éditeur officiel, 1974- . Quebec: Ministère des Communications [par le Bureau de l'Éditeur officiel]. irregular.

Primarily a sales catalog; supersedes *Publications...* 1967-74. Beginning 1986, an irregular annual publication entitled *Catalogue (Québec Province)* has been published by Les Publications du Québec. A similar selected, annotated list was entitled *Choix de publications gouvernementales.*
R015.714 Q30A or
CA2 PQ CO10 C12 GOVT

AM48 Liste bimestrielle des publications du gouvernement du Québec, 1988- . Québec: Les publications du Québec. bi-monthly.

Continues *Liste mensuelle des publications du gouvernement du Québec,* 1983-1987. *Liste annuelle des périodiques du gouvernement du Québec,* (1983/84- . annual) (R015.714053 Q3LA) lists periodicals issued by Quebec government, with ISSN numbers, source, frequency, etc.
CA2 PQ CO10 L32 GOVT

AM49 Livres blancs et livres verts au Québec, 1964-1981. Comp. by Gaston Deschenes. Québec: Bibliothèque de l'Assemblée Nationale, 1981. 58 p.

Lists *White Papers* and *Green Papers* produced by Quebec government.
CA2 PQ XL1 B08 GOVT

AM50 Theriault, Yvon. **Les publications parlementaires hier et d'aujourd'hui.** 2d ed. Québec: Assemblée Nationale, 1982. 32 p.

English title: *The Parliamentary Publications Past and Present* (1983) Useful introduction, and list of publications produced in Quebec from 1792 through 1983.
R015.714053 Q3L or
CA2 PQ CO100 L31 GOVT

ONTARIO

AM51 Bishop, Olga B. **Publications of the Government of Ontario, 1867-1900.** Toronto: Ministry of Government Services, 1976. 409 p.

A chronological list by government division with historical information included. Author, title, subject index and a library location provided. Earlier publications for Ontario can be found in Bishop's bibliographies covering the period 1791 to 1867 (see AM35 and AM36).
R015.713 B622P or
CA2 ON GS76 P73 GOVT

AM52 MacTaggart, Hazel I. **Publications of the Government of Ontario, 1901-1955.** Toronto: University of Toronto Press for the Queen's Printer, 1964. 303 p.

A checklist compiled for the Ontario Library Association. Arranged by issuing department with author, title, subject index and library locations.
R015.713 M175 or
CA2 ON GS64 P73 GOVT

AM53 MacTaggart, Hazel I. and Kenneth E. Sundquist. **Publications of the Government of Ontario, 1956-1971: A Checklist.** Toronto: Ministry of Government Services, 1975. 410 p.

Continues AM52, and the coverage is continued by *Ontario Government Publications: Monthly Checklist.*
R015.713 M175A or
CA2 ON GS75 P73 GOVT

AM54 Ontario Government Publications: Monthly Checklist, 1972- . Prepared by Research and Information Services, Legislative Library 1979- . Toronto: Ministry of Government Services. monthly.

Annual Catalogue, 1979- . Publisher varies. From Jan. 1984, incorporates *Catalogue des publications en française du gouvernement de l'Ontario,* published semi-annually from 1979–1983.
R015.713 O59G   or   CA2ON O53 GOVT

AM55 Select Committees of the Legislative Assembly of Ontario: 1867-1978: A Checklist of Reports. Comp. by Eleanor Barnes. Toronto: Legislative Library, 1983. 86 p.

Records reports of 109 select committees presented from Confederation to 1978. Provides historical background to committees, even if no reports issued. Notes committee chairperson and members' names. Locations of reports included. Indexed.
R354.713 B261S

WESTERN PROVINCES

AM56 Manitoba Government Publications Monthly Checklist, 1970- . Winnipeg: Legislative Libreary. monthly.

Title and publisher varies. Cumulated annually.
R015.712 M278A   or
Z1373.5 M3 M32 GOVT

AM57 Checklist of Saskatchewan Government Publications, 1979- . Regina: Legislative Library. annual.

Supplemented by *Saskatchewan Government Publications,* 1979-   (bimonthly), 1984- (monthly).
R015.7124 S252C   or   CA2 SAYL C37 GOVT

AM58 Alberta Government Publications, 1973- . Edmonton: Alberta Public Affairs Bureau. annual

Title varies. Formerly also quarterly. Also available is *List of Alberta Publications and Legislation,* (Public Affairs Bureau, 1987- annual).
R015.7123 A333PA   or
CA2 ALPB P71 GOVT

AM59 Forsyth, Joseph. Government Publications Relating to Alberta: A Bibliography of Publications of the Government of Alberta from 1905-1968, and of the Government of Canada Relating to the Province of Alberta from 1867 to 1968. 8 vols. University Microfilms, 1973. (Thesis submitted for Fellowship of the Library Association, 1971).

See also *MacDonald* (AM63) for pre-1905 publications.
Z1392 A4F67 GOVT

AM60 Holmes, Marjorie C. Publications of the Government of British Columbia, 1871-1947. Victoria: Provincial Library, 1950. 254 p.

Publications arranged by issuing departments with extensive notes on departments.
R015.711 H75   or   Z1373.5 B8H6 GOVT

AM61 Lowther, Barbara. A Bibliography of British Columbia: Laying the Foundations, 1849-1899. Victoria: University of Victoria, 1968. 328 p.

See related titles (AD54). Includes government publications of the two colonies of Vancouver Island and British Columbia, and after their union in 1866, of the united colony of B.C. to 1871, when the province entered Confederation.
R015.711 B582

AM62 Publications Catalogue [British Columbia], 1989- . Victoria: Crown Publications, Inc. annual.

Continues *Queen's Printer Publications Catalogue* (1988- semi-annual) and *British Columbia Government Publications Monthly Checklist*, 1970-198?.
R015.711 B862BA   or
CA2 BCPS Q76 GOVT

TERRITORIAL GOVERNMENTS

AM63 MacDonald, Christine. **Publications of the Government of the North-West Territories, 1867-1905 And of the Province of Saskatchewan, 1905-1952**. Regina: Legislative Library, 1952. 110 p.

Alberta was included in the Territories until 1905. Arranged by issuing body with author/subject index.
R015.712 M13   or   Z1373.5 N6M32 GOVT

AM64 Northwest Territories. **Publications Catalogue [Northwest Territories]**, 1977- . Yellowknife: Dept of Information, Publications and Production Division, 1978- . irregular annual.

Title varies.
R015.712 M13   or   Z1373.5 N6M32 GOVT

AM65 Yukon Bibliography. See AD57 for full entry information.
Includes some government publications.
Z1392 Y8L6

Parliamentary Publications - Canada

AM66 Canada. House of Commons. **Debates: Official Report**, 1875- . [Hansard]. Ottawa: Queen's Printer. daily, sessional

Official records of the debates, printed while House is in session. Oral questions and responses from Question Period are available online (1979-). Bound index published at the ned of session. Debates for the years 1867-1870, not officially recorded, were collated from available sources and published under the auspices of the Library of Parliament. *Debates of the Legislative Assembly of United Canada* (1844-1867) (CA CPX D24 GOVT) are also in process.
CA1 X1 D23 GOVT

AM67 Canada. House of Commons. **Journals / Journaux**, 1867- . Ottawa: Queen's Printer. sessional.

Published in bilingual format since 1967. Compiled from the edited and corrected version of the daily *Votes and Proceedings*. Indexed in final volume for each session.
CA1 X2 J53 GOVT

AM68 Canada. Senate. **Debates**, 1871- . Ottawa: Queen's Printer. sessional

Indexed at end of each session. As with House of Commons, Senate debates for 1867–1870 have been collated from unofficial sources.
CA 1 Y1 D32 GOVT

AM69 Canada. Senate. **Journals of the Senate of Canada / Journaux du Sénat du Canada,** 1867- . Ottawa: Queen's Printer. sessional.

Compiled from the edited and corrected version of the daily *Minutes of Proceedings*. Bilingual since 1967.
CA1 Y2 J79 GOVT

AM70 Canada. **Sessional Papers of the Dominion of Canada, 1867-1925.** 923 vols. Ottawa: Queen's Printer, 1867-1925.

Includes most papers put before Parliament and ordered printed, with the exception of committee reports, which were printed as appendices in the *Journals* of each House. Several volumes for each session, each with alphabetical and numerical lists of papers.
CA1 YS S27 GOVT

AM71 Canada. **Annual Departmental Reports of the Dominion of Canada, 1925-1930.** Ottawa: King's Printer, 1926-1930.

Included departmental reports formerly published in the *Sessional Papers*, along with reports of some commissions. Annual reports now published separately.
CA 1 YS S28 GOVT

AM72 Revised Statutes of Canada, 1985. 16 vols. Ottawa: Supply and Services, 1985.

Includes 8 volumes of statutes plus: *Appendices* (1 volume); *Table of Concordance* (1 volume); *Index* (1 volume) with English and French index volumes published separately, and *Supplements*, with Acts passed between January 1, 1985 and December 12, 1988 (volumes). On the latter date *RSC* 1985 was proclaimed in force. Consolidates all federal statutes in force as of December 31, 1984, arranged by subject *Chapters*. Available online. Supplemented by *Statutes of Canada* (1867-), published at the end of each Parliamentary session. New statutes are listed in *Canada Gazette*, Pt. III.
R348.71 C212R   or
CA1 YX41 1985 R27 GOVT

AM73 Consolidated Regulations of Canada, 1978. 19 vols. Ottawa: Queen's Printer [for the Statute Revision Commission], 1978.

All regulations in force at December 31, 1977 consolidated into subject areas. Full text of regulations in force, as of 31 August, 1983, available online as *Statutory Orders and Regulations* (SOR). Updated in *Canada Gazette, Part II*. Regulations in force since publication of *CRC 1978* are indexed in *Consolidated Index of Statutory Instruments* (quarterly).
R348.71025 C212C   or   Ca1 YX100 1978 S75 GOVT

AM74 Canada Gazette, 1867- .   Ottawa: Queen's Printer, in 3 pts.

From December 13, 1974, in three parts. *Pt. 1*: published every Saturday, contains notices of a general character, proclamations, certain Orders-in-Council and various other classes of statutory notices. *Pt. 2*: published on the second Wednesday of the month with special edictions as required, contains all regulations and statutory instruments required to be published. *Pt. 3*: published irregularly, contains the *Public Acts* of Canada and certain other ancillary publications, proclamations and updated *Tables of Public Statutes*.
CA1 YX99 G193 GOVT

Legislative Publications - Ontario

Provincial legislative publications follow a pattern similar to that of Ontario, which are described below.

AM75   Revised Statutes of Ontario, 1980. Being a Revision and Consolidation of the Public General Acts of the Legislature of Ontario, Published under the Authority of the *Statutes Revision Act*, 1979. Toronto: Queen's Printer, [1981-82].

Statutes are published sessionally in *Statutes of the Province of Ontario* (1867-). Access is provided by *Cumulative Index to Revised Statutes of Ontario Amended to December 31, 1984* (2 vols. Toronto: Queen's Printer, 1985).
R348.713 O59   or
CA2 ON YX41 84R27 GOVT

AM76   Revised Regulations of Ontario 1980. A Revision and Consolidation of Regulations Published under the Authority of the *Regulations Revision Act*, 1979. 8 vols. Toronto: Queen's Printer, 1980.

Supplement 1982. 2 vols.   New Regulations are published in the *Ontario Gazette*. Available online.
R348.713 O59R   or
CA2ON YX51 80 R59 GOVT

AM77 Ontario. Legislative Assembly. **Debates,** 1947- . Toronto: Queen's Printer. daily.

Published when Assembly is sitting. Continues *Debates: Newspaper Hansard ("Scrapbook Debates")*, 1867-1946, (Toronto: Dept. of Public Records and Archives) (CA2 ONX1 D23 MFM GOVT), microfilm of the contemporary newspaper reports of the debates in the Ontario Legislature.
CA2 ONX1 D23 GOVT

AM78 Ontario. Legislative Assembly. **Journals of the Legislative Assembly of Ontario,** 1867/68- . Toronto: Queen's Printer. sessional.

Compiled from *Votes and Proceedings of the Legislative Assembly...* (1930-) (CA2 ONX5 V78 GOVT).
CA2 ONX2 J53 GOVT

AM79   Ontario Gazette, 1884- . Toronto: Queen's Printer. weekly.
CA2 ONYX99 G19 GOVT

AM80   Ontario Sessional Papers, 1868–1948. Toronto: Queen's Printer. sessional.
CA2 ONYS S26 GOVT

Great Britain

Organization of Government

AM81   Britain: An Official Handbook, 1949/50- London: HMSO. annual.

Provides information on Britain in general, and includes a chapter on the government. See AH22 for full entry.
UK1 SI51 B65 GOVT

Guides to the Literature

AM82 Butcher, David. **Official Publications in Britain.** London: Clive Bingley, 1983. 161 p.

A concise introduction designed as a library science text.
015.41 B983P   or   Z2009 B97 GOVT

AM83 Ford, Percy. **A Guide to Parliamentary Papers: What They Are, How to Find Them, How to Use Them.** 3d ed. Totowa, NJ: Rowman and Littlefield, 1972. 87 p.
Brief but useful introduction.
R025.173 F711G3

AM84 Ollé, James G. H. **An Introduction to British Government Publications.** 2d ed. London: Association of Assistant Librarians, 1973. 175 p.
A standard text which provides an introduction to the entire range of British government publications. Emphasizes those published by HMSO.
025.173 O49I2   or   Z2009 O4 GOVT

AM85 Pemberton, John E. **British Official Publications.** 2d rev. ed. Oxford: Pergamon, 1973. 328 p.
Useful information not covered in the briefer guides. Emphasizes Parliamentary publications.
015.42 P394B2   or   Z2009 P45 GOVT(1971)

AM86 Richard, Stephen. **Directory of British Official Publications: A Guide to Sources.** 2d ed. London: Mansell, 1984. 431 p.
Lists some 1,300 British organizations which issue official publications themselves, rather than through HMSO. Notes types of publications issued, subjects covered, restrictions on availability. Includes names of contacts, addresses, telephone and telex numbers. Includes Northern Ireland, Scotland, Wales and Britain. Provides information on HMSO as well.
Z2009 R537 GOVT

AM87 Rodgers, Frank. **A Guide to British Government Publications.** New York: Wilson, 1980. 750 p.
Extensive coverage of both Parliamentary and executive publications, with background information on issuing bodies.
015.41 R691G   or   Z2009 R63 GOVT

Bibliographies and Indexes

AM88 British Government Publications: An Index by Chairmen and Authors. Comp. by Stephen Richard. London: Library Association, 1974–1984.
4 volumes have been published to date, covering the period 1800–1982. More recent chairmen can be found indexed in *Annual Catalogues* (AM96) and in *Committee Reports Published by HMSO; Indexed by Chairmen* (UK1 SO C56 GOVT)
Z2009 R535 GOVT

AM89 **Checklist of British Official Serial Publications.** 12th ed. Comp. by Hazel Finnie. London: British Library, 1987. 74 p.
Arrangement by serial title, gives frequency and availability and notes titles that have ceased since previous (1980) edition. Indexed by names of issuing bodies. Older serial titles can be found in earlier editions of this work, and in *Serial Publications in the British Parliamentary Papers, 1900–1968: A Bibliography* by Frank Rodgers (ALA, 1971) (Z2009 R64 GOVT).
Z2009 C5 GOVT

AM90   **Finding List of British Royal Commission Reports, 1860–1935.** Comp. by Arthur Harrison Cole. Cambridge, MA: Harvard University Press, 1935. 66 p.

Chronological arrangement under broad subject headings. Continued by Sectional List no. 59 *Royal Commissions (AM96n)*.
015.42 C689   or   Z2009 C68 GOVT

AM91   [Ford Lists].
Percy and Grace Ford compiled a number of *Select Lists* and *Breviates* of Parliamentary Papers, emphasizing social, economic, and political affairs as found in policy documents, reports of committees and Royal Commissions. These follow *Hansard's Catalogue and Breviate of Parliamentary Papers* (AM92) in chronological order. The *Breviates* provide information on the contents of the papers. In recent years, the lists have been continued as part of the *Southampton University Series in Parliamentary Papers*, and edited by Diana Marshallsay. The following titles have been published:

Select List of British Parliamentary Papers 1833–1899 (Oxford: Blackwell, 1953; Z2009 A1F63 GOVT).

A Breviate of Parliamentary Papers 1900–1916: The Foundation of the Welfare State (Oxford: Blackwell, 1957; Z2009 A1F56 GOVT).

A Breviate of Parliamentary Papers 1917–1939 (Oxford: Blackwell, 1961; Z2009 A1F57 GOVT).

A Breviate of Parliamentary Papers 1940–1954: War and Reconstruction (Oxford: Blackwell, 1961; Z2009 A1 F58 GOVT).

Select List of British Parliamentary Papers 1955–1964. (Shannon: Irish University Press, 1970; Z2009 A1F66 GOVT)

Ford List of British Parliamentary Papers 1965–1974: Together with Specialist Commentaries (Nendeln, Liechtenstein: KTO Press, 1979; Z2009 A1 F59 GOVT)

Ford List of British Parliamentary Papers 1974–1983: Together with Specialist Commentaries (Cambridge: Chadwyck-Healey, 1989; Z2009 A1 F593 GOVT)

AM92   Hansard's Catalogue and Breviate of Parliamentary Papers 1696–1834. Reprinted in Facsimile with an Introduction by P. Ford. Oxford: Basil Blackwell, 1953. 220 p.
Arranged by subject with detailed analysis of contents. Updated by the *Ford Lists* (see AM91).
342.42 AG786

AM93   Index to British Parliamentary Papers on Canada and Canadian Boundary, 1800-1899. Dublin: Irish University Press, 1974. 159 p.
Index by subject, person, and place, of Parliamentary Papers concerned with the colonies, in the Irish University Press series of British Parliamentary Papers. Can be used with other collections as well. Does not completely supersede *Guide to the Principal Parliamentary Papers Relating to the Dominions, 1812-1911.* (comp. by Margaret Adam, Edinburgh: Oliver and Boyd, 1913) (Z2021 C7A3 GOVT).
Z2009 I74 GOVT

AM94   Numerical Finding List of British Command Papers Published 1933-1961/62. Comp. by Edward Di Roma and S.A. Rosenthal. [New York]: New York Public Library, 1967. 148 p.

Command Papers, which are an assorted group of departmental and Royal Commission reports, government policy documents and treaties, are listed by number, providing quick reference to locations in sets of sessional papers. See *Walford* (AC5) for information on access to these papers in other periods.
015.42 D599   or   Z2009 D5 GOVT

AM95   Subject Catalogue of the House of Commons Parliamentary Papers, 1801-1900. 5 vols. Comp. by Peter Cockton. Cambridge: Chadwyck-Healey, 1988.

Provides a comprehensive listing in a thematic subject catalogue, covering the entire output of the 19th century. Arrangement is chronological within 19 subject groups (e.g. Population and Demography; Agriculture and Landed Society). Companion to Chadwyck-Healey's microfiche collection of 90,000 19th century papers, but can be used with other collections. Complements but does not replace existing indexes to 19th century sessional papers.
Z2019 C63 GOVT

Catalogues

AM96 Great Britain. HMSO. **HMSO Annual Catalogue,** 1922- . London: HMSO, 1923- . annual.

Lists publications of the year. Continues *Government Publications of* (Year), and earlier titles. Supplemented by *Daily List* and *HMSO Monthly Catalogue*. Five year consolidated indexes have been published since 1936/40, but more convenient is *Cumulative Index to the Annual Catalogues of Her Majesty's Stationery Office Publications 1922–1972* (2 vols., Carrollton Press, 1976) (UK1 SO1 S71 GOVT), which includes a useful introduction to British government publishing.   It merges 23 separate annual and quinquennial indexes and provides subject, author and title indexing. A photo-reproduction of the HMSO catalogues 1920–1970 and the consolidated indexes for 1936–1970 has been published as *Catalogues and Indexes of British Government Publications* (5 vols., Chadwyck-Healey, 1974). HMSO also publishes *HMSO Publications in Print on MIcrofiche*, and *Sectional Lists*, which are useful bibliographies of official publications arranged by subject or organization (UK1 SO1 S71 GOVT).
UK1 SO L35 GOVT

AM97   Catalogue of British Official Publications Not Published by HMSO, 1980-   Cambridge: Chadwyck-Healey, 1981- . monthly.

Includes the publications of over 400 government departments, nationalized industries, research institutions, quasi-autonomous non-governmental organizations, and other official bodies. Includes monographs, serials, newspapers and publicity items, atlases and some maps; excludes items which editors judge to be too ephemeral, too specialized, or groups of items well catalogued elsewhere (e.g. maps). Available online; microfiche document delivery service.
Z2009 C37 GOVT

United States

Organization of Government

AM98   Congressional Quarterly Almanac, 1945- . Washington: Congressional Quarterly, Inc. annual.

"Compendium of legislation" with comprehensive coverage of events, legislation, votes,

major issues of the year in Congress. Statistical comparisons with previous years. Available online on *Washington Alert Service*. CQ also publishes *Congressional Quarterly Weekly Report* (JK1 C152 GOVT) which provides current information on Congressional activities, and a number of other guides and directories.
JK1 C66 GOVT

AM99 Encyclopedia of Governmental Advisory Organizations, 1973- . Detroit: Gale Research. irregular.

(7th ed. 1990-91). Provides directory information, history, authority, program, membership, and other information on nearly 6,000 Presidential and Congressional advisory committees, interagency committees and other government related boards etc. Cross-referenced, with personnel, publications, agency and key word indexes. Supplemented between editions by *New Governmental Advisory Organizations*, which includes updated information and new listings.
JK468 C7E5 GOVT

AM100 Federal Statistical Directory: The Guide to Personnel and Data Sources. 28th ed. Comp. by William Evinger. Phoenix, AZ: Oryx Press, 1987. 127 p.

Lists over 4,000 persons who work on or with federal statistics. Covers main statistical agencies, such as Economic Research Service, National Agricultural Statistics Service, Bureau of the Census, and the Center for Educational Statistics. Evinger has also compiled *Federal Statistical Data Bases: A Comprehensive Catalog...* (Oryx, 1988) (HA37 U55E84 GOVT). Access to the statistics themselves can be obtained using *American Statistics Index* (see CA64).
HA37 U55E85 GOVT

AM101 Official Congressional Directory, 1809- . Washington: GPO. annual.

Identifies members of House of Representatives and Senate for each state, with biographical information. Lists Members of Congressional committees, major officers of Executive branch departments and agencies, with biographical information on members of Cabinet, and diplomatic and consular offices. Includes addresses, telephone numbers, and maps of Congressional districts.
US1 XY C59 GOVT

AM102 United States Government Manual, 1935- . Washington: GPO. annual.

Official handbook of U.S. federal government. Provides comprehensive information on the departments and agencies of the executive, judicial, and legislative branches of government. Also covers quasi-official boards, committees and commissions. Includes history, statement of purpose and role, description of programs and activities, a list of principal officials, and a "sources of information" section for each agency.
US1 GS85 U57 GOVT

Bibliographies and Guides to the Literature

AM103 Andriot, John L. Guide to U.S. Government Publications, 1962- . McLean, VA: Documents Index. annual.

Format varies. Formerly titled (until 1972) *Guide to U.S. Government Serials and Periodicals*. A comprehensive listing of publications arranged by Superintendent of Documents classification scheme, with separate agency and title indexes. Includes both serial and monographic publications. Published by the same publisher is *Guide to U.S. Government Statistics*, edited by Donna Andriot and Jay Andriot, an annotated

guide to government statistical publications which is published irregularly, (latest edition 1989) (Z7554 U5G8 GOVT).
Z1223 Z7G82 GOVT

AM104 Bailey, William G. **Guide to Popular U.S. Government Publications.** 2d ed. Englewood, CO: Libraries Unlimited, 1990. 313 p.

Includes over 1,500 recent popular, serial, and best-selling titles arranged by subject, with brief annotations. Many publications are available free of charge and a listing of these can be found in *Free Publications from U.S. Government Agenices: A Guide* by Michael Spencer (Libraries Unlimited, 1989) (Z688 G6S62 GOVT).
Z1223 Z7S34 GOVT

AM105 D'Aleo, Richard. **FEDFIND: Your Key to Finding Federal Government Information: A Directory of Information Sources, Products and Services.** 2d ed. Springfield, MA: ICUC Press, 1986. 480 p.

"A catalog of finding aids to information by and about the federal government including private sector products."
R353 D139F2 or Z1223 Z7D3 GOVT

AM106 **The Federal Data Base Finder: A Directory of Free and Fee-Based Data Bases and Files Available from the Government.** 1984- . Kensington, MD: Information USA. irregular.

(3d ed, 1990) Comprehensive listing of datafiles in all formats, disk, tape, online, and CD-ROM. Arrangement by agency, sub-arranged by name of database. Subject index. Databases described, with contact names.
QA76.9 D32F4 PASR

AM107 **Government Reference Books,** 1968/69- . Comp. by LeRoy C. Schwarzkopf. Englewood, CO: Libraries Unlimited. biennial.

Includes atlases, bibliographies, catalogs, compendiums, dictionaries, directories, guides, handbooks, indexes and other reference aids issued by U.S. federal government. Complemented by Schwarzkopf's *Government Reference Serials* listing annual reports, plus some biennial, semi-annual and quarterly publications. (Libraries Unlimited, 1988) (Z1223 Z7S3335 GOVT).
R015.73 AG73 or Z1223 Z7G68 GOVT

AM108 Morehead, Joe. **Introduction to United States Public Documents.** 3d ed. Littleton, CO: Libraries Unlimited, 1983. 377 p.

An account of the basic sources and bibliographic structure of U.S. federal government publications; emphasis is on current sources. Describes administrative machinery, activities of agencies such as GPO, NTIS, ERIC.
015.73 M813 or Z1223 Z7M67 GOVT

AM109 Robinson, Judith Schiek. **Subject Guide to U.S. Government Reference Sources.** 2d ed. Littleton, CO: Libraries Unlimited, 1985. 333 p.

Guide to "significant resources, including seminal works, unique historical works, comprehensive titles and sources of first resort for reference searches." Subject approach is also available in Wiley J. William's *Subject Guide to Major United States Government Publications*, (2d ed. ALA, 1987) (Z1223 Z9I3 GOVT).
Z1223 Z7 R63 GOVT

AM110 Robinson, Judith Schiek. **Tapping the Government Grapevine: The User-Friendly Guide to U.S. Government Information Sources.** Phoenix, AZ: Oryx Press, 1988. 193 p.

Discusses information sources for types of literature, with suggestions for searching and problems in accessing the information. Designed for the uninitiated.
R025.1734 R662T   or   Z1223 Z7R633 GOVT

AM111   Sears, Jean L. and Marilyn K. Moody. **Using Government Publications.** 2 vols. Phoenix, AZ: Oryx Press, 1985–1986.
Volume 1: *Searching by Subjects and Agencies* (1985); Volume 2: *Finding Statistics and Using Special Techniques* (1986). Organized by subject or agency, provides search strategies, bibliographical checklists.
R015.73 S439U   or   Z1223 Z7S4 GOVT

AM112   Smallwood, Carol. **A Guide to Selected Federal Agency Programs and Publications for Librarians and Teachers.** Littleton, CO: Libraries Unlimited, 1986. 321 p.
Surveys more than 200 federal agencies whose services and materials "will benefit librarians and teachers." Provides directory information and objectives for each agency, and an annotated list of publications and audiovisual materials. Agencies frequently publish catalogs of their publications, these are listed in Steven Zink's *United States Government Publications Catalogs* (Special Libraries Assn., 1988) (Z1223 A12 Z56 GOVT).
Z7688 G6S53 GOVT

AM113   Zwirn, Jerrold **Congressional Publications and Proceedings: Research on Legislation, Budgets and Treaties.** 2d ed. Englewood, CO: Libraries Unlimited, 1988. 299 p.
Explains the legislative process and the printed information of Congress, including hearings, reports, debates, budgets, etc., with guidelines for access. Also by the same author is *Access to U.S. Government Information: Guide to Executive and Legislative Authors and Authority* (Greenwood Press, 1989) (Z1223 Z7Z57 GOVT).
027.65 I98C2   or   JK1067 Z85 GOVT

Abstracts and Indexes

AM114   **American Statistics Index,** 1973- monthly.
Indexes and abstracts federal government publications of all types which contain statistics. See CA64 for full information.
Z7554 U5A54 GOVT

AM115   Congressional Information Service. **Index to Publications of the United States Congress,** 1970- . Washington: Congressional Information Service. monthly.
Quarterly cumulative index, annual cumulations (*CIS Annual*). Cumulative indexes 1970-74, 1975-78, 1979–82, 1983–86. Also known as *CIS Index*. Each monthly issue contains an abstracts volume and a separately bound index volume. *CIS Index* provides in-depth indexing to the contents of Congressional committee publications, including hearings, reports, documents, prints, and special publications. Annual cumulation, *CIS/Annual*, also includes legislative history citations for public laws enacted during the year. Available on CD-ROM on *Congressional Masterfile*, along with a number of other CIS products, including *CIS US Serial Set Index 1789–1969*, which indexes the *Serial Set*, the most important historical collection of U.S. government publications. Most documents indexed by CIS are available from the publisher on microfiche.
Z1223 A2C138/C14 GOVT

AM116 **Index to United States Government Periodicals,** 1974- . Chicago: Infordata International. quarterly.

Cumulates annually in fourth quarter. Cumulations for 1972 and 1973 also published. Indexes almost 200 periodicals, by author and subject. Serves as a general index because of the wide range of subject matter covered by government periodicals.
Z1223 Z9I53 GOVT

AM117 U.S. National Technical Information Service. **Government Reports Announcements and Index,**

Major indexing and abstracting service covering U.S. government sponsored research and development reports, as well as those of foreign countries. Complements and does not overlap significantly with *Monthly Catalog* (AM122). See DA32 for additional information.
Z7791 U5316 BMER; ENGR

Catalogues

The following are arranged in chronological order.

AM118 Poore, Benjamin Perley. **A Descriptive Catalogue of the Government Publications of the United States, September 5, 1774 – March 4, 1881.** 2 vols. Washington: GPO, 1885. Reprint/New York: Johnson, 1962.

Incomplete but still useful for this period. Arranged chronologically with brief annotations; indexed by subject, personal author and government agency.
R015.73 P823   or   US1GP Y5 D21 GOVT

AM119 **Checklist of United States Public Documents, 1789-1909.** 3d ed. rev. and enl. Washington: GPO, 1911. 1707 p. Reprint/ New York: Kraus, 1962.

Reproduced shelf list of the Public Documents Department Library. Originally planned as 2 vol. set. The second (index) volume was never published. Microfilm edition, *Checklist 76*, (Historical Documents Institute, 1976) includes and updates original to 1976. *Cumulative Title Index to U.S. Public Documents, 1789–1976* is a 5 volume hardcover index to the microfilm.
R015.73 U58C   or   US1 GPll C37 GOVT

AM120 Ames, John G. **Comprehensive Index to the Publications of the United States Government, 1881-1893.** 2 vols. Washington: GPO, 1905. Reprint/Johnson, 1962.

Each page in three columns. The middle column provides the main arrangement, alphabetical by keyword, usually a catchword from an inverted title. The first column cites issuing agency; the third column has the classification number, with personal name index.
R015.73 U58   or   US1 GP05 C53 GOVT

AM121 **Catalog of the Public Documents of Congress and of All Departments of the Government of the United States, 1893-1940.** 25 vols. Washington: GPO, 1896-1945. Reprint/ Hein.

A comprehensive record for the period.
US1 GP C16 GOVT

AM122 **Monthly Catalog of United States Government Publications,** 1895- . Washington: GPO. monthly.

Title varies. Lists documents by issuing agency. Since July 1976, publications are listed in full AACR format with LC subject headings. Entries arranged alphanumerically by Superintendent of Documents classification notation. From Dec. 1976, semi-annual and separate annual cumulative index volumes have been issued, with author, title, subject, series, reports, stock numbers, and title keyword indexes. Quinquennial indexes published commercially (1976–80, 1981-85, Oryx Press, 1987), entitled *GPO Monthly Catalog: Five Year Cumulated Index.*

Before July 1976, *MC* provided brief information with annual and some decennial and quinquennial indexes. Commercially published adjuncts to the pre-1976 *Monthly Catalog* include *Cumulative Subject Index to the Monthly Catalog of U.S. Government Publications 1895-1899* (2 vols.); *Cumulative Subject Index...1900-1971* (15 vols.); *Cumulative Personal Author Index...1941-1975* (5 vols).

Monthly Catalog is supplemented by *New Books* (bi-monthly unannotated list of all new titles); *U.S. Government Books* (quarterly annotated list of popular monograph and serial publications, including best sellers); and *Subject Bibliographies* (irregular series of topical bibliographies). *GPO Sales Publications Reference File* (PRF) is a microfiche in-print listing. *Monthly Catalog* is available online and on CD-ROM.
US1 GP M51 GOVT

State Government Publications

AM123 **Book of the States,** 1935- . Lexington, KY: Council of State Governments. biennial.

Reference work on state government with information on legislatures, elections, and statistics.
JK23403 B6 GOVT

AM124 **Monthly Checklist of State Publications,** 1910- . Prepared by the Library of Congress. Washington: GPO. monthly.

Bibliographical information on state government publications received at the Library of Congress.
Z1223.5 A1U5 GOVT

AM125 **State Legislative Sourcebook: A resource Guide to Legislative Information in the Fifty States,** 1986- . Topeka KS: Government Research Service. annual.

Information about each legislature, citations to state handbooks and rulebooks. Availability of legislative publications and directory information sources noted.
KF90 S72 LAWR

AN   INTERGOVERNMENTAL PUBLICATIONS

Directories which provide information on intergovernmental organizations can be found in *Political Science* Section CD, and in *Annuals, Handbooks and Directories*, Section AH. International statistical sources can be found in CA31 - CA67.

Multi-Organizational

Guides to the Literature

AN1 **Directory of International Statistics,** Volume 1, 1982. See CA32 for full entry information.

AN2 **International Documents for the 80's: Their Role and Use; Proceedings of the Second World Symposium on International Documentation, Brussels, 1980.** Ed. by Theodore D. Dimitrov and Luciana Marulli-Koenig. Pleasantville, NY: UNIFO Publishers, 1982. 570 p.
  A compendium of reports and papers. Covers sources, acquisition, organization, and utilization of international documents and archives of international organizations. Papers submitted by international organizations are on microfiche.
Includes subject and author indexes.
025 W927P mix   or   Z1008 W66 mix GOVT

AN3 **International Information: Documents, Publications and Information Systems of International Governmental Organizations.** Ed. by Peter I. Hajnal. Englewood, CO: Libraries Unlimited, 1988. 339 p.
  A compendium of essays examining the nature of IGO's, their role as publishers, the problems of bibliographic control, collection development and library arrangement of IGO documents and publications, reference and information work, citation forms, IGO documentation in microform, and computerized information systems. Concludes with case studies of use and users of IGO documentation. Includes bibliography and index.
025.2706 I615I   or   Z688 I57I56 GOVT

Bibliographies and Indexes

AN4 **Documents of International Organizations: A Selected Bibliography.** Boston: World Peace Foundation. Vol. 1-3, No. 4. (November 1947-September 1950.)
  Covers material issued by IGO's within and outside the UN system. Includes cumulative table of contents. Partly fills the indexing gap

for UN documents and publications prior to 1950.
Z6464 I6D6 GOVT

AN5**Index to International Statistics**, 1983- See CA33 for full entry information.
HA154 I64 GOVT

AN6**International Bibliography: Publications of Intergovernmental Organizations**, 1973- . Millwood, NY: Kraus International Publications. quarterly.

Current-awareness bibliography of publications of organizations in the UN system and other IGO's. In two parts: "Bibliographic Record" (annotated list of selected sales publications and free material), "Periodicals Record" (annotated entries or tables of contents of current issues of selected IGO periodicals). Supersedes *International Bibliography, Information, Documentation* (Vols. 1-10; 1973-1982).
Z6481 I6 GOVT

AN7**World Bibliography of International Documentation.** 2 vols. Compiled and edited by Theodore D. Dimitrov. Pleasantville, NY: UNIFO Publishers, 1981.

Lists monographs, journal articles and other material by and about the UN system and other IGO's. Also covers material on international relations.
Z6464 I6D56 GOVT

* * * *

United Nations System

Guides to the Literature

AN8 Advisory Committee for the Co-ordination of Information Systems [of the United Nations System of Organizations]. **Directory of United Nations Databases and Information Services.** 4th ed. New York: United Nations, 1990. 484 p.

A guide to 872 databases, and information systems and services of thirty-nine organizations in the UN system. In three sections: 1) description of the functions and structure of the thirty-nine organizations, with lists of databases and information services; 2) description of the information services; 3) description of the databases. Includes name/acronym index, and subject indexes in English, French and Spanish.
R025.04025 D598U

AN9 Advisory Committee for the Co-ordination of Information Systems [of the United Nations System of Organizations]. **Directory of United Nations Serial Publications.** New York: United Nations, 1988. 500 p.

Covers some 4,000 serial publications, including annual reports, published by thirty-eight UN organizations. The main listing is by key title, with each entry giving publisher, place, dates and frequency, subject descriptors and other bibliographic information, indicating other language versions when available. Includes indexes by organization, subject and ISSN, and a list of publication offices and libraries of the UN system of organizations.
UN9 CIS D37 GOVT

AN10 Fetzer, Mary K. **United Nations Documents and Publications: A Research Guide.** Occasional Papers, no. 76-5. New Brunswick, NJ: Rutgers University, Graduate School of Library Service, 1978. 61 p.

Describes UN depository libraries, major indexes, types of documents and publications, and research problems. Discusses UN resolutions, voting records, speeches, and treaties. Includes bibliography and index.
341.23 F42U   or   JX1977.8 D6F47 GOVT

AN11 Hajnal, Peter I. **Guide to Unesco.** London; Rome; NY: Oceana, 1983. 578 p.

An overview of Unesco's evolution, structure and work, with detailed discussion of programming, conferences, documentation and publishing, other information activities, and normative action. Includes an annotated bibliography of works by and about Unesco, a selection of basic texts, and index.
341.767 H154G   or   AS4 U83H33 GOVT

AN12 Hajnal, Peter I. **Guide to United Nations Organization, Documentation and Publishing for Students, Researchers, Librarians.** Dobbs Ferry, NJ: Oceana, 1978. 450 p.

An overview of the structure, functions and evolution of the UN, and a detailed description of the pattern of UN documentation and publishing. Includes an annotated bibliography of works by and about the UN, a selection of texts, and a brief survey of other organizations of the UN system.
341.23 H154G   or   JX1977 H22 GOVT

AN13 United Nations. **United Nations Documentation: A Brief Guide.** New York: United Nations, 1981. 51 p.

A practical guide to UN documents, their categories, numbering, distribution, availability and bibliographic control. Includes information about documents in microform, suggestions for organizing and maintaining UN document collections, and a select bibliography of guides to UN documentation.
UN2 LI 74U55A GOVT

Bibliographies and Indexes

AN14 **The Complete Reference Guide to United Nations Sales Publications, 1946–1978.** 2 vols. Ed. by Mary E. Birchfield and Jacqueline Coolman. Pleasantville, NY: UNIFO Publishers, 1982.

Vol. 1 of this cumulative guide lists publications by UN document series symbol, with full bibliographic information. Vol. 2 contains indexes by keyword, title, and sales number. Updated by lists of new sales publications in *UNDOC* and by sales catalogues.
Z6485 Z9U52 GOVT

AN15 Unesco. **Bibliography of Publications Issued by Unesco or under Its Auspices: The First Twenty-five Years, 1946 to 1971.** Paris: Unesco, 1973. 385 p.

Covers some 5,500 monographs and serials published by or with the assistance of Unesco. Lists official publications but excludes documents proper. Arranged by Universal Decimal Classification. Includes author and title indexes.
UN9 ES 73B36 GOVT

AN16 Unesco. Computerized Documentation System. **Unesco List of Documents and Publications.** 1972- . Paris: Unesco. quarterly; annual, multi-year cumulation.

Covers Unesco publications as well as documents of the General Conference, Executive Board, "main series" and "working series"

documents, and most of the other categories of Unesco material. Includes subject, personal name, meeting and corporate body, title and series, and conference indexes. Overlaps with and continues *List of Unesco Documents and Publications.*
UN9 ES730 U54 GOVT

AN17 Unesco. Division of the Unesco Library, Archives and Documentation Services. **Bibliography of Publications on Unesco.** Paris: Unesco, 1984. 433 p.

Lists over 3,300 monographs, theses, contributions to books, and periodical articles about Unesco but not issued by that organization. Arranged by country of publication. Includes subject and author indexes and a list of descriptors used.
UN9 ES722 84B36 GOVT

AN18 United Nations. Dag Hammarskjold Library. **UNDOC: Current Index; United Nations Documents Index.** 1979- . New York: United Nations. quarterly; annual cumulation (on microfiche, 1984-).

Covers nonrestricted UN documents and publications. Consists of a checklist arranged by document series symbol and giving full bibliographic information, and author, title and subject indexes. Also includes lists of maps, sales publications and new document series symbols. Supersedes *UNDEX: United Nations Documents Index* (1970–1979, 10 issues yearly); and *United Nations Documents Index* (1950-1973, monthly).
UN2 LI U51 GOVT

AN19 United Nations. Dag Hammarskjold Library. **United Nations Sales Publications, 1972–1977: Cumulative List with Indexes.** New York: United Nations, 1978. 149 p.

A chronological list of UN sales publications, subarranged by sales number. Includes subject, title, author, and UN document series symbol indexes.
UN2 LI11 78B27 GOVT

AN20 United Nations. Department of Public Information. **Ten Years of United Nations Publications, 1945 to 1955: A Complete Catalogue.** New York: United Nations, 1955. 270 p.

Covers UN monographic and periodical publications and official records, as well as selected League of Nations material.
UN6 PI 55T29 GOVT

AN21 United Nations. Library. **Check List of United Nations Documents.** 20 vols. New York: United Nations, 1946–1953.

Partially fills the gap for the period 1946–1949. For general indexes to UN documents and publications after 1950, see *UNDOC: Current Index; United Nations Documents Index* (AN18).
Z6481 A5 GOVT

AN22 United Nations. Sales Section. **United Nations Publications Catalogue, 1990–1991.** New York: United Nations, 1989. 144 p.

Latest issue of a periodic catalog of UN publications in print. Updated by semi-annual and monthly supplements.
UN2 CS30 C17 GOVT

Encyclopedias, Dictionaries and Handbooks

AN23 Osmanczyk, Edmund Jan. **The Encyclopedia of the United Nations and International Relations.** 2d. ed. New York; Philadelphia; London: Taylor and Francis, 1990. 1220 p.

A compendium of information on the UN system and other international organizations, on a large number of international treaties and agreements (providing many full or partial texts), on UN member states, and on political economic, military, diplomatic and legal concepts. Includes bibliographic notes and indexes.
JX1977 O8 GOVT

AN24 United Nations. Dag Hammarskjold Library. **United Nations Document Series Symbols, 1945–1977; Cumulative List with Indexes.** Bibliographical Series, No.5/Rev.3. New York: United Nations, 1978. 312 p.

A listing of series symbols (the principal numbering scheme for UN documents), with each entry providing the name of the issuing organ, period during which the symbol was used, restricted distribution of documents where applicable, and subsequent and other related symbols. Includes alphabetical subject/title index. Updated by: *United Nations Document Series Symbols, 1978–1984* (New York: UN, 1986). Further updated by listings in *UNDOC*.
UN2 LI11 U55 GOVT

AN25 United Nations. Department of International Economic and Social Affairs. **Macrothesaurus for Information Processing in the Field of Economic and Social Development.** 3d ed. Prepared by Jean Viet. New York: United Nations: United Nations/Organisation for Economic Co-operation and Development, 1985. 347 p.

A list of economic and social terms, indicating broader, narrower and related terms, and other relationships. In four parts: 1) alphabetical list of terms in English, with French and Spanish equivalents; 2) descriptor groups; 3) hierarchical index; 4) KWOC index.
ZZ EC M14 GOVT

AN26 **United Nations Handbook.** 1961- . Wellington, New Zealand: Ministry of Foreign Affairs. annual.

A concise survey of the constitutions, structure, membership and other characteristics of the UN system of organizations. Title varies: *United Nations and Specialized Agencies Handbook* (1961-67); *United Nations and Related Agencies Handbook* (1968-1972).
NJ1 EA U56 GOVT

AN27 **Yearbook of International Organizations,** 1948-   See AH12 for full entry information.

European Communities

Guides to the Literature

AN28 Jeffries, John. **A Guide to the Official Publications of the European Communities.** 2d ed. London: Mansell, 1981. 318 p.

A survey of official publishing and publications of the European Communities, grouped by issuing institution. Chapters include a list of bibliographic aids, appendices containing bibliography, and other lists. Includes index.
015.4 AJ47G   or   Z2000 J4 GOVT

AN29 Thomson, Ian. **The Documentation of the European Communities: A Guide.** London: Mansell, 1989. 382 p.

Describes the structure and documentation of European Community institutions and organizations, and cites printed EC material available to the public as of 1988. Includes information about online services, statistical and other tables,

and index. Should be used as a companion volume to *Jeffries*, above.
Z7165 E8T47 GOVT

Bibliographies and Indexes

AN30 European Communities. Commission. **Documents,** 1985?- . Luxembourg: Office for Official Publications of the European Communities. monthly; semiannual, annual cumulation.

Covers COM (Commission of the EC) documents, reports of the European Parliament, and opinions and reports of the Economic and Social Committee. In two parts: classified subject index; alphabetical keyword index. Title varies.
ZZ EM380 P73 GOVT

AN31 European Communities. Commission. **Publications of the European Communities,** 1974- . Luxembourg: Office for Official Publications of the European Communities. quarterly; annual cumulation.

Subject list of free and priced publications of the EC. Includes classified subject and periodical lists; alphabetical title/series index. Title varies.
ZZ EM380 P74 GOVT

AN32 European Communities. Statistical Office. **Eurostat Catalogue: Publications and Electronic Services,** 198?- . Luxembourg: Office for Official Publications of the European Communities.

Classified by eight "statistical themes": general; economy and finance; population and social conditions; energy and industry; agriculture, forestry and fisheries; foreign trade; services and transport; miscellaneous. Indicates availability of microfiche and electronic information.
ZZ EM10 C12 GOVT

Organisation for Economic Co-operation and Development

Bibliographies

AN33 Organisation for Economic Co-operation and Development. **Catalogue of Microfiches of English Monographs Available in the Micro-Library of OECD at the 31st of July 1981,** Paris: OECD, 1981. 10 microfiches.

Reverse chronological list of monographic publications of the OECD and its predecessor, the OEEC (Organisation for European Economic Co-operation). Updated by supplement of April 1983 (1 microfiche). Also available is a *Catalogue of Microfiches of English General Publications* (1983, 2 microfiches) which lists materials which are distributed free of charge.
ZZ ED C18 mfe GOVT

AN34 Organisation for Economic Co-operation and Development. **Catalogue of Microfiches of Periodicals Available in the Micro-Library of OECD at the 1st of October 1982.** Paris: OECD, 1982. 12 microfiches.

Alphabetical list of periodical titles issued in English and French. Gives detailed holdings for each volume, and title changes.
ZZ ED C19 mfe GOVT

AN35 Organisation for Economic Co-operation and Development. **Catalogue of Publications on Sale,** 1964- . Paris: OECD. annual; supplements.

This sales catalogue groups publications by subject, with author/title index. The only publicly available bibliographic source for OECD as a whole.
ZZ ED C16 GOVT

Part B

HUMANITIES

BA GENERAL REFERENCE IN THE HUMANITIES

This section contains reference sources that cover general disciplines in the humanities. More specialized sources are listed by discipline. See also Part A *General Reference* which has several sections which include materials in the humanities. See specifically Section AC *Selection Aids* which includes reviewing media and other tools which evaluate publications. Biographical information for the humanities can be found in Section AL *Biography*, which includes general biographical sources, and those covering authors.

Guides to the Literature

BA1 Blazek, Ron and Elizabeth Smith Aversa. **The Humanities: A Selective Guide to Information Sources.** 3d ed. Englewood, CO: Libraries Unlimited, 1988. 323 p.
Introductory chapters discuss humanities scholarship and most important general reference sources. Resource chapters selectively cover reference works and databases from philosophy, religion, visual and performing arts, language and literature. Access chapters discuss bibliographic access and control, user and use studies, and the research environment.
R001.3 AA724H3   or   Z5579 R63

Bibliographies and Indexes

BA2 American Humanities Index, 1975- . Troy, NY: Whitston Publishing. quarterly, with annual cumulation.
"An index to creative, critical, and scholarly journals in the arts and humanities." Some overlap with other indexing sources, but provides unique coverage of state and regional literary reviews, newsletters, and journals devoted to individual authors, and little magazines. Author/title entries, with works about an author appearing after primary entries by the author. Includes book reviews of more than 500 words.
AI3 A278

BA3 Arts and Humanities Citation Index, 1975- . Philadelphia: Institute for Scientific Information. semi-annual and annual cumulation.
Coverage from more than 6,000 of the world's leading journals in literature, history, language, religion, philosophy, drama and theatre, art and architecture, music, classics, dance, folklore and the media; many indexed fully, the remainder selectively. In addition to the usual citation indexing, *AHCI* includes works of art (poems, painting, films, etc) as indexing terms when

those works are the subject of the article. Available online as *Arts & Humanities Search*. See DA22 for description of arrangement.
AI3 A278

BA4 **British Humanities Index,** 1962- quarterly. Covers archaealogy, architecture, art, books and publishing, folkore, language, music, philosophy. See AF6 for full entry information.

BA5 **Current Contents: Arts and Humanities,** 1979- . Philadelphia: Institute for Scientific Information. weekly.

Contains contents pages for each issue of over 1,300 journals. Multi-authored works are selectively included. Covers the same fields as *AHCI* (BA3) Available on diskette, and online as *Current Contents Search ARTS*.

BA6 **Directory of Published Proceedings. SSH: Social Sciences and Humanities.** 1968- quarterly. See CA1 for full entry information.

BA7 **Dissertation Abstracts International.** Section A: The Humanities and Social Sciences. 1979- biweekly. See AF42 for full entry Information.

BA8 **Essay and General Literature Index,** 1900- semi-annual. Indexes essay collections with an emphasis on humanities, literature, and critical works. See AF37 for full entry information.

BA9 **Humanities Index,** 1974- . New York: H.W. Wilson. quarterly with annual cumulation.

Indexes 345 English language periodicals in art, archaeology and classical studies, area studies, dance, drama, film, folklore, history, journalism and communications, language and literature, music, performing arts, philosophy, religion amd theology, and related areas. Alphabetical subject/author index, with extensive cross-referencing. Original works of fiction, shorts stories, poetry and drama indexed by author and by genre, e.g. "Fiction - English language". Reviews listed by form, e.g. "Ballet Reviews". Book reviews listed separately at end.
 Available online and on CD-ROM.
AI3 H8

BA10 **An Index to Book Reviews in the Humanities,** 1960- . Williamston, MI: Philip Thomson. annual, 1963-.

From 1960–1971, indexing was selective. From 1971, indexes all book reviews in 700 journals in the arts, performing arts, literature, philosophy, language, travel, etc., with the exception of children's books. Includes biography, memoirs. Retrospective coverage of book reviews can be found in *Combined Retrospective Index to Book Reviews in Humanities Journals, 1802–1974* (10 vols, Research Publications, 1983–84) (Z1035 A1C63), which is particularly valuable for early book reviews not indexed elsewhere. Volumes 1-9 is arranged alphabetically by authors of books reviewed, then by titles. Reviewers are indexed where information available. Volume 10 is the title index. Book reviews can also be found in book reviewing media (see AC15 - AC35).
AI3 I63

Encyclopedias, Dictionaries, and Directories

BA11 **Benét's Reader's Encyclopedia.** 3d ed. New York: Harper and Row, 1987. 1091 p.

Earlier editions entitled *Reader's Encyclopedia*. Includes biographical notes on writers, artists, musicians, philosophers, and historical figures; plot and character synopses; discussion of myth, folklore, legends; description of movements, schools, place names etc. Literary terms, allusions defined. Does not completely supersede second edition (1960).
R803 B465 R3   or   PN41 B4

BA12   Brewer's Dictionary of Phrase and Fable. 14th ed. Ed. by Ivor H. Evans. London: Cassell, 1989. 1264 p.
First published by E.C. Brewer in 1870 and many times revised as a standard reference handbook with short entries on the source of many literary topics and allusions.
R803 B84B12 (Centenary edition, 1970)

BA13   Directory of Grants in the Humanities, 1986- . Phoenix AZ: Oryx Press. annual.
International directory of over 2,500 programs of private and governmental funding sources in all areas of humanities. See also *Handbook of Grants and Subsidies of the Federal and Provincial Governments*, (CC31), a looseleaf publication updated regularly, which contains funding sources available in all fields, including the arts and humanities, to Canadian individuals, businesses and organizations.
AZ188 U5 D56

BA14   Oxford Illustrated Encyclopedia of the Arts. Ed. by John Julius Norwich. New York: Oxford University Press, 1990. 449 p.
Covers architecture; decorative arts; film; literature; music; photography; theatre; and visual arts. Entries are short, with many cross references. Individual volumes do not have indexes or bibliographies.
NX70 O94 ROMU

*   *   *   *

BB   PHILOSOPHY

Guides to the Literature

BB1 Bynagle, Hans E. **Philosophy: A Guide to the Reference Literature.** Littleton, CO: Libraries Unlimited, 1986. 170 p.

A comprehensive annotated and classified guide to the reference literature, including coverage of general tools such as bibliographies, dictionaries, encyclopedias, indexes, and handbooks and specialized tools such as databases, concordances, core journals, biographical sources, research centers, and professional and other philosophical associations.
Z7125 B97 ROBA

BB2 De George, Richard T. **The Philosopher's Guide: To Sources, Research Tools, Professional Life, and Related Fields.** Lawrence, KS: Regents Press of Kansas, 1980. 261 p.

Classified guide to materials in philosophy supplemented by sections on research tools in related fields, and general reference sources. Some titles with brief annotations.
Z7125 D445

BB3 Mathien, Thomas. **Bibliography of Philosophy in Canada: A Research Guide / Bibliographie de la philosophie au Canada: une guide à recherche.** Kingston, ON: Ronald P. Frye & Co. 1989. 157 p.

This bibliography includes an annotated checklist of secondary sources on Canadian philosophy, selected bibliographies of English Canadian philosophers active prior to 1950, and a list of Canadian periodicals which contain articles of philosophical relevance.
Z7129 C3C38

BB4 Tice, Terrence N. and Thomas P. Slavens. **Research Guide to Philosophy.** Chicago: American Library Association, 1983. 608 p.

Bibliographic essays on the history of philosophy, individual philosophers, and areas of philosophical inquiry, followed by an annotated list of reference works. Author/ title, subject indexes.
R107 T555R

Bibliographies, Indexes and Abstracts

BB5 Bibliographie de la philosophie, 1954- . Paris: Vrin. quarterly.

Abstracts of important new monographs in a classified order. Original language for English, French, German, Italian, and Spanish books; in English or French for others.
Z7127 B5

BB6 A Bibliography of Philosophical Bibliographies. Ed. by Herbert Guerry. Westport, CT: Greenwood Press, 1977. 332 p.

In two parts: bibliographies of individual philosophers; subject bibliographies.
Z7125 A1G83

BB7 The Philosopher's Index: A Retrospective Index to Non-U.S. English Language Publications from 1940. 3 vols. Bowling Green, OH: Philosophy Documentation Center, Bowling Green State University, 1980.

Provides coverage of the philosophical literature from 1940 to the beginnings of indexing in the quarterly, (BB9); articles published, 1940-66; books published, 1940-78. Available online.
Z7127 P45

BB8 The Philosopher's Index: A Retrospective Index to U.S. Publications from 1940. 3 vols. Bowling Green, OH: Philosophy Documentation Center, Bowling Green State University, 1978.

"Contains information on approximately 16,000 articles published in the U.S. during 1940–1966 and approximately 5,000 books published in the U.S. during 1940–1976." Available online.
Z7127 P46

BB9 The Philosopher's Index: An International Index to Philosophical Periodicals and Books, 1967- . Bowling Green, OH: Philosophy Documentation Center, Bowling Green State University. quarterly, with annual cumulation.

An index, with abstracts of books in English, and articles from major journals in English, French, German, Spanish, and Italian; selected journals in other languages. Available online (1940-), excepting book reviews. Online searching of journal literature in philosophy can also be obtained through the *Humanities Index* database (BA9).

The abstracting service, *Bulletin signalétique: philosophie*, (1947- Paris: Centre Nationale de la Recherche Scientifique) (Z7127 F72), aims to provide exhaustive coverage of current international serial publication in philosophy and allied disciplines.
Z7127 P47

BB10 Rand, Benjamin. **Bibliography of Philosophy, Psychology and Cognate Subjects.** 2 vols. New York: Macmillan, 1905. Reprinted: New York: Peter Smith, 1949.

An important classifed bibliography of books, articles published up to 1902. Covers history of philosophy, bibliographies of individual philosophers of all periods, systematic philosophy, logic, philosophy of religion, ethics and psychology. No author index.
Z7125 R3(1905)

BB11 Répertoire bibliographique de la philosophie, 1949- . Louvain: Editions de l'Institut Superieur de Philosophie. quarterly.

Comprehensive classified list of current philosophical literature in English, Latin, and seven European languages. Covers books, articles, review articles. Indexes for book reviews, and authors appear in the November issue.
Z7127 R42

BB12 Varet, Gilbert. **Manuel de bibliographie philosophique.** 2 vols. Paris: Presses universitaires de France, 1956.

A selective bibliography containing approximately 25,000 entries of books, articles in many languages. Volume 1 covers basic works in philosophy; Volume 2 covers the philosophy of other disciplines. Emphasis is on the period 1914-1934. Extended by G.A. de Brie's

Bibliographia Philosophia, 1934-1945 (2 vols, Bruxelles: Spectrum, 1950-54) (Z7125 B7), a comprehensive bibliography in twelve languages.
Z7125 V3

Encyclopedias and Dictionaries

BB13 **The Concise Encyclopedia of Western Philosophy and Philosophers.** 3d ed. Ed. by James Urmson. Boston: Unwin Hyman, 1989. 331 p.
An encyclopedia for the non-specialist reader. Brief articles deal with the most important individuals and theories.
B41 U7

BB14 **Dictionary of the History of Ideas: Studies of Selected Pivotal Ideas.** 4 vols. Ed. by Philip P. Wiener. New York: Scribner's, 1973–74. Separate *Index*, 479 p.
An interdisciplinary approach to intellectual history. Significant concepts are explored by scholarly contributors in long essays with bibliographies. Index provides name and subject access.
B823.3 D5

BB15 **The Encyclopedia of Philosophy.** 8 vols. Ed. by Paul Edwards. New York: Macmillan and Free Press, 1967. Reissue 8 vols in 4, 1972.
A comprehensive, authoritative encyclopedia with articles by noted scholars. Broad scope, written in a readable style, with bibliographies and index. Largely supersedes James M. Baldwin's *Dictionary of Philosophy and Psychology* (1901-05; Reprinted, Gloucester MA: Peter Smith, 1960, 3 vols in 4).
R103 E56 (1967)

BB16 Lacey, A.R. **A Dictionary of Philosophy.** London: Routledge, 1976. 239 p.
"A pocket encyclopedia of philosophy ... with a bias toward explaining terminology. Epistemology and Logic occupy far more space than, say, politics or aesthetics." Many entries include bibliographies.
B41 L3

BB17 **A Dictionary of Philosophy.** Rev 2d ed. Ed. by Jennifer Speake. New York: St Martin's Press. 1984. 380 p.
Concise definitions of terms and brief articles on major concepts, movements, philosophers. More extensive coverage of Eastern topics is found in *Dictionary of Philosophy and Religion: Eastern and Western Thought* by William L. Reese (Humanities Press, 1980) (B41 R43).
B41 D52

Directories of Philosophers

BB18 **Directory of American Philosophers,** 1962/63- . Bowling Green, OH: Philosophy Documentation Center, Bowling Green State University. biennial.
(15th ed, 1990-91). Provides up-to-date information on philosophical activities in the U.S. and Canada, including names, addresses, university departments, assistantships, centers and institutes, societies, journals and publishers.
B935 D5

BB19 **International Directory of Philosophy and Philosophers,** 1966- . Bowling Green, OH: Philosophy Documentation Center, Bowling Green State University. irregular.

(7th ed, 1990–92). Companion to BB18 for Europe, Central and South America, Asia, Africa, and Australia.
B35 I55

BB20 Bales, Eugene F. **A Ready Reference to Philosophy East and West.** Lanham, MD: University Press of America, 1987. 289 p.

A non-technical treatment designed mainly for undergraduate students.
B72 B34

Histories of Philosophy

BB21 Brehier, Emile. **The History of Philosophy.** 7 vols. Chicago: University of Chicago Press, 1963-69.

Originally published in French (1926-32). A standard history of the development of philosophic thought from the Hellenic period to the early twentieth century.
B77 B72 ROBA

BB22 Coppleston, Frederick. **A History of Philosophy.** 8 vols. London: Burns, Oates and Washbourne Ltd. 1946-66. Rev. ed. Garden City, NY: Image Books, 1962–67. Supplementary Volume 9: *Maine de Biran to Sartre* (Paramus, NJ: Newman Press, 1975).

Written by a noted Jesuit scholar. The approach is chronological; each volume includes a bibliography and index.
B72 C6 ROBA

BB23 **A History of Western Philosophy.** 5 vols. Notre Dame, IN: Notre Dame University Press, 1963–71. Volumes 1 and 2 by Ralph M. McInerny; Volumes 3 to 5 by A. Robert Caponigri.

A history of Western philosophy from the pre-Socratics to the contemporary era.
B72.H55 SMC

BB24 **World Philosophy: Essay-Reviews of 225 Major Works.** 5 vols. Ed. by Frank N. Magill and Ian P. McGreal. Englewood Cliffs, NJ: Salem Press, 1982.

Contains review essays of 225 philosophical classics, beginning with the pre-Socratics to 1971. Each essay includes a critical discussion of the "principal ideas advanced", pertinent literature, and additional recommended reading. An enlargment and elaboration of the two-volume *Masterpieces of World Philosophy in Summary Form* (Harper & Row, 1981)(B21 M3 ROBA).
B21 M3 ROBA

BC   RELIGION

General Religions

Bibliographies and Guides to the Literature

BC1 Kiehl, Erich H. **Building Your Biblical Studies Library: A Survey of Current Resources.** St. Louis, MO: Concordia Publishing House, 1988. 151 p.
   Guide to the most authoritative biblical resources for church library collections.

BC2 **Religion and Society in North America: An Annotated Bibliography.** Ed. by Robert deV. Brunkow. Santa Barbara, CA: ABC-Clio, 1983. 515 p.
   Contains over 4,300 abstracts of periodical articles relating to the history of religion in the U.S. and Canada since the 17th century. Indexed.
   R7831 R44 ROBA

BC3 **Religious Books, 1876–1982.** 4 vols. New York: R.R. Bowker, 1983.
   List over 130,000 titles covering world religions and subjects of interest to religious scholars. Organized by subject, with author and title indexes. This work has been updated by *Religious and Inspirational Books and Serials in Print* (5th ed, 1987) (Z7751 R3822 KNOX). No new editions of this work are planned.
   Z7751 R436

BC4 **Religious Studies Review: A Quarterly Review of Publications in the Field of Religion and Related Disciplines,** 1975- Macon, GA: Council of Societies for the Study of Religion. quarterly.
   Issues contain detailed reviews of recent publications of all religions.
   A7 KNOX

BC5 Wilson, John F. and Thomas P. Slavens. **Research Guide to Religious Studies.** Chicago: American Library Association, 1982. 192 p.
   Provides an introduction to religious scholarship and an annotated list of reference works in bibliographic essays. A similar guide is *Library Research Guide to Religion and Theology: Illustrated Search Strategy and Sources* by James R. Kennedy (Pierian Press, 1984) ((BL41 K45).
   BL41 W56

Abstracts and Indexes

BC6 **Bulletin signalétique: histoire et sciences des religions,** 1947- . Paris: Centre Nationale de la Recherche Scientifique. quarterly.

International coverage of religious periodicals with annotations in French. The annual *International Bibliography of the History of Religions*, 1954- (Brill) (Z7833 I53) provides access to the scientific study of religions in books and periodicals.
Z7127 F72

BC7 **Old Testament Abstracts,** 1978- . Washington: Catholic Biblical Association of America. 3 issues per year.

Contains English-language abstracts of articles on Old Testament scholarship from over 350 international journals. *New Testament Abstracts* (1956- Weston School of Theology, 3 issues per year) (BS410 N35), is similar in format and scope to *Old Testament Abstracts*, and provides abstracts to articles in over 200 international Catholic, Protestant and Jewish periodicals. Both works have book review sections, and an annual index in the third issue.
BS410 O42

BC8 **Religion Index One: Periodicals,** 1949- . Chicago: American Theological Library Association, 1953- semi-annual with biennial cumulation.

Continues *Index to Religious Periodical Literature: An Author Subject Index to Periodical Literature* (1949/52-1977). Contains abstracts from more than 450 international journals from many denominations; organized by subject with subject, author and editor indexes. *Religion Index Two: Multi-Author Works*, (1976-) (Z7751 R43) provides access to scholarly works on religious and theological topics. Subject, author indexes.
Z7753 A52

BC9 **Religious and Theological Abstracts,** 1958- . Myerstown, PA: Religious and Theological Abstracts. quarterly.

Abstracts in English for articles from more than 200 journals in various languages. Nonsectarian, scholarly approach. Classified arrangement with annual author, subject, scripture index.
BR1 R286

Encyclopedias and Dictionaries, Handbooks and Directories

BC10 **Abingdon Dictionary of Living Religions.** Ed. by Keith Crim. Nashville, TN: Abingdon, 1981. 830 p.

Provides articles on the historical development, beliefs, terms and phrases, personalities, sacred writings, holy sites, and observance of religions that are practiced today. Major articles are included for the larger religions. Includes bibliographies
BL31 A24

BC11 Diagram Group. **Religions on File.** New York: Facts on File, 1990. var. pg. looseleaf binder.

Covers religions of Hinduism, Buddhism, Judaism, Christianity, Islam and 2 othe Asian religions. Foundational facts, concepts, dates, and beliefs are provided, along with maps, chronologies, timelines, calendars, and other illustrations. Looseleaf format allows for easy reproduction of the copyright-free materials.
BL82 R45 TRIF

BC12 Dictionary of Comparative Religion. Ed. by S.G.F. Brandon. New York: Scribner, 1970. 704 p.

Concise articles, many with bibliographies, written by specialists. Synoptic and general index.
BL34 D54

BC13 The Encyclopedia of American Religions: Religious Creeds: A Compilation of More Than 450 Creeds, Confessions, Statements of Faith, and Summaries of Doctrine. Ed. by Gordon Melton. Detroit: Gale Research, 1988. 838 p.

Provides information about the various religious doctrines in the United States.
BT990 E58 VUER

BC14 The Encyclopedia of Bioethics. 4 vols. New York: Free Press, 1978.

An interdisciplinary approach to ethical and legal problems (abortion, organ transplants, in vitro fertilization) current in philosophy, science and religion. Coverage of concepts, traditions, historical perspective with scientific summary. The *Encyclopaedia of Religion and Ethics* (13 vols. Ed. by James Hastings. T.&T. Clark, 1908-52) (BL31 E5) is now dated but still of interest for historical perspective.
QH332 E52 BMER

BC15 The Encyclopedia of Religion. Ed. by Mircea Eliade. 16 vols. New York: Macmillan, 1987.

Comprehensive encyclopedia covering the world's religions. Includes 2,750 signed articles of varying length, and a further 150 articles featuring biographies. All articles are written by scholars and include bibliographies. Topics covered include the history of religious traditions, Western and non-Western; cross- cultural themes, symbols, legends, rituals, religious beliefs, literature, terms, concepts, religious institutions, etc. Volume 16 is a detailed index.
BL31 E46

BC16 The Encyclopedia of Unbelief. Ed. by G. Stein. Buffalo, NY: Prometheus Books, 1985. 819 p.

Articles and bibliographies covering philosophy, history and biography of aspects of unbelief - from atheism to scepticism. Appendix lists periodicals on this topic.
BL2705 E53

BC17 The Encyclopedia of World Faiths: An Illustrated Survey of the World's Living Religions. Ed. by P. Bishop and M. Darton. New York: Facts on File, 1988. 352 p.

Covers the history, beliefs, writings, ethics, rituals and worship and present day organization of 12 major religions, including Judaism, Zorastrianism, Christianity, Islam, Baha'i, Hinduism, Jainism, Buddhism, Sikhism, Confucianism, Taosim, and Shinto. Additional chapters on the new religious movements in the West and conclusions are provided.
BL80.2 E55 TRIF

BC18 The Facts on File Dictionary of Religions. Ed. by John R. Hinnells. New York: Facts on File, 1984. 550 p.

Provides definitions of technical terms, beliefs, people and places, of world religions, with sections on "living" religions, astrology and magic, secular alternatives, and historical origins of religions. Emphasizes non-Christian religions. Detailed bibliographies and a comparative synoptic index are included. Published as *The Penguin Dictionary of Religions* in the U.K. Hinnells has also published the *Handbook of Living Religions* (Viking Penguin, 1984) (BL80.2

H275 TRIN), which surveys 20th century religions, covering history, practices, teachings, etc., and including maps, graphs, bibliographies.
R291.03 F142F

BC19 Gross, Ernie. **This Day in Religion.** New York: Neal-Schuman, 1990. 294 p.

Records events in religious history for each day of the calendar year. Major emphasis is on Christianity, with some coverage for Eastern religions and Judaism. Indexed.
BR149 G66 VUER

BC20 A Reader's Guide to the Great Religions. 2d ed. Ed. by Charles J. Adams. New York: Free Press, 1977. 521 p.

Includes 13 chapters discussing primitive religion, the ancient world, religions of Mexico and of Central and South America, religions of China, Hinduism, Buddhism, the Sikhs, the Jains, religions of Japan, early and classical Judaism, medieval and modern Judaism, Christianity, and Islam. Appendix outlines the history of religions, and includes reference lists.
Z7833 A35

BC21 Who's Who in Religion. 3d ed. Chicago: Marquis Who's Who, 1985. 439 p.

Includes religious leaders and professionals in the U.S. and Canada. Brief biographical information includes religious or secular occupation, denomination, vital statistics, creative works, activities, awards, and address.
BL72 R4 KNOX

Quotations

BC22 A Dictionary of Religious and Spiritual Quotations. Comp. by Geoffrey Parrinder. London: Routledge, 1990. 218 p.

Classified collection of more than 3,000 quotations on 177 topics, taken from Old and New Testaments, the Koran, philosophers, theologians, poets, sociologists and even skeptics through the ages. Judeo-Christian, Islamic, Eastern and aboriginal religions are all covered. Another work is *Dictionary of Religious Quotations*, edited by M. Pepper (London: André Deutsch, 1989).
PN6084 R3D4

BC23 Speake, J. **Biblical Quotations.** New York: Facts on File, 1983. 203 p.

Arranged in order of Old and New Testaments and employs the King James Version. Another definitive quotation work is K. Mcleish's *Longman Guide to Bible Quotations* (Harlow, Essex, Longman, 1986) which includes over 2,000 quotations arranged in 3 sections: Old Testament, New Testament, and Apocrypha, and further subdivided by book. *The Complete Book of Bible Quotations* by M.L. Levine (Bedrick Books, 1986) (BS432 C635 VUPR) lists 5,000 quotations from the King James Version arranged under 800 subject headings.
R220.52036 B582B   or   BS391.2 S63 ROBA

Buddhism

BC24 Humphreys, Christmas. **A Popular Dictionary of Buddhism.** Totowa, NJ: Rowman and Littlefield, 1984. 224 p.

First published in 1976. Glossary of approximately 1,000 people, places, terms and concepts for English speaking students of Buddhism.
BQ130 H856 VUPR

BC25 Reynolds, F.E. **Guide to Buddhist Religion.** Boston, MA: G.K. Hall, 1981. 415 p.

Guide to works on the historical development, religious thought, texts, beliefs, religious practices, mythology, etc. of the Buddhist religion.
Z7860 R48

Hinduism

BC26 Bell, David J. **Guide to Hindu Religion.** Boston: G.K. Hall, 1981. 461 p.

Annotated bibliography, broad in scope and comprehensive in coverage.
Z7835 B8G84

BC27 **Hinduism: A Select Bibliography.** Ed. by Satyaprakash. Atlantic Highlands, NJ: Humanities Press, 1984. 352 p.

Bibliography on Hinduism covering the years 1962–1983, includes over 11,000 entries from books, articles, research papers, and major Indian newspapers. Includes lists of periodicals and publishers in this area.
Z7835 B8A45

BC28 Rai, Priya Muhar. **Sikhism and the Sikhs: An Annotated Bibliography.** New York: Greenwood Press, 1989. 257 p.

A comprehensive, and updated bibliography of 1,150 entries covering Sikh history, gurus, scriptures, politics and socioeconomic conditions, listed in books and journal articles in English since 1965. Updates *A Select Bibliography of the Sikhs and Sikhism* by Ganda Singh (1965) and *Sikh Studies* by Hakim Singh (1982) (Z3207 P8S57).
Z7835 S54R34

Islam

BC29 Geddes, C.L. **Guide to Reference Books for Islamic Studies.** Denver, CO: American Institute of Islamic Studies, 1985. 429 p.

Includes 1,069 entries listing reference works on the history, culture, society and faith of Muslim people from Muhammed to 1924.
Z7835 M6G46

BC30 Glasse, Cyril. **The Concise Encyclopedia of Islam.** San Francisco, CA: Harper and Row, 1989. 472 p.

One volume encyclopedia with entries in single alphabetical sequence by an American Muslim scholar. Appendices include maps showing historical progress of Islam, branches of Islam, and genealogies. Also includes a chronology and bibliography, but no subject index. The more comprehensive *Encyclopedia of Islam*, (Leiden, E.J. Brill), currently in progress, is now complete to volume 6, (Mahk-Mid). This is an authoritative and scholarly work treating Islamic life, lands, and people. (DS37 E5).
BP40 G42 VUER

BC31 **The Holy Qur'an** 5 vols. Washington: Islam International Publications, 1989.

Complete reference on the Islamic faith containing the complete text of the *Qur'an*. Covers 1,400 years of historic research, written by western, oriental and middle eastern Islamic scholars. Indexed, with concordance and bibliography. Hanna Kassis' *Concordance of the Qur'an* (University of California Press, 1983) (BP133 K37), lists terms and concepts used in the *Qur'an*.
TPL

BC32 **Index Islamicus 1906–1955: A Catalogue of Articles on Islamic Subjects in Periodicals and Other Subjects in Periodicals and Other Collective Publications.** Comp. by J.D. Pearson and J.F. Ashton. Cambridge: Heffer, 1958. 1st supp. *1956–60* (1962); 2d supp. *1961-65* (1967); 3d supp. *1966–70* (1972); 4th supp.

1971-75 (1977); 5th supp. *1976-80* (2 vols, 1983).

Comprehensive bibliographic work covering worldwide Islamic literature in Western languages. After the publication of the fourth supplement in 1977, the work has been updated in *The Quarterly Index Islamicus*, which includes books, articles and papers on Islamic subjects taken from more than 1,300 periodicals. The fifth supplement cumulates volumes 1-5 of the *Quarterly*. Another work providing coverage before 1905 is *Index Islamicus 1665-1905: A Bibliography of Articles in Islamic Subjects in Periodicals* by Wolfgang Behn (Adiyok, 1989) (ZM835 M6L59).
Z7835 M6L62

Judaism

BC33 Brisman, Shimeon. **A History and Guide to Judaic Encyclopedias and Lexicons.** Cincinnati, OH: Hebrew Union College Press, 1987. 502 p.

Bibliographic guide identifies and evaluates the many Judaic encyclopedias and lexicons published since the 19th century. Includes over 360 entries, with brief annotation. Indexed.
PS102.5 B75 SMC

BC34 **Encyclopedia Judaica.** 16 vols. New York: Macmillan, 1972. *Yearbook*, 1973-.

Presents a scholarly, comprehensive picture of Jewish life and knowledge. Most of the 25,000 articles are signed; bibliographies emphasize English language material. *Decennial Book, 1973-1982: Events of 1972-1981* includes material from the yearbooks with additional information (Jerusalem: Encyclopedia Judaica, 1983). Other encyclopedias include: *The Encyclopedia of Judaism*, edited by Geoffrey Wigoder (Macmillan, 1989, 768 p.) (BM50 E63 TRIF), which identifies and defines the major terms, institutions, traditions, and individuals associated with the Jewish religion; and *The Jewish Encyclopedia*, (reprinted 1976 by Gordon Press from the original 1901-06 Funk & Wagnalls edition), in 12 volumes, which is a comprehensive work on "the history, religion, literature, and customs of the Jewish people from the earliest times to present day" (subtitle).
DS102.8 E55

BC35 Frank, R.S. and W. Wollheim. **The Book of Jewish Books: A Reader's Guide to Judaism.** New York: Harper & Row, 1986. 320 p.

Annotated bibliography listing over 500 books on the Bible, Jewish thought, Jewish history, the Holocaust, Israel, prayer books, etc. Essays on each section are included.
BM561 B66 SCAR

BC36 Kaplan, Jonathan. **International Bibliography of Jewish History and Thought.** New York: K.G. Saur, 1984. 483 p.

Lists over 2,000 works in the field of Jewish studies published in Hebrew or various European languages.
Z6372 K36

BC37 Steinsaltz, Adin. **The Talmud: The Steinsaltz Edition.** 3 vols. New York: Random, 1989- in progress.

New translation of the *Talmud*, making the oral law, legends, and philosophy of the Talmud more accessible to English-speaking people. Includes commentary and a 323 page *Reference Guide*, which explains the nature of the Talmud, the history, language, and chronology.
BM499.5 E4 TRIN

Alternative Movements

BC38 Melton, J.G. **Encyclopedic Handbook of Cults in America.** New York: Garland, 1986. 272 p.

Lists alternative or non-conventional religious movements across the United States. Includes established cults, new age movement, counter-cult groups, and violence associated with cults.
BL2525 M45

BC39 **The New Age Encyclopedia.** 1st ed. Ed. by J. Gordon Melton et al. Detroit: Gale Research Inc., 1990. 586 p.

Subtitled: *A Guide to the Beliefs, Concepts, Terms, People and Organizations That Make Up the New Global Movement Toward Spiritual Development, Health and Healing, Higher Consciousness, and Related Subjects.* Includes over 300 descriptive entries in one alphabetical sequence, with keyword index. Useful source for information on subject areas not well covered in more traditional reference sources. Entries range from "Channeling" to "MacLaine, Shirley" to "Seth".
BP605 N48 M45 SMCR

Christianity

Bibliographies and Indexes

BC40 Blumhofer, Edith L. and Joel A. Carpenter. **Twentieth-Century Evangelicalism: A Guide to the Sources.** New York: Garland, 1990. 384 p.

Contains 1,572 annotated entries listing reference works, archives, periodicals, publishers, etc. dealing with evangelicalism. *The Reader's Guide to the Best Evangelical Books* (Harper & Row, 1982), which includes books published between 1950 and 1980 written for and by evangelicals, is another useful guide.
BR1644 V6B48 WYLR

BC41 **Christian Periodical Index,** 1958- . Prep. by Librarians of the Association of Christian Librarians. Buffalo, NY: The Association. quarterly with annual and triennial cumulations.

Index to 60 evangelical and fundamentalist periodicals, most from the U.S. Includes an index to subject and authors, and a book review section.

BC42 Gorman, G.E. **Theological and Religious Reference Materials.** 4 vols. Westport, CT: Greenwood Press, 1984- in progress.

Annotated bibliography of reference works for Biblical and religious studies. Volume 1 titled *General Resources and Biblical Studies*; Volume 2 *Practical Theology*; Volume 3 *Systematic Theology and Church History*; and volume 4 (forthcoming) *Comparative Theology*.
Z7770 G66

BC43 McCage, James P. **A Critical Guide to Catholic Reference Books.** 3d ed. Englewood, CO: Libraries Unlimited, 1989. 323 p.

Comprehensive annotated guide to over 1,500 international reference works relating to Catholicism in the areas of Church liturgy and theological disciplines, and social sciences works with a Catholic perspective.
Z7837 M23

BC44 **The Papal Encyclicals, 1740–1981.** 5 vols. Ed. by Sister Claudia Carlen. Ann Arbor: Pierian Press, 1981.

Includes 280 encyclical letters, bulls, and briefs written by the Popes, beginning with

Benedict XIV to Pope John Paul II in 1981. Arranged in chronological order, with a full bibliography of commentaries provided. Extensive subject index.

A second work, *Papal Pronouncements, 1740-1978* (2 volumes) (BX850 C37 Ref REGC) catalogs 5,200 papal pronouncements (encyclicals, apostolic constitutions, addresses, and other major papal documents) beginning with Benedict XIV and concluding with John Paul I (1978) arranged by date of issue. Each pronouncement includes date, title, subject, information concerning the circumstances of the writing, type of document, concise summary of the issues and subjects addressed, and bibliographic sources. Extensive subject index and title index.
BX860 C37 SMCR

Dictionaries

BC45 **The Dictionary of Bible and Religion.** Ed. by William H. Gentz. Nashville, TN: Abingdon, 1986. 1147 p.

Concise reference work to 2,800 biblical subjects and religious matters covering the history and teachings of Christianity and other world religions. Liberal and conservative viewpoints are both represented. Cross-referenced with indexes.
BR95 P46 GENR

BC46 **A Dictionary of Christian Spirituality.** 2d ed. London: SCM Press, 1983. 400 p.

Published as *Westminster Dictionary of Christian Spirituality* in the U.S. Standard reference work which includes 358 signed articles on spiritual concepts, practices, schools and important persons.
BX4488 D5 KNOX

BC47 Erickson, Millard J. **Concise Dictionary of Christian Theology.** Grand Rapids, MI: Baker Book House, 1986. 187 p.

A handy, quick-reference guide to theological terms, major theologians, and selected aspects of philosophy and church history. *The Westminster Dictionary of Christian Theology* (1983) (BR95 W494 VUPR), is a similar work, but with a more liberal perspective.
BR95 E75 TRIF

BC48 Metford, J.C.J. **Dictionary of Christian Lore and Legend.** New York: W.W. Norton, 1983. 272 p.

Includes over 1,700 brief definitions of Christian tradition as found in literature, music, and the arts. Examples of entries include ceremony, Christian calendar, Christian symbols, saints, artistic expression of biblical stories, etc. Illustrated, with cross-references.
BR95 M48

BC49 **New Dictionary of Theology.** Ed. by Sinclair B. Ferguson and David F. Wright. Downers Grove, IL: Inter-Varsity Press, 1988. 738 p.

A dictionary covering theological thought and definitions, written in easily understandable terms for the lay reader. Signed articles are long, and include bibliographies. Two related works are *Concise Theological Dictionary*, edited by K. Rahner (Burns & Oates, 1983) (BX841 R313) which contains brief explanations to the most important concepts of modern Catholic dogmatic theology, and *The New Dictionary of Theology* edited by J. Komonchak (Michael Glazier, 1987) (BR95 N39 SMCR) which presents Roman Catholic theology in light of teachings from the Second Vatican Council.
BR95 N38

BC50 **The Westminster Dictionary of Christian Ethics.** Ed. by James F. Childress. Philadelphia: Westminster Press, 1986. 678 p.

Revision of *Dictionary of Christian Ethics* by John Macquarrie (1967). Contributors from around the world, including Canada, have written essays on major developments in science, medicine and health care, and bioethical issues such as abortion, euthanasia, handicapped, etc., as well as traditional ethical concepts from the Old and New Testaments, and philosophy.
BJ1199 W47 TRIF

Encyclopedias

BC51 **Encyclopedia of Biblical and Christian Ethics.** Ed. by R.K. Harrison. Nashville, TN: Thomas Nelson, 1987. 472 p.

Essays on biblical terms and issues followed by bibliographical references, covering a broad range of topics from Kant to perjury to sin, and other ethical issues such as heart transplantation and the Ku Klux Klan.
BJ1199 E53

BC52 **New Catholic Encyclopedia.** 15 vols. New York: McGraw Hill, 1967. *2 Supplements*, vol. 16-17, 1974-79.

Not a revision of the *Catholic Encyclopedia* (1907-14), but a new comprehensive work, ecumenical in outlook. Subtitle reads: "An International Work of Reference on the Teachings, History, Organization and Activities of the Catholic Church, and on All Institutions, Religions, Philosophies and Scientific and Cultural Developments Affecting the Catholic Church from Its Beginning to the Present." Some 17,000 signed articles by specialists, with bibliographies, illustrations and material on the arts, sciences. Supplements add new material and update articles in the main set.
BX841 N44

BC53 **World Christian Encyclopedia: A Comparative Survey of Churches and Religions in the Modern World, AD 1900–2000.** Ed. by D.B. Barrett. Nairobi: Oxford University Press, 1982. 1010 p.

Encyclopedia covering many aspects of Christianity as found in 20,800 denominations around the world. Country-by-country surveys, chronologies, directory information, etc. provides information on the types and activities of organized Christianity in the context of all other religions. Selected bibliographies included. Part 7 "Survey" includes a breakdown of Christians and other religions in an alphabetical listing.
BR95 W67

Biographical Sources and Directories

BC54 Butler, Alban. **Butler's Lives of the Saints.** 2d ed. 4 vols. Ed. by H. Thurston and D. Attwater. Montreal: Palm Publishers, 1987.

The homilies and lives of more obscure saints are omitted. John Delaney's *Dictionary of Saints* (Kaye and Ward, 1980) (BX4655.8 D44) is a more popular treatment without sources or index. *Butler's Lives of Patron Saints*, ed. by Michael Walsh (Burns & Oates, 1987) (BX4654 B8 REGIS) should be specially noted since it contains an "Index of Devotions" listing a variety of subjects with patron saint(s). *Oxford Dictionary of Saints* (Oxford, 1978) (BR1710 F3) by D.H. Farmer lists English saints and saints venerated in England.
BX4655 B8

BC55 A Handbook of Christian Theologians. Ed. by Dean Peerman and Martin Marty. Nashville, TN: Abingdon, 1984. 735 p.

Includes detailed essays on major theological figures from 1970-1980s such as Teilhard de Chardin, Karl Rahner, Han Kung, and others. A survey of theological thought is included.
BT28 H33 TRIF

BC56 Kelly, J.N.D. **The Oxford Dictionary of Popes.** New York: Oxford University Press, 1986. 347 p.

Includes 263 popes and 39 anti-popes from St. Peter to John Paul II. Concise biographical information with bibliographical references.
BX955.2 K45

BC57 World Council of Churches. **Handbook: Member Churches.** 2d rev. ed. Geneva: World Council of Churches, 1985. 289 p.

Compendium of information on churches, national and religious councils of churches and Christian world communions. Lists over 300 Christian churches by continent, region and country, with addresses, number of members, pastors, publications, etc. Indexed.
BX6 W78 A4 VUEM

BC58 Yearbook of American and Canadian Churches, 1916- . Nashville, TN: Abingdon Press. annual.

Statistical and directory information on over 250 religious institutions and organizations. Includes inter-church committees and organizations. Includes 3 year Church calendar in each issue plus topical and analytical essays.
BR513 Y4 VUEM

The Bible

BC59 The New Oxford Annotated Bible. New Revised Standard Version (NRSV). Ed. by Bruce Metzger and Roland Murphy. New York: Oxford University Press, 1973. 1564 p.

This Bible represents the most authoritative translation in English. Provides full introductions to the Old and New Testaments and the Apocrypha as well as comprehensive essays on the history, geography, and archaeology of the Holy Land. Written by foremost biblical scholars, includes essays on major sections of the Bible, expanded introductions to individual books, and a map section depicting the geography of the Holy Land in biblical times.
BS191 A1 1973B N43

Concordances

BC60 Strong, James. **The New Strong's Exhaustive Concordance of the Bible with Main Concordance; Appendix to the main concordance; Key verse comparison chart; Dictionary of the Hebrew Bible; Dictionary of the Greek Testament.** Nashville, TN: Nelson, 1984. var. pg.

Originally based on the *King James Version* (Authorized), this is a revised and updated edition, with new computer-produced type. New material includes Key Verse Comparison Chart listing approximately 1,800 important texts as they appear in six versions: *King James Version; New KJV: New American Standard Version (NASB); New International Version (NIV); the Revised Standard Version (RSV)* and *Today's English Bible (TEB)*. Originally published as *Exhaustive Concordance of the Bible* (Abingdon,

1890) (BS425 S8), 4 volumes in 1. A standard work reprinted in several editions.

Other concordances for editions of the Bible are:

An Analytical Concordance to the Revised Standard Version of the New Testament, compiled by C. Morrison. (Westminster Press, 1979) (BS425 E4). Relates the English translation to the original Greek text. Index/lexicon lists Greek words with all English translations in the *Revised Standard Version*.

Complete Concordance to the Bible, (Douay Version, 4th ed. rev. and enl.), edited by N.W. Thompson, and R. Stock (B. Herder, 1945). First published in 1942 as *Concordance to the Bible, Douay Version*.

Nelson's Complete Concordance of the New American Bible, edited by S.J. Hartdegen (Nelson, 1977) (BS425 H27) is a computer produced verbal concordance.

The NIV Exhaustive Concordance by Edward W. Goodrick and John R. Kohlenberger (Zondervan, 1990) (BS425 G62). The *New International Version (NIV)* of the Bible has become one of the twentieth century's major English translations. This work is the only exhaustive concordance to this version.

The NRSV Concordance Unabridged: Including the Apocryphal/Deuterocanonical Books by John R. Kohlenberger (Zondervan, 1991), which is the first concordance published for the *New Revised Standard Version of the Bible*. The *NRSV*, authorized by the National Council of Churches, is fast becoming one of the most popular "new" versions of the English-language Bible.
BS425 S8 WYLR

Encyclopedias and Dictionaries

BC61 A Dictionary of Biblical Interpretation. Ed. by R.J. Coggins and J.L. Houlden. Philadelphia: Trinity Press, 1990. 751 p.
    A dictionary about the interpretation of the Bible with over 350 entries covering schools, movements, and periods of interpretation, critical methods and terms (narrative criticism, feminist interpretation), influential interpreters, and the relation of the Bible with other disciplines. Bibliographies, cross-references, and subject and Scripture indexes are included.
BS440 D494

BC62 The Eerdmans Bible Dictionary. Ed. by Allen C. Myers. Grand Rapids, MI: Eerdmans, 1987. 1094 p.
    Includes 5,000 entries concerning people, places and things of the Bible, books of the Bible, and includes articles on major themes and ideas. Based on the Revised Standard Version of the Bible. Protestant viewpoint.
BS440 B5213

BC63 Harper's Bible Dictionary. Ed. by Paul J. Achtemeier. San Francisco, CA: Harper & Row, 1985. 1178 p.
    Single volume biblical dictionary which contains more than 3,500 entries covering biblical themes, places, people, and subjects.. A companion volume is *Harper's Bible Commentary*, (Harper & Row, 1988) (BS491.2 H37 ROBA), which includes general essays on the books of the Bible, as well as special topics. Nonsectarian, and can be used with any version of the Bible.
BS440 H237

BC64 Hastings, James. **Dictionary of the Bible: Dealing with its Language, Literature and Contents, Including Biblical Theology.** 5 vols. Edinburgh: T.&T. Clark, 1898–1904.

An older scholarly work based on the Authorized Version and Revised Authorized Version, including the Old Testament Apocrypha. A revised Hastings' *Dictionary of the Bible* (Scribner, 1963), edited by F.C. Grant and H.H. Rowley is based on the Revised Standard Version with cross references from the Revised and Authorized Versions.
BS440 H52 ROBA

BC65 **Illustrated Dictionary and Concordance of the Bible.** Ed. by Geoffrey Wigoder. New York: Macmillan, 1986. 1070 p.

Dictionary listing over 3,500 names of people, places, tribes, animals, plants, rituals, etc. found in the Bible. The concordance which is located in the margins next to the words, lists the biblical references to the words.
BS440 I56 TRIN

BC66 **The International Standard Bible Encyclopedia.** Rev. ed. 4 vols. Ed. by G.W. Bromiley. Grand Rapids, MI: Eerdmans, 1979–88.

A new edition of a classic work first published in 1915. Presented with a Protestant evangelical viewpoint. Includes signed articles written by Biblical scholars, within an alphabetical arrangement covering every person, place, event and item mentioned in Scripture. Entries on terms relating to theology or theological principles also included. Illustrated.
BS440 I6 VUPR

BC67 **The Interpreter's Dictionary of the Bible.** 4 vols. New York: Abingdon, 1962.

Subtitled: *An Illustrated Encyclopedia Identifying and Explaining All Proper Names and Significant Terms and Subjects in the Holy Scriptures, Including the Apocrypha, with Attention to Archaeological Discoveries and Researches into the Life and Faith of Ancient Times.* A comprehensive and authoritative work for modern Bible study; extensively illustrated.
BX440 I5

BC68 **New International Dictionary of Biblical Archaeology.** Ed. by E.M. Blaiklock and R. Harrison. Grand Rapids, MI: Zondervan, 1983. 485 p.

All articles except definitions are signed: many bibliographies and illustrations. *Encyclopedia of Archaeological Excavations in the Holy Land* (4 vols, Prentice Hall, 1975-78) (DS111 A2E5) is a detailed work translated from the Hebrew.
BS622 N48

BC69 **The Revell Bible Dictionary.** Old Tappan, NJ: Fleming H. Revell, 1990. 1156 p.

Includes all major historical, theological, geographical and literary topics found in the Bible, with charts, outlines, and illustrations. Conservative position is taken on many dates. Well indexed.

BC70 **Theological Dictionary of the New Testament.** Ed. by Gerhard Kittel and Gerhard Friedrich. Abridged in one volume by Geoffrey W. Bromiley. Grand Rapids, MI: Eerdmans, 1985. 1356 p.

The parent of this abridgement is the 10 volume work of the same title, published between 1964–1974 by Eerdmans, often referred to as "Kittel". This new work, known as "Little Kittel" retains the same number of entries, but focuses on biblical usage. All Greek and

Hebrew terms have been transliterated to make the work more accessible.
PA881 74713 KNOX

BC71 Theological Dictionary of the Old Testament. 6 vols. Grand Rapids, MI: Eerdmans. 1974- in progress.

A major work on the Old Testament, projected to be 12 volumes when complete. Written in dictionary format, translated from the German original *Theologisches Wörterbuch zum alten Testament*, also in process of publication.
BS440 B5713

BC72 Vine, W.E., Merrill F. Unger and William White. **An Expository Dictionary of Biblical Words.** Nashville, TN: Thomas Nelson, 1985. 755 p.

A compilation of two standard works: Unger and White's *Nelson's Expository Dictionary of the Old Testament* (1980), and W.E. Vine's *An Expository Dictionary of New Testament Words* (1983) (PA881 V5). This new work provides a reference to the Hebrew of the Old Testament and the Greek of the New Testament.
BS S37 E96 VUER

Handbooks

BC73 The Bible Almanac. Ed. by James I. Packer. Nashville, TN: Thomas Nelson, 1980. 765 p.

Information to assist in interpreting the Bible, e.g. coinage, weights, foods, means of travel, animal and vegetable life, social manners and customs, languages, etc. Indexed.
BS635.2 B48 STAS

BC74 Blair, Edward P. **The Illustrated Bible Handbook.** Nashville, TN: Abingdon, 1987. 538 p.

Revision of the *Abingdon Bible Handbook* (Abingdon, 1975) (BS475.2 B58). Addresses issues such as "The Bible Today", "The Bible in History", etc. Another handbook for Catholic study is *The Catholic Bible Study Handbook* by Jerome Kodell (Servant Publications, 1985), or for Protestants, *Eerdmans' Handbook to the Bible* (Eerdmans, 1983) (BS417 E35 VUER).
BS475.2 B5 ERIN

Atlases

BC75 The Macmillan Bible Atlas. Rev. ed. Ed. by Y. Aharoni, and M. Avi-Yonah. New York: Macmillan, 1977. 184 p.

Events in Biblical lands from 3000 BC to AD 200 shown in 264 maps; text by two Hebrew scholars.
G2230 A2 (1968)

BC76 Oxford Bible Atlas. 3d ed. Ed. by Herbert G. May. New York: Oxford University Press, 1984. 144 p.

Historical atlas which covers the period from 1025 BC to AD 70. Topical maps, tables, and accompanying essays on biblical history and archaeological findings complement the maps. Another work is *The Harper Atlas of the Bible* edited by James Pritchard (Harper & Row, 1987) (G2230 H97 TRIF), which relates Biblical incidents to Near Eastern history and culture from prehistoric to Byzantine Christian times.
BS630 O96

BC77 The Westminster Historical Atlas to the Bible. Rev. ed. Ed. by G.E. Wright, and F. Wilson. Philadelphia: Westminster Press, 1956. 130 p.
Authoritative work with good maps, extensive text.
BS630 W7 MAPL

Mythology and Folklore

BC78 Burkert, W. **Greek Religion in the Archaic and Classical Periods.** Oxford: Basil Blackwell, 1985. 512 p.
Survey discussing the literature and myth, art and archaelogy of what is presently known about the religions of the ancient Greeks. Includes bibliographies and indexes. A similar work for Roman life and religion from 100 BC to AD 100 is Lyttelton and Forman's *The Romans, Their Gods and Their Beliefs* (Orbis, 1984).

BC79 **Crowell's Handbook of Classical Mythology.** Comp. by Edward Tripp. New York: Thomas Y. Crowell, 1970. 631 p.
Myths of Greece and Rome with reference to literary sources and a pronouncing index. *Who's Who in Classical Mythology* (Weidenfeld Nicholson, 1973) (BL715 G68) by M. Grant and J. Haxel is similar in coverage, but includes genealogical trees and many illustrations.
BL303 T75 ROBA

BC80 **The Facts on File Encyclopedia of World Mythology and Legend.** New York: Facts on File, 1988. 807 p.
Includes more than 3,000 entries to world myth, fairy tale, and legend, arranged in an A-Z format. Includes a bibliography.
BL303 M45

BC81 Fowke, Ed. and C.H. Carpenter. **A Bibliography of Canadian Folklore in English.** Toronto: University of Toronto Press, 1981. 272 p.
Extensive bibliography, without annotations under headings such as folktales, superstitions, popular beliefs, folk art and material culture. Includes films and recordings.
Z5984 C2F69

BC82 Frazer, J.G. **The Golden Bough: A Study in Magic and Religion.** 3d ed. 13 vols. London: Macmillan Press, 1980.
Reprinted from the 1911-15 version. Encyclopedia covering primitive beliefs and customs, and their place in the history of religion. Indexed.
BL310 F7 ROBA

BC83 Grimal, Pierre. **The Dictionary of Classical Mythology.** 6th ed. New York: Basil Blackwell, 1986. 603 p.
A standard work written by a noted authority, Grimal provides alphabetized entries on gods and goddesses, heroes and mortals of Greek and Roman mythology. Entries are of varying length, footnotes and cross-references are provided, as well as 40 genealogical tables included in the appendix. *A Concise Dictionary of Classical Mythology* (Basil Blackwell, 1990) has shortened entries and focuses more on Greek and Roman myth, and excludes the illustrations and tables.
BL715 G7513

BC84 **Larousse World Mythology.** Rev. ed. Ed. by Pierre Grimal. London: Hamlyn, 1982. 569 p.
Essays cover the mythologies of many cultures from prehistoric times to the twentieth century.

Profusely illustrated with 40 colour plates and 600 black-and-white illustrations.
BL311 G963 ROBA (1965)

BC85 **Man, Myth and Magic: The Illustrated Encyclopedia of Mythology, Religion and the Unknown.** 12 vols. Freeport, NY: Marshall Cavendish, 1983.

Lengthy articles on many subjects in mythology, magic, and unusual religious beliefs. Includes many illustrations, and bibliographies with articles.
BF1411 M35

BC86 **Mythology: An Illustrated Encyclopedia.** Ed. by Richard Cavendish. New York: Rizzoli, 1980. 303 p.

Geographical arrangement with glossary, bibliography, index; lavishly illustrated. *A Guide to the Gods* (Morrow, 1982) (BL473 C37) by Richard Carlyon is also arranged geographically.
BL311 M95

BC87 **The Mythology of All Races.** 13 vols. Ed. by Louis H. Gray. Boston: Marshall Jones, 1916–32.

A comprehensive collection of myths presented and interpreted by specialists. Each volume represents a culture/geographic area, e.g. volume 1 "Greek and Roman", volume 10 "Oceania". Volume 13 is the index.
BL25 M8

BC88 Smith, R. **Mythologies of the World: A Guide to Sources.** Urbana, IL: National Council of Teachers of English, 1981. 347 p.

Bibliographical essays covering 6 broad geographical areas, subdivided by ethnic group and by type of material. A similar guide to sources on mythical creatures is *Mythical and Fabulous Creatures: A Source Book and Research Guide*, edited by M. South (Greenwood Press, 1987), which discusses in bibliographical essays, birds and beasts; human-animal composites; creatures of the night; and giants and fairies.
Z7836 S63 ROBA

BD   LITERATURE AND LANGUAGE

General Literature

Bibliographies and Guides to the Literature

BD1   Altick, Richard D. **The Art of Literary Research.** 3d ed. New York: W.W. Norton, 1981. 318 p.

Guide to the information sources in literature, and illustrating the principles and practices involved in literary research, bibliographic procedures, note taking, and library practices.
PR33 A4 SIGS

BD2   Anderson, G.L. **Asian Literature in English: A Guide to Information Sources.** Detroit: Gale Research, 1980. 336 p.

An annotated bibliography of literary works, critical studies and reference sources. Other guides in this extensive *American Literature, English Literature and World Literatures in English* series are *Indian Literature in English, 1827-1979* (1981) (Z3208 L5S56); *Australian Literature to 1900* (1980) (Z4021 A54); *Modern Australian Prose, 1901-1975* (1980) (Z4011 D38), *Modern English Canadian Prose* (1983), and *English Poetry 1660-1800: A Guide to Information Sources* (1982) (Z2014 P7M44).
Z3001 A63

BD3   **Annual Bibliography of English Language and Literature,** 1920– . London: Modern Humanities Research Association. annual.

An important annual bibliography listing books, pamphlets, articles, book reviews for English language and literature. Scope includes media, bibliography, folklore, computer applications. Arranged in two sections: language, and literature. Indexed by author and subject.
Z2011 M69

BD4   Baker, Nancy L. **A Research Guide for Undergraduate Students: English and American Literature.** 3d ed. New York: Modern Language Association of America, 1989. 60 p.

A "standard" in literary research, designed to provide students with an understanding of library use and online services available. Older, but still useful bibliographic guides include *A Guide to English and American Literature*, edited by Frederick W. Bateson and Harrison Meserole (Longman, 1976) (R820 AB329G2), which includes introductory chapters on literary periods, as well as important reference tools, and Richard Altick's *Selective Bibliography for the Study of English and American Literature* (6th ed, 1979) (Z2011 A4).
PR56 B34

BD5 Bracken, James K. **Reference Works in British and American Literature.** 2 vols. Englewood, CO: Libraries Unlimited, 1990-1991.

Volume 1: *English and American Literature* contains evaluative annotations of research guides, dictionaries, handbooks and histories, indexes and abstracts, bibliographies, biographical sources, and other reference materials; Volume 2: *English and American Writers* (1991) describes biographical reference works about writers.

BD6 **A Guide to Eastern Literatures.** Ed. by D.M. Lang. London: Weidenfeld and Nicolson, 1971. 500 p.

Essays, chiefly by Oriental scholars, at the University of London, on the history, trends, important writers in a variety of literatures (Arabic, Jewish, Turkish, Indian, Pakistani, Tibetan, Chinese, Japanese, Korean, Burmese). Bibliographies in each section. See also *A Guide to Oriental Classics* (3d ed, Columbia University Press, 1989) (Z7046 C65).
Z7046 L35

BD7 Harner, James L. **Literary Research Guide: A Guide to Reference Sources for the Study of Literatures in English and Related Topics.** New York: Modern Language Association of America, 1989. 737 p.

Designed to replace the standard work by Margaret Patterson *Literary Research Guide: An Evaluative, Annotated Bibliography of Important Reference Books and Periodicals on English, Irish, Scottish,...* (MLA, 1984). The work highlights essential reference sources published up to February 1989, and is arranged in 21 sections in topics relating to literature. Cross referenced, with name, subject and title indexes.
Z2011 H34

BD8 **Magill's Bibliographies,** 1989- . Englewood Cliffs, NJ: Salem Press. irregular.

Bibliographies, many on various literature themes, designed as a starting point for the non-specialist student researching a topic. Some titles published to date include: *Nineteenth Century American Poetry* (1989) (PS316 J37 SCAR); *Classical Greek and Roman Drama* (1989) (Z7018 D7F67 VUPR); and *Twentieth Century European Short Story* (1989) (PN3335 M48 SCAR).

BD9 **A New Reader's Guide To African Literature.** 2d ed. Ed. by H.M. Zell; C. Bundy, and V. Coulon. New York: Africana, 1983. 553 p.

Black African authors south of the Sahara writing in English, French and Portuguese. Annotated entries for reference materials, anthologies, criticism, collections, folklore, children's books, periodicals and belles lettres. Illustrated biographies of the most prominent authors; sources for African literature with publishers, booksellers, libraries listed.
PR 9798 Z4

BD10 **The Reader's Adviser.** 1986.

Volume 1 *The Best in American and British Fiction, Poetry, Essays, Literary Biography, Bibliography and Reference*; and Volume 2 *The Best in American and British Drama and World Literature in English Translation* contain information of interest to literature students. See AC14 for full entry information.

BD11 Thompson, George A. **Key Sources in Comparative and World Literature: An Annotated Guide to Reference Materials.** New York: Ungar, 1982. 383 p.

A basic handbook for Classical, European and Oriental literatures and literatures in English, including over 1,200 reference tools. Organized in chapters with access by editor/compiler, title, and subject indexes.
Z6511 T47

Abstracts and Indexes

BD12 Abstracts of English Studies, 1958– . Calgary, AB: University of Calgary. quarterly, 1981-.

Provides abstracts of articles published in international journals on British and world literature in English and other languages. Covers language and bibliography as well as themes, types, and periods of literature.
PR1 A25

BD13 Essay and General Literature Index, 1900- . semi-annual and annual.

Contains references to essays and articles in collections and anthologies. See AF37 for full entry information.

BD14 MLA International Bibliography of Books and Articles on the Modern Languages and Literature, 1921– . 2 vols. New York: Modern Language Association of America. annual.

Format varies. Standard bibliographic work used internationally as a source of critical information for languages and literatures around the world. Volume 1 contains the bibliographical citations in a classified arrangement with author index; Volume 2 provides a detailed subject index. In addition to a lengthy introduction to the use of this work, Volume 1 also contains five sections, referred to as "volumes", which are: Volume 1 "The Literature of English-speaking Nations"; Volume 2 "Foreign Language Literature" (European, Asian, African, and South American literatures); Volume 3, "Linguistics"; Volume 4, "General Literature:; and Volume 5, "Folklore". *MLA International Bibliography* indexes over 3,100 international journals and series, as well as proceedings, books, working papers, films, recordings, collections of essays, etc. Available online and on CD-ROM.
Z7006 M639 IND

BD15 Weiner, Alan R. and Spencer Means. **Literary Criticism Index.** Metuchen, NJ: Scarecrow Press, 1984. 685 p.

Index to 68 major checklists and bibliographies of literary criticism, including over 7,000 authors and 31,000 works. Arranged alphabetically by author, with cross references.
Z6511 W44

Reviews and Annuals

BD16 Magill's Literary Annual, 1977- . 2 vols. Englewood Cliffs, NJ: Salem Press. annual.

Reviews over 200 noteworthy books in all fields of literature, published in the United States during the year. Updates the 12 volume *Survey of Contemporary Literature* (MTRL), published in 1977, which analyzed the most significant novels, drama, short story collections, biographies, and other works published in the United States between 1953 and 1975.
MTRL LANG/LIT

BD17 Yearbook of Comparative and General Literature, 1952- . Bloomington, IN: Indiana University Press. annual.

Provides articles, biographical sketches, and news announcements useful for the study of comparative literature.
PN851 Y4O2 ROBA

BD18 Year's Work in English Studies, 1919– . London: J. Murray, published for the English Association. annual.
Brief critical survey of books and articles on English and American literature issued anywhere during the year. Each period discussed in a separate chapter by a specialist.
PE58 E6

19BD Year's Work in Modern Language Studies, 1929/30– . London: Modern Humanities Research Association. annual.
Brief critical surveys of books and articles on Latin, Romance, Celtic, Germanic and Slavonic languages and literatures.
PB1 Y45

Dictionaries, Encyclopedias, and Handbooks

BD20 Baldick, Chris. **The Concise Oxford Dictionary of Literary Terms.** New York: Oxford University Press, 1990. 246 p.
Includes over 1,000 brief definitions of literary terms, words, and phrases, mostly English, but some foreign expressions are included, from classical to contemporary times. Defintions explain usage, and provide etymological meanings if appropriate.
PN41 B26

BD21   Benét's Reader's Encyclopedia. 3d ed. 1987.

Includes entries for authors, titles, characters from literature, literary terms, and other relevant information.   See BA11 for full entry information.

BD22   The Cambridge Guide to Literature in English. Ed. by Ian Ousby. New York: Cambridge University Press, 1988. 1109 p.
Revision of an earlier edition with the title *The Cambridge Guide to English Literature* (1983) (PR85 C28). Covers English literature published internationally, with sections for literature of Canada, the U.S., Australia, New Zealand, Ireland, South Africa, the West Indies, and Nigeria. Works translated into English are not included. Entries include brief biographical data about world authors (although not extensively), definitions of literary terms, titles and characters of works, etc.
PR85 C29

BD23   Dictionary of Literary Themes and Motifs. 2 vols. Ed. by Jean-Charles Seigneuret. New York: Greenwood, 1988.
Entries include a short definition and the origin and historical background of key literary themes in Western literature. Includes topics such as adolescence, arcadia, apocalypse, family, and vampirism.
PN43 D48

BD24   Dictionary of Oriental Literatures. 3 vols. Ed. by J. Prusek. New York: Basic Books, 1974.
Volume I: *East Asia;* II: *South and South-East Asia;* III: *West Asia and North Africa.* Signed articles, many with bibliographies, about authors, literary forms and genres, schools of writing and movements. International list of contributors; many are Czechoslovakian.
PN 41 P75

BD25 Dictionary of World Literary Terms. Rev. ed. Ed. by Joseph Shipley. Boston: Writer, 1970. 466 p.

Formerly called *Dictionary of World Literature* (1943, 1953). Focus is on literary criticism. Part 1 defines terms, forms, types, techniques and genres. Part 2 contains major critical surveys of international criticism. Part 3 contains critical selections from an additional 25 countries.
PN41 S5

BD26 Encyclopedia of World Literature in the 20th Century. Rev. ed. 4 vols. Ed. by Leonard Klein. New York: Ungar, 1981-84.

Contains survey articles on national literatures, including Third World countries, with an emphasis on biographical/critical articles. Authors, literary movements, genres, movements in ideas, literature and related arts, are included.
PN771 E5

BD27 The Macmillan Guide to Modern World Literature. 3d ed. London: Macmillan, 1985. 1396 p.

Also published as *New Guide to Modern World Literature* (Peter Bedrick Books, 1985). Includes 33 chapters covering the literature of world nations and ethnic groups in the 20th century. Jean Albert Bédé's *Columbia Dictionary of Modern European Literature* (Columbia University Press, 1980) (PN41 C6), is a recognized standard work for comparative analyses of modern literature in European countries.
PN41 S48

BD28 Seymour-Smith, Martin. A Handbook to Literature. 5th ed. Ed. by H.C. Holman. New York: Macmillan, 1986. 647 p.

Explains, for the student of literature, over 1,500 "words and phrases peculiar to the study of English and American literature." Also includes the chronological "Outline to Literary History", and listings of Nobel and Pulitzer prizes. H. Shaw's *Dictionary of Literary Terms* (McGraw, 1972) (PN44.5 S46) and J.A. Cuddon's *A Dictionary of Literary Terms* (Deutsch, 1979) (PN41 C83) are also useful.
PN41 H6

Literary Criticism, Biographies, and Directories

BD29 Contemporary Literary Criticism: Yearbook, 1973– . Detroit: Gale Research. annual.

Continuation of the Gale Series BD37, BD38, BD42, and subtitled *The Year in Fiction, Poetry, Drama, and World Literature and the New Year's Authors, Prizewinners, Obituaries, and Works of Literary Biography*, CLC provides critical excerpts from books and periodicals of major authors living (or deceased) since 1960 and provides information on new publications and significant literary events of the year. Organized in five sections: 1) "The Year in Review" containing essays by literary figures who survey new works in fiction, poetry, drama, and world literature; 2) "New Authors", with excerpts of criticism of writers published for the first time in that year; 3) "Prizewinners" listing literary prizes and honours and information on recipients; 4) "Obituaries" of writers listed in earlier volumes of *CLC*; and 5) "Literary Biography" which lists criticisms of literary biographies.
PN94 C6

BD30 Critical Survey of Literary Theory. 4 vols. Ed. by Frank N. Magill. Englewood Cliffs, NJ: Salem Press, 1987.

Contains lengthy articles examining the theories of 265 literary critics, listing achievements; contributions; biography and bibliography.
PN45 C73

BD31 The Critical Temper: A Survey of Modern Criticism on English and American Literature from the Beginnings to the Twentieth Century. 3 vols. Ed. by Martin Tucker. New York: Ungar, 1969. *Supplement Volume 4*, 1979.

Presents excerpts from critical studies of world authors. Complements *The Library of Literary Criticism of English and American Authors Through the Beginning of the Twentieth Century* (4 vols, New York: Ungar, 1966) (PR83 M73), which covers authors from 680 to 1904.
R820.9 C934 or PR83 C764 ROBA

BD32 Cyclopedia of World Authors II. 4 vols. Ed. by Frank N. Magill. Englewood Cliffs, NJ: Salem Press, 1989.

Continues *Cyclopedia of World Authors* (1974, 3 vols). Biographical profiles of 711 authors surveyed in *Masterplots II* series (BD112), including updates on about 20% of authors in the 1974 edition. Authors selected have made "significant literary contributions, won awards or have continued to publish since the original series had been published". Combined, these works survey writers of classics to modern times. Each entry contains a brief biography with list of works published and a bibliography.
PN451 C93 VUPR

BD33 A Dictionary of Modern Critical Terms. Rev. ed. Ed. by Roger Fowler. New York: Routledge and Kegan Paul/Methuen, 1987. 262 p.

Dictionary/handbook which focuses on terms associated with literary criticism. Terms are described in lengthy articles in relation to each other and to modern criticism.
PN81 F68

BD34 European Writers. 14 vols. New York: Scribner's, 1983-1991.

Set covers European literature and writers from the Middle Ages through to the 20th century. Arranged chronologically by date of birth of the writer, and entries supply biographical information and notes on major world events during the lifetime. Includes novelists, poets, playwrights, and writers in other disciplines, including politics, philosophy, literary theory, etc.
PN501 E9

BD35 Great Writers of the English Language. 3 vols. Ed. by James Vinson. London: Macmillan, 1979.

Collection of biocritical essays of some 1,500 important writers from Anglo-Saxon period to the present day. Volume 1 covers poets, volume 2, novelists and prose writers, and volume 3, dramatists. Entries also include a list of bibliographies and critical studies. Coverage includes Commonwealth, American and African and Caribbean writers.
PR106 G64

BD36 Literary Criticism Index, 1984.

Index to 68 major checklists and bibliographies of literary criticism, including over 7,000 authors and 31,000 works. See BD15 for additional information.
Z6511 W44

BD37 Literature Criticism from 1400 to 1800. Detroit: Gale Research, 1984- in progress.

(Completed to Volume 13, 1990). Subtitled: *Excerpts from Criticism of the Works of Fifteenth, Sixteenth, Seventeenth, and Eighteenth-Century Novelists, Poets, Playwrights, Philosophers, and Other Creative Writers....* Compendium of critical opinion on world authors. Each volume covers 15 to 20 authors, with each entry containing a brief introduction to the author's works, followed by excerpts of published English-language criticism arranged in chronological order, a bibliography, and illustrations. Cumulative index for all published volumes is provided.
PN86 L53

BD38 Nineteenth-Century Literature Criticism. Detroit: Gale Research, 1981- in progress.
(Completed to Volume 30, 1991). Subtitled: *Excerpts from Criticism of the Works of Novelists, Poets, Playwrights, Short Story Writers, and Other Creative Writers who Died between 1800 and 1900....* Continues *Literature Criticism from 1400 to 1800* (above), with coverage of world authors who died during the nineteenth century. Each volume contains approximately 25 authors, listing a brief biographical sketch, list of works published, a chronological arrangement of excerpts from critics, and bibliography for further reading.
PN761 N5

BD39 The Nobel Prize Winners: Literature. 3 vols. Ed. by Frank N. Magill. Englewood Cliffs, NJ: Salem Press, 1987.
Essays, in chronological order, of each laureate up to 1987. Also includes photograph, reasons why the award was won, and a summary of the Nobel acceptance speech, and other relevant information, as well as a review of the major works, and critical works about the laureate. Author and title index included.
MTRL LANG/LIT

BD40 The Oxford Companion to English Literature. 5th ed., 1985.
A standard work, providing biographical sketches of some 3,000 authors born before 1939 with emphasis on twenthieth-century authors. See BD97 for full entry information.

BD41 Research Guide to Biography and Criticism. 2 vols. Ed. by Walton Beacham. Washington: Research Publishing, 1985.
A guide for students doing research in literary criticism. Contains biographical entries for many authors, listing a short chronology of the author's life, followed by a selected bibliography of biographical and autobiographical sources, many with evaluative comments.
Z2011 R47

BD42 Twentieth Century Literary Criticism. Detroit: Gale Research, 1978- in progress.
(Completed to Volume 39, 1991). Subtitled: *Excerpts from Criticism of the Works of Novelists, Poets, Playwrights, Short-story Writers....* Continues BD37 and BD38 above, listing authors who have lived (and died) between 1900 and 1960, and organized in the same format as the others. Contains cumulative title, author, and nationalities indexes.
PN771 T9

BD43 Twentieth Century Romance and Gothic Writers. 2d ed. Chicago: St. James Press, 1989. 856 p.
Part of a series of one volume biographical works on 20th century writers surveyed by genre. e.g. ... *Western Writers* (1982) (PS271 T84), ... *Children's Writers* (1989) (R028.5 T971T3). Series typically includes list of works and a brief, signed essay for each author.

Includes title index and references between names, pseudonyms etc.
PR888 L69T86

BD44   The Writer's Directory, 1971/72- . Chicago: St. James Press. biennial.

Listing of more than 17,000 living authors who write in English. Entries includes citizenship, year of birth, awards and appointments, complete bibliography and address. Indexed by subject, author and title. Contains information found in other specialized works, such as *Contemporary Poets*, *Contemporary Dramatists*, *Contemporary Novelists*, *Contemporary Literary Critics*.
PS1 W73

PSEUDONYMS

BD45   Dictionary of Literary Pseudonyms. 3d ed. Ed. by F. Atkinson. London: Clive Bingley, 1982. 305 p.

Useful for 20th century writers in English.
Z1041 A84

BD46 Halkett, Samuel and John Laing. **A Dictionary of Anonymous and Pseudonymous English Literature.** 3d ed. Ed. by John Horden. New York: Longman, 1980.

The most comprehensive index for identifying anonymous, pseudonymous works in the English language. The third edition was to be published in chronological volumes, however only Volume 1 covering the period 1475–1640 was published.
R014 AH17   or   Z1065 H17

BD47   Pseudonyms and Nicknames Dictionary, 3d ed. 2 vols. 1987.

Includes literary figures. See AL20 for full entry information.

Characters

BD48 Amos, William. **The Originals: Who's Really Who in Fiction.** London: Cape, 1985. 614 p.

Identifies almost 3,000 real-life personalities who served as models for fictional characters in novels, plays, essays and poetry in the past 400 years (Shakespeare to date), from many countries. Entries may include photographs of the real-life personality as well as brief biographical information. Indexed by characters.
PN56.4 A56

BD49   Cyclopedia of Literary Characters II. 4 vols. Ed. by Frank N. Magill. Englewood Cliffs, NJ: Salem Press, 1990.

Continues the two volume 1963 edition *Cyclopedia of Literary Characters* (PN44 M3). Describes over 12,000 new characters which appear in 1,667 titles in the *Masterplots II* series, (BD112). The 1963 edition contained profiles for over 16,000 characters from 1,300 classics of world literature. Indexed by character, title and author.
PN44 M3 Ref ERIN

Writer's Guides

BD50   Literary Market Place, 1940- annual.

Useful directory providing current listings of organizations, periodicals, publishing houses, involved in the placing, promotion, and marketing of literary works. See AB7 for full entry information.

BD51 The Writer's Handbook, 1936- . Boston: The Writer. annual.

Provides essays and articles on the art, craft, techniques and business of writing in the various forms: fiction, nonfiction, poetry, drama, television, children and young adults. Outlets for publication, such as magazines, are identified, as are prizes, organizations and agents. Kirk Polking's *Writing, A to Z: The Terms, Procedures, and Facts of the Writing Business* (Writers Digest, 1990) (PN141 W75) contains definitions of terms, and other advice for writers.
PN137 W74

BD52 Writer's Resource Guide. Ed. by Bernadine Clark. Cincinnati, OH: Writers Digest Books, 1983. 473 p.

A manual for writers discussing research practices for fiction and nonfiction, finding experts, conducting interviews, etc. Reading lists and organizations are listed.
PN146 W7

National Literatures

Canadian

BIBLIOGRAPHIES, INDEXES AND GUIDES

BD53 Brock Bibliography of Published Canadian Plays in English, 1766–1978. See BD141 for full entry information.

BD54 Canada's Playwrights: A Biographical Guide. See BD145 for full entry information.

BD55 Canadian Fiction: An Annotated Bibliography. See BD102 for full entry information.

BD56 Canadian Literature Index, 1985- . Ed. by Janet Fraser, Richard Hanson, and Nancy Cox. Toronto: ECW Press, 1987- . annual.

Provides comprehensive access to Canadian literature and literary criticism in 97 Canadian and international periodicals and in Canadian newspapers. Annotated entries arranged by author and subject. New edition for 1988 is forthcoming.
Z1375 C35

BD57 Comprehensive Bibliography of English-Canadian Short Stories, 1950-1963. 1988. See BD125 for full entry information.

BD58 Gnarowski, Michael. **A Concise Bibliography of English Canadian Literature.** Rev. ed. Toronto: McClelland and Stewart, 1978. 145 p.

Includes material to 1975; lists major works by date and type; plus criticism and studies of authors and their works.
Z1375 G525

BD59 Lecker, Robert. **The Annotated Bibliography of Canada's Major Authors.** 8 vols. Toronto: ECW Press, 1979- in progress.

(Completed to Volume 7, 1987). A bibliographical work providing comprehensive coverage of "major" Canadian authors and poets of the 19th and 20th centuries. Each volume is divided into two parts: Part 1: *Primary*, which lists books

and manuscripts, and contributions to periodicals; and Part 2: *Secondary*, which lists books and articles about the author, book reviews, audio-visual materials by and about the author, and awards and prizes received.
Z1375 L43

BD60 **Literary Archives Guide / Guide des archives littéraires.** Ottawa: National Archives of Canada, 1988. 59 p.

Bilingual guide to post-Confederation literary collections, including papers from poets, fiction and nonfiction writers, children's authors, journalists, editors, publishers, critics, and literary organizations. Arranged alphabetically by subject with information about the collection. *Literary Manuscripts at the National Library of Canada* (2d ed, 1990) (Z6621 N38N38), provides access to unpublished literature collections in the NLC collection. Arranged alphabetically by collection with information about extent, finding aids, and use.
Z1375 N37

BD61 Miska, John. **Ethnic and Native Canadian Literature: A Bibliography.** Toronto: University of Toronto Press, 1990. 445 p.

A bibliography of 5,500 references to primary and secondary material from earliest times to present day. Represents 65 nationality groups in more than 70 languages.
Z1376 E87M57

BD62 Moyles, R.G. **English Canadian Literature to 1900: A Guide to Information Sources.** Detroit: Gale Research, 1976. 346 p.

Critical annotations of reference works, travel literature, journals; critical comment in books and periodicals supplied for 12 major, 36 minor authors. One of 3 volumes on Canadian literature in the series 'American Literature ...'; others are P. Steven's *Modern English Canadian Poetry* (1978) (Z1377 P7S79) and Helen Hoy's *Modern English Canadian Prose* (1983) (BD106).
810.08 AM938E   or   Z1375 M693

BD63 Sirois, Antoine. **Bibliography of Studies in Comparative Canadian Literature, 1930–1987 / Bibliographies d'études de littérature canadienne comparée.** Sherbrooke PQ: Départment des lettres et communications, Université de Sherbrooke, [1989]. 130 p.

An enumerative, retrospective bibliography. Similar in format to the annual bibliography published in the journal *Canadian Review of Comparative Literature / Revue canadienne de littérature comparée.* Includes bibliographies and checklists, reference works, anthologies and collections, current periodicals, literary histories, comparative studies, comparisons of authors works, themes, literary genres, form, etc.
Z1377 F8B5

BD64 **Theses on English-Canadian Literature: Bibliography of Research Produced in Canada and Elsewhere from 1903 Forward.** Ed. by Apollonia Steele. Calgary, AB: University of Calgary Press, 1989. 505 p.

Index to 1,800 theses, dissertations, and other major academic papers on English-language Canadian literature published throughout the world, and in many languages. Author and subject arrangement, with call number from the collection at the University of Calgary Libraries.
Z5053 S74

BD65 Watters, Reginald E. **A Checklist of Canadian Literature and Background Materials, 1628–1960.** 2d ed. rev. Toronto: University of Toronto Press, 1972. 1085 p.

Record of the literature of English-speaking Canada up to 1960. In two parts; Part 1 records

all known titles of poetry, fiction, drama by anglophone Canadians to 1960; Part 2 selectively lists other books by Canadian authors which reveal the backgrounds of that literature and which are of value to the student of Canadian literature or culture. Includes categories for biographies, literary criticism, religion, etc.
R015.71 W346C2   or   Z1375 W3

HANDBOOKS

BD66 Canadian Writers and Their Works: Poetry and Fiction Series. 20 vols. Ed. by R. Lecker; J. David, and E. Quigley. Toronto: ECW Press, 1983-1991.
Essays outlining the development of Canadian fiction and poetry in the 19th and 20th centuries, each with biographical essays of authors, a discussion of the tradition and milieu in which the author worked, a critical assessment of their works, and a bibliography of primary and secondary sources.
PS 8141 C37 (Poetry); PS8187 C37 (Fiction)

BD67 Dictionnaire des oeuvres littéraires du Québec. 3 vols. Sous la direction de Maurice Lemire. Montreal: Fides, 1980.
Volumes are chronological, I: *Des origines à 1900*; II: *1900-1939*; III: *1940-1959*. An illustrated directory of major works; signed articles with bibliographies; index.
PS9015 D5

BD68 Fortin, Marcel, Yvan Lamonde and François Ricard. **Guide de la littérature québécoise.** Montreal: Boreal, 1988. 155 p.
An introduction to general works on Québécoise literature and specific genres.
Z1377 F8F67

BD69 Grandpré, Pierre de. **Histoire de la littérature française du Québec.** 4 vols. Montreal: Librairie Beauchemin, 1967-69.
Biographical and bibliographic approach to major literary figures, selected journalists and historians.
819 G754   or   PS9063 G733

BD70 Literary History of Canada: Canadian Literature in English. 2d ed. 3 vols. Ed. by Carl F. Klinck. Toronto: University of Toronto Press, 1976.
Signed essays on authors and literature; surveys of work on other disciplines, e.g. history, philosophy, religion, and the physical, biological and social sciences.
R819 K65L2   or   PS8063 K55

BD71 Moritz, Albert and Theresa Moritz. **The Oxford Illustrated Literary Guide to Canada.** Toronto: Oxford University Press, 1987. 246 p.
Survey of Canadian literary history in a geographical arrangement, noting authors' connections to places, i.e. birth, death, works, settings, or other literary connections such as journals published, literary memorials, archives, etc. Arrangement within larger communities is chronological, providing a history of literary activity. Indexed, and includes photographs. Similar information is available in John Robert Colombo's *Canadian Literary Landmarks* (Hounslow Press, 1984) (PS8087 C65)
PS8087 H67

BD72 New, W.H. **A History of Canadian Literature.** Basingstoke: Macmillan Education / New York: Amsterdam Books, 1989. 380 p.
A comprehensive survey placing Canadian literature within a historical, political and cultural context. Includes a discussion of early Indian

literature, the journals of explorers, and post-Confederation literature up to 1985. A bibliography is provided.
RS8063 N48   or   PS8063 N48

BD73   The Oxford Companion to Canadian Literature. Ed. by W. Toye. Toronto: Oxford University Press, 1983. 843 p.

Includes signed entries for authors, notable works, genres, themes, regional literatures, etc. Emphasis on modern writing in both English and French Canada. Cross references; no index. This work updates the literature portion of *The Oxford Companion to Canadian History and Literature* (1967, 1973) (CJ92).
R819 098P   or   PS8015 093

BD74   Profiles in Canadian Literature. Ed. by Jeffrey Heath. Toronto: Dundurn, 1980- in progress.

Provides biographical overviews of major Canadian authors. Arranged in four parts: critical evaluation; chronology; comments by and about the author; and bibliography. Volumes 1-4 and 6 are unbound; volume 5 is bound. Volumes 7 and 8 are forthcoming and will be bound.
PS8071 P76 SIGR

BD75 Union des Écrivains Québécois. **Dictionnaire des écrivains québecois contemporains.** Montreal: Québec/Amérique, 1983. 399 p.

Bio–bibliographies; illustrated.
PS8081 D53

BD76   Who's Who in Canadian Literature, Ed. by Gordon Ripley and Anne Mercer. Toronto: Reference Press. 1987. 360 p.

Directory of approximately 900 living Canadian poets, novelists, playwrights, short story writers, critics, editors, translators, and others active in the field of literature in Canada. Includes brief biographical information, and includes a list of winners for the Governor General's Literary Awards from 1937 to present. Companion to *Canadian Writers Since 1960: First Series* (Gale, 1987) (819 C212F) (see AL48).
PS8081 W56

American

BIBLIOGRAPHIES, INDEXES AND GUIDES

BD77   American Fiction to 1900: A Guide to Information Sources. See BD105 for full entry information.

BD78   American Literary Scholarship, 1963- . Durham, NC: Duke University Press. annual.

A reviewing journal of bibliographical essays analyzing research in American literature. All genres are included, as well as individual authors, with a special section on American literature pre 1800. Each volume is separately indexed.
PS3 A47 O2

BD79   American Prose and Criticism, 1820–1900: A Guide to Information Sources. Ed. by Elinor Hughes Partridge. Detroit: Gale, 1983. 575 p.

Identifies primary and secondary information sources on 19th century American nonfiction. A complementary work is *American Prose and Criticism, 1900–1950*, by Peter A. Brier (Gale,

1981) (Z1231 P8B74) (see *Dictionary of Literary Biography* series, AL55).
Z1231 P8P37

BD80 Blanck, Jacob N. **Bibliography of American Literature.** New Haven, CT: Yale University Press, 1955– in progress.

(Volume 8, 1990, names beginning with "W"). When completed, this series will provide descriptive bibliographies of approximately 300 selected American writers of literary interest, from the American Revolution to 1930. Entries list first editions, reprints containing textual or other changes, and a selected list of biographical, bibliographical and critical works. Includes illustrations, title pages, and library locations of copies. Complements work of early bibliographers Charles Evans (AD70) and Joseph Sabin (AD68).
R810.3 B641   or   Z1225 B55

BD81 Koster, Donald N. **American Literature and Language: A Guide to Information Sources.** Detroit: Gale Research, 1982. 396 p.

This annotated guide to secondary sources is Volume 13 of the *American Studies Information Guide* series. Other titles include *Afro-American Literature and Culture Since World War II* (1979) (Z1229 N39P4) by C.D. Peavy; *Jewish Writers of North American* (1981) (Z1299 J4N32) by I.B. Nadel.
Z1225 K68

BD82 Leary, Lewis Gaston. **Articles on American Literature, 1900-1950.** Durham, NC: Duke University Press, 1954. 437 p.

A bibliography listing works on all aspects of American literature. Updated by *Articles on American Literature, 1950–1967* (1970); *Articles on American Literature 1968–1975* (1979).
Z1225 L49

BD83 **Literary Writings in America: A Bibliography.** 8 vols. Millwood, NY: KTO Press, 1977.

Provides photographic reproductions of a card file at the University of Pennsylvania which listed almost 250,000 entries from magazines, literary histories, and other bibliographies of works written by 1,000 American writers between 1850 and 1940.
Z1225 L58

BD84 Nilon, Charles H. **Bibliography of Bibliographies in American Literature.** New York: R.R. Bowker, 1970. 483 p.

While dated, this work is still useful for identification of over 6,400 bibliographies, covering a period of 400 years, published in books, periodicals, and other forms. Organized by author, genre, and special subjects with a name and title index.
R810 AN712   or   Z1225 A1N5

BD85 **Reference Guide to American Literature.** 2d ed. Ed. by D.L. Kirkpatrick. Chicago, IL: St. James Press, 1987. 816 p.

Guide to bio-bibliographical information of American authors, including list of publications, and a bibliography of critical studies. A similar work is *Guide to American Literature* by Valmai Kirkham Fenster (Libraries Unlimited, 1983) (PS88 F45 SMCR), which also lists sources for 100 important American writers, and includes a section listing guides and reference works to American literature in general.
PS21 R44

*   *   *   *

HANDBOOKS

BD86 American Writers: A Collection of Literary Biographies. 4 vols, with 4 supplementary volumes. Ed. by Leonard Unger. New York: Scribner's, 1974-1981.

Critical essays discuss style, genre, contributions of 156 American poets, novelists, short story writers, playwrights, critics, and others from 17th century to present day. Includes bibliographies.
PS129 A55 ROBA

BD87 Annals of American Literature 1602-1983. Ed. by Richard Ludwig and Clifford Nault. New York: Oxford University Press, 1986. 342 p.

A chronology listing significant literary works in the United States, from 1602 to the present. Includes four genres of fiction, nonfiction, drama, and poetry, with a main alphabetical list of authors. Side columns indicate other major historical literary events beside the author entry. Other standards in the field include *Literary History of the United States*, (2 vols, 4th ed, Macmillan, 1974) (R810 AN712 PS88 L52) which is a survey from Colonial times to the present, and *The Cambridge History of American Literature* (4 vols, 1917-21/reprints 1933; 1967) (R810.9 C178).
PS94 L83

BD88 Modern American Literature. 4th ed. 5 vols. Ed. by Dorothy Nyren Curley. New York: Ungar, 1969-85.

Compilation of critical essays on prominent American authors covering the period 1900 to 1985. Includes original set (3 vols, 1969) and supplementary volumes (1976, 1985).
PS221 C8 VUPR

BD89 The Oxford Companion to American Literature. 5th ed. Ed. by James D. Hart. New York: Oxford University Press, 1983. 896 p.

Contains concise entries on American authors, listing major works, with brief analyses; descriptions of significant works in various genres; definitions; lists of societies, movements, awards, periodicals etc. *The Concise Oxford Companion to American Literature*, (1986) (PS21 H32), an abridged version, contains about half of the entries of the full work, with some revision to include women writers of note. Another handbook, *The Cambridge Handbook of American Literature* (Cambridge University Press, 1986) (PS21 C36), is similar to the *Concise Oxford*, covering movements, periodicals, plot summaries, biographical notes about authors, with bibliographies. Also includes a chronology of American literary and historical events, and a bibliography of important critical works published since 1930.
R810.3 H3204 (1965)   or   PS21 H3

British

BIBLIOGRAPHIES, INDEXES AND GUIDES

BD90 Index to British Literary Bibliography. 6 vols. Ed. by T.H. Howard–Hill. Oxford: Clarendon Press, 1969– in progress.

Bibliography of important works on the British literary tradition covering the period from 1475 to 1969. Volumes 1 to 5 include: 1: British literary bibliographies; 2: Shakespearian bibliography; 4–6: bibliography and textual criticism of authors, periods, and genres. Volume 6 contains the index.
Z2011 A1H68

BD91 The New Cambridge Bibliography of English Literature. 5 vols. Ed. by G. Watson, and I. Willison. Cambridge: University Press, 1969–77.

Revision of the *Cambridge Bibliography of English Literature* (5 volumes, University Press, 1940–57). Volumes 1–4 are arranged in chronological order: 600–1660; 1660–1800; 1800–1900; 1900–1950, with the index in volume 5. Entries arranged by period and form, then by authors. Differs from its predecessor by excluding Commonwealth literature and by limiting non–literary sections. Appears in abridged form as *The Shorter New Cambridge Bibliography of English Literature* (1981, 1622 p.) (Z2011 N45).
R820.3 AC178CA or Z2011 N45

HANDBOOKS

BD92 Baugh, Albert C. A Literary History of England. 2d ed. New York: Appleton, 1967. 1605 p.

A comprehensive history of English literature, including some Scottish and Irish writers, from earliest times to 1939.
R820.9 B346

BD93 British Writers. Ed. by Ian Scott-Kilvert. 8 vols. New York: Scribner's, 1979-1984. *Supplement* (1987).

Companion to *American Writers* (BD86). Includes signed essays of works by and about British authors from the time of William Langland to World War II. *Supplement* updates to post World War II.
PR85 B688 ROBA

*   *   *   *

BD94 The Cambridge History of English Literature. 15 vols. Cambridge: Cambridge University Press, 1907–27, reprint 1932.

This important history is arranged by period with each chapter written by a specialist. Covers period of earliest times to the end of the 19th century. Volume 15, the index, completes the set. Extensive bibliographies are provided in each volume. The reprint edition omitted the bibliographies. Also available is *The Concise Cambridge History of English Literature* (3d rev. ed, 1970) (PR85 S34 ROBA), edited by George Simpson, which has additional chapters on the literature of the English speaking world and of the U.S. at mid-century.
R820.9 C178 or PR83 C2

BD95 Gray, Martin. A Chronology of English Literature. Essex, U.K: Longman Group, 1989. 276 p.

Traces works of English literature in relation to historical events. Chronology of dates from earliest times (397 AD) to 1980. Includes appendices for book and literary awards and dates of version for the Bible. A similar work, edited by P.J. Smallwood, is *A Concise Chronology of English Literature* (Barnes and Noble, 1985) (PR83 S5 ROBA), which outlines important literary events within the context of British history, from 1875 (Chaucer) to 1975. Important world authors are included if they were of significance to the development of English literature.
PR87 G68

BD96 Modern British Literature. 5 vols. Ed. by Ruth Zabriskie Temple and Martin Tucker. New York: Ungar, 1966-1985.

Part of the *20th Century Literary Criticism* series BD42, originally published in three volumes in 1966, with a fourth volume published in 1975 and a fifth in 1985. Provides critical

references to works by British writers of the 20th century. Includes bibliographies of authors' separately published works.
PR473 T4 SCAR

BD97 **The Oxford Companion to English Literature.** 5th ed. Ed. by Margaret Drabble. New York: Oxford University Press, 1985. 1155 p.

The greatly revised fifth edition of this standard dictionary work includes brief biographies of some 3,000 authors born before 1939, many 20th century authors; genres, movements, and provides bibliographies. *The Concise Oxford Dictionary of English Literature* (1987) (PR19 C65 SIGR, 2d ed.) is an abridged version which summarizes periods of literary history and literary subjects.
R820.3 H34C4 or PR19 H3

BD98 **Oxford History of English Literature.** 13 vols. Oxford: Clarendon Press, 1945– in progress.

A scholarly, standard source for literary periods in England, from earliest times to modern times. Most recent publication is *The Victorian Novel* (1990).
R820.9 O98 or ROBA various call numbers

BD99 **St. James Reference Guide to English Literature.** 8 vols. Ed. by James Vinson and D.L. Kirkpatrick. Chicago: St. James, 1985.

An extensive reference work providing an introduction to British literature by period and by genre, with reading lists, and entries for over 1,200 writers. Volumes include: Volume 1: *The Beginnings and the Renaissance*; 2: *The Restoration and 18th Century*; 3: *The Romantic and Victorian Period: Excluding the Novel*; 4: *The Novel to 1800*; 5: *20th Century Poetry*; 6: *20th Century Fiction*; 7: *20th Century Drama*; and 8: *Commonwealth Literature*. International works are included in some volumes, particularly Volume 7, which includes American drama, and volume 8, which focuses on Commonwealth literature from West Indies, Canada, Australia, Africa, New Zealand, and India.
PR106 S7 SIGR

Literary Genres

Fiction

BIBLIOGRAPHIES AND GUIDES

BD100 Biagini, Mary K. with Judith Hartzler. **A Handbook of Contemporary Fiction for Public Libraries and School Libraries.** Metchuen, NJ: Scarecrow, 1989. 247 p.

Useful for reference and collection development. Part 1 contains a list of over 1,100 authors and titles organized by genre: romance, mystery, science fiction, westerns, historical fiction. Part 2 provides a list of world authors whose works have received critical acclaim. Bibliographies concerning each genre are provided.
808.83 AB567H

BD101 Davis, Barbara Kerr. **Read All Your Life: A Subject Guide to Fiction.** Jefferson, NC: McFarland, 1989. 286 p.

Subject analysis of serious fiction in five main themes: self, family, society and politics, religion, and philosophy. Intended as a resource for book discussion groups, literature classes, and readers of fiction, each entry includes a brief essay, excerpts of recommended novel, and a set of discussion questions. A similar work, but much different in form, is *The Bloomsbury Good Reading Guide* by Kenneth McLeish (London: Bloomsbury, 1990), (Z5916 M455 ROBA) which recommends more than 3,000 fictional works available in English written from ancient times to present day. Entries are by author or subject, and within entries are suggestions of similar or related titles. "Skein" or family tree charts lead readers to other works dealing with similar themes. Includes author and title index.

BD102 Fee, Margery. **Canadian Fiction: An Annotated Bibliography.** Toronto: Peter Martin, 1976. 170 p.

An annotated bibliography of pre-1973 Canadian fiction, designed as an introduction to the field. Authors are listed alphabetically within novel and short story sections.
Z1377 F4F44

BD103 Gardner, Frank M. **Sequels.** 9th ed. 2 vols. London: Association of Assistant Librarians, 1989.

Includes material published between 1950 to the end of 1988. Lists, by author, novels in which the same character appears, sequences of novels connected by theme, sequences of novels with historical or geographical connections, and non-fiction sequels, such as autobiographies. Volume 1 includes adult books; Volume 2 children's books. Janet Husband's *Sequels: An Annotated Guide to Novels in Series* (ALA, 1990) (Z5917 S44H87 ROBA) contains similar information.
Z6514 S4H52

BD104 Hinckley, Karen and Barbara Hinckley. **American Best Sellers: A Reader's Guide to Popular Fiction.** Bloomington, IN: Indiana University Press, 1989. 260 p.

A guide to the 468 best-selling fiction titles from 1965 to 1985. Each entry includes a plot synopsis, and biographical information about the author. Chapters classify best-sellers by topic and genre, highlight literary characters, patterns, trends and themes.
PS374 B45H56 ROBA

BD105 Kirby, David K. **American Fiction to 1900: A Guide to Information Sources.** Detroit: Gale Research, 1975. 296 p.

Guide listing major handbooks, periodicals, bibliographies, biographies, and critical studies covering American fiction in the 18th and 19th centuries. Continued by *American Fiction 1900–1950* by James Leslie Woodress (Gale, 1974) (Z1231 F4W64), which includes bibliographic information for 44 critically acclaimed writers during that period.
Z1231 F4K7

BD106 **Modern English Canadian Prose: A Guide to Information Sources.** Ed. by Helen Hoy. Detroit: Gale Research, 1983. 605 p.

A bibliography of 20th century Canadian fiction and poetry.
Z1377 F4H69

BD107 Moss, John. **A Reader's Guide to the Canadian Novel.** 2d ed. Toronto: McClelland and Stewart, 1987. 522 p.

Provides critical comments on 200 Canadian novels from 1769 to 1980, selected for their significance within the Canadian literary tradition. Arranged alphabetically by author.
PS8187 M67

BD108 Rosenberg, Betty. **Genreflecting: A Guide to Reading Interests in Genre Fiction.**

2d ed. Littleton, CO: Libraries Unlimited, 1986. 298 p.

A guide to currently available genre literature, including western, thriller, romance, science fiction, fantasy, and horror, listing best-selling, significant, or popular authors, and annotated lists of further readings (encyclopedias, manuals, associations, films, etc). Indexed by author and theme.
813 AR813G   or   PS374 P63R67 ROBA

CATALOGS AND INDEXES

BD109   Cumulated Fiction Index, 1945-1960. London: Association of Assistant Librarians, 1960.   552 p.   *Supplements* 1960–1969 (1970);   1970–1974 (1975); 1980-1984 (1985).

Indexes short story collections, anthologies, omnibus and condensed books. Updated with annual supplements.
R808.83 AC72   or   Z5916 C8

BD110   Fiction Catalog, 12th ed, 1991. Provides annotated references to the "best" novels published in that year. See AC11 for full entry information.

HANDBOOKS

BD111   Critical Survey of Long Fiction. Ed. by Frank N. Magill. Englewood Cliffs, NJ: Salem Press.

English Language Series (8 volumes, 1991) is a revision of the earlier published work (5 volumes, 1984), adding 25 new articles and revising most of the original articles. *Foreigh Language Series - Written in English* (5 volumes, 1984), examines 182 of the world's greatest foreign language novelists. The history of the novel for each language is also covered in separate essays.

There is also a 7 volume work *Critical Survey of Short Fiction* (1981) (PN3321 C7 ROBA), which examines short fiction writers from the oral tradition to modern times.
PR821 C7 ROBA

BD112   Masterplots II. 4 vols. Englewood Cliffs, NJ: Salem Press.

A major literary series covering all forms of literature. Published in various sets. Orginally published as the 12 volume *Masterplots* in 1976, which contained plot digests of over 2,000 of the greatest works published from 4000 BC to mid 20th century. Revisions to this work appeared in 1985 with *Masterplots: American Fiction* (3 volumes), which provided plot digests and critical evaluations to works written by authors from the U.S., Canada, and Central and South America;   and *Masterplots: British Fiction* (3 volumes),   which includes works written by authors from the British Commonwealth countries (except Canada).   In 1986 *Masterplots: European Fiction* (3 volumes), was published containing works written by authors from Europe, Russia and Asia.

Since 1986, *Masterplots II* has appeared with multi-volume sets for several genres, including *American Fiction Series* (4 volumes, 1986); *Short Story Series* (6 volumes, 1986); *British Commonwealth Fiction Series* (4 volumes, 1987); *World Fiction Series* (4 volumes, 1988); *Nonfiction Series* (4 volumes, 1989); *Drama Series* (1990); *Juvenile and Young Adult Fiction Series* (4 volumes, 1991); and *Poetry Series* (6 volumes, 1992 forthcoming).
PR881 M36

*   *   *   *

MYSTERY AND WESTERNS

BD113 Critical Survey of Mystery and Detective Fiction. 4 vols. Ed. by Frank N. Magill. Englewood Cliffs, NJ: Salem Press, 1988.

Standard source for brief overviews of mystery and detective fiction from the 19th century to the present. Volumes are arranged alphabetically by author, and include lengthy signed articles on over 280 authors, with biographical notes, plot types used, and list of principal characters created, contribution to the field, and an analysis of works. Bibliographies are included, and there are author, title, keyword, plot and character type indexes.
MTRL

BD114 Drew, Bernard A. **Western Series and Sequels: A Reference Guide.** New York: Garland, 1986. 173 p.

List of 375 western series published up to 1986. Includes settings in Canada, the French and Indian Wars, the Civil War, and the American West. Includes brief introduction to the genre. See also *Western Writers* (BD43n).
MTRL LANG/LIT

BD115 Hubin, Allen J. **Crime Fiction 1749–1980: A Comprehensive Bibliography.** New York: Garland, 1984. 712 p. *Supplement* 1981-1985 (1988), 260 p.

Comprehensive scholarly bibliography of mystery and detective fiction, providing information on 60,000 works; arranged by author with indexes by title, setting (primarily geographic), series, series character. The supplement adds an additional 6,900 new books and updates 4,300 entries in the original addition. The supplement also includes citations to films based on crime fiction, with indexes for movie titles, screenwriters and directors.
Z2041 F4H82

BD116 Murder in Print: A Guide to Two Centuries of Crime Fiction. London: Barn Owl Books. 1987. 244 p.

A successor to *Best Detective Fiction* (1975, PN3448 D4B3 SMC), examines 500 books: "milestone" works which are historically important, and others which the author believes important. Includes annotation, publication information, alternate titles, and pseudonyms.
Z5917 D5B36 ROBA

SCIENCE FICTION, FANTASY AND HORROR

BD117 Anatomy of Wonder: A Critical Guide to Science Fiction. 3d ed. Ed. by Neil Barron. New York: R.R. Bowker, 1987. 874 p.

Classified, annotated bibliography of 2,600 titles in three sections: English-language science fiction, foreign language science fiction, and research aids. Also includes articles which trace development of the genre from 1918-1986. Articles include annotated bibliographies. Subject, author, and title indexes.
Z5917 S36A52

BD118 Horror Literature: A Reader's Guide. Ed. by Neil Barron. New York: Garland, 1990. 596 p.

This work, and it's companion *Fantasy Literature: A Reader's Guide* (Garland, 1990) (PN3435 F35 ERIN), provide bibliographic essays on these genres, including an historical analysis, a selection of reference works, awards, arts, and selected annotated bibliographies.
Z5917 H65H67

BD119 Science Fiction & Fantasy Book Review Annual, 1988- . Westport, CT: Meckler. annual.

Compendium of critical book reviews of approximately 600 international works published in the science fiction, horror and fantasy genres each year. There are also survey articles, "The Year in...", identifying trends, movements and new books. Includes award winners, reading lists and an index.
PN3433 S35 ROBA

BD120 Science Fiction and Fantasy Reference Index, 1878-1985: An International Author and Subject Index to History and Criticism. 2 vols. Ed. by H.W. Hall. Detroit: Gale, 1987.

Comprehensive index to 19,000 international books, articles, essays, audiovisual materials and news items dealing with science fiction and fantasy covering the period of 1878 (Jules Verne) to 1985.

Updated in *Science Fiction and Fantasy Research Index*, (annual, Borgo Press, 1982-), which lists current research works. Quinquennial cumulations expected. Volumes 1-6 of the *Science Fiction and Fantasy Research Index*, covering the dates 1982 to 1985 appeared in cumulated form in the *Science Fiction and Fantasy Book Review Index 1980-1984* (BD121n).
Z5917 S36S3; H36

BD121 Science Fiction Book Review Index 1923-1973. Ed. by H.W. Hall. Detroit: Gale Research, 1975. 438 p.

Identifies reviews appearing in selected science fiction magazines, arranged alphabetically by author. Continued by *Science Fiction Book Review Index 1974-79* (Gale, 1981); and *Science Fiction and Fantasy Book Review Index 1980-1984* (Gale, (1986). This edition contains a section called *"Science Fiction and Fantasy Research Index"*, a compilation, for the years involved, of the annual publication of the same name (BD120n).
Z5917 S36 S19 Range 6A

BD122 Science Fiction, Fantasy, & Horror, 1985- . Oakland, CA: Locus Press. annual.

Originally titled *Science Fiction in Print, 1985*, includes author and title citations for all in-print English-language novels and short fiction in the field, organized according to broad subject categories. Appendices include a survey of publishing trends, cinema survey, bibliographic essay, and publishers addresses.
Z5917 S36S34 ROBA

BD123 Reader's Guide to Twentieth-Century Science Fiction. Comp. by Marilyn P. Fletcher. Chicago: American Library Association, 1989. 673 p.

Provides detailed coverage of major 20th century science fiction authors, including biographical information, analysis of themes and styles, and plot summaries of award-winning and major works. Lists of further readings in science fiction, appendices, and a title index are also provided.
R809.3876 R286R   or   PN3433.8 R44 VUPR

BD124 Wolfe, Gary K. **Critical Terms for Science Fiction and Fantasy: A Glossary and Guide to Scholarship.** Westport, CT: Greenwood Press, 1986. 162 p.

Provides definitions and commentaries for nearly 500 terms used in fantasy literature. Broader concepts are defined in short essays. Also has an introductory essay on the genre.
PN3435 W64 ROBA

SHORT STORIES

BD125 A Comprehensive Bibliography of English-Canadian Short Stories, 1950–1983. Comp. by Allan Weiss. Toronto: ECW Press, 1988. 973 p.

Bibliography of more than 24,000 short stories written in English by almost 5,000 authors, published between 1950 to 1983 in journals, newspapers, anthologies, and radio broadcasts. Describes the publishing history of each work. Arranged by author with title index.
Z1377 F4W44

BD126 Short Story Criticism: Excerpts from Criticism of the Works of Short Fiction Writers, 1988- . Detroit: Gale Research. volumes issued biennially.

Series surveys literary criticism of works by major short story authors from all nationalities and periods of literary history. Entries include brief biographical information, a critical introduction, and a list of works, followed by a chronological review of criticism. Bibliographies are also provided. Each volume includes 12-15 short story writers.
PN3373 S353 SCAR

BD127 Short Story Index: An Index to 60,000 Stories from 4,320 Collections. New York: H.W. Wilson, 1953. *Supplements* in quenquennial cumulations: 1950–54; 1955–58; 1959–63; 1974–78; 1979-83; 1984-88.

Includes stories, in English and English translation, published in periodicals and collections around the world in 1949 and earlier, with the supplements bringing the work up to 1988. There is also an annual work *Short Story Index* (1974-), which updates the supplements, and provides indexing of short stories published in collections or in periodicals indexed in *Readers' Guide* (AF17) and *Humanities Index* (BA9). Early 20th century short stories are indexed in Juliette Yaakov's *Short Story Index: Collections Indexed 1900-1978* (1979) (Z5917 S5 VUPR).
R808.83 AC77   or   Z5917 S5C6

Poetry

Additional works for poetry for children can be found in this section under "Children's Literature", BD162 - BD178.

BD128 The Columbia Granger's Index to Poetry. 9th ed. New York: Columbia University Press, 1990. 2082 p.

Formerly *Granger's Index to Poetry* until this 9th edition. Standard reference work which indexes poems, written in or translated into English, in anthologies. Indexed by first line, author and subject. Until the 7th edition (1982), *Granger's* was cumulative. The 8th edition (1986) resumed the cumulative format and this is continued in the 9th edition, which indexes anthologies published through the 20th century to 1989. Older editions of *Granger's* are still useful for titles deleted between editions.
R808.81 AG7515 (1982)   or   PN1021 G7

BD129 Critical Survey of Poetry Series. Ed. by Frank N. Magill. Englewood Cliffs, NJ: Salem Press.

The *English Language Series* (originally published 1982, and an 8 volume set forthcoming in 1992) includes articles on English-language poets, with bibliographies. The *Critical Survey of Poetry (Foreign Language Series - Written in English)* 5 volume set was published in 1984, and contains 190 foreign language poets, from Europe, the Far and Middle East, South America and the Third World. A

Supplement was published in 1987 which includes poets from all over the world not covered in the first two sets.
PR502 C85 SIGR (English Language)
MTRL (Foreign Language)

BD130 Deutsch, Babette. **Poetry Handbook: A Dictionary of Terms.** 4th ed. New York: Funk & Wagnalls, 1974. 203 p.

A standard work describing terms, with examples, used in the criticism, practice of poetry.
R808.1014 D486P4   or   PN44.5 D4

BD131 Guide to American Poetry Explication. 2 vols. Boston: G.K. Hall, 1989.

Bibliographic source for explication of American, including Canadian, poetry, since 1925, expanding the third edition of the standard work, *Poetry Explication: A Checklist of Interpretation Since 1925 of British and American Poems Past and Present*, by J.M. Kuntz (G.K. Hall, 1980) (Z2014 P7K8), which listed citations up to 1977. This edition extends coverage to December, 1987. Poets are listed alphabetically with a list of citations of explications under each poem. Volume 1 *Colonial and Nineteenth Century* by James Ruppert, covers pre-20th century poets; Volume 2 *Modern and Contemporary* by John Leo, the 20th century. British poetry, formerly covered in *Poetry Explication* is also to be published in separate volumes in the *Guide to British Poetry Explication*, each representing historical phases and movements. Volume 1: *Old English-Medieval* by Nancy Martinez (G.K. Hall, 1991) is the first to be published.
Z1231 P7G85

BD132 Hoffman, Herbert. **Hoffman's Index to Poetry: European and Latin American Poetry in Anthologies.** Metuchen, NJ: Scarecrow, 1985. 672 p.

Guide to anthologies of best-known European poetry, with over 14,000 poems written in French, German, Italian, Spanish, Portuguese, Polish, Russian, and Ukrainian by over 1,800 poets. Anthologies are available in the English-speaking world.
PN1022 H627

BD133   Index to Canadian Poetry in English. Ed. by Jane McQuarrie, Anne Mercer and Gordon Ripley. Toronto: Reference Press, 1984. 367 p.

Indexes over 7,000 poems in 51 collections written in the 19th and 20th centuries. French-Canadian poetry in English translation is also included. Another work is *Canadian Poetry in Selected English-Language Anthologies: An Index and Guide*, edited by Margery Fee (Dalhousie University School of Library Service, 1985) (R819.1 AF295C), which indexes by title and author, poems in "mainstream" anthologies.
R819.1 I38I

BD134   Master Index to Poetry: An Index to Poetry in Anthologies and Collections. 2 vols. Great Neck, NY: Poetry Index Press/Roth Publishing, 1988.

Contains analysis of 1,032 poetry book titles in 1,079 volumes, with a total inclusive list of 250,000 poems. The index can be used alone, or in conjunction with *Corefiche* (Poetry Index Press/Roth), which is a microfiche containing the full works of the volumes indexed in the *Master*

Index to Poetry. Most of the indexed titles predate 1950, with some from the 19th century. For current poetry, consult *Columbia Granger's Index to Poetry* (BD128).

BD135 Poetry Index Annual, 1982- . Great Neck, NY: Roth Publishing Inc. annual.

Index to poetry contained in international English-language published anthologies. Complements, but does not duplicate *Roth's American Poetry Annual* (BD138). Each annual edition supplements preceding issues.
PN1022 P63

BD136 Poetry Markets for Canadians, 1987- . Toronto: League of Canadian Poets. irregular annual.

Continues *Poetry Markets in Canada*, (1982-84). Lists Canadian book and periodical publishers which accept poetry, with some international publishers included. Also provides advice for submission, book contracts, a list of literary awards, and other resources. International directories include *Writer's Market* (1922- PN161 W83); *Poet's Market* (1985- PN1059 M3P6); *The International Directory of Little Magazines and Small Presses* (1974- Z6944 L5D5); and *Literary Market Place* (AB7, BD20).
PN161 P6 (1984) or MTRL LANG/LIT

BD137 Princeton Handbook of Poetic Terms. Ed. by Alex Preminger. Princeton, NJ: Princeton University Press, 1986. 309 p.

Abbreviated and updated form of *Princeton Encyclopedia of Poetry and Poetics* (1975). Contains 402 entries on poetic forms, prosody, rhetoric, genre and other topics. A similar work is Miller Williams' *Patterns of Poetry: An Encyclopedia of Forms* (Louisiana State University Press, 1986) (PN1042 W514).
PN1042 P75

BD138 Roth's American Poetry Annual: A Reference and Guide to Poetry Published in the United States... 1988- . Great Neck, NY: Roth Publishing. annual.

Cumulation of three other titles, *Annual Survey of American Poetry* (1985/86); *American Poetry Index* (1981-86); and *Annual Index to Poetry in Periodicals* (1984/86), this work is an index to poems that have been published in American journals and single author collections. Also includes news items, awards and prizes, directory information, etc. Complements *Poetry Index Annual* (BD135).
MTRL LANG/LIT

BD139 Who's Who in the League of Canadian Poets. 3d ed. Ed. by Stephen Scobie. Toronto: League of Canadian Poets, 1988. 227 p.

Biographical directory of over 200 published and performing poets in Canada, with photographs, list of awards, publications, and excerpts from critical comments.
PS8141 L42

*   *   *   *

Drama

BIBLIOGRAPHIES AND INDEXES

BD140 **American Drama Criticism.** 2d ed. Hamdon, CT: Shoe String Press, 1984. *Supplement*, I and II.

Index to play criticisms taken from 350 journals and 150 books.
Z1231 D7A54

BD141 **The Brock Bibliography of Published Canadian Plays in English, 1766–1978.** Ed. by Anton Wagner. Toronto: Playwrights Canada, 1980. 375 p.

An annotated bibliography of some 2,000 entries. *A Bibliography of English Language Theatre and Drama in Canada, 1800–1914* (University of Alberta, 1976) (Z1377 D7S44) by D. Sedgewick, and *Canadian Plays: A Supplementary Checklist to 1945* (Dalhousie University Library and School of Library Service, 1978) (Z1377 D7054) by P. O'Neill, are also useful.
R808.82 AB864B   or   Z1377 D7B72

BD142 Carpenter, Charles A. **Modern Drama Scholarship and Criticism 1966–1980: An International Bibliography.** Toronto: University of Toronto Press, 1986. 587 p.

A selective bibliography of modern world drama since Ibsen, containing over 27,000 entries from international sources, emphasizing plays and playwrights rather than performances and performers. Arranged by nationality and/or linguistic groups, including American, Canadian, British, Hispanic, Germanic, Italian, Eastern European, and other areas.
Z5781 C37

BD143 Forman, Robert J. **Classical Greek and Roman Drama: An Annotated Bibliography.** Pasadena, CA: Salem Press, 1989. 239 p.

Part of the *Magill Bibliographies* series (BD8), this work indexes basic translations, commentaries, and criticisms on classical plays and playwrights. An introductory essay on the evolution of classical drama is also included. Indexed.
Z7018 D7F67 VUPR

BD144 New York Public Library. Research Libraries. **Catalog of the Theatre and Drama Collections.** Boston: G.K. Hall, 1967. *Supplement* 1973; 1974.

In 3 parts: Part I: drama collection with author, cultural origin lists; theatre; Part II: theatre collection; Part III: non–book collection. Updated by the annual *Bibliographic Guide to Theatre Arts*, (G.K. Hall, 1975-) (Z5785 N43). See BG29n for more information.
Z5785 N4

HANDBOOKS

BD145 **Canada's Playwrights: A Biographical Guide.** Toronto: Canadian Theatre Review, 1980. 191 p.

Entry includes list of works with photo for more than 60 authors.
PS8081 C36

BD146 **Critical Survey of Drama.** Ed. by Frank N. Magill. Englewood Cliffs, NJ: Salem Press.

In two parts: *English Language Series* (6 volumes, 1985), which includes 220 English

language dramatists, and essays on dramatic genres, acting styles and techniques, and terms and movements. *Foreign Language Series* (6 volumes, 1986) lists 197 noteworthy dramatists of the Modern Genre, with one volume devoted to Classical, Greek and and Japanese Drama. Updated by the *Supplement* (1987).
PR623 C75 SCAR (English Language)
PN1625 C74 VUPR (Foreign Language)

BD147 Gassner, John and Edward Quinn. **The Reader's Encyclopedia of World Drama.** New York: Crowell, 1969. 1030 p.

Treats literary characteristics of drama, covering written works, authors, survey articles on drama developments in several countries, with brief bibliographies, biographies of major playwrights with critical evaluations, and summaries.
R809.2 G253R   or   PN1625 G3

BD148 **Major Modern Dramatists.** 2 vols. Ed. by Rita Stein. New York: Ungar, 1984-86.

Part of *Library of Literary Criticism* series. Provides excerpts of literary criticism from reviews, articles, and books, of international dramatists from Ibsen and late nineteenth-century realism up to the 1980's.
PN1861 M27 ROBA

BD149 **Masterplots II: Drama Series.** 4 vols. 1990.

Examination of 327 works of 20th century drama, mostly English-language, but many from around the world. Includes information about playwrights, with essays depicting the action, plot, issues, theatrical presentation, genre, of the play, with a reading list. See BD112 for full entry information.
PN6112.5 M37 TRIN

BD150 **McGraw-Hill Encyclopedia of World Drama.** 2d ed. 5 vols. New York: McGraw Hill, 1984.

A guide to major dramatists, with surveys on national, regional drama, non-Western dramatic traditions, influential directors, theatres and companies. Play title list, glossary, index.
PN1625 M3

BD151 Rinfret, Edouard G. **Le Theatre canadien d'expression française: répertoire analytique des origines à nos jours.** 4 vols. Ottawa: Leméac, 1975–78.

Arranged alphabetically by author with information on performance, cast, plot. Volumes 1–3 cover theatre and radio plays; volume 4, television plays.
Z1377 D7R5

BD152 Salem, James **Drury's Guide to Best Plays.** 4th ed. Metuchen, NJ: Scarecrow Press, 1987. 480 p.

Provides information about 1,500 plays from ancient times to 1984/85. Also includes "cast indexes", "selected subject" index, and lists of awards, popular plays for amateur productions, addresses of play publishers. A similar work is Joseph T. Shipley's *Crown Guide to the World's Great Plays: From Ancient Greece to Modern Times* (2d rev. ed, Crown, 1984) (PN6112.5 S45), which updates *Guide to Great Plays* (1956) and contains information about a selection of 750 great plays, from ancient times to present, with facts about the play's origin, significance, plot synopsis, stage history, leading players, and opinions of critics. Arranged by author, with title index.
Z5781 D8

PLAY INDEXES

BD153 Ireland, Norma. **Index to Full Length Plays, 1944 to 1964.** Boston: F.W. Faxon, 1965. 296 p.

Includes Author, title, and subject alphabetical index with author, adapter, number of acts and characters under the title entry. Continues R.G. Thomson's 1895–1944 *Indexes* (F.W. Faxon, 1946, 1956) (Z5781 T5).
R808.82 AT48   or   Z5781 T52

BD154 Keller, Dean H. **Index to Plays in Periodicals.** Rev. and expanded. Metuchen, NJ: Scarcrow, 1979. 824 p.

Author and title access to plays, published to 1976, in over 200 periodicals, chiefly American and British. Supplemented by *Index to Plays in Periodicals, 1977–1987* (1990), covering an additional 4,000 plays published in the same periodicals of the earlier edition.
Z5781 K43

BD155 Logasa, Hanna and Winifred Ver Nooy. **An Index to One Act Plays, 1900–1964.** 6 vols. Boston: F.W. Faxon, 1924–66.

Volume 1, 1900–23, other volumes as supplements, 1924–31; 1932–40; 1941–48; 1948–57; 1956–64. Third supplement adds radio plays; 4th adds TV plays. Index stresses plays for children, young people.
R808.82 AL83   or   Z5781 L83

BD156   **Play Index,** 1949– . New York: H.W. Wilson. irregular.

(Vol. 7, 1983-1987, 1988). Indexes single plays, collections, radio, TV plays, and plays for children. The 7 volumes provide access to more than 27,000 plays. *Plays: A Classified Guide to Play Selection* (Stacey Directories, annual) (PR1272 P6 1971-1986) lists reviews of new plays including full length comedies, dramas, one act plays, musicals, plays for young people, and pantomines. Includes information on where to obtain the scripts for acting and reading editions.
R808.82 AP722   or   Z5781 P53

BD157   **Ottemiller's Index to Plays in Collections: An Author and Title Index to Plays Appearing in Collections Published between 1900 and early 1985.** 7th ed. Ed. by Billie M. Connor. Metuchen, NJ: Scarecrow Press, 1986. 564 p.

Standard index to full-length plays published in international play collections. Organized by author, title indexes and a list of collection analyzed.
R808.82 AO8914   or   Z5781.O8

BD158 Sample, Gordon. **The Drama Scholars' Index to Plays and Filmscripts: A Guide to Plays and Filmscripts in Selected Anthologies, Series, and Periodicals.** 3 vols. Metuchen, NJ: Scarecrow Press, 1974-86.

Index of plays and filmscripts in anthologies, series, periodicals, in various languages.
Z5781 S17

Classical Literature

BD159 Classical and Medieval Literature Criticism: Excerpts from Criticism of the Works of World Authors from Classical Antiquity through the Fourteenth Century. 2 vols. Detroit: Gale Research, 1988.

Similar to other Gale works, *Twentieth Century Literature Criticism* (BD42); *Nineteenth Century Literature Criticism* (BD38); and *Shakespearean Criticism* (1984-1991)

(PR2965 S43). Provides commentary and an introduction to literature from antiquity to the fourteenth century, outlining major figures, authors, historical facts, and providing further resources.
PN511 C53 SMCR

BD160 Oxford Companion to Classical Literature. 2d ed. Ed. by M.C. Howatson. New York: Oxford University Press, 1989. 624 p.

Revision of the standard work by Sir Paul Harvey (1937). Written for the general reader, covers the period from 2200 BC to 529 AD. Articles provide information on authors, major works, historical and mythological figures, and topics of literary significance.
DF5 H3

Children's Literature

For information about children's authors see *Biography*, AL67 – AL72; for selection aids see AC36 – AC55.

Guides, Bibliographies, and Handbooks

BD161 Bingham, J. and G. Scholt. **Fifteen Centuries of Children's Literature.** Westport, CT: Greenwood Press, 1980. 540 p.

Subtitled: *An Annotated Chronology of British and American Works in Historical Context*, this work lists significant or representative books from the 6th century to 1945. A brief essay introduces each chapter which, for the period covered, includes references for historical background, development of books, attitudes to children and the chronology. In the appendixes, there is a list of secondary sources, and the book has author, illustrator, publishers of early works, and title index.
028.5 B613F

BD162 Children's Books in Print, 1969– . New York: R.R. Bowker. annual.

Supersedes *Children's Books for Schools and Libraries*. An author, title and illustrator index to the nearly 55,000 children's books available from U.S. publishers. The 1987/88 edition established a section on children's awards; the 1988/89 edition enlarged the section to cover more awards and to carry the information back a full decade. Canadian awards are included. (For related parent title, see AD76. For reference to equivalent U.K. children's books in print, see AD66.)

The annual *Children's Books in Print Subject Guide*, (1988/89–, R.R. Bowker) (R028.5 AC536AB) allocates the children's titles from *CBIP* into nearly 6,500 subject categories.
R028.5 AC536A

BD163 Children's Literature: A Guide to the Criticism. Ed. by L. Hendrickson. Boston: G.K. Hall, 1987. 664 p.

With author, title, subject index. Book is arranged in two parts. The first covers authors and their works; the second covers subjects, themes and genres. A descriptive word or two accompanies the entries which may be a book, article, ERIC report or dissertation. Concentrates exclusively on modern publication. *Writers for Children: Critical Studies of Major Authors Since the Seventeenth Century*, by J. Bingham, (Scribner's, 1988) (809.89282 W956 EDUC) covers a wider time range for fewer authors.
028.5AH498C

BD164 Early Canadian Children's Books, 1763–1840, and *1841-1867* (the Amtmann catalogues), 1976, 1977. See AD28 for full entry information.

BD165 Egoff, Sheila and Judith Saltman. **The New Republic of Childhood: A Critical Guide to Canadian Children's Literature in English.** 3d ed. Toronto: Oxford University Press, 1990. 378 p.

Previous editions, by Sheila Egoff, called *The Republic of Childhood*. Evaluative opinion and description of books in several genres which are primarily Canadian in content or authorship. J. Saltman's *Modern Canadian Children's Books* (Oxford University Press, 1987) (028.5 S178M) is a similar survey of English–language books.
028.5 E31R3

BD166 Fantasy Literature for Children and Young Adults: An Annotated Bibliography. 3d ed. By R.N. Lynn. New York: R.R. Bowker, 1989. 771 p.

Revised edition of *Fantasy for Children*, (2d ed, 1983). The major part contains over 3,000 novels and story collections for young people, grades 3 through 12. Entries are twentieth century, with a few exceptions, and exclude science fiction and horror. A second part is a research guide to authors. Related titles are *Anatomy of Wonder* (BD117), *Horror Literature* (BD118) and *Fantasy Literature* (BD118n).
R028.5 AL989F3

BD167 Fiction, Folklore, Fantasy & Poetry for Children, 1876–1985. 2 vols. New York: R.R. Bowker, 1986.

Volume 1: Authors, Illustrators Index. Volume 2: Titles, Awards Index. A massive reorganization taken from the *ABPR/BIP* (see AD75, AD76) database. Primarily useful as a source for identification of U.S. publishing and distribution of children's books with some additional information (awards), clarification (pseudonyms, syndicated writers) and corrections.
R808.068 AF448F

BD168 The History of Children's Literature: A Syllabus with Selected Bibliographies. Rev. and enl. by M. Hodges and S. Steinfirst. Chicago: American Library Association, 1980. 290 p.

At head of title: Elva S. Smith's *History ...*, recalling the first compiler of this bibliography which was intended as a course outline for children's librarians at the Carnegie Library, Pittsburgh. This new edition brings the material to the mid–1970s. A general bibliography and folklore references are also included. The work organizes the bibliographic citations under subjects (e.g. poetry, didactic writers) in a time frame from anglo–saxon times to the late nineteenth century.
028.5 AS64A

BD169 Meacham, Mary. **Information Sources in Children's Literature.** Westport, CT: Greenwood Press, 1978. 256 p.

Subtitled "A Practical Reference Guide for Children's Librarians, Elementary School Teachers, and Students of Children's Literature", this source, although not up-to-date, introduces books for the study of the literature as well as the books, indexes etc. for building of basic collections. Virginia Haviland's *Children's Literature: A Guide to Reference Sources* (Library of Congress, 1966 with supplements to 1969) (028.5 AH388) is the unsurpassed standard older source.
R028.52 M479I

BD170 The Oxford Companion to Children's Literature. Edited by H. Carpenter and M. Prichard. New York: Oxford University Press, 1984. 587 p.

Concise dictionary entries on British (broadly defined) and American children's literature with some reference to other countries, etc., and with limited information on educational works. Standard and traditional information is stressed; popular but nonstandard and post–1950s books must be well–known to be included.
R809.89282 C295P

BD171 Sutherland, Z. and M.H. Arbuthnot. **Children and Books.** 7th ed. Glenview, IL: Scott Foresman and Co., 1986. 751 p.

Describes children's books by type of literature (fiction, poetry, informational) with sections on using the books with children and issues in the area of children's materials. Although a standard college textbook in format and intention, this "guide" is perhaps the most widely known survey/textbook for modern curricular units on children's literature and is useful for general audiences wanting a survey of the subject. Similar texts are *Introduction to Children's Literature*, by J. Glazer and G. Williams, (McGraw–Hill, 1979) (028.5 G553I) or *Literature and the Child*, by B. Cullinan, (2d ed, Harcourt Brace Jovanovich, 1989) (028.5 C967L2). An older, shorter, but much–recommended standard discussion of worthy titles is Lillian H. Smith's *The Unreluctant Years* (A.L.A., 1953, reissued 1991) (028.5 S65A).
028.5A66C7

Indexes

BD172 A to Zoo: Subject Access to Children's Picture Books. 3d ed. Ed. by C.W. Lima and J.A. Lima. New York: R.R. Bowker, 1989. 939 p.

An introduction gives a brief history on the English language picture book. Provides selections of English-language picture books, both fiction and non-fiction, analyzed for their subject content, and indicating audience level from preschool to grade two. Many illustrations from the works are included. Title and illustrator index.
R028.5 AL732 A3

BD173 Index to Children's Poetry. Compiled by J.E. Brewton and S.W. Brewton. New York: H.W. Wilson, 1942. 966 p. *First Supplement* (1954); *Second Supplement* (1965).

A title, subject, author and first line index to poetry in anthologies collected for children and youth. Continued by the *Index to Poetry for Children and Young People* (BD176).
R808.81 AB848

BD174 Index to Fairy Tales, Myths and Legends. 2d ed. Compiled by M. Eastman. Boston: F.W. Faxon, 1926. 610 p. *Supplements* 1937; 1952; 1949–72; 1973–77; 1978–86.

Various compilers. *Fifth Supplement*, 1978–86 (1989), compiled by N.O. Ireland, and J.W. Sprug. This index is an alphabetical arrangement giving title, subject and author (if named in work) access to the fairy tales etc. that are in collections frequently found in libraries.
R398AE13

BD175 Index to Poetry for Children and Young People: 1964–1969. Edited by J.E. Brewton, S.W. Brewton, and G.M. Blackburn. New York: H.W. Wilson, 1972. 574 p. Supplements, 1970–75 (1978); 1976–81 (1983); 1982–87 (1989).

Continues the *Index to Children's Poetry* (BD174) as a single alphabet listing of title, subject, author and first index access to poetry in collections published in the years shown in the index's title. Collections include all types, e.g. a thematic anthology or the collected poems of one author.
R808.81 AB848

BD176 **Subject Index to Canadian Poetry in English for Children & Young People.** 2d ed. Comp. by Kathleen Snow. Ottawa: Canadian Library Association, 1986. 307 p.
Analyses 120 collections of Canadian poetry in English and in-print between 1976 and 1983. Entries are arranged by subject, with citation for title of poem and author, and location in collection where it can be found.
R809.1 S674S2

BD177 **Subject Index to Poetry for Children and Young People.** Compiled by V. Sell, and others. Chicago: American Library Association, 1957. 582 p. *Supplement*, 1957–75 (1977).
The 1957–75 supplement, edited by D.B. Frizzell, does not supersede the earlier edition, but is a much enlarged work. The original volume gives subject access to some 157 collections of poetry; the later work analyzes 263 anthologies on a wide variety of subjects.
R808.81 AA512

* * * *

Language

BD178 Collinge, N. E. **An Encyclopedia of Language.** London: Routledge, 1990. 1011 p.
Covers linguistics, evolutionary language, lexicography, language teaching, etc.
P106 E46 ROBA

BD179 Crystal, David. **The Cambridge Encyclopedia of Language.** New York: Cambridge University Press, 1987. 472 p.
Arranged in thematic sections with tables, maps, charts, and photographs.
P29 C84

BD180 Crystal, David. **A Dictionary of Linguistics and Phonetics.** 2d ed. New York: Basil Blackwell, 1985. 339 p.
Reflects recent developments in linguistic theory and applications.
PN29 C86

BD181 **International Handbook of Bilingualism and Bilingual Education.** Ed. by Christina Bratt Paulston. Westport, CT: Greenwood, 1988. 603 p.
Contains essays, bibliographies, author and language indexes.
P115 I58

BD182 **The World's Major Languages.** Ed. by Bernard Comrie. New York: Oxford University Press, 1987. 1025 p.
Articles by well known linguists describing fifty major languages and language families.
P121 W8

BE   ART AND ARCHITECTURE

Bibliographies and Guides to the Literature

BE1   Arntzen, E. and R. Rainwater. **Guide to the Literature of Art History.** Chicago: American Library Association, 1980. 616 p.

A guide to basic reference books and other resources for advanced research in art. More than 4,000 annotated titles divided into large categories by type of reference work and by the particular arts. Extensive list of serial publications. Donald Ehresmann's *Fine Arts: A Bibliographic Guide to Basic Reference Works, Histories and Handbooks*, (3d ed, Libraries Unlimited, 1990) covers some of the same territory plus other works such as topographic handbooks.
R709 AA767G   or   Z5931 A67

BE2   **Arts in America: A Bibliography.** 4 vols. Washington: Smithsonian Institution for the Archives of American Art, 1979.

Annotated bibliography of American art divided into 21 subject sections by individual contributors. These deal with individual media (including film, theatre, dance and music) and types of publications such as serials and visual resources. Index volume gives detailed access to artists and subjects.
Z5961 U5A77

BE3   **B.H.A.: Bibliography of the History of Art / Bibliographie d'histoire de l'art,** 1991– . Williamstown, MA: Getty Art History Information Program, Sterling and Francine Clark Art Institute. semi-annual.

Incorporates *RILA* (1973–1990) and *Répertoire d'art et d'archéologie* (1910–1990) with double the former references, and abstracts and subject indexes in English and French. Abstracts, books, exhibition catalogues, serials, congress reports, museum publications, and dissertations on western art, from late antiquity to the present. All three indexes are available online.

BE4   Freitag, Wolfgang. **Art Books: A Basic Bibliography of Monographs on Artists.** New York: Garland, 1985. 351 p.

Lists biographies, exhibition catalogues and oeuvre catalogues for 1,870 artists, i.e. painters, sculptors, architects and photographers.
Z5938 F73

BE5 Jones, Lois Swan. **Art Information: Research Methods and Resources.** 3d ed. Dubuque, IA, 1990. 373 p.

Discusses research strategies for students of art history, with approximately 19,000 bibliographic citations, and greatly expanded Canadian references. Principal headings are: Methodology; Bibliography of Research Sources; Research Centers. Fully indexed.

BE6 Lerner, Loren R. and Mary F. Williamson. **Art and Architecture in Canada: A Bibliography and Guide to the Literature to 1981 / Art et architecture au Canada: bibliographie et guide de la documentation à 1981.** 2 vols. Toronto: University of Toronto Press, 1991.

A classified bibliography with 9,555 entries citing books, exhibition catalogues, articles and theses, and lengthy annotations in English and/or French. Coverage includes decorative arts, crafts, and native arts. French and English subject indexes.
Z5961 C3L47

BE7 McKenzie, Karen and Mary F. Williamson. **The Art and Pictorial Press in Canada: Two Centuries of Art Magazines.** Toronto: Art Gallery of Ontario, 1979. 71 p.

Essays on Canadian art, architecture, photography, museum, and general pictorial and cultural magazines are followed by comprehensive checklists.
705.0971 A784A   or   N6540 A75 ROBA

BE8 National Gallery of Canada. **Catalogue of the Library of The National Gallery of Canada / Catalogue de la bibliothèque de la galerie nationale du Canada.** 8 vols. Boston: G.K. Hall, 1973. *Supplement,* 6 vols. 1981.

Entries for books, periodicals, art exhibition catalogues, art auction records, and artists' files, photocopied from the National Gallery Library's card catalogue.
Z5939 O88

Abstracts and Indexes

BE9 **Art Index,** 1929– . New York: H.W. Wilson. quarterly; annual cumulations.

Basic periodical index to articles, exhibition reviews, book reviews, illusrtations. Covers art, design, decorative arts, photography, and architecture periodicals, and museum bulletins from North American and Europe, but emphasis is on the U.S. Available online and on CD-ROM.
Z5937 A78

BE10 Art Institute of Chicago Ryerson Library. **Index to Art Periodicals.** 11 vols. Boston: G.K. Hall, 1962. *Supplement,* 1975.

Indexing starts in 1907. After publication of the *Art Index* (BE9) began in 1929 coverage changed to avoid duplication, and more foreign periodicals and museum bulletins were included.
Z5937 C55

BE11 **Artbibliographies modern,** Vol. 4, 1973– . Oxford, U.K.: Artbibliographies; Santa Barbara, CA: ABC-CLIO. semi-annual.

Volumes 1-3, 1970–1972, were titled *LOMA: Literature on Modern Art.* An international abstracting service for articles, exhibition catalogues, and, to a lesser degree, books. Currently concerned with art since 1900 except

for photography which is treated since its beginnings in the 1800s. Available online.
Z5937 A75

BE12 Frick Art Reference Library, New York. **Original Index to Art Periodicals.** 12 vols. Boston: G.K. Hall, 1983.

Indexes 84 periodicals between 1923 and 1969, held in the Frick Art Reference Library. Emphasis is on Western European and American art. Does not duplicate *Art Index* (BE9).
Z5937 F75

Encyclopedias and Dictionaries

BE13 Atkins, Robert. **Artspeak: A Guide to Contemporary Ideas, Movements, and Buzzwords.** New York: Abbeville, 1990. 176 p.

A source for explanations of terms in art today such as Postmodernism and Conceptual Art.
N6490 A93 ROBA

BE14 **Encyclopedia of World Art.** 15 vols. New York: McGraw-Hill, 1959–1968. *Supplements*: Vol. 16 (1983) and Vol. 17 (1987).

Still an authoratative work, with articles on styles and periods of art and architecture, individual countries, and well-known artists. Extensive bibliographies and analytical index.
R703 E56   or   N31 E533

BE15 Hall, James. **Dictionary of Subjects and Symbols in Art.** Rev. ed. London: John Murray, 1979. 349 p.

Explanations of themes and symbols in European art, beginning with classical Greece. Bibliography of iconographical studies and sources.
N33 H28

BE16 Mayer, Ralph. **A Dictionary of Art Terms and Techniques.** New York: Crowell, 1981. 464 p.

Explains terms encountered in the study and practice of the visual arts and in the literature. A similar work for artists and art terms is *Oxford Dictionary of Art* (Oxford University Press, 1988) (N33 O93). Materials and methods for reproducing historical and contemporary techniques are explained in Mayer's *The Artist's Handbook of Materials and Techniques* (5th ed, Viking, 1991).
N33 M468 ROMC

BE17 **McGraw-Hill Dictionary of Art.** 5 vols. Ed. by Bernard S. Myers. New York: McGraw Hill, 1969.

An illustrated general-purpose art encyclopedia, with entries for artists, styles, countries and definitions. The *Praeger Encyclopedia of Art* (5 volumes, New York: Praeger, 1971) (N33 P68 ROBA) is a similar work.
N33 M23

BE18 Munsterberg, Hugo. **Dictionary of Chinese and Japanese Art.** New York: Hacker Art Books, 1981. 354 p.

More than 5,000 definitions for persons, symbols, concepts, terms, materials, techniques, styles, places.
N7340 M818

* * * *

BE19 **The Oxford Companion to Twentieth Century Art.** Ed. by Harold Osborne. London: Oxford University Press, 1988. 800 p.

Articles on styles, groups, technical terms, countries. Substantive selective bibliographies organized by subject.
N6490 O94 (1981)

BE20 **The Thames and Hudson Dictionary of Art and Artists.** Rev. ed. Ed. by Nikos Stangos. London: Thames and Hudson, 1985. 352 p.

Biographies of artists; definitions of technical terms, processes, and movements, mainly in Western art since 1300.
N31 T47

Biographical Dictionaries

BE21 **Artist Biographies Master Index.** Detroit: Gale Research, 1986. 700 p.

"A consolidated index to more than 275,000 biographical sketches of artists living and dead, as they appear in a selection of the principal current and retrospective biographical dictionaries devoted to the fine and applied artists, including painters, sculptors, illustrators, designers, graphic artists, craftsmen, architects, and photographers."
N40 A78

BE22 Bénézit, Emmanuel. **Dictionnaire critique et documentaire des peintres, sculpteurs, dessinateurs et graveurs.** 10 vols. New ed. Paris: Grund, 1976.

The 1976 edition is not greatly changed from the original (1911–23) edition. Brief biographies of artists, eastern and western, from 5th century B.C. to mid-1900's. Entries usually list artist's most important works, some auction prices, and exhibitions.
NB40 B47

BE23 **Contemporary Artists.** 3d ed. London: St. James Press, 1989. 1059 p.

Entries for 750 artists, mostly living, include a biographical note, statement by the artist, list of exhibitions, bibliography, and short critical essay. Includes a few Canadians.
N6490 C68

BE24 Havlice, Patricia P. **Index to Artistic Biography.** 2 vols. Metuchen, NJ: Scarecrow Press, 1973. *Supplement*, 1981.

Basic volumes index artist biographies in 611 works in 10 languages. Supplement adds 70 titles, among them works on women artists, Japanese, Mexican, and Canadian artists.
N40 H38

BE25 **Larousse Dictionary of Painters.** New York: Larousse, 1981. 467 p.

Illustrated one-volume dictionary providing international coverage.
ND35 L3713

BE26 Petteys, Chris. **Dictionary of Women Artists: An International Dictionary of Women Artists Born before 1900.** Boston: G.K. Hall, 1985. 851 p.

While a complete work on Canadian women artists has not yet been published, *From Women's Eyes: Women Painters in Canada* by Dorothy Farr and Natalie Luckyj (Kingston, ON: Agnes Etherington Art Centre, 1976) (ND240 F3 ROBA) provides substantial information, with illustrations, on 46 artists from the 17th to 20th centuries.
N43 P47

BE27 Thieme, Ulrich, and Felix Becker. **Allgemeines Lexikon der Bildenden Kunstler von der Antike bis zur Gegenwart.** 37 vols. Leipzig: Seeman, 1907–50.

Authoritative dictionary for painters, engravers, sculptors of all periods through the end of the 19th century. Information is similar to that contained in *Bénézit* (BE22), but with the addition of extensive bibliographies. A new edition entitled *Allgemeines Kunstler-Lexikon: Die Bildenden Kunstler aller Zeiten und Volker* is underway (volume 4 has reached the letter "B") with future volumes to be published by K.G. Saur.
N40 T4

BE28 Vollmer, Hans. **Allgemeines Lexikon der Bildenden Kunstler des XX Jahrhunderts, unter Mitwirkung von Fachgelehrten des in- und Auslandes.** 6 vols. Leipzig: Seeman, 1953–62.

This set complements *Thieme-Becker* (BE27) for artists born after 1870.
N40 V6

BE29 Watson-Jones, Virginia. **Contemporary American Women Sculptors.** Phoenix, AZ: Oryx, 1986. 665 p.

Two-page biographical outlines on about 350 living sculptors including a few Canadians.
NB212 W37

BE30 Who's Who in American Art, 1935– . New York: R.R. Bowker. biennial.

Information on American, Canadian, Mexican artists, craftspeople, cartoonists, photographers, critics, historians, educators, and museum personnel. 11,534 entries in 1990 edition.
N6536 W5

BE31 Who's Who in Art: Biographies of Leading Men and Women in the World of Art Today, 1927– . London: Art Trade Press. irregular.

Emphasis is on Britain.
N40 W6

BE32 Who was Who in American Art: Compiled from the Original Thirty-four Volumes of *American Art Annual, Who's Who in Art: Biographies of American Artists Active from 1898–1947.* Ed. by Peter H. Falk. Madison, CT: Sound View Press, 1985. 707 p.

Where necessary, additional information has been added to that found in the original sources. Typical entry gives dates, education, memberships, awards, positions, exhibition list, writings, and notes on some works.
N6512 F26

BE33 Wood, Christopher. **Dictionary of Victorian Painters.** 2d rev. ed. Woodbridge, Suffolk: Antique Collector's Club, 1978. 764 p.

Biographical dictionary of over 11,000 artists working 1837–1901. Another work for the 19th and 20th centuries is *Dictionary of British Watercolour Artists up to 1920.* (2 vols, Poughkeepsie, NY: Apollo, 1986) (ND1928 M27) by H.L. Mallalieu.
ND467 W6

Biographical Dictionaries - Canada

BE34 Artists in Canada / Artistes au Canada: A Union List of Files / Une liste collective des dossiers. 3d ed. Ottawa: National Gallery of Canada, 1988. 776 p.

A list of Canadian artists based on artists files maintained by 24 Canadian libraries. Copies of the information contained in these files, e.g.

newspaper reviews, can be obtained from the institutions. Available online.
N6548 A77

BE35   Biographies of Inuit Artists, 1988– . 3d rev. ed. 4 vols. Mississauga, ON: Tuttavik. looseleaf service.

Exhaustive, regularly updated loose-leaf dictionary of Inuit artists who can be searched by name variations. Typical entry includes dates, exhibition list, collections, honours and selected references, and sometimes quotes from commentaries on artist's work.
E99 E7 B55 Ref ROMU

BE36   Harper, J. Russell. **Early Painters and Engravers in Canada.** Toronto: University of Toronto Press, 1970. 376 p.

Dictionary of more than 4,000 artists (no sculptors) born before 1867 or working in Canada before 1900.
ND248 H37

BE37   MacDonald, Colin S. **A Dictionary of Canadian Artists.** Ottawa: Canadian Paperbacks, 1967- in progress.

By 1990 covers artists A-Sadowski in 7 volumes. Information about the life and works of a wide range of artists is compiled from newspapers, books; periodicals, and exhibition catalogues.
R920.3 M135   or   N6548 M234

BE38   McMann, Evelyn de R. **Royal Canadian Academy of the Arts / Académie royale des arts du Canada: Exhibitions and Members 1880–1979.** Toronto: University of Toronto Press, 1981. 448 p.

A record of all works exhibited by more than 3,000 artists in the annual exhibitions of the R.C.A., drawn from the original catalogues. McMann covers the 90 years of the Montreal Spring Exhibitions in *Montreal Museum of Fine Arts, Formerly Art Association of Montreal: Spring Exhibition 1880–1970* (University of Toronto Press, 1988) (N6545 M36 ROBA).
N17 R618 M45

Directories

BE39   American Art Directory, 1898– . New York: R.R. Bowker. biennial.

(53rd ed, 1990/91).   Lists American and Canadian art galleries and museums, art libraries, arts councils, art schools, art magazines and newspapers, and art critics.   Subject and personnel indexes.
N17 R618 M45

BE40   The Directory of Museums and Living Displays. 3d ed.   New York: Stockton Press, 1985. 1047 p.

Very brief descriptive entries for museums in 170 countries.
AM1 D57

BE41   International Directory of Arts, 1952/53– . 2 vols. Frankfurt: Muller. biennial.

Lists museums and art galleries, universities and art schools, societies, artists, collectors, art and antique dealers, commercial galleries, publishers, restorers, periodicals and booksellers.
N50 I6

BE42   The Official Directory of Canadian Museums and Related Institutions / Répertoire officiel des musées Canadiens et

institutions connexes, 1984/85– . Ottawa: Canadian Museums Association. triennial.

Directory first appeared in 1978 as *Directory of Canadian Museums*. Listing for each institution under province and town includes names of curators and administrative personnel. Fully indexed.
R069.0971 D598DC   or   AM21 A2D52

BE43   The Official Museum Directory, 1971– . Wilmette, IL: National Register Publishing Co. with American Association of Museums. annual.

The 1990 edition lists approximately 6,700 U.S. museums and art galleries by state and city, with institutions and personnel indexes. Formerly called *Museums Directory of the United States and Canada*, and after the 1983 edition, Canadian entries are no longer included.
AM10 O438

Canadian Museums and Galleries

BE44   The Art Gallery of Ontario: Selected Works. Toronto: A.G.O., 1990.   463 p.

Works of art selected from all Gallery departments are given a one-page description and an illustration, usually in colour. Indexes by Department and by artist.

BE45   Burnett, David.   Masterpieces of Canadian Art From the National Gallery of Canada. Edmonton: Hurtig, 1990.   230 p.

One-page descriptions accompanied by colour reproductions of Canadian "masterpieces" from Thomas Davies (c1737–1812) to Joanne Tod (b1953).

BE46   Canadian   Watercolours   and Drawings in the Royal Ontario Museum. 2 vols.   Comp. by Mary Allodi.   Toronto: Royal Ontario Museum, 1974.

A catalogue of over 2,200 works on paper by 273 topographic and portrait artists of the 18th and 19th centuries. Biographical summaries. Indexes by place names and subjects. For part of the Coverdale collection of early Canadian art which was transferred from Canada Steamship Lines to the National Archives of Canada see *W.H. Coverdale Collection of Canadiana: Paintings, Water-colours and Drawings: Manoir Richelle Collection* (Ottawa: 1983) (N910 O72P8 ROBA).
ND1727 C2765 ROBA

BE47   The McMichael Canadian Art Collection. Kleinburg, ON: McMichael Canadian Art Collection; Toronto: McGraw-Hill Ryerson, 1989.   175 p.

A history of the collection which emphasizes the Group of Seven and Inuit art, together with biographies of several artists. Many colour plates.
N910 K57M35 ROBA

BE48 National Gallery of Canada. **Canadian Art.** Ottawa: National Gallery of Canada, 1988- (Catalogue of the National Gallery of Canada) in progress.

Volume 1: artists A-F, is the first of 4 projected volumes describing and illustrating all Canadian works in the Gallery's collection. Includes biographical summaries.
N6540 N38

*   *   *   *

BE49 National Gallery of Canada. **European and American Painting, Sculpture, and Decorative Art.** Ottawa: National Gallery of Canada, 1987- in progress.

Volume 1, the only one to appear so far, covers works of art in the Gallery collection, 1300–1800. Each volume consists of two parts: test and plates.
N910 O7A554 ROBA

General Histories of Art

BE50 Burnett, David and Marilyn Schiff. **Contemporary Canadian Art.** Edmonton: Hurtig, 1983. 300 p.

A history of Canadian art since World War II, with many colour plates. The past few years are documented in Mark A. Cheetham's *Remembering Postmodernism: Trends in Recent Canadian Art* (Oxford University Press, 1991). For art in Quebec of the 1940s to 1960s see Guy Robert's *L'Art au Quebec depuis 1940* (Montreal: Prese, 1973).
N6545 B77 ROBA

BE51 Hartt, Frederick. **Art: A History of Painting, Sculpture, Architecture.** 2d ed. 2 vols. Englewood Cliffs, NJ: Prentice-Hall; New York: Abrams, 1985.

A standard history along with H.W. Janson's *History of Art* (Abrams; Prentice-Hall, 1986) (N5300 J3); E.H.J. Gombrich's *The Story of Art* (Oxford: Phaidon, 1978), and *Gardner's Art Through the Ages* by Helen Gardner (Harcourt Brace, 1986) (N5300 G25 1970 ROBA), all of which have had numerous editions.
N5300 H283 ROBA

BE52 Hunter, Sam and John Jacobus. **Modern Art: Painting / Sculpture / Architecture.** 2d ed. Englewood Cliffs, NJ: Prentice-Hall, 1985. 408 p.

A history of modern art from the mid 1800s, with many colour illustrations. Bibliography and chronology. Modern art is studied chronologically from the point of view of significant art movements in H.H. Arnason's *History of Modern Art: Painting, Sculpture, Architecture, Photography* (Prentice-Hall and Abrams, 1986) (N6490 A713 ROBA).
N6447 H86 ROBA

Canada

BE53 Reid, Dennis. **A Concise History of Canadian Painting.** 2d ed. Toronto: Oxford University Press, 1988. 418 p.

Together with Russell Harper's *Painting in Canada: A History.* (University of Toronto Press, 1977) (ND240 H3 ROBA), are twin canons of the history of Canadian painting. Among Harper's many books see also *A People's Art: Primitive, Native, Provincial, and Folk Painting in Canada* (University of Toronto Press, 1974) (ND240 H32 ROBA). The one-hundred year history of the Royal Canadian Academy is recounted in Rebecca Sisler's *Passionate Spirits: A History of the Royal Canadian Academy of Arts, 1880–1980* (Toronto: Clarke, Irwin, 1980) (N17 R618S57 ROBA).
ND240 R45 ROBA

* * * *

Reproductions of Works of Art

BE54 Clapp, Jane. **Sculpture Index.** 2 vols. in 3. Metuchen, NJ: Scarecrow, 1970.

Indexes reproductions of sculpture of all countries appearing in 950 books, with emphasis on Europe and the Americas since 1900.
NB36 C55

BE55 Havlice, Patricia P. **World Painting Index.** 2 vols. Metuchen, NJ: Scarecrow, 1977. *Supplement*, 1973–1980. 2 vols. 1982.

Artist and title access to reproductions in 1,167 books and catalogues published 1940–1975. The supplement adds 617 titles.
ND45 H38

BE56 Parry, Pamela J. **Contemporary Art and Artists: An Introduction to Reproductions.** Westport, CT: Greenwood, 1978. 327 p.

Indexes 63 books from reproductions of works of art by artists active from 1940 to the mid-1970s.
N6490 P277

BE57 Smith, Lyn Wall and Nancy Moure. **Index to Reproductions of American Paintings Appearing in More than 400 Books Mostly Published Since 1960.** Metuchen, NJ: Scarecrow. 1977. 931 p.

Indexes over 3,000 reproductions of paintings by American artists by artist, title, and subject. A similar older work is Isabel S. Monro and Kate M. Monro's *Index to Reproductions of American Paintings: A Guide to Pictures Occurring In More than Eight Hundred Books* (H.W. Wilson, 1948 and *Supplement*, 1964) (ND205 M57 ROBA).
R759.13 AM752   or   ND205 S575

Art Auctions Records and Price Guides

BE58 Art Sales Index, 1984/85- . Poughkeepsie, NY: Apollo Book. annual.

Formerly *Annual Art Sales Index* (Weybridge, Surrey, 1968-1979). In two annual volumes indexes approximately 1,800 sales catalogues issued by 250 auctioneers worldwide. Available online as *ArtQuest*. Among numerous specialized art auction indexes are *Gordon's Print Price Annual* (New York: Martin Gordon, 1972-) and *The Index of Paintings Sold in the British Isles During the Nineteenth Century* (ABC-Clio, 1988-) (ND47 I5).

BE59 Canadian Art Sales Index, 1980- . Vancouver: Westbridge Publications. annual.

Priced list of paintings, watercolours, and drawings sold at auction in 16 auction houses across Canada. For prices of antiques and decorative arts see the annual *UNITT's Canadian Price Guide to Antiques and Collectables* (Peterborough, ON: Clock House Publications, 1968-).
N8670 C36 Can ROMC

Architecture

BE60 The Architectural Periodicals Index, 1972/73- . London: Sir Banister Fletcher Library, Royal Institute of British Architects, 1974–. quarterly.

Supersedes *RIBA Library Bulletin; RIBA Annual Review of Periodical Articles*. Indexes hundreds of journals from many countries in design, architecture, construction techniques, environmental studies, planning and research.

Full-text copies of articles are available from publisher.
Z5941 A7 ARCH

BE61 Architecture Series: Bibliography. Monticello, IL: Vance Bibliographies, 1978–1990. irregular.

Ceased at the end of 1990 with no. 2372. Separately issued bibliographies on architectural topics, geographical areas, and individual architects including Canadian. Cumulated author, title, subject indexes. The bibliographies have been compiled by the publishers and by various contributors, and the quality varies widely.
Z5941 A74

BE62 Columbia University. **Avery Index to Architectural Periodicals.** 2d ed. 15 vols. Boston: G.K. Hall, 1973. *Supplements* 1975–1989, 10 vols.

Indexing began in 1934 and earlier. Includes decorative arts, interior design, city planning and housing. The *Avery Index* is best accessed online via *RLIN*. The second edition and the 1975, 1977 supplements are available on microfiche.
Z5941 C62

BE63 Contemporary Architects. 2d ed. Chicago: St. James Press, 1987. 1038 p.

Entries for some 640 mostly living architects include biographical note, chronological list of works, bibliography, statement by the architect and brief essay. Information has been contributed by the architects themselves and hundreds of writers.
NA680 C646

BE64 A Dictionary of Architecture. Rev. and enl. Comp. by N. Pevsner. London: Penguin, 1975. 556 p.

Defines terms, describes national schools, styles, movements in world architecture. Includes biographies.
NA31 P49 ROBA

BE65 Ehresmann, Donald L. **Architecture: A Bibliographic Guide to Basic Reference Works, Histories, and Handbooks.** Littleton, CO: Libraries Unlimited, 1984. 338 p.

Annotated bibliography of the principal works on architecture published between 1875 and 1980 in English and Western European languages.
Z5941 E38

BE66 Fletcher, Banister. **A History of Architecture on the Comparative Method.** 19th ed. Rev. by J.C. Palmes. London: Athlone Press, 1975. 1390 p.

First published in 1896, but revisions have maintained its status as an authoritative survey of architectural styles and key buildings on all continents from ancient times to the early 20th century.
NA200 F63 (17th ed. 1961)

BE67 Kostof, Spiro. **A History of Architecture: Settings and Rituals.** New York and Oxford: Oxford University Press, 1985. 788 p.

A history of architecture and urbanism from the stone age to Postmodernism. Includes glossary.
NA200 K65 ROBA

BE68 Macmillan Encyclopedia of Architects. 4 vols. Ed. by Adolf K. Placzek. New York: Free Press; London: Collier Macmillan, 1982.

Biographical articles by many contributors on more than 2,400 architects from ancient times to the present. Articles include a list of works and bibliographies.
NA40 M25

Canada

BE69 Bergeron, Claude. **Index des périodiques d'architecture Canadiens: 1940–1980 / Canadian Architectural Periodicals Index: 1940–1980.** Québec: Presses de l'Université Laval, 1986. 518 p.

A detailed index to 9 Canadian architectural periodicals over a 40 year period. Separate sections provide access by building types, architects, and city or town.
Z5944 C3B47

BE70 Brosseau, Mathilde. **Gothic Revival in Canadian Architecture.** Ottawa: Parks Canada, 1980. 208 p.

Parks Canada has issued a series of studies of architectural styles in Canadian architecture in separate English and French editions. The others are: Nathalie Clerk's *Palladian Style in Canadian Architecture* (1984) (NA740 C5513 ROBA); Janet Wright's *Architecture of the Picturesque in Canada* (1984) (NA740 W74 ROBA); Leslie Maitland's *Neoclassical Architecture in Canada* (1984) (NA740 M35 ARCH); and Maitland's *The Queen Anne Revival Style in Canadian Architecture* (1990) (NA744 M35 ROBA).
NA744 B7 ARCH

BE71 Gowans, Alan. **Building Canada: An Architectural History of Canadian Life.** Rev. and enl. Toronto: Oxford University Press, 1966. 412 p.

Originally appeared in 1958 as *Looking At Architecture in Canada*. Still the standard work on architecture in Canada. *Québec: Trois siècles d'architecture* (Libre Expression, 1979) (NA474 A4N66 ROBA) by Luc Noppen, Claude Paulette and Michel Tremblay is a detailed study of architecture in Québec City. Ontario architectural styles and building types are outlined in John J.G. Blumenson's *Ontario Architecture: A Guide to Styles and Building Terms 1784 to the Present* (Markham, ON: Fitzhenry & Whiteside, 1990) (NA746 O6B6 ROBA).
NA740 G6 ROBA

BE72 Whiteson, Leon. **Modern Canadian Architecture.** Edmonton: Hurtig. 1983. 272 p.

A survey of Canadian architecture by region from the late 1960s. Includes biographical summaries and many colour plates.
NA745 W54 ROBA

Coins and Stamps

BE73 The Charlton Standard Catalogue of Canadian Coins, 1952- . Toronto: Charlton Press. annual.

Lists and illustrates tokens issued as substitutes for coins in British North America from 1794 to 1867.
R737.4971 C481C   or   CJ1861 S82

BE74 Morin, Cimon. **Canadian Philately: Bibliography and Index, 1864–1973 / Philatélie canadienne: bibliographie et index, 1864–1973.** Ottawa: National Library of Canada, 1979. 281 p. *Supplement*, 1983. 246 p.

Supplement extends bibliographic coverage to 1980. Includes books, catalogues and articles on Canadian postal history and philately. Author and subject indexes.
R383.23 AM858C   or   Z7164 P85 M6 ROBA

BE75 Room, Adrian. **Dictionary of Coin Names.** London: Routledge & Kegan Paul, 1987. 250 p.

Lists the official and unofficial popular names of nearly 1,000 worldwide coin denominations. Unfortunately, the loonie issued in the same year as this publication is not represented. An older standard dictionary of numismatic names and terms is Albert Frey's *A Dictionary of Numismatic Names: Their Official and Popular Designations* (various publishers) (CJ67 F7, 1947). First issued in 1917, and many times reprinted, the dictionary also contains a polyglot glossary for English, French, German, Italian and Swedish terms.   R.A.G. Carson's *Coins: Ancient, Mediaeval & Modern* (London: Hutchinson, 1970) (CJ75 C3) is another older standard reference dealing with the history and description of money and like objects arranged in different civilizations. There is a short section on the coinage of the New World. See also *The Macmillan Encyclopedic Dictionary of Numismatics* (Macmillan, 1982) (CJ69 D67) by Richard Doty, which defines and illustrates terms in world coinage.
CJ69 R66

BE76   **Standard Postage Stamp Catalogue,** 1973- . New York: Scott Publications. annual.

The 1991 edition is in 4 volumes. Formerly called *Scott's Standard Postage Stamp Catalogue.* For Canadian stamps consult Scott's *Specialized Catalogue of Canadian Stamps 1991* (Toronto: Unitrade, 1990) which is illustrated in colour, or Stanley Gibbon's *Stamp Catalogue,* Part I: British Commonwealth.
HE6226 S48

Costume

BE77 Arnold, Janet. **A Handbook of Costume.** London: Macmillan, 1973. 336 p.
Guide to visual, documentary and museum sources for costume study.
GT510 A75

BE78 Boucher, Francois. **Twenty Thousand Years of Fashion: The History of Costume & Personal Adornment.** Exp. ed. New York: Abrams, 1987. 356 p.

A study of costume from prehistoric times to the present, with over 1,000 illustrations. The British edition (Thames & Hudson, 1987) is titled *A History of Costume in the West* (GT510 B6713). Similar information can be found in *Fashion, From Ancient Egypt to the Present Day* by Mila Contini (Crescent Books, 1965) (GT513 C762 ROMU). Blanche Payne's *History of Costume: From the Ancient Egyptians to the Twentieth Century* (Harper Collins, 1965) (GT510 P35 ROBA) is a good general history.

BE79 Bruhn, Wolfgang and Max Wilke. **A Pictorial History of Costume: A Survey of Costume of All Periods and Peoples from Antiquity to Modern Times including National Costume in Europe and Non-European Countries.** New ed. New York: Crown, 1988. 74 + 200 p.

A history of costume from antiquity through the 19th century in a series of annotated colour plates. Useful for national and regional costume.
GT513 B763 ROBA (1973)

BE80 Collard, Eileen. **Clothing in English Canada Circa 1867 to 1907.** Burlington, ON: E. Collard, 1975. 72 p.

One of many books by the author on clothing worn by men, women and children in the English-speaking parts of Canada. Illustrated with original photographs, fashion plates, advertisements, and patterns that were in use during the period.
GT620 C636 ROBA

BE81 Davenport, Millia. **The Book of Costume.** 2 vols. in 1. New York: Crown, 1965. 958 p.

Authoritative information about costume and accessories from ancient times through the 19th century, with many illustrations from works of art.
GT513 D38 SMC

BE82 **The Dictionary of Costume.** Comp. by R. Turner Wilcox. New York: Macmillan, 1977. 406 p.

Describes clothing styles, terms, materials.
GT507 W5 ROBA (1969)

Decorative Arts and Design

BE83 **Contemporary Designers.** 2d ed. London: St. James Press, 1990. 641 p.

Entries for approximately 550 names involved in graphic, industrial, textile, fashion, and interior design. Entries written by 125 contributors include biography, list of representative designs, bibliography of books and writings by and about, artist's statement, one illustration, and brief critical essay.
NK1110 C66 (1984)

BE84 **Jackson's Silver & Gold Marks of England, Scotland & Ireland.** 3d ed. Ed. by Ian Pickford. Woodbridge, Suffolk: Antique Collectors' Club, 1989. 766 p.

Guide to British hallmarks and silversmiths' marks. Fully illustrated. For porcelain marks see William Chaffers' *Marks & Monograms on European and Oriental Pottery and Porcelain* (London: W. Reeves, 1965) (NK4215 C433 ROMU).
NK7143 A1J34 ROMC

BE85 **The Oxford Companion to the Decorative Arts.** Ed. by Harold Osborne. Oxford: Clarendon Press, 1985. 865 p.

Short entries and longer articles on the main fields of fine craftsmanship and minor crafts worldwide from ancient times to the 20th century.
NK30 O93 (1975)

BE86 **The Penguin Dictionary of Decorative Arts.** Ed. by J. Fleming and H. Honour. London: Viking, 1989. 935 p.

A concise guide to the decorative arts in Europe from the Middle Ages and in America from Colonial times to the present.
NK30 F54 (1977)

Canada

BE87 Chamberlain, Ken. **Design in Canada: 1940–1987, A Bibliography.** Richmond, BC: The author, 1988. 48 p.

An unannotated bibliography of books, pamphlets and periodical articles on commercial art and industrial design.

BE88 Collard, Elizabeth. **Nineteenth-Century Pottery and Porcelain in Canada.** 2d ed. Kingston: McGill-Queen's University Press, 1984. 477 p.

An exhaustive study of ceramic wares made in and used in Canada in the 19th century. Includes list of Canadian potters.
NK4029 C65 ROBA

BE89 King, Thomas B. **Glass in Canada.** Erin, ON: Boston Mills Press, 1987. 318 p.

A history of the glass industry in Canada. Includes lists of old glass companies, glassmakers, and bottle markings. Illustrated. Gerald Stevens' *Canadian Glass* (Toronto, 1967, and later editions as *Glass in Canada*) (NK5113 S844c ROMC) is still a classic in the field.
NK5113 K55 ROMU

BE90 Langdon, John E. **Canadian Silversmiths, 1700–1900.** Toronto: Stinehour, 1966. 249 p.

Alphabetical list of silversmiths with biographical summaries and illustrations of hallmarks. Indexes to silversmiths' initials, cities and towns, and punchmark designs.
NK7113 L273 ROMU

BE91 Lessard, Michel and Hugette Marquis. **Complete Guide to French Canadian Antiques.** New York: Hart Publishing Co., 1974. 255 p.

Translated from *Encyclopédie des antiquités du Québec: Trois siècles de production artisanale* (Editions de l'Homme, 1971) (NK842 Q3L4 ROBA). A well-illustrated guide to furniture, glass, ceramics, metalwork and a wide range of Québec collectibles. Glossary, index.
NK842 Q3L4 ROBA

BE92 Pain, Howard. **The Heritage of Upper Canadian Furniture: A Study in the Survival of Formal and Vernacular Styles from Britain, America and Europe, 1780–1900.** Toronto: Van Nostrand Reinhold, 1978. 548 p.

A compendium of early Ontario furniture presented by type (chairs, tables, chests, etc.) Hundreds of annotated illustrations. A similar work on Quebec furniture is Jean Palardy's *Furniture of French Canada* (Macmillan, 1963), and for Maritime furniture Charles Foss's *Cabinet Makers of the Eastern Seaboard* (Toronto: M.F. Feheley, 1977) (NK2441 F68 ROBA).
E10 3446 RBSC

BE93 Webster, Donald D. **The Book of Canadian Antiques.** Toronto: McGraw Hill Ryerson, 1974. 352 p.

Essays by leading authorities on furniture, toys, tools, glass, ceramics, textiles, books, photography, etc. Numerous illustrations.
NK841 W42

Graphic Arts

BE94 Bridson, Gavin D.R. and Geoffrey Wakeman. **Printmaking & Picture Printing: A Bibliographical Guide to Artistic & Industrial Techniques in Britain 1750–1900.** Oxford, U.K: Plough Press, 1984. 250 p.

Covers the technical literature of the many varied methods and media developed in Britain for printing illustrations and prints. Classified under broad and narrow headings, each of which begins with an explanation of the particular process. Indexes to processes and authors.
NE850 B75 ROMC

BE95 **Contemporary Graphic Artists: A Biographical, Bibliographical, and Critical Guide to Current Illustrators, Animators, Cartoonists, Designers, and other Graphic Artists.** 3 vols. Detroit: Gale, 1986–1988.

Each volume in this series deals with approximately 100 artists, providing detailed information about their work, writings, exhibitions, and biographical and critical sources.
NC45 C66 ROBA

BE96 Mason, Lauris. **Old Master Print References: A Selected Bibliography.** White Plains, NY: Kraus International, 1986. 279 p.

A listing by artist of 3,000 citations to catalogues raisonnés, checklists, articles, and catalogues concerned with prints by "old masters". Printmakers of more recent times are dealt with in *Print Reference Sources: A Selected Bibliography, 18th-20th Centuries* by Mason and Ludman (KTO Press, 1979) (Z5947 A3M37).
NE850 M376 SCAR

BE97 Riggs, Timothy A. **The Print Council Index to Oeuvre-Catalogues of Prints by European and American Artists.** Millwood, NY: Kraus International, 1983. 834 p.

For each artist provides references to books, exhibitions catalogues and periodical articles containing complete lists of prints by the artist.
Z5947 A3R53

BE98 **Who's Who in Graphic Art: An Illustrated World Review of the Leading Contemporary Graphic and Typograhic Designers, Illustrators and Cartoonists.** 2d ed. Ed. by W. Amstrutz. Dubendorf, Switzerland: De Clivo, 1982. 891 p.

Individual chapters are devoted to 42 countries, including Canada. Each begins with an overview of graphic design followed by short biographies and a portrait of representative graphic artists. Index to artists' names, and bibliographies.
NC45 W5

Canada

BE99 Ainslie, Patricia. **Images of the Land: Canadian Block Prints 1919–1945.** Calgary: Glenbow Museum, 1984. 165 p.

A detailed survey of block prints made by 63 Canadian artists during an international revival of the art form between the wars. Includes biographies of the artists and over 200 illustrations, several in colour. Twenty early 20th century printmakers of Quebec are covered in Denis Martin's *Printmaking in Quebec, 1900–1950* (Musée du Québec, 1990) (NE542 M87a ROMC).
NE541 I434 ROBA

BE100 Allodi, Mary. **Printmaking in Canada: The Earliest Views and Portraits / Les débuts de l'estampe imprimé au Canada: vues et portraits.** Toronto: Royal Ontario Museum, 1980. 244 p.

A fully-illustrated survey of separately-issued engravings and lithographs printed up to 1850 in Canada. Includes index of artists, printmakers, and publishers.
NE541 A66 ROBA

BE101 Stacey, Robert. **The Canadian Poster Book: 100 Years of the Poster in Canada.** Toronto: Methuen, 1979. 86 p.

A well-illustrated oversize history of Canadian posters arranged according to themes, with information about artists and designers. Extensive list of "Selected References."
NC1807 C35S75 ROBA

Photography

BE102 Browne, Turner. **The Macmillan Biographical Encyclopedia of Photographic Artists & Innovators.** New York: Macmillan, 1983. 722 p.

Biographical information about more than 2,000 photographers around the world from the 1830s to the present. Entries include a career summary, list of publications, and collections owning their work.
TR139 B767

BE103 **Contemporary Photographers.** 2d ed. Ed. by Colin Naylor. Chicago: St. James, 1988. 1145 p.

Entries on 750 photographers include biographical note, exhibition list, bibliography, personal statement, and critique.
TR139 C663

BE104 **Encyclopedia of Photography.** New York: Crown, 1984. 607 p.

Issued by the International Center of Photography in New York. More than 1,300 entries address all aspects of photography including technical, theoreticall, aesthetic, commercial, and individual photographers.
TR9 E54 SCAR

BE105 **Index to American Photographic Collections.** 2d ed. Ed. by Andrew H. Eskind and Greg Drake. Boston: G.K. Hall, 1990.

540 American institutions have contributed information about their photographic collections which has been compiled at the International Museum of Photography in Rochester, NY. Separate indexes for institutions with lists of their collections, and for photographers.
TR12 M4 ENGR (1982)

BE106 Johnson, William. **Nineteenth-Century Photography: An Annotated Bibliography, 1839–1879.** Boston: G.K. Hall, 1990. 962 p.

Brings together nearly 21,000 references to books and articles about photography from 1839 to 1879. Entries under the names of photographers often include a biographical summary.
Z7134 J64 ENGR

BE107 Moss, Martha. **Photography Books Index: A Subject Guide to Photo Anthologies.** Metuchen, NJ: Scarecrow, 1980. 286 p. *Photography Books Index II*, 1985. 261 p.

Provides access by photographer and subject to illustrations in 22 photo-anthologies and exhibition catalogues in Volume I, with a further 28 titles in Volume II. Selection of titles includes portraiture, fashion, nature, and photojournalism.

BE108 Newhall, Beaumont. **The History of Photography from 1839 to the Present.** 5th rev. ed. New York: Museum of Modern Art, 1982. 319 p.

A well-illustrated general history of photography. For the origins and beginning decades of the medium consult Helmut Gernsheim's *Origins of Photography* (3d rev. ed. Thomas & Hudson, 1983) (TR15 G37 ENGI).
TR15 N47 SIGS

Canada

BE109 Contemporary Canadian Photography from the Collection of the National Film Board. Edmonton: Hurtig, 1984. 176 p.

A selection of photographs from the Stills Division of the N.F.B. The notes describing the photographs include biographical summaries of the photographers.
TR654 C65 ENGI

BE110 Greenhill, Ralph and Andrew Birrell. **Canadian Photography, 1839–1920.** Toronto: Coach House Press, 1979. 184 p.

An illustrated history focusing on the pioneers of Canadian photography. The photoanthology *Private Realms of Light: Canadian Amateur Photography 1839–1940* (Fitzhenry & Whiteside, 1984) (TR26 P75 ROMC) includes photographers' biographies and a bibliography.
TR26 G74 ENGI

BE111 Public Archives of Canada. **Guide to Canadian Photographic Archives / Guide des archives photographiques Canadiennes.** Ottawa: The Archives, 1984. 727 p.

Descriptions of thousands of collections of historical photographs in 139 Canadian archives and libraries. Indexes to subjects, and to individual repositories with lists of collections.
Z7137 A32

BF MUSIC

Bibliographies and Guides to the Literature

BF1 Brockman, William S. **Music: A Guide to the Reference Literature.** Litteton, CO: Libraries Unlimited, 1987. 254 p.
   A selective guide to 559 important current and retrospective sources of information, with emphasis on works in English. Annotations are descriptive, evaluative, and comparative.
R780 AB864M   or   ML113 B85

BF2 Duckles, Vincent and Michael H. Keller. **Music Reference and Research Materials: An Annotated Bibliography.** 4th ed. New York: Schirmer Books, 1988. 714 p.
   An important music bibliography, with over 3,200 entries, and indexes to authors, titles and subjects.
R780 AD835 M4   or   ML113 D83

BF3 Harris, Ernest E. **Music Education: A Guide to Information Sources.** Detroit: Gale Research, 1978. 566 p.
   A comprehensive guide to the bibliographic structure of this interdisciplinary field.
ML19 H37

BF4 Hefele, Bernhard. **Jazz-Bibliography: International Literature on Jazz, Blues, Spirituals, Gospel and Ragtime Music with a Selected List of Works on the Social and Cultural Background from the Beginning to the Present.** Munich: K.G. Saur, 1981. 368 p.
   Includes 6,600 entries arranged by topic, with an index of names.
ML128 J3H43

BF5 Hoffman, Frank W. **The Literature of Rock, 1954–1978.** Metuchen, NJ: Scarecrow Press, 1981. 337 p. Supplement: *The Literature of Rock, II, 1979–83*, 1986, 2 vols.
   Includes annotated bibliographies, lists of periodicals covering the genre and basic rock recordings; indexed by artist and trend.
ML128 R6H62

BF6 Jackson, Roland. **Performance Practice, Medieval to Contemporary: A Bibliographic Guide.** New York: Garland, 1988. 518 p.

Contains nearly 1,400 citations of articles, books, dissertations, and introductions to editions, arranged in historical periods, and indexed by author and title. The bibliography emphasizes titles since 1960, when the issue of how musical works were originally performed in their own time began to be a major concern for musical scholars.
ML128 P235J3

BF7 Parker, Mary Ann. **G.F. Handel: A Guide to Research.** New York: Garland, 1988. 294 p.

One of a series by Garland entitled *Composer Resource Manuals*, which offer selective annotated bibliographies, lists of works, and guide to scholarly organizations and library resources.
ML134 H16P37

BF8 **A Small Basic Music Library: Essential Scores and Books.** 2d ed. Ed. by Pauline Shaw Bayne. Comp. by the Music Library Association. Chicago: American Library Association, 1983. 357 p.

A guide for small and medium-sized libraries.
780 AM987B2 or ML113 B3

Bibliographies and Indexes of Music

BF9 Berkowitz, Freda P. **Popular Titles and Subtitles of Musical Compositions.** 2d ed. Metuchen, NJ: Scarecrow Press, 1975. 209 p.

Identifies (by original title, opus number, key, etc.) over 700 nicknamed works.
ML113 B39

BF10 De Charms, Desirée and Paul F. Breed. **Songs in Collections: An Index.** Detroit: Information Service, 1966. 588 p.

Continues the work of Sears *Song Index*, (BF19), indexing 9,493 songs in 411 collections. Arranged by composer, or by title under nationality for anonymous and folk songs. Indexed by title and first line.
ML128 S3D37

BF11 Fuld, James J. **The Book of World Famous Music: Classical, Popular and Folk.** 3d ed. rev. and enl. New York: Dover, 1985. 714 p.

Information about 1,100 of the most familiar compositions of the western world, from *Happy Birthday* to Beethoven's *Ninth*: themes in musical notation, detailed commentary on the bibliographic sources, composers, and performance history of the works. Name and title indexes.
ML113 F8

BF12 Havlice, Patricia. **Popular Song Index.** Metuchen, NJ: Scarecrow Press, 1975. 933 p. *Supplements* 1978–1989, 3 vols.

Locates folk and pop songs, children's songs, spirituals, blues, and sea chanteys in several hundred anthologies published since 1940. Indexed by titles, first lines, first lines of choruses, and composers and lyricists.
ML128 S3H4

BF13 Heyer, Anna H. **Historical Sets, Collected Editions, and Monuments of Music: A Guide to their Contents.** 3d ed. 2 vols. Chicago: American Library Association, 1980.

Indexes, by composer and title, the contents of scholarly editions of early music in series, collected works of individual composers, and important publishers' series. A new edition of this essential guide is in preparation using computers, with distribution expected in an electronic format.
ML113 H52

BF14 Hinson, Maurice. **Guide to the Pianist's Repertoire.** 2d ed. Bloomington: Indiana University Press, 1987. 856 p.

An example of a type of reference tool designed for the performer: a list of available music, with publisher information, and indication of style, and level of difficulty.
ML128 P3H5

BF15 Lewine, Richard and Alfred Simon. **Songs of the Theatre.** New York: H.W. Wilson, 1984. 897 p.

A title listing of 17,000 songs from American shows, 1891–1983, with a chronology, extensive information about the original stage productions, a list of film and television productions, and a name index.
ML128 S3L55

BF16 **Music in Print Series,** 1974- . Philadelphia: Musicdata. irregular.

The series lists specific available editions of scores and parts, based on information supplied by international publishers. Entries are arranged by composer and title, with appropriate cross-references, indexing, and publishers' directory. The basic volumes cover: Sacred choral music, Secular choral music, Organ music, Classical vocal music, Orchestral music, and String music. In addition to occasional re-editions of these six titles, there is a general annual supplement (1979-), and in 1988 Master composer and Master title indexes were issued.
ML128 MUSI

BF17 **Répertoire international des sources musicales.** 1960- . Munich: Henle.

RISM is a major tool for locating musical sources, sponsored by the International Musicological Society and the International Association of Music Libraries. The aim is a "catalogue of all available musical works, writings about music, and textbooks on music from all countries... to 1800." Series A and B have introductions in English, French, and German, and for each entry, descriptive bibliography, and location symbols identifying copies in libraries. Each volume is appropriately indexed. Series A/I lists music publications, 1500–1800, containing music by a single composer. Series A/II lists manuscripts attributed to single composers. It exists as a database with microfiche indexes, in progress. Series B covers manuscripts and printed editions of collections of music by various composers, and writings on music. Series C comprises directories of collections of significant holdings, with information on services and bibliographic references.
ML113 I6

BF18 Ryom, Peter. **Répertoire des oeuvres d'Antonio Vivaldi: les compositions instrumentales.** Copenhagen: Engstrom & Sodring, 1986. 726 p.

An example of a thematic catalogue, in which works are organized and numbered either chronologically, or as in this case, by form and instrumentation, and identified by "incipits", musical citations of the opening notes. There is also information about the autograph source(s), manuscript copies and early and scholarly editions, and references to literature.
ML134 V7R97

BF19 Sears, Minnie E. **Song Index: An Index to More Than 12,000 Songs in 177 Song Collections.** New York: H.W. Wilson, 1926. *Supplement ... 7,000 Songs in 104 Collections*, 1934.

Entries for title, first line, composer, and author, in one alphabet. Classified and alphabetical listings of the song collections indexed.
ML128 S3S4

BF20 Shapiro, Nat and Bruce Pollock. **Popular Music, 1920–1979: A Revised Cumulation.** 3 vols. Detroit: Gale Research, 1985.

An annotated index of over 18,000 American popular songs, with introductory essays, indexes of lyricists and composers, awards and important performances, and list of publishers. Continued by volumes covering 1980–1984, and 1985 to the present, supplemented by *Popular Music, 1900–1919*, edited by Barbara Cohen-Stratyner.
ML120 U5S5

Library Catalogues

BF21 British Library. Dept. of Printed Books. **The Catalogue of Printed Music in the British Library to 1980.** 62 vols. London: K.G. Saur, 1981-87.

Includes approximately one million entries for items in the British Library collection.
ML136 L8B71

BF22 Canadian Music Centre. **Acquisitions.** 1984- . Toronto: CMC. annual.

Annual listing of new scores by Canadian concert music composers, added to the Centre's library. The 1990 catalogue also describes tapes of electro-acoustic pieces. The CMC previously issued occasional catalogues by genre, e.g. *Canadian Chamber Music* (ML120 C3 C456 1980) and *Catalogue of Canadian Choral Music* (ML120 C3C355 1978).
ML136 T6C362

BF23 Library of Congress. National Union Catalog. **Library of Congress Catalogs: Music, Books on Music and Sound Recordings,** 1973- . Washington: Library of Congress. semi-annual with annual cumulation. microfiche. Cumulated ed. *1973-77* (8 vols); *1978-80* (8 vols).

Includes scores, sheet music, libretti, books about music and musicians, and sound recordings of a musical, educational, literary or political nature.
ML136 U5L4602 MUSI; GENR (1978-86)

BF24 New York Public Library. Reference Dept. **Dictionary Catalog of the Music Collection.** 2d ed. 45 vols. Boston: G.K. Hall, 1984.

Photo-duplication of the card catalogue of one of the great American music libraries. Books, pamphlets, scores, and analytics for articles in festschriften, periodicals, etc., all in one alphabet including names, titles, and subjects. The second edition incorporates the first edition (1964) and its supplements, 1964-1971 (1973) and 35,000 entries not previously listed. Updated by the annual *Bibliographic Guide to Music*, 1975–.
ML136 N5N573 (1964, 1973)

Abstracts and Indexes

BF25 Bull, Storm. **Index to Biographies of Contemporary Composers.** 3 vols. New York: Scarecrow Press, 1964-1987.

Indexes 273 reference works (dictionaries, who's whos, periodical indexes, etc.) indicating sources of biographical information on 16,000 twentieth-century composers.
ML105 B8

BF26 The Music Index: The Key to Current Music Periodical Literature. 1949- . Detroit: Information Coordinators. monthly with annual or biennial cumulations.

Indexes 500 music periodicals from around the world in all fields of music, by subject and author. The last decade is available on CD-ROM.

BF27 RILM: Abstracts of Music Literature, 1967- . New York: International RILM Center. quarterly.

Abstracts of international scholarly literature on music, including monographs, articles, dissertation, reviews, etc. Classified arrangement, with an annual name, title, and subject index; cumulative indexes every five years. Available online from 1971.
ML113 R14 MUSI

Encyclopedias and Dictionaries

BF28 Barlow, Harold and Sam Morgenstern. **A Dictionary of Musical Themes.** Rev. ed. New York: Crown, 1975. 642 p.

Lists 10,000 themes from instrumental works, in musical notation, arranged alphabetically by composer. Indexed by title and by themes in letter notation. The companion, *A Dictionary of Opera and Song Themes* (1976) (ML128 V7B28 MUSI) covers 8,000 vocal works, and has additional indexing by title and first line of text.
ML128 I65B3

BF29 Encyclopedia of Music In Canada. Ed. by Helmut Kallmann, Gilles Potvin and Kenneth Winters. Toronto: University of Toronto Press, 1981. 1076 p.

Includes over 3,000 signed entries for individuals, organizations and topics in concert, jazz, popular and traditional music, with bibliographies, discographies and illustrations. Articles are extensively cross-referenced and there is an index to names not covered by individual articles. It was also issued in French. A second edition is in preparation.
ML106 C3E6

BF30 Die Musik in Geschichte und Gegenwart: Allgemeine Enzyklopädie der Musik. 17 vols. Kassel: Barenreiter Verlag, 1949-67. *Supplement* 1973-79. *Register* 1986.

Scholarly, comprehensive articles on music and musicians, contributed by specialists throughout the world, with well-organized lists of composers' works and bibliographies. Many useful illustrations, some in colour. The Register (Index) is extensive.
ML100 M92

BF31 The New Grove Dictionary of Music and Musicians. 20 vols. London: Macmillan, 1980.

Grove's Dictionary was published in five editions (1879-1961). *The New Grove* is the standard music encyclopedia in English, containing entries on music history, theory and practice, instruments and terms. Biographical entries include lists of works and bibliographies. Several of the bibliographical articles are the best available surveys, e.g. "Bibliography of Music", "Collections, private", "Dictionaries and Encyclopedias", "Libraries", "Periodicals" and "Sources". There is an index to ethnomusicological terms, but no general index. *The New Grove* was typeset by computer, and parts of it have been revised and reissued as monographs: about 100 composer biographies, several titles on individual musical instruments, and specialized volumes such as *Music Printing and Publishing* (ML112 M87) and *Performance Practice* (ML457 P457).

The Norton/Grove Concise Encyclopedia of Music, edited by Stanley Sadie (Norton, 1988) is a concise version of *NGDMM*. Includes over 10,000 short entries in dictionary form, in all areas of music.

Other *New Grove Dictionaries* include *The New Grove Dictionary of Musical Instruments* (BF32), *The New Grove Dictionary of American Music* (4 vols, 1986) (ML101 U6N48 MUSI); *The New Grove Dictionary of Jazz* (2 vols, 1988) (ML102 J3N48 MUSI); and forthcoming (1992) *The New Grove Dictionary of Opera* (4 vols).
ML100 G88863

BF32 The New Grove Dictionary of Musical Instruments. 3 vols. Ed. by Stanley Sadie. London: Macmillan, 1984.

Articles on western and non-western, classical, folk and ethnic, historical and modern instruments, their makers and performance practices, with extensive cross-references, illustrations and bibliographies. Many articles are based on *The New Grove* (BF31), but have been largely rewritten.
ML102 I5N48

BF33 The New Harvard Dictionary of Music. Ed. by Don Michael Randel. Cambridge, MA: Belknap Press, 1986. 942 p.

Completely revised edition of a standard English-language source for non-biographical information: musical terms, brief historical articles, with good, basic bibliographies.
ML100 R3

Biographical Dictionaries

BF34 Baker's Biographical Dictionary of Musicians. 8th ed. Rev. by Nicholas Slonimsky. New York: Schirmer, 1991. approx. 2500 p.

The most authoritative biographical dictionary in English, covering musical figures of all periods and countries, mainly in the field of art music, with concise lists of musical and literary works. The editor's style, an integration of irony and pedantry, makes it also the most entertaining of all music reference works.
ML105 B16

BF35 Cohen, Aaron I. International Encyclopedia of Women Composers. 2d ed. 2 vols. New York: Books & Music (USA), 1987.

Brief biographies and lists of works for over 6,000 composers. Appendix of listings by country and century. Illustrations, discography, and extensive bibliography.
ML105 C7

BF36 Compositeurs canadiens contemporains. Dir. par Louise Laplante. Montreal: Les Presses de l'Université du Québec, 1977. 382 p.

Biographies of 160 prominent composers, with complete lists of works and bibliographies. Revised version of English edition published in 1975: *Contemporary Canadian Composers*, edited by Keith Macmillan and John Beckwith. A recent supplementary title is *Directory of Associate Composers / Répertoire des compositeurs agréés*, issued in looseleaf format by the Canadian Music Centre in 1989. Includes 199 composers who answered a questionnaire; others are omitted. All entries are the same length, so the ones on senior composers are sketchy.
ML390 C738

BF37 International Who's Who in Music, and Musicians' Directory, in the Classical and Light Classical Fields, 1935- . Cambridge: IWWM. triennial.

(12th ed, 1990) Includes resumes with addresses for 7,500 living musicians, musicologists, critics, etc, from information supplied by the subjects. Appended lists of orchestras, libraries, educational institutions, and competitions.
ML106 G7W442

Popular Music

BF38 Feather, Leonard. **The Encyclopedia of Jazz in the Seventies.** New York: Horizon Press, 1976. 393 p.

Supplements *The Encyclopedia of Jazz* (1962), and *The Encyclopedia of Jazz in the Sixties* (1966). All works include short essays on the history, sociology, and general state of jazz, biographies of jazz musicians with emphasis on their recording activities, and results of jazz polls.
ML105 F36

BF39 Green, Stanley. **Encyclopedia of the Musical Theatre.** New York: Dodd Mead, 1976. 488 p.

Subtitled: *An Updated Reference Guide to over 2,000 Performers, Writers, Directors, Productions, and Songs of the Musical Stage, Both in New York and London.* Includes bibliography, discography, lists of awards, and long runs.
ML102 M88G7

BF40 Kinkle, Roger D. **The Complete Encyclopedia of Popular Music and Jazz, 1900–1950.** 4 vols. New Rochelle: Arlington House, 1974.

Volume 1 chronologically lists significant pieces; Volumes 2-3 include biographies, alphabetically, with lists of works and recordings; Volume 4 indexes names, titles and popular songs, with lists of winners of polls and prizes.
ML102 P66K5

BF41 Stambler, Irwin and Grelun Landon. **Encyclopedia of Folk, Country, and Western Music.** 2d ed. New York: St. Martin's Press, 1983. 902 p.

Detailed biographies of performers, concentrating on the most commercially successful; selective discography and bibliography; lists of awards.
ML102 F66S7

BF42 Stambler, Irwin. **Encyclopedia of Pop, Rock, and Soul.** Rev. ed. New York: St. Martin's Press, 1989. 881 p.

Biographical entries for significant and representative figures in popular music of the 1950s-1980s, with discographical information, illustrations and lists of awards.
ML102 P66S8

Opera

BF43 **Kobbe's Complete Opera Book.** 10th ed. Ed. and rev. by the Earl of Harewood. London: Bodley Head, 1978. 1404 p.

The standard plot summary book, arranged historically, treating over 300 works, including information on their composition and early performances, with musical examples.
MT95 K52

BF44 Loewenberg, Alfred. **Annals of Opera, 1597–1940, Compiled From the Original Sources.** 3d ed. rev. Totowa, NJ: Rowman and Littlefield, 1978. 1756 columns.

A chronology of nearly 4,000 operas, by year of first performance, with indexes to title, composer, librettist, and other names, places, and subjects.
ML102 O6L6

BF45 **New Grove Dictionary of Opera.** 4 vols. Ed. by Stanley Sadie. Forthcoming 1992. See BF31n.

Hymnology

BF46 Diehl, Katherine S. **Hymns and Tunes: An Index.** New York: Scarecrow Press, 1966. 1185 p.

Index to hymns from the 78 twentieth century hymnals, chiefly Protestant, but include a few Catholic and Jewish hymns. Access to hymns by first line and author, to tunes by composer, melody, name.
BV305 D5

BF47 Julian, John. **A Dictionary of Hymnology, Setting Forth the Origin and History of Christian Hymns of all Ages and Nations.** Rev. ed. 2 vols. New York: Dover, 1957.

Biographical, historical and bibliographical entries on authors, titles, and subjects of hymn texts: originally published 1907.
BV305 J8

Directories

BF48 **Computing in Musicology: A Directory of Research.** 1989- . Ed. by Walter B. Hewlett and Eleanor Selfridge-Field. Menlo Park, CA: Center for Computer Assisted Research in the Humanities. annual.

Contains a list of current scholarly activities and practical applications, e.g. music printing. Issued 1985-1988 under the title *Directory of Computer Assisted Research in Musicology*.
ML19 D57

BF49 **Music Directory Canada,** 1983- . Toronto: CM Books. biennial 1984-.

A music industry guide, organized in 40 categories, among them booking agencies, music education, music photographers, night clubs, and record producers. Based mainly on response from listed organizations and institutions.
ML21 M8174

BF50 **Musical America International Directory of the Performing Arts,** 1986- . New York: ABC Consumer Magazines. annual.

Lists performing organizations, music schools, festivals, contests, publishers, magazines, etc, mainly in North America. Continues *Musical America: Annual Directory*, and was first issued as a special number of *Musical America*.
ML12 M882

*   *   *   *

Histories of Music

BF51 Grout, Donald J. and Claude V. Palicsa. **A History of Western Music.** 4th ed. New York: Norton, 1988. 910 p.

Standard college textbook, with numerous musical and photographic illustrations. Annotated bibliography, chronology of musical and historical events, and glossary of terms. The publisher has also issued a complementary music anthology, *The Norton Scores*, and set of LP recordings.
ML160 G87

BF52 McGee, Timothy J. **The Music of Canada.** New York: Norton, 1985. 257 p.

A survey of activity from the French settlement in the early seventeenth century, up to the early 1980s, with a separate chapter on music of the indigenous peoples. Designed for the general reader, or as a textbook, with musical analyses and illustrations, an anthology of scores, and an appendix of readings, recordings and films.
ML205 M27

BF53 **The New Oxford History of Music.** 11 vols. London: Oxford University Press, 1954- in progress.

Each volume contains essays by authoritative scholars, edited by a specialist in the period. Volumes 1-10, covering *Ancient and Oriental Music*, up to *The Modern Age (1890-1960)* have been issued, and also a second edition of Volume 2 *Early Medieval Music*. The volume of chronological tables and a general index is yet to be issued. Except for Volume 1, the coverage is of western art music. *The Concise Oxford History of Music*, by Gerald Abraham (Oxford, 1979) (ML160 A26) is a general history with extensive biographical references and index.
ML160 N44

BF54 **The Prentice-Hall History of Music Series.** Englewood Cliffs, NJ: Prentice-Hall, 1965- in progress.

An unnumbered publisher's series of a dozen short surveys covering traditional music as well as major historical periods of western music. Designed as textbooks, they include recommended readings and discographies. Examples are *Nineteenth-century Romanticism in Music*, by Rey M. Longyear, (3d ed, 1988) (ML196 L65); *Music in the United States: A Historical Introduction*, by H. Wiley Hitchcock, (1988) (ML200 H58); and *Music in the Renaissance*, by Howard M. Brown (ML172 B86).
various call numbers

BF55 Strunk, W. Oliver. **Source Readings in Music History From Classical Antiquity through the Romantic Era.** New York: Norton, 1950. 919 p.

English translations of 87 excerpts from the writings of theorists, composers, teachers, performers, and critics, arranged chronologically.
ML160 S89

Discographies

BF56 **Bibliography of Discographies.** 3 vols. New York: R.R. Bowker, 1977-83.

Entries for monographs, and for discographies appearing as articles, or appended to articles. Volume 1, *Classical Music*, by Michael H. Gray and Gerald D. Gibson, is supplemented by *Classical Music Discographies, 1976–1988: A Bibliography*, also by Michael H. Gray,

(Greenwood Press, 1989). Volume 2, *Jazz*, by Daniel Allen includes jazz, blues, ragtime, gospel, and rhythm and blues. Volume 3, *Popular Music*, by Michael H. Gray, covers pop, rock, country, and film and musical theatre discographies.
ML113 G77

BF57 Litchfield, Jack. **Canadian Jazz Discography, 1916–1980.** Toronto: University of Toronto Press, 1982. 945 p.

For improved music, the recording is the predominant form in which the music exists. This is an example of a contemporary systematic discography, including artists biographies, and for each recording, other performers, city and date of session, label name and number, and titles and composers of selections played.
ML156.4 J3L58

BF58 Myers, Kurtz. **Index to Record Reviews: Based on Material Originally Published in** *Notes, The Quarterly Journal of the Music Library Association.* 7 vols. Boston: G.K. Hall, 1978-89.

A guide to critical writing about classical music recordings in about 50 periodicals and other sources, from 1949 to 1987. Organized by composer, with indexes for performers and manufacturers' numbers. Continued in the *Notes* column "Index to CD and Record Reviews" now compiled by Richard LeSueur.
ML156.9 M89

BF59 **The New Penguin Guide to Compact Discs and Cassettes.** Ed. by Edward Greenfield, Robert Layton, and Ivan March. London: Penguin, 1988. 1366 p.

A selective survey of available classical (they use the term "permanent") music, with comprehensive discographical and performance information, and the authors' opinionated evaluations. Supplemented in 1989 by a *Yearbook*.
ML156.2 G723

BF60 OPUS. 1990- . Chatsworth, CA: ABC Consumer Magazines. quarterly.

This is the latest manifestation of *Schwann*, listing, mainly by composer, classical recordings in all formats available currently in the United States. *Artist Issue* appears annually. Another title, *Spectrum* (1990-) covers all other music types. *Inmusic* (1990-) is a monthly companion magazine for all new releases.

BF61 Phonolog Reporter, 1948- . San Diego, CA: Trade Service Publications. weekly. looseleaf.

An index of currently available recordings, useful for libraries for locating recordings of individual popular songs.
ML156 P56

BG   PERFORMING ARTS

Performing Arts

Bibliographies and Guides to the Literature

BG1 **Performing Arts Books, 1876–1981: Including an International Index of Current Serial Publications.** New York: R.R. Bowker, 1981. 1656 p.

Lists items catalogued by the Library of Congress since 1876 in all areas of the performing arts. Main entry under more than 12,000 subjects with access through topical outline of subjects, author and title index. Serials listed by subject with title index.
Z6935 P43

BG2 Whalon, Marion K. **Performing Arts Research: A Guide to Information Sources.** Detroit: Gale Research, 1976. 280 p.

This is Volume 1 of the *Performing Arts Information Guide Series*. Covers reference sources including guides and bibliographies, dictionaries, directories, encyclopedias, finding lists, play indexes, review sources, etc.
R790 AW552P   or   Z6935 W5

Directories, Handbooks and Biographical Sources

BG3 Association of Canadian Television and Radio Artists. **Face to Face with Talent.** 10th ed. Toronto: ACTRA, 1989. 582 p.

A directory of members of *ACTRA* and *Equity*, with portraits.
PN1573 C3A88

BG4 **BASELINE.** New York: Baseline Inc. Database. Updated daily.

Comprehensive coverage of U.S. entertainment industry, with emphasis on movies, theatre, and individuals. Covers film and television productions, awards, etc. Provides full text of entertainment newspapers.

BG5 **Contemporary Theatre, Film, and Television: A Biographical Guide Featuring Performers, Directors, Writers, Producers, Designers Managers, Choreographers,**

Technicians, Composers, Executives, Dancers, and Critics in the United States and Canada, 1984- . 2 vols. Detroit, Gale Research. annual.

Supersedes *Who's Who in the Theatre* (1912–1981, Gale) (PN2012 W5), which included biographies of people from all areas of the theatre, and playbills; and *Who Was Who in the Theatre, 1912–1976* (4 vols, Gale, 1978), which included biographies of deceased or inactive individuals who had been listed in the *Who's Who* volumes. Volume 8 (1990) of *Contemporary Theatre, Film, and Television* contains cumulated index to Volumes 1-8, and to *WWT* (1st-17th eds.) and *Who Was Who*.. . *CTFT* provides expanded coverage with biographical sketches of individuals currently employed, and prominent retirees. Emphasis on Americans.
PN2012 C65

BG6 Creative Canada: A Biographical Dictionary of Twentieth Century Creative and Performing Artists. 2 vols. Toronto: University of Toronto Press, 1971-72.

Includes about 1,000 biographees, both then living or deceased whether native-born or not, who have contributed to Canadian culture.
R920.3 C912

BG7 Index to Characters in the Performing Arts. 4 vols. in 6. Comp. by Harold S. Sharp and Marjorie Z. Sharp. Metuchen, NJ: Scarecrow Press, 1966–73.

A dictionary of major and minor characters in plays, operas, musicals, ballet, and in radio and television.
PN 1579 S45 ROBA

BG8 The Lively Arts Information Directory: A Guide to the Fields of Music, Dance, Theatre, Film, Radio and Television for the United States and Canada. 2d ed. Detroit: Gale Research, 1985. 1040 p.

Covers over 9,000 organizations, grant sources, and foundations. Additional information on grants and subsidies available for performing arts in Canada can be found in the *Handbook of Grants and Subsidies of the Federal and Provincial Governments*. See CC31 for full entry information.
PN 2289 L55

BG9 Performing Arts Biography Master Index: A Consolidated Index to over 270,000 Biographical Sketches of Persons Living and Dead. 2d. ed. Ed. by Barbara McNeil and Miranda Herbert. Detroit: Gale Research, 1981. 701 p.

Guide to biographical citations in over 100 reference sources covering a wide range of performing arts. Very concise; variant forms of names are not consolidated. Updated information can be found in *Biography and Genealogy Master Index* (AL6). Obituaries can be found in *Variety Obituaries 1905–1986* (12 vols, Garland, 1988) (PN1583 V35).
PN1583 M37

BG10 Performing Arts Resources, 1974- . New York: The Theatre Library Association. annual.

Articles deal with notable collections in libraries and archives, collection management, and topics of interest to theatre research.
Z675 T36P4

BG11 Sourcebook for the Performing Arts: A Directory of Collections, Resources, Scholars, and Critics in Theatre, Film, and Television. Comp. by Anthony Slide, and others. Westport, CT: Greenwood, 1988. 227 p.

Profiles institutions with major collections, and provides directory information. Includes biographical information on academics, archivists, critics, librarians, historians and scholars. Also includes information on bookshops, periodicals, publishers, organizations in the U.S. *Performing Arts Libraries and Museums of the World / Bibliothèques et musées des arts du spectacle dans le monde* (Paris: Centre Nationale de la Recherche Scientifique, 1984) (Z675 T36I5 (1967) ROBA) describes collections held in museums and libraries worldwide.
PN2289 S54

BG12 Who's Who in Entertainment, 1989/90. 1st ed. Wilmette, IL: Marquis Who's Who, 1989. 712 p.

Contains 17,000 biographical sketches of individuals who work in the entertainment industry in North America. Includes both prominent performers and those who work behind the scenes, for example, actors, musicians, composers, cinematographers, dancers, film directors and producers, broadcast executives, engineers, video specialists, radio and television personalities, clowns, etc.
PN1583 W56

Dance

Bibliographies, Catalogues and Indexes

BG13 Collier, Clifford and Pierre Guilmette. **Dance Resources in Canadian Libraries.** Research Collections in Canadian Libraries, No. 8. Ottawa: National Library of Canada, 1982. 136 p.

Includes a bibliography of reference sources on dance and a list of serials with locations. Dance collections in libraries and archives are described and access noted.
R026 R432 v.8

BG14 Magriel, Paul David. **A Bibliography of Dancing: A List of Books and Articles on the Dance and Related Subjects.** New York: H.W. Wilson, 1936. *Supplement 1936-40*, 1941. Reprint/ Blom, 1966.

Standard work with over 4,300 entries covering ballet, related music, mime, folk and national dance, costume, and decoration. Classified list, partly annotated, with indexing for author, subjects, analytics.
Z7514 D2M2 ROBA

BG15 New York Public Library. Research Libraries. Performing Arts Research Center. **Dictionary Catalog of the Dance Collection.** 10 vols. Boston: G.K. Hall, 1973.

Catalogue of a collection, often described as the world's most comprehensive resource of print and non-print, on the dance. Especially strong on folk dance and religious and ritualistic dance. Lists over 10,000 items including, books, dance scores, films, letters, manuscripts, pamphlets, periodicals, scrapbooks, and tapes. Supplemented annually by *The Bibliographic Guide to Dance* (1975- G.K. Hall) (Z7514 D2B5), which lists all material catalogued during the year at NYPL.
Z7514 D2N48

BG16 Studwell, William E. and David A. Hamilton. **Ballet Plot Index: A Guide to Locating Plots and Descriptions of Ballets and Associated Material.** New York: Garlland, 1987. 249 p.

Indexes 54 books in several Western languages, published between 1926 and 1982,

which provide information on 1,600 ballets, of all periods.
GV1790 A1 S77 ROBA

Dictionaries, Encyclopedias and Handbooks

BG17 Balanchine, George. **Complete Stories of the Great Ballets.** Rev. and enl. ed. New York: Doubleday, 1977. 838 p.

Contains synopses of over 4,200 ballets of classic stature or lasting importance. Also includes sections on history, chronology, careers, a glossary, discography, bibliography, and notes on dancers and choreography.
R792.8 B171C2

BG18 Beaumont, Cyril William. **Complete Book of Ballets: A Guide to the Principal Ballets of the Nineteenth and Twentieth Centuries.** Rev. ed. London: G.P. Putnam, 1951. 1106 p.

First published 1938, with supplements 1945, 1954, 1955. Provides synopses of almost 200 important ballets, in chronological order under name of choreographer. Includes information about author, composer, designer, date and cast of first performace, with excerpts of reviews of that performance.
GV1787 B35 (1941)

BG19 Cohen-Stratyner, Barbara. **Biographical Dictionary of Dance.** New York: Schirmer Books/Macmillan, 1982. 970 p.

Includes nearly 3,000 individuals, including performers, choreographers, composers, designers, impresarios, theorists, and teachers from "the last four centuries of dance history in Europe and the Americas, embracing a wide range of dance and theatrical genres." Most useful for information on little-known personalities not included in other sources.
GB1785 A1C58

BG20 **The Concise Oxford Dictionary of Ballet.** 2d ed. Ed. by Horst Koegler. New York: Oxford University Press, 1982. 459 p.

Comprehensive coverage of dance, including modern and ethnic, as well as ballet, and of dancers, companies, and terms. Concise entries, some with bibliographical notes. Somewhat less comprehensive is G. B. Wilson's *A Dictionary of Ballet* (3d ed, Black, 1974) (GV1585 W5 ROBA), which includes 2,500 entries covering classical ballet, modern dance, and Spanish and Indian dances. *Dictionary of Ballet Terms* by Leo Kersley and Janet Sinclair (3d ed, Black, 1973) (GV1585 K45) is another standard.
GV1585 K62

BG21 **The Dance Encyclopedia.** Rev. and enl. ed. Comp. by Anatole Chujoy and Phyllis Manchester. New York: Simon & Schuster, 1967. 992 p.

Treats all aspects of dance, emphasizing ballet, including history, stage, design, criticism, choreography. Most entries are brief; some long signed articles by specialists. Updated somewhat by *The Encyclopedia of Dance and Ballet*, edited by Mary Clarke and David Vaughan (Putnam, 1977) (GV1588 E5 ROBA), which puts greater emphasis on more contemporary dance styles.
GV1585 C5

BG22 **The Dance Handbook.** Ed. by Allen Robertson and Donald Hutera. Boston: G.K. Hall, 1990. 278 p.

Covers Western ballet and modern dance. Broad chronological arrangement, with factual data, critical evaluation, bibliography of books,

films and videos, and list of periodicals, festivals, companies worldwide.
MTRL ARTS

BG23 Grant, Gail. **Technical Manual and Dictionary of Classical Ballet.** 3d ed. New York: Dover, 1982. 127p.

Provides definitions of dance terms, with pronunciations, with line drawings of main positions. More information on technique can be found in *Classical Ballet Technique* by Gretchen Ward Warren (University of South Florida Press, 1989) (GV1788 W37 ROBA) which in addition to photographs and discussion, includes glossary, pronunciation guide, and bibliography.
GV1787 G68 (1967) ROBA

BG24 **International Dictionary of Ballet.** 2 vols. Ed. by Martha Bremser. Chicago: St. James, 1991.

Covers individual ballets, ballet companies, individual dancers, choreographers, composers, teachers, etc. Information on ballets includes details of first performances. Lists publications about ballets and individuals. Illustrated.
MTRL ARTS

BG25 McDonough, Don. **The Complete Guide to Modern Dance.** New York: Doubleday, 1976. 534 p.

Biographical sketches, descriptions of work and chronologies of over 100 choreographers, arranged alphabetically within broad time frames. Also includes a chronology of modern dance development and events, a bibliography and index.
GV1783 M26 ROBA

Theatre

This section deals with theatre production. For drama, as a literary genre, see BD140 - BD158.

Bibliographies

BG26 Baker, Blanche M. **Theatre and Allied Arts.** New York: H.W. Wilson, 1952. 536 p. Reprint/Blom, 1967.

Subtitled: *A Guide to Books Dealing with the History, Criticism, and Technic of the Drama and Theatre and Related Arts and Crafts.* Contains about 6,000 titles, annotated and arranged in three sections on drama, theatre and actors; stagecraft and allied art; miscellany. Though dated, still heavily used. Some sections are updated in bibliographies such as Richard Stoddard's *Stage, Scenery, Machinery and Lighting* (Gale, 1977) (Z5784 S8S79), and his *Theatre and Cinema Architecture* (Gale, 1978) (Z5784 S8S82).
R792 AB167   or   Z5781 B18

BG27 Ball, John and Richard Plant. **A Bibliography of Canadian Theatre History: The Beginnings to 1984.** New ed. Toronto: ECW Press, 1991. 600 p.

Cumulates and brings forward earlier volume covering 1583–1975 and a supplement 1975–1976 (The Playwrights' Co-op, 1976, 1979). Approximately 10,000 entries for books, articles, essays on theatre history in French and English Canada, little theatres, festivals, technical details, and biographies. Indexed by author and subject.
Z1377 D7B35/B52 (1976)

BG28 **International Bibliography of Theatre,** 1981-85. Ed. by Benito Ortolani New York: Theatre Research Data Center, Brooklyn College, City University of New York. annual.

Listed brief annotations for international theatre books, chapters, dissertations, articles, and documents published during the year. The 1985 edition included items not covered in previous volumes, and contained vastly expanded subject access. Now ceased.
Z5781 I56

BG29 New York Public Library. The Research Libraries. **Catalog of the Theatre and Drama Collections.** 51 vols. Boston: G. K. Hall, 1967–1976. Supplements, 1973, 1974.

Part 1, *Drama Collection: Author Listing* (6 volumes) and *Listing by Cultural Origin* (6 volumes) lists plays published separately or in anthologies and periodicals; Part II, *Theatre Collections: Books on the Theatre* (9 vols) relating to acting, biography, theatre history; Part III, *Non-Book Collection* (30 vols) lists programs, photographs, portraits, press clippings, and other ephemera. Catalogue includes materials in the NYPL collection, with theatre broadly interpreted to include stage, cinema, radio, television, nightclub performances, carnivals, circuses, and magic shows. Supplemented annually by *Bibliographic Guide to Theatre Arts* (1976-) (Z5785 N43), which lists items newly catalogued at NYPL, including non-book materials, and additional entries from LC-MARC tapes.
Z5785 N4

Annuals and Directories

BG30 **Canada on Stage: Canadian Theatre Review Yearbook,** 1974- . Toronto: PACT Communication Centre for the Faculty of Fine Arts, York University. irregular annual.

Well illustrated review of the year's theatrical activity including festivals, summer and youth theatre, and awards. Indexed. After a delay in publication, the 1986/88 edition will be published in Fall, 1991, and will be updated on an irregular basis.
PN2304 C26 ROBA (to 1981) or MTRL ARTS

BG31 **The Dramatist's Bible.** Ed. by A. Delaplaine. Chicago: St. James Press, 1989. 222 p.

Directory of production organizations in the U.S., Canada, and United Kingdom, as well as agents, publishers.
PN2289 D69

BG32 **Theatre Companies of the World.** 2 vols. Ed. by Colby H. Kullman and William C. Young. New York: Greenwood Press, 1986.

Survey of some 300 theatre companies. Arranged by region, country. Information on each company's philosophy, history, performing style, location, facilities, directors, programs, performance schedules. Separate U.S. volume planned.
PN2052 T48

BG33 **The Theatre Listing: A Directory of English Language Canadian Theatres from Coast to Coast,** 1989- . Toronto: PACT Communication Centre. annual.

Title varies, formerly *Behind the Scenes* (1986) (PN2304 B44), which updated *Playwright's Guide to Canadian Non-Profit Professional Theatre* (1984) (PN2304 P434, ROBA). Comprehensive guide to professional theatres, both profit and nonprofit, which respond to requests for information, and theatre-related

resources. Arranged by province, includes theatre companies, festivals, professional development, rehearsal spaces, agencies, publications, federal and provincial government agencies, etc.
PN2304 B44 (1986)   or   MTRL ARTS

BG34   Theatre World, 1944/45- . New York: Theatre World / Crown. annual.

Covers the theatre season. Factual information on theatre productions in the United States, particularly Broadway. Notes agents, authors, cast lists, composers, designers, directors, producers, song titles, technicians, theatres. Illustrated and indexed. Another long running standard which provides similar information, and includes digests and evaluations of selected plays is *Best Plays of [year] and Yearbook of the Drama in America* (1920- annual, Dodd Mead) (PN 6112 B45 ROBA), whose title has recently changed to *The Burns Mantle Theatre Yearbook* (Applause Theatre Book Publishers, 1990-).
PN2277 N5D32

Dictionaries, Encyclopedias and Handbooks

BG35   The Cambridge Guide to World Theatre. Ed. by Martin Banham. Cambridge University Press, 1988. 1104 p.

"Comprehensive review of history and present practice of theatre in all parts of the world." Signed articles of varying length. Illustrated.
PN2035 C27

BG36   A Companion to the Medieval Theatre. Ed. by Ronald W. Vince. Westport, CT: Greenwood Press, 1989. 420 p.

Covers theatrical forms and genres, including dance and music, personal names, places, production, staging, with an emphasis on performance. Covers the period A.D. 900 to 1500. Both long and short articles, cross referenced, and indexed by personal name, place, titles, subject.
PN2152 C66

BG37   Enciclopedia dello spettacolo. 9 vols. Rome: Maschere, 1954–62. *Aggiornamento 1955–65*, Rome: Union Editorale, 1966. *Indice Repertorio*, 1968.

A definitive work on staged entertainment including drama, opera, operetta, musicals, dance, variety, pantomime, puppetry, circus, and the media. Signed articles, many illustrations and bibliographies. Supplement primarily a biographical dictionary.
PN1625 E7

BG38   Hodgson, Terry. The Drama Dictionary. New York: New Amsterdam, 1989. 432 p.

Handbook of information on dramatic practice, theory, and criticism, with emphasis on the working terminology of the theatre.
PN1625 H58

BG39 Leonard, William T. **Theatre: Stage to Screen to Television.** 2 vols. Metuchen, NJ: Scarecrow Press, 1981.

Arranged by play's title with synopsis, comment and details of stage performances, operas, ballets, screen and television versions. Indexed by composer, lyricist, librettist, author, and playwright. Excludes Greek classics, Shakespeare, Gilbert and Sullivan. See also *Filmed Books and Plays* (BG62).
PN2189 L44

BG40 **The Oxford Companion to Canadian Theatre.** Ed. by Eugene Benson, and L. W. Connolly. Toronto: Oxford University Press, 1989. 662 p.

Covers the development of English and French theatre in Canada. Includes signed entries by prominent scholars on all aspects of the theatre including actors, directors, designers, companies, playwrights, genres, and provincial and territorial activity. A similar work for the United States is *Oxford Companion to American Theatre*, edited by Gerald Bordman (1984) (PN2289 B6 SIGR).
PN2301 O94

BG41 **The Oxford Companion to the Theatre.** Ed. by Phyllis Hartnoll. London: Oxford University Press, 1983. 934 p.

Concise, authoritative, literate articles on all aspects of the theatre, stressing the stage and performance rather than drama as a literary form. Coverage is international.
PN2035 H3

Reviews

BG42 **The New York Times Theatre Reviews,** 1870/1919- . New York: New York Times, 1975-. biennial, 1971-.

1870–1919 (6 volumes, 1976); *1920–1970* (10 volumes, 1971), final volumes in each set are indexes. Productions anywhere which are reviewed in the *NYT* are reprinted chronologically, plus appendices of awards and detailed indexes of titles, companies, personal names. Reviews from other New York newspapers and periodicals are found in *New York Theatre Critics Reviews* (weekly, 1940-) (PN1601 N4).
PN1581 N4/N38/N42

BG43 Salem, James M. **A Guide to Critical Reviews.** Metuchen, NJ: Scarecrow Press, 1966–1982.

Part I: *American Drama 1909–1982* (3d ed, 1984); Part II: *The Musical, 1909–1974 (2d ed, 1976)*; Part III: *Foreign Drama, 1909–1977,* (2d ed, 1979); Part IV: *The Screenplay from The Jazz Singer to Dr. Strangelove* (1971), and Part IV *Supplement One: 1963–1980* (1982). Citations to reviews in periodicals and brief information about production history. Indexed by title, author, adaptors. *Selected Theatre Criticism* edited by Anthony Slide (3 vols, Scarecrow, 1985-86) (PN2277 N5S44) is a collection of reviews of the New York stage, reprinted in their entirety, selected from 10 periodicals and covering 1900–1950.
Z5781 S16

Cinema and Film

This section includes works about film as a performing art. Catalogues and indexes of films and videos, and selection aids designed specifically for libraries can be found in Section AG *Audiovisual Materials*.

Bibliographies and Guides

BG44 Armour, Robert A. **Film: A Reference Guide.** Westport, CT: Greenwood, 1980. 251 p.

Bibliographic essays on sources for history, production, genres, actors, films. Subject and author indexes.
PN1993.45 A75

BG45 **A Bibliography of Reference Works for Cinema Studies.** Comp. by Ian Crellin. Toronto: Audiovisual Library, University of Toronto, 1990. 70 p.

Provides annotated entries for English-language film reference material, with locations at the central libraries of the University of Toronto. Author/title index.
R791.4 AU5893B

BG46 Dyment, Alan R. **The Literature of the Film: A Bibliographical Guide to the Film as Art and Entertainment, 1936–1970.** London: White Lion, 1975. 398 p.

Classified, annotated bibliography of approximately 1,300 English language items. Author and title indexes. Approximately the same period is covered in *The Film Book Bibliography, 1940–1975* by Jack Ellis and others (Scarecrow, 1979) (Z5784 E44), an unannotated list of English language titles.
Z5784 M9D88

BG47 **The Film Index: A Bibliography.** 3 vols. New York: Museum of Modern Art Film Library/ Wilson, 1941 / White Plains, NY: Kraus, 1985.

Volume 1, edited by Harold Leonard (1941); Volumes 2 and 3 published 1985. Includes citations to books and articles published to 1936, with an emphasis on silent movies. Updated by *The New Film Index* (BG52).
Z5784 M9W75

BG48 Fisher, Kim N. **On the Screen: A Film Television and Video Research Guide.** Littleton, CO: Libraries Unlimited, 1986. 209 p.

Guide to the literature on artistic and entertainment films and videos, including items published 1960–1983. Emphasizes American films.
Z5784 M9E535

BG49 Rehrauer, G. **The Macmillan Film Bibliography: A Critical Guide to the Literature of the Motion Picture.** 2 vols. New York: Macmillan, 1982.

Supersedes *Cinema Booklist* and *Supplement*(s) (1972–1977). Volume 1 contains brief reviews of over 6,700 English language film books arranged alphabetically by title. Volume 2 is an index for access by subject, author, script.
Z5784 M9R423

Abstracts and Indexes

BG50 Film Literature Index, 1974- . Albany, NY: Filmdex. quarterly.

Subject and author index to international film and television/video literature in more than 300 periodicals. Indexes individual performers, screenwriters, etc; includes film and book reviews.
Z5784 M9F45

BG51 **International Index to Film Periodicals: An Annotated Guide.** 1972- . London: International Federation of Film Archives (FIAF). annual.

Annotated index to approximately 85 key international film periodicals, covering general subjects, individual films, and biographies. Entries for countries, festivals. Indexed by directors, authors. Also available on microfiche: 1972–1986, 1987–1990, 1991 supplements (bimonthly). IFFA also publishes *International Index to Television Periodicals: An Annotated Guide* (1979/80-).
Z5784 M9I5

BG52 McCann, Richard Dyer and Edward S. Perry. **The New Film Index: A Bibliography**

of Magazine Articles in English 1930–1970. New York: Dutton, 1975. 522 p.

Designed to fill gap between *The Film Index* (BG47) and *Film Literature Index* (BG50). Indexes some 12,000 articles with brief notes; classified arrangement with author index. The same period is also covered in *Retrospective Index to Film Periodicals, 1930–1971*, by Linda Batty, (R.R. Bowker, 1975) (Z5784 M9B39); and in *The Critical Index: A Bibliography of Articles on Film in English, 1946–1973*, by John C. Gerlach, (New York: Teachers College Press, 1974) (Z5784 M9G47), which covers U.S., British, and Canadian journals.
Z5784 M9M29

BG53 Schuster, Mel. **Motion Picture Performers: A Bibliography of Magazine and Periodical Articles, 1900–1969.** Metuchen, NJ: Scarecrow Press, 1971. 702 p. *Supplement, 1970–1974*, 1976.

Articles from popular English language magazines. Useful for locating obscure figures, as well as major performers. Schuster also compiled *Motion Picture Directors: A Bibliography of Magazine and Periodical Articles, 1900–1972* (Scarecrow, 1973) (Z5784 M9S34).
Z5784 M9S35/2

Encyclopedias and Dictionaries

BG54 Boussinot, Roger. **L'encyclopédie du Cinéma.** 2 vols. Paris: Bordas, 1980.

An international guide to films, performers, technical terms.
PN1993.45 B6

BG55 **Cinema: A Critical Dictionary: The Major Film-Makers.** 2 vols. Ed. by Richard Roud. London: Secker & Warburg, 1980.

Signed essays on directors, genres, national schools covering 1895 to 1975. Indexes for names and film titles.
PN1993.45 C5

BG56 **Le Dictionnaire du cinéma québécois.** Ed. by Michel Coulombe and Marcel Jean. Montreal: Boréal, 1988. 530 p.

Signed entries covering important individuals and organizations in Québécois cinema as well as definitions of cinematic terms. Lists 333 significant films made in Quebec.
PN1993.5 C32Q45

BG57 **International Dictionary of Films and Filmmakers.** 2d ed. 5 vols. Ed. by Nicholas Thomas. London: St. James Press, 1990- in progress.

Volume 1: *Films* (1990) is the first volume to be published. Includes 626 films which "represent the current concerns of North American, British, and West European film scholarship." Many important foreign films have also been included. Entries include production and release information, credits, bibliographies, and signed critical commentaries. Also includes a list of films by director. Until second edition is completed, the first edition of this work, (5 vols, St. James, 1884–1988) is still useful for its coverage of directors, filmmakers, writers, performing and production artists.
PN1997.8 I6

BG58 Katz, Ephraim. **Film Encyclopedia: The Most Comprehensive Encyclopedia of World Cinema in One Volume.** New York: Harper Row, 1990. 1278 p.

(1st ed, 1979). Brief entries cover individuals, film industry events, national cinema, and definitions of technical terms. Includes comprehensive

filmographies for directors and stars.
PN1993.45 K34 (1979)

BG59 Konigsberg, Ira. **The Complete Film Dictionary.** New York: New American Library, 1987. 420 p.

Comprehensive dictionary of some 3,000 technical terms relating to filmmaking. Illustrated. L.N. Ensign's *The Complete Dictionary of Television and Film* (Stein and Day, 1985) (PN1992.18 E57) seeks to standardize the language of film.
PN1993.45 K66

BG60 **The New York Times Encyclopedia of Film.** 13 vols. Ed. by Gene Brown. New York: Times Books, 1984.

Chronological arrangement of articles which appeared in the *NYT* from 1896–1979. Includes feature articles, news items, interviews, etc. Indexed in volume 12. Excludes reviews, which are reprinted in *New York Times Film Reviews* (BG79).
PN1993 N465 ROBA

Directories and Handbooks

BG61 Aros, Andrew A. **Title Guide to the Talkies: A Comprehensive Listing of 16,000 Feature Length Films from October, 1927, until December, 1963.** 2 vols. New York: Scarecrow Press, 1965.

Information on the literary sources of feature films. Alphabetical listing of films, with information on screenwriters, and the novels, plays, short stories, on which the films are based. Supplemented by *A Title Guide to the Talkies, 1964 Through 1974* (1977); and ... *1975 Through 1984,* (1986) (PN1998 A6695, ROBA) which includes more foreign films, and information about novelizations. Richard B. Dimmitt published *An Actor Guide to the Talkies: A Comprehensive Listing of 8,000 Feature-Length Films from January 1948 until Decmeber 1964* (2 vols, Scarecrow, 1967) which was also updated by Aros through 1974 (Scarecrow, 1977) (PN1998 A6694). The *Actor Guide* lists casts for films, with name index.
PN1998 A6695 ROBA

BG62 Enser, A.G.S. **Filmed Books and Plays: A List of Books & Plays From Which Films Have Been Made, 1928–1986.** Rev. ed. Aldershot, U.K: Gower, 1987. 770 p.

English-language films based on books and plays. Access by title of film, original title, change of original title, and author. See also *Theatre: Stage to Screen to Television* (BG39), and *A Title Guide to the Talkies* (BG61).
Z5784 M9E55

BG63 **Film Canada Yearbook,** 1986- . Toronto: Cine-communications. annual.

Supersedes *Canadian Film Digest Yearbook* (1971/72–1985, Canadian Film Digest) (PN1993.5 C3C2 ROBA). Lists production companies, distributors, exhibitors of films in Canada. Covers television, video, government agencies, unions, guilds, awards, festivals, film courses, publications.
PN1993.5 C3C22

BG64 Halliwell, Leslie. **Halliwell's Filmgoer's Companion.** 9th ed. London: Grafton Books, 1988. 786 p.

Incorporates *The Filmgoer's Book of Quotes*, and *Halliwell's Movie Quiz*. A quick reference aid, emphasizing British and American films with particular emphasis on the 1930s and 40s. Also useful, *Halliwell's Film Guide* (7th ed, Harper & Row, 1989) (PN1993.45 H27), which

lists films by title and includes critical quotes with notes on video availability.
PN1993.45 H3

BG65 **International Film Guide,** 1966- . London: Tantivy. annual.

Surveys film production in more than 50 countries, with reviews of important films and books, festivals, and awards. Also lists directory information for bookstores, archives, schools.
PN1993.3 I544

BG66 **International Motion Picture Almanac,** 1919-. New York: Quigley. annual.

Contains a wide range of information about mostly U.S. individuals, companies, suppliers, agents, the press, censorship, etc. Includes miscellaneous facts and statistics.
PN1993.3 I55

BG67 **Magill's Survey of Cinema.** Ed. by Frank Magill. Englewood Cliffs, NJ: Salem Press, 1980- in progress.

Includes *English Language Films: First Series* (4 volumes); *Second Series* (6 volumes, 1981); *Silent Films* (3 volumes, 1982); *Foreign Language Films* (8 volumes, 1985), and *Annual Indexes*, 1982- . Films are listed alphabetically with brief details of production and players, followed by signed critical essays. Indexes provide access to directors, screenwriters, performers, etc. Supplemented by *Magill's Cinema Annual* (1982-) which covers selected films of the previous year, with list of awards and obituaries. Both available online.
PN1993.45 M3/3 ROBA

BG68 Morris, Peter. **The Film Companion.** Toronto: Irwin, 1984. 335 p.

"Comprehensive guide to more than 650 Canadian films and film-makers." Film entries include synopses, credits, critical comments and references. Biographical information covers about 300 producers, directors, writers, editors, animators, composers, etc. Covers some 1,900 films - shorts to features. Includes cross references, bibliography.
PN1993.5 C3M65

BG69 Nowlan, Robert A. and Gwendolyn Wright Nowlan. **Movie Characters of Leading Performers of the Sound Era.** Chicago: American Library Assn, 1990. 396 p.

Includes biographical information on actors, list of key roles with character and film names, and information about the role.
R791.43 N948M

BG70 **Science Fiction, Horror & Fantasy Film and Television Credits.** 2 vols. Comp. by Harris M. Lentz. Jefferson, NC: McFarland, 1983. *Supplement* (1989).

Subtitled: *Over 10,000 Actors, Actresses, Directors, Producers, Screenwriters, Cinematographers, Art Directors, and Make-up, Special Effects, Costume and Other People; Plus Full Cross References from All Films and TV Shows.* Volume 1: *The People*; Volume 2: *The Films and Shows.*
PN1995.9 S26L46

BG71 Truitt, Evelyn M. **Who Was Who on Screen.** 3d ed. New York: R.R. Bowker, 1983. 788 p.

Brief biographies and filmographies for more than 13,000 screen personalities, mostly American, British, German, and French, who died between 1905 and 1982.
PN1998 A2T73

BG72 **World Film Directors.** 2 vols. Ed. by John Wakeman. New York: H.W. Wilson, 1987–1988.

Volume 1: *1890–1945*, Volume 2: *1945–1985*. Long entries with bibliographies, filmographies, on 419 major filmmakers worldwide. Can be supplemented by Michael Singer's *Film Directors: A Complete Guide* (Santa Barbara, CA: Lone Eagle, 1983- annual) (PN1998 A155 VUPR), which provides international coverage of more than 1,800 living directors.
PN1998.2 W67

Reviews

BG73 **AFVA Evaluations,** 1988- . La Grange Park, IL: American Film & Video Association. looseleaf.

Continues *EFLA Evaluations* (1948–1987). Critical evaluations summarize content, technical quality, and give suggestions for audience use.
791.4375 A110 OISE or PN1995.9 E9542 AVL

BG74 Bowles, S.E. **Index to Critical Film Reviews in British and American Film Periodicals Together with: Index to Critical Reviews of Books about Film.** 3 vols. in 2. New York: B. Franklin, 1974–75.

Covers 1930–1972. Arranged by film or book title with indexes for directors, authors and reviewers.
PN1995 B68 ROBA

BG75 **Film Review Index.** 2 vols. Edited by Patricia King Hanson and Stephen I. Hanson. Phoenix, AZ: Oryx Press, 1986.

Volume 1, *1882–1949*; Volume 2, *1950–1985*. Reviews of 6,000 films in reference works and in popular magazines, trade journals, scholarly publications are cited. Arranged alphabetically by film title, indexed by director, year, country of origin.
791.43016 F497 OISE

BG76 **Guide to Critical Reviews, Part IV: The Screenplay from *The Jazz Singer* to *Dr. Strangelove*,** (1971, 1982). Cites reviews in popular periodicals. See BG43 for full entry information.

BG77 **Media Review Digest,** 1973- . Ann Arbor, MI: Pierian Press. annual, with semi-annual supplements.

Continues *Multi-Media Review Index* (1970–72). An annual index to, and digest of, reviews, evaluations, and descriptions of all forms of non-book media appearing in over 145 periodicals and reviewing services. Has films, (feature and short, some non-U.S.), filmstrips, videocassettes, records, tapes, slides, globes, charts, kits and games etc. Includes several indexes, a "Film Awards and Prizes" section, and a mediagraphy.
791.43016 M489 OISE

BG78 **The Motion Picture Guide.** 12 vols. Ed. by Jay Robert Nash and Stanley Ralph Ross. Chicago: Cinebooks, 1985–1987. annual updates.

Lists and rates over 50,000 English language (and significant foreign) films released theatrically, and on videocassette between 1927–1984, with concise reviews. Volume 10 covers silent films (1910–1936). Indexes in volumes 11 and 12, by alternate title, series, awards. Continued by *The Motion Picture Guide Annual* (Bowker, 1986-).
PN1993 M67

BG79 The New York Times Film Reviews, 1913–1968. 6 vols. New York: New York Times and Arno Press, 1970- Biennial supplements 1969/70- New York: Garland.

Volume 6 is *Cumulated Index 1913–1968*. Reviews published in the *NYT* of some 17,000 films arranged chronologically in order of publication. Film and name indexes in volume 6. *Film Review Annual* (Englewood, NJ: Ozer, 1981-) (PN1993 F5) contains complete reviews from selected magazines and newspapers of feature films released in the U.S. during the year.
PN1995 N48, N4834

BG80 Variety Film Reviews, 1907–1989. 20 vols. New York: R.R. Bowker, 1989-90.

Volume 20 covers 1987–1989. Volume 16 is index to 1907–1980. Chronological arrangement of complete reproductions of original reviews of feature-length films printed in *Variety*. Lists cast, credits, running time, first showing, country of origin, etc.

Radio and Television

BG81 Dunning, John. **Tune in Yesterday: The Ultimate Encyclopedia of Old-Time Radio, 1925–1976.** Englewood Cliffs, NJ: Prentice Hall, 1976. 703 p.

Includes articles on radio shows from the period, with background information, biographies. Index of names. *Radio Soundtracks: A Reference Guide*, edited by Michael R. Pitts (2d ed, Scarecrow, 1986) (PN1991.9 P58) provides information on radio programs from the 1920s to the 1960s which are available on tape.
PN1991.3 U6D8

BG82 Halliwell, Leslie with Philip Purser. **Halliwell's Television Companion.** 3d ed. London: Grafton Books, 1986. 941 p.

More than 12,000 entries, for Britain, U.S., on series, TV movies, performers, networks and technical terms. Excludes news and sports.
PN1992.3 G7H36

BG83 International Index to Television Periodicals see BG51n for information.

BG84 International Television & Video Almanac, 1987- . New York: Quigley. annual.

Continues *International Television Almanac* (1956–1986). Similar to *International Motion Picture Almanac* (BG66). Includes review of the television year, statistics, awards, provides information on shows, networks, stations, features, and individuals. Covers home video companies, products, technicians, programs. Includes a who's who section.
HE8698 I552

BG85 The New York Times Encyclopedia of Television. Ed. by Les Brown. New York: Times Books, 1977. 492 p.

Entries on the history, technology, programs, stars, executives, legal landmarks, rating system, etc. of the medium.
PN1992.18 B7

BG86 Radio and Television: A Selected, Annotated Bibliography. Comp. by William E. McCavitt. Metuchen, NJ: Scarecrow, 1978. 229 p. *Supplement One: 1977–1981* (1982), *Supplement Two: 1982–1986* (1989).

Second supplement edited by Peter K. Pringle and Helen Clinton. Annotated bibliography covering the years from 1926 in a classified arrangement under broad subject headings.

Part C
SOCIAL SCIENCES

CA GENERAL REFERENCE IN THE SOCIAL SCIENCES

For selection aids for the Social Sciences, see Section AC, *Selection Aids*.

Bibliographies and Guides to the Literature

CA1 **Directory of Published Proceedings. SSH: Social Sciences, Humanities,** 1968- . Harrison, NY: Interdok. quarterly, with annual and four year cumulations.

Worldwide. Lists published proceedings chronologically by conference date (year and month), with subject and sponsor indexes. Four year cumulations include editor and location indexes. Does not provide access to individual papers within published proceedings.
Z7166 D56

CA2 **International Bibliography of the Social Sciences,** 1955- . London: Routledge, Chapman and Hall, 1988- . annual.

Previously published by Unesco, now produced by the British Library of Political and Economic Science. Published in four annual subject volumes: *International Bibliography of Economics*, (1952-) (Z7164 E2I58); *International Bibliography of Political Science*, (1953-) (Z7163 I64); *International Bibliography of Social and Cultural Anthropology*, (1955-) (Z7161 I593); and *International Bibliography of Sociology*, (1955-) (Z7161 I594). Beginning with 1988 volumes, to be issued with "improved currency, enhanced indexing, and wider coverage to over 1,500 monographs and periodicals." International coverage, including developing world and Eastern European publications. Available online. Routledge has published a *Thematic List of Descriptors* for each discipline, (1989).

CA3 Li, Tz-chung. **Social Science Reference Sources: A Practical Guide.** 2d ed. Westport, CT: Greenwood Press, 1990. 590 p.

Part 1 covers social sciences in general; part 2 has chapters on types of materials in major subdisciplines. Lists 2,200 references sources in anthropology, business, cultural anthropology, economics, education, geography, history, law, political science, psychology, and sociology. Includes name and title indexes.
300 AL693S (1980)   or   Z7161 A1L5

CA4 A London Bibliography of the Social Sciences: Being the Subject Catalogue of the British Library of Political and Economic Science at the School of Economics. 4 vols. London: Mansell, 1931–32. *Supplement*(s) Vol. 5- 1929–73; annual 1974-.

Catalogues the holdings of the British Library of Political and Economic Science and the Edward Fry Library of International Law. Prior to Volume 7 included holdings of other libraries as well. Largest subject bibliography of its kind, the BLPES's greatest collection strength is in economics, political science, law, but bibliography includes all areas of social sciences. The annual supplements are the most comprehensive record of each year's monographic publications, and include discussion papers, occasional papers, government, IGO, and private organization publications as well. Provides brief bibliographical details with subject access only, no author index.
Z7161 L84

CA5 The Social Sciences: Cross Disciplinary Guide to Selected Sources. Ed. by Nancy L. Herron. Englewood, CO: Libraries Unlimited, 1989. 287. p.

Part 1 covers general reference sources applicable across all disciplines; part 2 contains essays by subject specialists on the literatures of anthropology, economics and business, history, law and legal issues, political science, and sociology. Part 3 covers disciplines "emerging" as social sciences: education, psychology, communications; and part 4 covers geography, statistics, and demographics. Includes 768 annotated citations.
R300 AS678S

CA6 Webb, William. **Sources of Information in the Social Sciences: A Guide to the Literature.** 3d ed. Chicago: American Library Association, 1986. 707 p.

Supersedes earlier editions by Carl M. White. The standard guide to the literature, it systematically provides critical and descriptive annotated citations to the more than 8,000 items in the literatures of anthropology, education, economics, geography, history, political science, psychology, and sociology.
R300 AW583SA3

Abstracts and Indexes, Periodical Directories, and Union Lists

CA7 **ASSIA: Applied Social Science Index and Abstracts,** 1987- . London: Library Association. 6 issues a year.

Covers more than 500 journals from 16 countries (80% U.K., U.S.), to provide inter-disciplinary approach to literature of behavioural and social sciences. Arranged by subject, using chain indexing, with concise abstracts. Available online.
Z7163 A66

CA8 **Current Contents: Social and Behavioral Sciences,** 1969- weekly.

A current awareness service of contents pages from over 1,330 journals, approximately 150 per week. Issues include tables of contents of new multi-authored books. Title word index, author index and addresses. Available online and on diskette. See DA15 for full information.
PER diskette

CA9 **Dissertation Abstracts International,** Section A: *The Humanities and Social Sciences*, 1938- monthly. See AF42 for full entry information.

CA10 Essay and General Literature Index, 1900- semi-annual.

Indexes essay collections in the social sciences. See AF37 for full entry information.

CA11 Index to Social Sciences and Humanities Proceedings, 1979- . Philadelphia: Institute for Scientific Information. quarterly with annual cumulation.

Indexes about 21,000 individiual papers from published proceedings of worldwide conferences each year. Covers most "significant" proceedings each year, but with considerable time delay. Conference proceedings which are not published are not included. Seven indexes: contents of proceedings; category; author/editor; sponsor; meeting location; subject; corporate. Some papers available from I.S.I.
Z7151 I524

CA12 PAIS International in Print, 1990- monthly. Formerly **Public Affairs Information Service Bulletin,** 1915-.

Indexes worldwide literature covering many social science topics. See AF15 for full entry information.

CA13 Social Sciences Citation Index, 1966- . Philadelphia: Institute for Scientific Information. 3 issues per year and annual cumulation.

Coverage of 4,700 titles in the social and behavioural sciences, 1,400 fully and 3,000 selectively. In 3 parts: 1) *Source Index,* a standard index of articles arranged by author with each entry followed by a brief list of the references cited in that article; 2) *Citation Index,* which provides access by the names of authors whose works are cited in the references or footnotes of the articles indexed in the *Source Index.* It includes a corporate index for conferences and author's affiliation. 3) *Permuterm Subject Index,* which indexes every important word in the title of each item. Topics in psychology, public health, anthropology are indexed in *Arts and Humanities Citation Index* (BA3). Available online as *Social SciSearch.* For additional information see DA22.
Z7161 S65 (IND)3

CA14 Social Sciences Index, 1975- . New York: H.W. Wilson. quarterly with annual cumulation.

Supersedes *Social Sciences & Humanities Index* (1965–74). Comprehensive coverage of 350 English language periodicals in anthropology, area studies, community health and medical care, economics, ethnic studies, geography, gerontology, international relations, law and criminology, minority studies, planning and public administration, police science and corrections, policy sciences, political science, psychology and psychiatry, social work and public welfare, sociology, and urban studies. Covers both applied and theoretical aspects of disciplines. Extensive cross references, full bibliographical data. Includes a separate index to reviews of current books in social sciences. Available online and on CD-ROM. Book reviews for earlier periods are indexed in *Combined Retrospective Index to Book Reviews in Scholarly Journals 1886–1974* (see AC35), which covers 359 journals in history, political science, and sociology.
IND

CA15 Union List of Serials in the Social Sciences and Humanities held by Canadian Libraries, 1990- annual. See AE21 for full entry information.

CA16 **World List of Social Science Periodicals / Liste mondiale des périodiques specialisés dans les sciences sociales.** 7th ed. Paris: Unesco, 1986. 818 p.

Over 3,500 entries from 107 countries listed by country of origin, with title, subject and geographic indexes. Includes "scientific" periodicals, e.g. those containing research, field studies, or articles by scholars or specialists. Also lists secondary periodicals that contain bibliographies or abstracts of articles in primary periodicals. Updated semi-annually in the *International Social Science Journal*.
Z7163 U522

Encyclopedias and Dictionaries

CA17 **Encyclopaedia of the Social Sciences.** 15 vols. Ed. by E.R.A. Seligman. New York: Macmillan, 1930-34. Reprinted/ 5 vols., Encyclopaedia Britannica.

A classic work with scholarly essays covering the history of the social sciences in general, and anthropology, economics, law, penology, politics, and sociology. Still useful for history, biography (4,000 biographies) and as documentation of the state of the art for social sciences in the 1930s.
R303 E56

CA18 Gould J. and W.K. Kolb. **A Dictionary of the Social Sciences.** New York: Free Press, 1964. 761 p.

Published under auspices of Unesco. Authoritative standard for about 1,000 major concepts which are defined and described. Provides historical/analytical background. Cross references. Though dated, still valid and not superseded.
H41 G6

CA19 **International Encyclopedia of the Social Sciences.** 19 vols. Ed. by D.L. Sills. New York: Macmillan and The Free Press, 1968-1991. Reissue/ 8 vols. (1977).

Does not supersede its predecessor (CA17). Emphasizes analysis, research methodology, and comparative information, with bibliographies, in the central social sciences: anthropology, economics, political science, psychology and sociology. Volume 18 is *Biographical Supplement* (1980) adds biographies not included here or in CA17, and Volume 19 *Quotations* (1991), cites quotations of noted social scientists.
R303 I61

CA20 Miller, P.M. and M.J. Wilson. **A Dictionary of Social Sciences Methods.** New York: J. Wiley, 1983. 124 p.

Current research methods in empirical social sciences are explained and put in context.
H41 M54

CA21 Reading, Hugo F. **A Dictionary of the Social Sciences.** London: Routledge & Kegan Paul, 1977. 231 p.

Provides very brief definitions of over 7,500 terms for all social sciences except economics and linguistics.
H41 R42

CA22 **The Social Science Encyclopedia.** Ed. by Adam Kuper and Jessica M. Kuper. London: Routledge & Kegan Paul, 1985. 896 p.

Articles contributed by 500 scholars from 25 countries (mostly U.S., U.K.) cover all main disciplines, related disciplines, and problems in the social sciences. Covers theories, methods, issues, defines specialized terms, includes biographies. Spin-off publications include *Key*

Thinkers Past and Present (1987) which contains biographies of social theorists.
H41 S63

CA23 Wolman, Benjamin. **Dictionary of Behavioral Science.** 2d ed. San Diego, CA: Academic Press, 1989. 370p.

Defines 20,000 terms in anthropology, education, human relations, neuroscience, physiology, psychology, psychiatry, social work, and statistics. Includes historical, biographical information. Definitions are technical and complex.
BF31 W64

Directories

CA24 **American Men and Women of Science: Social and Behavioral Sciences.** 13th ed. 2 vols. New York: R.R. Bowker, 1978.

Biographies of over 24,000 persons. Discipline, geographic indexes. More recent information can be located using *Biography and Genealogy Master Index* (AL6) and the encylopedias noted above.
Q141 A48

CA25 **Canadian Register of Research and Researchers in the Social Sciences.** London: University of Western Ontario, Social Sciences Computing Laboratory. database.

Provides information on members of Canadian social sciences research community including biographical information, professional qualifications, specialization, current research, and information about projects, publications, reports, grey literature. Covers all social sciences including interdisciplinary Canadian and environmental studies. Available online only as *CANREG*.

CA26 **Canadian Social Science Data Archive.** Downsview, ON: Institute for Social Research, York University, 1985. 136 p. loose-leaf.

Guide to the holdings of the largest social science data archive in Canada. Outlines means of access and descriptions of databases held. New edition in progress.
R300 AC212C

CA27 **Directory of Social Science Research Centres and Institutes at Canadian Universities / Répertoire des centres et instituts de recherche en science sociale dans les universités canadiennes.** Rev. ed. Ottawa: University of Ottawa Press for Social Science Federation of Canada, 1987. 196 p.

Information on about 200 centres and institutes and their activities and publications.
H62.5 C3D5

CA28 **Forthcoming International Scientific and Technical Conferences.** 1966- quarterly.

Includes information on conferences in the social sciences, law, statistics. See DA69 for full entry information.

CA29 **World Directory of Social Science Institutions / Répertoire mondial des institutions de sciences sociales: Research, Advanced Training, Documentation, Professional Bodies.** 4th ed. Paris: Unesco, 1985. 905 p.

List of 1,932 international bodies, associations and institutions. Arranged by country, includes directory information and indicates size of staff, type (public/private), field of study. Unesco also prepares *Selective Inventory of Social Science Information and Documentation Services* (3d ed, 1988), which lists libraries and research institutes

which create and disseminate information; and the *Directory of Social Science Information Courses*, (London: Berg Publishers, 1988) (R020.71 D598S).
R300.72 R425R (1977)   or
UN9 ES95 W52   GOVT

CA30   World Meetings: Social and Behavioral Sciences, Human Services, and Management, 1971- . New York: Macmillan. quarterly.

A companion to *World Meetings: United States* and *World Meetings Outside US and Canada* (DA72). A two year registry of forthcoming meetings with locations, dates, sponsors, etc.
AS8 U75

Statistical Information

This section covers statistical guides, compilations and indexes covering international, Canadian, British, and American statistics. Materials on statistical science are found in *Mathematics*, Section DB.

International

BIBLIOGRAPHIES AND INDEXES

CA31   DataMap: Index of Published Tables of Statistical Data. Phoenix, AZ: Oryx Press, 1989. 787 p.

Cross-index of 13,000 tables of statistical data found in 27 published sources chosen for breadth of coverage and wide use in libraries. Sources include 16 U.S. government, 6 international, and 5 privately published almanacs.
Z7552 D37 GOVT

CA32   Directory of International Statistics. 2 vols. New York: United Nations. Statistical Office, 1982- in progress.

Volume 1 is a guide to statistical series issued by the UN system and several other IGO's, and to databases of economic and social statistics. Volume 2, in preparation, will provide information on the organization and responsibilities of statistical services of the UN system and of other IGOs.
UN2 S13 75 M561 GOVT

CA33   Index to International Statistics, 1983- . Washington: Congressional Information Service.

Catalogues, abstracts and indexes statistical publications of all major intergovernmental organizations, including United Nations main and subsidiary bodies, regional commissions and specialized agencies; the European Community; Organization for Economic Cooperation and Development; etc. Includes indexes by subject, names, geographic areas, categories, titles, issuing sources and report numbers. Most items indexed are available from publisher on microfiche. Available online, and on CD-ROM on *Statistical Masterfile*.
HA154 I64 GOVT

CA34   Statistics Europe: Sources for Social, Economic and Market Research. 5th ed. Comp. by Joan M. Harvey. Beckenham, U.K: CBD Research; Detroit: Gale Research, 1987. 320 p.

Covers 2,427 current print sources, arranged by country. Includes information on central statistical offices and other sources of statistical publications. Companion volumes are *Statistics Asia and Australasia*, (1983) (Z7554 A7H37 ROBA); *Statistics Africa*, (1978) (Z7554 A34H37 ROBA); and *Statistics America*, (1980) (Z7554 A5H37 ROBA).
Z7554 E83H3

CA35 Statistics Sources: A Subject Guide to Data on Industrial, Business, Social, Educational, Financial and Other Topics for the United States and Internationally. 15th ed. 2 vols. Ed. by Jacqueline Wasserman O'Brien and Steven R. Wasserman. Detroit: Gale Research, 1991.

A "finding guide" of over 2,000 international statistics sources, both published and unpublished sources, and print and non-print, on over 20,000 topics. Includes a selected bibliography of key sources which describes statistical compendia from governmental and nongovernmental sources.
R310 AS797S11 (1988) or Z7551 S84

CA36 Westfall, Gloria. **Bibliography of Official Statistical Yearbooks and Bulletins.** Alexandria VA: Chadwyck-Healey, 1986. 247 p.

Lists 374 general official statistics yearbooks from 191 countries. Arranged by region and country with descriptions of contents, sources and prices. Excludes publications of international organizations. Information on non-official statistics can be found in *International Directory of Non-Official Statistics Sources* (London: Euromonitor, 1990) which lists some 1,000 (mostly U.S.) sources issued by non-governmental organizations.
Z7551 W47 GOVT

COMPENDIA

CA37 European Historical Statistics, 1750-1975. 2d rev. ed. Ed. by B.R. Mitchell. New York: Facts on File, 1980. 868 p.

Summarizes data from wide variety of sources in statistical tables arranged in subject areas, e.g. population, labour force, external trade, prices, etc. for the countries of Europe. Sources of statistics documented.
HA1107 M5

CA38 International Historical Statistics: The Americas and Australasia. Ed. by R. B. Mitchell. Detroit: Gale Research, 1983. 949 p.

Summarizes data from a wide variety of sources, covering North and South America, Australia, and New Zealand. Companion volumes are *International Historical Statistics: Africa and Asia*, (New York University Press, 1982) (HA4675 M55 SIGR) and *European Historical Statistics, 1750-1975* (CA37). Statistical tables in subject areas: e.g. climate, population, industry, education, national accounts, etc. Sources of data noted.
HA155 M58 GOVT

CA40 Kurian, George T. **New Book of World Rankings.** 3d ed. New York: Facts on File, 1991. 324 p.

Includes descriptions of countries, and ranking under 349 subject headings.
HN25 K87 (1984)

CA41 Mulhall, Michael George. **Dictionary of Statistics.** 4th ed. London: Routledge, 1985.

Reprint of original 1899 ed. Not a dictionary but a compilation of statistics from the time of

Emperor Diocletian (ca. 300 A.D.) to 1898. *New Dictionary of Statistics* (1911) (HA46 M952) supplements to 1909.
HA46 M94 ROBA

CA42 Unesco Statistical Yearbook / Annuaire statistique, 1962- . New York: Unesco, 1963- annual.

Statistics of population, education, science and technology, publishing, culture and communication, films and broadcasting. Data series are presented subject-by-subject in some 100 tables covering over 200 countries and territories. *Unesco Statistical Digest* (1981-) provides the data by country (UN9 ES S72 GOVT).
R311.3 U58S (1976) or
UN9 ES 718 S79 GOVT

CA43 United Nations. Statistical Office. **Demographic Yearbook / Annuaire démographique,** 1948- . New York: United Nations, 1949- . annual

"A comprehensive collection of international demographic statistics" for about 220 countries or areas. *Demographic Yearbook: Historical Supplement* (1979) includes time series covering 1948-78.
UN2 S30 D29 GOVT

CA44 United Nations. Statistical Office. **Statistical Yearbook / Annuaire statistique,** 1948- . New York: United Nations, 1949- annual.

"A comprehensive compendium of the most important internationally comparable data." Statistics are updated in *Monthly Bulletin of Statistics* (1947-) (UN2 S30 M51 GOVT). More detailed information on specific subjects is published by the specialized agencies (e.g. *Unesco Statistical Yearbook* (CA42), and *Yearbook of Labour Statistics* (CC24n)). *World Statistics in Brief: United Nations Statistical Pocketbook* (1976-) (UN2 S22 W57 GOVT) is a compact compilation of basic statistics for 167 nations.
R311.3 U580 (1981) or UN2 S30 S81 GOVT

CA45 The World in Figures: Editorial Information Compiled from *The Economist*. 5th ed. London: Hodder Stoughton, 1987. 296 p.

Detailed figures are provided for each country of the world; arranged by subject and by country. Comparative statistics are arranged by subject in Victor Showers' *World Facts and Figures* (3d ed, Wiley, 1989) (G109 S52) which covers countries, cities and geographic and cultural features.
HA161 W67 GOVT

CA46 World Tables. 3d ed. 2 vols. Baltimore MD: Published for the World Bank by Johns Hopkins University Press, 1983.

Includes time series of basic economic and social variables by country, and by groups of countries. Updated in the annual *World Development Report* (UN9 MG W53 GOVT).
UN9 MG W57 GOVT

Canada

CA47 Annotated Bibliography of Canadian Demography 1966–1982. Comp. by Lokky Wai, Suzanne Shiel and T. R. Balakrishnan. London, ON: Centre for Population Studies. University of Western Ontario, 1984. 314 p. Supplemented annuallly with *Updates*, 1985- .

Comprehensive annotated bibliography of scholarly materials on Canadian population, including journal articles, books, research monographs, dissertations, and government

publications. Supplemented by the annual *Updates of the Annotated Bibliography...* (1985-). Those covering 1983–1984, 1984–85, 1986 and 1987 and new annotations covering 1988 and 1989 have been published as *Annotated Bibliography of Canadian Demography 1983–1989*, (1990) (Z7164 D3W312). Beginning in 1986, annotations covering less scholarly material are also included. Arranged by author, with subject, and name indexes.
Z7164 D3W3

CA48 Canadian Statistics Index, 1985- . Toronto: Micromedia. annual.

Indexes statistical publications of federal, provincial, and municipal governments, public and private organizations, and commercial publishers. Also indexes statistical information in commercial and trade magazines. Arranged by issuing agency, with subject index. Items indexed can be obtained on microfiche from publisher. Available online as *CSI*.
HA741 C43 GOVT

CA50 Leacy, F.H. **Historical Statistics of Canada.** 2d ed. Ottawa: Statistics Canada, in joint sponsorhsip with Social Science Federation of Canada, 1983. 800 p.

Political, social and economic statistics from 1867-1975 (some tables to 1976, 1977).
R317.1 H673H2

CA51 Statistics Canada. **Bibliography of Federal Data Sources Excluding Statistics Canada.** Ottawa: Supply and Services, 1982. 189 p.

Provides information on sources of social and economic data produced on a regular basis by other federal departments and agencies.
R015.71 B582B

CA52 Statistics Canada. **Canada Year Book: Review of Economic, Social and Political Developments in Canada,** 1905- annual. See AH15 for full entry information.
R317.1 C212   or   HA74C32

CA53 Statistics Canada. **Canadian Economic Observer / L'observateur économique canadienne.** 1988- . Ottawa: Statistics Canada. monthly, with supplementary bulletins. Annual supplement: *Historical Statistical Supplement.*

Formerly titled *Canadian Statistical Review* (1926-1988). Each monthly issue includes a statistical summary by sector and an index to the tables. In addition there is a discussion of current economic conditions, economic and statistical events, and a feature article. A list of recent feature articles is provided as well. Articles or overviews which first appear here are sometimes separately published. The *Canadian Economic Observer: Historical Statistical Supplement* (1988-) (CA1 BS11 C210 GOVT) is an annual companion volume to *CEO* which contains historical annual series to correspond to those published in the monthly tables.

Information in *CEO* is retrieved from *CANSIM*, see CA55, and data is cross-referenced to the *CANSIM* identifier for the unadjusted or seasonally adjusted monthly or quarterly data. Available online and on CD-ROM.
PER

CA54 Statistics Canada. **Canadian Social Trends,** 1986- . Ottawa: Statistics Canada. quarterly.

Includes latest figures for major social indicators.
CA1 BS11 C0 O8 GOVT

CA55 Statistics Canada. **CANSIM (Canadian Socio-Economic Information Management System).** Ottawa: Statistics Canada. database.

CANSIM is Statistics Canada's information retrieval system providing access to it's computerized databases. *Time Series Data Base* (*CANSIM* Main Base) contains data relating to the system of national accounts, labour, manufacturing, construction, trade, agriculture and finance, and selected economic and social data. Business, economic and social data are also available on the *Cross Classified Data Base* (XCL). Census data for a variety of geographical areas are available on the *Census Summary Data System* (CSDS) for all census years since 1961. Time Series and 1986 census data are also available on CD-ROM on *CANSIM Disc*, and *1986 Census Profile*, respectively. The *CANSIM Main Base Series Directory* (3 vols.) (R050 C212CB) is a detailed guide to Time Series data. The *CANSIM Cross-Classified Table Directory* is a guide to the data on XCL. *CANSIM MiniBase* is a subset of the main CANSIM base, which contains significant data series of interest to economic researchers in Canada.

CA56 Statistics Canada. **Census Handbook / Recensement Canada.** Ottawa: Statistics Canada, 1988. 150 p.

Includes brief history of census taking, introduction to geography of the census, information on how variables are derived, how 1986 census differs from its predecessors, and on new products and services. Statistics Canada also published *Products and Services*, (1988) which describes 1986 census products available from the 100% and 20% data bases. Descriptions are to the table level. In addition the 1986 Census *Dictionary* (1988) provides definitions of concepts related to the universe, variables, geographic divisions of the 1986 census data base. A series of *User's Guides to 1986 Census Data* have been published which describe the collection, processing and validation of 1986 census data. Each *User's Guide* covers a different subject, e.g. *Industry*, *Families*, *Ethnic Origin*, etc.
R317.1 C212R

CA57 Statistics Canada. **Census of Canada, 1850/51- .** Ottawa: Statistics Canada, 1852- decennial; quinquennial.

Census data for 1986 has been issued. Data for the 1991 census will begin to be available in late 1991. Data are available in print, on microfiche, on computer tapes, and on CD-ROM (see CA55). Specialized tabulations are produced on a fee basis.
R317.1 C212P   or   CA1 BS GOVT

CA58 Statistics Canada. **Focus on Canada.** Ottawa: Statistics Canada. 1989-91.

Series of 16 profiles of Canadians, including such titles as *Canada's Seniors*; *Women and the Labour Force*; *Educational Attainment*; *Canada's Linguistic Profile*; *Canada's Farm Population*. Each separately authored report, about 35 pages in length, is based on data from the 1986 census and includes statistical data, and summary conclusion.
R317.2 C212R   or   CA1 BS98 C212 GOVT

CA59 Statistics Canada. **Historical Catalogue of Statistics Canada Publications, 1918–1980.** Ottawa: Supply and Services, 1982. 337 p.

Replaces all earlier catalogues. Lists all publications of the Dominion Bureau of Statistics and its successor Statistics Canada to December 31, 1980.
R015.71 C21GT

CA60 Statistics Canada. **Market Research Handbook,** 1975- annual.

A source of information and reference for analysis of Canadian markets. See CC23 for full entry information.

CA61 Statistics Canada. **Statistics Canada Catalogue,** 1930- . Ottawa: Statistics Canada. annual.

Name changed with 1986–1988 edition to *Current Publications Index.* Lists publications available for sale from the Publications Section; and mapping services available from the Geography Division. Also lists publicly available micro-data files. Includes author/title and subject indexes. Available online and on CD-ROM as *StatCan Reference.* Over 500 popular titles selected from the *Catalogue* are listed annually in *Statistics Canada Publications List* (1990-); arranged by subject with no indexing.
R015.71 C21

Great Britain

CA62 **British Historical Statistics.** Comp. by R.B. Mitchell. New York: Cambridge University Press, 1988. 886 p.

Replaces *Abstract of British Historical Statistics* (1962), and *Second Abstract...* (1971). Includes economic statistics.
HA1134 M58 GOVT

CA63 Great Britain. Central Statistical Office. **Annual Abstract of Statistics,** 1840- . London: HMSO, 1854- . annual.

Contains the most often requested time series for vital statistics, social and economic topics; supplemented by *Monthly Digest of Statistics.*

R314.2 G786A(1982) or UK1 CB40 S71 GOVT

United States

CA64 **American Statistics Index,** 1973- . Bethesda, MD: Congressional Information Service. monthly, with annual cumulation.

Multi-year cumulative indexes: *1974–1979, 1980–1984, 1985–1988.* Indexes and abstracts the contents of federal government publications of all types, which contain statistics. Each monthly issue contains an index volume and a separately bound abstract volume, with data indexed by subject, name, type of data breakdown, agency report number. Most publications indexed are available from publisher on microfiche. Available online, and on CD-ROM or *Statistical Masterfile.* For information on statistical organizations of U.S. government, see *Federal Statistical Directory* (AM100).
Z7554 U5A54 GOVT

CA65 **Statistical Abstract of the United States,** 1878- . Washington: Bureau of the Census, 1879- . annual.

Comprehensive data book for statistics on social, political, and economic organisations of the United States, with international statistics included as well. Sources are given for all statistics. Supplemented by *County and City Data Book* (1949- irreg.), and *State and Metropolitan Area Data Book,* (1979- irregular). Retrospective economic, geographic, political and social statistics from 1610 to 1970 can be found in *Historical Statistics of the United States Colonial Times to 1970* , (1975, 2 volumes (R317.3 U58HA). *Statistical Abstract* is available online on *STATPACK,* which also includes statistical information from a number of government agency publications, such as *Agricultural*

Statistics, *Area Wage Surveys*, *Survey of Current Business*, etc.
R317.3 U58S (1985)   or
US1 CM100 S71 GOVT

CA66   Statistical Reference Index, 1980- . Bethesda, MD: Congressional Information Service. monthly with annual cumulation.

Statistics produced by private sector organisations and state governments in the U.S. are indexed and abstracted. Covers publications of associations, institutes, business and commercial publishers, state government agencies, research centres and universities. Available online, and on CD-ROM on *Statistical Masterfile*. Most documents indexed can be obtained from publisher on microfiche.

CA67   United States. Bureau of the Census. **Census Catalog and Guide,** 1947- . Washington: GPO. annual.

Name changed from *Bureau of the Census Catalog* in 1985. Cumulative catalogue describing all products of the Census Bureau issued since 1980. Supplemented by *Monthly Product Announcements*. For a retrospective bibliography, see *Bureau of the Census Catalog of Publications: 1790–1972*, (GPO, 1974), in 2 parts: 1, *1790–1945*; 2, *1945–1972*.
US1 CM100 C21 GOVT

Urban Materials and Information

CA68   Artibise, Alan F.J. and Gilbert A. Stelter **Canada's Urban Past: A Bibliography to 1980 and Guide to Canadian Urban Studies.** Vancouver: University of British Columbia Press, 1981. 396 p.

Includes over 7,000 articles, books, reports. General material by topic and specific materials by geographic areas. The "guide" section deals with research approaches and resources of all types.
Z7164 U7A77

CA69   Bannister, David and Laurie Pickup. **Urban Transport and Planning: A Bibliography with Abstracts.** London: Mansell, 1989. 354 p.

Brief abstracts arranged in broad subject areas.
Z7164 U72B36

CA70   Chandler, Tertius. **Four Thousand Years of Urban Growth: An Historical Census.** Lewiston, NY: St. David's University Press, 1987. 656 p.

Covers urban populations from 2250 B.C. to 1975. Concentrates on population estimating for ancient cities. Includes outline maps and tables, index of place names, bibliography.
HB2161 C46

CA71   Cities of the United States: A Compilation of Current Information on Economic, Cultural, Geographic, and Social Conditions.

Each volume is devoted to a different region: *The Midwest*; *The Northeast*; *The South*; *The West*. Each city is described using standard comparable data (population, history, geography, economy, transportation, health care, etc.). Gale Research has also published *Cities of the World* (4 vols, 1985) (G153.4 C57), which contains information on cultural, geographical, political conditions in the countries and cities in: Volume 1) *Africa*; Volume 2) *Western Hemisphere* (does not include U.S.); Volume 3) *Europe and the Mediterranean Middle East*; and Volume 4)

Asia, the Pacific and Asiatic Middle East. These are based on the U.S. Department of State's *Post Reports.*
HT123 C48297

CA72 Council of Planning Librarians. **CPL Bibliographies,** 1979- . Chicago: Council. 10 per year.

Continues *Exchange Bibliographies,* (1959–79), with *Comprehensive Index* (1979). Originally published irregularly. A series of bibliographies on many aspects of regional and urban planning and problems, and a wide range of related fields. Topics are international in scope.
Z5942 C682

CA73 **Index to Current Urban Documents,** 1972- . Westport, CT: Greenwood Press. quarterly with annual cumulation.

Indexes local government documents issued by the largest cities, and counties in the U.S., and by 24 Canadian cities in 10 provinces. Geographical organization, with subject index. Documents indexed are available from *Urban Documents Microfiche Collection* (Greenwood Press).
Z7164 L8I5 GOVT

CA74 **Index to Municipal Data.** Ottawa: Statistics Canada, 1983. 553 p.

Lists Statistics Canada sources of published data for Canadian municipalities in 2 parts, those over 10,000 in population, and those under 10,000. Includes an annotated list of sources, plus a guide to unpublished data and a bibliography of related reference sources.
CA1 BS11 C515 GOVT

CA75 **Microlog: Canadian Research Index,** 1979- monthly.

Indexes and abstracts publications from all levels of government, including urban, regional, etc. See AM31 for full entry information.

CA76 **The Municipal Year Book,** 1934- . Washington: International City Management Association. annual.

Volumes include five year cumulative indexes. "The authoritative source book of urban data and development." Profiles individual cities, counties in the U.S. Covers intergovernmental relations, salaries of officials, directory and information sources, statistical tables. *Reference* section includes sources of information, directories, etc. Information on cities in the U.K. can be found in *Municipal Year Book and Public Service Directory* (London, Municipal Journal) (JS3003 M82).
R352.073 M966M   or   JS301 M8

CA77 **Sage Urban Studies Abstracts,** 1973- . Beverly Hills, CA: Sage. quarterly with annual cumulation.

Informative abstracts of a wide range of books, articles, pamphlets, government documents, speeches, and reports on all areas of urban studies, arranged by subject. Indexed. Sage also publishes the *Urban Affairs Annual Reviews,* (1967-) (HT108 U7O3).
HT51 S24

CA78 Sayegh, Kamal. **Housing: A Multi-Disciplinary Dictionary.** Ottawa: ABCD Academy Books, 1987. 626 p.

Comprehensive dictionary with definitions of 28,000 terms. Designed to assist users ranging from tenants and sociologists, to contractors, architects, politicians.
HD7287 S29

CA79 Urban and Regional References, 1945-1969. 7th ed. Ottawa: Canadian Council on Urban and Regional Research, 1970. 796 p. *Supplement*(s) 1970-75.

Now of historical interest only. Covers general sources; physical, population, and social characteristics; urban regional settlement and development; economics, transportation and communication; government and administration. Subject arrangement; author, geographic indexes. R301.36A AC212U7

CB   ECONOMICS

For reference sources related to finance and banking see *Business*, Section CC.

Bibliographies and Guides to the Literature

CB1 **Business and Economics Books, 1876–1983.** 1983. 4 vols. See CC7 for full entry information.

CB2 **Canadian Business and Economics: A Guide to Sources of Information,** 1984. New edition forthcoming December 1991. See CC6 for full entry.

CB3 **Economic Books Current Selections,** 1974– . Pittsburgh, PA: Dept. of Economics, University of Pittsburgh. quarterly.

An annotated list of all English language economics books, arranged by subject. Author index.
Z7164 E2E3

CB4 **Economics and Business: An International Annotated Bibliography,** 1984 (vol. 29)- . New York: Gordon and Breach. quarterly.

Formerly *Economic Selections* (1964-1984) (Pittsburgh University, Dept. of Economics), which superseded *Economics Library Selection* (1954-1962) (Johns Hopkins University). Entries are arranged under subject and include short, non-evaluative annotations. Includes author index. Frequent time lag in publication.
Z7164 E2E3243

CB5 **Economics Working Papers: A Bibliography,** 1973– . Ed. by J. Fletcher. Dobbs Ferry, NY: TRANS-Media. semi-annual.

An international bibliography which provides subject coverage to advanced drafts of unpublished papers from over 400 universities or other institutions around the world in the fields of economics, management and business, demography, urban studies, and politics. Contains subject, series, and author indexes. Microforms of the papers are available for about half the drafts.
Z7164 E2E33 BUSI

CB6 Fletcher, John. **Information Sources in Economics.** 2d ed. Stoneham, MA: Butterworths, 1984. 382 p.

Provides an overview of the literature, including literature searching; reference tools; unpublished materials; databases and databanks; British, American, and international official publications; statistics and a wide range of

economics topics.
Z7164 E2U8

CB7 International Bibliography of Economics / Bibliographie internationale de science économique, 1952– . London: Tavistock Publications. annual.

Classified bibliography of books, articles, research reports. Author index; separate English and French subject indexes. *Thematic List of Descriptors: Economics* (Routledge, 1989) (Z7164 E2I583) has been compiled for use when searching the *IBSS*. Available online as part of Unesco's *International Bibliography of the Social Sciences* (CA2).
Z7164 E2I58

CB8 The Journal of Economic Literature, 1963– . Nashville, TN: American Economic Association. quarterly.

A review and current awareness journal. Book reviews; annotated list of new books; contents of current journals with subject index to articles, and selected abstracts with author index to subject list. Available online. Bibliographic sections available on CD-ROM on *EconLit*.
HB1 J676

CB9 New Practical Guide to Canadian Political Economy, 1985.

Topics include resources, finance, foreign investments, and industrial and commerical policy. See CD10 for full entry information.

Abstracts and Indexes

CB10 Index of Economic Articles in Journals and Collective Volumes, 1961- . 2 vols. Nashville, TN: American Economic Association. annual with 3-6 year publication delay.

(Vol. 29/1987, 1990). Lists articles published in English or with English summaries in over 300 international economic journals and collective volumes. Volume 1 contains over 300 subject categories with a subject guide; Volume 2 is an alphabetical author index. No cumulative index. Updated by the *Journal of Economic Literature*. Available online and on CD-ROM as *EconLit*.
Z7164 E2 I45

Other abstracts and indexes which contain information related to economics are: **Business Periodicals Index,** (CC17), **Canadian Business Index,** (CC18), and **PAIS,** (AF15).

Encyclopedias and Dictionaries

CB11 Block, Walter and Michael Walker. **Lexicon of Economic Thought.** Vancouver: Fraser Institute, 1989. 390 p.

One to two page articles and economic analyses on 176 socioeconomic topics from a Canadian perspective. Includes Sunday shopping, airline deregulation, tax freedom day.
HB61 W34

CB12 Crane, David. **A Dictionary of Canadian Economics.** Edmonton: Hurtig, 1980. 372 p.

Intended as "a convenient source of information about our economic institutions, about traditional economic and business terms and about the ideas of major economists and schools of economic thought."
HC112 C7

CB13 **Dictionary of Business and Economics**, 1984. See CC34 for full entry.

CB14 **Encyclopedia of Economics.** Ed. by Douglas Greenwald. New York: McGraw-Hill Book Company, 1982. 1070 p.
  Detailed entries with references for further reading. Name and subject index.
HB61 E55 SIGR

CB15 Gilpin, Alan. **Dictionary of Economics and Financial Markets.** 5th ed. London: Butterworths, 1986. 245 p.
  Primarily for students and economists. A British slant.
HB61 G47

CB16 **The McGraw-Hill Dictionary of Modern Economics: A Handbook of Terms and Organizations.** 3d ed. New York: McGraw-Hill, 1983. 632 p.
  Provides definitions of 1,425 frequently used terms, and descriptions of 235 organizations and agencies.
R330.3 M147 (1965)   or   HB61 M3

CB17 **The MIT Dictionary of Modern Economics.** 3d ed. Ed. by David W. Pearce. Cambridge, MA: MIT Press, 1986. 462 p.
  2,600 terms defined. Useful for researchers and students.
HB61 M2

CB18 **The New Palgrave: A Dictionary of Economics.** 4 vols. Ed. by John Eatwell, Murray Milgate and Peter Newman. New York: Stockton Press, 1988.
  Update of a classic work, *Dictionary of Political Economy* by R.H.I. Palgrave. Biographies of well-known economists, and topics such as money, arbitrage, interest rates and option pricing.
HB61 P17

CB19 **Who's Who in Economics: A Biographical Dictionary of Major Economists 1700–1986.** 2d ed. Ed. by Mark Blaug. Cambridge, MA: MIT Press, 1986. 935 p.
  Over 1,400 entries for economists, both living and deceased, and from around the world, are provided. Brief entries include birth/death dates, current/previous position, degrees, awards, fields of interest, and contributions. Indexed by specialty and by country of residence.
HB76 W4

Statistical Handbooks

See also Statistical Information listed in Section CA, *Social Sciences*, CA31 - CA67.

CB20 Moore, Geoffrey H. and Melita H. Moore. **International Economic Indicators: A Sourcebook.** Westport, CT: Greenwood Press, 1985. 372 p.
  Description of economic indicators available in Canada, U.S., Japan, and OECD countries.
HC59 M56716 GOVT

CB21 **World Economic Data.** 2d ed. Ed. by Rose Schumacher. Santa Barbara, CA: ABC-Clio, 1989. 257 p.
  Statistical compendium providing extensive economic data for over 170 countries, arranged in chart form to allow for national comparisons. A section on world currency rates and conversion charts is included. Data on U.S. foreign

trade with other nations in 1986 is also provided. Based on information provided in *Kaleidoscope: Current World Database* (AF33).
HC59 W643 ROBA (1987)

CB22 World Economic Survey, 1955- . New York: United Nations. annual.
Study of the world economy in terms of growth, current policies, international trade and payments and international capital flows to developing countries.
UN2 C W52 GOVT

CB23 World Index of Economic Forecasts: Including Industry Tendency Surveys and Development Plans. 3d ed. Ed. by Robert Fildes. New York: Stockton Press, 1988. 563 p.
Guide to the use of macroeconomic forecasts; index of organizations involved with economic forecasting. Includes an annotated list of economic development plans by country.
HB3730 W66

Atlases

CB24 Historical Atlas of Canada III: Addressing the Twentieth Century, 1990.
This work is useful as an economic atlas. See CJ87 for full entry information.

CC BUSINESS

Bibliographies and Guides to the Literature

CC1 **Access Canada 1990: Micromedia's Directory of Canadian Information Sources,** 1990.

Updates the *Browning Directory of Canadian Business Information* (Browning Associates, 1987). Contains bibliographic information to sources in many subject areas, including business. See AH1 for full entry information.

CC2 Baker Library. [Harvard University. Graduate School of Business Administration]. **Harvard Business School Core Collection,** 1990– . Boston: Baker Library. annual.

Formerly *Core Collection: An Author and Subject Guide* (1969-89). Updated by *Recent Additions to Baker Library* (10/year) which also serves as a selection aid. Baker Library is the major research library for material in business, economics, business administration etc. Its *Author Title Subject Catalog* (G.K. Hall) (Z7165 C81 H248) and *First Supplement* (1974) make available the library's holdings from its beginning, before 1850, to 1974. Baker Library also published *Business Reference Sources: An Annotated Guide for Harvard Business Students* (Rev. ed. 1987) (650 AH339).
Z7164 C81 H25626 BUSI

CC3 Balachandran, M. **A Guide to Statistical Sources in Money, Banking, and Finance.** Phoenix, AZ: Oryx Press, 1988. 119 p.

Includes serial sources available in hardcopy and on database on banking and monetary statistics primarily for U.S. states and regions, but also includes foreign countries. Arrangement is geographical with publisher, subject and title indexes.
Z7164 F5B23

CC4 **Basic Business Library: Core Resources.** 2d ed. Ed. by Bernard S. Schlessinger. Phoenix, AZ: Oryx Press, 1989. 278 p.

Includes a selected core list of publications, a bibliography of literature on business reference and business libraries, and essays on business reference sources and services. Sources are evaluative.
027.69 AB311B2

CC5 **Books and Periodicals Online: A Guide to Publication Contents of Business and Legal Databases,** 1987- semi-annual.

Useful for determining what sections of journals and some books are indexed in various databases. See AB30 for full entry information.

CC6 Brown, Barbara E. **Canadian Business and Economics: A Guide to Sources of Information / Economique et commerce au Canada: Sources d'information.** Rev. ed. Ottawa: Canadian Library Association, 1984. 469 p. New edition forthcoming December 1991.

Includes over 7,000 government, nongovernment books, periodicals and services arranged by subject. Some entries are annotated. Indexed by author, title, publisher, series.
R330 AB877C2

CC7 **Business and Economics Books, 1876–1983.** 4 vols. New York: R.R. Bowker, 1983.

Comprehensive listing of over 140,000 publications from the Bowker database. Full bibliographic information; author, subject indexes.
Z7164 C81B927

CC8 **Directory of Periodicals Online: Indexed, Abstracted & Full-text, News, Law and Business,** 1985- irregular.

Alphabetical list of periodicals covering law, business and general news available online in North America. Lists publishing information and database coverage. Organized by database and by subject. See AE5 for full entry information.

CC9 **FINDEX: The Directory of Market Research Reports, Studies and Surveys,** 1979- . Bethesda, MD: Cambridge Information Group Directories. annual.

International directory listing abstracts of 12,500 published market research reports, surveys, directories, databases, etc. Arranged by industry and company. Includes title, publisher, subject, geographic and company indexes. Semi-annual updates and phone service updates available. Available online. Incorporates *The Directory of U.S. and Canadian Marketing Surveys and Services.*
Z7164 M18F5 BUSI (5th ed)

CC10 Geahigan, Priscilla C. **U.S. and Canadian Businesses, 1955 to 1987: A Bibliography.** Metuchen, NJ: Scarecrow Press, Inc., 1988. 589 p.

Bibliography of business histories arranged by industry. Includes company name, personal name and personal author indexes.
Z7164 C81G32

CC11 **Information Sources in Finance and Banking.** 2 vols. Ed. by R.G. Lester and J. Cropley. London: Bowker/Saur, 1990- in progress.

Volume 1, *Data Sources*, is a guide to published information sources in fields of banking and finance, arranged by subject. Volume 2, *Evaluating Financial Information*, forthcoming.

CC12 Land, Brian. **Sources of Information for Canadian Business.** 4th ed. Ottawa: Canadian Chamber of Commerce, 1985. 108 p.

A general overview of print and online business information sources with emphasis on Canadian content. New edition forthcoming, 1992.
R650 L253 BA4

CC13 Lavin, Michael R. **Business Information: How to Find it, How to Use it.** Phoenix, AZ: Oryx Press, 1987. 299 p.

Written for researchers, chapters provide detailed descriptions of sources, explaining how and why they are used. Topics discussed include searching Registered Trade Marks and business law sources. Includes discussion of business concepts. Similar works include *Competitor*

Intelligence: How to Get It; How to Use It (Wiley, 1985) (MTRL), and *Monitoring the Competition: Find Out What's Really Going on over There* (Wiley, 1988) (MTRL) both by Leonard Fuld.
R650 AL412B

CC14 Strauss, Diane Wheeler. **Handbook of Business Information: A Guide for Librarians, Students, and Researchers.** Englewood, CO: Libraries Unlimited, Inc., 1988. 537 p.

Range of basic reference sources, directories, periodicals and newspapers, looseleaf services, government information, statistics, vertical file material and online databases. Covers subjects of marketing; accounting; taxation; money, credit and banking; investments; stocks; bonds; mutual funds; futures and options; insurance; and real estate. Includes sample pages from various sources. American business sources are emphasized.
R330 AS912H

Abstracts, Indexes, and Databases

CC15 ABI/INFORM, 1971- . Louisville, KY: UMI/Data Courier. database. updated monthly.

ABI/INFORM, the most comprehensive of general business databases, provides detailed abstracts articles from more than 800 major international business and management journals. Used for management, administration and general business information. Available online and on CD-ROM as *ABI/INFORM ONdisc*. ONdisc provides fulltext of articles from selected journals in the index. A complementary database is *Management Contents* (1974- Information Access), which indexes conference proceedings, transactions and research reports, in addition to journals, and covers areas of corporate intelligence, labour relations, market research and business law. Available in print form as *Business Publications Index and Abstracts* (Gale Research, 1983- monthly) (HF5001 B87 ROBA 1983-85). Another database produced by Information Access is *The Business Index*, which provides citations to articles in over 1,000 popular business and legal journals, including *Barron's, Wall Street Journal*, and the business and financial sections of *The New York Times*.

CC16 The Accountants Index, 1921- . New York: American Institute of Certified Public Accountants. monthly with annual cumulation.

Provides citations to English-language periodicals, books, pamphlets, government documents and reports in accounting and related business and finance subjects. Contents reflect the changing information needs and interest of CPA's worldwide. Available online.
Z7164 C81A5

CC17 Business Periodicals Index, 1958- . New York: H.W. Wilson. monthly with annual cumulation.

Standard business index to approximately 345 business periodicals, mostly American, covering all areas of business, with executive and company information. Useful for general business and management information. Book reviews are listed separately at end of issues. Available online and on CD-ROM.
Z7164 C81 B983 BUSI

CC18 Canadian Business Index, 1975- . Toronto: Micromedia. monthly, annual cumulation.

Formerly *Canadian Business Periodicals Index*. Indexes over 170 Canadian serials in business, industry, economics, related fields.

Also indexes *Financial Post, Financial Times,* and business items in *The Globe and Mail.* Separate subject, corporate and personal name indexes. Available online and on CD-ROM on *Canadian Business and Current Affairs* (AF2). From 1991, some abstracts are included.
Z7164 C81 C242 BUSI

CC19 Canadian Statistics Index, 1985- annual.

Federal government agencies produce statistics of interest to business and industries. Particularly useful for market research, import and export statistics, etc. See CA48 for full entry information.

CC20 Index of Industrial Relations Literature, 1976– . Kingston, ON: Research Reference Library, Industrial Relations Centre, Queen's University. annual.

Emphasis on applied and policy-oriented trends and emerging issues in the broader industrial relations field.
K33 I49 Ind. LAWP

CC21 Predicasts F & S Index, 1979– . Cleveland, OH: Predicasts. weekly (U.S.); monthly; with annual cumulations.

Predicasts is a major supplier of business information in both print and electronic forms, and is regarded as the primary source for current product information, technological developments, corporate mergers and acquisitions, etc. *Predicasts F & S Indexes* are published in three sections: Europe, International, and United States. The International volumes provide citations to articles from periodicals, newspapers, trade publications and special reports, on recent business (i.e. product and industry) developments in Canada, Latin America, Africa, the Middle East, Asia and Oceania. The U.S. volume provides similar information, and is divided into two sections: *Industries and Products*, which is organized using a format similar to the Standard Industrial Classification system, and *Companies*, which is an alphabetical list of companies. A subject index is published several months after the weekly editions. Available online as *PTS F&S Indexes* (1972-). Other Predicast publications include *Predicasts Forecasts* (1980- quarterly), which cites projections for markets, products and industry in the U.S.; *PROMPT (Predicasts Overview of Markets and Technology)*; *Predi-Briefs (Cleveland)* (1961- monthly), which lists article abstracts in 29 industries; and *Predicast F & S Index of Corporate Change* (vol. 17 1981-) which covers U.S. business changes, mergers, bankruptcies, joint ventures, etc. in 1,500 business sources. Most are available online.
MTRL BU/SS

Statistical Handbooks

CC22 Canadian Markets: Complete Demographics for Canadian Urban Markets. 1925– . Toronto: Financial Post Information Service, 1986- . annual.

Name varies; formerly *Financial Post Survey of Markets*. Provides demographic and economic profiles on Canadian urban markets, buying power indices, retail sales, provincial comparisons and special features. Covers regions across Canada based on Census information. Data is supplied by Statistics Canada, Revenue Canada, Compusearch Market and Social Research Ltd, Canadian Advertising Rates and Data, and the Bureau of Broadcast Measurement.
R330.971 C212D

CC23 Statistics Canada. **Market Research Handbook / Récueil statistique des études de marche,** 1975– . Ottawa: Merchandising and Services Division, Statistics Canada. annual.

Provides statistical information and reference material useful in analyzing Canadian markets, from local to national levels. Also includes sections on Canada's position in world trade; and comparative sections on Canada with U.S.; women in the labour force; and service industry.
R330.971 C212M   or   CA1 BS63 C224 GOVT

CC24   Year Book of Labour Statistics: Retrospective Edition on Population Censuses 1945-1989. Washington: International Labour Office, 1990. 1959 p.

Contains population census data for 184 countries and territories for the period 1945-1989 which can be analyzed to determine participation of the labour force in nearly every country in the world. Data has been collected from the annual *Yearbook of Labour Statistics* (1936-) (UN9 LY21 GOVT).
HD4826 I63 O3 BUSI   or   UN9 LY22 GOVT

Handbooks

CC25   ABC Assistance to Business in Canada: Federal/ Provincial. Ottawa: Federal Business Development Bank, 1987. 409 p.

Handbook of business assistance programs available from the federal government, including a supplement for provincial programs offered by Ontario. Arranged by granting body; especially useful for small businesses. This publication will no longer be published.
MTRL BU/SS

CC26   Annual Salary Survey, 1980- . 6 vols. Vancouver: Peat Marwick, Stevenson & Kellog. annual.

Formerly *An Annual Study of Compensation Across Canada* published by Stevenson & Kellog. Contains salary ranges for clerical to CEO positions in various industries in regions across Canada. Volumes include: *Information Systems Report; Engineering & Technical Report; Executive Compensation Report; Production and Distribution Report; Administrative and Finance Report;* and *Sales & Marketing Report.*
MTRL BU/SS

CC27   Canadian Classification and Dictionary of Occupations. 7 vols. Ottawa: Employment and Immigration Canada, Occupational and Career Information Branch, 1971, with revised volumes.

The *CCDO* is a detailed guide to occupational descriptions reflecting the work performed by Canadians, indicating significant duties, educational requirements, aptitude factors, etc. Organized by Major Group (occupations defined broadly), then further subdivided with each subgroup assigned a numbered code.

Originally published in 1971, it is now available in 7 colour-coded volumes: Volume 1 (yellow) is a reprint of the 1971 work listing occupational groups that have not been revised. Volumes 2-6 contain revised occupational groups. Volume 7 (red), published annually, is the *CCDO Guide*, (R331.7 C212CC) which contains the complete index to the job and occupational titles in *CCDO*, and a list of new *CCDO* occupational descriptions.

A related source offering information on future occupational labour markets and educational requirements is *Job Futures: An Occupational Outlook* (annual, 2 vols) (R331.12409 M1J62, CA1 MI GOVT), which presents a five year overview of present and future labour market conditions in some 100 fields at the post-secondary level, and for specific occupations. Available in print, looseleaf and diskette formats.

The *Canadian Standard Industrial Classification for Companies and Enterprises 1980* published by Statistics Canada (1986) (CA1 BS12 C570 GOVT), is used by business in compiling corporation financial statistics and profits. It outlines job descriptions in 18 main industrial sectors which are associated with the production and delivery of goods and services.
CA1 M1 C11 GOVT

CC28 Cheveldayoff, Wayne. **The Business Page: How to Read It and Understand the Economy.** 2d ed. Ottawa: Deneua, 1980. 320 p.

Guide to basic economics and financial data for the general reader.
HC115 C49 BUSI

CC29 de Stricker, Ulla and Jane I. Dysart. **Business Online: A Canadian Guide.** Toronto: John Wiley in association with the Canadian Institute of Chartered Accountants, 1989.

Guide to online searching. Provides descriptions of Canadian databases and examples of how they can be used.
025.0665 D477B or HF5548.2 D48

CC30 **Handbook for Professional Managers.** Ed. by L.R. Bittel and J.E. Ramsey. New York: McGraw-Hill, 1985. 1000 p.

Intended to "provide managers with clear explanations of fundamental concepts and widely practised techniques, and specific advice about how to apply them successfully." Includes over 200 articles in 50 broad subject areas, many with bibliographies. Updates *Encyclopedia of Professional Management* (1978). Another useful source is *The Encyclopedia of Management*, by Carl Heyel (3d ed, 1982, Van Nostrand Reinhold) (HD19 H4).
HD30.15 E5

CC31 **Handbook of Grants and Subsidies of the Federal and Provincial Governments.** Farnham, PQ: Canadian Research and Publication Centre. monthly updates. looseleaf.

Consists of two looseleaf binders: federal and provincial. Provides descriptions of grants and subsidies available for private enterprise, including contact names, and outline of requirements.
HD3646 H35 AERO or MTRL BU/SS

CC32 **McGoldrick's Canadian Customs Tariff "Harmonized System",** 69th ed. 1961- . Montreal: McMullin. annual.

Provides customs, tariffs, rates of duty and general customs information for Canada. Continues *McGoldrick's Canadian Customs & Excise Tariff*.
HJ6092 A6M322

CC33 Monty, Vivienne. **The Canadian Small Business Handbook.** Don Mills, ON: CCH Canadian, 1985. 152 p.

Guide to establishing and running a small business. Includes resource material for small business. New edition available shortly.
R658.022 M814C or HD62.7 M65 Ref BUSI

Encyclopedias and Dictionaries

CC34 Ammer, C. and D. Ammer. **Dictionary of Business and Economics.** Rev. and expanded. New York: Free Press, 1984. 507 p.

Intended for the general reader as well as the student; covers a broad range of terms and concepts.
HB61 A53

CC35 Encyclopedia of Banking and Finance. 9th ed. rev. and exp. Ed. by Glenn G. Munn. Rolling Meadows, IL: Bankers Publishings, 1991. 1097 p.

Classic encyclopedia of banking and finance, providing definitions of banking, finance and related insurance terms, with illustrations of usage. Also includes lengthly articles on banking and finance topics. Includes bibliographies.
HG151 M8 BUSI (8th ed, 1983)

CC36 Fitch, Thomas P. **Dictionary of Banking Terms.** Hauppauge, NY: Barron's Educational Series, 1990. 698 p.

Traditional terms and recent changes in investment and commercial banking terminology are reflected in this dictionary. Cross-referenced, with a list of abbreviations and acronyms.
HG151 F57 SCAR

CC37 Troy, Leo. **Key Business Ratios,** 1963- . Toronto: Dun & Bradstreet Canada. annual.

Provides operating and financial averages for Canadian corporations comparing ratios across industries. Similar to the annual American Dun & Bradstreet's *Industry Norms and Key Business Ratios*, Robert Morris Associate's *Annual Statement Studies*, and the *Almanac of Business and Industrial Financial Ratios* (Prentice-Hall) (HF5681 R25A5 BUSI).
HD2807 K4 ERIN

Directories

Canada

CC38 The Blue Book of Canadian Business, 1976– . Toronto: Canadian Newspaper Services International. annual.

Standard reference source for information and data on major Canadian businesses. Section 1 profiles over 100 leading public and private Canadian companies in all areas; Section 2 ranks major companies in terms of sales, assets, net income, advertising expenses, etc; and Section 3 offers current information on companies listed in the directory, including address, ownership and legal structure, size, nature of business, key executives.
R658.1145 B658B or HD2808 B6

CC39 Canadian Key Business Directory, 1974– . Toronto: Dun & Bradstreet Canada. annual.

A listing of 20,000 companies with $1 million or more net worth, $10 million plus sales, or 100 or more employees. Dun & Bradstreet also publish *Guide to Canadian Manufacturers* (1979–) (T12.5 C2G84 BUSI) which lists market information on 10,000 manufacturing companies. Current information for more than 357,000 public and private companies in Canada in all industry sectors is available online through *Canadian Dun's Market Identifiers (CDMI)*.
HF 5071 C38 O2

CC40 Canadian Marketing Goldbook, 1989- . Toronto: Goldbook Productions. annual.

Canada's national guide to services and suppliers for the communications industry. Over 20,000 current listings of company names,

addresses, and telephone numbers most frequently called by marketing professionals.
HF5415.12 C35C337

CC41   Canadian Mines Handbook, 1931– .
Willowdale, ON: International Press Publications. annual.

Includes 2,500 mining companies, listing stock exchange information, company information, comments on operations and financial conditions. Also includes a list of producing mines, conversion tables, mineral production exports, list of producers of metals and minerals, and Canadian mining area maps.
HG5159 M4C302 BUSI

CC42   Canadian Trade Index, 1900– .
Toronto: Canadian Manufacturers' Association. annual.

Directory of Canadian manufacturers, arranged in two parts: by region (by province and city), and by product, using Canadian Standard Industrial Classification code. Available online.
T12.5 C2C25 BUSI

CC43   Directory of Canadian Manufacturers, 1985– . 2 vols. Ottawa: : Business Opportunities Sourcing System, Industry, Science and Technology. annual.

Issued in 2 volumes: Volume 1, titled as above, listing manufacturing companies in Canada; and Volume 2, *Directory of Canadian Made Products,* (HF5071 D6), which lists products manufactured in Canada. Entries in volume 1 list the full name, address and telephone and fax number of the company, number of staff, sales information, and parent country, and where the company exports to. In volume 2, each product has a list of companies with address, telephone and fax numbers. Both volumes have sections on export statistics, and the data on the number of manufacturers within each product area. A list of winners in the Canada Awards for Business Excellence is also included. Updated by supplements. Another directory useful for business professionals is the BOSS *Directory of Canadian Management Consultants* (HD69 C6D57).
HF1040.9 C2D57

CC44   Directory of Labour Organizations in Canada / Répertoire des organisations de travailleurs au Canada, 1911– . Ottawa: Ministry of Labour. annual.

Includes information on national, international unions, local organizations and central congresses with names and address of principal officers. Summary statistics on union membership, etc.
HD6523 D57

CC45   The Financial Post 500: Canada's Largest Corporations, 1964– . Toronto: Financial Post. annual.

Subtitle varies. Issued as a journal each summer as a supplement to *The Financial Post. Canadian Business* issues a list of the Corporate 500 in June or July and *The Globe and Mail* issues the *Report On Business 1000* as the June issue of *Report on Business Magazine.*
HD2807 F54 SCAR

CC46   Franchise Annual: The Original Franchise Handbook and Directory, 1969– .
Lewiston, NY: Information Press. annual.

Directory of over 4,200 Canadian and U.S. franchise opportunities.
HF5429.3 F7 BUSI

CC47 Fraser's Canadian Trade Directory, 1913– . 4 vols. Toronto: Fraser's Trade Directories. annual.

Includes product classifications, trade names index and a brief list of all foreign firms with agent in Canada.
R670 F842   or   HF3223 F7

CC48 Guide to Canadian Financial Services Industry, 1986– . Toronto: Financial Times of Canada. annual.

Directory of institutions and individuals involved in the financial services industry. Corporate profiles and executive and director biographies, government regulators, industry associations, and larger accounting firms are included.
R332.102571 G946G   or   HG68 G85

CC49 KOMPASS Canada: Register of Canadian Industry and Trade, 1990– . 2 vols. Toronto: Micromedia. annual.

Includes classified listing of products and services manufactured in Canada and profiles of 15,000 Canadian companies. The KOMPASS network produces international directories for 120 countries, including: *KOMPASS U.S.; KOMPASS U.K.; KOMPASS France; KOMPASS: Register of Hong Kong Industry and Commerce*; *KOMPASS Switzerland*. Useful for establishing trade contacts and determining manufacturers of similar products within the country and around the world. Available online.
MTRL BU/SS

CC50 Report on Business Canada Company Handbook, 1989– . Toronto: InfoGlobe. annual.

Provides brief summaries, including descriptive and financial information, of the Toronto Stock Exchange 300 companies.
HF5071 R46

CC51 Scott's Industrial Series, 1958– . Oakville, ON: Scott's Industrial Directories. biennial.

In four volumes covers Atlantic region, Quebec, Ontario and Western Region. Designed for industrial sales, listing manufacturers and exporters. Main arrangement is geographical by community, with company, product indexes.
R670 S431   or   HC117 O6S223

CC52 Survey of Industrials, 1985– . Toronto: Maclean Hunter Research Bureau. annual.

Name changed from *Financial Post Survey of Industrials* with the 1985 edition. Financial information on all Canadian public industrial corporations and mutual funds. *The Financial Post Survey of Mines and Energy Resources* (R338.7622 S963S) is a similar compilation for that area.
R338 F491   or   HG5151 F53

United States

CC53 Dun & Bradstreet. **The Million Dollar Directory,** 1979– . 6 vols. Parsippany, NJ: Dun's Marketing Services. annual.

First three volumes list approximately 160,000 American companies having an indicated net worth exceeding $500,000. Volumes 4 and 5 are geographic and industry indexes. Volume 6 *Top 50,000 Companies*, lists companies with an

indicated net worth of more than $1,850,000.
HC102 D8

CC54   Dun's Directory of Service Companies. Dun's Marketing Services, 1989. 3094 p.

Provides information on 50,000 U.S. service businesses that employ 50 or more people. One of several of Dun's business reference series. Others include: *Dun's Industrial Guide*; *Dun's Europa*; *Dun's Consultants Directory*.

CC55   Moody's Bank & Finance Manual, 1955– . New York: Moody's Investors Services. annual.   Supplement: *News Reports*. semi-weekly.

One of the many services from Moody's. Other manuals are *Industrials* (1954-); *OTC Industrials* (1970-); *Municipal and Government* (1955-); *Public Utility* (1954-); and *Transportation* (1954-). Entries have a brief history of company, description of plants and products, list of officers, financial information (balance sheets, dividends). Available online and on CD-ROM.
R332.6 M817 (1987)   or   HG4961 M65

CC56   Standard & Poor's Register of Corporations, Directors and Executives, 1928– . 3 vols. New York: Standard & Poor's. annual. cumulative *Supplement* 3 times a year.

Canadian and U.S. coverage. Volume 1 lists 45,000 U.S. and Canadian businesses, including address and telephone, principal officers, bank and law firms retained, SIC codes for products and services, annual sales, number of employees, and the exchange listed on (if public company). Volume 2 contains biographical information on officers, directors and trustees of businesses listed in Volume 1. Volume 3 includes SIC Codes indexes, geographical indexes and a corporate family index. Complements, but does not overlap, *Million Dollar Directory* (CC53) or *Thomas Register* (CC57). Available online and on CD-ROM as part of *Standard & Poor's Corporations*.
HG4057 A43

CC57   Thomas Register of American Manufacturers and Thomas Register Catalog File, 1905– . 25 vols. New York: Thomas. annual.

The standard American buyer's guide providing information on more than 50,000 classes of products made in U.S. and Canada, the businesses that make them, and the locations of production. Over 152,000 public and private companies are listed. The multi-volume set is divided into volumes covering products and services, profiles, and catalogs of companies. Available online and on CD-ROM.
R670 T463T   or   T12 T6

CC58   Ward's Business Directory of U.S. Private & Public Companies, 1989- . 3 vols. Detroit: Gale Research. annual

Formerly *Ward's Business Directory*, revised in a new format to include over 92,000 U.S. private and public companies. Arranged in 3 volumes: Volume 1: Over 11.5 million in sales; Volume 2: From .5 to 11.5 million in sales; Volume 3: Ranked by industry. For information on private companies, another source is *Macmillan Directory of Leading Private Companies* (4th ed, 1989, National Register Publishing), which lists over 4,300 large private parent companies in the U.S.
R338 W266W

*   *   *   *

International

CC59 Bankers Almanac and Yearbook, 1844- . 3 vols. London: U.K: Thomas Skinner. annual.

Standard work for information about international banks, listed by country. Emphasis on British banks. Another standard directory is *Polk's World Bank Directory* (1895-, 2 parts, Nashville), which covers U.S. and foreign banks with branches in the U.S.
R332.1025 B218B   or   HG1536 B3

CC60 Business Organizations, Agencies, and Publications Directory. 5th ed. Ed. by Sandra MacRitchie. Detroit: Gale Research, 1990. 1231 p.

Contains more than 23,500 entries of business publications, organizations, and agencies that promote, coordinate, and service business and industry worldwide. Expanded international coverage.
MTRL BU/SS

CC61 Directory of Corporate Affiliations. 1973- . Wilmette, IL: National Register Publishing. annual.

Provides corporate relationship data for over 6,000 parent companies and over 80,000 affiliates and subsidiaries from all over the world. More than 40% of database covers non-U.S. companies. Available online.
R658.1146 D598D (1987)   or   HG4057 A22

CC62 Directory of [year] Japanese-Affiliated Companies in USA & Canada, 1969- . Tokyo: JETRO; distr. Detroit: Gale Research. triennial.

(1991-92 edition, 1991). JETRO (Japan External Trade Association) publishes this work, which includes some 6,900 corporations and restaurants in North America. Includes name of business, parent company, nature of operation, address and fax numbers, executives, etc. Detailed indexed and appendices.

CC63 International Directory of Company Histories. 5 vols. London: St. James, 1989- in progress.

When completed, the five volumes will cover some 1,200 major businesses (sales of over $2 billion U.S.) from North and South America, Australia, Europe, and Asia. Volume 1 (1989) covered businesses relating to "Advertising - Drugs"; Volume 2 (1990) "Electronics - Food". Provides name, address, public/private, detailed company history.
HD2721 I57

CC64 Who Owns Whom, 1958- . 4 vols. in 6. London: Dun & Bradstreet International. annual.

Provides company connections, subsidiaries, parent companies, nationalized industries and state holding companies. Volumes for United Kingdon & Republic of Ireland, Continental Europe, North America, Australia and the Far East.
R658.1146 W678W   or   HG4271 Z5W5

Biographical Sources

CC65 The Financial Post Directory of Directors, 1930– . Toronto: Financial Post. annual.
   Lists directors, executives with their positions, directorships, and addresses for Canadian companies.
HG4090 Z5D5

CC66 Who's Who in Canada, 1910- biennial.
   Includes Canadian business leaders, usually with portraits. See AL35 for full entry information.

CC67 Who's Who in Canadian Finance 1979/80– . Toronto: Trans-Canada Press. annual.
   Brief biographical information on Canada's top financial executives (numbering over 5,500) in financial institutions, banks and other companies. Appendices list professional bodies and associations, and sectoral rankings by size of companies for financial industries. A similar source is *Who's Who in Canadian Business* (1980-, International Press) (HF5071 W5). Financial executive information can also be found in the annual *Directory of Canadian Chartered Accountants* (Canadian Institute of Chartered Accountants, 1949-) (HF5616 C2D8).
HG68 W64

CC68 Who's Who in Finance and Industry, 1936– . Chicago: Marquis. biennial.
   Comprehensive coverage of 21,000 North American and international professionals who are currently active and well-known in business.
R920.3 W927S   or   HF3023 A2W5

Business Service Publications

CC69   Canadian companies such as *CCH Canadian Ltd, Richard de Boo, Canada Law Book*, and *Carswell* publish looseleaf legal publications such as *Canadian Tax Reporter* (LAWL) and *Business Law Reports* (LAWL). Consolidation is occurring since *Thomson Publications* has purchased both *Richard de Boo* and *Carswell*.

CC70 Consumer and Corporate Affairs Microfiche, Ottawa: Canada. Department of Consumer and Corporate Affairs. weekly.
   Annual reports on microfiche for all federally incorporated companies with sales greater than $25 million or assets greater than $15 million.
MTRL BU/SS

CC71 Corporate and Industry Research Reports (CIRR), 1990- . New York: R.R. Bowker. microfiche service.
   Provides access to more than 30,000 corporate and economic reports on some 10,000 American companies, 1,000 foreign companies, 5,000 products or brands, and over 610 industries worldwide. Prepared by economists and analysts from 68 securities and investment firms. Articles from 300 periodicals are also included. An index to the microfiche reports are available in print in the quarterly *CIRR Index*, and abstracts and indexes are available online and on CD-ROM.

CC72 Dun & Bradstreet of Canada. **Reference Book,** 1859– . Toronto: Dun & Bradstreet. biennial.
   Credit rating guide to Canadian companies; arranged by province, by city, by company

name, "for confidential use of subscribers [to Dun & Bradstreet] only."

CC73   Financial Post Corporation Service, 1929– . Toronto: Maclean Hunter. annual.

Card service for investment information on Canadian securities. Financial Post also has online databases for Canadian corporate data, dividends, mutual funds, securities, stock profiles, and bonds.
HD2809 F56 BUSI

CC74   Insider: Canadian Companies, Toronto: Micromedia. weekly. microfiche.

Microfiche subscription service for reports filed with the U.S. Securities Exchange Commission by some 3,000 companies listed on the Toronto Stock Exchange. *Disclosure: U.S. Companies* (Distributed by Micromedia) is a service for reports of U.S. corporations.

Consumer Information

CC75   Canadian Consumer, 1971- . Ottawa: Consumer's Association. monthly.

Provides consumer product information and consumer related information of interest to Canadians. French edition called *Le consommateur canadien*.
MTRL BU/SS

CC76   Consumer Reports, 1936- . Mount Vernon, NY: Consumers Union. monthly.

Provides results of product tests, investigations of consumer services from automobiles and appliances to food and cleaning products. December issue is an annual buying guide. Available online and on CD-ROM from 1985.
TX335 A1C602

CC77   Consumer Sourcebook: A Subject Guide... 5th ed. Ed. by Kay Gill and Robert Wilson. Detroit: Gale Research, 1988. 473 p.

A directory and comprehensive listing of over 6,200 government organizations, information centers, clearinghouses, associations and institutions which have print sources of information available for consumer protection and guidance. Arranged by subject category with a master name and keyword index. Company and trade names are now covered in Gale's *Trade Names Dictionary* (1986, 5th ed.) (T223 V4A22 BUSI). Gale also published *Consumer Product and Manufacturer Ratings 1961–1990* (2 vols, 1991) which has data and quality analysis for 150,000 individual consumer products.

CC78   Consumers Index to Product Evaluations and Information Sources, 1973- . Ann Arbor, MI: Pierian Press. quarterly with annual cumulation.

"Aimed at general consumer, business office and educational or library community." Indexes articles from a variety of journals, ranging from *Archery World* to *Yachting*, and including *Consumer Reports*, *Consumer's Research*. Focus is on finance, health and well-being of buyer.
MTRL BU/SS

CD   POLITICAL SCIENCE

This section covers political science and public administration, international relations, peace and disarmament, and human rights. Information on government can also be found in sections AM and AN. Section AH *Annuals, Handbooks and Directories* lists many sources which provide factual, statistical, and directory information about governments.

Bibliographies and Guides to the Literature

CD1   Foreign Affairs Bibliography: A Selected and Annotated List of Books on International Relations, 1919/32 - 1962/72. 5 vols. New York: Harper for Council on Foreign Relations, 1933–1976.

Based on bibliographies which were published in the journal, *Foreign Affairs*, with critical annotations. *Foreign Affairs 50 Year Bibliography* (Bowker, 1972) (Z65463 F74) is a selective bibliography of "outstanding" items published 1920–1970, taken from *Foreign Affairs Bibliography*, some with new annotations. Z6463 F73

CD2   Holler, Frederick L.   **Information Sources of Political Science.** 4th ed. Santa Barbara, CA: ABC-Clio, 1986. 417 p.

Includes annotated entries on more than 2,400 bibliographies and reference works in political science.   Part 1 offers a political reference theory which provides a conceptual framework for identifying and accessing political science information. Part 2 covers reference sources by type and by subject. Arranged in seven sections: general reference, social sciences, American government, politics and public law, international relations and organizations, comparative and area studies of politics and government, political theory and public administration. Indexed by author, title, subject, and type of reference work. *Political Science: A Guide to Reference and Information Sources* by Henry E. York (Libraries Unlimited, 1990) (R320 AY61P) is less

comprehensive, concentrating on material published between 1980 and 1987.
Z7161 H64

CD3 Information Sources in Politics and Political Science: A Survey Worldwide. Ed. by Dermont Englefield and Gavin Drewry. London: Butterworths, 1984. 509 p.

Includes 24 bibliographic essays citing English language works. British emphasis with a global scope. Subject index.
Z7161 I526

CD4 International Bibliography of Political Science / Bibliographie internationale de science politique, 1953- . Paris: Unesco. annual.

Classified bibliography of books and articles, with worldwide coverage focusing on political science, political thought, government and public administration, government process, international relations, and area studies. Selective coverage of 2,000 journals. Available online as part of Unesco's *International Bibliography of the Social Sciences*, (CA2).
Z7163 I64

CD5 Martin, Daniel W. **The Guide to the Foundations of Public Administration.** New York: Marcel Dekker, 1989. 454 p.

Bibliographical essays attempt to put works discussed into a context. Covers mostly American works and American public administration.

Public Administration: A Bibliographic Guide to the Literature, by Howard E. McCurdy (Dekker, 1986) (Z7164 A2M29 ROBA) is useful as an orientation to the literature, listing about 12,000 frequently cited titles in 33 specialized areas of study within public administration, emphasizing theories and concepts.
Z7164 A2M27

Canada

CD6 A Bibliography of Works on Canadian Foreign Relations, 1945–1970. Comp. by Donald M. Page. Toronto: Canadian Institute of International Relations, [1973]. 442 p. *Supplement*(s): *1971–1975* (1977); *1976–1980* (1982). *1981–1985* (1987).

Beginning 1976-, edited by Jane R. Barrett, with Jane Beaumont. Covers literature of, and about, the period 1945–1970. Supplements bring date of coverage forward. Organized by broad subject area, with name and subject indexes. No annotations. Includes Canadian and foreign monographs, articles, theses, research papers, government publications, conference papers, and selected departmental press releases. Beginning 1980, available online as *Canadian Foreign Relations CFR* (1980-) on *Canadian Business and Current Affairs* (AF2).
Z6465 C2P3

CD7 Canadian Public Administration: Bibliography / Administration publique canadienne: bibliographie. Comp. by W. E. Grasham, and Julien Germain. Toronto: Institute of Public Administration of Canada, 1972. 261 p. *Supplement*(s) published every 3 or 4 years, 1971- .

Supplement 5 1983–85 (1990), edited by V.

Segsworth, and J. M. Alain. Includes books, articles, theses, government publications in public administration, broadly defined. Topical arrangement.
Z7165 C2G72

CD8 **Contemporary Canadian Politics: An Annotated Bibliography, 1970–1987.** Comp. by Gregory Mahler. Westport, CT: Greenwood Press, 1988. 400 p.

Wide ranging bibliography of 3,738 books, articles, and government publications, published between 1970 and 1987, which are concerned with contemporary political issues. Some entries briefly annotated.
Z7165 C2M28

CD9 Heggie, Grace F. **Canadian Political Parties, 1867–1968: A Historical Bibliography.** Toronto: Macmillan, 1977. 603 p.

Includes 8,850 annotated references for popular and scholarly works, published before 1970, on the development of federal politics. Peter Weinrich's *Social Protest from the Left in Canada, 1870–1970*, (University of Toronto Press, 1982) (Z1387 S66W44), attempts to cover all publications of the CCF, NDP, Communist, Socialist, and labour parties, trade unions and various movements.
Z7165 C2H4

CD10 **The New Practical Guide to Canadian Political Economy.** Ed. by Daniel Drache, and Wallace Clement. Toronto: James Lorimer, 1985. 243 p.

Bibliographical essay, followed by bibliographies of books and articles arranged topically. Topics covered include resources and staples, women, Quebec, class, multinationals, provinces and regions, culture and ideology, etc. Author index.
Z7165 C2C53

CD11 **Theses in Canadian Political Studies / Thèses canadiennes en science politique.** Kingston, ON: Canadian Political Science Association, 1970.

Supplements, entitled *Theses in Canadian Political Science*, bring coverage to 1985/87- . Includes theses completed and in progress at Canadian and foreign universities. A supplement of the *Canadian Journal of Political Science*.
320.971 C212   or   Z7161 T44

Abstracts and Indexes

CD12 **ABC POL SCI: Advanced Bibliography of Contents: Political Science and Government,** 1969- . Santa Barbara, CA: ABC-Clio. 5 issues a year. annual cumulative author and subject index; quinquennial cumulative indexes.

Index, Volumes 1-15 cover 1969-1983. Provides contents pages from about 300 journals. Permuted title and author indexes in each issue. Contents pages of political science journals can also be found in *Current Contents: Social and Behavioral Sciences* (CA8)
Z7163 A13 (1969–1986)   ROBA

CD13 **Combined Retrospective Index to Journals in Political Science, 1886–1974.** 8 vols. Arlington, VA: Carrolllton Press, 1978.

Indexes 15,000 articles from mostly English language journals, in the areas of political science, sociology, and history. Volume 1 covers international affairs and organizations, laws, trade and finance; Volume 2 covers methodology and theoretical approaches; Volumes 3 to 6 cover public administration. Arrangement by keyword, with author index in Volumes 7 and 8.

CD14 International Political Science Abstracts / Documentation politique internationale, 1951- . Paris: International Political Science Association. bimonthly.

Frequency varies. Published under the auspices of the International Social Science Council in cooperation with the International Committee for Social Science Documentation and with the financial support of Unesco. Selective, authoritative source which provides abstracts of scholarly and significant books, reports, and articles from 600 journals, produced worldwide. Titles translated into English or French, abstracts in French for all but English language articles. Subject index in each issue. Annual author and cumulated subject indexes. Usually published about three years after date of coverage.
JA36 I5

CD15 Political Science Abstracts, Annual Supplement, 1980- . New York: IFI/Plenum. annual.

Continues *Universal Reference System: Political Science*, (13 vols. in 36, 1967-1979, Princeton Research) (Z6461 U663 ROBA), which was a comprehensive index to books articles pamphlets, with each volume covering a different subject. Each issue of *Political Science Abstracts* briefly abstracts about 10,000 books and articles annually. Subject, author indexes.
Z6461 U6632 (1980–1986) ROBA

CD16 PAIS International in Print, 1991- . monthly.

Continues *Public Affairs Information Service Bulletin* (1915–1980) and *PAIS Foreign Language Index* (1968/71–1990). Covers public administration, international affairs. See AF15 for full entry information.

CD17 Rohn, Peter H. **World Treaty Index.** 2d ed. 5 vols. Santa Barbara, CA: ABC-Clio, 1984.

Indexes more than 44,500 bilateral and multilateral treaties signed by 120 countries since 1900. Provides names of signatories, dates, subject and language, and citation to location of full text. Indexed by names of parties, subject. Volume 1, *Reference Volume*, includes introduction, thesaurus, and *Treaty Profiles* which provide a statistical analysis of treaties. For descriptions of treaties in specific subject areas (e.g. disarmament, international economic cooperation, etc.) see *Treaties and Alliances of the World* (5th ed, Gale Research, 1990) (JX4005 T72). See also *Major International Treaties Since 1945* (CD31).
JX171 R63 GOVT

CD18 Sage Public Administration Abstracts, 1974- . Beverly Hills, CA: Sage Publications. quarterly.

Selectively abstracts about 200 journals in both theoretical and practical aspects of public administration. Includes journals on comparative administration, financing and budgeting, organizational behaviour, personnel, etc. Subject and title indexes.
MTRL BU/SS

CD19 **United States Political Science Documents,** 1975- . 2 vols. Pittsburgh, PA: University of Pittsburgh. annual.

Indexes and abstracts every article in 120 scholarly American political science, and some social science, journals. Indexes about 4,000 journals annually by subject, author, journal title, proper name, and geographic location. Available online with quarterly updates.
Z7163 U58

Encyclopedias and Dictionaries

CD20 **Blackwell Encyclopedia of Political Thought.** New York: Blackwell, 1987. 570 p.

Along with *Blackwell Encyclopedia of Political Institutions* (1987) (JA61 B56), provides information on political institutions, theories, ideas. Contains both short entries and long essays, with a British emphasis. Includes bibliographies, cross references, detailed index.
JA61 B7

CD21 Chandler, Ralph C. and Jack C. Plano. **The Public Administration Dictionary.** 2d ed. Santa Barbara, CA: ABC-CLIO, 1988. 430 p.

Definitions arranged alphabetically within seven subject chapters: fundamentals of public administration, public policy, public management, bureaucracy and administrative organization, personnel administration, financial administration, public law and regulation. Indexed.
JA61 C45

CD22 Evans, Graham and Jeffrey Newnham. **The Dictionary of World Politics: A Reference Guide to Concepts, Ideas, and Institutions.** New York: Harvester Wheatsheaf, 1990. 449 p.

"A guide to terms needed to understand world politics and those likely to be found in specialized texts and journals." Not intended to be comprehensive, includes long definitions, and a select bibliography of sources referred to in definitions.
JA61 E85

CD24 McMenemy, John. **The Language of Canadian Politics: A Guide to Important Terms and Concepts.** Toronto: Wiley, 1980. 294 p.

Intended to provide "a comprehensive summary of terms and concepts in Canadian government and politics, with references to some of the current or standard academic works on these subjects."
JA61 M36

CD25 Pepermans, Raymond. **Vocabulaire de l'administration publique et de la gestion / Public Administration and Management Vocabulary.** Terminology Bulletin 194. Ottawa: Supply and Services, 1990. 775 p.

Issued by the Translation Bureau, Terminology and Linguistic Services Directorate. "Includes the terminology used in the Canadian Public Service as well as private sector terms that have become part of public administration vocabulary." Contains 7,000 entries under English terms, with French equivalents; 2,400 definitions in English or French; and a French-English glossary. Similar *Terminology Bulletins* have been issued in a wide variety of subject areas.
JA61 P47

CD26 Plano, Jack C. and Roy Olton. **The International Relations Dictionary.** 4th ed. Santa Barbara, CA: ABC-Clio, 1988. 446 p.

Dictionary of concepts, theories, specific facts, events, and institutions, designed for use by students, teachers. Includes a "guide to major concepts" and terms grouped into subject chapters and then arranged so as to link information. Includes definitions and "significance" for each term. ABC-Clio has also published a series of political dictionaries such as *The European Political Dictionary*, (1985) (JN12 R65); *The Soviet and East European Political Dictinary*, (1984); and other volumes covering the Middle East; Latin America; and Africa. The series is edited by Jack Plano, who is also the author of *The Dictionary of Political Analysis* (ABC-Clio, 1982) (JA61 P57) and *The American Political Dictionary* (7th ed, Holt, Rinehart and Winston, 1985) (JK9 P55).
JX1226 P65

CD27 Shafritz, Jay. **The Dorsey Dictionary of American Government and Politics.** Chicago: The Dorsey Press, 1988. 661 p.

Comprehensive dictionary with four thousand alphabetical entries covering national, state, or local govenment politics. Includes illustrations, photographs, lists, charts, excerpts, directory information, and bibliographic references. Appendices include the U.S. *Constitution*; and guides to federal government documents, statistical information, and online databases; and "key concepts" organized by subject. Unusual terminology used in American politics can be found in *Safire's Political Dictionary* (3d ed. Random House, 1978) (JK9 S2), which gives meanings and origins of words, with cross-references, and a name index.
JK9 S42

* * * *

Annuals, Directories, Handbooks and Atlases

International

CD28   **Europa Year Book**, 1926- 2 vols. annual.

Provides concise descriptions of nations and intergovernment organizations, and lists officials, diplomatic representatives. See AH23 for full entry information. *The International Directory of Government* (1990) (JF37 I58) is a spinoff of *Europa*. It provides directory information, including fax numbers, of national government officials and agencies for all countries.
JN1 E852

CD29   **Everyone's United Nations.** 10th Ed. New York: United Nations. 1986.

Titled *Everyman's United Nations* until 1979. Basic reference on the organization and role of the United Nations and its agencies, including peacekeeping, disarmament, human rights, international law etc. This edition focuses on 1978 to 1985, continuing the coverage in previous editions. Includes text of *United Nations Charter*, *Universal Declaration of Human Rights*, etc.
R341.13 U58E9   or   UN6 PI E87 GOVT

CD30   **Facts on File World Political Almanac.** Comp. by Chris Cook. New York: Facts on File, 1989. 453 p.

Provides factual information about national and world politics since World War II. Covers international political organizations and individual countries, with information on legislatures, constitutions, treaties, political parties, elections, etc. Provides a dictionary of political events, a

glossary of political terms, and biographies of important political figures.
D843 C5797 ROBA

CD31 Grenville, J.A.S. and Bernard Wasserstein. **The Major International Treaties since 1945: A History and Guide with Texts.** New York: Routledge, Chpaman & Hall/ London: Methuen, 1987. 528 p.

Companion volume to Grenville's *The Major International Treaties 1914–1945* (1987) (JX71 G74, GOVT). The two volumes update Grenville's earlier work, *Major International Treaties 1914–1973* (1973). See also *World Treaty Index* (CD17).
JX171 G745

CD32 **Parliaments of the World: A Comparative Reference Compendium.** 2d ed. 2 vols. Aldershot, U.K.: Gower; New York: Facts on File, 1986.

Based on comprehensive survey of 83 parliaments, conducted by the Inter-Parliamentary Union. Includes membership, rules of procedure, proceedings, committees, legislative process, budget, parliamentary libraries, etc., in a tabular arrangement.
JF511 P37

CD33 Political Handbook of the World, 1927-1970, 1975- . Binghamton, NY: CSA Publications. annual.

1982-83 and 1984-85 combined issues. Publisher varies. Published for the Council of Foreign Relations. Articles on countries give basic statistics, information on news media, government and politics. Covers political parties, including both legal and illegal revolutionary groups. Articles on intergovernmental organizations provide information on officers, membership, origin, and development.
JF37 P6

CD34 Kruschke, Earl R. and Byron M. Jackson. **The Public Policy Dictionary.** Santa Barbara, CA: ABC-Clio, 1987. 159 p.

Intended to define terms which provide a basic knowledge of the field; covers the nature, formulation, implementation, types of public policy, and evaluation of its impact. Definitions and significance provided, in U.S. context.
H97 K78

CD34 **Political Parties of the World.** 3d ed. Ed. by Alan J. Day. Chicago: St. James, 1988. 776 p.

Arranged by country, includes address, leader, orientation, date of founding, history, structure, membership, and other particulars for each political party. Appendix covers international party organizations. Indexed by names of individuals and parties. A similar work, edited by George E. DeLury, is *World Encyclopedia of Political Systems and Parties* (2d ed. Facts on File, 1987) (JA61 W67).
JF2051 D39

CD35 Statesman's Year-Book, 1864- annual.

Similar to *Europa World Year Book*, but more concise. Includes information on history, government, geography, defense, etc. of countries, with bibliography. See AH25 for full entry information.
JA 51.57

CD36 Strategic Atlas: Comparative Geopolitics of the World's Powers, 1990.
Graphical display of global political, military and economic issues from a variety of national perspectives. See AK20 for full entry information.
G1046 F1 C43413 MAPL

CD37 Worldmark Encyclopedia of the Nations, 1988.
See CJ56 for full entry information.

CD38 Worldwide Government Directory, 1983- . Bethesda, MD: Cambridge Publications. irregular
Formerly *Lambert's Worldwide Government Directory*. Covers over 170 countries, listing names, addresses etc. of officials in major ministries, departments and branches of government, heads of state, cabinet officers, in addition to general information about each country. Covers intergovernmental organizations as well. Available online.
JF37 L343

CD39 Yearbook of the United Nations, 1946/47- . New York: United Nations. Office of Public Information. annual.
Annual review with documentary references, of the activities of the U.N. and its agencies. Published about three years behind date of coverage. Updated quarterly in *U.N. Chronicle*.
R341.13 U58Y (1976) or UN6 PI Y27 GOVT

* * * *

Annuals, Directories and Handbooks

Canada

CD40 Campbell, Colin. **Canadian Political Facts, 1945-1976.** Toronto: Methuen, 1977. 151 p.
A useful compilation despite some inaccuracies.
JL78 1977 C34

CD41 Canada, the State of the Federation, 1985- . Kingston, ON: Institute of Intergovernmental Relations, Queen's University. annual.
Continues *Year in Review: Intergovernmental Relations in Canada*, which superseded *Federal Year in Review* (1978/79–1984). Annual review of federal-provincial relations in Canada and related policy issues. Arranged by topic, with an overview of the state of the relationship for the year. Includes a chronology of events, bibliography and index, and may include appendices. The topic has also been covered by Darrel R. Reid's *Bibliography of Canadian and Comparative Federalism 1980–1985* (Institute of Intergovernmental Relations, 1988) (Z7164 F4R44).
JL27 C468 GOVT

CD42 Canadian Annual Review of Politics and Public Affairs. 1960- . Toronto: University of Toronto Press. annual.
Titled *Canadian Annual Review* until 1970. Contains objective essays in two sections: *Federal Perspective* which covers parliament and politics, Ottawa and the provinces (and territories), national economy, external affairs and defence, and military and security issues; and *Provincial Perspective* which covers provincial

issues, by province. Includes obituaries, and an index of names. An earlier similar work was *Canadian Annual Review of Public Affairs, 1901-38* (35 volumes, Canadian Review Co, 1903-40) (971 C212A), which reviewed the year's events and listed Canadian books published for the year.
R971 C212AB   or   F5003 C327

CD43   The Canadian Directory of Parliament, 1867–1967. Ed. by J. K. Johnson. Ottawa: Public Archives of Canada, 1968. 731 p.
The standard biographical reference work on past members of Parliament. Brief factual information.
R920.3 C212C   or   CA1 AK68 C212   GOVT

CD44   Canadian Parliamentary Guide, 1962- annual.
Includes biographical information about federal, provincial and territorial legislators, the judiciary, diplomatic corps, commissions and boards, public service officials, and the parliamentary press gallary. Includes federal election results from 1867. See AM11 for full entry information.
JL5 A3

CD45   Canadian Representatives Abroad, 1951- . Ottawa: Supply and Services. annual.
Includes offices, office address, phone and fax numbers. Arranged by country and city. Yellow page index.
JX1729 A2A353   or   CA1 EA C161   GOVT

CD46   DeLong, Linwood. **A Guide to Canadian Diplomatic Relations 1925–1983.** Ottawa: Canadian Library Association, 1985. 58 p.

Countries with which Canada has, or has had, diplomatic relations are listed in alphabetical order. Includes information on date of recognition, establishment of relations, first Canadian mission or legations, mission closures, termination of relations, etc.
JX1729 D45   ROBA

CD47   Feigert, Frank.   **Canada Votes 1935–1988.** Durham, NC: Duke University Press, 1989. 351 p.
Supplements and verifies Howard A. Scarrow's *Canada Votes* (New Orleans, Hauser Press, 1962) (JL193 S35) which covered federal elections 1928–1958, and provincial elections 1920–1960. Feigert provides statistical results of federal elections at the national, regional and provincial/territorial levels.
JL193 A54

CD48   Guide to Canadian Ministries Since Confederation, July 1, 1867–February 1, 1982. Ottawa: Supply and Services, 1982. 326 p.
Prepared by Public Archives of Canada. Part 1: Chronological list of ministries, with alphabetical lists of departments, giving name and dates of ministers. Part 2: Appendix, an alphabetical list of ministers, with names and dates of ministries held.
R354.7104 G946G

Great Britain

CD49   Butler, David and Gareth Butler. **British Political Facts 1900-1985.** 6th ed. New York: St. Martin's Press, 1986. 536 p.
Provides basic facts and statistics on British government, including social and economic statistics. Covers national, regional and local

politics. Bibliography of major sources for research on British politics. *The Almanac of British Politics*, (3d ed., Croom Helm, 1987) profiles each parliamentary seat or constituency and provides electoral data. Arranged geographically.
DA566 B87

United States

CD50 **The Almanac of American Politics 1990.** 10th ed. Washington: National Journal, 1989. 1482 p.

Major source for current political information. Provides state-by-state and district-by-district analysis, with statistical and electoral data. Provides information on the 1988 presidential election and on the 101st Congress. First edition was 1972 and intervening editions provide a continuum of data. Available online.
JK1012 A44   GOVT

CD51 **Encyclopedia of American Political History: Studies of the Principal Movements and Ideas.** 3 vols. New York: Scribner, 1984.

Provides an overview of American politics from the beginning, including political and social issues, in long signed articles. Includes bibliographies, subject and name indexes. Information on individual political parties can be found in *Political Parties and Elections in the United States: An Encyclopedia*, edited by Sandy Maisel (Garland, 1990).
E183 E5

CD52 **Who's Who in American Politics,** 1967- .   New Yok: R.R. Bowker, 1989. biennial.

Provides biographical information on 24,000 Americans active in politics, based on questionaires completed by biographees. Bowker has published other similar biographical works such as *Who's Who in South African Politics* (3d ed, 1990) (DT779.954 G37); and *Who's Who in European Politics* (1990).
E747 W52

Peace and Disarmament

CD53 Atkins, Stephen E. **Arms Control and Disarmament, Defense and Military, International Security and Peace: An Annotated Guide to Sources, 1980-1986.** Santa Barbara, CA: ABC-CLIO, 1988. 411 p.

Annotated list of 1,596 mostly English language reference sources, and "monographs, hearings, papers, serials, and miscellaneous other materials." Does not include journal articles.
Z6464 D6A75

CD54 **Canada and International Peace and Security: A Bibliography / Le Canada, la paix et la securité internationales: une bibliographie.** Ottawa: Canadian Institute for International Peace and Security, 1990. 434 p.

Covers items published in Canada from January 1985 through December, 1989, including articles, theses, government publications, conference papers, and newsletters. Includes citations of non-Canadian works if written by Canadians or covering Canadian interests. Annual updates planned.
Z6464 Z9C23

CD55 Elliot, Jeffrey and Robert Reginald. **Arms Control, Disarmament, and Military Security Dictionary.** Santa Barbara, CA: ABC-Clio, 1989. 349 p.

Gives definitions and significance of terms which are arranged in subject areas; e.g. war and peace, military security, arms race, nuclear proliferation. Includes bibliographic notes, index.
JX1974 E47

CD56 **International Peace Directory.** Ed. by T. Woodhouse. Plymoth, U.K: Northcote, 1988. 188 p.

Covers peace movements worldwide and includes addresses, membership and publications, affiliations, function, meetings, objectives, volunteer placements, etc., if applicable. Indexed. *Peace Movements of the World* edited by Alan J. Day (Longman, 1986) (JX1905 P426) identifes more than 500 international and national peace movements. The *Canadian Peace Directory*, (Canadian Peace Alliance, 1988) (JX1905.5 C35), is "an annotated guide to more than 500 Canadian peace and disarmament organizations" (subtitle). American groups, both national and local, are listed in the *Peace Resource Book* (Ballinger, 1988) (JX1904 A152), which also includes guides to peace related literature, educational programs, and peace issues and strategies. A *World Directory of Peach Research and Training Institutions* is also available (Berg/Unesco, 1989) (JX1904.5 W67).
JX1905.5 I58

CD57 Jones, Peter. **Peacekeeping: An Annotated Bibliography.** Kingston, ON: Ronald P. Frye, 1989. 192 p.

Annotated guide to English language articles and essays published since World War II on international peacekeeping. Emphasizes Canadian materials. Arranged by subject.
Z6483 A7 J65

CD58 **Peace Research Abstracts Journal,** 1964- . Dundas, ON: Peach Research Institute. monthly.

Abstracts books and articles on many subjects relating to disarmament, peace, war, and international relations. Classified arrangement, author index in each issue. Annual author and subject indexes.
JX1901 P43

CD59 Stockholm International Peace Research Institute. **SIPRI Yearbook: World Armaments and Disarmament,** 1969- . New York: Oxford University Press. annual.

Various publishers. Until 1987, titled *World Armaments and Disarmament: The SIPRI Yearbook*. Provides information on weapons and technology, military expenditures, the arms trade, armed conflict, and developments in arms control. Includes numerous notes and references, tables and charts, chronology of events, glossary, acronyms list, etc. The *United Nations Disarmament Yearbook* (United Nations, 1966-) (UN2 B15 U55 GOVT) focuses on activities of the U.N. with respect to disarmament.
UA10 W672

CD60 **World Encyclopedia of Peace.** 4 vols. Ed. by Ervin Laszlo and Jong Youl Yoo. London: Pergamon, 1986.

Volumes 1 and 2 include alphabetically arranged articles; Volume 3 includes treaties in full, chronology of the peace movement, and bibliographical sketches of Nobel prize winners; Volume 4 contains a directory of peace institutes

and organizations, annotated list of journals, and index. Focuses on peace research and activism, covers human rights and arms control and disarmament.
JX1952 W63

Human Rights

CD61 Donnelly, Jack and Rhoda E. Howard. **International Handbook of Human Rights.** Westport, CT: Greennwood, 1987. 495 p.

Reviews human rights practices in 19 countries, including Canada, with bibliographic notes and suggested readings for each country. Also includes a selected bibliography.
JC571 I587 ROBA

CD62 Yearbook on Human Rights, 1946- . New York: United Nations. annual.

Covers all members of the United Nations and all trust territories. Provides overview on human rights in each country. Includes citations to UN documents, resolutions etc. Publication not current, and volumes appear several years after date of coverage.
UN2 A50 Y23 GOVT

CE LAW

Guides to Legal Research

CE1 Banks, Margaret A. **Using a Law Library: A Guide for Students and Lawyers in Common Law Province of Canada.** 5th ed. Toronto: Carswell, 1991. 249 p.

The most comprehensive guide to the organization and use of legal materials for all commonwealth jurisdictions. A section on computer assisted legal research is included.
340.0971 B218U4 (1985) or KF240 B3 LAW (1985)

CE2 Blackburn, Rae. **Guide to Research Using *The Canadian Abridgement*.** Toronto: Carswell, 1989. 179 p.

The Canadian Abridgement, a comprehensive system for legal research, contains digests of court and administrative tribunal decisions in the common law provinces, and decisions of federal cases decided in Quebec.
Dig. Can. LAW

CE3 **The CLIC Guide to Computer Assisted Legal Research.** Ottawa: Canadian Law Information Council, 1988/89. 153 p.

Provides detailed instruction to the three major Canadian online legal retrieval systems: *QL; CAN/LAW;* and *SOQUII*.
340.072 C738C4

CE4 Cohen, Morris L., Robert C. Berring and Kent C. Olson. **How to Find the Law.** 9th ed. St. Paul, MN: West Publishing, 1989. 570 p.

A standard guide to American legal research.
KF240 H62 LAW

CE5 Dane, Jean. **How to Use a Law Library.** 2d ed. London: Sweet & Maxwell, 1987. 274 p.

A basic guide to legal research using British materials. Another guide to legal research in the United Kingdom suitable for librarians and law students is *Legal Research in England and Wales* by John Jeffries and Christine Mishkin (Legal Information Resources, 1990) (KF240 J36 LAWR).
KF240 D36 LAW

CE6 **Encyclopedia of Legal Information Sources.** 2d ed. Ed. by Paul Wasserman. Detroit: Gale Research, 1991. 624 p.

A comprehensive bibliographic guide to approximately 19,000 citations for publications, organizations and other sources of information on 460 law related subjects. Includes live, print and electronic information sources, mostly American.
KF1 E53 LAWR

CE7 Guide to International Legal Research. Stoneham, MA: Butterworths, 1990. 400 p.

This guide was the winner of the Joseph L. Andrews Award of the American Association of Law Libraries and was first published as a double issue of *The George Washington Journal of International Law and Economics*, volume 20, numbers 1 and 2. The editorial staff have since updated the 1988 version. This is an authoritative research tool in international legal research.
JX1297 G84 LAWR

CE8 Information Sources of Law. Ed. by R.G. Logan. Boston: Butterworths Legal Publications, 1986. 370 p.

A compact introduction to print and online legal research sources written in essay format with bibliographies. Emphasis on the United Kingdom.
KF240 I53 LAWR

CE9 Jacobstein, J. Myron and Roy M. Mersky. **Fundamentals of Legal Research.** 5th ed. Westbury, NY: Foundation Press, 1990. 734 p.

Formerly *Pollack's Fundamentals of Legal Research*. Covers U.S. and Commonwealth jurisdictions.
KF240 J3 LAWR

CE10 MacEllven, Douglas. **Legal Research Handbook.** 2d ed. Toronto: Butterworths, 1986. 440 p.

A complete guide to all current sources of Canadian law.
304.072 M141L2 or KF240 M23 LAW

CE11 Raistick, D. **Lawyers' Law Books.** 2d ed. London: Professional Books, 1985. 604 p.

A practical guide to standard legal literature.
KF1 R34 LAWR

CE12 Yogis, John A., Innis M. Christie and Michael Iosipescu. **Legal Writing and Research Manual.** 3d ed. Toronto: Butterworths, 1988. 224 p.

Practical manual of primary and secondary materials, with emphasis on Canadian and English sources.
KF240 Y6 LAW

Bibliographies and Union Lists

CE13 A Bibliography of Bibliographies of Legal Materials. 4 vols. Ed. by Margaret Howell. Woodbridges, NJ: New Jersey Appellate Printing Co. Inc., 1969. *Supplement* 1972.

Based on the law collection at Rutgers University. Includes independently published bibliographies, articles and monographs with bibliographic notes, essays and references not indexed in any other source. Although dated, it is invaluable for historical research.

CE14 Bibliography of Commonwealth Law Reports. Ed. by Wallace Breem and Sally Phillips. London: Mansell Publishing, 1991. 332 p.

An enumerative bibliography of all published law report titles issued by Commonwealth jurisdictions.
K38 B74 LAWR

CE15 Books and Periodicals Online: A Guide to Publication Contents of Business and Legal Databases, 1987- semi-annual.

Lists the indexed sections in journals, books (e.g. articles, editorials, chapters, etc.). See AB30 for full entry information. See also *Directory of Periodicals Online*, (1985-), which contains a list of law journals available online in the part for *News, Law and Business*. See AE5 for full entry information.

CE16 Boult, Reynauld. **A Bibliography of Canadian Law / Bibliographie du droit canadien.** 2d ed. Ottawa: Canadian Law Information Council, 1977. 661 p. *Supplement* 1982.

A valuable search tool to access over 11,000 articles, treatises and texts dealing with all aspects of Canadian law.
R340.0971 AB764A   or   Z6458 C2B6

CE17 Checklist of Law Reports and Statutes in Canadian Law Libraries / Listes de contrôle des recueils de jurisprudence et des statuts dans les bibliothèques de droit du Canada. 4 vols. Ottawa: Resources Survey Division, National Library of Canada. 1977.

Although fourteen years out of date, these four volumes, which cover Canadian, American, U.K., and Irish Republic law reports and Canadian statutes, are still useful reference tools and comprise a union list of holdings in Canadian law libraries. Supplementation is planned.
R348 AC212C   or   Z6458 C2088 CRIM

CE18 Jenner, Catherine. **Bibliography of Legal Materials for Non-Law Librarians.** Toronto: [Ontario] Ministry of Citizenship & Culture, 1984. 158 p.

"A selected annotated list of lay legal material for Ontario Public Libraries."
R340.0971 AJ54B   or   KF1 J46 LAW

CE19 Law Books in Print: Books in English Published Throughout the World and In Print, 1957- . 6 vols. Dobbs Ferry, NY: Glanville Publishers. irregular.

(6th ed, 1990) Includes English language law books, looseleaf services, cassettes, microforms, software, CD-ROMS, court reports, published in the U.K., Western Europe, the Commonwealth, and former Commonwealth countries. Supplemented three times per year with *Law Books Published*. Also available is *International Legal Books in Print: An Annotated Bibliography 1990/91* (2 vols, Saur) (K38 I56 LAW) and *Bowker's Law Books and Serials in Print: A Multimedia Sourcebook*, (3 vols, 1990-, annual with quarterly updates) (KF1 B68 LAW), which lists over 70,000 legal resources including books, serials, microfiche, audiovisual, software, and databases. A retrospective bibliography of legal books is also published by Bowker, *Law Books, 1876–1981* (4 vols, 1981) (K38 L392 LAW).
KF1 J33 (5th, 1987) LAW

CE20 Law Books in Review, 1974- . Dobbs Ferry, NY: Glanville Publishers. quarterly with annual cumulations.

Critical reviews of new and forthcoming law books and related titles.
K33 L38 LAWP

CE21 Legal Bibliography of the British Commonwealth of Nations. 2d ed. 7 vols. Ed. by W.H. Maxwell et al. London: Sweet & Maxwell, 1955–64.

The standard bibliography of the British Commonwealth.
Z6458 G7L44

CE22 Mitchell Mary E. **Periodicals in Canadian Law Libraries: A Union List.** 1987- . 4th ed. Vancouver: University of British Columbia Law Library. Updated with microfiche supplements.
KF4 C34 Ref LAWC

Abstracts and Indexes

CE23 **Current Law Index,** 1980- . Menlo Park, CA: Information Access Corporation. monthly with annual cumulation.

Indexes over 700 legal publications. Access is provided by subject, author/title, case name and official and popular name of statutes. Book reviews are included. Available online and on CD-ROM as *Legal Resource Index*.
K33 C877

CE24 **Index to Canadian Legal Literature.** 1981- . Toronto: Carswell. quarterly with annual cumulation.

Published in association with the Canadian Association of Law Libraries and the Canadian Law Information Council. Lists "current monographs, learned articles, book reviews, case comments and annotations, government documents, and audio-visual materials on Canadian legal subjects", organized by subject in a bilingual format.
Indexes CAN LAW

CE25 **Index to Canadian Legal Periodical Literature,** 1963/65- . Montreal: Canadian Association of Law Libraries. quarterly with annual cumulation.

Indexes articles, case comments, and book reviews from 60 Canadian periodicals. Relevant cassettes and essays published in book format are also included.
K33 I52 LAWP

CE26 **Index to Foreign Legal Periodicals,** 1960- . London: Institute of Advanced Legal Studies, University of London. quarterly with annual cumulation.

This publication indexes all articles dealing with public and private international law, comparative law and municipal law of all countries, excluding the United States and Commonwealth countries.
K33 I552 LAWP

CE27 **Index to Legal Periodicals,** 1926- . New York: H.W. Wilson. monthly with annual cumulations.

Indexes 570 standard legal journals published in English from United States, Canada, Ireland, Australia, New Zealand and the United Kingdom. Available online and CD-ROM.
K33 I559 LAWP

CE28 **Index to Periodical Articles Related to Law,** 1958- . Dobbs Ferry, NY: Glanville Publishers Inc. quarterly.

Indexes all articles concerned with legal issues published internationally and which are not indexed in *Index to Legal Periodicals*. Also available is a 30 year cumulation covering 1958–1988 (4 vols, 1989).
Z6453 I64 CRIM

CE29 Legal Journals Index, 1986- . Hebden Bridge, West Yorkshire, U.K: Legal Information Resources Ltd. annual.

This index covers all journal titles published in the U.K. which are devoted to law or frequently contain articles on legal topics.
K33 L446 LAWP

Encyclopedias and Handbooks

CE30 Davis, Louis B.Z. **Canadian Constitutional Law Handbook: Leading Statements, Principles and Precedents.** Aurora, ON: Canada Law Book, 1985. 1056 p.

A reference source to Canadian constitutional law principles and related statements from 1949 to 1985.
KF4482 D38 LAW

CE31 The Legal Desk Book, 1988- . Toronto: Carswell. annual.

Formerly called *The Laywer's Desk Book* (1982-87). Provides list of resources and factual information of interest to legal researchers, including directories of courts, judges, law associations, government bodies, sources of legal information, sections on the Law Society of Upper Canada, and the legal profession, and on statutes. Reflects Ontario court reform.
KF195 ZB3 L28 LAWR

CE32 The Oxford Companion to Law. Ed. by David M. Walker. Oxford: Clarendon Press, 1980. 1366 p.

An invaluable reference tool.
K48 W34 LAWR

Dictionaries and Glossaries

CE33 Black, Henry Campbell. **Black's Law Dictionary: Definitions of the Terms and Phrases of American and English Jurisprudence, Ancient & Modern.** 6th ed. St. Paul, MN: West Publishing Co, 1990. 1657 p.

A standard dictionary for legal terms and phrases found in statutes or judicial opinions, or English words used in a legal context.
R340.03 B627 (4th ed.) or
KF156 B53 LAWR

CE34 A Concise Dictionary of Law. 2d ed. New York: Oxford University Press, 1990. 448 p.

Deals with contemporary law in England and Wales. Useful for nonlawyers. Includes over 3,400 entry articles, many of extended length.
KF156 C66 LAWR

CE35 Dictionary of Canadian Law. Toronto: Carswell / Thomson Professional Publishing Canada, 1991, 1184 p.

Comprehensive, single volume legal dictionary created from Canadian legal sources (federal and provincial statutes, legal texts). Includes over 25,000 terms, with Latin terms and maxims. Indexed.

CE36 The Dictionary of English Law. 2d ed. 2 vols. Ed. by Earl Jowitt. London: Sweet & Maxwell, 1977.

Reflects the reorganization of the British court system and remodelling of local and central government. Excludes Scottish legal terms.
KJ8757 D5

CE37 **The Encyclopedia of Words and Phrases, Legal Maxims: Canada 1825–1985.** 4th ed. 3 vols. Don Mills, ON: Richard De Boo, 1986-. loose-leaf.

Standard Canadian authority which provides meaning of words and phrases, legal and otherwise, from Canadian judicial decisions. Provides references to cases and decisions.
KF156 E5 LAWR

CE38 Goulet, Cyrille. **Collection of Definitions in Federal Statutes / Recueil des définitions des lois fédérales.** 2d ed. Ottawa: Dept. of the Secretary of State of Canada, 1989. 981 p.
KF156 G68 LAWR

CE39 **Mozley and Whiteley's Law Dictionary.** 10th ed. Ed. by R.H. Ivamy. London: Butterworths, 1988. 510 p.

Contains over 3,000 legal terms and references of past and present use, including terms used in the commercial and business world.
KF156 M6 LAWR

CE40 **Osborn's Concise Law Dictionary.** 7th ed. London: Sweet & Maxwell, 1983. 390 p.

Provides definitions to British legal terms, with reference to case law and legislation.
KF156 O8 LAWR

CE41 **Stroud's Judicial Dictionary of Words and Phrases.** 5th ed. 5 vols. London: Sweet & Maxwell, 1986.

A "dictionary of the English language ... so far as that language has received interpretation by the Judges." (preface).
KF156 S8 LAWR

Directories

CE42 **Canadian Law List,** 1951 - Aurora, ON: Canada Law Book Inc. annual.

Complete listing of lawyers in Canada. Absorbed *Carswell's Directory of Canadian Lawyers*.
KF195 ZA2C3 LAWC

CE43 **Canadian Legal Directory.** 1911- . Don Mills, ON: Richard De Boo. annual.

Annual directory of Canadian legal practictioners, judges, government officials, and academics.
KF195 ZA2C28 LAWR

CE44 **Law and Legal Information Directory.** 6th ed. 2 vols. Detroit: Gale Research, 1991.

Includes descriptions of institutions, services and facilities, organized within 25 chapters, for U.S. and international organizations, bar associations, law schools, legal periodicals, etc. Emphasis is on U.S. legal system.

CE45 **Martindale - Hubbell Law Directory,** 1931- . 8 vols. New Providence, NJ: Martindale - Hubbell. annual.

Volumes 1-7 lists attorneys and law firms in Canada and the U.S. with some international representation. Arranged geographically by state/province and alphabetically by city.

Includes brief biographical history, legal ability, and recommendations rating for each attorney, and for law firms, lists biographical information on members of the firm, areas of law practice, representative clients, and references. Also lists special services available by nonlawyer organizations, eg. banks, litigation and support services, title search companies, etc. Law schools and trademark lawyers rosters for Canada and the U.S. are included. Volume 8 consists of digests of major state laws, patent, trademark and copyright laws, international conventions, etc. Now available online and on CD-ROM. A more selective reference is *The Martindale-Hubbell Bar Register* (1917-) which lists pre-eminent law firms in the U.S. Inclusion is highly selective. A *Martindale-Hubbell Law Digest* (1991-) is also available (KF190 M3 LAWR).
KF190 M3 LAWR

Legal Systems

CE46 Gall, Gerald L. **The Canadian Legal System.** 3d ed. Toronto: Carswell, 1990. 444 p.

A standard text which is particulary useful for the select bibliographies at the end of each chapter, and a chapter on the Quebec legal system.
KF385 ZA2G3 LAW

CE47 **International Encyclopedia of Comparative Law.** 17 vols. New York: Oceana. 1971- in progress.

A major work, still in progress. Offers comparative analyses of the main issues in civil and commercial law throughout the world. Volume 2 of this encyclopedia discusses the legal systems of the world. A useful guide to the basis of the different systems of law.
K530 I62 LAWR

Statutory Materials

CE48 **Canadian Encyclopedic Digest (Ontario),** 1926- . 38 vols. Toronto: Carswell. quarterly updates.

(3d ed, 1984-) *C.E.D.* is "a complete statement of the federal laws of Canada and the provincial laws of Ontario." Includes a *Research Guide and Key*. Also available is *Canadian Encyclopedic Digest (Western)*, which covers federal and Manitoba, Alberta, Saskatchewan, and British Columbia. A shorter, 1 volume alternative to this work is *Anger's Digest of Canadian Law*, by William Anger (20th ed, 1987) (KF889 A85 LAW).
DIG CAN LAW

CE49 **Corpus Juris Secundum,** 1936- . 101 vols, in 147. St. Paul, MN: West Publishing Co., 1963-.

Subtitle reads: "A complete restatement of the entire American law as developed by all reported cases, 1658 to date." Kept up-to-date by cumulative annual parts and recompiled volumes. *General Index* (5 vols) published in 1981.
DIG US Enc LAW

CE50 **Halsbury's Laws of England.** 4th ed. 56 vols. London: Butterworths, 1973- in progress. *Annual Abridgement*, 1974-; *Cumulative Supplement* (2 vols, 1989); updated monthly.

The definitive encyclopedic treatment of the laws of England arranged in an alphabetical arrangement. Includes case law, statutues, consolidated table of cases.
DIG GB LAW

CE51 Nyberg, Cheryl. **Subject Compilations of State Laws 1988–1990: An Annotated Bibliography.** Urbana, IL: Carol Boast & Cheryl Nyberg, 1991. 595 p.

Originally published in 1981 by Carol Boast and Lynn Foster as *Subject Compilations of State Laws: Research Guide and Annotated Bibliography* (Westport, CT: Greenwood Press) and updated for 1979–1983 (1984), 1983–1985 (1986), and 1985–1988 (1989). Sources selected are from legal periodicals, looseleaf services, federal and state documents, and U.S. Supreme Court decisions.
KF1 N93 LAW

CE52 Schultz, Jon S. **Comparative Statutory Sources: U.S., Canadian, Multinational.** 3d ed. Buffalo, NY: William S. Hein, 1987. 177 p.

A comparison of statutes of multiple jurisdictions.
KF1 S35 LAW

CE53 **Updating Statutes and Regulations for all Canadian Jurisdictions.** 3d ed. Ed. by Mary Jane T. Sinclair. Ottawa: Canadian Law Information Council, 1989. 70 p.

A step-by-step guide outlining procedures required to update federal and provincial acts and regulations.
025.1734 H847H3   or   KF90 S45 LAWR

CF ANTHROPOLOGY AND ETHNOLOGY

Bibliographies, Guides to the Literature, and Catalogues

CF1 **Anthropology Journals and Serials: An Analytical Guide.** Ed. by John T. Williams. Westport, CT: Greenwood Press, 1986. 182 p.

Lists 404 currently published English-language serials with detailed annotations. Includes title, subject and geographical indexes. *Serial Publications in Anthropology* (2d ed, Redgrave, 1982) (Z5112 L53) provides publishing information on over 4,000 titles, but does not provide annotations.
Z5112 W54

CF2 Brown, Samuel R. **Finding the Source in Sociology and Anthropology: A Thesaurus-Index to the Reference Collection.** Westport, CT: Greenwood, 1987. 269 p.

A guide to 586 reference sources. Entries are unannotated, but are arranged by subject. Includes a thesaurus/index.
Z7164 S68 B78 ROBA

CF3 Gravel, Pierre Bettez. **Anthropological Fieldwork: An Annotated Bibliography.** New York: Garland, 1988. 241 p.

A selective bibliography of books, chapters in books, and periodical articles written between 1925 and 1986 on the methodology and techniques of fieldwork. International coverage.
GN346 G75 ERIN

CF4 Harvard University. Peabody Museum of Archaeology and Ethnology Library. **Author and Subject Catalogues of the Library of the Peabody Museum, Authors,** 27 vols. **Subjects** 27 vols. Boston: G.K. Hall, 1963. *Supplements* 1-4, 1970-79: **Authors** 14 vols; **Subjects** 16 vols.

Records the holdings of this outstanding anthropology collection, founded in the 1860s. Includes analytic entries from periodicals, conference proceedings, pamphlets, festchriften, as well as monographs. Entries are reproductions of library cataloguing cards. The collection emphasizes American archaeology and ethnology, including Mexico and Central America. The main set of the catalogue includes material to 1962; supplements add material from 1962 to 1977.

The Library at the Peabody Museum has now been renamed the Tozzer Library, and continues to collect materials from all over the world. Since 1982, the catalogues have not included periodical literature. A second edition of the catalogues was published by G.K. Hall in 1988 on microfiche, and contains the entire card catalogue through July 1986 (G.K. Hall).

This second edition is now supplemented by the annual *Bibliographic Guide to Anthropology and Archaeology*, (1987-) (Z5134 H374) which contains full cataloguing information compiled from OCLC records for books and other materials on topics related to cultural anthropology, physical anthropology, archaeology and linguistics in the Tozzer Library.

The *Tozzer Library Index to Anthropological Subject Headings* (G.K. Hall, 1981) (Z5134 H3722) lists subject headings for ethnic groups, languages and major archaeological sites, as well as other headings, used in the catalog in the Library.
Z5134 H37

CF5 **HRAF Source Bibliography,** 1954- . 2 vols. New Haven, CT: Human Relations Area Files. looseleaf.

Includes all books, articles and manuscripts processed for HRAF (Human Relations Area Files). HRAF includes primary source material arranged by culture, geographic area and cultural traits. Use of HRAF is outlined in Robert O Lagacé's *Nature and Use of the HRAF Files: A Research and Teaching Guide* (HRAF, 1974) (300 L172N). Items in HRAF are numbered according to George Murdock's *Outline of Cultural Materials* (5th rev. ed, 1987) (GN345.3 O98 ROMU) which functions as a subject index to HRAF. Also by Murdock is *Outline of World Cultures* (6th ed, HRAF, 1983) (GN345.3 M87) which provides an outline of the organization and classification of the known cultures of the world. Available online and on CD-ROM as *HRAF Data Archive* (1989-), a full-text database covering 1800 to the present.
R300 AH918H   or   Z7164 S667H82

CF6 **International Bibliography of Social and Cultural Anthropology / Bibliographie internationale d'anthropologie sociale et culturelle,** 1955- . Prepared by the International Committee for Social Sciences Documentation in cooperation with the International Congress of Anthropological and Ethnological Sciences. London: Tavistock Publications. annual.

Classified bibliography of books and articles with an emphasis on sociocultural anthropology. Author index, separate English and French subject indexes. Available online as part of *International Bibliography of the Social Sciences* (CA2).
Z7161 I593

CF7 Kemper, Robert V. and John F.S. Phinney. **The History of Anthropology: A Research Bibliography.** New York: Garland, 1977. 212 p.

An introduction to research on the development of anthropology as a science and a profession. The 2,439 entries list general reference and bibliographical sources, background works, and works in modern anthropology and related social sciences. A more specialized work is *Ecce Homo: An Annotated Bibliographic History of Physical Anthropology* (Greenwood Press, 1986) (Z5118 S7S64), which lists books and articles published since ancient times, concentrating on various aspects of physical anthropology.
Z5111 K44

Abstracts, Indexes and Reviews

CF8 **Abstracts in Anthropology**, 1970- . Farmingdale, NY: Baywood Publishing. 2 volumes, 8 issues per year.

Includes references to books, articles and conference papers in archaeology; cultural, physical anthropology; linguistics. International in scope but English language materials predominate. Author and subject indexes.
GN1 A17

CF9 **Annual Review of Anthropology**, 1972- . Palo Alto, CA: Annual Reviews. annual.

Describes and evaluates current literature in the field, with chapters written by specialists on topics of current interest in physical, social and cultural anthropology. Bibliographies at end of chapters have international coverage, with many references in English. Formerly called *Biennial Review of Anthropology* (1959-71). *Reviews in Anthropology* (1974-, Redgrave, quarterly), (GN1 R43) publishes reviews of new books in the field.
GN1 A56

CF10 **Anthropological Index**, 1983- . London: Royal Anthropological Institute. quarterly.

Supersedes *Anthropological Index to Current Periodicals in the Library of the Royal Anthropological Institute* (1963-76), and *Anthropological Index to Current Periodicals in the Museum of Mankind Library* (1977-83). Covers archaeology, enthnomusicology, physical anthropology, human biology, cultural anthropology, and ethnography and linguistics. Subarranged by topic under geographical areas.
Z5112 A52

CF11 **Anthropological Literature: An Index to Periodical Articles and Essays**, 1979- . Comp. by Tozzer Library. South Salem, NY: Redgrave. quarterly. 1979-1983 5 vols. in 6; 1984-88 published in microfiche only. 1989- quarterly in paper.

International coverage of serial publications, symposia, collections of readings, festchriften, arranged in 5 broad sections: Cultural/social; Archaeology; Biological/Physical; Linguistics; and General Method, Theory. Covers archaeology up to Roman times. Indexes for author, archaeological site and culture, ethnic and linguistic groups, and geographics. Until 1982 periodical articles were also indexed in the *Catalogue of the Library of the Peabody Museum* (CF4).
Z5112 A56/A562   and   Z7 A574 Mfe

Encyclopedias and Dictionaries

CF12 **The Cambridge Encyclopedia of Archaeology**. Ed. by Andrew Sherratt. New York: Crown Publishers/Cambridge University Press, 1980. 495 p.

Contains signed articles on major themes in archaeology, such as early empires of the western old world, the postglacial evolution, and the development of modern archaeology. Illustrations, cross references, and indexes are included.
CC165 C3

CF13 **Encyclopedia of Anthropology.** Ed. by David Hunter and Phillip Whitten. New York: Harper & Row, 1976. 411 p.

Contains almost 1,400 short articles dealing with concepts, language, theories and leading figures in anthropology; entries on topics in related fields are also included.
GN11 E52

CF14 **Encyclopedia of Human Evolution and Prehistory.** Ed. by I. Tattersall. New York: Garland Publishing, 1988. 603 p.

Provides comprehensive coverage of human evolution and prehistoric archaeology. Covers fossils and primates, archaeological sites, methodology. Includes bibliographies, maps, and charts. Cross-referenced but not indexed.
GN281 E53

CF15 **The Facts on File Dictionary of Archaeology.** 1984. See CF53 for full entry information.

CF16 **The Illustrated Encyclopedia of Mankind.** 2d rev. ed. 22 vols. New York: Marshall Cavendish, 1989.

An extensive anthropological record depicting the lives and customs of the peoples of the world. Articles are signed and include over 4,200 coloured illustrations.
GN307 I44 SCAR   or   GN307 I44 (1984)

CF17 Pearson, Roger. **Anthropological Glossary.** Malabar, FL: R.E. Krieger, 1985. 282 p.

A dictionary with wide scope, listing over 4,000 entries, and excluding biographies. More extensive than Charlotte Seymour-Smith's *Dictionary of Anthropology* (G.K. Hall, 1986) (GN11 D48 VUPR), which contains concise articles on concepts and terms in social and cultural anthropology. Published in England as *Macmillan Dictionary of Anthropology* (Macmillan).
GN11 P48

Atlases

CF18 **The Atlas of Mankind.** Chicago: Rand McNally, 1982. 191 p.

Provides articles on major concepts of sociocultural anthropology, such as kinship, marriage and taboo, languages, food production, and other topics. Ethnographic groups are described in the "Peoples of the World" section, which is arranged in 11 regions. Included are maps of language distribution, land use, diagrams of populations and religious practices, and an historical time bar depicting important dates. Also includes a glossary, and general and place name indexes.
GN25 A8 MAPL

CF19 Hawkes, Jacquetta Hopkins. **The Atlas of Early Man.** New York: St. Martin's, 1976. 255 p.

Illustrates the development of early man, from 40,000 BC to AD 500, with maps, illustrations, colour photographs, and a chart for various regions of the world depicting the state of economy, main centres, events and developments, people, religion, technology and inventions, architecture, and art. While dated, it remains the only comprehensive source of information of many early archaeological sites from all over the world.
CB311 M35

CF20 Price, David H. **Atlas of World Cultures: A Geographical Guide to Ethnographic Literature.** Newbury Park, CA: Sage Publications, 1989. 156 p.

A useful work for students of cultural anthropology and ethnic studies who wish to identify cultural/ethnic groups. This work contains geographical and bibliographical information on 3,500 worldwide cultural groups and consists of 41 maps, a bibliography and a culture index. The culture index lists individual cultural groups. Used in conjunction with the Human Relations Area Files, (HRAF) (CF5), and with George Murdock's *Atlas of World Cultures* (University of Pittsburgh Press, 1981) (GN345.3 M86 ROBA), formerly *Ethnographic Atlas* (1967), which identifies and provides brief facts on 563 societies frequently cited in ethnographic literature.
G1046 E1P7 MAPL

Biographical and Directory Sources

CF21 **The Archaeologists' Year Book: An Introductory Directory of Archaeology and Anthropology.** Poole, Dorset, U.K: Dolphin Press, 1977. 312 p.

Contains directory information of interest to archaeologists and anthropologists, such as museums, international universities and schools, governmental departments, societies and associations, research groups, and book reviews.
CC120 A67

CF22 **Biographical Directory of Anthropologists Born Before 1920.** Comp. by Library-Anthropology Resource Group and edited by Thomas Mann. New York: Garland, 1988. 245 p.

Contains 3,488 short biographical entries on well-known anthropologists born before 1920, with birth/death dates, professional information, and a summary of contributions made to the field. Bibliographical references are provided if available. Indexed.
GN20 B56

CF23 **Guide to Departments of Anthropology,** 1969/70- . Washington: American Anthropological Association. annual.

(28th ed, 1989/90) Covers the U.S. and Canada, including academic departments, museum and research departments (with list of faculty and staff). Lists PhD theses presented for the year. *The Guide to Departments of Sociology, Anthropology and Archaeology in Universities and Museums in Canada* (National Museum of Man, 1986/87) (GN44 C3H47 ROMU) is another useful directory.

Information on research and funding in anthropology is found in *Funding for Anthropological Research* by Karen Cantrell (Oryx Press, 1986) (GN42 F86).
GN43 A2G82

CF24 **International Directory of Anthropologists.** 5th ed. Chicago: University of Chicago Press, 1975. 496 p.

While dated, provides information on 4,752 anthropologists, listing affiliation, research performed, publications. Includes geographic, subject/methodology, institution/residence indexes. *Women Anthropologists: A Biographical Directory* (Greenwood Press, 1988) (GN20 W63) by Ute Gacs focuses on 20th century women anthropologists.
GN20 I5

Ethnic Studies

CF25   Canadian Ethnic Groups Bibliography. 2d ed. Ottawa: Department of Secretary of State, 1985. 96 p.

A complete listing of material held by the Library of the Department of the Secretary of State. Contains over 700 entries of monographs, directories and periodicals as of March, 1985 covering ethno-cultural communities in Canada. Also available is *Multicultural Information: Selected Bibliography of Ministry Materials* (Ontario Ministry of Citizenship and Culture) (305.80971 AM961N 1984; R016.3058 M961 1985), which is a bibliography of books and periodicals on the topic of multiculturalism in Canada, with chapters on immigrant women, Francophone Canadians, Native peoples, and individual ethnic groups in Canada.
Z1395 E8C35

CF26   A Directory of International Migration Study Centers, Research Programs and Library Resources. Ed. by Diana Zimmerman. Staten Island, NY: Center for Migration Studies of New York, 1987. 299 p.

Directory arranged alphabetically, including information on research activity, projects, publications, library, and addresses.

CF27   Guide to Multicultural Resources. Ed. by Charles Taylor. Madison, WI: NMCC Publications, 1986. 378 p.

A directory listing ethnic minority organizations; institutions covering Afro-American, Hispanic America, and Native American resources; and ethnic studies and human rights organizations. Some publications listed. There are two similar publications published in Canada which relate specifically to the Toronto population, including: *Multicultural Information Resources: A Guide to Metropolitan Toronto* (Cross Cultural Communication Centre, 1987) (305.809713 H477M), which is a guide to libraries, resource centres and community agencies in Toronto which produce or collect information on multicultural topics, and *Toronto Immigrant Services Directory*, (3d ed, Cross Cultural Communication Centre, 1988) (R361.9713 T686T3), which lists organizations, agencies, community information centres, etc, available to ethnic groups, with full descriptions of services, contact names and numbers.
Z1361 E4T39

CF28   Index to Afro-American Reference Resources. Ed. by Rosemary M. Stevenson. Westport, CT: Greenwood Press, 1988. 315 p.

Lists reference sources published in U.S., Canada, Caribbean, and South America. Selectively includes materials on black experiences in Africa, Asia, and Europe. Author and title indexes.
Z1361 N39S77

CF29   International Handbook on Race and Race Relations. Ed. by Jay Sigler. Westport, CT: Greenwood Press, 1987. 483 p.

Contains descriptive essays on race relations in 20 countries written by experts. Appendix includes data on population in each country.
HT1521 I485

CF30   World Directory of Minorities. Ed. by the Minorities Rights Group. Chicago: St. James Press, 1989. 427 p.

Describes over 160 minority groups in 11 world regions. In Canada, it covers Japanese-Canadians, Indians and Métis, Inuits, and French-Canadians. Appendix of primary sources,

maps, cross-references. Indexed.
JC311 W67

Native Peoples

Bibliographies and Guides to the Literature

CF31 Abler, Thomas and Sally M. Weaver. **A Canadian Indian Bibliography, 1969-1970.** Toronto: University of Toronto Press, 1974. 732 p.

An annotated bibliography listing books, monographs, journal articles, unpublished papers, reports, federal and provincial government documents. Includes a case law digest as "an attempt to bring together all case law relating to Indian legal questions decided since 1 July, 1867."
Z1209A9 VUER   or   Z1209.2 C2A64

CF32 Corley, Nora T. **Resources for Native Peoples Studies.** Research Collections in Canadian Libraries: Special Studies, No. 9. Ottawa: Resources Survey Division, National Library of Canada, 1984. 342 p.

In English, French language reverse; a directory of Canadian libraries with native studies holdings, a union list of periodicals and bibliography of reference and other relevant materials.
R026 R342

CF33 Hirschfelder, Arlene. **Guide to Research on North American Indians.** Chicago: American Library Association, 1983. 330 p.

Selected, annotated guide to about 1,100 English-language books, articles, government documents and other written materials in 27 fields. The "goal is to present a selection of scholarly materials in the various disciplines." Includes material on some Canadian, Central and South American native peoples, but emphasis is on U.S. peoples.
Z1209.2 N67H57

CF34 **Index to Literature on the American Indian,** 1970- . San Francisco: Indian Historian Press, 1972-. annual.

An author and subject index to articles and books published in U.S. and Canada on American Indians.
Z1209 I6

CF35 Haas, M.L. **Indians of North America: Methods and Sources for Library Research.** Hamden, CT: Shoestring Press, 1983. 160 p.

Provides a guide to library methodology and library research reference tools. Includes an annotated bibliography organized by subject, as well as lists of books for individual tribes.
Z1209 H22

CF36 Martin, Marlene M. **Ethnographic Bibliography of North America.** 4th ed Supplement 1973-1987. 3 vols. New Haven, CT: Human Relations Area Files Press, 1990.

Supplement to the 4th edition (1975), covering the period 1973 to 1987. Includes 25,000 citations to international literature in the form of books, articles, government publications and reports describing the cultures and ways of life of North American native peoples. Ethnic group, author, and subject indexes.
Z1209 M8 (1975)

CF37 Meikeljohn, Christopher. **The Native Peoples of Canada: An Annotated Bibliography of Population, Biology, Health and Illness.** Ottawa: National Museums of Canada, 1988. 570 p.

Supersedes *Annotated Bibliography of the Physical Anthropology and Human Biology of Canadian Eskimos and Indians* (Department of Anthropology, University of Toronto, 1971) (Z1210 E7M38).
Z1209.2 C2M4 NEWC (1986)

CF38 Newberry Library. Edward E. Ayer Collection. **Dictionary Catalog of the Edward E. Ayer Collection of Americana and American Indians in the Newberry Library.** 16 vols. Boston: G.K. Hall, 1961. *Supplement*, 3 vols, 1970; 4 vols, 1980.

Extensive collection contains research material on early history of the Americas, Hawaii and the Philippines.
Z1209 N48

CF39 Newberry Library Center for the History of the American Indian. **Indian Bibliographical Series.** Bloomington, IN: Indiana University Press, 1976-1983.

A multi-volume series covering a wide variety of topics in a standard format. Each volume includes a bibliographical essay and a list of books and periodicals, rated according to level of suitability (e.g. beginner, advanced, etc.) Titles include *Canadian Indian Policy: A Critical Bibliography* by Robert Surtees (1982) (Z1209.2 C2S9).
various call numbers

CF40 **Resource Reading List 1990: Annotated Bibliography of Resources by and about Native People.** Comp. by Catherine Verrall and Patricia McDowell. Toronto: Canadian Alliance in Solidarity with the Native Peoples, 1990. 157 p.

Identifies "most useful books and other resources" which are in-print, most published, written or produced by native peoples. Includes adult books arranged in topic categories, teaching resources, books for children, youth.
Z1209.2 C2V47

CF41 Wai, Lokky. **Native Peoples of Canada in Contemporary Society: A Demographic and Socioeconomic Bibliography.** London, ON: Population Studies Centre, University of Western Ontario, 1989. 82 p.

Covers Métis, Inuit, status and non-status Indians. Includes books, articles, dissertations, reports, working papers, and government publications. Library locations noted. Subject and name indexes.
Z1209.2 C2W34

CF42 Whiteside, Don. **Aboriginal People: A Selected Bibliography Concerning Canada's First People.** Ottawa: National Indian Brotherhood, 1973. 345 p.

Emphasizes unpublished speeches, reports, work of native peoples.
Z1209.2 C2W45

Encyclopedias and Dictionaries

CF43 **Handbook of North American Indians.** 20 vols. Washington: Smithsonian Institute, 1978- in progress.

Completed to volume 15. Volumes are not published in chronological order, e.g. Volume 7 published 1990, volume 15, 1978. "An encyclopedic summary of what is known about the prehistory, history, and cultures of the aboriginal peoples of North America." Regions are treated separately (e.g. Volume 15 Indians of the Northeast, which includes information on 75 Indian tribes who lived in southeastern Canada and north-east USA). Includes many illustrations, bibliographies, and indexes.

Also available is the 16 volume work *Handbook of Middle American Indians* (University of Texas Press, 1964-76) (F1434 H3 VUPR), with supplement *Archaeology*, 1981, each volume including essays by specialists on the life, customs, arts and culture, environmental influences, language, anthropology, etc, of the groups comprising the Middle American Indians; and the *Handbook of South American Indians* (Smithsonian Institution, 1946-1959) (E51 S8 VUPT), a 7 volume set describing South American Indians.
E77 H25

CF44 Jenness, Diamond. **The Indians of Canada.** 7th ed. Ottawa: National Museum, 1979. 432 p.

A broad overview of Canadian Indians and Inuit. Includes chapters on economic conditions, social and political organization, and religion.
R970.1 J54   or   E78 C2J4

CF45 Klein, Barry T. **Reference Encyclopedia of the American Indian.** 5th ed. West Nyack, NY: Todd Publications, 1990. 1078 p.

Bibliography of 4,500 titles, directory information and biographical information about American Indians. Includes a section for Canadian native people.
E76 2R4

CF46 Waldman, Carl. **Atlas of North American Indians.** New York: Facts on File, 1985. 276 p.

Includes over 100 maps. There is also a chronology of North American Indian history, a list of Canadian and American tribes, a directory of Indian museums and archaeological sites, and a list of locations and reservations of tribes. Waldman has also published *Encyclopedia of Native American Tribes* (Facts on File, 1988) (E76.2 W35), which discusses 140 tribes with information on tribal culture, history, present day situation.
E77 W34

Archaeology

Bibliographies and Guides

CF47 Ellis, Linda. **Laboratory Techniques in Archaeology: A Guide to the Literature, 1920-1980.** New York: Garland, 1982. 419 p.

A bibliography of over 3,700 international sources dealing with the application of science to archaeology. Problem areas such as remote sensing, environmental reconstruction, data management, and other topics are included. Indexes for author, geographic area, method of analysis, and type of material analyzed are provided.
Z5131 E43

CF48 Heizer, Robert Fleming and others. **Archaeology: A Bibliographical Guide to the Basic Literature.** New York: Garland, 1980. 434 p.

Bibliography of over 4,800 English-language reference and research aids published up to 1979 for New World archaeology, with some coverage on Old World, African and Asian archaeology.
Z5131 H44

CF49 Woodhead, Peter. **Keyguide to Information Sources in Archaeology.** New York: Mansell, 1985. 219 p.

Bibliography identifying reference materials and nontraditional sources of information for students of archaeology. A general historical overview of the development of the subject, with a directory of international organizations in also provided.
CC120 W66

Encyclopedias and Dictionaries

CF50 Bray, W. and D. Trump. **Penguin Dictionary of Archaeology.** 2d rev. ed. London, Allen Lane: Penguin Press, 1982. 283 p.

Contains 1,600 entries, arranged alphabetically, on archaeological terms, sites, techniques and prehistoric peoples. A good, nonspecialized guide to archaeological terms and concepts. A more technical dictionary is Ruth Whitehouse's *The Facts on File Dictionary of Archaeology* (Facts on File, 1983) (CC70 F32 ROBA), published in Britain as *The Macmillan Dictionary of Archaeology*, which contains worldwide coverage of archaeological terms with concise definitions. See also *New International Dictionary of Biblical Archaeology* (BC68), which includes articles and definitions and illustrations of archaeological terms relating to Biblical archaeology.
CC70 B73

CF51 **The Cambridge Encyclopedia of Archaeology.** Ed. by Andrew Sherratt. New York: Crown/Cambridge University Press, 1980. 495 p.

A general interest encyclopedic work with 64 chapters, each written by a specialist and including a bibliography. Organized in three sections, the first on modern archaeology, second on archaeological periods, regions, and empires, and the third on frameworks, dating, and distribution. Indexed.
CC70 F32

CF52 **Concise Encyclopedia of Archaeology.** 3d ed. London: Hutchinson, 1974. 430 p.

A reference source for archaeologists or students, with entries for discoveries and techniques, especially those outside Greece and Rome and medieval Europe.
CC70 C6

CF53 **The Facts on File Dictionary of Archaeology.** Ed. by Ruth D. Whitehouse. New York: Facts on File, 1983. 597 p.

Covers sites, terminology, archaeological techniques, and individuals in 3,500 entries written by professional archaeologists. Worldwide coverage, and includes discussion of field work and methodology. Cross references, bibliography.
CC70 F32 ROBA

CF54 **Historical Dictionary of North American Archaeology.** Ed. by Edward B. Jelks. Westport, CT: Greenwood Press, 1988. 760 p.

A guide to prehistoric Indian cultures, sites, and artifacts of North America. Information about each site indicates who excavated it, the date of excavation, artifacts and features noted, and cultural affiliations identified. Detailed 150 page bibliography is included, as well as an index.
E77.9 H57

CF55 **Larousse Encyclopedia of Archaeology.** 3d ed. Ed. by G. Charles-Picard. London: Hamlyn, 1987. 432 p.

Written for the non-specialist, with many illustrations, describes the development of archaeology, with chapters on various periods from different parts of the world.
CC165 C4313

Atlases

See also section on Atlases, CF18 - CF20.

CF56 **The Atlas of Archaeology.** London: Macdonald, 1982. 240 p.
Provides information on archaeological sites from various periods and from all over the world. Maps, glossary, and an index are included.
CC165 A83 MAPL

CF57 Coe, Michael and others. **Atlas of Ancient America.** New York: Facts on File, 1986. 240 p.
Written for non-specialists, this work summarizes New World archaeology theories, concepts, and knowledge. Divided into six parts, 1) "The New World" presents an overview of cultures and the environment, early exploration, and discovery of North America, 2) "The First Americans", which discusses movement of peoples into the New World, 3) "North America", 4) "Mesoamerica", 5) "South America", and 6) "The Living Heritage", which summarizes to present-day cultures. Illustrated with black and white and colour photographs, with a detailed gazetteer and a subject index.
E61 C66 MAPL

CF58 **Atlas of Classical Archaeology.** Ed. by M. Finley. New York: McGraw Hill, 1977. 256 p.

Covering the period 1000 BC to 500 AD, provides descriptions of the major cities of antiquity. Descriptions of archaeological sites include maps, plans, photographs of art found at the site, and a short bibliography. An appendix includes a chronological table, a list of Roman emperors, a glossary, and illustrations of Greek vase types, and Greek architectural types. Indexed.
G1046 E15A8 MAPL

CF59 **Hammond Past Worlds: The Times Atlas of Archaeology.** Maplewood, NJ: Hammond, 1988. 319 p.
Current and balanced worldwide coverage. Maps and text arranged chronologically and subdivided regionally. Published in Britain as *Pasts Worlds: The Time Atlas of Archaeology* (Times Books, 1989) (G1046 E15P3 MAPL fo).
MTRL HIST

CF60 Whitehouse, David. **Archaeological Atlas of the World.** London: Thames and Hudson, 1975. 272 p.
Contains maps of archaeological sites, mostly in Europe. Useful for discerning locations of sites. A short bibliography and an index are provided.
G1046 E15W5 MAPL

CF61 **The World Atlas of Archaeology.** Boston: G.K. Hall, 1985. 423 p.
Arranged by region, and subdivided by subject, articles provide information on human life from earliest times. Includes a useful glossary, as well as colour photographs and maps.
G1046 E15G7813 SIGR

CG   SOCIOLOGY AND RELATED TOPICS

Bibliographies and Guides to the Literature

CG1   Aby, Stephen H. **Sociology: A Guide to Reference and Information Sources.** Littleton, CO: Libraries Unlimited, 1987. 231 p.

Lists over 600 major reference sources in sociology and the related social sciences published between 1970 and 1986, including indexes, bibliographies, dictionaries, and other reference sources. Entries have short annotations with some critical analysis. Author/title and subject indexes. Another bibliographic guide, which includes a thesaurus-index to works in sociology and the related field of anthropology, is *Finding the Source in Sociology and Anthropology* (see CF2).
Z7164 S68 A24

CG2   **International Bibliography of Sociology / Bibliographie internationale de sociologie,** 1951– . London: Tavistock. annual.

A classified bibliography of books and articles, with author index and separate English, French subject indexes. Annotations are not included. Available online as part of *International Bibliography of the Social Sciences* (see CA2).
Z7161 I594

CG3   McMillan, Patricia and James R. Kennedy. **Library Research Guide to Sociology: Illustrated Search Strategy and Sources.** Library Research Guides, no. 5. Ann Arbor, MI: Pierian Press, 1981. 69 p.

Presents a good introduction to the library and outlines a research strategy for the beginning researcher.
HM15 M38

CG4 Wepsiec, Jan. **Sociology: An International Bibliography of Serial Publications, 1880–1980.** London: Mansell, 1983. 183 p.

An alphabetical list of 2,300 sociology and other journals in the social sciences covering sociological topics. Numerous cross-references and subject index.
Z7164 S68W47

Abstracts, Indexes and Reviews

CG5 **Annual Review of Sociology,** 1975– . Palo Alto, CA: Annual Reviews. annual.

Substantial scholarly articles on current problems in a variety of areas. Extensive bibliographies. Subject index with cumulative author index.
HM1 A766

CG6 **Contemporary Sociology: A Journal of Reviews,** 1972– . Washington: American Sociological Association. bimonthly.

Includes reviews and critical discussions of recent works in sociology and related disciplines under broad subject headings. Selection reflects important issues which merit the attention of sociologists. Annual index.
HM1 C65

CG7 **Cumulative Index of Sociology Journals 1971–1985.** Comp. by Judith C. Lantz. Washington: American Sociological Association, 1987. 763 p.

Provides an author and subject index to articles, book reviews and review essays contained in 10 A.S.A. sociology journals published between the years 1971 to 1985.
Z7164 S68 L36

CG8 **Social Sciences Index,** 1975- quarterly.

Contains many citations to articles of a sociological nature. See CA14 for full entry information.

CG9 **Sociological Abstracts,** 1952– . New York: Sociological Abstracts. five issues per year.

Sponsored in part by the International Sociological Association. Non-evaluative abstracts in a classified arrangement by broad subjects with subdivisions; author, subject indexes. Each issue has the section "International Reviews of Publications in Sociology", a bibliography of book reviews from the journals abstracted. Available online and on CD-ROM as *SocioFile*.
HM1 S67

Encyclopedias and Dictionaries

CG10 Bardis, P.D. **Dictionary of Quotations in Sociology.** Westport, CT: Greenwood Press, 1985. 356 p.

Provides quotations from history and from all fields of knowledge on nearly 200 concepts in sociology, from "Abortion" to "World, Third". Quotations are in chronological order. Quotation includes identification of the author, source, and date, if known. Indexed by name and subject.
HM17 B37 ROBA

CG11 Boudon, Raymond and Francois Bourricand. **A Critical Dictionary of Sociology.** Chicago: University of Chicago Press, 1989. 438 p.

Includes bibliographic essays on 73 selective sociological concepts, theories and leaders. Indexed.
HM17 B6813

CG12 Encyclopedia of Sociology. 2d ed. Guilford, CT: DPG Reference Pub, 1981. 317 p.

Includes over 1,300 brief definitions, articles and descriptions of social theories, institutions, topics, and leading figures in historical and contemporary sociology. Includes a bibliography of current publications.
HM17 E5

CG13 Handbook of Sociology. Ed. by N.J. Smelser. Newbury Park, CA: Sage Publications Ltd, 1988. 824 p.

Supersedes *Handbook of Modern Sociology* by R.E.L. Faris (1964). Contains lengthy bibliographies and name/subject indexes.
HM51 H249

CG14 International Encyclopedia of Population. 2 vols. Ed. by John A. Ross. New York: Free Press, 1982.

Companion to *International Encyclopedia of the Social Sciences* (CA19) and *International Encyclopedia of Statistics* (2 vols, 1978) (HA17 I63). Covers demography, fertility, marriage, mortality, morbidity and migration. Geographic coverage in separate articles for the 11 most populated countries of the world, and Canada. Subject index.
HB849.2 I55

CG15 International Encyclopedia of Sociology. Ed. by Michael Mann. New York: Continuum, 1984. 434 p.

This is the U.S. version of the *Macmillan Student Encyclopedia of Sociology*. British and American emphasis. Entries are signed. Includes historical, developmental and biographical information.
HM17 I53

Aging

Bibliographies and Guides, and Abstracts and Indexes

CG16 Brazil, Mary Jo. **Building Library Collections on Aging: A Selection Guide and Core List.** Santa Barbara, CA: ABC-Clio, 1990. 174 p.

Organized in two parts: part one provides advice for nonlibrarians in selecting books, journals and government documents, as well as lists of organizations and publishers. Part two lists 400 core collection items.

Another collection development resource is Shirley B. Hesslein's *Serials on Aging: An Analytical Guide* (Greenwood Press, 1986) (Z7164 O4H47), which is an annotated bibliography listing a broad range of international serials. Arranged in general disciplinary areas, then by topic with geographical, publisher, title, and subject indexes.
025.2761267 AB827B

CG17 Current Literature on Aging, 1957– . Washington: National Council on Aging. quarterly.

Indexes and abstracts selected books and journals, government documents and conference proceedings on gerontology from NCOA's library. Subject arrangement. Cumulated author/subject indexes in last issue each year.
Z7164 O4N35

CG18 Gerontological Abstracts, 1976- Ann Arbor, MI: University Information Services. bi-monthly.

Citations to biological, clinical and social aspects of aging. Another source is *Abstracts in Social Gerontology*, (1990- , Sage Publications) (Z7164 O4N352).

CG19 Harris, Diana K. **The Sociology of Aging: An Annotated Bibliography and Sourcebook.** 2d ed. New York: Harper & Row, 1990. 510 p.

List of English language monographs, book chapters and periodical articles published in the 1980's which deal with sociology of aging. An earlier edition (1985) covered works published between 1960 and 1980.
Z7164 O4H36

Dictionaries and Encyclopedias

CG20 Harris, Diana K. **Dictionary of Gerontology.** Westport, CT: Greenwood Press, 1988. 201 p.

Provides definitions of terminology in the area of gerontology found in the literature of the social and physical sciences. Intended for students, researchers and practitioners.
HQ1061 H338

CG21 Maddox, G.L. **The Encyclopedia of Aging.** New York: Springer Publishing Co., 1987. 890 p.

Articles of varying length on more than 400 topics concerning aging. Includes bibliography and subject index. R.G. Binstock's *Handbook of Aging and the Social Sciences* (2d ed. Van Nostrand Reinhold Company, 1985) (HQ1061 H336 ROBA) provides information and bibliographies for many aspects of aging and society.
HQ1061 E53

Animal Rights

CG22 Magel, Charles R. **Keyguide to Information Sources in Animal Rights.** Jefferson, NC: McFarland, 1989. 281 p.

A bibliographic guide with an overview to the literature and philosophy of the animal rights movement. Includes essays on current topics, with bibliographies; a detailed annotated bibliography on many topics; and a directory of animal rights organizations.
Z7164 C45M36 SIGR

Child Abuse

CG23 Sexual Abuse of Children in the 1980's: Ten Essays and an Annotated Bibliography. Ed. by Benjamin Schlesinger. Toronto: University of Toronto Press, 1986. 201 p.

A sequel to *Sexual Abuse of Children: A Resource Guide and Annotated Bibliography* (1982). Essays are reprinted from a variety of sources published between 1982 and 1985. Bibliographic entries are arranged by topic and include Canadian government reports, newsletters, and public service publications. Includes a list of clearinghouses and research centers.
Z7164 C5S38

CG24 Wells, Dorothy P. and Charles R. Carroll. **Child Abuse: An Annotated Bibliography.** Metuchen, NJ: Scarecrow Press, 1980. 450 p.

Concentrates "on physical and psychological abuse and intentional neglect." Includes books, articles, audio-visual materials, mostly published 1962–1976. Organized by subject with author index.
Z7164 C5W37

Death

CG25 Bleckman, Isaac A. **Death and Dying A to Z: A Loose-leaf Encyclopedic Handbook on Death and Dying and Related Topics.** 1980- . New York: Croner Pubs. quarterly updates.

Provides concise explanations of current trends and the historical background of the concept of death. Definitions of special terms, tables of facts and figures, directories of organizations and services, and bibliographies on various topics are also provided.

CG26 **Encyclopedia of Death.** Ed. by Robert Kastenbaum and Beatrice Kastenbaum. Phoenix, AZ: Oryx Press, 1989. 295 p.

Includes over 130 articles covering topics from trends in attitudes, to philosophical and theological themes. Social sciences and biomedical topics are also included. Bibliographies are included with articles. Includes subject index.
HQ1073 E54

CG27 Wass, Hannelore. **Death Education II: An Annotated Resource Guide.** Washington: Hemisphere Publishing Corp, 1985. 467 p.

The compilers have continued and expanded their earlier bibliographic work, *Death Education: An Annotated Resource Guide* (1980). Annotations are detailed and critical.
HQ1073 D42

Drugs and Alcholism

CG28 **Directory of Alcohol and Drug Treatment Resources of Ontario,** 1981- . Toronto: Addiction Research Foundation. annual.

Directory of drug and alcohol treatment centres in Ontario, listing treatment type, services available, and populations serviced. Indexed geographically and by service.
HV5283 C22 D57 BMER

CG29 **Drug Abuse Bibliography,** 1970- . Troy, NY: Whitston Publishing. annual.

Supplement to *Drugs of Addiction and Non-Addiction, Their Use and Abuse: A Comprehensive Bibliography 1960–1969* (1970) (Z7164 N17 M45 BMER), compiled by Joseph Menditto. Included are citations to books, monographs, pamphlets and periodical articles.
Z7164 N17M6 O2 BMER

CG30 Fay, John J. **The Alcohol / Drug Abuse Dictionary and Encyclopedia.** Springfield, IL: Charles Thomas, 1988. 167 p.

Designed for professional and layperson. Includes over 1,400 terms, phrases and concepts related to drug and alcohol abuse. Includes street jargon. Bibliography and appendixes are also provided.
RC564 F39 BMER

CG31 O'Brien, Robert and Morris Chafetz. **The Encyclopedia of Drug Abuse.** New York: Facts on File, 1984. 454 p.

Provides information in an international framework of the medical, physical, psychological, political and legal aspects of drug abuse. Expands upon another work, *The Encyclopedia*

of Alcoholism, by the same authors (Facts on File, 1982).
HV5804 O24

CG32 **Statistics on Alcohol and Drug Use in Canada and Other Countries,** 1982- . 2 vols. Toronto: Addiction Research Foundation. irregular.

(1989 latest edition) Volume 1 deals with alcohol use; volume 2 with drug use. Trends in Canada are compared with statistics from around the world.
CA2 ONH 85-1989 S71 GOVT

Marriage and the Family

CG33 Cline, Ruth K. **Focus on Families: A Reference Handbook.** Santa Barbara, CA: ABC-Clio, 1990. 233 p.

Provides information and resources on a variety of family issues, including stepfamilies, divorce, children of divorce, child abuse, etc. Topical essays explain concepts, provide definitions, and cite statistics, and are followed by annotated bibliographies to fiction, nonfiction and nonprint materials. Organization, subject, title and author indexes included.

CG34 DiCanio, Margaret. **The Encyclopedia of Marriage, Divorce and the Family.** New York: Facts on File, 1989. 607 p.

Over 500 entries dealing with marriage and the family, arranged in alphabetical order. Entries are in the form of brief essays, with bibliographies. Indexed.
HQ9 D38

CG35 **Inventory of Marriage and Family Literature,** 1973/74- . Minneapolis, MN: National Council Family Relations, 1975- . annual.

Lists "all relevant articles published in professional journals" on marriage and the family. Continues the *International Bibliography of Research in Marriage and the Family*, a comprehensive collection prepared for the Minnesota Family Center (2 vols, University of Minnesota Press, 1967–74) (Z7164 M2I58), covering the period of 1900–1972.
Z7164 M2I59

CG36 **Sage Family Studies Abstracts,** 1979- . Beverly Hills, CA: Sage Publications. quarterly.

Each issue contains some 250 abstracts of important recent books, articles, etc. on marriage, the family, sex roles, counselling, etc. Broad subject arrangement with author, subject indexes.
HQ536 S23

CG37 Schlesinger, Benjamin. **The One-Parent Family in the 1980s: Perspective and Annotated Bibliography 1978–1984.** 5th ed. Toronto: University of Toronto Press, 1985. 284 p.

Surveys various aspects of single parent families and provides annotated bibliographies. Other similar bibliographies are: *Families in Transition: An Annotated Bibliography* by Judith DeBoard Sadler, (Archon Books/Shoe String Press, 1988) (Z5118 F2S23), which is a guide to information on the changing pattern of family structures listing short annotations on almost 1,000 resources published between 1975–1987; and *Child Care: An Annotated Bibliography* published by the International

Labour Office (Washington, 1990) (016.362712 C536 Ref OISE) which cites international sources published between 1978 and 1988 dealing with the issues of women's work and care of children.
Z5118 F2S36

Sex and Sex Roles

CG38 **Encyclopedia of Homosexuality.** 2 vols. Ed. by Wayne R. Dynes. New York: Garland, 1990.

Presents 770 articles on many topics. Dynes has also published *Homosexuality: A Research Guide*, (Garland, 1987) (Z7164 S42 D96) which includes citations and evaluative annotations to 5,000 research studies, some back to the 19th century, classified under 24 broad categories such as women's studies, history, psychology, law, etc. International in scope.
HQ76.25 E53 VUER

CG39 Frayser, Suzanne G. and Thomas J. Whitby. **Studies in Human Sexuality: A Selected Guide.** Littleton, CO: Libraries Unlimited, 1987. 442 p.

Guide to over 600 works on human sexuality. Includes biological, medical, psychological, sociological, political aspects of sexuality. Arranged by subject with brief annotations. Author, title and subject indexes.
Z7164 S42 F73

*   *   *   *

Social Work

Bibliographies, Abstracts and Indexes

CG40 **Human Resources Abstracts,** 1966– . Beverly Hills, CA: Sage Publications. quarterly.

Formerly *Poverty and Human Resources Abstracts*. Contains references to works in the areas of human, social, and manpower problems, slum rehabilitation, job development training, compensatory education, minority group problems and rural poverty. Arranged by subject with author and subject indexes.
Z7165 U5P222

CG41 Moscovitch, A., T. Jennisen and P. Findlay. **The Welfare State in Canada: A Selected Bibliography, 1840 to 1978.** Waterloo, ON: Wilfrid Laurier University Press, 1983. 246 p.

Part one generally treats the origin and administration of the welfare state in Canada, including statistical sources. Part two covers areas of policy, such as unemployment, prisons, child and family welfare, and health care. Subject and author indexes.
Z7164 C4M6

CG42 **Social Work Research & Abstracts,** 1977– . Albany, NY: National Association of Social Workers. quarterly; annual cumulation.

Supersedes *Abstracts for Social Workers, 1965–1977*. Arranged by broad topics for areas of service, social policy and action, methods, the profession, history and related fields. Author, subject indexes.
HV1 A272

Dictionaries, Encyclopedias, and Directories

CG43 Barker, Robert L. **The Social Work Dictionary.** Silver Spring, MD: National Association of Social Workers, 1987. 207 p.

Intended for use by social workers working within the professional community. Contains brief explanations for over 3,000 medical, sociological, political and jargon terms that are used in the literature of related disciplines. Future editions of the work are planned.
HV12 B37

CG44 Directory of Community Services in Metropolitan Toronto. 1972– . Toronto: Community Information Centre of Metropolitan Toronto. annual.

Also known as *"The Blue Book"*, includes services provided by major social service and government agencies in Toronto. Organizations listed alphabetically, with subject index. Similar works available in other large communities.
HV110 T6C6

CG45 The Encyclopedia of Social Work. 18th ed. 2 vols. Ed. by Anne Minahan. Silver Spring, MD: National Association of Social Workers, 1987. Supplement: *Face of the Nation 1987*.

Contains articles on many problems and activities in social welfare, biographies of outstanding social workers, statistical tables and an agency directory. Articles arranged by subject and include bibliographies. A statistical supplement provides international demographic characteristics, with many graphs and charts, current through the first half of the 1980s. American emphasis.
HV35 S6A

Women's Studies

Bibliographies and Guides, and Abstracts and Indexes

CG46 Ballou, Patricia K. **Women: A Bibliography of Bibliographies.** 2d ed. Boston: G.K. Hall, 1986. 288 p.

First published in 1980. Provides annotations to 906 bibliographies found in books, journal articles, pamphlets, microforms, and documents published between 1970 and June 1985, some with annotations. Maureen Ritchie's *Women's Studies: A Checklist of Bibliographies* (Mansell, 1980) (Z7961 A1R58 ROBA) includes bibliographies published to 1980.
Z7961 A1B34

CG47 Building Women's Studies Collections: A Resource Guide. Ed. by Joan Ariel. Middletown, CT: Association of College and Research Libraries, 1987. 48 p.

Includes English language materials from the U.S. and some from Canada, Britain, and Europe. Descriptive annotations of bibliographies, review sources, publishers' catalogues, dissertations and reports.
HQ1181 U5B844 SCAR

CG48 Carter, Sarah and Maureen Ritchie. **Women's Studies: A Guide to Information Sources.** Jefferson, NC: McFarland & Co, 1990. 278 p.

Contains 1,076 annotated entries from 1978 to 1988. Arranged in three sections: general reference material; areas of the world; and special topics. Includes English language reference monographs and serials. Other helpful guides to

the literature include *Women's Studies: A Recommended Core Bibliography 1980–1985* by Catherine R. Loeb (Libraries Unlimited, 1987) (Z7963 F44L63); and Susan Searing's *Introduction to Library Research in Women's Studies* (Westview Press, 1985) (Z7961 S42).
Z961 C37

CG49 Light, Beth. **True Daughters of the North: Canadian Women's History, An Annotated Bibliography.** Toronto: Ontario Institute for Studies in Education, 1980. 210 p.

The sources listed include "both primary and secondary by which Canadians may ... improve their understanding of women's experience and role in the creation of the modern community." Organized by topic under broad chronological headings. Another bibliography is C. Mazur and S. Pepper's *Women in Canada: A Bibliography 1965–1982*, (Ontario Institute for Studies in Education, 1984) (Z7964 C3H37).
Z7964 C3L54

CG50 **Resources for Feminist Research / Documentation sur la recherche féministe,** 1972– . Toronto: Department of Sociology, Ontario Institute for Studies in Education. quarterly.

"An interdisciplinary, international periodical of research on women and sex roles... (also) book reviews, bibliographies." Two issues each year are on specific themes, others focus on book reviews. Author, subject indexes. The *Canadian Feminist Thesaurus*, compiled by The Canadian Women's Indexing Group (OISE, 1990) (Z695.1 W65C36), provides a vocabulary for access to the literature of Canadian feminism; bilingual and reflects Canadian usage.
HQ1101 C32

CG51 **Studies on Women Abstracts,** 1983– . Abingdon, Oxfordshire: Carfax Publishing Co. bimonthly.

Covers books and journal articles in all main areas of women's studies. Author and subject indexes, cumulated annually. Another abstracting publication is *Women's Studies Abstracts* (1972-, Rush Publishing, quarterly) (HQ1101 W4), which provides abstracts of articles in specialized and general periodicals.
HQ1101 S78

Directories

CG52 **Canadian Women's Directory / Annuaire des femmes du Canada.** Ed. by Jacquie Manthorne. Montreal: Les Éditions Communiqu'Elles, 1987. 308 p.

Bilingual directory listing almost 2,000 advisory councils, publishers, and national and regional women's groups and associations. Arranged geographically by province, and by subject, with a title index. *Making a World of Difference: A Directory of Women in Canada Specializing in Global Issues / Les femmes s'en melent*, (1990) (HQ1455 A3A34), published by Vehicule Press of Montreal, is a directory of Canadian women (community activitists, economists, theologians, journalists, teachers, feminists) who are active in global issues affecting women. Entries provide brief biographical data with addresses and phone numbers. Includes geographic and subject indexes.
HQ1883 A66

CG53 Directory of Federal Government Programs and Services for Women. Ottawa: Status of Women Canada, [1989]. 162 p.

Guide to services and programs available for women through the federal government in areas of work and labour, education, social services and health, legal matters, culture, native women, multicultural services for immigrants and voluntary groups.
R354.7100813 D597D

CG54 Ireland, Norma Olin. **Index to Women of the World from Ancient to Modern Times: A Supplement.** Metuchen, NY: Scarecrow Press, 1988. 774 p.

A supplement to the 1970 reference work of the same name. Index to notable women from biblical times to the present. Entries list birth and death dates, nationality, occupation, followed by citations to further information.
Z7963 B6I73

CG55 Women's Movements of the World: An International Directory and Reference Guide. Ed. by Sally Shreir. Phoenix, AZ: Oryx Press, 1988. 384 p.

Guide to the current status of women's issues and organizations throughout the world. Organized by country, each entry provides brief analysis of the women's movement in that country, followed by a list of organizations and government agencies dealing with women's issues. International organizations are listed in the final chapter. *Women in the Third World: A Directory of Resources* (Orbis Books, 1987) (Z7964 D44 F76 ROBA) contains annotated entries to selected resources about women in the Third World. Indexed by organization, individuals, titles, geographical areas and subject.
HQ1883 W56

CG56 The World Who's Who of Women, 1973- . Cambridge: International Biographical Centre. irregular.

(10th ed, 1990) A who's who of women who have achieved fame in many areas of accomplishment (academe, business, entertainment, government, sports, etc.). Short entries with photographs. For additional biographical information on women, see AL14.
MTRL BU/SS

CH   PSCYCHOLOGY

Bibliographies and Guides to the Literature

CH1 **Bibliographic Guide to Psychology,** 1975- . Boston: G.K. Hall. annual.

Lists all material catalogued each year by the New York Public Library and the Library of Congress in LC classification BF. Covers psychology, parapsychology and occult sciences. Arranged by main entry.

CH2 McInnis, Raymond G. **Research Guide for Psychology.** Westport, CT: Greenwood Press, 1982. 604 p.

Intended as "a research guide that contains the principal information sources in a logically integrated and critically analytical format." Bibliographical essays in 16 topical sections; with an additional chapter on general works by type. Lists works published to the end of 1979. Author, title, subject indexes.
Z7201 M35 ROBA

CH3 Osier, Donald V. and Robert H. Wozniak. **A Century of Serial Publications in Psychology 1850–1950: An International Bibliography.** Millwood, NY: Kraus International, 1984. 805 p.

Provides information on publishing histories of a wide range of psychology and psychology-related journals and monograph series. International coverage. Information on current journals can be found in *Journals in Psychology: A Resource Listing for Authors* (2d ed, American Psychological Association, 1989) (016.1505 J86 Ref OISE), which is a guide to 233 English-language periodicals. Indexed by subject areas of interest.
Z7203 O8

CH4 **PsycBOOKS,** 1987- .   5 vols. Washington: American Psychological Association. annual.

PsycBOOKS complements *PsycINFO* (CH9) by providing access to the 30% of published information in psychology which is published in books. The annual volumes cite more than 1,000 books and almost 6,000 chapters in edited books covering basic and applied experimental psychology; developmental, personality, and social psychology; professional psychology, disorders and treatment; educational and health psychology. Also includes author, subject, publisher, and book title indexes.

CH5 Reed, Jeffrey G. and Pam M. Baxter. **Library Use: A Handbook for Psychology.** Washington: American Psychological Association, 1983. 137 p.

Designed as a guide to library research for undergraduates. Includes information on library resources and how to use them. Covers indexing and abstracting services, U.S. government publications, computerized searching, current awareness sources, tests and measurement, and biographical sources. Includes instructions on literature searching and a discussion on selecting and defining topics for student papers. Complementing this work is *Library Research Guide to Psychology: Illustrated Search Strategy and Sources* by Nancy Douglas and Nathan Baum (Pierian Press, 1984) (BF76.5 D63), which provides similar information.
BF76.8 R43

Abstracts and Indexes

CH6 **Child Development Abstracts and Bibliography,** 1927- . Chicago: University of Chicago Press for the Society for Research in Child Development. 3 issues per year.

Abstracts of periodical articles arranged by broad subject; book reviews arranged by author. Author and subject indexes; cumulated indexes in last issue.
HQ750 A1C47

CH7 **Current Contents: Social and Behavioral Sciences,** 1969- weekly.

Provides tables of contents of journals in psychology, psychiatry, education, sociology, and other areas. See DA15 for full entry information.

CH8 **Psychological Abstracts: Nonevaluative Summaries of the Serial Literature in Psychology and Related Disciplines,** 1927- . Arlington, VA: American Psychological Association. monthly.

Each issue contains about 3,000 abstracts of articles published in over 1,400 international journals organized by broad subject areas and subdivided into specific topics, with author and brief subject indexes. Cumulative indexes appear quarterly, with annual subject and author indexes. Cumulative indexes are also published triennially. Covers all areas of psychology, as well as anthropology, education, management and sociology. Available online and on CD-ROM on *PsycINFO* (CH9).
BF1 P65

CH9 **PsycINFO,** 1974- . Arlington, VA: American Psychological Association. databases. updated quarterly.

Database version of *Psychological Abstracts* (CH8). Several quarterly current awareness publications are produced from the *PsycINFO* database, including *PsycSCAN: Applied Psychology* (1981–); *PsycSCAN: Clinical Psychology* (1980-); *PsycSCAN: Developmental Psychology* (1982-); and *PsycSCAN: Learning and Communication Disorders and Mental Retardation* (1982-). Issues contain abstracts of journal articles, arranged by journal title.
Thesaurus of Psychological Index Terms

(5th ed, 1988, American Psychological Association) (Z695.1 P65T4) is helpful in accessing *PsycINFO*.

Reviews and Annuals

CH10 **L'année psychologique**, 1894- . Paris, Presses Universitaires de France. semi-annual.

Contains critical reviews of international current research in chosen areas of psychology. Reviews are in French with abstracts in English. Also includes evaluative book reviews, written in French.
BF2 A6 PRRH

CH11 **Annual Review of Psychology**, 1950- . Palo Alto, CA: Annual Reviews. annual.

Each review covers a variety of topics in essay format, each with an extensive bibliography. Some areas of psychology are covered annually, some biennially, and others less frequently. Essays are international, reviewing research conducted around the world. Includes author and subject indexes, with a five-year cumulative list of articles arranged in a classified format.
BF30 A56

CH12 **Contemporary Psychology: A Journal of Reviews**, 1956- . Arlington, VA: American Psychological Association. monthly.

Each issue provides critical reviews of some 60 new scholarly and professional books and films in the areas of psychology and psychiatry, public opinion, and animal behaviour, published in English in the U.S. Includes an annual author and reviewer index.
BF1 C53 PRRH

CH13 **The Psychological Bulletin**, 1904- . Arlington, VA: American Psychological Association. bimonthly.

Each issue includes evaluative reviews of research literature in all areas of psychology.
BF1 P68O2 PRRH

Encyclopedias and Dictionaries, Manuals, and Handbooks

CH14 Bruno, Frank. **Dictionary of Key Words in Psychology.** London: Routledge & Kegan Paul, 1986. 275 p.

Defines current and frequently used psychological terms with examples of use and "connections" to broader concepts. Includes bibliography and brief biographies.
BF31 B78 ROBA

CH15 Campbell, Robert Jean. **Psychiatric Dictionary.** 6th ed. New York: Oxford University Press, 1989. 811 p.

First published in 1940. Earlier editions edited by Leland E. Hinsic and Jacob Shatzky. Takes into account *DSM-III* (CH16) and reflects many changes and technological advances since the 1970 edition.
RC437 H5 BMER

CH16 **Diagnostic and Statistical Manual of Mental Disorders: DSM-III-R.** 3d ed, rev. Washington: American Psychiatric Association, 1987. 567 p.

DSM-III is widely accepted in the U.S. as the language of the mental health field. This revision of *DSM-III*, third edition, provides "clear descriptions of diagnostic categories in order to enable clinicians and investigators to

diagnose, communicate about, and treat the various mental disorders." Includes classification codes, diagnostic categories, decision trees for differential diagnosis, a glossary of terms, etc.
RC455.2 C4D54 BMER

CH17 Dictionary of Behavioral Science. 2d ed., 1989.

Contains terms relevant to psychology. See CA23 for full entry information.

CH18 Encyclopedia of Occultism and Parapsychology. 2d ed. 3 vols. Ed. by Leslie Shepard. Detroit: Gale, 1984.

Contains articles of varying length on the occult sciences, magic, demonology, superstitions, spiritism, mysticism, metaphysics, psychical science, and parapsychology, many with bibliographies. Based on *Encyclopedia of Occultism* by Lewis Spence (London, 1920), and *Encyclopaedia of Psychic Science* by Nandor Fodor, (London, 1934), with revisions and additional information. Includes biographical data on prominent individuals and personalities in the field. Cross referenced with subject and general indexes.
BF1407 E518

CH19 Encyclopedia of Psychology. 4 vols. Ed. by R.J. Corsini. New York: J. Wiley, 1984.

Volumes 1-3 contain separate articles on some 2,150 topics and persons, including descriptions of tests and summary of psychology worldwide. Volume 4 contains bibliography. Cross-referenced with subject index. Also available is an abridged edition, the *Concise Encyclopedia of Psychology* (Wiley, 1987, 1242 p.) (BF31 E553 VUPR), which eliminates or condenses bibliographical and biographical material, but does add new information and updates material in the larger set.
BF31 E5545

CH20 The Encyclopedic Dictionary of Psychology. Ed. by Rom Harré and Roger Lamb. London: Blackwell Reference; Cambridge, MA: MIT Press, 1983. 718 p.

Covers the broad range of psychological topics. Alphabetical organization with cross references and index for improved access. Many articles include bibliographies. Harré and Lamb have also published *The Dictionary of Personality and Social Psychology* (Blackwell, 1986) (HM251 D53).
BF31 E555

CH21 International Encyclopedia of Psychiatry, Psychology, Psychoanalysis & Neurology. 12 vols. Ed. by Benjamin B. Wolman. New York: Van Nostrand, 1977. *Progress Volume*, (Aesculapius Publishers, 1983).

Includes nearly 2,000 signed articles by specialists. Volume 12 contains an extensive bibliography, though few items are later than 1974. The *Progress Volume* focuses on new developments.
RC334 I57

CH22 Longman Dictionary of Psychology and Psychiatry. Ed. by Robert M. Goldenson. New York: Longman, 1984. 815 p.

Comprehensive dictionary with over 21,000 brief entries. Emphasis is on current terms, but also includes older terms with historical value. Includes definitions of disorders found in *DSM-III* (CH16) and appendices include classification codes and lists of test and therapy entries.
BF31 L66

CH23 Popplestone, John A. and Marion White McPherson. **Dictionary of Concepts in General Psychology.** Westport, CT: Greenwood Press, 1988. 380 p.

Contains essays examining about 50 concepts in behavioural psychology. Includes cross references, sources of additional information, and name and subject indexes.
BF31 P665

CH24 Stratton, P. and N. Hayes. **A Student's Dictionary of Psychology.** New York: Routledge, Chapman & Hall, 1988. 216 p.

Defines basic terms used in contemporary psychology with emphasis on clinical, experimental and theoretical psychology and statistics and measurement. Includes flowcharts, tables, drawings, etc. to clarify difficult ideas. Stuart Smith's *The International Dictionary of Psychology* (New York: Continuum, 1989) (BF31 S87 ROBA), published in England as *Macmillan Dictionary of Psychology*, covers similar terminology but with few illustrations.
MTRL BU/SS

CH25 Zusne, Leonard. **Biographical Dictionary of Psychology.** Westport, CT: Greenwood Press, 1984. 563 p.

Revised edition of *Names in the History of Psychology: A Biographical Sourcebook* (1975). Provides brief biographical information on 627 deceased psychologists.
BF109 A1 Z85

* * * *

Tests and Measurement

CH26 **The Tenth Mental Measurements Yearbook.** Ed. by Jane Close Conoley and Jack J. Kramer. Lincoln, NB: University of Nebraska Press, 1989. 1014 p. *Supplement* 1990, 321 p.

Does not supersede the earlier editions. Contains information (test title, group for whom intended, date of publication, validity and reliability data, length, time of administration, publisher, etc.) on new and revised tests that have been printed since the *Ninth Mental Measurements Yearbook* (1985). Tests are reviewed by experts in psychometrics and test evaluation. See also *Tests in Print* (CH28).
Z58144 P3B932

CH27 **Test Critiques.** 8 vols. Ed. by Daniel Keyser and Richard C. Sweetland. Kansas City, MO: Test Corporation of America, 1984-1991.

Provides reviews and critiques of tests frequently used in psychology, education and business, discussing application, administration, scoring, and interpretation. Validity and reliability studies are cited, along with other relevant sources.
BF176 T419

CH28 **Tests in Print III: An Index to Tests, Test Reviews, and the Literature of Specific Tests.** Ed. by James V. Mitchell. Lincoln, NE: Buros Institute of Mental Measurements, University of Nebraska-Lincoln, 1983. 714 p.

A companion to *Mental Measurements Yearbook* (CH26), provides "descriptive listings and references, without reviews, of commercially published tests that are in print and available for

purchase and use... [and] a comprehensive index to the contents of *Mental Measurements Yearbooks*." Includes 2,672 tests.
Z5814 E9T47

Directories

CH29 **Directory of the American Psychological Association,** 1918- . Washington: American Psychological Association. quadrennial.

A comprehensive current listing of some 54,000 members of the APA; providing education, specialty, employment information. Includes a geographical index. Supplemented annually by the *APA Membership Register*.
BF11 A67

CH30 **Directory of the Canadian Psychological Association,** 1960- . Montreal: C.P.A. annual.

Lists current members, present, past officers of the Canadian Psychological Association.
BF30 C35

CH31 **International Directory of Psychologists Exclusive of the U.S.A.** 4th ed. Amsterdam: North-Holland Publishing, 1985.

Lists more than 32,000 psychologists worldwide, excluding Americans, who are listed in the APA *Directory* (CH29). Arranged by country.
BF109 A1I5 BMER

CH32 **Psychware Sourcebook.** 2d ed. Ed. by Samuel E. Krug. Kansas City, MO: Test Corporation of America, 1987. 457 p.

Lists some 300 computer based assessment products for use in psychology, eduction and business, noting supplier, category, publications, sale restrictions and pricing. Products are described, with samples.
155.28 K94P Ref OISE

CI   EDUCATION

Bibliographies and Guides to the Literature

CI1 Auster, Ethel. **Reference Sources on Canadian Education: An Annotated Bibliography.** OISE Bibliography Series, No. 3. Toronto: Ontario Institute for Studies in Education, 1978. 114 p.
 Lists selected reference sources arranged by subject. Includes author-title index.
R370.971 AA934R   or   016.370971 A934R Ref OISE

CI2 Buttlar, Lois J. **Education: A Guide to Reference and Information Sources.** Englewood, CO: Libraries Unlimited, 1989. 258 p.
 Provides descriptions of mainly American sources of information in education and related fields. Lists over 900 print sources as well as online databases, major research centres and organizations, and periodical titles.
R370 AB988E   or   011.02 R988E Ref OISE

CI3 Finley, E.G. **Education in Canada: A Bibliography / L'education au Canada: une bibliographie.** 2 vols. Toronto: Dundurn Press, 1989.
 Contains over 14,000 items, in English and French, related to the development of education in Canada from the seventeenth century to the early 1980s. Includes books, theses, reports, research studies, and government documents. Arranged by author, title, and subject. Also available on diskettes and machine-readable magnetic tape.
R370.971 AF513E   or
016.370971 F513E Ref OISE

CI4 Harris, Robin S. and others. **A Bibliography of Higher Education in Canada / Bibliographie de l'enseignement supérieur au Canada.** Studies in Higher Education in Canada. Toronto: University of Toronto Press, 1960. 158 p. *Supplement* 1965; 1971; 1981.

Series title varies. Entries are arranged under broad headings with subdivisions. Includes books, periodical articles, theses and reports.
R378.71 AH315   or   016.37871 H315B Ref OISE

CI5 Woodbury, Marda. **A Guide to Sources of Educational Information.** 2d ed. Arlington, VA: Information Resources Press, 1982. 430 p.
"The coverage is largely current and American." A guide to the research process, printed research tools, special subject, instructional materials, and non-print sources.
370 AW885G (1976)   or
016.37 W885G Ref OISE

Abstracts and Indexes

CI6 British Education Index, 1954- . Leeds, U.K: Leeds University Press. quarterly with annual cumulation.
"Aims to list and analyse the content of all articles of permanent educational interest in a wide range of English language periodicals published in the British Isles, together with certain internationally published periodicals." Articles indexed by subject and by author. Available online.
370 B862 Ref OISE

CI7 CD:Education, 1991- . Toronto: Micromedia. CD-ROM. quarterly discs.
Combines several key educational databases including: *Canadian Education Index* (CI8), *CEA Handbook/Ki-es-ki* (CI30), and *ONTERIS*, the Ontario Ministry of Education database, which include publications and materials from the Ministry, OISE, boards of education, faculties of education, teachers' associations, TV Ontario, and other educational agencies.
OISE

CI8 Canadian Education Index / Répertoire canadien sur l'education, 1965- . Toronto: Micromedia Ltd. 3 issues / year; annual cumulation.
Provides an author and a subject index to over 200 Canadian education periodicals as well as books, reports, theses, book reviews, and curriculum documents. Abstracts provided for all reports and monographs and selected theses in a separate section arranged by title. Available online and on CD-ROM. *Canadian Education Thesaurus*, edited by Michelle Hudon (Micromedia, 1988) (R025.4937 C2124) is the subject authority file for *CEI*.
016.37 C2124 Ref OISE

CI9 Contents Pages in Education, 1986- . Abingdon, U.K: Carfax Publishing. monthly.
An international current awareness service showing the content pages of over 600 education journals. Contents pages arranged alphabetically by journal titles; also includes author and subject index.
016.3705 C761 Ref OISE

CI10 Current Index to Journals in Education, 1969- . Phoenix, AZ: Oryx Press [for ERIC], 1979- . monthly, semi-annual cumulation.

CIJE indexes over 700 journals, including some indexed in *Education Index*, CI11. Main entry section arranged by broad subject area; also indexed by subject, author and journal name. Short abstracts provided for all entries. Available online and on CD-ROM.
050.16 C9765 Ref OISE

CI11 **Education Index: A Cumulative Author Subject Index to a Selected List of Educational Periodicals and Yearbooks,** 1929- . New York: H.W. Wilson. monthly; with quarterly, annual cumulations.

Indexes by subject and author about 330 journal titles, including some also indexed by *CIJE*, CI10. Important yearbooks, proceedings, and selected U.S. government publications included. Separate list of book reviews. Available online and on CD-ROM.
370 E24 Ref OISE

CI12 ERIC (Educational Resources Information Center). See entry numbers CI10 and CI13 for *Current Index to Journals in Education* and *Resources in Education* for full bibliographic information.

CI13 **Resources in Education,** 1975- . Washington: GPO [for ERIC, National Institute of Education, U.S. Dept. of Education]. monthly; semi-annual cumulative index.

Formerly titled *Research in Education*, 1966–1974. Indexes research, conference papers, and other types of mainly unpublished material collected by ERIC clearinghouses. Provides subject, author, institution, and publication type index. Detailed abstracts provided for all entries. Available online and on CD-ROM.
370.78 R4342 Ref OISE

Encyclopedias and Dictionaries, Annuals, and Handbooks

CI14 **Educational Media and Technology Yearbook,** Vol. 11, 1985- . Littleton, CO: Libraries Unlimited. annual.

Provides essays that give an overview of the field of educational media and technology. Each year focuses on a particular theme. Essays arranged by broad subject category, with author, title, subject, and organizational index.
AV 371.3078 E2422 OISE

CI15 **Encyclopedia of Education.** 10 vols. Ed. by L.C. Deighton. New York: Macmillan, 1970.

Provides more than 1,000 articles dealing with history, theory, research, philosophy and structure of education. Useful from an historical point of view.
370.3 E563 Ref OISE

CI16 **Encyclopedia of Educational Research.** 5th ed. 4 vols. Ed. by Harold E. Mitzel. New York: Free Press, 1982.

Sponsored by the American Educational Research Association. Substantial articles cover 18 broad topics, most with extensive bibliographies. Name and topical index.
370.78 E56 Ref OISE

CI17 **Encyclopedia of Special Education.** 3 vols. Ed. by Cecil R. Reynolds and Lester Mann. New York: John Wiley, 1987.

"A reference for the education of the handicapped and other exceptional children and adults."
371.903 E56 Ref OISE

CI18 Good, Carter, V. **Dictionary of Education.** 3d ed. New York: McGraw Hill, 1973. 681 p.

Defines technical, professional terms and concepts in education, as well as terms in related fields.
370.3 G646D Ref OISE

CI19 The International Encyclopedia of Education: Research and Studies. 1st ed. 10 vols. Ed. by Torsten Husén and T. Neville Postlethwaite. Oxford: Pergamon Press, 1985. *Supplementary Volumes*, 1989- .

Contains 1,448 well-documented articles that present an overview of educational developments worldwide since 1960. Volume 10 contains a subject index, based on key words in the articles, as well as an author index and a classified list of entries. *Advances in Education* (1987-) (various call numbers) is a series of handbooks and encyclopedias developed primarily from this encyclopedia.
370.3 I61 Ref OISE

CI20 The International Encyclopedia of Higher Education. 10 vols. San Francisco: Jossey Bass, 1977.

"A first attempt to bring together all major aspects of international higher education." Substantial articles on subject and geographic areas. Name and subject indexes.
378.003 I61 Ref OISE

CI21 International Handbook of Women's Education. Ed. by Gail P. Kelly. New York: Greenwood Press, 1989. 657 p.

Compares information on women's education across a broad spectrum of countries. Discusses history, current status, and outcomes of women's schooling. Arranged geographically. Includes an essay on worldwide trends in women's education and a bibliography.
376 I61 Ref OISE

CI22 International Higher Education: An Encyclopedia. 2 vols. Ed. by Philip G. Altbach. New York: Garland Publishing, 1991.

Includes 67 essays by scholars in the field dealing with topics such as academic freedom, costs of higher education, graduate education, university reform, and women in higher education. Also provides coverage of 51 major nations and smaller countries with important developments in higher education.
OISE   or   LB15 I59

CI23 An Overview of Canadian Education. 3d ed. Toronto: Canadian Education Association, 1984. 56 p.

Provides a "brief, general overview of education in Canada, describing how it is structured and supported as well as common principles and practices." New edition in progress.
370.971 G2860 Ref OISE

CI24 Page, G.T., J.B. Thomas and A.R. Marshall. **International Dictionary of Education.** London: Kogan Page, 1977. 381 p.

Over 10,000 brief entries for all aspects and levels of education. International terminology with wide coverage of national and international organizations and associations.
370.3 P132I Ref OISE

CI25 Palmer, James C. **Dictionary of Educational Acronyms, Abbreviations, and Initialisms.** 2d ed. Phoenix, AZ: Oryx Press, 1985. 97 p.

Provides a listing of acronyms and other short forms found in documents, journal articles, and monographs in the field of education. First section arranged alphabetically by acronym; the second lists unabbreviated forms.
370.3 P174D Ref OISE

CI26 Shafritz, Jay H., Richard P. Koeppe and Elizabeth W. Soper. **The Facts on File Dictionary of Education.** New York: Facts on File, 1988. 503 p.

A comprehensive, very much American-oriented dictionary of "words, terms, phrases, processes, names, laws, and court cases" of interest to those in the field of education.
370.3 S525F Ref OISE

CI27 **World Education Encyclopedia.** 3 vols. Ed. by George Thomas Kurian. New York: Facts on File, 1988.

"Designed as a descriptive survey of the national educational systems of the world." Countries divided into major and minor categories with information on each provided following a standardized format.
370.3 W927 Ref OISE

Directories

CI28 **American Universities and Colleges,** 1928- . Hawthorne, N.Y: Walter de Gruyter. irregular.

Provides a detailed overview of 1,900 accredited institutions of higher education in the U.S. that offer a baccalaureate or higher degree. Also offers a large section providing a description of accreditation activities in 40 professional fields. Includes a general and an institutional index. Appendices provide additional statistics on earned degrees and summary data on enrollment, teaching staff, etc. for each institution.
378.73025 A5128 Ref OISE

CI29 Ashley, Thomas. **Directory of Canadian Private Residential Schools.** Toronto: Methuen, 1986. 461 p.

A guide for parents providing descriptions and list of programs for private residential schools in Canada, or schools abroad owned or operated by Canadians. Other directories for Canadian private schools are: *Directory of Member Schools*, published by the Canadian Association of Independent Schools, (1989-) (371.0202571 C2124D Ref OISE); and *Peterson's Guide to Independent Secondary Schools* (Peterson's Guides, 1988-) (373.2220257 P4851 Ref OISE), which lists American and Canadian private schools.
371.0202571 T482 D Ref OISE

CI30 **The CEA Handbook,** 1970- . Toronto: Canadian Education Association. annual.

Known in French as "*Le ki-es-ki*", this bilingual handbook lists officials of provincial education departments, school boards, teacher education institutions, universities and community colleges, and education organizations. Available on CD-ROM on *CD-Education* (CI7). Provincial directories are also available, such as the *Directory of Education / Annuaire de l'administration scolaire* (L906 O6A34), published by the Ontario Ministry of Education, which lists publicly supported schools, school boards, and education officials, organized by geographic area.
371.2006271 C2124C Ref OISE

CI31 **Commonwealth Universities Yearbook: A Directory to the Universities of**

the Commonwealth and the Handbook of Their Association, 1914- . 4 vols. London: Association of Commonwealth Universities. annual.

Under each country lists principal officers, teaching staff, and general information on each institution granting degrees. For larger countries, there is an article on the university system. Indexed by institution and topics, by subjects of study, and by names.
378.0025 C734 Ref OISE

CI33   Directory of Canadian Universities / Répertoire des universités canadiennes, 1958- . Ottawa: Association of Universities and Colleges of Canada. biennial.

Comprehensive guide to Canadian universities including information on history, programs of study, admission requirements, tuition fees, academic year, grading system, research facilities, etc. Arranged alphabetically by institution with an index by program. A companion volume is *Universities Telephone Directory: A Guide to Academic and Administrative Officers at Canadian Universities* (1989-) (LB2341.8 C2D562).

Popular guide books providing descriptive comments about Canadian universities include: *Linda Frum's Guide to Canadian Universities* (rev. ed, Key Porter Books, 1990) (L905 F78), which reviews 42 universities and six affiliated colleges across Canada accroding to tuition, residences, enrolment, etc;   Danton O'Day's *How to Succeed at University* (2d ed, Canadian Scholar's Press, 1990) (LB1049 O38 Ref ERIN), which is a directory of universities and a student guide to methods of study, orientation activities, and report writing, and *The Student's Guide to Ontario Universities*, by Dyanne Gibson (University of Toronto Press, 1990) (L906 O6G44), similar to *Frum's* but highlighting only the 17 universities in Ontario.
378.71025 D598 Ref OISE   or   L905 C423

CI34   The Education Authorities Directory and Annual, 1968- . Redhill, U.K: School Government Publishing Company. annual.

Comprehensive list of government departments, local education authorities, middle and secondary schools, universities, polytechnics, teacher training institutions, special schools, and educational organizations and publishers in Great Britain. Includes a section on Commonwealth education departments and universities.
370.942025 E24 Ref OISE

CI35   Gourman, Jack. The Gourman Report: A Rating of Undergraduate Programs in American and International Universities. 7th ed. Los Angeles, CA: National Education Standards, 1989.

This directory, and it's companion *The Gourman Report: A Rating of Graduate and Professional Programs in American and International Universities* (5th ed, 1989) (LA228.5 G68), rank universities and programs on a scale of 1 to 5. While highly controversial because of Gourman's refusal to divulge his methods of determining the value assigned, they are still frequently consulted.
LB2341 G62

CI36   International Handbook of Universities and Other Institutions of Higher Education, 1959- . Paris: International Association of Universities. triennial.

Complements *Commonwealth Universities Yearbook* (CI31) and *American Universities and Colleges*, (CI28). Covers institutions of higher education in all other parts of the world.
378.0025 I614 Ref OISE

CI37   The National Faculty Directory, 1970- . 4 vols. Detroit: Gale Research. annual.

"An alphabetical list, with addresses, of about 597,000 members of teaching faculties at junior colleges, colleges and universities in the U.S. and at selected Canadian institutions." From 1984, an annual supplement of changes and new entries published.
R378.12 N277N (1988)   or   378.12025 N277 Ref OISE

CI38   Patterson's American Education, 1904- . Mount Prospect, IL: Educational Directories. annual.

Comprehensive list of public school districts, public secondary schools, private and parochial secondary schools, and post-secondary institutions in the U.S. School systems arranged by state and town; other institutions by specialty. A similar directory of American elementary public schools is *Patterson's Elementary Education* (1989-) (372.20573 P318 Ref OISE).
370.973025 P318 Ref OISE

CI39   Peterson's Guides. Princeton, NJ: Peterson's Guides. annual.

Series of directories to assist in choosing independent secondary schools, community and junior colleges, undergraduate and graduate university courses, professional programs, scholarships, student aid, etc. in the U.S. Also available on CD-ROM are *Peterson's College DBase* which profiles degree granting institutions in the U.S. and Canada, and *Peterson's Gradline*, which profiles graduate and professional programs in the U.S. and Canada.

Other major directories include *Lovejoy's College Guide* (Monarch Press, biennial) (LA226 L6); *The College Blue Book* (Macmillan, biennial) (LA226 C685), which lists colleges and universities in Canada and the U.S., and *The Right College* (Arco, 1990-) (L901 R54), which has information on over 1,500 U.S. and Canadian post-secondary schools. See also *The Gourman Reports*, CI35.
various call numbers

CI40   Study Abroad, 1948- . Paris: Unesco. biennial.

(27th ed, 1991) A trilingual (English, French, Spanish) publication outlining opportunities for students to take post-secondary education and training (short-term courses, professional in very field - humanities, social sciences, technology, communications) in 124 countries. There is practical information on duration of courses, admissions, fees and costs of living, and, in some instances, facilities for the physically disadvantaged. Editions are intended to cover three academic years, e.g. 1991/92 to 1993/94.
LB 2338 S86

CI41   World of Learning, 1947- . London: Europa. annual.

Organized by country with brief information on learned societies, libraries, museums, galleries, universities and colleges. Introductory section on international bodies. Indexed by institution.
060 W927 Ref OISE

Education Statistics

CI42   Digest of Education Statistics, 1962- . Washington: U.S. Department of Education, Office of Educational Research and Improvement; National Center for Education Statistics. annual.

Major source of American education statistics from kindergarten to graduate school. To be included material must be national in scope and

"of current interest and value." Also includes a guide to statistical sources.
370.973021 D5723 Ref OISE

CI43   Fact Book on Higher Education, 1984/85- . New York: American Council on Education. annual.

Provides U.S. statistical information in 8 areas relevant to higher education: demographic and economic; enrollment; institutions; finance; faculty and staff; students; earned degrees; and student aid.
378.73 F1422 Ref OISE

CI44   Statistics Canada. **Education Statistics Bulletin,** 1984- . Ottawa: Statistics Canada, Education, Culture and Tourism Division. irregular.

The statistical series, *81 Series*, for education publications, including serials and monographs. Examples include *Financial Statistics of Education; Education in Canada: A Statistical Review; Universities, Enrolment and Degrees*. Continues *Service Bulletin* (1979-83).
CA1 BS 81 C992 GOVT

CI45   Trends: The Canadian University in Profile. Ottawa: Association of Universities and College of Canada, 1990. 119 p.

Replaces the *Compendium of University Statistics*. Includes statistical information, text and graphics highlighting the important trends in Canadian universities, such as enrolment figures, degrees granted, faculty, finances, and research. Also published in French.
378.71 T794 Ref OISE

CJ HISTORY AND AREA STUDIES

The *History* section is divided into two parts: **General World History**, CJ1 - CJ51, which, in addition to listing the standard reference sources for history, includes historical time periods, such as Ancient History (CJ28 - CJ34), Medieval and Renaissance History (CJ35 - CJ43), and Modern World History (CJ44- CJ51); and **Area Studies**, CJ52-163, which lists current and historical reference works for regions and countries of the world.

GENERAL WORLD HISTORY

Bibliographies and Guides to the Literature

CJ1 American Historical Association. **Guide to Historical Literature.** New York: Macmillan, 1961. 962 p.

Dated, but useful as an annotated guide to important literature in all historical fields. Entries arranged by time period and/or geographic areas. Foreign language materials are included (all annotations in English). Subject-author index, but no direct access by title. Another guide is *Student's Guide to History* by Jules Benjamin (St. Martin's Press, 1987) (D16.3 B4 VUPT)
Z6201 A55

CJ2 Havlice, Patricia. **Oral History: A Reference Guide and Annotated Bibliography.** Jefferson, NC: McFarland, 1985. 140 p.

Extensive bibliography of books, articles and dissertations published since the 1930s, with most titles from the 1970s and 1980s. Some Canadian and British titles are included. Provides directory information on societies and journals of the oral history movement.
Z6201 H38

CJ3 **Historical Periodicals Directory.** 5 vols. Ed. by Eric H. Boehm and others. Santa Barbara, CA: ABC-Clio, 1981-1986.

This 5 volume set provides citations to worldwide historical periodicals, annuals and serials. Volume 1 covers United States and Canada; Volume 2, Europe; Volume 3, Eastern Europe and USSR; Volume 4, Latin America and West Indies; and Volume 5, Australia and New Zealand. A cumulative subject and geographical index is provided to all volumes in Volume 5.
Z6205 H654

CJ4 **Historiography: An Annotated Bibliography of Journal Articles, Books, and Dissertations.** 2 vols. Ed. by Susan K. Kinnell. Santa Barbara, CA: ABC-Clio, 1987.

Comprehensive coverage of world writings on historiography published from 1970 to 1985. Volume 1 concentrates on the different methodologies and schools of historiography. Volume 2 is arranged by geographic area. The work is "by far the most detailed recent compilation of books, dissertations, and journal articles on all aspects of world historical writing."
Z6208 H5H57

CJ5 **International Bibliography of Historical Sciences,** 1926- . Ed. by International Committee of Historical Sciences. New York: K.G. Saur. annual.

Selective coverage of international historical articles and monographs. Arranged by subject, with name and geographical indexes. There is an approximate four year time lag between years of coverage and publication of volume: Volume 55, 1986 is the latest published.
Z6205 I62

CJ6 Poulton, H.J. and M.S. Howland. **The Historian's Handbook: A Descriptive Guide to Reference Works.** Norman, OK: University of Oklahoma Press, 1977. 304 p.

Basic reference and research titles in history and important titles in allied fields are introduced in bibliographic essays. Covers some 970 international titles. Elizabeth Frick's *Library Research Guide to History: Illustrated Search Strategy and Sources* (Pierian Press, 1980) (D16 F87) is a guide covering materials and methods.
R900 AP876H

Abstracts and Indexes

CJ7 **America: History and Life,** 1964- . Santa Barbara, CA: ABC-Clio. quarterly with annual cumulation.

North American counterpart to *Historical Abstracts* (CJ8). Covers prehistory to present, and scope includes all aspects of U.S. and Canadian history, culture, area studies and current events. Consists of four parts: Part A: contains English language abstracts from over 2,000 serial publications published internationally; Part B: an index to book reviews; Part C: "American History Bibliography", which is further divided into six parts: North America, Canada, U.S. National History to 1945; U.S. National History since 1945; U.S. State and Local History; and History, the Humanities, and Social Sciences. Part C includes abstracts and book reviews in Parts A and B. Part D is the annual index to all four parts. Available online.
E171 A54 O2

CJ8 **Historical Abstracts,** 1955- . Santa Barbara, CA: ABC-Clio. quarterly; cumulative annual index; quinquennial index.

Abstracts over 2,000 historical serials worldwide covering all areas except North America. Published in two parts. Part A: Modern History Abstracts, 1450-1914. Part B: Twentieth Century Abstracts, 1914 to the Present. Subject, biographic, geographic permuted index. From 1980 includes citations for books, theses, selected journals. Available online.
D299 H5

CJ9 **Recently Published Articles,** 1976- . Washington, American Historical Association. 3 issues per year.

Formerly included in the *American Historical Review*. International coverage with citations in general and geographic sections.
Z6205 R4

Encyclopedias, Dictionaries and Handbooks

CJ10 Barzun, Jacques and Henry F. Graff. **The Modern Researcher.** 4th ed. New York: Harcourt, Brace, Jovanovich, 1985. 450 p.

Standard handbook for history students, but also useful for those in other disciplines. Covers techniques of research and writing. Basic reference tools for U.S. history discussed.
D13 B334

CJ11 **Blackwell Dictionary of Historians.** Ed. by John Cannon. New York: Blackwell, 1988. 480 p.

Biographical information on 450 historians as well as essays on 25 nations and 40 historiographical subjects.
D14 B58

CJ12 Cook, Chris. **Dictionary of Historical Terms.** 2d ed. London: Macmillan, 1989. 350 p.

Covers 2,000 historical terms from the fall of the Roman Empire to the present. Global in scope, but emphasis is Western Europe, North America. Military history, politics, economics and religion is emphasized, with few entries for cultural or social concepts, persons or places.
D9 C67

CJ13 **Encyclopedia of Historic Places.** 2 vols. Ed. by Courtlandt Canby. New York: Facts on File, 1984.

Detailed coverage on all geographic locations of historical significance, from ancient times to present.
D9 C29

CJ14 Langer, William L. **The New Illustrated Encyclopedia of World History: Ancient, Medieval, and Modern History Chronologically Arranged.** 2 vols. New York: Abrams, 1975.

An illustrated edition of the earlier *Encyclopedia of World History* (5th ed, 1972), this reference work is considered to be a "historian's Bible". Covers world developments, arranged by period and geographical area, up to 1970 with a chapter on historical events of this century, including space exploration and technological advances.
D21 L28

CJ15 **Macmillan Concise Dictionary of World History.** Comp. by Bruce Wetterau. New York: Macmillan, 1983. 867 p.

Coverage of over 10,000 people, places, and events in history. Chronologies for major events, countries and wars are included.
D9 W47

CJ16 McEvedy, Colin. **The Macmillan World History Factfinder.** New York: Macmillan, 1985. 208 p.

Reviews world history in eight major sections covering "Ancient World", "Feudal Age in Western Europe", to the "Triumph of Technology". Each section includes historical tables, introductory essays, maps and illustrations.
MTRL GIS

Chronologies, Outlines, and Tables

CJ17 **Everyman's Dictionary of Dates.** 7th rev. ed. Ed. by Audrey Butler. London: Dent, 1987. 631 p.

Identifies and provides key dates for people, places, institutions, ideas, movements, events, etc. of major historical significance. Universal in scope, with British emphasis. 7th ed. includes a 73 page "Chronology of Events" section.
D9 D5 (1971 6th ed)

CJ18 Freeman-Grenville, G.S.P. **Chronology of World History: A Calendar of Principal Events from 3000 BC to AD 1976.** 2d ed. London: Rex Collings, 1978. 746 p.

A chronology of world history from 3100 B.C. to 1976, with an emphasis on developments and dates outside of the Western world. Similar to S.H. Steinberg's *Historical Tables 58 BC-AD 1985* (CJ22) and *The People's Chronology*, (CJ21) but includes an extensive index. Arranged in tabular fashion in six columns, making the information easily accessible.
D11 F75

CJ19 Grun, Bernard. **Timetables of History: A Historical Linkage of People and Events.** New York: Simon & Schuster, 1987. 688 p.

Covers historical figures and events from 5000 BC to present day, in all areas of interest. Arranged in parallel columns for comparison purposes.
D11 G78

CJ20 **Newnes Dictionary of Dates,** 2d rev. ed. 1966. See AH53 for full entry information.

CJ21 **The People's Chronology: A Year-by-Year Record of Human Events from Prehistory to the Present.** Ed. by James Trage. New York: Holt, Rinehart & Winston, 1979. 1206 p.

Contains over 30,000 entries covering events in areas from political affairs to technology to environment and food and drink. Symbols are used to assist user in locating information.
D11 T83

CJ22 Steinberg, S.H. **Historical Tables 58 BC- AD 1985.** 11th ed. Updated by John Paxton. New York: Garland, 1987. 320 p.

A chronological table of political, economic, and cultural events. Includes noteworthy events of world history from 58 BC to 1985.
D11 S83 (10th ed)

CJ23 **World Almanac Dictionary of Dates.** Ed. by Lawrence Urdang. New York: Longman, 1982. 318 p.

Includes over 10,000 events in world history from B.C. to present times arranged alphabetically by topic or name. All fields are included, with emphasis on popular interests in the 20th century.
D9 W73

Atlases

CJ24 **Harper Atlas of World History.** Toronto: Fitzhenry & Whiteside, 1987. 340 p.

Attractive and colourful atlas covering all time periods. Includes maps, photographs, and charts as well as explanatory notes and chronologies.
G1030 G68513 MapL

CJ25 **Rand McNally Atlas of World History.** Rev. ed. Ed. by R.I. Moore. Chicago: Rand McNally, 1987. 191 p.

Covers period from the Ice Age to 1986. Maps are large and clear and deal with specific time periods or movements (e.g. Reformation). Text is informative and references to additional literature are provided.
MTRL MAPS

CJ26 Shepherd, William R. **Shepherd's Historical Atlas.** 9th ed. New York: Harper & Row, 1973. 115 p.

Covers world history from ancient Egypt (3000 BC-252 BC) to 1964, with emphasis on Europe and North America.
G1030 S4

CJ27 **The Times Atlas of World History.** 3d ed. Ed. by Geoffrey Barraclough. London: Times Books Limited, 1989. 358 p.

Including over 600 maps and illustrations, this work aims to cover world historical geography with an emphasis on broad movements and worldwide events rather than national changes. Divided into seven chronological stages, from "early man" to "global civilization." An extensive chronology preceeding the atlas, a glossary, and an index of historical place names is included.
G1030 T54 Atlases

Ancient History

CJ28 **Atlas of Classical History.** Ed. by J.A. Talbert. London: Croom Helm, 1985. 217 p.

An atlas of classical history to the time of Constantine. Geared to high school and undergraduate students. Includes major archaeological sites and extensive mapping of the classical world.
G1033 A83

CJ29 **Atlas of the Greek and Roman World in Antiquity.** Ed. by N.G.L. Hammond. Park Ridge, NJ: Noyes Press, 1981. 56 p.

Contains 46 high quality maps covering the Greco-Roman world from Neolithic Age to 500 A.D. Maps for political organization, economic resources, trade routes, climate, geology, and excavated archaeological sites are included. Written for the more advanced reader. A less detailed work suitable for the nonspecialist is *Ancient History Atlas 1700BC to 565 AD* (3d ed, London: Weidenfeld & Nicolson) (G1033 G65 MAPL).
G1033 A84 MAPL

CJ30 **Cambridge Ancient History Series.** 3d ed. 12 vols. Cambridge: Cambridge University Press, 1970- in progress.

The standard, comprehensive reference for ancient history. The twelve volumes cover the time period from Prehistory and the Early Middle East (Volume 1), to Assyrian and Babylonian Empires, the Greek World, Persian Empire, Hellenistic World, Rome and Mediterranean, Roman Republic, Augustine Empire, and the Imperial Crisis 324 A.D. in Volume 12. Extensive bibliographies and index in each volume. Plates are published in separate volumes. New volumes are still published as Part I or Part II of an established volume, e.g. Volume 7 Part 2 *The Rise of Rome to 220 B.C.* (2d ed, 1990).
D57 C25

CJ31 **Chronology of the Ancient World.** 2d ed. Ed. by E.J. Bickerman. Ithaca, NY: Cornell University Press, 1980. 223 p.

Written for advanced scholars in ancient history. Includes calendars, and chronological tables of rulers, etc. to 476 A.D. Also provides information on the evolution of the Julian calendar, and ancient calendars, and answers the question of how to date events in ancient times.
D54.5 B5

CJ32 Grant, Michael. **Guide to the Ancient World: A Dictionary of Classical Place Names.** New York: H.W. Wilson, 1986. 736 p.

Provides background information, such as history, geography, archaelogy, art, mythology, etc, and maps of important places of the ancient Greek, Roman and Etruscan empires. Includes 900 essays, arranged alphabetically by placename, with extensive bibliography. Suitable for the nonspecialist reader. A more detailed and scholarly work is *The Princeton Encyclopedia of Classical Sites* (1976, Princeton University Press) (DE59 P7).
DE25 G72

CJ33 **Oxford Classical Dictionary.** 2d ed. Ed. by N.G.L. Hammond, Oxford: Clarendon Press, 1970. 1176 p.

Standard reference work provides brief entries of events in Roman and Greek culture, including bibliographical references. Longer articles are included for major events or people. Can be used in conjunction with *New Century Classical Handbook*, edited by Catherine Avery (Appleton-Crofts, 1962) (DE5 N4 ROBA), or *Who's Who in the Ancient World: A Handbook to the Survivors of the Greek and Roman Classics*, (Penguin, 1973) (DE7 R33 ROBA).
DE5 O9

CJ34 **Who Was Who in the Greek World 776 BC - 30 BC.** Ed. by Diana Bowder. Ithaca, NY: Cornell University Press, 1982. 227 p.

A similar reference work is also available for Roman history called *Who Was Who in the Roman World 753 BC – AD 476*, also edited by Diana Bowder (Cornell University Press, 1980) (DG203 W45).
DF208 W56

Medieval History

Bibliographies and Guides to the Literature

CJ35 Boyce, Gray C. **Literature of Medieval History, 1930–1975.** 5 vols. New York: Kraus, 1981.

A supplement to Louis Paetow's *Guide to the Study of Medieval History* (Kraus, 1980 reprint of c1917) (Z6203 P19 VUCR). Sponsored by the Medieval Academy of America. A comprehensive guide to the literature written between 1930 and 1975, especially for Western Europe and excluding works specifically on English history. Organized in three parts: 1) General Works, Reference, Auxiliary; 2) General Histories, Chronologically; 3) Medieval Culture to 1500. The semi-annual *International Medieval Bibliography* (1967-, University of Leeds) (Z6203 I6) updates Boyce's work. It covers periodical literature, essays, etc. published throughout the world in all areas of the European Middle Ages (AD 450 - 1500). Over 3,000 periodicals are included each year.
Z6203 B6

CJ36 Caenegem, R.C. van. **Guide to the Sources of Medieval History.** New York: Elsevier, 1978. 428 p.

A comprehensive guide to medieval history, with an emphasis on Western European sources.
D116 M4 ROBA

CJ37 Crosby, Everett. **Medieval Studies: A Bibliographical Guide.** New York: Garland Publications, 1983. 1131 p.

Contains approximately 9,000 entries covering reference sources and secondary literature on the Middle Ages in Europe between the 3rd and 5th centuries A.D.
Z5579.5 C76

CJ38 Powell, James M. **Medieval Studies: An Introduction.** Syracuse, NY: Syracuse University Press, 1976. 389 p.

This work is a useful starting point for student research into Western culture before 1500 AD. Chapters cover various aspects of medieval studies, and summarize state of current knowledge and recent trends in scholarship. Bibliographies up to 1974 are included.
D116 M4 ROBA

Dictionaries, Encyclopedias, Handbooks, and Atlases

CJ39 **Cambridge Medieval History.** 8 vols / 6 vols. Cambridge: Cambridge University Press, 1911–1936.

The 8 volumes cover the period from Christian Roman Empire to the close of the Middle Ages. Written by experts with bibliographic references included. A second edition of Volume 4, published in 2 parts (1966-67), is a reworking of the earlier volume 4, *The Byzantine Empire.*
D117 C3

CJ40 **Chronology of the Medieval World 800–1491.** Ed. by R.L. Storey. London: Barrie and Jenkins, 1973. 705 p.

List of political events and social and cultural happenings. European emphasis, with coverage of other continents, if available.
D118 S855 VUPR

CJ41 **Dictionary of the Middle Ages.** 12 vols. Ed. by John R. Strayer. New York: Scribners, 1982-1989.

Includes over 5,000 entries, ranging from brief definitions to major articles; bibliographies primarily in English language. Index to the set is available as Volume 13. Other works in the same area include Joseph Dahmus' *Dictionary of Medieval Civilization* (Macmillan, 1984) (CB351 D24), and Aryeh Grabois' *Illustrated Encyclopedia of Medieval Civilization* (Oxford University Press, 1988) (D102 O94 ROBA).
D114 D5

CJ42 Holmes, George. **Oxford Illustrated History of Medieval Europe.** Toronto: Oxford University Press, 1988. 398 p.

Covers time-period from the fall of the Roman Empire to the dawn of the Renaissance. Includes maps, tables, and bibliographies. A scholarly reference work which is a useful introduction to the history of countries and cultures in the European/Mediterranean area.
D102 O94 ROBA

CJ43 Platt, Colin. **The Atlas of Medieval Man.** New York: St. Martin's Press, 1980. 256 p.

Analytical encyclopedia/atlas of the Middle Ages, covering the period 1000 to 1400 AD, and each major global region. The historical evolution of each region is traced, with maps and illustrations included. Other similar works

include Donald Matthew's *Atlas of Medieval Europe* (Facts on File, 1983) (CB351 M293 MAPL).
CB351 P587

Modern History

Encyclopedias and Handbooks

CJ44 Cook, Chris and John Stevenson. **The Longman Handbook of Modern European History 1763 to 1985.** White Plains, NY: Longman, 1987. 435 p.
 Covers the political, economic, and diplomatic history for Germany, Austria-Hungary, Italy, and Spain. Great Britain is covered in *Longman Handbook of Modern British History 1914-1980*. Major events, statistics, topic bibliographies, and an index makes this work a useful introduction to European history.
940.2 C771L OISE

CJ45 Cook, Chris and John Stevenson. **The Longman Handbook of World History Since 1914.** London: Longman Publishing, 1991. 480 p.
 Designed for student and general reader as a handy reference work for facts and figures of modern world history from World War I to the late 1980's. Political chronologies and government information and international organizations are included.

CJ46 Gibbons, S.R. **Handbook of Modern History: World History Since 1870.** New York: Longman, 1986. 270 p.
 Contains 450 articles on events, personalities, organizations, political ideas and concepts, and important scientific cultural influences. Arranged alphabetically with cross references.
D395 G53 ROBA

CJ47 **Larousse Encyclopedia of Modern History from 1500 to the Present Day.** New rev.ed. Ed. by Marcel Dunan. Middlesex, UK: Spring Books, 1987. 437 p.
 Contains 23 chapters of continuous narrative of European history from 1500 to 1980.
D209 H5153 VUPR (1964)

CJ48 **The New Cambridge Modern History.** 13 vols. plus Atlas. Cambridge: Cambridge University Press, 1957-79.
 Covers period from the Renaissance (1493-1520) to 1945. Separate indexes in each volume with no cumulation.
D208 C16

Chronologies, Outlines, and Tables

CJ49 Clifton, Daniel. **Chronicle of the 20th Century.** Mount Kisco, NY: Chronicle Publications, 1987. 1357 p.
 Published in 13 languages and in 15 countries, each adapted to suit national readership. Covers events on a month-by-month basis from January 1900 to December 1987. Cross references link events. Includes a detailed analytical index.
D427 C47 ROBA

CJ50 de Ford, Miriam Allen and Joan S. Jackson. **Who Was When? A Dictionary of Contemporaries.** 3d ed. New York: H.W. Wilson, 1976. 184 p.

This well-known quick reference work provides access to over 10,000 historical figures between 500 BC and 1974. Information is arranged in chronological order and in field of subject expertise. Birth and death dates are included. Indexed.
CT103 D4

CJ51 **20th Century.** 20 vols. Ed. by A.J.P. Taylor and J.M. Roberts. 1979 ed. revised by R. Cross. Milwaukee, WI: Purnell Reference Books, 1979.

This 20 volume work updates the 10-volume set published in 1971-72 under the title *Purnell's History of the 20th Century*. It is a thematical, chronological, illustrated history of world events from 1900 to the late 1970s. Included signed articles on many topics including race, terrorism, women, energy crisis, and civil rights. Some attention is given to the arts, music, literature, science, and popular culture, but the major emphasis is on world political, military and economic events. A general index and a thematic bibliography is appended to Volume 20.
D421 P78

AREA STUDIES

Multinational

CJ52 Statistical information of a historical nature can be found in several sources, including **International Historical Statistics: The Americas and Australiasia** 1983, **International Historical Statistics: Africa and Asia,** 1982, and **European Historical Statistics, 1750-1975,** 1980. See CA38 and CA38n and CA37 respectively, for full entry information.

CJ53 **The Europa World Year Book,** 1926- . 2 vols. London: Europa. annual.

Provides a world survey of 300 countries. Also available are volumes for various regions, including: *Western Europe* (CJ119); *The Far East and Australasia* (CJ148); *Middle East & North Africa* (CJ138); *Africa South of the Sahara* (CJ145); *South America, Central America & The Caribbean* (CJ117); *The USA and Canada* (CJ60). The *International Directory of Government* (CD28n) is also published by Europa.
JN1 E85

CJ54 **Handbooks to the Modern World,** 2d ed. 7 vols. New York: Facts on File, 1988- in progress.

A series describing regions of the world, including statistics, basic information on geography and population, the media and social welfare, and articles, written by noted international scholars, providing an overview of regional and national problems and concerns. Published volumes include: *Western Europe* (CJ118); *The Soviet Union and Eastern Europe* (CJ133); *The Middle East* (CJ137); *Asia and the Pacific* (CJ151); *Africa* (CJ144). Forthcoming volumes include: *The United States and Canada*; and *Latin America and the Caribbean.*

CJ55 Kurian, George Thomas. **Encyclopedia of the Third World.** 3d ed. 3 vols. New York: Facts on File, 1987.

Considered to be the most comprehensive reference compendium on important topics concerning the Third World. Volume 1 covers major international organizations and countries from A-G; Volume 2 and 3 cover the remaining countries. Coverage includes 124 developing countries (aligned and non-aligned), but excludes

China and Taiwan. Entries include basic facts and geographic, political, economic and social information, and summarize various other subjects, including budget, constitution, defense, ethnic composition, food, language, etc.). Selective bibliography and comprehensive index are also provided. Companion volumes include *Encyclopedia of the First World* (2 vols, 1990) (G63 K87), which consists of survey of 26 advanced countries and six European ministates, and *Encyclopedia of the Second World* (1990), which covers communist countries. *EFW* and *ESW* are arranged in a format similar to *ETW*. All three are comparable to *Europa World Year Book* (CJ53), but include longer essays and focus less on history and more on social issues.

Kurian has also written *Glossary of the Third World: Words For Understanding Third World Peoples and Cultures* (1989) (HC59.7 K873).
HC59.7 K87

CJ56   Worldmark Encyclopedia of the Nations. 7th ed.   5 vols.   New York: Worldmark, 1988.

A practical guide to the geographic, historical, political, social and economic status of 176 nations, their international relationships, and the United Nations system. Volume 1: *The United Nations*; Volume 2: *Africa*; Volume 3: *The Americas*; Volume 4: *Asia and Oceania*; and Volume 5: *Europe*.
G103 W65

CJ57   World Bibliographical Series, 1978- .   Santa Barbara, CA: CLIO Press. irregular.

Series will eventually cover every country in the world, each in a separate volume. Volumes include annotated entries on works dealing withthe country's history, geography, economy, and politics, and with its people, their culture, customs, religion and social organization. See for example CJ149n *China*.
various call numbers

North America

CJ58   Bibliographic Guide to North American History, 1977- .   Boston, MA: G.K. Hall. annual.

Lists books, serials and other non-book materials catalogued during the year by the New York Public Library and the Library of Congress on all aspects of U.S. and Canadian history. Main entries provide the full bibliographic record. Additional entries feature a more condensed format.
Z1250 N483

CJ59   Directory: Historical Agencies in North America. 13th ed.   Ed. by Betty Pease Smith. Nashville, TN: American Association for State and Local History, 1986.   686 p.

Comprehensive guide to information to local historical and genealogical organizations in Canada and the United States, with material on oral history centers, folklore societies, living history gorups, libraries, and archival depositories. Two separate sections for Canada and the United States, with geographical arrangement within each section. Entries list address and phone numbers, publications, staff, etc. Index is included.
E172 D572

CJ60 **The USA and Canada.** 1st ed. London: Europa, 1990.

Aim is "to provide a comprehensive guide to the political, economic and social structures, and international roles of these ... nations." More comprehensive than *Europa World Year Book* (CJ53). Included for each country is a historical and political chronology, bibliographic essays on social, economic and political issues, statistical data and basic directory information.
E158 U17

Canada

Bibliographies and Guides and Primary Sources

CJ61 **Access Canada: Micromedia's Directory of Canadian Information Resources**, 1990.

Comprehensive list of sources for current information about Canada and things Canadian; essentially a directory of directories. See AH1 for full entry information.

CJ62 Aiken, Barbara B. **Local Histories of Ontario Municipalities, 1951–1977: A Bibliography.** Toronto: Ontario Library Association, 1978. 120 p. *Supplement* 1977-1987, 1989.

Cites 1,700 local histories in alphabetical order by municipality. The 1977-1987 supplement includes 1,050 new titles.
Z1392 O6A 48

CJ63 Aubin, Paul and Paul-André Linteau. **Bibliographie de l'histoire du Québec et du Canada.** 1981- . Québec: Institut Québécois de Recherche sur la Culture,

Each two volume set includes citations to journal articles, books and dissertations relating to the history of Quebec and Canada published during the time period. Entries are arranged by systematic, analytic and author classifications. No attempt is made to judge importance or scientific value. Covers 1946–1965; 1966–1975; 1976–1980.
Z1382 A79

CJ64 Bishop, Olga, Barbara Irwin and Clara G. Miller. **Bibliography of Ontario History, 1867-1976: Cultural, Economic, Political, Social.** 2 vols. Toronto: University of Toronto Press, 1980.

A revision and expansion of *Ontario Since 1867: A Bibliography* (Ministry of Colleges and Universities, 1973). A comprehensive list of printed items; some 15,000 bibliographies, monographs, pamphlets, articles and theses. Includes library location and author, title, subject index. Continued by *The Bibliography of Ontario History, 1976–1986* (Dundurn Press, 1989) (Z1392 O5B54 ROBA), which provides a subject arrangement of academic and popular publications on Ontario history. Also includes references to pre-Confederation period. Incorporates *Annual Bibliography of Ontario History 1980–1985* (016.9713 A615).
R971.3 AB622B

CJ65 Bliss, J.M. **Canadian History in Documents, 1763-1966.** Toronto: Ryerson, 1966. 397 p.

A collection of primary historical sources. Supersedes *A Source-book of Canadian History: Selected Documents and Personal Papers* by J.H.S. Reid, (rev. ed, Longman, 1964) (F5004 R4 ROBA).
R971 B649 or F5004 B55 ROBA

CJ66 Canadian Historical Documents Series. 3 vols. Scarborough, ON: Prentice-Hall of Canada, [1965-66].

Identifies and describes important historical documents in Canadian history. Volume 1: *The French Régime* (F5057 N53 ROBA); Volume 2: *Pre-Confederation* (F5067 W3 ROBA); and Volume 3: *Confederation to 1949* (F5080 B86 ROBA).

CJ67 Canadian Local Histories to 1950: A Bibliography. Toronto: University of Toronto Press, 1967-1978.

Volume 1: *The Atlantic Provinces: Newfoundland, Nova Scotia, New Brunswick, Prince Edward Island*, (1967) by William F.E. Morley. Volume 2: *La Province de Québec* (1971) by W.F.E. Morley and A. Beaulieu. Volume 3: *Ontario and the Canadian North* (1978) by W.F.E. Morley.
Z1392 M37M6

CJ68 Cooke, O.A. **The Canadian Military Experience 1867-1983: A Bibliography.** 2d ed. Ottawa: Directorate of History, Department of National Defence, 1984. 329 p.

Bibliography of military works, arranged by era and by naval, land, and air forces. Indexed by subject, person, branch of service, formations, and units.
Z1395 M5C66

CJ69 Canadian Studies: Foreign Publications and Theses / Études canadiennes: publications et thèses étrangères. 3d ed. Prep. by Linda M. Jones. Ottawa: International Council for Canadian Studies for External Affairs Canada, 1989. 175 p.
Z1385 M65

CJ70 Doctoral Research on Canada and Canadians 1889-1983, 1986. See AF43 for full entry information

CJ71 Guide du chercheur en histoire canadienne. Québec: Presses de L'Université Laval, 1986. 808 p.

An extensive guide to reference and general sources of Canadian historical materials. Arranged by type of source (e.g. archival materials, government documents, etc.) Includes subject and author indexes.
Z1382 G85

CJ72 The History of Canada: An Annotated Bibliography. Ed. by Dwight L. Smith. Santa Barbara, CA: ABC-Clio, 1983. 327 p.

An annotated bibliography of periodical literature relating to Canadian history and life, from prehistory to 1983. Articles derived from the database *America: History and Life* (CJ7).
Z1382 H57

CJ73 Interdisciplinary Approaches to Canadian Society: A Guide to the Literature. Ed. by Alan F.J. Artibise. Montreal: Published for the Association for Canadian Studies by McGill-Queen's University Press, 1990. 156 p.

Provides methodological and bibliographic summary and themes of interest for study in Canada, including native, ethnic, religious, and labour studies.
F5050 I58 SIGR; ROBA

CJ74 A Reader's Guide to Canadian History. 2 vols. Toronto: University of Toronto Press, 1982.

A guide to, and critical assessment of, articles,

papers, books on the topic of Canadian history. Chapters are organized around regional and thematic topics, and are written in essay format. Volume 1: *Beginnings to Confederation*, edited by D.A. Muisel, is a largely regional approach. Volume 2: *Confederation to the Present*, edited by J.L. Granatstein and Paul Stevens has both topical and regional chapters. Volume 2 was previously published as *Canada Since 1867: A Bibliographical Guide* (1977).
Z1382 R4

CJ75 **Register of Post-Graduate Dissertations in Progress in History and Related Subjects / Répertoire des thèses en cours portant sur des sujets d'histoire et autres sujets connexes, 1966- .** Ottawa: Canadian Historical Association. annual.

A guide to work in progress, mainly in Canada. Broad chronological and geographical arrangement. Name index.
Z6201 C3

CJ76 **Review of Historical Publications Relating to Canada.** 22 vols. Toronto: University of Toronto Press, 1897–1919.

An annual survey of reviews of books and papers on Canadian history in the broad sense. Continued in *Canadian Historical Review*.
F5000 R4

CJ77 Thibault, Claude. **Bibliographia Canadiana.** Don Mills, ON: Longman, 1973. 795 p.

A chronological and topical bibliography of over 25,000 entries for printed items on Canadian history. In four parts: sources for research; French colonial regime; British North America; Dominion of Canada. Not annotated.
Z1382 T45

CJ78 Waterston, Elizabeth. **The Travellers: Canada to 1900.** Guelph: University of Guelph, 1989. 321 p.

"Annotated list of over 700 reports on Canada, published in English and written by travellers before 1900." Arranged in chronological order, covering the period 1577 to 1900; includes material published after 1900 if written before 1900.
Z1382 W37

Encyclopedias, Dictionaries, Handbooks, and Atlases

CJ79 Bercuson, David J. and J.L. Granatstein. **The Collins Dictionary of Canadian History: 1867 to the Present.** Don Mills, ON: Collins, 1988. 270 p.

Includes some 1,600 concise entries on topics ranging from politics to agriculture, a chronological timeline, and appendices listing government officials at various levels, statistical information, election results, etc.
F5010 B47

CJ80 **Canada's North: The Reference Manual,** 1983- . Ottawa: Indian and North Affairs Canada: Canadian Government Publication Centre, Supply and Services. looseleaf.

Information about the Yukon and Northwest Territories, updated on a continuing basis. Topics include physical environment, people, history, native organizations, land claims, government, renewable resources, transportation, communications, socio-economic issues. Charts, maps, tables and other statistical information complement text. References are provided at the end of each section.
F5903 C38

CJ81 The Canadian Centenary Series: A History of Canada. 18 vols. Ed. by W.L. Morton and D.G. Creighton. Toronto: McClelland & Stewart, 1963-79.

Series intended to be the "definitive history of Canada". Volumes cover the period of early voyages and exploration from the north, 1000-1632 to the opening of Canada's north, and Canadian politics 1939-1957. Volumes 4, 15 and 17 were never published.
various call numbers

CJ82 The Canadian Encyclopedia. 2d ed. 4 vols. Ed. in Chief James H. Marsh. Edmonton, AB: Hurtig Publishing, 1988.

Continues, rather than updates, the first edition of this work, published in 1985. The second edition includes almost 10,000 alphabetical entries written by recognized scholars. Designed to "provide an intricate sketch of Canada" in "all aspects of life in Canada, of all regions, over a vast time scale from the geological formation of the ancient rocks of the Shield to the most recent political events" (introduction). Includes articles for literature and arts, regional and ethnic diversities, politics, foreign policy, economic, social and linguistic problems, biographies, geography, flora and fauna. Bibliographies are provided at the end of many entries. Includes colour photographs. *The Junior Encyclopedia of Canada*, also edited by James H. Marsh, (5 vols, Hurtig, 1990), contains 4,100 entries about Canada and Canadians, written for young students. See AI18 for more information.
F5010 C35

CJ83 Chronicle of Canada. Ed. by Elizabeth Abbott. Montreal: Chronicle Publications, 1990. 980 p.

A chronicle of Canada's history, from earliest prehistoric times to December, 1989. History is told in newspaper-type articles, with headlines, place and datelines, and is written through the eyes of a contemporary journalist, in a factual rather than interpretative manner. Chronologies of important events are listed beside the articles in a separate column. Contains many colour illustrations, portraits, and maps. Indexed.
F5010 C47

CJ84 Colombo, John Robert. **999 Questions About Canada.** Toronto: Doubleday, 1989. 390 p.

Companion volume to his earlier work *1001 Questions About Canada* (1986). Written in a question and answer format, the work explores Canadian cultural facts and traditions. Includes a keyword index.
F5052 Q4C653

CJ85 Gentilcore, R. Louis and C. Grant Head. **Ontario's History in Maps.** Toronto: University of Toronto Press, 1984. 304 p.

Illustrates the political and social development of the province from the first European settlement to the early 20th century. Presents a wide variety of maps including copper engravings, water colours and satellite transmissions. Each map is accompanied by extensive descriptive notes. Includes a list of references and a cartobibliographic essay by Joan Winearls.
G1146 S1 G46 Atlas Stand

CJ86 Guide to Canadian Diplomatic Relations 1925-1983, 1985. See CD46 for full entry information.

CJ87 Historical Atlas of Canada. 3 vols. Ed. by R. Cole Harris. Cartographer Geoffrey J. Matthews. Toronto: University of Toronto Press, 1987-1990.

This 3 volume historical atlas set offers full-colour maps, paintings and other illustrations to provide a portrait of Canada showing the development of the country from pre-historical times until 1961. Volume 1: *From the Beginning to 1800*; Volume 2: *The Nineteenth Century*; Volume 3: *Addressing the Twentieth Century*.
FO G116 S1 H56

CJ88 **The Illustrated History of Canada.** Ed. by Craig Brown. Toronto: Lester & Orpen Dennys, 1987. 574 p.

Describes the national history of Canada beginning with Native peoples at the time of European contact, through pre-Confederation, the 19th century of nation building, and the 20th century up to 1987. Chapters are written by noted Canadian historians. Social history and Canada's role in international communities are discussed. Illustrated.
F5055 I55 ROBA

CJ89 Kowaliczko, Beatrice. **Canadian Studies Data.** Ottawa: Association for Canadian Studies, 1990. 255 p.

Also called *Directory of Canadian, Québec and Regional Studies in Canada*. French edition available. The Association has also published *Directory of Funding Sources for Canadian Studies* (1988).
F5006 K68 ROBA

CJ90 Myers, Jay. **The Fitzhenry & Whiteside Book of Canadian Facts and Dates.** Markham, ON: Fitzhenry & Whiteside, 1986. 354 p.

Designed to be a quick reference work and fact-finder as well as a narrative history book, this chronology covers the period from prefifteenth century to 1984. Subject and name indexes are provided.
F5010 M94

CJ91 Shortt, Adam and Arthur G. Doughty. **Canada and its Provinces: A History of the Canadian People and their Institutions.** 23 vols. Toronto: Publisher's Association of Canada, 1913–1917.

A comprehensive work covering history, political, economic and cultural development of Canada. Volume 23 contains the index and bibliography.
F5011 S57

CJ92 Story, Norah. **The Oxford Companion to Canadian History and Literature.** Toronto: Oxford University Press, 1967. 935 p. *Supplement*, ed. by William Toye (1973).

Source for information on Canadian historical figures, political and constitutional issues, forts, important places, and subjects such as voyages of discovery, fur trade, arctic exploration, political parties, and fiction, including legends and tales of native peoples. Includes bibliographies. *Supplement* updates for works published between 1967 and 1972, and includes biographical articles for writers who came into prominence in the same period. The Literature portion has been updated by *The Oxford Companion to Canadian Literature* (1983), edited by William Toye (BD73). There has been no update to the history portion.
R971.03 S887   or   PS8015 S7

CJ93 Trudel, Marcel. **Atlas de la Nouvelle France / An Atlas of New France.** 2d ed. Quebec: Presses de l'Université Laval, 1973. 219 p.

Reproductions of maps relating to the history of French Canada. A revision of *Atlas historique du Canada français des origines à 1867* (1961).
G1116 S2T69 ATLAS (1968)

United States

Bibliographies and Guides and Primary Sources

CJ94 **American Studies: An Annotated Bibliography.** 3 vols. Ed. by Jack Salzman. New York: Cambridge University Press, 1986. *Supplement* 1984-1988, 1990.

Covers the period 1900-1983, with over 6,000 entries. The three volume work is a revision of the 1982 *American Studies: An Annotated Bibliography of Works on the Civilization of the United States.* Covers thematic topics such as history, literature, political science, science. The 1990 supplement adds an additional 3,500 works.
Z1361 C6A436

CJ95 Beers, Henry P. **Bibliographies in American History, 1942–1978: Guide to Materials for Research.** 2 vols. Woodbridge, CT: Research Publications, 1982.

Broad coverage. Volume 1 is organized by topic; Volume 2, geographically. Name/subject index included.
Z1236 A1B4

CJ96 Commager, Henry S. **Documents of American History.** 9th ed. 2 vols. New York: Appleton, 1973.

A selection of important U.S. documents, arranged chronologically with notes and bibliographic references.
E173 C66 SIGS

CJ97 **A Guide to the Study of the United States of America: Representative Books Reflecting the Development of American Life and Thought.** Washington: Library of Congress, 1960. 1193 p. Supplement, 1956–1965 (1976).

Full bibliographic information for each entry with descriptive, evaluative annotations.
R016.9173 U58 or Z1215 U53

CJ98 **Guide to the Study of United States History Outside the U.S., 1945–1980.** 5 vols. White Plains, NY: Kraus International Publications, 1985.

The first part, containing 3 volumes, consists of narrative essays on the teaching of U.S. history in foreign countries. Coverage of the world's major countries is provided. The second part is an annotated bibliography of monographs, articles, essays, dissertations, covering 1945-1980 on the subject of U.S. history, and all of which were published outside of the U.S. Compiled by historians and librarians worldwide.
E175.8 G84

CJ99 **Harvard Guide to American History.** 2d ed. 2 vols. Ed. by F. Freidel. Cambridge, MA: Belknap Press, 1974.

A standard general guide. Volume 1 contains section on research methods and materials, biographies and personal records, with area histories, and histories of special subjects. Volume 2 is arranged in chronological order beginning with 1789 and ending in June, 1970. Author/subject index included.
Z1236 F77 VUPR

CJ100 Prucha, Francis P. **Handbook for Research in American History: A Guide to Bibliographies and Other Reference Works.** Lincoln, NB: University of Nebraska Press, 1987. 289 p.

Useful as a general introductory guide to American history, covering such areas as

American historical bibliography, immigrations, ethnic groups, etc. Many entries are not annotated.
Z1236 P78

CJ101 Writings on American History. 53 vols. Washington: American Historical Association, 1902-1961. annual, 1973/74-.

Originally published as part of the American Historical Association's *Annual Report*, *Writings on American History* was an annual publication covering the years 1902 to 1961, missing only 1904-05, and 1941-47. *Writings* was a classified list of books and articles published during the year in question that had value for a researcher studying U.S. history from primitive times to the recent past. Indexes varied year to year, with some years having name/place and subject indexes and other years having only name and place index. From 1962–1973, subtitled: *A Subject Bibliography of Articles* and included journal articles only.
Z1236 W77

Abstracts and Indexes

CJ102 America, History and Life, 1964- . annual, quarterly 1989-.

See CJ7 for full entry information. One spin-off of this reference work is *Women in American History: A Bibliography*, edited by Cynthia Harrison (ABC-Clio, 1975-85) in 2 volumes: 1964-1977; 1978-1984 (Z7964 U49H365), which includes nearly 3,400 abstracts taken from *American, History and Life*. This bibliography is one of the best sources for historical scholarly periodical literature about women.
E171 A54

Encyclopedias, Dictionaries, Handbooks and Atlases

CJ103 Album of American History. 6 vols. Ed. by James Truslow Adams. New York: Scribner's, 1969.

This well-known work is a pictorial chronicle of American history, covering various aspects of American cultural and political life. Volume 1 covers the colonial period. Volume 2 illustrates the years 1783 to 1853. Volume 3 covers 1853-1893; Volume 4 1893-1917; Volume 5 is a pictorial history of 1917 to 1953; and Volume 6 completes the work to 1968. Includes some 6,300 pictures; a general index is provided.
E178.5 A48 (1961) SCC

CJ104 Almanac of American History. Ed. by Arthur Schlesinger. New York: Putnam, 1983. 623 p.

Covers American history from the year 989 to 1982. Arranged in 5 mains sections, each including an overview, chronology of significant events, and descriptions of noteworthy individuals. Indexed.
E174.5 A45

CJ105 Dictionary of American History. Rev. ed. 8 vols. New York: Scribner's, 1976-78.

Concise articles on aspects of American history covering cultural, economic, industrial, political and social history. No biographies. The *Scribner Desk Dictionary of American History*, is an abridged version of this work, containing shortened entries. Arrangement is alphabetical by subject. Biographical entries are excluded. Companion volume is *Atlas of American History* (2d rev ed, Scribner, 1984)

(E179.5A3 (1978)), which presents, in a chronological format, the exploration and colonization of the U.S. to its emergence as a world power.
E174 A43

CJ106 Encyclopedia of American Facts and Dates. 8th ed. New York: Harper & Row, 1987. 1006 p.

Tabular arrangement of over 15,000 facts and dates, arranged chronologically.
E174.5 C3

CJ107 Encyclopedia of American History. 6th ed. Ed. by R.B. Morris and J.B. Morris. New York: Harper and Row, 1982. 1285 p.

Purpose is to provide "in a single handy volume the essential historical facts about American life and institutions" in a comprehensive manner. Serves as a standard source on this subject.
E174.5 E52

CJ108 Encyclopedia USA: The Encyclopedia of the United States of America Past and Present. 50 vols. Ed. by R. Alton Lee and Archie P. McDonald. Gulf Breeze, FL: Academic International Press, 1983- in progress (3 volumes per year).

A projected 50 volume set, aimed at describing American events, individuals, institutions, and movements in American history from the European discovery to the present era in an essay style format.

CJ109 Historical Atlas of the United States. Ed. by Wilbur E. Garrett. Washington: National Geographic Society, 1988. 289 p.

Using photographs, maps, texts, diagrams, examines facets of American history. Divided thematically and chronologically.
G1201 S1N3 Fo

CJ110 Historical Statistics of the United States, Colonial Times to 1970, See CA66n for information.

Latin America and the Caribbean

Bibliographies and Guides

CJ111 A Bibliography of Latin American Bibliographies. Ed. by Arthur E. Gropp. Metuchen, NJ: Scarecrow Press, 1968. 515 p. *Supplements*: 1971 (1965-69); 1979 (1969-74); 1982 (1975-79); and 1987 (1980-84). annual updates.

The original 1968 edition contains over 7,200 unannotated entries to bibliographic monographs published to 1964. Updated annually under the sponsorship of SALALM (Seminar on the Acquisition of Latin American Library Materials). Gropp also edited *A Bibliography of Latin American Bibliographies Published in Periodicals* (2 vols, Scarecrow, 1976), which included almost 9,700 items published between 1929-1965. Supplements and annual updates list both monographs and periodical articles.
Z1601 A2 G7624

CJ112 Grieb, Kenneth J. Central America in the Nineteenth and Twentieth Centuries: An Annotated Bibliography. Boston: G.K. Hall, 1988. 573 p.

This annotated interdisciplinary bibliography covers the period of 1810 to 1980, emphasizing the social sciences, and provides a selective guide to books dealing with Central America since independence. Annotations are in English, although many of the books are written in Spanish. Five countries, Guatemala, Honduras, El Salvador, Nicaragua and Costa Rica, are included; Panama is not. The author has published another useful work called *Research Guide to Central America and the Caribbean* (University of Wisconsim Press, 1985) (Z1595 R47) which identifies archival resources that focus on this region.
Z1437 G74

CJ113 Latin American Studies: A Basic Guide to Sources. 2d ed. Ed. by Robert A McNeil. Metuchen, NJ: Scarecrow Press, 1990. 458 p.

A guide to research in the social sciences and humanities. Details resources available, identifies major reference works. *Latin America and the Caribbean: A Directory of Resources* (Orbis, 1986) (F1601 F46) lists organizations, books, periodicals, audiovisuals, and other resources.
Z1601 L324

Encyclopedias, Handbooks, and Atlases

CJ114 The Atlas of Central America and the Caribbean. Ed. by the Diagram Group. New York: Macmillan, 1985. 144 p.

Arranged in three parts with a bibliography and an index. Part One describes the region's lands, seas, climate, vegetation, wildlife, and prehistory; Part Two "Central America" highlights each country and provides an overview of comparative statistics between the countries (population size, land use, economic situations, etc.); Part Three "The Caribbean" follows a similar format to that in Part Two. All parts include charts, graphs, and diagrams.
G1550 D5 MAPL

CJ115 The Cambridge Encyclopedia of Latin American and the Caribbean. Ed. by Simon Collier et al. New York: Cambridge University Press, 1985. 456 p.

An encyclopedic introduction containing 82 brief articles covering the physical environment, economy, people, history, politics and society, and culture. Articles do not focus on specific countries. Includes bibliographies, maps, tables and charts.
F1406 C36

CJ116 Handbook of Latin American Studies, 1935- . Austin, TX: University of Texas Press, 1980- . annual.

An annotated guide to material published in the social sciences and humanities compiled by scholars. Beginning with volume 36, even numbered issues cover humanities, odd numbers cover social sciences.
Z1605 H23

CJ117 South America, Central America and the Caribbean, 1985- . London: Europa. annual.

Similar in format to other Europa regional yearbooks (see CJ53). Includes background notes and essays on current issues in the region (e.g. economy, dictatorship, social change), description of regional organizations, and a survey of each country including statistical data. Much of the information is also found in *The Europa World Year Book.*
F1408.29 S68

Western Europe

CJ118 Western Europe. Ed. by Richard Mayne. New York: Facts on File, 1986. 699 p.

Part of the *Handbooks to the Modern World* series, (CJ54). Contains current information in the form of essays on problems facing European countries. Includes comparative tables and charts for the 27 states of Europe. Political, economic and social issues, and information on the structure and function of major organizations, such as the European Economic Community, are included.
D967 W47 SCAR

CJ119 Western Europe: A Political and Economic Survey, 1988- . London: Europa Publications. biennial.

Contains information on all member countries of the European Communities and European Free Trade Association, including Cyprus, Malta and Turkey, for a total of 33 countries. Each country chapter contains information on geography, recent history and politics, economics, social issues, media, transportation and tourism. More comprehensive than *Europa World Year Book* CJ53, but with less statistical data.
D1050 W48 VUPR

Great Britain

Bibliographies and Guides and Primary Sources

CJ120 Conference on British Studies. **Bibliographical Handbooks,** 1968- . Cambridge: Cambridge University Press. irregular.

Bibliographical coverage by period. Less detailed than the Oxford series, *Sources of Literature of English History* (CJ122). Includes periodical articles and other printed sources. Intended for scholars as a basis for research. Volumes include: Volume 1: *Anglo Norman England, 1066–1154* (1969); Volume 2: *High Middle Ages in England, 1154–1377* (1978); Volume 3: *Tudor England, 1485–1603* (1968); Volume 4: *Restoration England 1660–1689* (1971); Volume 5: *Victorian England 1837–1901* (1970); and Volume 6: *Modern England 1901–1984* (1987).
VUPR various call numbers

CJ121 English Historical Documents. 13 vols. London: Eyre, 1953- in progress. 2d ed. 1979- in progress.

Completed to Volume 12 as of 1991. An extensive collection of original documents for British history, 500 AD to 1914. Notes, references, introductory essay in each volume.
DA26 E56 ROBA

CJ122 Gross, Charles. **Sources and Literature of English History from the Earliest Times to about 1485.** 2d ed. Oxford, NY: Clarendon Press, 1975. 1103 p.

The original 1915 bibliography was revised and published in this second edition in 1975. To update British history, the Royal Historical Society of Great Britain and the American Historical Association jointly sponsored the compilation of companion volumes to cover all British history. These updates form the *Bibliography of British History* series, and include volumes covering the Tudor and Stuart revised in 1959 and 1970; the 18th century volume revised in 1977, as well as the 1851-1914 volume (1976) and the 1789-1851 period (1977).
Z2018 R28

CJ123 Royal Historical Society. **Annual Bibliography of British and Irish History,** 1976- . Brighton, England for the Royal Historical Society and with the Institute of Historical Research by Harvester Press. annual.

Includes brief citations to books and journal articles on British and Irish history published during the previous year in British and non-British sources. Citations are arranged into thirteen broad sections by geographic area and time period, then subdivided by subject. Beginning with the 1988 volume, material is arranged in alphabetical order by author's name within each subsection. Comprehensive author and subject indexes. Designed to provide interim coverage for *Writings on British History* (CJ124), during its lengthy publishing delays.
Z2016 A6

CJ124 Writings on British History, London: Royal Historical Society. *1901-33* (5 vols in 7, 1933). Supplements: *1934-1945* (8 vols, 1937-60); *1946-48* (1973); *1949-51* (1975); *1952-54* (1975); *1955-57* (1977); *1958-59* (1977); *1960-61* (1978); *1962-64* (1979); *1965-66* (1981); *1967-68* (1982); *1969-70* (1984); *1971-72* (1985); *1973-74* (1986).

The original 7 volume set was a bibliography of books and articles published between 1901 and 1933 on British history covering the period from 450 AD to 1914. Volumes included: Volume 1: *Auxiliary Sciences and General Works*; Volume 2: *The Middle Ages, 450–1485*; Volume 3: *The Tudor and Stuart Periods, 1485–1714*; Volume 4: *The Eighteenth Century, 1714–1815*; and Volume 5: *1815-1914* and appendix. Supplements to this work have been published, as noted, and since 1973/74, appear in irregularly published annuals, and now include works published on British history from 450 AD to 1939. There is a considerable time-lag in publication. See *Annual Bibliography of British and Irish History* (CJ123) for interim coverage.
Z2016 R88

Encyclopedias, Dictionaries, and Handbooks

CJ125 The Cambridge Historical Encyclopedia of Great Britain and Ireland. Cambridge: Cambridge University Press, 1985. 392 p.

A basic one-volume historical encyclopedia including a combination of 61 interpretative essays and many brief data-type entries. Well illustrated with photographs, drawings and maps. Includes a "who's who" section, and a subject index. Another useful work is *Steinberg's Dictionary of British History* (2d ed, London: E. Arnold, 1970) (DA34 S7), which includes historical essays on Britain and her colonies.
DA34 C28

CJ126 Cook, Chris and John Stevenson. **British Historical Facts, 1688-1760.** New York: St. Martins Press, 1988. 252 p.

Topical arrangement in 14 chapters, including the monarchy, parliament, elections, religion, treaties, armed forces, law and order, colonies, economy, social developments. Includes a chronology. Continued by *British Historical Facts 1760-1830* (1980), with sections for foreign affairs, radicalism, trade unions, the press; and *British Historical Facts 1830-1900* (1975), with a list of all who held any official office between 1830-1900. All works include bibliographies.
DA 498 C66

Eastern Europe

Bibliographies

CJ127 Horecky, Paul. **Russia and the Soviet Union: A Bibliographic Guide to Western-Language Publications.** Chicago: University of Chicago Press, 1965. 473 p.
Comprehensive survey with evaluative annotations. Companion volumes are *East Central Europe* (1969) and *Southeastern Europe* (1969). Updated by Stephen M. Horak's *Russia, the USSR and Eastern Europe: A Bibliographic Guide to English Language Publications 1964–1974* (1978), *1975–1980* (1982), and *1981-1985* (1987), (Z2483 H54).
Z2491 H64 ROBA

Encyclopedias and Handbooks

CJ128 de Mowbray, Stephen. **Key Facts in Soviet History.** London: Printer Publishers with John Spiers, 1990- in progress.
Only the first volume has been published, as of 1991. Volume 1: *1917 to 22 June 1941*, provides a chronology in Soviet history within the years outlined, with a list of references.
DK40 D46

CJ129 **Encyclopedia of Ukraine.** Ed. by Voldoymyr Juijovyc. Prepared for the Canadian Institute of Ukraine Studies. Toronto: University of Toronto Press, 1984- in progress.
Translation, revision and updating of Ukrainian language *Entsyklopediia ukrainoznaovstva: slovnykova chastyna* (1981-). A source of balanced information on Ukraine and Ukrainians. Includes illustrations, maps, colour plates.
DK508.2 E613

CJ130 **Great Soviet Encyclopedia,** 3d ed, 32 vols, 1973-1983. See AI25 for full entry information.

CJ131 Shaw, Warren and David Pryce. **Encyclopedia of the USSR 1905 to the Present: Lenin to Gorbachev.** London: Cassell Publishers, 1990. 351 p.
Provides detailed background information on political and economic events in the Soviet Union between the 1905 revolution to early 1990. Includes a chronology and biographies.
DK246 S52

CJ132 **The Soviet Union.** 3d ed. Ed. by Daniel C. Diller. Washington: Congressional Quarterly, 1990. 352 p.
Handbook on the current affairs of the Soviet Union, with brief and accurate entries on a wide range of topics. Historical aspects of Imperial Russia, and the Stalin, Khrushchev and Brezhnev eras are covered, as well as reform of the system, economy, foreign policy, ethnicity, U.S.-Soviet relations. Covers events up to mid-1990, just before the coup. Includes appendixes, illustrations.
DK246 S68 ROBA

CJ133 **The Soviet Union and Eastern Europe.** Ed. by George Schopflin. New York: Facts on File, 1986. 638 p.
Part of the *Handbooks to the Modern World* series (CJ54). Provides information and analysis on the Soviet Union and Eastern Europe. Political histories, economic, social, religious and cultural problems of each country are examined in depth by leading authorities.
DK17 S64 UNIV

Middle East / Near East / North Africa

Bibliographies and Guides

CJ134 Littlefield, David. **The Islamic Near East and North Africa: An Annotated Guide to Books in English for Non-Specialists.** Littleton, CO: Libraries Unlimited, 1977. 375 p.

Lists over 1,600 annotated entries arranged by country and by subject.
Z3013 L58

Encyclopedias, Handbooks, and Atlases

CJ135 **Atlas of the Middle East.** Ed. by Moshe Brawer. New York: Macmillan, 1988. 140 p.

Encyclopedic atlas covering all countries of the Middle East with the exception of Algeria, Tunisia, and Morocco. Includes thematic and physical maps, charts, diagrams and tables. Part One examines the physical, economic, social, and cultural geography of the region; Part Two examines each country separately. Includes bibliographies.
G2205 K33 MAPL

CJ136 **The Cambridge Encyclopedia of the Middle East and North Africa.** Ed. by Trevor Mostyn. New York: Cambridge University Press, 1988. 504 p.

Information on the history, society and culture of the area from Morocco to Afghanistan and Turkey to Djibouti and Somalia. Includes illustrations and maps.
DS44 C37

CJ137 **The Middle East.** Rev. ed. Ed. by Michael Adams. New York: Facts on File, 1988. 865 p.

Part of the *Handbooks to the Modern World* series, (CJ54). Examines, in lengthy articles, the general background of the Middle East as well as the historical, social, and economic sources of various problems, including the Arab-Israeli conflict, the Palestinian problem, and modernization. Also includes statistical information. Each country has a separate section for political affairs, economic issues, technological change, foreign aid, and social problems.
DS44 A32

CJ138 **The Middle East and North Africa,** 11th ed, 1964/65- . London: Europa. annual.

Similar to other Europa publications, contains detailed essays and statistical data for all countries in the Middle East. Arranged in 3 sections: "General Survey", "Regional Organizations", and "Country Surveys", with additional coverage of timely topics, e.g. natural gas, Islamic politics, etc. Includes bibliographies.
DS41 M45

CJ139 **A Middle East Studies Handbook.** Ed. by Jere L. Bacharach. Seattle: University of Washington Press, 1984. 160 p.

Updates an earlier titled work *A Near East Studies Handbook: 570-1974* (1974). Includes all countries in Southwest Asia and Egypt, covering the time period 570 to 1983. Provides detailed information in the form of charts and maps on dynasties and rulers, chronology of events, and historical atlases, as well as a glossary of terms.
DS61 B3

Africa

Bibliographies and Guides

CJ140 **Africa Since 1914: A Historical Bibliography.** Santa Barbara, CA: ABC-Clio, 1985. 402 p.

A bibliography which includes 4,329 articles published in scholarly journals between 1973-1982 which relate to Africa after 1914. Many articles focus on politics, society, history, and economics. Abstracts and index provided.
Z3501 A44

CJ141 **African Book Publishing Record,** 1975- . Oxford, U.K: Hans Zell. quarterly.

Lists new and forthcoming books published in Africa.
Z3503 A35

CJ142 **International African Bibliography 1973-1978: Books, Articles and Papers in African Studies.** London: Mansell, 1982. 343 p.

This volume represents a cumulation of 24 issues of *International African Bibliography* with 3,000 additional entries. Continuted by the journal *International African Bibliography: Current Books, Articles and Papers in African Studies* (1971- Mansell, quarterly). Since 1984, another bibliography, sponsored by the International African Institute, which is no longer affiliated with *IAB*, has been published on an annual basis called *Africa Bibliography* (Z3503 A27). This work records current publications (periodical articles, books and essays in edited volumes) in the social sciences, humanities and arts for the whole continent of Africa and the islands.
Z3501 I53

CJ143 Scheven, Yvette. **Bibliographies for African Studies 1970–1986.** London: Hans Zell, 1988. 615 p.

Written by one of Africana's foremost bibliographers contains annotated bibliographies relating to sub-Saharan Africa, arranged topically and geographically with detailed index.
Z3501 A1S34

Encyclopedias, Dictionaries, Handbooks, and Atlases

CJ144 **Africa.** Rev. ed. 2 vols. Ed. by Sean Moroney. New York: Facts on File, 1989.

Part of the *Handbooks to the Modern World* series (CJ54). Written in 3 sections, including general information on the country, the people, geography, political system, etc; statistical information; and essays, written by noted scholars, on the state of political, economic and social affairs. Not as detailed as *Africa South of the Sahara* (CJ145), but does provide coverage of North Africa, while the latter does not.
DT3 A24

CJ145 **Africa South of the Sahara,** 1971- . London: Europa Publications. annual.

Contains a wealth of detailed historical, political, economic and statistical information on the nations of sub-Saharan Africa. Much of the information is based on the *Europa World Year Book* (CJ53).
JQ1870 A1A4

CJ146 The **Cambridge Encyclopedia of Africa** New York: Cambridge University Press, 1981. 492 p.

Thematic arrangement covering land, people, history, nations, problems.
DT3 C35

CJ147 Historical Atlas of Africa. Ed. by J.F. Ade Ajayi and Michael Crowder. New York: Cambridge University Press, 1985. 173 p.

Contains over 300 coloured maps of three types: event maps which provide information on places and events; process maps which show historical processes; and quantitative maps using numeric data. Some describe African physical features, animals, languages, while others relate to the political, economic and social history of Africa from earliest times to modern times. Detailed index is provided. This atlas updates an earlier work *An Atlas of African History* by J.D. Fage (2d ed. 1978).
G2446 S1H56 MAPL fo

Far East and Australasia

CJ148 The Far East and Australasia. 1969- . London: Europa Publications. annual.

Information about countries in Asia, Australia, new Zealand, Pacific Islands, and the Soviet Union in Asia. Covers political and economic events of the previous year with background material for various regions. Directory of "international organizations and research bodies active in Asia and the Pacific is also included."
DS1 F37

*   *   *   *

Asia

Bibliographies

CJ149 An Annotated Bibliography of Selected Chinese Reference Works. 3d ed. Compiled by Ssu-yu Teng and Knight Biggerstaf. Cambridge, MA: Harvard University Press, 1971. 250 p.

A standard annotated bibliographical work in this field. Material is arranged under eight broad subject categories. Current bibliographies have been edited by Peter Cheng, including *China* (Clio Press, 1983) (Z3101 C39), which is part of the *World Bibliographical Series* (CJ57), and which contains citations to 1,450 English language books published between 1970 to 1982; and *Current Books on China 1983-1988: An Annotated Bibliography* (Garland, 1990) (Z3106 C45), with brief annotations on some 500 English language books arranged in 25 subject areas.
Z1035 T32 SIGS

CJ150 Bibliography of Asian Studies. 1948- . Ann Arbor, MI: Association for Asian Studies. annual.

(1984 edition, 1988) Publication of this work is several years after date covered in work. Lists periodical articles and books and other materials, such as conference proceedings, arranged geographically and then by subject, with subheadings for type of work (e.g. bibliographies, etc). Entries are not annotated, but the work is indexed.
Z3001 B5

Encyclopedias, Handbooks, and Atlases

CJ151 Asia and the Pacific. 2 vols. Ed. by Robert H. Taylor. New York: Facts on File, 1991.

Part of the *Handbooks to the Modern World* series, (CJ54). Similar to other handbooks, it provides a survey of the country and people, and discusses current social, economic and political issues.
DS5 A79

CJ152 The Cambridge Encyclopedia of India, Pakistan, Bangladesh, Sri Lanka, Nepal, Bhutan, and the Maldives. New York: Cambridge University Press, 1989. 520 p.

A standard work for information on South Asia. Well illustrated.
DS334.9 C36

CJ153 China Facts and Figures, 1978- . Gulf Breeze, FL: Academic International Press. annual.

Each issue contains updated information and statistical data on the PRC obtained from a variety of sources, including official, international, private and scholarly works.
DS701 C26 Ref ERIN

CJ154 The Contemporary Atlas of China. Ed. by Nathan Sivin. Boston: Houghton Mifflin, 1988. 200 p.

Includes regional maps, photographs, charts, diagrams, and drawings, as well as chapters on the history, society and culture of China. Statistical data is provided for China's natural resources, agriculture, industry, trade, economy, transportation, and defense, etc. up to 1988.
G2305 C986 MAPL fo

CJ155 Encyclopedia of Asian History. 4 vols. Ed. by Ainslie Embree. New York: Scribner's, 1988.

All entries, written by leading scholars in the field, provide detailed information on events, countries, and people from Iran and Central Asia to Japan and the Philippines over the past 5,000 years. Short bibliographies and brief prefaces plus an extensive index make this work a valuable reference resource.
DS31 E53

CJ156 A Historical Atlas of South Asia. Ed. by Joseph Schwartzberg. Chicago: University of Chicago Press, 1978. 352 p.

This work is a cartographic record of South Asia (Afghanistan to Burma; India to the Maldives), from earliest times to 1978. Includes 650 coloured maps, charts, tables, photographs and drawings. Arranged chronologically. There is an index and a classified bibliography.
G2261 S1H5 MAPL FO

CJ157 Information China: The Comprehensive and Authoritative Reference Source of New China. 3 vols. New York: Pergamon Press, 1989.

Comprehensive and current survey of Modern China, with articles on cultural, economic, social, and political life in the country. Statistical data in the "China in Figures" section, maps, colour

illustrations, and symbols are included. Another encyclopedic work is *The Cambridge Encyclopedia of China* (Cambridge University Press, 1982) (DS705 C35).
DS706 I5

CJ158   Kodansha Encyclopedia of Japan.
9 vols. Tokyo; New York: Kodansha, 1983. *Supplement*, 1987.

Comprehensive encyclopedic work covering all aspects of Japanese society, including Japanese history, art and literature, technology, politics, economics, etc. Includes many lengthy articles written by Japanese scholars.
DS805 K598

CJ159 The Times of India Directory and Yearbook, Including Who's Who. 1914- . Middlesex, U.K: Bennet Coleman & Company. irregular annual.

Latest edition 1984. Chapters discuss the country, nature and resources, agro-based industries, education and science, welfare programmes, demography, trade and industry, finance, communications, politics, etc. There is also *India Who's Who* (19th ed, 1988/89) (New Delhi: Infa Publications, irregular annual) (DS434 I45), which has approximately 5,000 entries for people in India who have made a significant contribution in their field.
DS405 T5 (1984)

Australia and New Zealand

CJ160   Australians: A Historical Library. 10 vols. Ed. by Alan D. Gilbert. New York: Cambridge University Press, 1987.

Guide to the history of Australia, including a wide range of factual and statistical information with over 3,000 illustrations. An atlas volume, a historical dictionary, a chronological listing of events since 1788, a guide to historical places, and a guide to bibliographical and library sources are also included. Entries are essays written by well-known scholars. A similar work is *Concise Encyclopedia of Australia* (David Bateman, 1989) (DU90 C64 SCAR (1984)).
DU96 A87

CJ161   The Illustrated Encyclopedia of New Zealand. Rev. ed. Ed. by Gordon McLauchlan. Auckland, New Zealand: David Bateman, 1989. 1448 p.

Revision of *New Zealand Encyclopedia* (1984) (DU405 B37 ROBA). Provides information on the history, national identity, etc. on New Zealand. Includes many colour illustrations.
DU408 I45

Arctic

CJ162   Arctic Bibliography, 1953-1975. 16 vols. Prepared by Arctic Institute of North America. Montreal: McGill - Queen's University Press.

Scholarly resource containing citations and abstracts to world literature (i.e. books, journal articles, government reports in the language of origin (many non-English) in polar research. Topics covered include Inuit, archaeology, economic and social conditions, physics, geology, mapping, ethnography, etc. Detailed subject and locality index. The original work was published in 3 volumes, and updated with volume 4 to cover works published 1950-52; subsequent annual volumes (volumes 6-16) listed then current material and older works not previously listed in the set. Now ceased.
Z6005 P7A7 GEOL

CJ163 Catalogue of the Library of the Arctic Institute of North America, (Montreal). 1968. 4 vols. Boston: G.K. Hall. *Supplements:* 1971 (1 vol); 1974 (2 vols); 1980 (3 vols).

This catalogue represents one of the largest collections devoted to polar regions, with particular strength in the Arctic, sub-Arctic regions. Main set describes the 9,000 books, 20,000 pamphlets and reprints with 1,200 periodical titles, and many analytic entries for periodical contents.
Z6005 P7A75

CK GEOGRAPHY

For additional information on cartography and gazetteers, see Section AK, *Maps and Atlases*.

Bibliographies and Guides to the Literature

CK1 American Geographical Society of New York. **Research Catalogue.** 1962. 15 vols. Boston: G.K. Hall. *First Supplement*, 2 vols, 1972; *Topical Catalogue*, 2 vols, 1974; *Second Supplement*, 2 vols, 1978.

The most comprehensive retrospective bibliography in the field of geography. Includes articles as well as books and government documents and pamphlets held by the American Geographical Society. Continued by *Current Geographical Publications: Additions to the Research Catalogue of the American Geographical Society* (1938-, 10 issues per year) (Z6009 A49).
Z6009 A5

CK2 **A Bibliography of Geographic Thought.** Ed. by Catherine L. Brown and James O. Wheeler. Westport, CT: Greenwood Press, 1989. 520 p.

Bibliography of English-language works published in books and periodicals within the past 25 years on the history and philosophy of geography. Entries are not annotated. Indexes for subject and author.
Z6001 B75

CK3 Brewer, James Gordon. **The Literature of Geography: A Guide to Its Organization and Use.** 2d ed. Hamden, CT: Linnet Books, 1978. 264 p.

A guide to the standard sources in geography, describing the structure of the literature, and reference works, periodicals, statistics, government publications, geographical methodology. A complementary work is *A Guide to Information Sources in the Geographical Sciences*, edited by Stephen Goddard (Barnes and Noble, 1983) (Z6001 G84), which provides bibliographic essays describing the subfields of geography, including systematic approaches, tools used, and regional information.
Z6001 B74

CK4 Dunbar, Gary S. **The History of Modern Geography: An Annotated Bibliography of Selected Works.** New York: Garland, 1985. 386 p.

Includes over 1,700 annotated entries to information sources in modern general and systematic geography from the mid 18th century to present day. Coverage includes works in English, French, German, Italian, Spanish, Dutch, Norwegian, Swedish, and Portuguese, and

translations of works published in Slavic and Oriental languages.
Z6001 D86

CK5 **A Geographical Bibliography for American Libraries.** Ed. by Chauncy D. Harris. Washington: Association of American Geographers and National Geographical Society, 1985. 437 p.

Includes over 2,900 annotated entries for mostly English language geographical reference sources for theory and methodology and specific fields (human, applied, regional) of geography. Emphasizes works published 1970 to 1984 with selective inclusion of earlier works of enduring value.
Z6001 G38

CK6 Harris, Chauncy Dennison. **Bibliography of Geography.** 2 parts. Chicago: University of Chicago, Department of Geography, 1976-84.

Annotated entries of geographical bibliographies, both current and retrospective, published since 1969. Part 1 consists of general introduction; Part 2 contains five sections: United States, Soviet Union, The Americas, Europe, and Africa, Asia, Australia, and the Pacific.
Z6001 H313

CK7 Hill, A. David and Regina McCormick. **Geography: A Resource Book for Secondary Schools.** Santa Barbara, CA: ABC-Clio, 1989. 387 p.

Guide and handbook for geographical information, useful as a starting point for students, teachers, and librarians. Includes chapters on geographical methods, the history of geography, geographic data, a directory of associations, agencies, and organizations, a list of reference works. There is also a section on maps, charts, diagrams and other images used by geographers.
910.7073 H645 EDUC

CK8 **International List of Geographical Serials.** 3d ed. Ed. by Chauncy Harris. Chicago: University of Chicago, Department of Geography, 1980. 457 p.

Lists 3,500 international serial titles with geographical content, listing publication information, frequency, brief descriptions. Current material can be found in the quarterly journal of the American Geographical Society *Geographical Review*, which annually reviews new journals.

Harris also published *Annotated World List of Selected Current Geographical Serials* (Chicago, 4th ed, 1980), (Z6003 H28) which summarizes 443 of the most scholarly geographical journals.
Z6003 H375

Abstracts and Indexes and Databases

CK9 **Bibliographie géographique internationale,** 1891- . Paris: Laboratoire d'Information et de Documentation en Géographie, Centre National de la Recherche Scientifique. quarterly.

The best international current bibliography covering modern geography. Abstracts are in French, with English headings and table of contents.
Z6001 B57

CK10 **GEOBASE,** 1980- . Norwich, U.K: Geo Abstracts. database. updated monthly.

Provides abstracts to worldwide literature on geography, geology, ecology, and other topics from 2,000 geographical journals, books, conference proceedings, and reports. Print versions include *Geographical Abstracts* (CK11), *International Development Abstracts*, *Geological Abstracts* (DG13), and *Ecological Abstracts* (DK13).

CK11 Geographical Abstracts, 1989- . Norwich, U.K: Elsevier/Geo Abstracts.

Title varies. Formerly *Geomorphological Abstracts* (1960-65), *Geographical Abstracts* (1966-73), and *Geo Abstracts* (1974-88). Covers physical, social, historical regional geography and urban planning. Published in two parts: *Human Geography*, and *Physical Geography*. Available online as *GeoBase* (CK10).
G1 G32942

Encyclopedias and Dictionaries

CK12 Clark, Audrey N. **Longman Dictionary of Geography: Human and Physical.** White Plains, NY: Longman, 1985. 724 p.

Definitions of more than 10,500 terms used in physical and human geography, including techniques, philosophical viewpoints, environmental resources, commercial products, and regional and local terms.
G63 C56

CK13 The Encyclopaedic Dictionary of Physical Geography. Ed. by Andrew Goudie. New York: Basil Blackwell, 1985. 528 p.

Dictionary which includes long signed articles and brief definitions on all aspects of physical geography, including geomorphology, climatology, soil geography and other areas. Includes diagrams, tables, photographs, maps, and an extensive index.
GB10 E53

CK14 Goodall, Brian. **The Facts on File Dictionary of Human Geography.** New York: Facts on File, 1987. 509 p.

Includes over 3,500 entries of varying length on terms and concepts used in human geography (human awareness, values, experiences). Other dictionaries in the same area are: *Dictionary of Human Geography* (2d ed, Blackwell, 1986) (GF4 D52), which also has lengthy definitions and bibliographic references; and Robert Larkin's *Dictionary of Concepts in Human Geography* (Greenwood, 1983) (GF4 L37), which provides more advanced definitions.
GF4 G66

CK15 Huber, Thomas P. **Dictionary of Concepts in Physical Geography.** New York: Greenwood Press, 1988. 291 p.

Detailed, lengthy articles covering terms and concepts in the field of physical geography, which provide bibliographic references to many of the topics. Complements *Encyclopaedic Dictionary of Physical Geography* (CK13).
GB10 H82

CK16 Illustrated Encyclopedia of World Geography. 11 vols. Oxford University Press, 1990- in progress.

Four volumes completed, 1991. Volume 1: *The Earth's Natural Forces* (GB54.5 E27 SCAR), provides a survey of the origins of the solar system and our planet, and discusses topics relating to climate and geology; Volume 2: *World Government* (JF51 W65 SCAR), includes information on government systems, and topical issues such as human rights and the arms race. Other volumes include Volume 3 *Nature's Last Strongholds* (QH75 N3559 SCAR) and Volume 4 *Plant Life* (QK101 P55 SCAR). Text focuses on regional concerns in countries and regions, rather than on comparisons between each. Written for the general reader, includes colour photographs, maps and diagrams. Future volumes include *People and Cultures; Planet Management; The World Economy.*

CK17 Modern Geography: An Encyclopedic Survey. Ed. by Gary S. Dunbar. New York: Garland, 1991. 219 p.

Provides an "overview of developments in geography" since 1890. Covers evolution of the discipline, concepts, individuals, institutions. Signed entries are arranged topically, and include bibliographies.
G63 M57 ROBA

CK18 Webster's New Geographical Dictionary. Rev. ed., 1984. See AK51 for full entry information.

Directories and Biographical Sources

CK19 The Discoverers: An Encyclopedia of Explorers and Exploration. Ed. by Helen Delpar. New York: McGraw-Hill, 1980. 471 p.

Includes biographical information on 15th-20th century explorers, information about geographical regions and their importance in exploration, and various subjects relating to exploration.
G200 D53

CK20 Geographers: Biobibliographical Studies, 1977- . Ed. by Thomas W. Freedman. Rutherford, NJ: Publishers Distribution Center. annual.

Index to articles, studies and obituaries about prominent international geographers who have made major contributions to the development of geographical thought and of geography as an academic discipline.
G67 G36

CK21 Orbis Geographicus: World Directory of Geography, 1960- . Wiesbaden: Franz Steiner Verlag. irregular.

(1980/84). Lists academic departments, societies, research institutions, map collections, and authorities in various fields, and a listing of geographers by country. For Canada and the United States, see also *Guide to Departments of Geography in the United States and Canada* (Association of American Geographers, 1984- annual) (G76.5 U5G82), which lists graduate geography programs in universities, admission requirements, financial aid available, and faculty areas of specialty.
G64 O7

Travel Guides

CK22 Franck, Irene. **To the Ends of the Earth: The Great Travel and Trade Routes of Human History.** New York: Facts on File, 1984. 472 p.

Guide to 45 historic land and water passages that are frequently travelled by tourists. Includes descriptions of the route's commercial and historic importance in past and present times with maps and colour photographs.
HE 323 F73 ROMU

CK23 Hayes, Greg and Joan Wright. **Going Places: The Guide to Travel Guides.** Boston: Harvard Common Press, 1988. 772 p.

Annotated bibliography of some 3,000 English-language travel guides in all areas and all interests. Lists titles that have been published between 1982 and 1988 for regions of the world. Reviews well-known travel guide series such as Fodor's, Fielding's, Rand McNally, and others. Includes geographical and subject indexes.
Z6011 H39

CK24 Hecker, Helen. **Travel for the Disabled: A Handbook of Travel Resources and 500 Worldwide Access Guides.** Portland, OR: Twin Peaks Press, 1985. 185 p.

Guide to accessible places in the U.S. and Canada, and internationally, for handicapped persons, including motels, parks, campgrounds, etc. Information on means of travel (train, airplanes, buses, etc.) is also provided.
MTRL HIS

CK25 **International Handbook of National Parks and Nature Reserves.** Ed. by Craig Allin. New York: Greenwood Press, 1990. 539 p.

Comparative descriptions of national parks and nature preserves in 25 countries. Arranged geographically and includes history, parks and reserves, and administration for each country. Includes bibliographies, maps, index.
SB481 I475 BMED

CK26 **Worldwide Travel Information Contact Book,** 1991- . Detroit: Gale Research. biennial.

Includes government agencies, tourism boards, associations, travel agencies, tour operators, mapping agencies, automobile clubs, railways, park authorities, wildlife departments, mountain and ski clubs, tourist newspapers and magazines, chambers of commerce, local and regional information centres, embassies and travel bureaus abroad. Arranged by country. Includes address, phone, and fax numbers.
MTRL HIS

CL   SPORTS AND GAMES

Bibliographies

CL1   **SportBiblio.** Ottawa: Sport Information Resource Centre. irregular series.

A specialized bibliography series on current topics in sports, such as *Ethics in Sports, Employee Fitness, Strength Training for Youth*, and drugs in sports (*Drug File*), etc. Bibliographies contain over 200 references.

Another bibliographic resource published by SIRC is *Sport and Recreation for the Disabled: A Bibliography 1984–1989* edited by Richard Stark (Z7514 H36S7).

Abstracts, Indexes, and Databases

CL2   **SPORT Database,** 1974- . Gloucester, ON: Sport Information Resource Centre. database.

SIRC (Sport Information Resource Centre) is recognized as a world leader in the field of sport information. *SPORT Database* contains over 270,000 bibliographic references to the world's practical and research literature on sport and fitness available in magazine and journal articles, books, theses, conference papers, and unpublished papers. Topics included are multi-disciplinary, and include sports medicine, biomechanics, physical fitness, and coaching, as well as individual and team sports. As of June, 1991, *SPORT Database* includes the *Sport and Leisure* database from the University of Waterloo, containing over 18,000 abstracts to research literature for the social and psycho-social aspects of sports, games, dance, etc.

SPORT Database is available in print form as *SportSearch* (September, 1985-) (Z7513 S75). Formerly *Sport and Recreation Index* (1974–84); and *Sport and Fitness Index* (1984–85), this index is published monthly with some combined issues. *SPORT Database* is also available on CD-ROM as *SPORT Discus*.

SPORT Thesaurus (1990) contains over 8,000 index terms and 2,000 cross references used in the *SPORT Database*, and is useful for online searching. Also available from SIRC is the *SPORT Database User Aid* manual.

Encyclopedias, Dictionaries, and Handbooks

CL3 Cuddon, J.A. **The International Dictionary of Sports and Games.** New York: Schocken, 1980. 870 p.

Brief definition, history, etymology, rules and other pertinent information on major sports and games. Includes a chronology of events from 5200 B.C. to A.D. 1979. Official and slang terminology are also included.
GV567 C8

CL4 **The Guinness Sports Record Book.** 1972- . Ed. by David Boehm. New York: Sterling Publishing. annual.

Formerly titled *Guinness Book of Sports Records: Winners and Champions*. Contains records and statistics for all sporting events, professional and non-professional, from earliest times to present. Organized alphabetically by sport. Each entry gives brief history of the sport, followed by records, winners, record holders. Includes useful charts, tables, and some photographs. Subject, but no name, index.
MTRL SCI/TECH

CL5 **The Information Please Sports Almanac,** 1989- . Boston: Houghton Mifflin. annual.

Provides statistical updates and information on sporting events, primarily American events, but does include international sports as well.
MTRL SCI/TECH

CL6 **The Rule Book.** New York: St. Martin's Press, 1983. 430 p.

Extensive examination of international sporting rules of over 50 sports, equipment and playing surfaces specified by the governing bodies and associations of each major sport. Explains acronyms and terminology. Jess White's *Sports Rules Encyclopedia* (2d ed, Leisure Press, 1990) provides an overview of sports rules from an American perspective, with an emphasis on team sports. Canadian official rules for sports are available by contacting the national associations for individual sports.
GV731 R75

CL7 Wallechinsky, David. **The Complete Book of the Olympics.** New York: Viking Press, 1984. 628 p.

Information about the Olympics from the start of the modern games up to 1980. Organized by summer or winter events, then by type of sport and event. Includes photographs of famous athletes and stories about their achievements.
GV721.5 W25

CL8 **The World of Games: Their Origins and History, How to Play Them and How to Make Them.** Ed. by Jack Botermans, Tony Burrett and others. New York: Facts on File, 1989. 240 p.

Provides historical information on more than 150 games that have been played throughout the world, including how they were developed, how they are played, and how to make them. Includes illustrations.
MTRL SCI/TECH

Directories

CL9 Ferguson, Bob. **Who's Who in Canadian Sports.** Toronto: Summerhill Press, 1985. 354 p.

Unique source of information about Canadian athletes, including over 2,800 individuals in amateur and professional sports, including athletes, coaches and administrators. Features include a list of Canadian Olympic teams, and a list of members of all the halls of fame in Canada. Indexed with cross references, with a "Glossary of Terms".
GV697 A1F46

CL10 Sports Federation of Canada. **Sports Directory / Répertoire récréation,** 1982- . Ottawa: National Printers [Ottawa] Inc. annual.

Source of information on who's who and where of Canadian amateur and professional sports. Also includes brief entries about sports associations and organizations, listing all athletic groups, federal and provincial, amateur and professional, with contact names, addresses and telephone numbers. Major sports awards, halls of fame, government agencies are also listed. Sports for the disabled and educational bodies are included. A similar directory is *Canadian Fitness Sourcebook: Organizations & Resource Materials* (Gloucester, ON: The Program, 1988) (GV510 C2C36), which also lists federal and provincial/territorial sport and fitness organizations, government departments, nonprofit agencies, and membership associations and includes resource materials and teaching kits available and a directory of equipment suppliers.
GV585 S73

CL11 Sports Market Place, 1980- . Princeton, NJ: Sportsguide. annual.

Information regarding the business side of professional and amateur sports, such as data for U.S., Canadian, and international associations, professional teams and leagues, and event sponsoring organizations. Television and radio broadcasters and marketing and promotion services are included. Entries list names, addresses, description of the organization, membership, publications, etc. Also lists popular magazines for each sporting event, suppliers of sporting equipment.

Specialized Handbooks and Directories

Baseball

CL12 Reichler, Joseph. **The Baseball Encyclopedia: The Complete and Official Record of Major League Baseball.** 8th ed. New York: Macmillan, 1990. 2600 p.

Published triennially, this is a comprehensive source for baseball statistics, information on current players, and analyses of world series, playoffs, and All-Star games. Baseball fans can also obtain current information from *Baseball America's Almanac*, and *Baseball America's Directory*, two annual reference sources produced by the newspaper with the same name. The *Almanac* provides team and player statistics for major and minor league teams in the U.S. and Canada, as well as Mexican, Japanese, and Winter leagues. The *Directory* lists names, addresses and telephone numbers of teams and

officials, and provides a schedule of games, call letters and frequencies of broadcast stations, and a list of ballparks.
MTRL SCI/TECH

Football

CL13   The Canadian Football League Facts, Figures and Records, 1987- . Markham, ON: McClelland & Stewart. annual.

Comprehensive guide to Canadian professional football, including statistics, historical information, stadium facts, playoff and Grey Cup game records, player profiles, and many illustrations on the Canadian aspect of this sport.
MTRL SCI/TECH

CL14   The Official NFL Encyclopedia, 4th ed. New York: New American Library, 1986. 544 p.

Provides historical and statistical information about the 28 NFL teams and an overview of professional football in the United States. A similar encyclopedic work is *The Sports Encyclopedia: Pro Football*, (St. Martins Press, 1987). Annual reference sources for this sport include the *Football Register* and the *Pro Football Guide*, both published by The Sporting News. The *Register* contains biographical and statistical information on all NFL players and coaches; the *Guide* is a compilation of statistics, draft information, player rosters, schedules, etc. for the NFL season.
MTRL SCI/TECH

Hockey

CL15   The Hockey Encyclopedia. Ed. by Stan Fischler and Shirley Walton Fischler. New York: Macmillan, 1983. 720 p.

Regarded as "the bible of the hockey world", with information dating back to the earliest beginnings of the NHL and supplying player and team records to 1983. Covers North American professional hockey. Updated information can be found in *The National Hockey League Official Guide & Record Book*, published annually by Running Press, which includes statistics, schedule of games, names of coaches, captains, and general managers, list of individual and team records, etc., or the *Hockey Guide* and *Hockey Register* (both published annually by The Sporting News) which provide extensive coverage of hockey: the *Guide* providing schedules, draft information, team directories, and statistics, while the *Register* provides information on all NHL players for the year covered.
MTRL SCI/TECH

Part D
SCIENCE AND TECHNOLOGY

DA GENERAL REFERENCE IN SCIENCE AND TECHNOLOGY

For Selection Aids for Science and Technology, please refer to *Selection Aids*, Section AC.

Bibliographies and Guides to the Literature

DA1 Abstracts and Indexes in Science and Technology: A Descriptive Guide. 1985. 2d ed. Ed. by D.B. Owen. Metuchen, NJ: Scarecrow Press. 235 p.
 Describes about 200 of the abstracts and indexes titles most frequently used in science and technology; entries are in broad discipline categories.
R050 A097A2   or   Z74093 O95 PASR, ENGR

DA2 Handbooks and Tables in Science and Technology. 1983. 2d ed. Ed. by R.H. Powell. Phoenix, AZ: Oryx Press. 304 p.
 Comprehensive annotated list of about 2,000 science and technology handbooks (tabulated data, physical constants, properties of materials etc.). Indexed by subject and author.
Z7405 T3H35 PASR

DA3 Hurt, Charlie D. 1988. Information Sources in Science and Technology. Englewood, CO: Libraries Unlimited. 362 p.
 This guide attempts an identification of the major and most useful items in the pure and applied sciences. Some 2,000 annotated entries are subarranged by form (bibliographies, encyclopedias, etc.) within 17 subject sections (history of science, physics, biomedical sciences, zoology, etc.).
R500 AH19571   or   Z7401 H85 PASR

DA4 Publications of the National Research Council of Canada, 1916–1981. Ottawa: National Research Council Canada. annual and various cumulations.
 A cumulative listing of work done in NRCC's laboratories, and other publications. Discontinued in hardcopy; continued online as *NRCPUBS*.
Z5055 C2N3 BMER

DA5 **Pure and Applied Science Books 1876–1982.** 1982. 6 vols. New York: R.R. Bowker.

Bibliography of over 220,000 titles in science and technology published and distributed in the U.S. Arranged by subject, author, and title.
Z7401 P89 ENGR

DA6 **Science and Technology Annual Reference Review,** 1989- annual.

Reviews science and technology reference books. See AC7 for full entry information.

DA7 **Science Books & Films,** 1965- . 5 issues per year.

Evaluates science trade, text, and reference books for all age groups. See AC25 for full entry information.

DA8 **Scientific and Technical Books and Serials in Print,** 1978- . New York: R.R. Bowker. annual.

Formerly *Scientific and Technical Books in Print*. Arranged by subject with author and title access, this spinoff from *BIP* (AD76) and *Ulrich's* (AE13) contains about 125,000 books and 18,000 serials in the physical and biological sciences and in applied technology and engineering. Introductory matter has general article on publishing and information resources in science and technology.
Z7401 S38 PASR; ENGR

DA9 **Scientific and Technical Information Sources.** 1987. 2d ed. Comp. by Ching-Chih Chen. Cambridge, MA: MIT Press. 824 p.

A guide to resources primarily published post-1976. Work is most useful for science and engineering librarians and library school students.
R500 AC518S2 or Z4701 C48 ENGR; BMER

Periodicals and Union Lists

DA10 **Directory of Periodicals Online: Science and Technology,** 1985- irregular.

Provides list of science and technology periodicals available online in North America on English-language commerical databases. Lists publishing information and information on database coverage. Organized by database and by subject. See AE5 for full entry information.
Z7403 D56 PASR; ENGR

DA11 **Union List of Scientific Serials in Canadian Libraries.** See AE20 for full entry information.

DA12 **World List of Scientific Periodicals Published in the Years 1900–1960.** 1963-1965. 4th ed. 3 vols. London: Butterworths.

A comprehensive union list of almost 60,000 science and technology periodicals held in British libraries for the period 1900 to 1960. After 1960, updates were incorporated into *British Union Catalogue of Periodicals: New Periodical Titles* (1964-1980) (R050 AB862A), and continued by *Serials in the British Library* (AE19).
500 AW927 or Z7403 W92 PASR

*   *   *   *

Abstracts and Indexes

DA13 Applied Science and Technology Index, 1913- . New York: Wilson. monthly with annual cumulation.

Subject access to 250 English language professional, scholarly journals as well as many general audience and semi-popular journals overlapping slightly with *General Science Index* (DA18). Available online and on CD-ROM.
Z7913 I7 ENGR

DA14 Composite Index for CRC Handbooks. 1977. 2d ed. Cleveland, OH: CRC Press. 1111 p.

Indexes all 57 CRC handbooks. A new edition is in press.
QD65 C74 ENGR

DA15 Current Contents, 1958- . Philadelphia: Institute for Scientific Information. weekly.

A "current awareness" alerting service separately published in seven editions. Each weekly issue (or edition) reproduces tables of contents from most recent issues of journals and outstanding books in the relevant fields. Five of the seven sections are in the sciences (*Life Sciences* (1958-); *Clinical Medicine* (1973-); *Agriculture, Biology, & Environmental Sciences* (1970-); *Physical, Chemical & Earth Sciences* (1961-); *Engineering, Technology & Applied Sciences* (1970-). Each issue contains a subject index, author index and address directory. The publishers directory in each issue is for the publishers whose journals are covered in that week. The *Current Contents Address Directory* (1961-87) has ceased publication. The machine-readable *Current Contents on Diskette*, (1991-) provides abstracts.
BMED; PASR; FLIS; ENGR

DA16 Current Technology Index, 1981- . monthly. See DL17 for full entry information.

DA17 Engineering Index, 1884- . monthly. See DL21 for full entry information.

DA18 General Science Index, 1978- . New York: H.W. Wilson. monthly with annual cumulation.

A cumulative subject index. Coverage has gradually grown to over 100 journals of general interest to readers of science. There is a cross-section of important, scholarly journals as well as the better-known magazines for wide and popular reading. Available online and on CD-ROM.
Z7401 G46 PASR

DA19 INSPEC, 1969- . London: Institution of Electrical Engineers. Database. monthly updates.

The *INSPEC* database contains citations and abstracts of international technical literature in the areas of physics, electrical engineering, electronics and telecommunications, control technology, computers and computing, and information technology. Corresponds to *Science Abstracts* (see DA21).
PASR or PHYS

DA20 Referativnyi Zhurnal, 1953- . Moscow: Akademiya Nauk SSSR, VINITI. irregular annual.

"The most comprehensive of abstracting services, producing over one million abstracts and references each year", some in English, in 70 sections in pure and applied sciences. Time lag of six to seven months.
various call numbers

DA21 Science Abstracts, 1898- . 4 series. London: Feilden Pub. for Institution of Electrical Engineers (IEE) / Piscataway, NJ: IEEE. monthly.

A major international service for a broad range of physical, mathematical, engineering sciences abstracting periodicals, papers, etc. The separately titled series (parts) are: *A: Physics Abstracts*, 1898-; *B: Electrical and Electronic Abstracts*, 1966-; *C: Computer and Control Abstracts*, 1966-; *D: IT Focus*, 1983- [information Technology].

Titles of foreign language articles and abstracts (varying in length with series, 100-300 words) are in English and often signed. Annual detailed author and subject indexes appear with usually quinquennial cumulations. Available online as *INSPEC*, (DA19).
PASR

DA22 Science Citation Index, 1945- . Philadelphia: Institute for Scientific Information. bimonthly with annual cumulation. Two decennial cumulations, 1945–1954; 1955–1964. Thereafter quinquennial cumulations pattern, most recent is 1985–1989.

Institute for Scientific Information started *SCI* in 1961, and has since expanded coverage back to 1945. The decennial cumulations cover, respectively, about 750,000 and 1 million journal items, from some 500 science journals. Coverage since 1964 reflects the increase in science publishing. *SCI* is the oldest and largest of the three citation indexes (*SCI*; *Social Sciences CI* (see CA13); *Art & Humanities CI* (see BA3)) produced by ISI. In a year, *SCI* includes well over .5 million items from 3,100 leading journals plus itemizing the contents of many monographs.

SCI lists every substantive item in each journal indexed, and provides access to the contained information through an author (i.e., the *Source*) index; title/keyword permuted (i.e. rotated) index, and citation index. The permuted terms index and the citation volumes have author, co-author and corporate name references to full bibliographic data in the *Source* volume. *SCI* covers clinical medicine; life sciences; physics; chemistry; earth and agricultural sciences; engineering, technology and applied sciences; mathematics and computer science. From 1975, *Journal Citation Reports* (Z7401 S366) analyzes journals as an aid to collection management; the report ranks journals according to various citation and other measures. Versions of these reports usually appear in *Current Contents* (DA15). *SCI* is available online, and on CD-ROM as *SciSearch*. From 1991 citation indexes for specific disciplines are available on CD-ROM. Those for neuroscience, chemistry and biotechnology include abstracts.

Index to Scientific Reviews, 1974- (Z7403 I54 BMER) is a semi-annual cumulation of review articles identified in *SCI*. For large research libraries, *ISR* provides multidisciplinary display of scientific review literature.
Z7401 S365 BMER

Conference Papers and Proceedings

DA23   Bibliographic Guide to Conference Publications, 1975- . 2 vols. Boston: G.K. Hall. annual.
A dictionary catalog of entries catalogued by the Research Libraries of the New York Public Library and LC/MARC records during the year. All languages included.
Z5051 B5 BMER

DA24   Conference Papers Index, Vol. 6, 1978- . Bethesda, MD: Cambridge Scientific Abstracts, 1988-. monthly with cumulative annual index.
Supersedes *Current Programs*, 1973-1977. Annual index separately available. Cites research papers worldwide given at scientific, medical and technological conferences. Sections for title, registry number, date, location, language, sponsor of conference. With author and subject index. Available online.
Z7409 C6 BMER

DA25   Directory of Published Proceedings. Series: SEMT: Science, Engineering, Medicine, Technology, 1965- . Harrison, NY: InterDok. 10 issues / year with annual cumulation.
Worldwide. Lists proceedings chronologically by conference date (year and month) with indexes for editor, location, subject/sponsor.
Z7409 D56 PASR

DA26   Index to Scientific & Technical Proceedings, 1978- . Philadelphia: Institute for Scientific Information. monthly with semi-annual cumulation.
ISTP provides multi-disciplinary coverage of well over 4,000 conferences and the some 125,000 papers generated at the conferences. Entries provide complete bibliographic description and contents table for papers; six indexes (conference topic; sponsor of conference; keyword subject; author/editor; organizational affiliation of author; location of conference). *Index to Scientific & Technical Proceedings & Books*, (1978-) (*ISI/ISTP&B*) is an online service combining *ISTP* with *Index to Scientific Book Contents*, (1985-). *ISBC's* annual 2 volume cumulation indexes about 2,000 multi-authored books at the chapter level each year.
Z7409 I56 BMER

Translations

DA27   Canadian Index of Scientific Translations. Ottawa: National Research Council Canada / Canada Institute for Scientific and Technical Information.
A request service, i.e. not a publicly available print/online source. CISTI's *Index* contains references to over .5 million translated documents available from several world centres.

DA28   Index Translationum, 1948- . annual. See AF47 for full entry information.

DA29   World Translations Index, 1987- . Delft, Netherlands: International Translations Centre. 10 issues / year.
Title varies; supersedes *World Transindex* and *Translations Register Index* (1967-1986) (Z7403 W34 BMER). Source and author listing to translations available (and reported to the ITC) for all fields of science and technology,

including articles, patents, standards. Translations noted are primarily from East European and Asiatic languages into Western languages. Available online.
Z7403 W94 PASR

Theses, Research and Technical Reports

DA30 Current Research in Britain, 1985- , annual. See AF40 for full entry information.

DA31 Dissertation Abstracts International: B: The Sciences and Engineering, Vol. 30, 1969- . monthly. See AF42 for full entry information.
Subtitle for *B* varies, formerly *Physical Sciences and Engineering*. Arranged by subject categories with keyword and author indexes. Microform, ondisc availability. (See also AF45 for *Canadian Theses*.)
Z5053 D513 O2 BMER

DA32 Government Reports Announcements And Index, Vol. 75, no. 7, 1975- . Springfield, VA: National Technical Information Service. biweekly.
Titles varies. Supersedes *Government Reports Announcement* and *Government Reports Index*. An abstract journal covering U.S. government sponsored research and development reports. Arranged by subject and indexed by corporate author, personal author, subject, contract number, accession report number. Annual cumulated index. Available online as *NTIS*.
Weekly Government Abstracts is a current awareness bulletin. The National Technical Information Service, established 1970, within the U.S. Department of Commerce is a major supplier of science and technology information, and the central source for the public sale of U.S. and foreign government sponsored research (including some patented information, development and engineering reports, analyses prepared by national, local government agencies, their contractors or grantees). NTIS publishes subject bibliographies, directories and weekly alerting services (newsletters) for various fields in technology, science.
Z7916 U5316 BMER; ENGR

Patents and Trademarks

DA33 The Patent Office Record / La gazette du bureau des brevets, 1873- . Ottawa: CGPC, Supply and Services. weekly.
Formerly *The Canadian Patent Office Record*. Numbered entries are in classes according to the Patent Office Domestic Classification scheme. An outline of the main classes is in the first January issue each year. Index of inventors and patentees in each issue, with annual cumulative index. Separate indexing aids, e.g. *Subject Matter Index*, *Class Schedules* and *Class Listings* aid searching the *POR* pre-1982. Selected drawings and abstracts once carried in the *POR* no longer appear.
Canada's *POR* follows the pattern of U.K., U.S. patent gazettes. Great Britain's weekly notice is in the *Official Journal (Patents)*, (#2196 1931-) (Patent Office) (MTRL); U.S. notices are in the weekly *Official Gazette of the United States Patent Office*, (V931 Feb 1975-) (Superintendent of Documents) (MTRL); *The INPADOC Patent Gazette*, (1973-) (Vienna: International Patents Documentation Center) (available online) collates information from

gazettes and journals of 45 countries, and publishes various indexes to aid in bringing related patents together.

For an understanding of the patent process in Canada, the *Manual of Patent Office Practice* (Supply and Services) (T226 K6C3 ENGR) supplies information and instructions.
T226 A2 PASS, BMED; MTRL

DA34 Trade Marks Journal / Journal des marques de commerce, 1953- . Ottawa: CGPC, Supply and Services. weekly.

Trade mark is shown; arranged by registration number with statement on wares, service to which mark applies; also amendments, cancellations, extensions. Trademarks can also be searched online through several databases. In Canada, the *Canadian Trade Marks* database is available.
MTRL SCI/TECH

DA35 World Patents Index, 1963- . London: Derwent Publications. database. updated weekly.

"Supplies titles and other details [patent number, journal citation, patent equivalents, etc.] of general, mechanical, electrical, and chemical patents, covering the patent literature of leading industrial countries." Cumulation of *World Patents Index* (weekly); *World Patents Abstracts*, *Chemical Patents Index*, and *Electrical Patents Index*.

Standards

DA36 Access to Standards Information. 1986. Geneva: International Organization of Standards. 102 p.

(English or French edition.) Intended as an aid to information about standards and technical regulations worldwide. Describes print and electronic reference aids, gives addresses of organizations and laboratories, with meanings of initials and certification marks. Organized by broad subject with a number of geographical listings.
389.6 A169A or T59 A36 ENGR

DA37 American Society for Testing and Materials. **Annual Book of ASTM Standards,** 1939- . Philadelphia, PA: ASTM. annual.

(1991 ed, 67 vols.) Voluntary standards for materials, products, systems, services. Each type or group is in a separate volume. Comprehensive indexes to this multivolume set.
TA401 A653 ENGR

DA38 Directory and Index of Standards / Répertoire des normes, 1977- . Ottawa: Standards Council of Canada. annual, 1987-.

(12th ed, 1991). At head of title: *National Standards System...* Bilingual and containing the titles of more than 6,500 standards published by the five Canadian standards writing organizations. Includes national and organization standards. The index of standards permutes title under all significant keywords. Material in the annual is current as of March 31 of the year of issue. Information on standards published or changed after that date is available from the Standards Council of Canda and in *Consensus* (1973-), a quarterly published by SCC. *Consensus* lists the standards approved as national each quarter year, and lists recently published ISO, IEC, and other standard cumulations. A companion publication, *The Catalog of National Standards*, (1987-) (6th ed, 1991) accompanies the *Directory*.
Z7914 A22N38 ENGR

DA39 KWIC Index of International Standards. 1991. Geneva: International Organization for Standardization. 694 p.

A single source to help in identifying all standards (over 7,500) published by 24 international bodies. All titles are permuted on keywords. Two criteria for inclusion of a standard are establishment of technical requirements of importance to international exchange and emanation from recognized international organization.
TA368 K28 ENGR (3d ed, 1987)

Handbooks, Encyclopedias and Yearbooks

DA40 The Cambridge Guide to the Material World. 1985. Ed. by R. M. J. Cotterill. Cambridge/New York: Cambridge University Press. 352 p.

Discusses the physical, chemical and biological properties of materials such as metals, minerals, plastics, glass, ceramics and crystals.
QC173.3 C66 PASR

DA41 Encyclopedia of Physical Science and Technology. 1987. 15 vols. Ed. by Robert A. Meyers. Orlando, FL: Academic Press.

Volume 15 is the subject index to this set on the physical sciences (robotics, electronics, computers, materials, mathematics, earth and related chemical sciences, etc.). Signed articles with cross references are intended for the scientific community and general readers with a science background. The *Encyclopedia of Physical Science and Technology Yearbook*, 1989- (Q123 E4972 ENGR) is a supplement to the encyclopedia and an annual review of topical subjects in the physical sciences.
Q123 E497 ENGR

DA42 Handbook of Chemistry and Physics, 1913- . Boca Raton, FL: CRC Press. irregular annual.

Subtitled *"A Ready Reference Book of Chemical and Physical Data"*, and also known as the *CRC Handbook*, this concise summary of definitions, formula, tables, measurements, and miscellaneous data is a standard authoritative general reference work crossing several fields of science and technology. Extensive subject index. There is a student's edition of the *CRC Handbook* (1st ed, 1988) (QD65 H313 PASS), and CRC Press (originally the Chemical Rubber Co.) produces many specialized, standard handbooks for the various science and technology disciplines.
QD65 H3 PASR

DA43 McGraw-Hill Encyclopedia of Science and Technology. 1987. 6th ed. 20 vols. New York: McGraw Hill.

Volume 20 is the index to this comprehensive work covering all branches of physical, natural and applied science. Arranged alphabetically; signed articles are usually short with cross references to more specific subjects. Articles group material under subheadings, and longer articles have bibliographies. Supplemented by a *Yearbook of Science and Technology*, 1962- (Q121 M32 PASS). A concise version for the high school and college audience is the *McGraw Hill Concise Encyclopedia of Science and Technology*, (1989) (Q121 M324).
Q121 M3 BMER

DA44 Science Year: The World Book Science Annual, 1965- . Chicago: World Book. annual.

A supplement to *The World Book Encyclopedia*, (AI15). Contains feature articles on selected topics, and a review of major scientific developments for the year. Includes biographies,

obituaries, lists of awards and prizes. Geared to upper elementary, high school interests.
R505.8 S416

DA45 Van Nostrand's Scientific Encyclopedia. 1989. 7th ed. 2 vols. Ed. by D. M. Considine. New York: Van Nostrand Reinhold.

Long a one volume standard, enlarged and in this edition with an index in Volume 2. Alphabetically arranged articles assume scientific readership; longer articles signed, most articles brief, with cross references, tables, bibliographies. Emphasizes the physical sciences, but with any new field or newer technologies (e.g. genetic discoveries) and information science represented.
Q121 V3 PASR, ENGR

DA46 Yearbook of Science and the Future, 1969- . Chicago: Encyclopaedia Britannica. annual.

Title varies, spine title *Science and the Future*; formerly *Britannica Yearbook of ...* . A science supplement to the *New Encyclopaedia Britannica* (AI8), emphasizing American scientific accomplishments. Has feature articles, and other shorter special reports and articles. With some emphasis on school interests, the review of the year is well illustrated and supported with references, etc. Lists annual awards, prizes in science.
Z1 Y43 SIGR

Encyclopedias - Children's and Young Adults

DA47 The New Book of Popular Science. 1924- . 6 vols. New York: Grolier. annual.

Title varies, formerly *The Book of Popular Science*. Annual issuance and revision. Topics are treated under broad subject headings and designed to correspond to an upper elementary science curriculum. Explanations are nontechnical with many illustrations for an audience at the elementary and secondary school level. Volume 6 has bibliography and index.
R503 B724   or   Z162 N48 SCC (1982)

DA48 World of Science Encyclopedia. 24 vols. Chicago: Encyclopaedia Britannica.

First issued in 1989, this set supersedes the 1984 *Science & Technology Illustrated: World Around Us* set in 28 volumes. Volumes 23 and 24 are an *Illustrated Dictionary of Science* and index to set. Volumes are by subject with individual titles, e.g. physical geography is volume 6 with the title "Face of the Earth". Intended for readers at the grade six level and up through secondary school.

Dictionaries

DA49 Acronyms, Initialisms and Abbreviations Dictionary, 1960- irregular. See AJ34 for full entry information.

DA50 Chambers Dictionary of Science and Technology. 1988. Ed. by P.M. Walker. Edinburgh: Chambers. 1000 p.

Comprehensive, with few illustrations and assuming a knowledge of the physical and applied sciences.
Q123 D53 PASR

DA51 Concise Science Dictionary. 1984. New York: Oxford University Press. 758 p.

Contains over 7,000 entries in physics, chemistry, biology, earth sciences, astronomy and mathematics. Not as detailed as *McGraw Hill Dictionary of Science and Technology*, but useful.
Q123 C68 PASR

DA52 A Dictionary of Named Effects and Laws in Chemistry, Physics and Mathematics. 1980. 4th ed. Ed. by D.W.G. Ballentyne and D. R. Lovett. London: Chapman and Hall. 350 p.

Arrangement is alphabetical by name of the effect or law with explanations, formulae and illustrations.
Q123 B3 PASR

DA53 Dictionary of Scientific Units Including Dimensionless Numbers and Scales. 1986. 5th ed. London: Chapman and Hall/Methuen. 222 p.

A comprehensive dictionary with information on over 850 topics, with appendices for physical constants, weights and measures, conversion factors, etc.
QC82 J4 BMED, ENGR

DA54 Hammond-Barnhart Dictionary of Science. 1986. Ed. by R.K. Barnhart with S. Steinmetz. Maplewood, NJ: Hammond. 740 p.

Title varies, formerly *American Heritage Dictionary of Science*. Over 16,000 entries defined and identified as to broad descipline (e.g. biology, chemistry). Definitions within the general physical and biological sciences range from basic through fairly sophisticated but are intended for the general reader. Typical of dictionaries designed for layreaders is the *Harper Dictionary of Science in Everyday Language: Scientific Terms Explained So You Can Really Understand Them* (Harper & Row, 1988) (Q123 S36 SCAR), by Herman and Leo Schneider, which defines and illustrates some 200 items in an easy to read manner.
A123 B35 PASR

DA55 McGraw-Hill Dictionary of Scientific and Technical Terms. 1988. 4th ed. New York: McGraw Hill. 2200 p.

A comprehensive dictionary with brief information on over 100,000 entries; abbreviations and multiple definitions are given.
Q123 M34 VUPR

Bilingual Dictionaries

DA56 Dictionary of Science & Technology: English-French/French-English. 1979–80. 2 vols. Ed. by A.F. Dorian. New York: Elsevier Scientific.

Detailed, comprehensive coverage of some 150,000 terms.
Z123 D668 BMER; ENGR

DA57 Dictionary of Technology: English-German/German-English. 1984–85. 5th ed. rev. 2 vols. New York: Elsevier Scientific.

Volumes may be purchased independently; each volume has its own lexicon, abbreviations and acronyms. Oriented to the English speaker working with German, and needing equivalents for translation in applied fields from data processing, construction engineering, ceramics, to forestry, transport and machinery.
Q123 D68 PASR

DA58 Harrap's French and English Science Dictionary. 1985. London: Harrap. 320 p.

Covers 30,000 commonly used terms; designed for the general reader rather than the translator or scientist.

Histories and Chronologies

DA59 Asimov's Chronology of Science & Discovery. 1989. New York: Harper & Row. 768 p.

"How science has shaped the world and how the world has affected science from 4,000,000 BC to the present." A popular chronicling of science and technology advances with indication of historical, social and cultural context. Similar to *Asimov's* is *Breakthroughs: A Chronology of Great Achievements in Science and Mathematics 1200–1930*, edited by C.L. Parkinson (G.K. Hall, 1985) (Q125 P39 PASR). *Breakthrough's* is a chronology which places several thousand events in a timeline under broad disciplines written for a nontechnical audience.
Q125 A765 PASR

DA60 Dictionary of the History of Science. 1981. Ed. by W.F. Bynum. New York: Princeton University Press. 494 p.

Brief encyclopedic entries placing concepts from five centuries of Western natural science in context of their development. A comparable work is *A Dictionary of Concepts in the Philosophy of Science*, edited by P.T. Durbin (Greenwood, 1988) (Q174.7 D87 PASR) which provides the historical context for about one hundred concepts with any additional information such as contemporary status, debate.
Q125 B98 PASR

DA61 Milestones in Science and Technology: The Ready Reference Guide to Discoveries, Inventions and Facts. 1987. Comp. by E. Mount and B. List. Phoenix, AZ: Oryx Press. 141 p.

Approximately 1,000 brief descriptions of science and technology inventions and discoveries from prehistoric times to the 1980s. With indexes for broad discipline, year, inventors and their nationalities.
Q199 M68 PASR; ENGR

Biographical Sources

DA62 American Men & Women of Science. 1988/89. 17th ed. 8 vols. New York: R.R. Bowker.

Titles varies; 12th-16th editions subtitled *American Men and Women of Science: Physical and Biological Sciences*. Provides general coverage of living scientists in physical and biological sciences including mathematics, engineering, public health, environmental and earth sciences, statistics, computer sciences.
Volumes 1-7 alphabetically lists scientists, including Canadians, giving personal, educational, professional data. Non-citizens who have or who are working in North America are also listed. Volume 8 is an index by discipline. Various spinoff titles from each edition including *American Men and Women of Science: Physics, Astronomy*, and *American Men and Women of Science: Consultants* which identifies persons available as experts, researchers, etc. Available online.

A retrospective companion volume is the *Biographical Dictionary of American Science: 17th Through 19th Centuries* (1979, Greenwood) (Q141 E37 BMER).
R509.2 A512A14   or   Q141 A482

DA63 **Asimov's Biographical Encyclopedia of Science and Technology.** 1982. 2d rev. ed. General editor I. Asimov. New York: Doubleday. 941 p.

Subtitled "The Lives and Achievements of 1510 Great Scientists from Ancient Times to the Present, Chronologically Arranged," the articles are primarily concerned with achievements. Compare *Concise Dictionary of Scientific Biography* (DA65n) which covers more scientists but with less depth.
Q141 A74 ENGR

DA64 **The Biographical Dictionary of Scientists.** 1984–85. 6 vols. Ed. by D. Abbott. New York: Harper & Row.

A British publication (Blond Educational) with brief sketches for approximately 200 persons in each volume. Volumes are about 200 pages, and each is devoted to a broad discipline (astronomers, biologists, chemists, physicists, engineers and inventors, mathematicians). With name and subject indexes.
Q141 B5 PASR

DA65 **Dictionary of Scientific Biography.** 1970-90. 18 vols. in 10. New York: Scribner.

Different editions appear in various volume numbers. Published for the American Council of Learned Societies and intended as a parallel to the *DAB* (AL36) and *DNB* (AL13). The *DSB* includes persons of all periods, places who have contributed to the advancement of natural sciences and mathematics. No living persons included. There is a *Concise DSB* (1981) (Q141 C55 ENGR). J. Carvill's *Famous Names in Engineering* (1981, Butterworths) (Q141 C37 ENGR) is also useful for identification.
Q141 D53 SIGR

DA66 **Modern Scientists and Engineers.** 1982. 3 vols. New York: McGraw Hill.

Autobiographical entries (for the most part) from over 1,100 of the world's achievers in scientific fields. Topical index and bibliographies included. Another source, *Who's Who in Science in Europe: A Biographical Guide in Science, Technology, Agriculture, and Medicine* (5th ed. 3 vols, Detroit, 1988) (Q145 W5 PASR), lists a wide range of scientists with biographical information.
Q141 M15

DA67 **Who's Who in Technology,** 1986- . Detroit: Gale Research, 1989- . irregular annual.

(6th ed, 2 vols, 1989). Formerly *Who's Who in Technology Today*. In this edition, entries are arranged alphabetically. Includes 38,000 North American men and women. Separate index volume provides access by 46 technical disciplines, areas of expertise, locations, employees.
T39 W5 ENGR

Directories

DA68 **Directory of Federally Supported Research in Universities,** 1972/73 - 1987/88. 3 vols. Ottawa: National Research Council Canada and Canada Institute for Scientific and Technical Information.

An annual listing of university-based projects reported by federal government funding agencies. Print copy discontinued with 16th edition (1987/88). Available online.
Q180 C2D5 PASR

DA69 Forthcoming International Scientific and Technical Conferences, 1966- . Oxford: Learned Information. quarterly.

Compiled by Aslib and the London Department of Education and Science. Chronological arrangement with three indexes for subject, location, organization. Coverage is broader than name implies, including social sciences (law, statistics, library and information science).
Q10 F67 PASR

DA70 Scientific and Technical Societies of Canada. 1988. Ottawa: National Research Council Canada and Canada Institute for Scientific and Technical Information. biennial.

Information given in language (English or French) of society. Discontinued with 1988 issue. Information contained in the *Directory of Associations in Canada* (AH6).
Q21 S37 ENGR   or   Q21 N34 PASR

DA71 World Guide to Scientific Associations and Learned Societies. 1990. 5th ed. Ed. by M. Sachs. Handbook of Information Documentation and Information, vol. 13. Munich/London/New York: K.G. Saur. 702 p.

Over 17,000 national and international groups in science, culture, and technology, arranged by name under country headings. With indexes for subject, name and publications. A somewhat comparable directory is *Scientific And Technical Organizations and Agencies Directory* (2d ed, 1987 with inter-annual supplement; Gale Research), edited by M.L. Young. *STOAD* has keyword and name indexes to its 15,000 entries which emphasizes U.S. coverage for governmental, educational, corporate and smaller organizations including libraries. Includes Canada, and has some international coverage for areas such as standards, patents, various research centres, etc.
Q145 W67

DA72 World Meetings Outside United States and Canada, 1968- . New York: Macmillan. quarterly.

A two-year registry of future medical, scientific, technical meetings. Indexed by date, keyword, deadline, location, sponsor. Also *World Meetings: Medicine* and *World Meetings: United States and Canada* (1963- quarterly) (Q10 T44O2 BMER), which lists meetings in North America.
Q101 W6 O2 PASR

DB   MATHEMATICS

Bibliographies and Guides to the Literature

DB1 May K.O. 1973. **Bibliography and Research Manual of the History of Mathematics.** Toronto: University of Toronto Press. 818 p.
  Extensive annotated bibliography of over 31,000 items from books, periodicals and other secondary literature.
Z6651 M35 BMER

DB2 Schaaf, William L. 1987. **High School Mathematics Library.** 8th ed. Reston, VA: National Council of Teachers of Mathematics. 83 p.
  Well-known (1st ed. 1960) brief bibliography of some 1,000 titles under topical headings. Useful also to public and college libraries despite the title.
R510.16 S291H (4th ed)

Abstracts, Indexes and Databases

DB3 **CompuMath Citation Index, (CMCI),** 1976– . Philadelphia, PA: Institute for Scientific Information. 3/year.
  A spinoff from *Science Citation Index* (see DA22) and in the same format, this index takes a multidisciplinary approach to the literature of computer science, math, statistics and operational research, plus other related fields. Available online as *Computer and Mathematics Search* (1980-, updated weekly).

DB4 **Current Mathematical Publications,** 1969– . Providence, RI: American Mathematical Society. 17/year.
  A list of new and upcoming publications. Available online and on CD-ROM (see *MATHSCI*, DB6).
QA1 C65 SCAR

DB5 **Mathematical Reviews: A Reviewing Journal Covering the World Literature of Mathematical Research,** 1940– . Providence, RI: American Mathematical Society. monthly.
  Abstracts in four languages (English, French, German, Italian) of international literature, arranged by subject. Also available online and on CD-ROM (see *MATHSCI* DB6).
QA1 M424 PASR

DB6 **MATHSCI,** 1959– . Providence, RI: American Mathematical Society. monthly.

This is an online version of several math and computer services: *ACM Guide to Computing Literature* (DC2n); *Computing Reviews* (DC2); *Current Mathematical Publications*; and *Mathematical Reviews*. The CD-ROM version is *MATHSCI DISC* (1989– semi-annual), which contains *Mathematical Reviews*, (1985–), plus over 60,000 entries from *Current Mathematical Publications*.

Handbooks

DB7 Bronshtein, I.N. 1985. **Handbook of Mathematics.** 3d rev. ed. New York: Van Nostrand Reinhold. 973 p.

Based on the well-known German *Taschenbuch der Mathematik*, this volume covers all major fields at an advanced level.
QA40 B713 PASR

DB8 Burington, Richard S. 1973. **Handbook of Mathematical Tables and Formulas.** 5th ed. New York: McGraw-Hill. 500 p.

Well established (1st ed. 1933) handbook consisting of two parts: part 1 has formulas and theorems of math, physics, engineering, etc.; part 2 has tables of logarithms, trigonometry, and probability distributions.
QA47 B8 SCC

DB9 **CRC Handbook of Mathematical Sciences.** 1987. 6th ed. Ed. by W.H. Beyer. Boca Raton, FL: CRC Press. 860 p.

Extensive collection of tables and formulae for all areas of mathematics, with explanations of the main formulae and equations and notes on their use.
QA47 H323 PASR

DB10 **CRC Handbook of Tables for Probability and Statistics.** 1988. 2d ed. Ed. by W.H. Beyer. Boca Raton, FL: CRC Press. 656 p.

Reprint of the original 1968 edition containing tables for use in statistical and probability distributions. Tables are accompanied by explanations of formulae.
QA276.25 B48 PASR

DB11 **CRC Standard Mathematical Tables.** 1987. 28th ed. Ed. by W.H. Beyer. Boca Raton, FL: CRC Press. 674 p.

A wide selection of tabulated data intended to aid engineers, teachers, and students as well as mathematicians. Includes conversion factors, constants, formulae, and diagrams.
QA47 C2 BMER

DB12 **Handbook of Applicable Mathematics.** 1980–1985. 6 vols. in 8 parts. Ed. by Walter Ledermann et al. New York: Wiley.

Set provides thorough coverage to specific areas of applied mathematics: algebra, probability, numerical methods, analysis, geometry and combinatorics, and statistics.
QA36 H36 PASC

DB13 Spiegel, Murray R. 1968. **Mathematical Handbook of Formulas and Tables.** New York: McGraw-Hill. 271 p.

Part of the *Schaum's Outline Series*, this handbook offers 60 tables and over 2,400 formulas from both elementary and advanced mathematics.
QA41 S75 SCC

DB14 Tuma, Jan J. 1987. **Engineering Mathematics Handbook: Definitions, Theorems, Formulas, Tables.** 3d ed. New York: McGraw-Hill, 498 p.

Arranged in five sections according to the field of math covered, this handbook is aimed at practicing engineers, scientists, and architects.
TA332 T85 ENGR

Encyclopedias and Dictionaries

DB15 Bendrick, Jeanne. 1989. **Mathematics Illustrated Dictionary: Facts, Figures, and People.** Rev. ed. New York: Franklin Watts. 247 p.

Dictionary of mathematical terms, concepts, processes, and people. Includes tables for formulas and mathematical symbols, logs, metric system. Illustrated.
QA5 B4 PASR (1980)

DB16 Clapham, Christopher. 1990. **Concise Dictionary of Mathematics.** New York: Oxford University Press. 203 p.

Brief but authoritative definitions.

DB17 **Dictionary of Named Effects and Laws in Chemistry, Physics and Mathematics.** 1980, 4th ed. See DA52 for full entry information.

DB18 Dunham, William. 1990. **Journey Through Genius: The Great Theorems of Mathematics.** New York: Wiley. 300 p.

Not strictly a dictionary, but an entertaining historical account of famous discoveries through history, from Pythagoras to Einstein.
QA21 D78 PASC

DB19 **Encyclopedia of Mathematics.** 1987– . 10 vols. Ed. by M. Hazewinkel. Dordrecht, Netherlands: Kluwer Academic, in progress. (6 vols. to 1991).

An updated and annotated translation of the *Soviet Mathematical Encyclopedia*, to be issued in 10 volumes with volume 10 a comprehensive index.
QA5 M37213 PASR

DB20 **Encyclopedia of Mathematics and Its Applications.** 1984–1987. 30 vols. New York: Cambridge University Press.

A series of very comprehensive surveys, with each volume devoted to a major area of current research or application. Two recently published volumes in this series are: Volume 32: *Basic Hypergeometric Series* by George Gasper (1990) (QA353 H9G37 PASC), and Volume 34: *Volterra Integral and Functional Equations*, by Gustaf Gripenberg (1990) (QA431 G76 PASC).

DB21 **Encyclopedia of Statistical Sciences.** 1982–88. 9 vols. Ed. by Samuel Kotz and others. New York: Wiley.

A wide survey of the many fields in which statistical methods play a role, from actuarial science to zoology, with useful bibliographies and an index in volume 9.
QA276.14 E5

DB22 **Encyclopedic Dictionary of Mathematics.** 1987. 2d ed. 4 vols. Comp. by the Mathematical Society of Japan. Cambridge, MA: MIT Press.

A translation of the third Japanese edition. Compact, yet comprehensive, with 450 numbered articles arranged alphabetically, and much historical and biographical information. Volume 4

contains a name index and classified list of articles.
QA5 N5 PASR

DB23 Mathematics Dictionary. 1976. 4th ed. Ed. by G. James and R.C. James. New York: Van Nostrand Reinhold. 509 p.

Covers all branches of mathematics, with an index in German, French, Spanish, and Russian.
QA5 J3 PASR

DB24 McGraw-Hill Dictionary of Physics and Mathematics. 1978. Ed. by D.N. Lapedes. New York: McGraw-Hill. 1074 p.

Over 20,000 brief definitions in math, physics, optics, electronics, control systems, etc. show the close relationship many fields have with mathematics.
QC5 M23 PASR

DB25 VNR Concise Encyclopedia of Mathematics. 1989. 2d American ed. Ed. by W. Gellert et al. New York: Van Nostrand Reinhold. 776 p.

Translation of a German edition. Lengthy articles on key topics in elementary and advanced mathematics, with effective use of colour to highlight critical points, and a set of colour plates at the end, including pictures of famous mathematicians.
QA40 K5415 PASR

DB26 World of Mathematics: A Small Library of the Literature of Mathematics from Ah-mose the Scribe to Albert Einstein. 1988. 4 vols. Ed. by James R. Newman. Redmond, WA: Microsoft Press.

Reprint of the original 1956 edition. Unique anthology of 133 selections, many by the original discoverers, on mathematics and its history, philosophy, and applications. Contains a detailed index in volume 4.
QA3 N48 PASC

Histories, Biographies and Directories

DB27 Bell, Eric Temple. 1986. Men of Mathematics. New York: Simon & Schuster. 590 p.

Reprint of original 1937 edition. Contains 34 detailed individual biographies, ranging from Zeno (5th Century B.C.) to Poincaré (d. 1912).
QA28 B4 PASC

DB28 Biographical Dictionary of Scientists: Mathematicians. 1986. Ed. by David Abbott. New York: Bedrick Books. 175 p.

One of a series of collective biographies in different fields of science. Contains brief biographies with a useful index by area of expertise at the back.
Q141 B5 PASR

DB29 Kline, Morris. 1990. Mathematical Thought from Ancient to Modern Times. 3 vols. New York: Oxford University Press.

Reprint of original 1972 edition. A thorough survey of major mathematical developments in the West from ancient times (Mesopotamia) to the 1930s. Arranged in loose chronological order in chapters.
QA21 K516 PASC

DB30 Struik, D.J. 1986. **Source Book of Mathematics, 1200–1800.** Princeton, NJ: Princeton University Press. 427 p.

Reprint of original 1969 edition. Divided by chapters into broad subject and contains valuable excerpts from key mathematical works from the Renaissance to 1800. Authors represented include Descartes, Euler, Newton, and more.
QA21 S88 PASR

DB31 **World Directory of Mathematicians,** 1958– . Ed. by the International Mathematical Union. Providence, RI: American Mathematical Society. quadrennial.

(8th ed., 1986) Alphabetical name and address list of 40,000 mathematicians from 83 countries. Also has a geographical index.
QA30 W67 PASR

DC   COMPUTER SCIENCE

For additional references to computer and information science, refer to the section on the Information Industry in Section AB, (AB19 to AB42).

Bibliographies and Guides to the Literature

DC1   Computing Information Directory, 1990. 7th ed. Ed. by D. M. Hildebrandt. Federal Way, WA: Pedaro Inc.

Wide ranging resource for computing literature, listing journals, university newsletters, some books and indexes, software and hardware review resources, and appendices of computer languages, publishers, and computer career literature.
R001.64 AM996C7   or   Z5640 C65 PASR

DC2   Computing Reviews, 1960– . New York: Association for Computing Machinery. monthly.

Brief reviews in classified arrangement of current publications in all areas of computer science, including hardware, software, systems organization, and theory. Available online on *MATHSCI* (see DB6). The annual index to *Computing Reviews* is the *ACM Guide to Computing Literature* (1964-), which is a bibliographic listing with six separate indexes of over 20,000 entries. Book reviews for current literature can be found in *Computer Book Review* (1983- Honolulu: Maeventec), a bi-monthly looseleaf format periodical which provides capsule reviews and ratings of popular trade titles in computer literature.
PER   or   QA76 C68O2 ENGR

DC3   Cortada, James W.   1990. Bibliographic Guide to the History of Computing, Computers, and the Information Processing Industry. New York: Greenwood Press. 644 p.

Citations to books, journals, proceedings, technical papers and industry surveys. Includes chapters on reference and introductory materials, the history and origins of modern computing, hardware developments from 1939-1980s, programming languages, software and applications and information processing industry.
R004.09 AC827P   or   Z5640 C67 ENGR

Abstracts, Indexes and Databases

DC4   Computer & Control Abstracts, 1966– . London / Piscataway, NJ: IEEE. monthly; semi-annual cumulative indexes.

Covers international literature organized by

subject with brief abstracts. Listings include publication details for acquisition purposes, and cover over 3,500 journals plus conference proceedings, books, and reports. Cumulated index every four years. Available as "Series C" of *Science Abstracts* (DA21); and available online as part of *INSPEC* (DA19).
TJ212 C56 ENGR

DC5 **Computer Database,** 1983– . Foster City, CA: Information Access Co. weekly.
Full text articles from over 70 periodicals. Available on CD-ROM and online.

DC6 **Computer Library,** 1988– . New York: Ziff Communications. weekly.
CD-ROM issued monthly. Each disk contains 12 months worth of full text articles from about 130 periodicals.

DC7 **CompuMath Citation Index,** 1976- 3 issues per year. See DB3 for full entry information.

DC8 **Computer Literature Index: Subject/Author Index to Computer and Data Processing Literature.** Vol. 10, 1980– . Phoenix, AZ: Applied Computer Research Inc. quarterly. annual cumulation.
Formerly titled *Quarterly Bibliography of Computers and Data Processing*, (1971–79). Indexes computer related trade publications, general business and management periodicals, and publications of computer oriented associations. Subject arrangment, author and publisher indexes.

DC9 **Microcomputer Index,** 1980– . Medford, NJ: Learned Information Inc. quarterly with annual index.
Detailed index by subject and application, with abstracts to about 80 popular computer magazines. Includes sections on book reviews, hardware and software reviews, and new product announcements. Available online.
IND

Annuals and Handbooks

DC10 **Advances in Computers,** 1960– . San Diego, CA: Academic Press. annual.
Comprehensive monographic series covering the latest research in computer science. Each issue averages over 300 pages.
QA76 A3 ENGS

DC11 **Annual Review of Computer Science,** 1986– . Ed. by J.F. Traub. Palo Alto, CA: Annual Reviews Inc. annual.
Numerous expert authors contribute articles on advances in specific fields. Extensive bibliographies.
QA75.5 A54 ENGS

DC12 **Fundamentals Handbook of Electrical and Computer Engineering,** 1982-83. 3 vols. See DL64 for full entry information.

DC13 **Handbook of Artificial Intelligence.** 1981–89. 4 vols. Ed. by Avron Barr. Reading, MA: Addison-Wesley.
Example of a comprehensive and authoritative

source on one field of computer science, written by a team of experts in AI.
Q335 H36 PASC

DC14 Handbook of Computers and Computing. 1984. Ed. by A.H. Seidman and Ivan Flores. New York: Van Nostrand Reinhold. 874 p.

Fifty articles arranged under six subject areas, with a thorough index. Intended for professionals and students with a technical background.
QA76.5 H3544 PASC

Encyclopedias and Dictionaries

DC15 Computer Science Source Book. 1988. New York: McGraw Hill. 370 p.

Compiled from the *McGraw Hill Encyclopedia of Science and Technology* (6th ed, 1987) (DA43), covering computer topics of a technical nature.

DC16 Cortada, James W. 1987. **Historical Dictionary of Data Processing.** 3 vols. Westport, CT: Greenwood Press.

Organized into three volumes: Volume 1: *Organizations*; Volume 2: *Technology*; Volume 3: *Biographies*. Each volume has articles in an alphabetical encyclopedia style arrangement, with an index in each.
QA76.15 C66 PASC

DC17 Dictionary of Computing, 1990. 3d ed. Ed. by Valerie Illingworth. New York: Oxford University Press. 510 p.

Contains about 4,500 terms used in all fields of computing, with many acronyms and lengthy and detailed definitions included.
QA76.15 D526 PASR

DC18 Dictionary of Data Communications. 1985. 2d ed. Ed. by Charles Sippl. New York: Halsted Press. 532 p.

Formerly *Data Communications Dictionary* (1976). Technical definitions assume background in the field of data communications.
QA76.15 S516 ENGR

DC19 Dictionary of Data Processing: Including Applications in Industry, Administration and Business. 1987. 5th ed. Ed. by A. Wittmann and J. Klos. New York: Elsevier. 358 p.

Provides equivalent usages of over 5,500 terms used in data processing in English, followed by its French and German equivalent. Useful for those involved in international research in this area.
QA76.15 W57 BMER (4th ed.)

DC20 Edmunds, Robert A. 1987. **The Prentice-Hall Encyclopedia of Information Technology.** Englewood Cliffs, NJ: Prentice-Hall. 590 p.

Written for business people without an information technology background. Provides 146 articles on various subjects including communications networks, memory, personal computers, programs, word processing, robotics, etc. Explains technical vocabulary. Indexed.
QA76.15 E184 PASR

DC21 Encyclopedia of Computer Science and Technology, 1975– . 16 vols. with *Supplements* (6 to 1990). Ed. by J. Belzer. New York: Marcel Dekker. irregular.

Technical articles written by experts discussing issues in the area of computer technology and research, including database design, LANs, optical character recognition, cryptologic research, image enhancement and processing, etc.
QA76.15 E5 PASR

DC22 Encyclopedia of Microcomputers, 1987– . 6 vols. to 1991. Ed. by Allen Kent and J.G. Williams. New York: Marcel Dekker. in progress.

Complements DC21 with lengthy technical articles on all aspects of microcomputers, including hardware, software, history, organizations, and applications. Volumes appear approximately two per year.
QA76.15 E53 ENGR

DC23 Hordeski, Michael F. 1990. **Illustrated Dictionary of Microcomputers.** 3d ed. Blue Ridge Summit, PA: TAB Books Inc. 442 p.

Thorough coverage of all fields involved in microcomputers, from microelectronics to trademarked software names. Well illustrated, with an Appendix showing electronic symbols.
TK7885 A2H67 ENGR (2d ed.)

DC24 McGraw-Hill Encyclopedia of Electronics and Computers. 1988. 2d ed. See DL54 for full entry information.

DC25 Meadows, A.J. 1987. **Dictionary of Computing and Information Technology.** 3d ed. London: Kogan Page. 281 p.

Contains succinct definitions of terms currently used in the computer and information industry, with articles on major topics. Cross referenced.
R001.503 D554D3

Directories and Buying Guides

DC26 Computer Industry Almanac, 1987– . Incline Village, NV: Computer Industry Almanac. annual.

Comprehensive directory to people, companies, products and trends in the industry. Lists award winners, publications, associations, users, groups, etc.

DC27 Computer Publishers and Publications: An International Directory and Yearbook, 1984– irregular annual. See AB23 for full entry information.

DC28 Directory of Computer Software and Services. 1990. Ottawa: Software, Systems and Services Division, Information Technologies Industry Branch. var. pg.

Also called *BOSS Directory of Computer Software and Services*. Contains a list of directories of the computer software industry in Canada.
R338.47005 D589D

DC29 InfoWorld Consumer Product Review 1990, Volume 2: A Year of Hardware and Software Reviews. 1990. New York: Brady Books.

Current reviews of hardware and software compiled from the weekly magazine *InfoWorld*.

Has a companion publication, the *Software Buyer's Guide*, which reviews and ranks popular business programs such as spreadsheets, databases, and desktop publishers.
QA76.9 E94 I53 PASR

DC30 The Software Catalog: Microcomputers, 1983- . New York: Elsevier. semi-annual with updates.

Provides information about the availability, applications, prices and compatibility of over 25,000 software programs for all major micros. Other editions of *Software Catalog* include *Minicomputers, Business Software, Science and Engineering*, (QA76.6 S577ENGR); *Health Professions* (R858 S63 BMER); and *Systems Software*. Available online. Also available is *Software Publishers' Catalogs Annual* (microfiche, Meckler, 1983/84-), with over 2,000 catalogues of U.S. and Canadian Software publishers.
R005.36 S681S

DC31 The Software Encyclopedia. 1985/86- . 2 vols. New York: R.R. Bowker. annual.

Annotated list of over 21,000 software programs. Indexed by publisher, title, compatible system and application. Available online as *Microcomputer Software Guide Online*.
QA76.753 S63 ENGS

DC32 Software Reviews on File, 1985- . New York: Facts on File, Inc. monthly with annual index.

Looseleaf service which compiles abstracts of software reviews appearing in over 150 popular and professional computer journals. Features software for all major microcomputer systems and for business, school, library, or home use.
371.33453 S6815 OISE

DC33 Truett, Carol. 1990. **Microcomputer Software Sources: A Guide for Buyers, Libraries, Programmers, Business People and Educators**. See AB29 for full entry information.

DD ASTRONOMY

See also *Engineering*, Section DL for entries relating to aeronautical and aerospace engineering, and astronautical sciences.

Guides to the Literature

DD1 Lusis, Andy. 1986. **Astronomy and Astronautics: An Enthusiast's Guide to Books and Periodicals.** New York: Facts on File. 292 p.

Annotated bibliography of books and periodicals published since 1977, with a few older classics included, in the area of astronomy and astronautics. Includes author/title/subject indexes. Updates Robert Seal's *Guide to the Literature of Astronomy* (Libraries Unlimited, 1977) (Z5151 S4 PASR), and *A Bibliography of Astronomy, 1970–1979* (Libraries Unlimited, 1982) (Z5151 S38 PASR). Another bibliography is *History of Modern Astronomy and Astrophysics* edited by David H. DeVorkin (Garland, 1982) (Z5154 H58 D48 PASC), which includes selected popular and scholarly works beginning with the invention of the telescope.
Z5151 L87 PASR

Abstracts and Indexes

DD2 **Astronomy and Astrophysics Abstracts,** 1969- . Berlin: Springer. semi-annual.

Supersedes *Astronomischer Jahresbericht* 1899–1969. International in scope with abstracts primarily in English (some in French or German). Arranged by broad subject categories with author, subject indexes.
QB1 A8875 PASR

DD3 **International Aerospace Abstracts,** 1961- semi-monthly. Companion volume to *STAR* (DD4) covering technical report literature. See DL26 for full entry information.

DD4 **Scientific and Technical Aerospace Reports (STAR),** 1963- semi-monthly.

Entries on astronomy, astrophysics, lunar and planetary exploration, solar physics, and space radiation can be found in *STAR* under the heading "Space Sciences." For full entry information, see DL32.

Reviews and Annuals

DD5 Advances in Astronautical Sciences, 1957- . annual. See DL34 for full entry information.

DD6 Annual Review of Astronomy and Astrophysics, 1963- . Palo Alto, CA: Annual Reviews. annual
 Broad technical survey for the professional astronomer.
QB1 A2884 O2 PASS

DD7 Progress in Astronautics and Aeronautics, 1960- annual. See DL47 for full entry information.

DD8 Vistas in Astronomy, 1955- . Oxford: Pergamon Press. annual.
 Each volume generally covers a specific field. For example, Volume 19, Part 4: *From Newton to Black Holes.*
QB3 V56 PASS

Encyclopedias and Dictionaries

DD9 Biographical Dictionary of Scientists: Astronomers. 1984. Ed. by David Abbott. New York: Bedrick Books. 204 p.
 Concise biographies (one-half to two pages) of more than 200 worldwide astronomers from past to present. Includes glossary, author/subject index, and photographs.
Q141 B5 PASR

DD10 The Cambridge Encyclopedia of Space. 1990. Ed. by Michael Rycroft. New York: Cambridge University Press. 386 p.
 New edition of *The Cambridge Encyclopaedia of Astronomy* (1977) (QB43.2 C35 PASR), which was a definitive sourcebook. A treatise for lay people on modern astronomy and astrophysics. Includes a discussion of international space exploration from 1961-62 to the launch of the Hubbel Space Telescope in 1990, sections on space technology, exploration of the solar system, living in space and uses, now and in the future, of Earth orbiting satellites and space stations. Tables, colour photographs, diagrams, as well as a bibliography and glossary are provided.
TL788 E7713 ENGR

DD11 Encyclopedia of Astronomy and Astrophysics. 1989. Ed. by Robert A. Meyers. San Diego, CA: Academic Press. 807 p.
 Compendium of 42 articles, each written by an expert in the field. Provides "comprehensive indepth and yet concise treatment at an advanced level of the latest in fundamental astronomy and astrophysics theory, instrumentation, and observations of the solar system, stars, and stellar systems." Provides glossaries, historical background, basic theory, status of current research, and future prospects, and short bibliographies in each article.
 An encyclopedia written for the lay person by Patrick Moore is *The International Encyclopedia of Astronomy* (Orion Books/Crown, 1987) (QB14 I58 PASR) which contains over 2,500 short entries, written by leading authorities, in all topics in astronomy. Six longer essays discuss superclusters, pulsars and moons, space exploration, interstellar matter, superclusters, and the big bang. Illustrated, with charts and tables.
QB14 E53 PASR

DD12 The Facts on File Dictionary of Astronomy. 1985. 2d ed. Ed. by Valerie Illingworth. New York: Facts on File, 437 p.

Includes information on standard terms, abbreviations, theories and laws, equipment, and celestial bodies, as well as organizations, agencies, and observatories. New techniques and instruments, satellites and probes are described. A shorter, well-illustrated dictionary, *Longman Illustrated Dictionary of Astronomy and Astronautics: The Terminology of Space* by Ian Ridpath (Longman, 1987) contains entries on the solar system, tides, eclipses, the Earth, planets, stars, astrophysics, and astronautics.
QB14 F23 SIGS

DD13 Glossary of Astronomy and Astrophysics. 1982. 2d ed. rev. and enl. Ed. by Jeanne Hopkins. Chicago: University of Chicago Press. 196 p.

A comprehensive dictionary of astronomical and astrophysical terms. Wide range of definitions, from the simplistic to those intelligible only to experts.
QB14 H66 PASR

DD14 Illustrated Encyclopedia of Space Technology: A Comprehensive History of Space Exploration. 1985. 4th ed. Ed. by Kenneth Gatland. New York: Harmony. 301 p.

A one-volume encyclopedia covering the space age. Includes photographs, drawings, diagrams, and maps, along with a glossary, index, and chronology from 360 B.C. through 1980. Space exploration is well covered in Richard S. Lewis' *Illustrated Encyclopedia of the Universe* (Harmony, 1983) (QB501.2 L48 SCC) and also includes colour illustrations, drawings, and brief bibliographies.

Dictionary of Space edited by Malcolm Plant (Longman, 1986) (QB497 P53 PASR) is a concise dictionary of space and space technology terms, persons, organizations and abbreviations.
TL788 I44 SCC

DD15 Magill's Survey of Science: Space Exploration Series. 1989. 5 vols. Englewood Cliffs, NJ: Salem Press.

Series of 350 lengthy essays outlining the discoveries, exploration and technological developments in space from 1950 to the Challenger disaster, with some information on current projects. Topics such as space travel, black holes, solar systems, astronauts, and missions are discussed. Essays include bibliographies.

DD16 McGraw-Hill Encyclopedia of Astronomy. 1983. Ed. by Sybil P. Parker. New York: McGraw-Hill. 450 p.

Includes over 200 articles on theoretical, observational, and experimental aspects of astronomy. Concise definitions, as well as photographs, figures, and biographical sketches are provided. Based on the *McGraw-Hill Encyclopedia of Science and Technology* (DA43).
Q121 M3 PASR

DD17 Room, Adrian. 1988. **Dictionary of Astronomical Names.** New York: Routledge, Chapman & Hall. 282 p.

Information on the origins of stars, planets and other celestial objects. Provides essays on the history of astronomical names and on the persons of the 16-20th centuries who played a role in naming heavenly bodies. Arrangement is alphabetical under popular rather than scientific name. Includes glossary and appendices for lunar and asteroid names.
QB14 R66 Ref ERIN

Guides for Amateur Astronomers

DD18 Dickinson, Terence. 1989. **Nightwatch: An Equinox Guide to Viewing the Universe.** Camden East, ON: Camden House. 159 p.

Written by a noted Canadian astronomer, this is a basic guide for amateur astronomers. Dickinson has also written a guide for children, *Exploring the Night Sky: The Equinox Astronomy Guide for Beginners* (Camden House, 1987) (520 D553 E FLIS JC).
QB63 D52 SIGS

DD19 Pasachoff, Jay. 1983. **Field Guide to the Stars and Planets.** 2d ed. Boston: Houghton Mifflin. 473 p.

Written by a noted authority, includes planets, the sun, comets, asteroids, and meteors. *Peterson First Guide to the Solar System*, also by Pasachoff, (Houghton Mifflin, 1990), is an abridged version of *Field Guide*, and adds photographs and data gathered by U.S. spacecraft over the past two decades to assist amateur astronomers.
QB64 M4 SCC

DD20 Sidgwick, John Benson and James Muirden. 1980. **Amateur Astronomer's Handbook.** 4th ed. Hillside, NJ: Enslow. 568 p.

Standard guide which covers most topics in a basic manner, and includes many illustrations. Another amateur guide intended for those interested in setting up a systematic study of the sky, and which includes tables, lists or recurring phenomena, reading lists, and a glossary is James Muirden's *Astronomy Handbook* (Prentice-Hall, 1984) (QB44 S558 PASR).
QB44 S558 SCC

Handbooks

DD21 Allen, C.W. 1973. **Astrophysical Quantities.** 3d ed. London: Athlone. 310 p.

Includes experimental, theoretical values, constants, conversion factors. Intended for advanced students and professional astronomers. *Astrophysical Formulae: A Compendium for the Physicist and Astrophysicist* by Kenneth Lang (2d ed., 1986, Springer/Verlag) (QB461 L36 PASC) complements *Astrophysical Quantities*, with formulae, derivations, applications, rather than lists of data.
QB461 A564 PASC

DD22 Apparent Places of Fundamental Stars, 1940- . Heidelberg: Astronomisches Rechen-Institut. annual.

Lists the mean and apparent location for over 1,500 stars, giving right ascension and declination, mean place, magnitutde, and spectral class. Useful for amateur and professional astronomers.
QB9 I5 PASS

DD23 The Astronomical Almanac, 1981- . Washington: U.S. Government Printing Office/ London: HMSO. annual.

Supersedes *American Ephemeris and Nautical Almanac* (Washington: US GPO, 1852-1980) (QB8 U6 PASS) and *Astronomical Ephemeris* (HMSO) (QB8 G6 PASS). Standard tool for professional and advanced amateur astronomers. Contains detailed tabular predictions for astronomical phenomena, primarily in the solar system.
QB8 U6A77 PASR

DD24 Hoffleit, Dorrit. 1982. **Bright Star Catalogue.** 4th ed. New Haven, CT: Yale University Observatory. 472 p.

Catalogue of over 9,000 stars suitable for professional or advanced amateur astronomers. Includes name, number, infrared source, equatorial coordinates for 1900 and 2000, spectral class, and rotational velocity. Compiled through to 1979.

DD25 Huchtmeier, W.K. and O.-G. Richter. 1989. **A General Catalog of HI Observations of Galaxies: The Reference Catalog.** New York: Springer/Verlag. 350 p.

Compilation of all known published observations of external galaxies in the spectral line of neutral hydrogen (HI). Contains 19,976 entries for 10,308 galaxies covering the period 1954 to 1988. References, author index.
QB857 H83 PASC

DD26 Luginbuhl, Christian B., and Brian A. Skiff. 1989. **Observing Handbook and Catalogue of Deep Sky Objects.** New York: Cambridge University Press. 352 p.

Describes 2,050 nonstellar objects found in the 68 constellations north of -50 degrees declination. Alphabetical arrangement by constellation name, and includes information on each galaxy, star cluster, and nebula.
QB64 L84 PASR

DD27 Malin, David. 1984. **Catalogue of the Universe.** London: Cambridge University Press. 288 p.

This work includes photographs, with background and historical information on galaxies, stars, and planets, especially on those in the southern celestial orbits.
QB816 M34 PASC

DD28 Marsden, Brian G. 1983. **Catalog of Cometary Orbits.** Hillside, NJ: Enslow Publishers. 96 p.

Provides comprehensive orbital data on 1,109 "cometary apparitions" for observers, theoreticians, and historians. The catalog is divided into six parts: "General Catalog", "Names and Observational Intervals", "References and Notes", "Appearance of Periodic Comets", "Nongravitational Parameters", and "Statistical Tables".
QB357 M3 PASC

DD29 **Master List of Nonstellar Optical Astronomical Objects.** 1980. Ed. by Robert S. Dixon and George Sonneborn. Columbus, OH: Ohio State University Press. 835 p.

Consolidates 85,000 listings from 270 catalogues of nonstellar objects for professional and amateur astronomers, engineers, physicists.
QB65 D56 PASR

DD30 **NGC 2000.0: The Complete New General Catalogue and Index Catalogues of Nebulae and Star Clusters by J.L.E. Dreyer.** 1988. Ed. by Roger Sinnott. Cambridge, MA: Sky Publishing and New York: Cambridge University Press. 273 p.

Dreyer's NGC and its indexes originally published between 1888 and 1908 lists 13,226 deep sky objects, mostly non-stellar. This new version lists all its celestial objects in one place, with no need to refer to appendices. A classic reference for professional and amateur astronomers. Available on diskette.
QB853 D58 PASC

DD31 **Norton's 2000.0 Star Atlas and Reference Handbook.** 1989. 18th ed. Ed. by Ian Ridpath. New York: John Wiley. 179 p.

New edition of a classic work. Includes star catalog and charts updated to 2000 AD. Four main chapters: "Position and Time"; "Practical Astronomy"; "The Solar System"; and "Stars, Nebulae and Galaxies".
QB65 N7 PASC

DD32 Observer's Handbook, 1907- . Toronto: Royal Astronomical Society of Canada. annual.

(1990, 83th ed.) Tables of data for the year for Canadian observers. Includes a list of some Canadian observatories and planetaria.
QB64 R6 PASR

DD33 Star Catalog. 1971. 4 vols. Washington: Smithsonian Institution.

This master catalog for the epoch and equinox of 1950.0 giving positions and motions of 258,997 stars. Available in machine readable form.
QB6 S57 PASC

DD34 Stars and Stellar Systems: Compendium of Astronomy and Astrophysics Series. 1982. 9 vols. Ed. by G.P. Kuiper and B.M. Middlehurst. Chicago: University of Chicago Press.

Volume titles include *Telescopes, Astronomical Techniques, Basic Astronomical Data, Clusters and Binaries, Galactic Structures, Stellar Atmospheres, Nebular and Interstellar Matter, Stellar Structure* and *Galaxies and the Universe*.

DD35 Stars, Galaxies, Cosmos: A Catalog of Astronomical Anomalies. 1987. Comp. by William R. Corliss. Glen Arm, MD: Sourcebook Project. 240 p.

Includes 817 references, illustrations, and indexes to unusual phenomena relating to stars and extended objects, quasars, the cosmos, and galaxies. Description of the anomaly, possible explanations, related phenomena, and the author's rating of the phenomena in light of substantiating data and scientific theories, is included.
QB52 C67 DUNO

DD36 Webb Society Deep-Sky Observer's Handbook. 1987. 2d ed. 7 vols. Hillside, NJ: Enslow.

Volume 1: *Double Stars*, Volume 2: *Planetary and Gaseous Nebulae*, Volume 3: *Open and Globular Clusters*, Volume 4: *Galaxies*, Volume 5: *Clusters of Galaxies*, Volume 6: *Anonymous Galaxies*, and Volume 7: *The Southern Sky*. Each of the 7 volumes includes a review article, background information, positions, magnitudes, charts, and various other information for the experienced observer.
QB64 W36 SCAR

DD37 Zombeck, Martin. 1990. **Handbook of Space Astronomy and Astrophysics.** 2d ed. New York: Cambridge University Press. 300 p.

A compilation of often inaccessible information in tables, graphs and formulas for use across a broad range of the physical sciences. Information is provided for all aspects of astronomy and astrophysics, the earth's atmosphere and environment, relativity and atomic physics.
QB64 Z65 PASR (1982)

Atlases

DD38 The Cambridge Atlas of Astronomy. 1988. 2d ed. Ed. by Jean Audouze and Guy Israel. New York: Cambridge University Press. 431 p.

Aimed at educated laypersons, more encyclopedic than atlas. Arranged in broad subject categories, subdivided into specific topics with overviews and drawings, charts, photographs.
QB65 G6813 PASR

DD39 Moore, Patrick. 1983. **Atlas of the Solar System.** New York: Rand McNally. 464 p.

A combination of historical perspective and current thought and knowledge on the planets, their satellites, and the sun. Includes a glossary, tables, bibliographies and an index. Another atlas in the same field is Paul Doherty's *Atlas of the Planets* (McGraw-Hill, 1980) (QB601 D634 PASC) which is a detailed guide to the planets and solar system with useful information for the amateur observer.
QB501 M687 SCC

DD40 **Palomar Observatory Sky Survey.** 1949-1955. Pasadena, CA: California Institute of Technology.

Consists of high quality red and blue sensitive photographs covering the entire sky - 33 degrees to + 90 degrees declination. Comprehensive coverage.
DUNO Atlas

DD41 Tully, R. Brent and J. Richard Fisher. 1987. **Nearby Galaxies Atlas.** New York: Cambridge University Press, 1987. var. pg.

"This atlas represents almost the first attempt to map the structure of our environment on a scale significatnly larger than the Milky Way Galaxy." Using colour sky maps, over 2,300 nearby galaxies are analyzed.
QB857 T841 ROMU

DD42 Vehrenberg, Hans. 1983. **Atlas of Deep-Sky Splendors.** 4th ed. New York: Cambridge University Press. 240 p.

Contains photographic charts and a description of all Messier objects and more than 300 celestial wonders. Sections on the Messier catalog, Lacaille's catalog, and Schmidt's contributions to astronomical photography are included. Originally published in 1965 as *Mein Messier-Buch*.
QB65 V413 SCC

DD43 Wray, James D. 1988. **The Color Atlas of Galaxies.** New York: Cambridge University Press. 189 p.

Contains colour photographs of more than 600 star systems photographed at McDonald Observatory in Texas and two other observatories. Address the development of star systems. Colour photographs of galaxies are useful to study their evolution.
QB857 W73 PASC

Directories

DD44 Marx, Siegfried. 1982. **Observatories of the World.** New York: Van Nostrand. 200 p.

Directory of optical and radio astronomical observatories. Meteorological and seismic observatories are excluded. Arrangement is by country, subdivided by optical or radio. Information consists of founding date, location, list of equipment, and programs.
QB81 M3913 PASC

DE   PHYSICS

Bibliographies and Guides to the Literature

DE1 Heilbron, J.L. and B.R. Wheaton. 1981. **Literature on the History of Physics in the 20th Century.** Berkeley, CA: Office of the History of Science and Technology, University of California. 485 p.

Comprehensive bibliography on all types of physics literature, arranged by subject. Supplemented by *The History of Modern Physics: An International Bibliography* (Garland, 1983) (Z7141 B677 ROBA) which concentrates on non-English publications.
Z7141 H45 PASC

DE2 Home, R.W. 1984. **The History of Classical Physics: A Selected, Annotated Bibliography.** New York: Garland, 1984. 324 p.

Covers current writings on history of classical physics in more than 1,300 entries, citing general bibliographies, bibliographies of individual scientists collected works, correspondence and histories.
Z7141 H65 PASR

DE3 Information Sources in Physics. 1985. 2d ed. Ed. by Dennis F. Shaw. London: K.G. Saur. 456 p.

A descriptive guide to the physics literature. Various indexing and abstracting services and sources available in physics are discussed. Name index and subject/title indexes provided.
Z7141 I53 PASC

Abstracts, Indexes and Databases

DE4 CINDA 86 (1982–1986): The Index to Literature and Computer Files on Microscopic Neutron Data. 1986. Vienna: International Atomic Energy Agency. 444 p. *Supplement*, 1986, 116 p.

Aimed at physicists and other researchers. *Computer Index of Neutron Data* contains "bibliographical references to measurements, calculations, reviews and other microscopic neutron data.

DE5 Current Contents: Physical, Chemical and Earth Sciences, 1961- weekly. See DA15 for full entry information.

DE6 Current Papers in Physics, 1966- . London: Institution of Electrical Engineers. bimonthly.

A current awareness service consisting of titles of research articles from the world's physics journals. Available online through *INSPEC*, see DA19
QC1 C85 SCAR

DE7 Current Physics Index, 1975- . New York: American Institute of Physics. quarterly.

Provides information about physics research appearing in journals published by the American Institute of Physics. Arranged by subject, the entries include title, author, affiliation, and bibliographic description. AIP also publishes *General Physics Advance Abstracts* (semi-monthly), which is available online as *SPIN (Searchable Physics Information Notices)*, and *Physical Review Abstracts* as current awareness services.
QC1 C86 PASR

DE8 INIS Atomindex: An International Abstracting Service. 1970- . Vienna: International Atomic Energy Agency. monthly. 1976- . semi-monthly.

Partially supersedes *Nuclear Science Abstracts* and IAEA's *List of References on Atomic Energy*. A cooperative effort of over 60 countries and international organizations contributing to the International Nuclear Information System. Main section classed by subject. Covers economic, legal and social aspects as well as scientific works. Includes books, journal literature, patents, technical reports and standards. Available online and on CD-ROM. Many *INIS* reports are available on microfilm document delivery.
Z5160 I18 PASR

DE9 Physics Abstracts, 1898- . London: Institute of Electrical Engineers. semi-monthly.

In 1941 *Physics Abstracts* became Section A of *Science Abstracts*, (DA21). Provides comprehensive international coverage of all physics literature including books, journals, technical reports, dissertations, patents and conference papers. Available online as part of *INSPEC*, DA19.
QC1 P4843 PASR

DE10 Physics Briefs, 1979- . New York: American Institute of Physics. semi-monthly.

This journal covers many areas of physics. Coverage is international, and books, journals, technical reports, theses, patents and conference papers are included. Journals are abstracted completely. More timely than *Physics Abstracts* (above), but not as complete. Available online.
QC1 P83 PASR

Reviews and Annuals

DE11 Advances in Electronics and Electron Physics, 1954- irregular, 2-3 issues per year. See DL38 for full entry information.

DE12 Advances in Nuclear Science and Technology, 1962- annual.

Includes articles summarizing current trends in nuclear physics. See DL42 for full entry information.

DE13 Annual Review of Nuclear and Particle Science, Vol. 28-, 1978- . Palo Alto, CA: Annual Reviews. annual.

Reviews of recent significant developments, with extensive bibliographies. Author and subject indexes are included. Formerly *Annual Review of Nuclear Science* (1952–1977).
QC770 A52 PHYS

DE14 Reports on Progress in Physics, 1934- . London: Institute of Physics and Physical Society. monthly with cumulated annual index.
Indexes a variety of abstracting services for current research literature in physics.
QC1 R37 PHYS

DE15 Reviews of Modern Physics, 1929- . New York: American Institute of Physics. quarterly.
Reviews advanced level articles in current research.
ZC1 R37 PHYS

Encyclopedias and Dictionaries

DE16 Cambridge Illustrated Thesaurus of Physics. 1984. Ed. by Teresa Richards. New York: Cambridge University Press. 256 p.
Useful for quick, short definitions in general physics. Cross-referenced and indexed.
QC5 R53 PASR

DE17 A Dictionary of Named Effects and Laws in Chemistry, Physics and Mathematics, 1980. 4th ed. See DA52 for full entry information.

DE18 Dictionary of the Physical Sciences. 1987. Ed. by Cesare Emiliani. New York: Oxford University Press. 365 p.
Contains definitions and tables in the physical sciences. Aimed at professionals.
Q123 E46 PASR

DE19 A Dictionary of Scientific Units: Including Dimensionless Numbers and Scales. 5th ed, 1986. See DA53 for full entry information.

DE20 Elsevier's Dictionary of Nuclear Science and Technology in Six Languages: English/American-French-Spanish-Italian-Dutch and German. 1970. 2nd rev. ed. Comp. by W.E. Clason. Amsterdam: Elsevier. 787 p.
Entries are listed by the English words followed by equivalent in tabular arrangement. Separate index for each languages refers to the English word.
QC772 E4 PASR

DE21 Encyclopaedic Dictionary of Physics: General, Nuclear, Solid State, Molecular Chemical, Metal and Vacuum Physics, Astronomy, Geophysics, Biophysics, and Related Subjects. 1961–64. 9 vols. *Supplement* 1966–75. 5 vols. Ed. by James Thewlis. New York: Pergamon. irregular.
Covers all aspects of physics and related areas such as mathematics, astronomy, chemistry and hydraulics for professionals. Updated with regular supplements. Terminology for students and non-professionals is also found in *Concise Dictionary of Physics and Related Subjects* (Pergamon, 1979) (QC5 T5 PASC).
QC5 E5 PASR

DE22 **Encyclopedia of Physics.** 1991. 2d ed. Ed. by Rita G. Lerner and George L. Trigg. New York: VCH. 1408 p.

Authoritative coverage of physics, astrophysics and related topics for graduate students and professionals. Some articles assume advanced levels of mathematics and physics. *Concise Encyclopedia of Solid State Physics* (1983) is a spinoff. The *Encyclopedia of Physics* (3d ed, Van Nostrand Reinhold, 1985), edited by Robert M. Besancon is a concise one volume encyclopedia covering all areas of physics with articles written by experts and geared to varying levels of readers, depending on the subject covered.
QC5 E545 ENGR

DE23 **The Facts on File Dictionary of Physics.** 1988. rev. ed. Ed. by John Daintith. New York: Facts on File. 235 p.

Short informative entries for novices in physics.
QC5 F34 SMCR

DE24 **McGraw-Hill Encyclopedia of Physics.** 1983. Ed. by Sybil P. Parker. New York: McGraw-Hill. 1343 p.

Covers all areas of classical and modern physics and related topics in mathematics.
QD5 M36 PASR

Handbooks

DE25 **American Institute of Physics Handbook.** 1972. 3d ed. Ed. by Bruce Billings. New York: McGraw-Hill. var. pg.

Respected handbook which provides tables, reference materials, and descriptions of areas by leaders in individual fields. Each section covers a field of physics, from definitions and concepts through the many subtopics of that particular field. Detailed index.
QC61 A5 PASR

DE26 **Astrophysical Quantities.** 1973. 3d ed.

This work and the companion *Astrophysical Formulae: A Compendium for the Physicist and Astrophysicist* contain values, constants and conversion factors for physicists. See DD21 for full entry information.

DE27 **Handbook of Chemistry and Physics,** 1913- . Boca Raton, FL: CRC Press. irregular annual.

(71st ed, 1990). Subtitled *A Ready Reference Book of Chemical and Physical Data*, and also know as *The CRC Handbook*. Useful as a concise summary of major definitions, formulas, tables and examples of elementary and intermediate technical physics. Extensive subject index.
QD65 H3 PHYS

DE28 **Handbook of Physical Calculations.** 1983. 2d ed. Ed. by J.J. Tuma. New York: McGraw Hill. 512 p.

Provides information, definitions, formulas, charts, and tables of elementary and intermediate technological physics.
QC61 T85 PASR

DE29 **Tables of Physical and Chemical Constants and Some Mathematical Functions.** 1986. 15th ed. Ed. by G.W.C. Kaye and T.H. Laby. London: Longman. 320 p.

In addition to tables, includes introductions to

each section, notes to the literature with sources of tables and background information. All tables in SI units.
QC61 K3 PASR

Directories and Biographical Sources

DE30 **Biographical Dictionary of Scientists: Physicists.** 1984. Ed. by David Abbott. New York: Bedrick. 212 p.

Covers ancient to contemporary physicists in one-half to two page biographies.
QC15 B56 PASR

DE31 **The Nobel Prize Winners: Physics.** 1989. Ed. by Frank Magill. 3 vols. Pasadena, CA: Salem Press.

Includes information on physics prize winners from the first award through to 1988. Introductory information and history of the Nobel Prize for physics is followed by chapter for each of the winners, including biographical information, a description of the work involved in the prize, a summary of the presentation speech, and a bibliography of further reading.

DE32 **World Nuclear Directory.** 1981- . Detroit: Gale Research. irregular.

(8th ed, 1988). Directory of organizations and laboratories which are carrying out or funding research and development projects within nuclear science. Alphabetical arrangement.
QC770 W6522 ENGR

DF CHEMISTRY AND CHEMICAL ENGINEERING

See also *Engineering*, Section DL, for additional titles in Chemical Engineering.

Bibliographies and Guides to the Literature

DF1 Anthony, A. 1979. **Guide to Basic Information Sources in Chemistry.** New York: Jeffrey Norton. 219 p.
  A useful introduction for students or librarians.
QD8.5 A57 PASR; ENGR

DF2 Dorman, Phae H. 1988. **Chemical Industries: An Information Sourcebook.** Phoenix, AZ: Oryx Press. 95 p.
  An annotated bibliography written for chemical manufacturers listing over 550 English-language sources of business information required for chemical market analyses. Organized by industry group. Indexed.
Z5521 D65 ENGR

DF3 Maizell, Robert E. 1987. **How to Find Chemical Information: A Guide for Practicing Chemists, Educators, and Students.** 2d ed. New York: John Wiley. 402 p.
  Covers all aspects in chemistry, online databases, marketing and business information, patent information, etc.
QD8.5 M34 ENGR

DF4 Ray, Martyn S. 1990. **Chemical Engineering Bibliography (1967–1988).** Park Ridge, NJ: Noyes. 887 p.
  Contains references to over 20,000 articles indexed from 40 major chemical engineering journals. Organized by subject with a detailed subject index.
Z7914 C4R35 ENGR

Abstracts, Indexes and Databases

DF5 **Analytical Abstracts,** 1954- . London: Chemical Society. monthly with annual index.

Covers all areas of analytical chemistry in a broad subject arrangement. Over 12,000 abstracts of books and papers are included each year. Cumulative index available. Available online 1980-.
QD71 A49 PRSR

DF6 **CCINFO databases,** 1986- . Hamilton, ON: Canadian Centre for Occupational Health and Safety.

The Canadian Centre for Occupational Health and Safety (CCOHS) provides a computerized information service called *CCINFO* to government, management and labour for occupational health and safety concerns. The service is available online as *CCINFOline* and on CD-ROM as *CCINFOdisc*. There are over 45 databases available on *CCINFOline*. Access to *CCINFOdisc* is available through four series: Series A1 *MSDS* (Material Safety Data Sheets); Series A2 *CHEM Data*; Series B1 *OHS Source*; and Series B2 *OHS Data*; each series containing a selection of databases. *CHEMINFO* (DF11), a major database source of chemical information, and *RTECS* (DF15n) are available online and on Series AI and A2 on *CCINFOdisc*.

DF7 **Chemical Abstracts,** 1907- . Columbus, OH: American Chemical Society. weekly.

CA annually provides over 500,000 abstracts from over 14,000 international journals, patents, conference proceedings, government research reports, books and dissertations. Organized in 80 subject areas including applied, organic, inorganic, physical, analytical chemistry, and chemical engineering, etc. Even numbered weekly issues contain applied chemistry and chemical engineering; odd numbered issues contain organic and biochemical sections. Indexes cumulate semi-annually and annually. Available online, (1967-). Other online services are *CA Previews* (1988-) which provides citations to documents that will be published in the printed publication; *CA Index Guide* (1967-) which lists equivalent substance names derived from the *CA Collective Indexes*; *CA Registry File* (1957-) which contains names and formula information for over 9 million substances identified by Chemical Abstracts Service (CAS); and *CA Search* (1967-) which contains bibliographic data and *CA* entries, and CAS Registry Numbers.
QD1 C45 BMER; ENGR

DF8 **Chemical Abstracts Service Source Index [CASSI],** 1970- . Columbus, OH: Chemical Abstracts Service. quarterly.

CASSI contains bibliographical descriptions for source literature of chemical sciences contained in 360 U.S. libraries and 28 international libraries with key to library holdings. Available online covering CAS publications from 1907 and including some citations from international databases back to 1830.
Z5523 C5 PASR

DF9 **Chemical Engineering Abstracts,** 1982- . Nottingham, U.K: Royal Society of Chemistry. monthly with annual cumulation.

Abstracts for over 4,500 entries each year, organized in 22 sections, including heat transfer, diffusional operations, reactors, plant equipment. Available online and on CD-ROM as *CEBA* (Chemical Engineering and Biotechnical Abstracts) (1989-).
TP155 C36 ENGR

DF10 Chemical Titles, 1961- . Columbus, OH: Chemical Abstracts Service. bi-weekly.

Current awareness service which provides citations to research papers from over 800 international periodicals in the area of pure and applied chemistry. KWIC and author indexes included. Available online.
CHEM

DF11 CHEMINFO, 1986- . Hamilton, ON: Canadian Centre for Occupational Health and Safety. database. updated quarterly.

Available on *CCINFOline* or *CCINFOdisc* (DF6). Includes information on pure chemicals, natural substances and mixtures resulting from industrial processes. Data identifies each chemical, describes physical properties, uses and occurences and chemical reactivity; also provides information on health hazards, first aid, protective procedures and WHMIS criteria.

DF12 Current Abstracts of Chemistry and Index Chemicus, 1970- . Philadelphia: Institute for Scientific Information. weekly.

Current Abstracts in Chemistry absorbed *Index Chemicus* (1960–69) in 1970. The work now contains abstracts from approximately 100 major journals. Abstracts state chemical structure examined in the article. Quarterly and annual indexes for author, subject, biological activity, corporate, and corporate indexes. Also contains an "Alert to Labelled Compounds" section. A 22 year cumulation is available on microform for 1960–81. Available online.
Z5523 I62 CHEM

DF13 Current Chemical Reactions (CCR), 1979- . Philadelphia: Institute for Scientific Information. monthly with annual cumulation.

Provides abstracts to articles in over 100 organic chemistry and pharmaceutical journals and books. Brief descriptions as to the type of reaction are included in abstracts. Contains author, journal, corporate and subject indexes, which are cumulated annually. Available online.
QD501 C85 CHEM

DF14 Current Contents: Physical, Chemical and Earth Sciences, 1961- . weekly. See DA15 for full entry information.

DF15 TOXLINE, 1965- . Bethesda, MD: National Library of Medicine. Database.

Citations, taken from a variety of sources, including *Chemical Abstracts* and *MEDLINE*, on the pharmacological, biochemical, physiological and toxicological effects of drugs and other chemicals; human and animal toxicity; pesticides; environmental chemicals and pollutants, etc. Also available on *Pollution/Toxicology CD-ROM (PolTox)*, DK18. Other databases with similar information are *RTECS (Registry of Toxic Effects of Chemical Substances Database)*, available on *CCINFO* (see DK19), and *IRPTC/Legal* (Health and Welfare Canada, 1988-), (DK19n).

Reviews and Annuals

DF16 Advances in Chemical Engineering, 1956- . irregular annual. See DL37 for full entry information.

DF17 Annual Reports on the Progress of Chemistry, 1905- . 3 sections. London: Royal Society of Chemistry. annual.

Consists of three sections: A: *Inorganic Chemistry*; B: *Organic Chemistry*; C: *Physical Chemistry*. Each section containing articles

documenting the significant advances in the major fields of chemistry during the year.
QD146 A56 PASS; CHEM (Section A)
QD241 A56 PASS; CHEM (Section B)
QD450 A56 PASS; CHEM (Section C)

DF18 Chemical Reviews, 1924- . Washington: American Chemical Society. bimonthly.
Review articles with extensive bibliographies written by specialists in their fields highlighting new current research and progress in chemistry. Cumulative indexes provided.
QD1 C58 CHEM

Encyclopedias and Dictionaries

DF19 Alger, Mark S.M. 1989. **Polymer Science Dictionary.** New York: Elsevier Science Publishing. 532 p.
Comprehensive reference tool explaining the terminology of polymer science, excluding technological areas. Covers molecular biology, polymer chemistry, physics. Includes structural formulas, with appendices for SI units and conversion factors.
QD382.3 A52 PASC

DF20 Concise Chemical and Technical Dictionary. 1986. 4th ed. Ed. by H. Bennett. New York: Chemical Publishing. 1271 p.
Contains brief descriptions to 100,000 terms used in all fields of scientific and technical development, including chemicals, drugs, trade names, propietary products, etc. Useful for laypersons or practicing chemists.
QD5 B4 PASR

DF21 Concise Encyclopedia of Biochemistry. 1988. 2d ed. New York: Walter de Gruyter. 649 p.
Brief entries of concepts and terms in biochemistry written for an advanced audience. Includes some longer essays with references, as well as diagrams of chemical structures, and tables of chemical properties.
QD415 A25B713 BMER

DF22 A Dictionary of Named Effects and Laws in Chemistry, Physics and Mathematics, 1980, 4th ed. See DA52 for full entry information.

DF23 Dictionary of Organic Compounds. 1982- in progress. 5th ed. 8 vols. London: Chapman & Hall.
Subtitled: *The constitution of physical, chemical, and other properties of the principal carbon compounds and their derivatives together with the relative literature.* Contains data on 150,000 of common and important organic compounds. Indexed.
QD251 D495 PASR

DF24 Encyclopedia of Chemical Processing and Design, 1976- in progress. New York: Marcel Dekker.
Projected to be 45 volumes when complete. Currently completed to Volume 36 (1991). Comprehensive encyclopedia with lengthy articles which emphasize the design of equipment, systems, control used in chemical processing. Complements the more theoretical *Kirk-Othmer Encyclopedia of Chemical Technology* (DF32).
TP9 E66 ENGR

DF25 Encyclopedia of Polymer Science and Engineering. 1985-1990. 2d ed. 17 vols plus supplement and index. See DL51 for full entry information.

DF26 The Facts on File Dictionary of Chemistry. 1988. Rev. ed. Ed. by John Daintith. New York: Facts on File. 249 p.

Provides definitions for the layperson for 2,500 terms used in chemistry, such as basic chemical reactions and applications. Also discusses issues in chemistry, such as acid rain and heavy metal pollution. Daintith has also published the *Concise Dictionary of Chemistry*, (Oxford University Press, 1985) which provides short and easy-to-understand terms in the fields of chemistry, physical chemistry and biochemistry.
QD5 F23 CHEM

DF27 Gardner's Chemical Synonyms and Trade Names. 1987. 9th ed. Brookfield, VT: Gower Publishing. 1081 p.

A standard quick-reference dictionary of commerical chemical synonyms and trade names, primarily for agricultural chemicals, petrochemicals, and pharmaceuticals.
TP9 G28 ENGR

DF28 Grant & Hackh's Chemical Dictionary. 1987. 5th ed. New York: McGraw Hill. 641 p.

Contains definitions and information on over 50,000 terms used in chemical formulas, as well as trade names, inventors and scientists, and concepts associated with mineralogy, physics, agriculture, biology, pharmacology, and medicine. Covers information in biotechnology, cytotoxic drugs, and space science. Tables and illustrations are also included.
QD5 H3 PASR

DF29 Hawley's Condensed Chemical Dictionary. 1987. 11th ed. Ed. by N. Irving Sax. New York: Van Nostrand Reinhold. 1288 p.

Classic chemical dictionary with concise, factual, chemical information and data on over 20,000 entries. Classes of compounds; trademarked products; chemical concepts, phenomena, and reactions; large-scale chemical processes, applications and equipment; biographies of well-known chemists; and information on technical societies and trade associations are included. Entries reflect concern over environmental and health aspects of chemicals and energy sources.
QD5 C5 PASR; ENGR

DF30 The International Encyclopedia of Physical Chemistry and Chemical Physics, 1960- in progress. London: Pergamon Press.

A massive work of over 100 volumes to date, providing a comprehensive account of all aspects of the domain of science between chemistry and physics. Primarily for the graduate and research worker. Theoretical, rather than practical aspects are emphasized. Organized in 20 general topic groups, each with several volumes.
QD453 I5 CHEM; PASR

DF31 International Union of Pure and Applied Chemistry. 1987. **Compendium of Chemical Terminology: IUPAC Recommendations.** Comp. by V. Gold. Oxford, U.K: Blackwell Scientific. 456 p.

Definitions of over 3,000 chemical terms with references to sources published by IUPAC.
QD5 C48 PASR

DF32 Kirk Othmer Encyclopedia of Chemical Technology, 1978-1984. 3d ed. 26 vols, including *Supplement* and *Index.* New York: John Wiley.

Authoritative coverage of chemical engineering. Each volume is self-contained, and presents lengthy signed articles with tables, figures, and bibliographies. Complements the multi-volume *Encyclopedia of Chemical Processing and Design* (DF23). Available online and on CD-ROM. A single volume version is *Kirk-Othmer Concise Encyclopedia of Chemical Technology* (1985) (TP9 K54 SIGR).
T9 E685 PASR

DF33 McGraw-Hill Dictionary of Chemical Terms. 1984. New York: McGraw Hill. 470 p.

Provides definitions to over 6,000 general chemical terms found in the *McGraw Hill Dictionary of Scientific and Technical Terms* (DA55). A related publication, *McGraw Hill Dictionary of Chemistry* (McGraw Hill, 1984) (QD5 M357 ENGR), provides definitions, also derived from the *Dictionary of Scientific and Technical Terms*, for more than 9,000 terms in theoretical and applied chemistry, drawing from related disciplines such as biochemistry, chemical engineering, physical chemistry, etc.
MTRL

DF34 Ullmann's Encyclopedia of Industrial Chemistry. 1985- in progress. 5th ed. Ed. by Wolfgang Gerhartz. New York: VCH.

Originally published in German (4th ed, 1984), version projected to be 38 volumes. Each volume contains a list of contents, cross references, a table of symbols and units, conversion factors, and a periodic table of the elements. Articles are written by experts and are illustrated with charts, diagrams, and tables. An index to published volumes is also available.
TP9 U4413 ENGR

DF35 Van Nostrand Reinhold Encyclopedia of Chemistry. 1984. 4th ed. Ed. by Douglas Considine. New York: Van Nostrand Reinhold. 1082 p.

Contains 1,300 bibliographic essays on many general chemical concepts written at an intermediate level. A detailed subject index is provided.
QD5 E58 ENGR; PASR

DF36 Winter, Ruth. 1984. **A Consumer's Dictionary of Cosmetic Ingredients.** New York: Crown. 282 p.

Provides definitions of common ingredients found in cosmetics written for the consumer interested in preservatives, coloring agents, fragrances, acids, etc., and possible harmful effects.
MTRL

Handbooks

DF37 Cambridge Guide to the Material World, 1985.

Contains information about physical, chemical, and biological properties. See DA40 for full entry information.

DF38 **Canadian Chemical Register.** 1987. 2 vols. Ottawa: Industry, Science and Technology Canada.

A definitive list in 2 volumes of the manufactured chemicals, manufacturers, and manufacturing plants in Canada. Volume 1 lists manufacturers with the chemicals (by common and chemical name) produced; Volume 2 lists of chemicals followed by manufacturer.
TP12 C24 ENGR

DF39 **The Chemical Formulary: Collections of Commerical Formulas for Making Thousands of Products in Many Fields,** 1933- . New York: Chemical Publishing. annual.

Contains current formulas for products such as adhesives, foods and beverages, cosmetics, detergents, drugs, polishes, resins, etc.
TP151 C53 PASR; ENGR

DF40 Cross-Reference Index of Hazardous Chemicals, Synonyms, and CAS Registry Numbers, 1990.

Provides a means for identifying hazardous chemical substances based on the substance name commonly used in chemistry and by industry. See DK25 for full entry information.

DF41 **Dangerous Properties of Industrial Materials.** 1989. 7th ed. 3 vols. See DL112 for full entry information.

DF42 Flick, Ernest W. 1989. **Cosmetic and Toiletry Formulations.** 2d ed. Park Ridge, NJ: Noyes Publications. 971 p.

Covers over 1,800 products. For each raw material, percentage by weight, suggested method of preparation and manufacturer are given.
TP983 F55 ENGR

DF43 **Handbook of Applied Chemistry.** 1983. 3d ed. Washington: Hemisphere Publishing Corporation and New York: McGraw Hill. var. pg.

Originally published in German. Chapters cover fundamentals of inorganic and organic chemistry, industrial production processes for base and primary chemicals, technical service and development in plastics, fibres, detergents and nuclear chemistry, oil and coal as chemical feedstocks, and biopolymers.
TP151 H5813 ENGR

DF44 **Handbook of Chemistry and Physics,** 1913- . Boca Raton, FL: CRC Press. irregular annual.

(71st ed, 1990). Subtitled *A Ready Reference Book of Chemical and Physical Data*, and also known as *The CRC Handbook*, this is a standard authoritative reference work in chemistry containing major definitions, formulas, tables, and examples of elementary and intermediate technical chemistry.
QD65 H3 PASR; CHEM; ENGR: PHYS

DF45 **Handbook of Polymer Science and Technology.** 1989. 4 vols. Ed. by Nicholas Cheremisinoff. New York: Marcel Dekker.

Each volume contains articles discussing the theoretical foundations of polymer science and related manufacturing concepts, processing operations, and specialty applications. Includes bibliographies and subject indexes in each volume. *Polymer Handbook* (3d ed, Wiley, 1989) (QD281 P6B68 PASR), edited by J. Brandrup, contains tables for chemists in this field, including: nomenclature rules for polymers; data and constants needed for synthetic work and thermodynamic studies of polymerization; physical constants; and solid state properties of polymers. The *Index of Polymer Trade Names* (VCH, 1987) (TP156 P6I55 ENGR) is an alphabetical list of

trade names for over 24,000 polymers, monomers, and substances used in the production of polymers.
QD388 H36 PASC; ENGR

DF46 Lange's Handbook of Chemistry. 1985. 13th ed. Ed. by John A. Dean. New York: McGraw Hill. 1792 p.

First published in 1934, this standard work contains values, formulas, facts, and figures in chemistry.
TP151 L3 ENGR

DF47 Perry's Chemical Engineer's Handbook. 1984. 6th ed. New York: McGraw Hill. var. pg.

Handbook of charts, tables and text in 27 sections covering various aspects of chemical engineering from fluid and particle mechanics to heat transmissions and biochemical engineering. A six volume reference series entitled *What Every Chemical Technologist Wants to Know About...*, compiled by Michael and Irene Ash (Chemical Publishing, 1988) (TP12 A75 ENGR), outlines trademark chemical products suitable for particular applications. Volumes include: *Emulsifiers and Wetting Agents; Dispersants, Solvents and Solubilizers; Plasticizers, Stabilizers and Thickeners; Conditioners, Emollients and Lubricants; Resins;* and *Polymers and Plastics*.
TP151 P45 ENGR

DF48 Sax, N. Irving. 1987. **Hazardous Chemicals Desk Reference.** New York: Van Nostrand Reinhold. 1084 p.

Contains approximately 5,000 entries for materials (e.g chemicals, lubricants, drugs, soaps, pesticides) commonly found in industrial settings. Appendices include cross references to synonyms for materials names, and references to Chemical Abstracts Service registry numbers.

Another guide for the general public seeking information on the characteristics of, and protection against, the most common toxic chemicals in the workplace is *Hazardous Chemicals on File* (Facts on File, 1988, 3 vols.) (T55.3 H3N67 ENGI).
T55.3 H3533 ENGR

DF49 Shugar, Gershon J. and John Dean. 1990. **Chemist's Ready Reference Handbook.** New York: McGraw Hill. var. pg.

Handbook written for the practicing laboratory chemist, with instructions on lab techniques and procedures in chemical research and experiments. Includes diagrams, tables of data, and references to further information. Shugar has also written *Chemical Technician's Ready Reference Handbook* (McGraw Hill, 1990) (QD61 S58 ENGR; PASR).
QD65 S537 PASC

DF50 Tables of Physical and Chemical Constants and some Mathematical Functions. 1986. 15th ed. See DE29 for full entry information.

DF51 Verschueren, Karel. 1983. **Handbook of Environmental Data on Organic Chemicals.** 2d ed. New York: Van Nostrand Reinhold. 1310 p.

More than 1,000 organic chemicals included. Chemicals are arranged in alphabetical order with cross references to related terms.
TD196 O73V47 ENGR

* * * *

Directories and Biographical Sources

DF52 CHEM Sources - USA, 1958- . Ormond Beach, FL: Chemical Sources International. annual.

This directory and it's sister publication *Chem Sources - International* (1986- biennial), are chemical source directories which list chemicals, trade name products, industrial applications and product activities, a company directory, and agents and representatives and country indexes (in the International volume).
TP12 C312; C324 ENGR

DF53 Chemical Industry Directory, 1964- . Kent, U.K: Benn Businesss Information Services. annual.

International directory of chemical manufacturers, plant and laboratory equipment manufacturers, storage depots, associations, consultants, and other related information.
TP12 C34A ENGR

DF54 Chemical Research Faculties: An International Directory, 1988. Washington: American Chemical Society. 558 p.

Provides coverage on chemical research institutions in 107 countries, including those involved in chemical engineering, biochemistry, pharmaceutical/medicinal chemistry, toxicology, and polymer science. Complements the *Directory of Graduate Research* (American Chemical Society, 1989) (Z5525 U5A6 CHEM), which contains information on Canadian and American institutions.
Z5525 U5C53 PASR

DF55 The Nobel Prize Winners: Chemistry. 1990. 3 vols. Pasadena, CA: Salem Press.

Biographical articles and portraits of the 113 laureates listing award winner's area of concentration and Nobel lecture. Also includes an essay of the history of the Nobel prize in chemistry. Bibliographies are included.

DG   EARTH SCIENCES

Bibliographies and Guides to the Literature

DG1 **Arctic Bibliography**, 1953-1975. 16 vols. Prepared by the Arctic Institute of North America. Montreal: McGill-Queen's University Press. 6 issues per year.

Scholarly resource containing citations and abstracts to world literature in polar research in many areas, including geology, and mapping. See CJ162 for full entry information.

DG2 **Bibliography and Index of Geology**, 1969- . 4 vols. Alexandria, VA: American Geological Institute. monthly with annual cumulation.

The major reference tool in geology. Supersedes the *Bibliography and Index of Geology Exclusive of North America* (1933-68), and the *Bibliography of North American Geology* (1931-72), continuing the volume numbering of the former. A major indexing service for geology, providing worldwide coverage of more than 55,000 items annually in 29 fields of interest, including citations to both technical and nontechnical publications relating to the earth sciences. Covers monographs, textbooks, reports, articles in serials, guidebooks, abstracts of talks, maps, and theses in Canada and the U.S. Excludes book reviews. Translations are provided for non-English titles. Includes subject and author indexes. The *GeoRef Thesaurus and Guide to Indexing*, (American Geological Institute, 5th ed, 1989) (Z695.1 G45 G46 ESCR) provides an extensive set of terms useful for searching this bibliographical index. Available online and on CD-ROM as *GeoRef (Geological Reference File)*.
Z6031 G42 ESCR

DG3 **Bibliography of Economic Geology**, 1982- . London: Geosystems. bimonthly.

Formerly *Geocom Bulletin* (1968-81). References to over 5,000 items in the areas of regional geology, applied geology, mineral deposits, geochemistry, geoscience, and related topics each year. Contains subject, locational, stratigraphical, geographical and author indexes.
QE1 G123 PASR

DG4 **Catalogue of the Library of the Arctic Institute of North America, (Montreal)**, 1968. 4 vols. *Supplements:* 1971 (1 vol); 1974 (2 vols); 1980 (3 vols).

This catalogue represents one of the largest collections devoted to polar regions, with particular strength in the Arctic, sub-Arctic regions. Related titles are the *Arctic Bibliography* (DG1) and *ASTIS*, (DG6).
Z6005 P7A75

DG5 **How to Find Information on Canadian Natural Resources: A Guide to the Literature**, 1985.

Contains numerous references to works in earth sciences, including mineral resources, climate, and water resources. See DH5 for full entry information.

DG6 **Information Sources in the Earth Sciences.** 1989. 2d ed. New York: Bowker-Saur/K.G. Saur. 518 p.

Bibliographic essays describe specific fields of geology, identifying and evaluating resources, and listing major resources by country.
Z6031 W67 ESCR

DG7 Lakos, Amos A. and Andrew F. Cooper. 1987. **Strategic Minerals: A Bibliography.** Waterloo, ON: University of Waterloo Library. 132 p.

Bibliographic references to books, journals, technical reports, and U.S. and Canadian government documents in the area of resource politics, mineral economics and policy.
Z6736 L34 ENGR

DG8 Sarjeant, William A.S. 1980. **Geologists and the History of Geology: An International Bibliography from the Origins to 1978.** 5 vols. New York: Arno Press. *Supplement 1979–1984* (1987 2 vols). Malabar, FL: Krieger.

Contains an introduction and an extensive list of resources about geologists and geological events, historical accounts, museums and institutions concerned with geology, history of the petroleum industry, and other information. Indexes include geologists by nationality and specialty; authors; editors; and women geologists.
Z6031 S28 PASR;   Suppl: Z6021 S28 PASR

DG9 Ward, D.C. and M.W. Wheeler. 1981. **Geologic Reference Sources: A Subject and Regional Bibliography of Publications and Maps in the Geological Sciences.** 2d ed. Metuchen, NJ: Scarecrow Press. 560 p.

Introduction to the literature of geosciences; materials at both introductory and advanced levels.
Z6031 W3 PASR

Abstracts, Indexes and Databases

DG10 **ASTIS Current Awareness Bulletin,** 1978- . Calgary: Arctic Science and Technology Information System, University of Calgary. bimonthly with annual cumulation on microfiche.

Lists abstracts of over 2,500 items each year in areas of geography, geology, mineralogy, ice, petroleum, archaeology, etc.
ENGS current only

DG11 **Current Contents: Physical, Chemical and Earth Sciences**, 1961- weekly. See DA15 for full entry information.

DG12 Geoline, 1970- . Hannover, Germany: Deutsches Bundesanstalt für Geowissenschaften und Rohstoffe (BGR). database.

Citations and abstracts of the world's literature (reports, journals, dissertations, conference papers, books, maps) in geosciences, including geology, stratigraphy, tectonics, mineralogy, mining, environmental geology, soil sciences, etc. Abstracts in English, German or French. BGR also publishes *GEOS*, a database which comprises *Geoline, Hydroline,* and *Stimline*, covering hydrology, marine science and mineral resources.

DG13 Geological Abstracts, 1986- . Essex, U.K: Elsevier/Geo Abstracts. monthly with annual cumulation.

Formerly *Geophysics and Tectonics Abstracts* (1982-85); originally *Geophysical Abstracts* (1977-81). As of 1986-88 published in four parts: 1) Geophysics and Tectonics, 2) Economic Geology, 3) Palaeontology, and Stratigraphy, and 4) Sedimentary Geology. Includes annual and regional indexes. Available online on *GEOBASE* (CK10).
QE500 G3522 ESCR

DG14 Geomechanics Abstracts, 1977- . London: University of London Rock Mechanics Information Service. database.

Lists approximately 3,000 references and abstracts each year in more than 300 international journals, conference papers, technical reports, theses, and books dealing with rock and soil mechanics, related aspects of mining, civil engineering, geophysics, geology. A print version is published as part of the *International Journal of Rock Mechanics and Mining Sciences* (TA710 A1I522 ENGS) (Pergamon Press).

DG15 Geoscan, Ottawa: Canada. Department of Energy, Mines and Resources. database.

Citations to Canadian produced and Canadian-related geoscience information, with emphasis on geology, non-renewable energy, and mineral resources. Many unpublished federal and provincial government reports are included, as well as others published by geoscience agencies and the geoscience society. Covers period 1845 to present. Available online.

DG16 Geotechnical Abstracts, 1970- monthly. See DL23 for full entry information.

DG17 Geotitles Weekly, 1969- . London: Geosystems. weekly.

A comprehensive weekly classified international subject bibliography for all forms of geological literature. Cumulates monthly. Geographical, stratigraphical indexes, plus access by location, author, serial source. Covers both academic and economic fields of interest. Available online and on CD-ROM as *Geo-Archive*.
Z6032 G37 PASR

DG18 Hydro-Abstracts, 1980- . Minneapolis, MN: Environmental Hydrology Corp. monthly.

Contains over 2,000 abstracts per year found in reports, proceedings, bulletins, and other books in areas of water properties, groundwater, saline water conversion, water pollutants, quality control, demand, etc. Formerly *Water Resources Abstracts* (1968-79).
HD1691 W182

DG19 Index to Publications of the Geological Survey of Canada, 1961- . Ottawa: CGPC, Supply and Services [for the Geological Survey]. annual. Cumulated for 1959–74 (1975); 1975–79 (1980); 1980-84 (1985); 1985-87 (1989).

Lists publications by type (memoirs, bulletins, papers, maps, etc) and then chronologically. Includes a finding list by area (Canada, provinces, territories, NTS quadrants) and author index. There is a retrospective volume *Index of Publications of the Geological Survey of Canada, 1845–1958* (Queen's Printer, 1961) (Z6034 C19A4 PASR; MAPL).
Z6034 C19A4, A4112 MAPL

DG20 MNT (Mining Technology), 1973- . Ottawa: Canada Centre for Mineral and Energy Technology (CANMET). database.

Citations, with abstracts, to Canadian, or Canadian-related articles on mining. CANMET also publishes bibliographies of articles and scientific papers on mining, for example *Biotechnology Bibliographies* (1987) (R015.71 C21G).

DG21 Metals Abstracts, 1968- . Metals Park, OH: ASM International, Materials Information. monthly.

"World's foremost reference source on metallurgy", with international coverage from 1,800 journals and conference proceedings, books and reports of all aspects of metallurgy. Approximately 25,000 descriptive abstracts per year. Available online and on CD-ROM as *Metadex*.
TN1 M488 ENGR

DG22 Mineralogical Abstracts, 1920- . London: Mineralogical Society of Great Britain and Mineralogical Society of America. quarterly with annual indexes.

Includes approximately 5,500 abstracts in areas of mineralogy, geochemistry, meterorites, petrology, etc., in a subject arrangement with author and subject indexes.
QE351 M54 PASR

DG23 Oceanic Abstracts, 1964- . Bethesda, MD: Cambridge Scientific Abstracts. bimonthly with annual index.

Provides abstracts of worldwide technological literature on oceanic research, including marine biology, ecology, meteorology, marine pollution, marine resources, ships and shipping, etc. International technical journals, conference proceedings, government reports, trade publications and books are included. Available online and on CD-ROM as part of *Pollution/Toxicology CD-ROM*, DK18.
Z6004 P6 O255 PASR

Reviews and Annuals

DG24 Advances in Geophysics, 1952- . New York: Academic Press. irregular.

Each volume covers a particular topic, for example Volume 25 (1983) *Theory of Climate*; Volume 27 (1985) *Satellite Oceanic Remote Sensing*.
QC801 A283 GEOL

DG25 Canadian Minerals Yearbook, 1886- . Ottawa: Energy, Mines and Resources. annual.

Permanent official record of the Canadian mineral industry. Title varies. Contains comprehensive reports reviewing the events and assessing the outlook for the Canadian mineral industry and for commodities. Outline maps and statistical tables enhance the text.
TN26 A3422 ENGR; PASR

DG26 Earth Science Reviews, 1966- . Amsterdam: Elsevier. quarterly.

"Bridging gaps between research articles and textbooks" and international in scope, it includes reviews of new books, forthcoming events and recent journal contents of interest.
QE1 E14 GEOL

DG27 Geological Survey of Canada. **Current Research,** 1978- . Ottawa: Department of Energy, Mines and Resources. annual.

Supersedes *Current Research in the Geological Sciences in Canada*, (1950–1977). Series

containing full reports "comparable in scope and subject matter to those appearing in scientific journals and other serials." Arranged in five volumes: Part A: *Abstracts* (which includes abstracts and citations to full reports in the other volumes); Part B: *Eastern and Atlantic Canada*; Part C: *Canadian Shield*; Part D: *Interior Plains and Arctic Canada*; and Part E: *Cordillera and Pacific Margin*.
3401 C5 GSC Papers MAPL

DG28 United States. Bureau of Mines. **Minerals Yearbook,** 1932/33- . Washington: GPO. annual.
"A record of the performance of the world's mineral industry" for metals, minerals, fuels by type, mineral industries of the U.S. and other countries. A major statistical source.
TN23 U612 PASR

Encyclopedias and Dictionaries

DG29 Arem, Joel E. 1987. **Color Encyclopedia of Gemstones.** 2d ed. New York: Van Nostrand Reinhold. 248 p.
Descriptions of some 250 gems are presented. Basic properties such as chemical formula, crystallography, colour, luster, hardness, etc. are listed with additional comments where appropriate. Colour photographs accompany text.
QE392 A73 ROMU

DG30 The Cambridge Encyclopedia of Earth Sciences. 1981. Cambridge: Cambridge University Press. 496 p.
Collection of long, signed articles surveying different earth sciences. Includes a glossary, index, and bibliography.
QE262 C35 PASR

DG31 Challinor's Dictionary of Geology. 1986. 6th ed. Ed. by Antony Wyatt. New York: Oxford University Press. 374 p.
Contains 2,000 entries with British emphasis. Citations to geological literature are included.
QE5 C45 PASR

DG32 Concise Encyclopedia of Mineral Resources. 1989. Ed. by Donald D. Carr. Cambridge, MA: MIT Press. 426 p.
Comprehensive coverage of all aspects of mineral resources from geology and extraction to economics and manufacturing. Many of the articles are extracted from the *Encyclopedia of Materials Science and Engineering* (DL101). Articles are cross referenced and include bibliographies.
TA402 C66 SCAR

DG33 Dixon, Dougal. 1988. **The Macmillan Illustrated Encyclopedia of Dinosaurs and Prehistoric Animals: A Visual Who's Who of Prehistoric Life.** New York: Macmillan. 312 p.
A compendium describing almost 600 species of dinosaurs and other prehistoric animals, presented in chapters for main species (fishes, amphibians, reptiles, birds, mammals). Glossary, classification of vertebrates, bibliography, and an index are included. Another reference for the nonspecialist interested in dinosaurs is Helen Roney Sattler's *The Illustrated Dinosaur Dictionary* (Lothrop, Lee and Shepard, 1983). Almost 300 dinosaurs and terms used to describe them are included. A classification table of dinosaurs and a 12 page pictorial section with a chart of relationships showing the Mesozoic world are provided, in addition to drawings, a bibliography, and a table indicating locations in Canada and the U.S. where dinosaurs have been found.
QE841 M32 ROMU

DG34 Encyclopedia of Earth Sciences, 1966- in progress. 16 vols. New York: Van Nostrand Reinhold.

Series of single-volume encyclopedias on various subjects, each containing signed articles with bibliographic references. Subjects covered include oceanography (volume 1); paleontology (volume 7); beaches and coastal environment (volume 15) and solid earth geophysics (volume 16).

DG35 Geology of Canada. 1989- . 9 vols. Ed. by G.O. Wheeler. Ottawa: Geological Survey of Canada.

Presents the latest knowledge about the geology and geophysics of North America. The volumes in this set form part of the geological survey of America's *Geology of North America* series produced as part of the Decade of North American Geology Project. Volume 1 is *Quarternary Geology of Canada and Greenland* (1989) (QE696 Q37 ERIN).

DG36 Glossary of Geology. 1987. 3d ed. Ed. by Robert L. Bates. Alexandria, VA: American Geological Institute. 788 p.

Comprehensive dictionary to over 30,000 English-language geological terms used in North America. Includes references to geological literature.
QE5 A485 Ref ERIN

DG37 Lapidus, Dorothy Farris. 1987. **The Facts on File Dictionary of Geology and Geophysics.** New York: Facts on File. 347 p.

Contains more than 3,000 entries of varying length describing commonly used terms in the major subfields of geology. A companion to this work is *The Facts on File Dictionary of Marine Science*, (1988) (GC9 F28 BMER), covers terminology used to describe marine ecosystems, oceans, reefs, coastlines, waves, tides, marine plants and animals, and water chemistry. Appendices provide additional information, such as geological time periods, a chronology of significant marine history from 609 BC to 1977, a taxonomic chart, and a list of marine science research projects.
QE5 L29 PASR

DG38 Magill's Survey of Science: Earth Science Series. 1990. 5 vols. Ed. by Frank Magill. Pasadena, CA: Salem Press.

Contains 377 essays written by specialists in earth sciences covering the disciplines of geology, oceanography, meteorology, astronomy, geophysics, geochemistry, paleontology, hydrology, seismology, and soil science.
QE28 M33

DG39 McGraw-Hill Dictionary of Earth Sciences. 1984. New York: McGraw Hill. 837 p.

Consists of more than 15,000 terms commonly used in earth sciences, many taken from the *McGraw Hill Dictionary of Scientific and Technical Terms* (DA55). Includes synonyms, acronyms, and abbreviations.
QE5 M27 PASR

DG40 McGraw-Hill Encyclopedia of the Geological Sciences. 1988. 2d ed. New York: McGraw Hill. 722 p.

Articles selected from the sixth edition of the *McGraw Hill Encyclopedia of Science and Technology* (1987) (DA43), cover most of the major areas in geology in one convenient volume. A similar compilation is *McGraw Hill Encyclopedia of Ocean and Atmospheric Sciences* (1980) (GC9 M32 ROBA), which

contains selected articles from an earlier version of the same encyclopedia, with additional updated material.
QE5 M29 ESCR

DG41 Mitchell, Richard Scott. 1985. **Dictionary of Rocks.** New York: Van Nostrand Reinhold. 228 p.

Provides brief definitions of rock names. Rocks are classified by type, and name origins and dates are included when known. Cross references from local and trade names of rocks to the known and accepted form. Includes a glossary of descriptive petrologic terms. Photographs enhance the text.
QE423 M58 PASR

DG42 Multilingual Thesaurus of Geosciences. 1988. Elmsford, NY: Pergamon Press. 516 p.

Publication is intended to enable geoscience researchers to access international databases by providing geologic equivalents to approximately 5,000 terms in six languages (English, French, German, Russian, Spanish, and Italian). Columnar arrangement by English word.
Z695.1 G45 M84 PASR

DG43 Read, P.G. 1988. **Dictionary of Gemmology.** 2d ed. Stoneham, MA: Butterworths. 266 p.

Provides concise and comprehensive descriptions of gems, scientific terms, and techniques. Appendices include balance systems, colour, and clarity grading standards, sorting standards, units of measurement, tables of elements, table of flourescence of principal gemstones, and constant characteristics of principal gemstones.
QE392 R43 PASR

DG44 Roberts, Willard Lincoln. 1990. **Encyclopedia of Minerals.** 2d ed. New York: Van Nostrand Reinhold. 979 p.

An alphabetical arrangement of more than 3,200 descriptions of minerals, outlining properties of the mineral, and locations found. Black and white drawings and a center section with colour photographs for more than 300 minerals are included.
QE355 R6 ESCR

DG45 Thrush, Paul W. 1968. **Dictionary of Mining, Mineral and Related Terms.** Washington: U.S. Bureau of Mines. 1269 p.

The standard dictionary in the field with over 55,000 terms and 150,000 definitions relating to metal mining, coal mining, quarrying, geology, metallurgy, ceramics, minerals, etc.
TN9 T5 ENGR

DG46 van der Leeden, Frits. 1990. **The Water Encyclopedia.** 2d ed. Chelsea, MI: Lewis. 808 p.

More than 700 tables, charts, graphs, and illustrations reprinted from a number of sources, with only a minimal amount of text. Topics covered include climate, precipitation, water laws, etc. "Clean water" is emphasized, with only a portion of the work covering "wastewater". Moves from a general to more specific level in each topic. Indexed.
GB661 T64 BMER

Handbooks and Almanacs

DG47 **AGI Data Sheets: for Geology in the Field, Laboratory, and Office.** 1989. 3d ed. Ed. by J.T. Dutro Jr. Alexandria, VA: American Geological Institute. looseleaf.

Provides a wide range of information useful to geologists. Divided into 89 sections of varying length. Illustrated with black and white drawings; bibliography also included.
QE52 A36 ESCR (1983, 2d)

DG48   Audubon Society Field Guide to North American Rocks and Minerals. 1979. Ed. by Audubon Society staff and C.W. Chesterman. New York: Knopf. 850 p.

A pocket-sized guide which provides all relevant data necessary to identify 232 rocks and minerals, including chemistry, descriptions, etc. Colour plates included. Another similar publication is F.H. Pough's *A Field Guide to Rocks and Minerals* (4th ed, 1976, Houghton Mifflin) (QE367 P6 PASC), written for the amateur, and providing an introduction to the study of rocks and minerals and mineral descriptions with a glossary and bibliography. For Canada, consult the *Rocks & Minerals for the Collector* series by Ann Sabina (4 vols, Geological Survey of Canada, 1983-87) (ESCI), which describes mineral, rock and fossil occurrences in various areas of Canada.
QE443 C45 PASR

DG49   Cambridge Guide to the Material World, 1985.

Contains information about physical, chemical and biological properties. See DA40 for full entry information.

DG50   Catalogue of Canadian Minerals. 1983. Comp. by R.J. Traill. Ottawa: Dept. of Energy, Mines and Resources. 432 p.

List of Canadian mineral resources in alphabetical order.
QE376 A1 T7 SCC

DG51   CRC Handbook of Physical Properties of Rocks. 1982-84. 3 vols. Ed. by R.S. Carmichael. Boca Raton, FL: CRC Press.

Summarizes data in reports and other sources into one convenient handbook. Volume 1 covers mineral compositions of rocks; Volume 2 seismic velocities; and Volume 3 density of rocks and minerals. Each volume has an index and bibliography.
QE431.6 P5H3 GEOL

DG52   Geological Survey of Canada. 1976-1982. **Geology and Economic Minerals of Canada.** 5th ed. 3 vols. Ottawa: Energy, Mines and Resources Canada.

Reference text for scientists on Canadian geology. Contains information on the physiographic subdivisions of Canada, the Canadian mineral industry, and the geology and economic minerals of various regions (e.g. Canadian Shield) in Canada. Includes maps and correlation charts, diagrams and photographs, and a bibliography.
QE185 A43 SIGS

DG53   Grice, Joel D. 1989. **Famous Mineral Localities of Canada.** Markham, ON: Fitzhenry & Whiteside. 190 p.

Discusses 19 well-known Canadian mineral sites, how they were discovered, and why the particular minerals found there are important. A glossary and bibliography are provided.
QE376 G74 PASC

DG54   Handbook of Applied Meteorology. 1985. Ed. by David D. Houghton. New York: Wiley Interscience. 1461 p.

Intended for non-meteorologists, organized in five main sections: "basic information" about

circulation systems, severe weather, forecasting, and climatology; "measurements" for satellites, observing networks, ground-based systems, and various other techniques; "applications" for acid precipitation, agricultural and hydrological problems, and solar and wind energy; "societal impacts", particularly environmental and economic impacts; and "resources", including lists of publications, research centres, and sources of basic data. Appendices include a glossary, a list of abbreviations and acronyms, units of measurement, and climatic data for many locations in the world.
TA197 H36 ENGR

DG55 Lambert, David. 1988. **The Field Guide to Geology.** New York: Facts on File. 256 p.

Introductory handbook to earth sciences, consisting of diagrams and photographs on most aspects of geology. The text portion of each chapter is written in basic language. Includes a list of museums and geologic features around the world.
QE28 L35 Ref ROMU

DG56 Mangone, Gerard J. 1986. **Concise Marine Almanac.** New York: Van Nostrand Reinhold. 135 p.

Summary of maritime facts in seven major sections: measurements, geographic features, naval forces and ports, fisheries, marine mineral resources, and marine pollution.
TPL

DG57 Matlins, Antoinette Leonard. 1984. **The Complete Guide to Buying Gems: How to Buy Diamonds and Colored Gemstones with Confidence and Knowledge.** New York: Crown. 206 p.

Instructions provided on how to look at gems, noting colour, cut, flaws. Describes frauds and how to protect against them. One third of the work deals with diamonds. Diagrams illustrate cuts and compare sizes and weights. Gemstone chart included.
TPL

DG58 Metals Handbook. 1978-1989, 9th ed. 15 vols. See DL57 for full entry information.

DG59 Minerals Handbook [year]: Statistics and Analyses of the World's Mineral Industry, 1986/87- . New York: Stockton Press. biennial.

This handbook for nonspecialists provides an overview and statistical picture of 46 minerals and metals. Minerals are briefly summarized, and reserves, consumption and substitutes, prices and marketing information provided. Information is derived from *Minerals Yearbook*, (DG28), *Mineral Facts and Problems* (TN23 U5 ENGS), and *Mineral Commodity Summaries*.
HD9506 A1M55 ESCR

DG60 Pellant, Chris. 1990. **Rocks, Minerals and Fossils of the World.** Boston: Little, Brown. 175 p.

Descriptions and photographs of rocks, minerals, and fossils. Rocks are organized by type (igneous, metamorphic, and sedimentary) with brief descriptions for each type. 250 minerals are listed with major identifying characteristics, such as crystal shape, colour, luster, etc. Fossils are organized by type (corals, crinoids, trilobites and fish) and this section includes a discussion on fossil formation, fossil naming, and the role of fossils in the study of evolution.

Directories

DG61 **Earth and Astronomical Sciences Research Centres: A World Directory of Organizations and Programmes.** 1991. 2d ed. Ed. by Jennifer M. Fitch. Harlow, U.K: Longman. forthcoming.

Lists official research centers, industrial research and development laboratories, academic laboratories, national survey and meteorology teams, consultancies, and societies which are carrying out, funding, or promoting research and development activity.
QE40 E3 ESCI (1984)

DG62 O'Reilly. W. 1986. **International Directory to Geophysical Research.** New York: Elsevier Science Publishing. 122 p.

List of specialists in various fields of physics, arranged alphabetically with subject index. Includes business address and a short synopsis of research.
QC805 A2 O74 PASR

DH BIOLOGY

This section includes general biology, botany and horticulture, and zoology, including subsections on mammals, fish, birds, reptiles, insects, and pets, etc.

Biology

Bibliographies and Guides to the Literature

DH1 Davis, Elisabeth B. 1981. **Using the Biological Literature.** New York: Dekker. 286 p.
  Guide to the literature of biological sciences for university students covering broad subject fields in pure, not applied, biology.
QH303 D39 BMER

DH2 **Information Sources in the Life Sciences.** 1987. 3d ed. London, Boston: Butterworths. 191 p.
  Third edition of R.T. Bottle's *Use of Biological Literature* (2d ed, Butterworths, 1972) (QH-315 B67 SIGS). Provides an overview of the literature with separate chapters on biochemistry, biotechnology, botany, ecology, genetics, microbiology, zoology, and the history of biology. Covers secondary sources and databases.
QH315 B67 BMER

DH3 Kronick, David A. with Wendell D. Winters. 1985. **The Literature of the Life Sciences: Reading, Writing, Research.** Philadelphia: ISI Press. 219 p.
  Covers resources for research, including primary and secondary sources, with additional information on searching the literature, writing and publishing.
574 K933L or QH303.6 K76 BMER

DH4 Overmeier, Judith A. 1989. **The History of Biology: A Selected, Annotated Bibliography.** New York: Garland. 157 p.

Descriptive annotations of bibliographic essays, books, monographs, journal articles, conference proceedings and other published sources that summarize aspects of history of biological sciences. Includes biographies and autobiographies.
Z5320 O9 ROBA

DH5 Pal, Gabriel. 1985. **How to Find Information on Canadian Natural Resources: A Guide to the Literature.** Ottawa: Canadian Library Association. 182 p.

Covers significant sources of information, and methods of searching the Canadian literature of natural resources, including zoology, botany.
R333.7 AP153H   or   Z1395 N38P34 BMER

DH6 Smith, R..C. and W.M. Reid. 1980. **Smith's Guide to the Literature of the Life Sciences.** 9th ed. Minneapolis, MN: Burgess. 223 p.

A library guide covering the broad range of biological sciences, dealing with the literature, including databases, and literature problems in the field.
574 AS658 GE (1972)   or   Z7991 S5 BMER

Abstracts and Indexes

DH7 Biological Abstracts, 1926- . Philadelphia: Biosciences Information Service (BIOSIS). semi-monthly, semi-annual cumulative index.

The most comprehensive biological abstracting service available. Abstracts journals in the life sciences, by broad subjects with many subheadings. Life sciences are broadly defined to include related fields. Indexes in each issue for author, biosystem, generic concept, permuted subject. Available online and on CD-ROM as part of *BIOSIS Previews* (DH10).

Serials indexed are listed in *Serial Sources for the BIOSIS Database*, (1980-) (QH301 B3714 BMER); and *Serial Sources for the BIOSIS Previews Database* (1990-) (QH301 B37142 BMER).
QH301 B37 BMER

DH8   **Biological Abstracts / RRM,** 1980- . Philadelphia: Bioscience Information Service. monthly with semi-annual index.

Supersedes *BioResearch Index* (1967-1979). Acts as an index to research reports, reviews, patents, meetings, not covered by DH7. Available online an on CD-ROM as part of *BIOSIS Previews* (DH10).
Z5321 R5 BMER

DH9   **Biological and Agricultural Index,** 1916/18- . New York: H.W. Wilson. monthly, quarterly with annual cumulation.

Provides access to more than 200 English language journals in the life sciences, covering a wide range of pure and applied sciences. Also indexes symposia and conferences, and chapters of annual reviews, but is not meant to cover the research literature. Includes biographical information and a section on book reviews. Available online and on CD-ROM.
Z5073 A452 BMER

DH10 BIOSIS Previews, 1969- . Philadelphia: BIOSIS. database, updated weekly.

Citations to international literature concerning biology and biomedicine. Detailed coverage of animals from circadium rhythm and life cycles to veterinary science. Compilation of *Biological Abstracts, Biological Abstracts/RRM*, and *BIOSIS Previews*.

DH11 **CAB Abstracts**, 1973- . monthly. See DJ9 for full entry information.

DH12 **Current Awareness in Biological Sciences**, 1983- Oxford: Pergamon. monthly.
Supersedes *International Abstracts of Biological Sciences*, (1954–1983). Covers worldwide literature of biological sciences, including biochemistry, clinical chemistry, cell biology, genetics, microbiology, ecology, plant science, pharmacology, physiology, immunology, toxicology, cancer research, neuroscience, developmental biology, and endocrinology. Available online and on CD-ROM on *CAB Abstracts* (DJ9).
QH301 I632 BMER

DH13 **Current Contents: Life Sciences**, 1958- weekly; and **Current Contents: Agriculture, Biology and Environmental Sciences**, 1970- weekly. See DA15 for full entry.

DH14 **General Science Index**, 1978- monthly. See DA18 for full entry information.

DH15 **Microbiology Abstracts**, 1965- . Bethesda, MD: Cambridge Scientific Abstracts. monthly.
Issued in three sections: A: *Industrial and Applied Microbiology*; B: *General Microbiology and Bacteriology*; C: *Algology, Mycology, and Protozoology*. Available online and on CD-ROM.
QR1 I52 BMER

Reviews and Annuals

DH16 **Biological Reviews**, 1923- . London: Cambridge University Press. quarterly.
Comprehensive reviews of particular topics; extensive references.
QH1 B55 BMES

DH17 **Current Advances in Microbiology**, 1984- . New York: Pergamon. monthly.
Contains an index to articles, microbiological papers and reviews published around the world in the field of microbiology. Organized into 188 main areas. Available online through *CABS* database (DJ9).
Z5180 C8 BMER

Dictionaries

DH18 **Chamber's Biology Dictionary.** 1989. Ed. by Peter M.B. Walker. New York: Cambridge University Press. 324 p.
Over 10,000 definitions for novice biology students and generalists. Covers all areas of biology, with greatest emphasis in zoology. Also published as *Cambridge Dictionary of Biology* (1990).
QH 302.5 C46 VUPR

DH19 **The Facts on File Dictionary of Biology.** 1988. Rev. ed. Ed. by Elizabeth Tootill. New York: Facts on File. 326 p.
Broad coverage, including traditional fields and technical fields. Nontechncial definitions, cross-references.
QH13 F35 ESCR

DH20 Henderson's Dictionary of Biological Terms. 1989. 10th ed. New York: Wiley. 637 p.

Comprehensive, with over 22,000 concise, technical definitions, with useful appendices, including table of classification of plants and animals.
QH13 H4 BMER; ZOOL

DH21 King, Robert C. and William D. Stansfield. 1985. **Dictionary of Genetics.** 3d ed. New York: Oxford University Press. 480 p.

Reflects recent developments in and interdisciplinary nature of genetics. Includes 5,920 definitions and four appendices with classification of living organisms; common and scientific names of organisms; chronology of events with an index of scientists; and a list of periodicals cited in the literature. *Dictionary of Genetics and Cell Biology* by Norman Maclean (New York University Press, 1987) covers the terminology of these and related fields, and the appendices include taxonomic classification, lists of common and Latin names of organisms, numbers of chromosomes and amounts of DNA in key species.
QH431 K518 BMER

DH22 The Oxford Dictionary of Natural History. 1985. Ed. by Michael Allaby. New York: Oxford University Press. 688 p.

More than 12,000 short entries covering the inter-disciplinary vocabulary of natural history, including technical terms. Taxa of plant and animals listed to family level. Cross referenced. Also from the same publisher is *Concise Dictionary of Biology*, (1985) which is derived from the *Concise Science Dictionary* (DA51) with long definitions that assume no previous knowledge. Allaby has also edited *The Concise Oxford Dictionary of Zoology* (1991).
QH13 O9 BMER

DH23 Singleton, Paul and Diana Sainsbury. 1987. **Dictionary of Microbiology and Molecular Biology.** 2d ed. New York: Wiley. 1019 p.

First edition titled *Dictionary of Microbiology* (1978). Describes terms and provides references to review sources where the terms are extensively discussed. Appendixes include specific pathways, biosyntheses, and fermentation processes. Terminology of molecular biology is also found in *Dictionary of Biochemistry and Molecular Biology* by J. Stenesh. (2d ed, Wiley, 1989) (QP512 S73 BMER).
QR9 S56 BMER

Encyclopedias

DH24 The Cambridge Encyclopedia of Life Sciences. 1985. Ed. by Adrian Friday and David S. Ingram. New York: Cambridge University Press. 432 p.

Surveys "the current state of knowledge in biology." Thematically arranged in 3 parts: part 1 covers cells; organisms, genetics, behaviour, sociobiology, and ecology; part 2 describes various environments; part 3 covers evolution and fossils. Includes species and subject indexes, and a review of classification schemes. Illustrated.
QH307.2 C36 BMER

DH25 Comprehensive Biotechnology. 1985. 4 vols. See DL81 for full entry information.

DH26 Encylopedia of Bioethics, 1978. See BC14 for full entry information.

DH27 Encyclopedia of Human Biology. 1991. 8 vols. Ed. in chief, Renato Dulbecco. New York: Academic Press.

Presents an overview of topics in contemporary human biology (food toxicology, biocultural sex differences, malaria) written for a wide audience. Articles of varying lengths are written by noted specialists. Includes a cross-reference index.
QP11 E53 Ref SCAR

DH28 Encyclopedia of the Biological Sciences. 1970. 2d ed. Ed. by Peter Gray. New York: Van Nostrand Reinhold. 1027 p.

Includes signed articles on many aspects of the biological sciences, biophysics and biochemistry. Articles vary in length depending on the topic, and most include short bibliographies. Subject index.
QH13 G7 BMER

DH29 Illustrated Natural History of Canada. 1971-1974. 12 vols. Toronto: Natural Science of Canada.

Each separately titled volume covers a different area of Canada or topic, e.g. *The Great Lakes*; *The Nature of Fish*, giving a scientific lists of rocks, plants, etc. Designed for lay people. Includes bibliographies.
R500.971 I29

DH30 Magill's Survey of Science: Life Science Series. 1991. 6 vols. Englewood Cliffs, NJ: Salem Press.

Events and phenomena in biology, genetics, microbiology and related disciplines are examined in separate essays covering some 400 tropics. Methods of study, conclusions, significance considered. Annotated bibliographies with each essay.
QH 207.2 M34 Ref ERIN

Handbooks and Directories

DH31 Altman, P.L. and D.S. Dittmer. 1972–74. **Biology Data Book.** 3 vols. 2d ed. Washington: Federation of American Societies for Experimental Biology.

Contains basic reference data for biology in the form of quantitative and descriptive tables, charts, diagrams. The Federation also publishes specialized handbooks.
QH310 A38 BMED, ZOOL

DH32 CRC Handbook of Microbiology. 1977- 1988. 9 vols. in 10. 2d ed. Boca Raton, FL: CRC Press.

A comprehensive and current source of information on composition, activities and adverse effects of microorganisms. Volumes cover: *Bacteria; Fungi, Algae, Protozoa and Viruses; Microbial Composition; Microbial Products; Growth and Metabolism; Microbial Transformation; Genetics and Immunology; Toxins, Enzymes and Microbiotics*. Volumes include glossaries, bibliographies, a list of collections, and indexes. The *Practical Handbook of Microbiology*, edited by William O'Leary (CRC Press, 1989) (QR41.2 C2 BMED) is a one volume condensed version of this 9 volume set.
QR41.2 C2 BMED

DH33 Genetic Engineering and Biotechnology Related Firms Worldwide Directory. 1988/89. 7th ed. Kingston, NJ: Sittig & Noyes. 919 p.

Directory including comprehensive listings of research laboratories, and production plants as well as venture capital fund sources for genetic engineering and biotechnology in over 57 countries.
QH442 G44242 BMER

DH34 Life Sciences Organizations and Agencies Directory. 1988. Detroit: Gale Research. 864 p.

Subtitled *A Guide to Approximately 8,000 Organizations and Agencies...* Includes biology, microbiology, zoology, and agricultural sciences, environmental sciences, food sciences, veteranary sciences, and biotechnology. Covers U.S. and international associations, U.S. state and federal agencies, educational institutions, research centres, consulting firms, libraries, and botanical gardens.
QH321 L54 BMER

DH35 The Naturalists' Directory and Almanac International, 1877- . Baltimore, MD: World Natural History Publications. irregular annual.

Publisher varies. (Volume 45, 1990). Professional and amateur naturalists are listed geographically, with name, address, subject of interest. Also lists museums, societies, serials. A similar directory with emphasis on North America is *Naturalists Directory International*, (1975- PCL Publications, annual) (QH35 N3 BMES).
QH35 N3 BMER

DH36 Practical Handbook of Biochemistry and Molecular Biology. 1989. Boca Raton, FL: CRC Press. 601 p.

For the graduate student and research worker.

CRC Press also published *Handbook of Biochemistry and Molecular Biology* (3d ed. 9 vols, 1976) (AP514.2 H34 BMER).
QP514.2 P73 BMER, ZOOL

DH37 Statistical Tables for Biological, Agricultural and Medical Research. 1974. 6th ed. rev. and enl. Comp. by R.A. Fisher and F. Yates. New York: Hafner. 146 p. Reprint/ Longman, 1982.

Comprehensive collection of tables, with usefulness of each table explained. Bibliography on statistical methods appended. A standard statistical reference of wide applicability in scientific research.
HA33 F53 BMED, ZOOL

Botany and Horticulture

The following is list of sources dealing with the subject of botany, horticulture and home gardening. Additional information can also be found in *Agriculture*, Section DJ, which covers the area of food and food production.

Bibliographies and Guides, Abstracts, Indexes and Reviews

DH38 Botanical Reviews, 1935- . New York: Botanical Gardens. quarterly.

Interprets botanical progress in long review articles.
QK1 B56 BOTA

DH39 Davis, Elisabeth B. 1987. **Guide to Information Sources in the Botanical Sciences.** Littleton, CO: Libraries Unlimited. 175 p.

Selective coverage of some 600 reference sources, with annotations. Covers bibliographic tools (abstracts, indexes, databases): ready-reference sources (encyclopedias, dictionaries, handbooks, current awareness tools); additional sources of information (textbooks, histories, publishers).
Z5351 D28 ESCR

DH40 Excerpta Botanica, 1959- . Stuttgart, Germany: Fischer. quarterly.

A leading source for information in botany with annotations in English, French or German. In two parts: A) *Taxonomica et Chronologica*; and B) *Sociologica.* Includes periodical literature and books covering systematic botany, herbaria, gardens, museums, plant geography and ecology.
Z5356 A1E9 ESCS (Part A)
Z5354 E1E9 ESCS (Part B)

DH41 Horticultural Abstracts, 1931- . Wallingford, Oxon, U.K: CAB International. monthly with annual cumulation.

Includes approximately 10,000 abstracts each year for articles on all areas of horticulture, including fruits, vegetables (greenhouse and outdoor), ornamental plants, subtropical and tropical fruit and crops, as well as current research and applications. Available online on *CAB Abstracts* (DJ9).
SB1 H65 BOTA

DH42 Isaacson, Richard T. 1985. **Gardening: A Guide to the Literature.** New York: Garland. 198 p.

Bibliography, with annotations, of 700 books on gardening and horticulture covering regions across North America. Includes entries for reference works, landscape design, ornamentals, methods of growing and using plants, etc., as well as a section on periodicals and publications from various societies and specialty book sellers. Indexed.

Encyclopedias, Dictionaries and Handbooks

DH43 Audubon Society Field Guide to North American Wildflowers: Eastern Region. 1983. New York: Knopf. 887 p.

Together with *Audubon Society Field Guide to North American Wildflowers: Western Region* (Knopf, 1979) (QK110 S64 Ref ROMU), these guides provide information and illustrations on all wildflowers in North America. Indexed by common and scientific names.
MTRL SCI/TECH

DH44 Beckett, Kenneth A. with the Royal Horticultural Society. 1987. **The RHS Encyclopedia of House Plants Including Greenhouse Plants.** Topsfield, MA: Salem House. 491 p.

A comprehensive work "intended for serious collectors of plants". Sections include the history of house plants, plant origin, selection and cultivating, maintenance and propagation, pests and diseases. While title suggests indoor plants, some shrubs and trees are also included. The largest section includes entries for over 4,000 plant species, some not common in North America. Each entry includes a general description and growing requirements. Colour photographs for over 1,000 plant species, a glossary and index are provided.

Other guides to plants include *The American Horticultural Society Encyclopedia of Garden Plants* (Macmillan, 1989) (MTRL), a compendium of over 8,000 garden plants with thousands of colour illustrations, and *Reader's Digest Encyclopedia of Garden Plants and Flowers* (Reader's Digest, 1987, 4th ed.).

DH45 Davis, Brian. 1987. **The Gardener's Illustrated Encyclopedia of Trees & Shrubs: A Guide to More Than 2,000 Varieties.** Emmaus, PA: Rodale Press. 256 p.

Guide to over 2,000 trees and horticultural shrubs, with information on plant appearance, hardiness in temperatures, soil and light conditions, propagation, common problems, and typical growth patterns with colour photographs Another guide for the home gardener to the selection, care, and planting of popular North American trees, including flowering fruit trees, deciduous trees and shrubs, is *Taylor's Guide to Trees* (Houghton Mifflin, 1988) (SB435 T434 ARCH).
MTRL SCI/TECH

DH46 Eldin, Herbert. 1973. **Atlas of Plant Life.** New York: John Day. 128 p.

Atlas describing plant life found in each continent, including vegetation maps, climate descriptions, and the spread of plants by man. Indexed.
QK50 E3 BMED

DH47 **The Encyclopedia of Natural Insect and Disease Control: The Most Comprehensive Guide to Protecting Plants.** 1984. Emmaus, PA: Rodale Press. 490 p.

Guide to diseases and pests for garden plants.
MTRL SCI/TECH

DH48 Everett, T.H. 1980-82. **The New York Botanical Garden Illustrated Encyclopedia of Horticulture.** 10 vols. New York: Garland.

A comprehensive encyclopedic work which describes and evaluates more than 3,600 genera and 26,000 species of plant types found in Canada and the United States. Articles on fertilisers, propagation, pests and diseases, and tips for home gardening are also included.
SB317.58 E94 BMER

DH49 Gledhill, D. 1989. **The Names of Plants.** 2d ed. New York: Cambridge University Press. 202 p.

Includes an alphabetical glossary of scientific names of plants worldwide. Also includes information on the naming of plants, problems and rules of botanical nomenclature, the International Code of Nomenclature of Cultivate Plants, and botanical terminology. The *International Code of Botanical Nomenclature*, adopted by the Fourteenth International Botanical Congress, was published in 1988 (Koeltz Scientific Books, Konigstein, Germany) (QK96 I43 BOTA 1978).
QK96 G54 ESCI; ROMU

DH50 Horst, R. Kenneth. 1990. **Westcott's Plant Disease Handbook.** 5th ed. New York: Van Nostrand Reinhold. 953 p.

Standard reference for plant pathology provides information on more than 2,400 diseases and 1,200 plants, including flowers, shrubs, trees, vegetables and vines worldwide. Includes glossary, bibliography, index.
SB731 W47 SIGS (4th ed, 1979)

DH51 **HORTI,** Montreal: André Clouatre. database.

Contains information on 300 plant species in Canada, where they grow and optimum growing conditions.

DH52 Howes, F. 1975. **Dictionary of Useful and Everyday Plants and Their Common Names.** Cambridge: Cambridge University Press. 290 p.

This work, and John Willis' *Dictionary of the*

Flowering Plants and Ferns (Cambridge University Press, 1985) (QK45 W7 BMER 1973) combine to provide an overview of the plant world. Both are scholarly works listing terminology, trade and common names of plants, commercial plant produces, practical uses, origins, and other information.
QK45 H68 BOTA

DH53   Larousse Gardening and Gardens. 1990. Ed. by Pierre Anglade and others. New York: Facts on File. 624 p.

Translation of 1988 French edition. All aspects of gardening are covered with detailed technical information. Includes an encyclopedia of plants, including trees and a section on biographical information on botanists.

DH54   Little, R. John. 1980. **Dictionary of Botany.**   New York: Van Nostrand Reinhold. 400 p.

Short entries of a basic nature with some illustrations. A standard reference work first published in 1933, is *Hortus Third: A Concise Dictionary of Plants Cultivated in the United States and Canada* (3d ed, 1976) (SB45 B22 ROMU) which lists over 10,400 plants and botanists.
QK9 L735 BMER

DH55   Mulligan, Gerald A. and   Derek B. Munro. 1990. **Poisonous Plants of Canada.** Ottawa: Research Branch. Agriculture Canada. 96 p.

Catalogues Canadian plants (native and naturalized) which are poisonous to humans or animals, with descriptions, geographic ranges, toxic effects. Includes indexes of common and botanical names. Bibliography. A handbook to poisonous plants found around the world, particularly in Europe is *Colour Atlas of Poisonous Plants* by Dietrich Frohne (London: Wolfe, 1984) (QK100 F76 ROMU), which includes decorative and house plants, with many colour photographs.
R581.69 W959P

DH56   The Oxford Companion to Gardens. 1986.   New York: Oxford University Press. 635 p.

Covers gardens from earliest times to the present. Includes 1,500 scholarly entries by 170 international specialists.   Includes landscape architecture, important groups of plants, types of gardens with information on 700 significant gardens.
SB469.25 O95 BMED

DH57   Rodale's Encyclopedia of Indoor Gardening.   1980.   Ed. by A.M. Halpin. Emmaus, PA: Rodale Press. 902 p.

Contains information on tools and techniques of indoor gardening, plant types, special environments (greenhouses), and plant growth. Includes appendices with lists of societies and publishers in U.S. and Canada; a glossary; and two detailed indexes.
MTRL SCI/TECH

DH58 Scoggan, H.J. 1978-79. **The Flora of Canada.** 4 vols. Ottawa: National Museums of Canada.

Identifies 4,153 species of ferns and flowering plants found in Canada.
QK201 S39 BMED; BOTA; GEOL

DH59 Smith, Miranda and Anna Carr. 1988. **Rodale's Garden Insect, Disease & Weed Identification Guide.** Emmaus, PA: Rodale Press. 328 p.

Guide to over 200 common insects, diseases and weeds found in North American gardens, and the organic methods used to prevent and control them are described in detail. Illustrated with colour and black and white drawings, with tables and charts, glossary, and index to common and scientific names.
MTRL SCI/TECH

DH60 Rodale's Illustrated Encyclopedia of Herbs. 1987. Ed. by Claire Kowalchik. Emmaus, PA: Rodale Press, 1987. 545 p.

Description, usage, growing conditions and illustrations of herbs grown throughout the world.
MTRL SCI/TECH

DH61 Wyman, Donald. 1986. **Wyman's Gardening Encyclopedia.** 2d ed. New York: Macmillan. 1221 p.

A standard horticultural reference work for professionals and amateurs alike, which includes articles on all aspects of gardening, plants types, and related information, such as pesticide/herbicide use, and rules for importing plants.
SB450.95 W96 ARCH

Directories

DH62 Boivin, B. 1980. **Survey of Canadian Herbaria.** Québec: Université Laval. 187 p.

Brief description of 410 public and private herbaria, of which 160 are no longer in existence.
QK76 C2B65 BMED

DH63 Horticultural Research International: Directory of Horticultural Research Institutes and Their Activities in 63 Countries. 1986. 4th ed. Wageningen, Netherlands: International Society for Horticultural Science. 903 p.

A detailed directory of 16,650 horticultural scientists at 1,250 institutions in 63 countries around the world. Provides information on research stations, research currently in progress, and names of staff members. Chapters for each country describing growing conditions (rainfall, hours of sunlight, humidity, elevation, crops grown) also included.
SB44 I58 BMER (1973)

DH64 Index Herbariorum: Guide to the Location and Contents of the World's Public Herbaria. 1981. 7th ed. Utrecht: Bohn, Sheltema & Holkema. 452 p.
Lists herbaria and collectors.
QK75 I5 BOTA

DH65 North American Horticulture: A Reference Guide. 1982. New York: Scribner's. 367 p.

A directory of Canadian and American horticultural organizations, associations, government programs, and libraries arranged alphabetically by state with a section for Canada. Also includes a section on regulations for pesticide/herbicide usage, a list of awards and flower shows.
MTRL SCI/TECH

Zoology

Bibliographies, Abstracts and Indexes

DH66 Animal Behavior Abstracts, 1974- . Bethesda, MD: Cambridge Scientific Abstracts. quarterly.

An indexing and abstracting service with over 5,000 abstracts each year, covering communication, aggression, ethology, etc. Book reviews and notices of proceedings are included. Available online.
QL750 A53 BMER

DH67 Animal Identification: A Reference Guide. 1980. 3 vols. London: Natural History Section. British Museum. New York: Wiley.
Lists primary sources leading to identification of any animal from any part of the world.
Z994 T34A54 BMER

DH68 Aquatic Sciences and Fisheries Abstracts, 1971- . Bethesda, MD: Cambridge Scientific Abstracts. monthly with semi-annual index.
Formerly published in two parts, Part 1: *Biological Sciences and Living Resources*; Part 2: *Ocean Technology*. Revised into 3 parts: (1990) 1) *Living Resources*; 2) *Non-living Resources*; and 3) *Aquatic Pollution and Environmental Quality*. Reviews more than 5,000 journals and other source documents on all aspects relating to "biological sciences and the conservation and use of living resources as well as ocean technology, policy, and the use and conservation of non-living resources." Each issue contains 2,000 abstracts, with author, subject, taxonomic, and geographic indexes. Available online and on CD-ROM.
QH90 A64 ZOOL (part 1);
GC1 A68 PASR (part 2 and 3)

DH69 Database of Wildlife Research, 1974- . Zurich, Switzerland: Swiss Wildlife Information Service. database, updated quarterly.
An index to articles and books on international wildlife research, conservation and management, covering topics such as animal behaviour, diseases, ecology, population, etc. *The Wildlife Database* (1934- Julie Moore and Associates) indexes scientific literature on North American waterfowl, shore birds, game birds, birds of prey, oceanic birds, marine mammals, whales and bats, compiled from *Biological Abstracts, AGRICOLA, Zoological Record, Current Contents* and other sources.

DH70 Miller, Melanie Ann. 1986. **Birds: A Guide to the Literature.** New York: Garland. 887 p.
Attempts to cover the literature since 1800. Arranged by type of work (bibliographies, dictionaries), by topic, and by subject. Includes lists of works devoted to particular species and geographical areas.
MTRL SCI/TECH

DH71 Zoological Record, 1864- . London: Zoological Society of London. annual.
Title varies. Cites worldwide zoological literature with emphasis on systematic and taxonomic information. Arranged in three parts, 20 sections. Each section covers one genus with contents list, author, subject and systematic index. Available online.
Z7991 Z8 BMER

Encyclopedias, Dictionaries, Handbooks and Directories

GENERAL

DH72 Gamlin, Linda and Gail Vines. 1987. **Evolution of Life.** New York: Oxford University Press. 248 p.

Encyclopedic work dealing with evolution, genetics, and classification of life; the development of fungi, algae, lower invertebrates, arthropods, fish, amphibians, reptiles, birds and mammals; chemistry and the role of amino acids, enzymes, DNA; and the reproductive processes of fertilization, embryo growth and regeneration.
QH 308.2 G35 Ref ROMU

DH73 Grzimek's Encyclopedia of Evolution. 1977. Editor-in-chief Bernhard Grzimek. New York: Van Nostrand Reinhold. 560 p.

Grzimek's work is still useful and provides thorough and authoritative coverage of theories and research findings on evolutionary topics. This work is complementary to his *Animal Life Encyclopedia* (DH94n). A more recent work is *Encyclopedia of Evolution: Humanity's Search for its Origins* edited by Richard Milner (Facts on File, 1990) (GN281 M53 ERIN).
QE711.2 G79 BMER

DH74 Immelmann, Klaus and Colin Beer. 1989. **A Dictionary of Ethology.** Cambridge, MA: Harvard University Press. 336 p.

Based on earlier German language dictionaries by Klaus Immelman. Defines over 600 terms relating to animal behaviour and neighbouring disciplines, excluding highly technical terminology.
QL750.3 I4513 BMER; ZOOL

DH75 International Commission on Zoological Nomenclature. 1985. **Code international de nomenclature zoologique/International Code of Zoological Nomenclature.** 1985. 3d ed. Berkely, CA: University of California Press. 338 p.

Adopted by the 20th Congress of International Union of Biological Sciences, 1985.
QL353 I5 BMER

DH76 International Zoo Yearbook, 1959- . London: Zoological Society. annual.

Reviews recent developments and animal populations in zoos and aquaria around the world. A guide to zoos and aquariums in Canada and North America is *Lions and Tigers and Bears: A Guide to Zoological Parks, Visitor Farms, Nature Centers, and Marine Life Displays in the United States and Canada* by Jefferson Ulmer (Garland, 1984) (QL76.5 U6 U45 Ref ROMU).
QL76 I55O2 BMER, ZOOL

DH77 Leftwich, A. W. A. 1973. **Dictionary of Zoology.** 3d ed. London: Constable. 478 p.

Contains approximately 7,000 brief definitions of zoological terms, excluding medical and anatomical terms and elementary biological terms. Cross referenced with English names. Includes bibliography.
QL9 L4 BMER

DH78 Peterson Field Guide Series. 1947- . Boston: Houghton Mifflin.

A standard reference work in the sciences, some titles of interest for biologists include: *Animal Tracks* (Easton Press, 1985); *Field Guide to the Birds* (1980) (QL681 P45 BMER); *Field Guide to Western Reptiles and Amphibians* (2d ed, 1985) (QL651 S81 ROMU (1966)); and others.

DH79 Stokes, Donald W. 1986. **A Guide to Animal Tracking and Behavior.** Boston: Little Brown. 418 p.

Guide for the identification and discovery of North American animal tracks and trails and behaviour. The first section of the guide identifies mammal tracks, showing acutal size clear and unclear tracks; the second section describes the mammal's life and behaviour.
TPL

DH80 **Synopsis and Classification of Living Organisms.** 1982. 2 vols. Ed. by Sybil Parker. New York: McGraw Hill.

Compendium showing systematic positions of all living organisms, down to the family level. Includes over 8,300 brief articles arranged in taxonomic order with reference to the literature. Includes more than 8,000 articles written by 170 contributors from 12 countries writing in semi-technical language. Illustrated.
QH83 S78 BMER

DH81 **UFAW Handbook on the Care and Management of Laboratory Animals.** 1987. 6th ed. Comp. by Universities Federation For Animal Welfare. London: Longman. New York: Churchill Livingstone. 433 p.

Describes procedures for humane treatment of laboratory animals, including housing, transportation, anaesthesia, and euthanasia. *Alternatives to Laboratory Animals: ALTA* (FRAME: Fund for the Replacement of Animals in Medical Experiments, 1973- quarterly) (QH301 A48 PRRS) is an abstracting service covering aspects of the development, introduction, and use of alternatives to the use of laboratory animals in biomedical research and toxicity.
QL55 U65 BMED

INVERTEBRATES

DH82 Abbott, Tucker and Peter Dance. 1986. **Compendium of Seashells.** Melbourne, FL: American Malacologists. 411 p.

General handbook and identification guide written for the amateur shell collector, providing information and bibliographies. Includes photographs.
QL404 A23 BMER

DH83 **Comprehensive Insect Physiology, Biochemistry, and Pharmacology.** 1985. 13 vols. Oxford, U.K: Pergamon.

Compendium of 200 chapters summarizing the research and knowledge of insects from 1950 to mid 1982.
QL495 C64 ZOOL

DH84 The Insects and Arachnids of Canada, 1976- . Comp. by J.H. Martin. Ottawa: Agriculture Canada. irregular.

Series identifies and provides information on insects and arachnids found in Canada. Includes distribution maps.
QL476 C35 ROMU

DH85 Line, Les and others. 1983. **Audubon Society Book of Insects.** New York: Abrams. 260 p.

Survey of insects written for the general public. Includes many colour illustrations and an index of common and scientific names.
QL463 L44 ROMU

DH86 Scott, James A. 1986. **The Butterflies of North America: A Natural History and Field Guide.** Stanford, CA: Standford University Press. 583 p.

Covers identification, distribution, ecology, and behaviour of all 679 species found in Canada and the United States. Includes colour plates, illustrations, and line drawings, distribution maps, glossary and index. Another handbook which describes butterflies found in Europe is *Butterflies: A Colour Field Guide* (David & Charles, 1983) (MTRL).
QL548 S38 BMED

REPTILES AND AMPHIBIANS

DH87 **Amphibian Species of the World: A Taxonomic and Geographical Reference.** 1985. Ed. by Darrel R. Frost. Lawrence, KS: Allen Press. 732 p.

Dictionary for species names and taxonomic relationships, and a reference guide to the literature of herpetology and taxonomy, written by specialists from all over the world. Based on the International Code of Zoological Nomenclature.
QL645 A67 BMED

DH88 Cook, Francis R. 1984. **Introduction to Canadian Amphibians and Reptiles.** Ottawa: National Museum of Natural Sciences. 200 p.

Field guide to Caudata, Anura, Testudines, Squamata, with distribution maps. Covers habitats, characteristics, food etc. Includes information on pet care. Selective bibliography. International guides include *A Field Guide to the Reptiles and Amphibians of Britain and Europe* by E.N. Arnold (Collins, 1978) (QL658 A1A76 ROMU); R.L. Ditmars' classic *Reptiles of the World: The Crocodiles, Lizards, Snakes, Turtles and Tortoises of the Eastern and Western Hemisphere* (Lane, 1933) (QL641 D615 ROMU); and David Alderton's *Turtles and Tortoises of the World* (Facts on File, 1988) (C5 A43 SCAR).
QL654 C63 BMED

DH89 **The Encyclopedia of Reptiles and Amphibians.** 1986. Ed. by Tim R. Halliday, and Kraig Adler. New York: Facts on File. 143 p.

Summarizes information on biology and classification of species. Arranged by classes, with chapters on each order, with representative species described. Includes illustrations, glossary, selective bibliography, and index. *The Completely Illustrated Atlas of Reptiles and Amphibians for the Terrarium* by Frizt Jurgen Obst (T.F.H. Publications, 1988) (QL640.7 O28 ROMU) contains illustrated entries on all aspects of the care and maintenance of reptiles and amphibians in terraria.
QL640.7 E83 ROMU

DH90 Mehrtens, John M. 1987. **Living Snakes of the World in Color.** New York: Sterling Publishing. 480 p.

An identification guide to hundreds of snakes, with colour photographs.
QL666 O6M44 ROMU

MAMMALS

DH91 Banfield, W. F. 1977. **The Mammals of Canada.** Toronto: University of Toronto Press for the National Museum of Natural Sciences. 438 p.

Covers 196 species of animals, excluding fossils, known to have occurred since historical times in Canada or its coastal waters.
QL721 B34 BMER

DH92 **The Encyclopedia of Mammals.** 1984. Ed. by David Macdonald. New York: Facts on File. 895 p.

Covers about 4,000 important and unique species in 700 articles by international scholars. Includes evolutionary facts, appearance, social patterns, and environmental concerns. Illustrations show animals in habitats. Provides classification schedules, charts etc. *Walker's Mammals of the World* (4th ed, Johns Hopkins University Press, 1983) (QL703 W22 BMER) provides similar information.
QL703 E53 SIGR

DH93 Forsyth, Adrian. 1985. **Mammals of the Canadian Wild.** Camden East, ON: Camden House. 351 p.

U.S. edition entitled *Mammals of the American North*. Guide to mammals of the North American continent, arranged by species. Provides description, range, and behaviour. Illustrated, with glossary, bibliography, and index.
QL715 F67 SIGS

DH94 **Grzimek's Encyclopedia of Mammals.** 1989. 2d ed. 5 vols. Ed. by Bernhard Grzimek. New York: McGraw-Hill.

New edition of the *Mammals* section of the 13 volume *Grzimek's Animal Life Encyclopedia* (Van Nostrand Reinhold, 1972-76, first published in German in 1964) (QL45 G813 BMER). Complete coverage of mammals, including domesticated species and humans. Volume 1 contains general introduction to mammal evolution, anatomy, physiology, ethology and environmental issues. Entries grouped by order and include description of species habits and habitat. Well illustrated, with standardized charts. Each volume separately indexed, with no comprehensive index to the set. Includes guide to English, French, and German common names.
QL701 G7913 BMER

DH95 **The Illustrated Encyclopedia of Wildlife.** 1991. 15 vols. Chicago: Encyclopaedia Britannica.

Volumes 1-5: *Mammals*; Volumes 6-8: *Birds*; Volume 9: *Reptiles/Amphibians*; Volume 10: *Fishes*; Volumes 11-15 *Invertebrates*. Index in Volume 15. Animals grouped by order and family. Includes more than 7,000 illustrations and maps.

DH96 **Mammal Species of the World: Taxonomic and Geographic References.** 1982. Ed. by James H. Honacki, Kenneth E. Kinman, and James W. Koeppl. Lawrence, KA: Allen Press and the Association of Systematics Collections. 694 p.

Comprehensive and detailed taxonomic and geographic listing of all mammals species of the world.
QL708 M35 BMED

DH97 Wolfheim, Jaclyn H. 1983. **Primates of the World: Distribution, Abundance, and Conservation.** Seattle, WA: University of Washington Press. 831 p.

Describes the distribution, numbers, habitats and factors facing the primate species living in the wild. Another work is this area is Michael Kavanagh's *Complete Guide to Monkeys, Apes, and Other Primates* (Viking Press, 1983) (QL737 P9K38 SCC) which is a survey and classification guide to primates.
QL737 P9W64 BMED

BIRDS

DH98 **A Bird-finding Guide to Canada.** 1984. Ed. by James C. Finlay. Edmonton: Hurtig. 387 p.

Twelve chapters cover each province and territory, with descriptions of areas where birds can be sighted. Emphasis is on areas in parks or near urban areas, rather than wilderness.
QL685 B57 ROMU

DH99 **A Dictionary of Birds.** 1985. Ed. by Bruce Campbell, and Elizabeth Lack. Vermillion, SD: Buteo Books for British Ornithologists' Union. 670 p.

Supersedes *A New Dictionary of Birds*, edited by A. Landsborough Thomsom (McGraw-Hill, 1964). Articles range from brief definitions to several pages. Covers all aspects of ornithology, and also includes such subjects as birds in music, and birds in the Bible. Illlustrated, with bibliographies. *The Encyclopedia of Birds*, edited by Christopher M. Perrins, and Alex Middleton (Facts on File, 1985) (QL673 E53 SCAR; ERIN) is not as comprehensive as *The Dictionary of Birds*, but provides informative and detailed coverage of bird families, with illustrations.
QL672.2 D53 SCAR

DH100 Godfrey, W. Earl. 1986. **The Birds of Canada.** Rev ed. Ottawa: Nation Museum of Natural Sciences / National Museums of Canada. 595 p.

Appearance, measurements, field marks, habitat, nesting habits, and range provided for each species. Includes colour plates and pictures, line drawings, maps of breeding distribution, flight silhouettes. Consistent with American Ornithological Union checklist.
R598.2971 G583B   or   QL685 G6 ERIN Ref

DH101 **Handbook of North American Birds.** 1962- . New Haven, CN: Yale University Press.

Volume 1, *Loons Through Flamingoes*, (1962); Volumes 2-3, *Waterfowl*, (1976); Volumes 4-5 cover condors, eagles, falcons, hawks, kites, vultures, etc. (1988). Written at a scholarly level, but accessible to the layperson, the articles are based on comprehensive review of the literature and primary research by their authors. Extensive bibliographies. Taxonomic arrangement, with descriptions, subspecies, field identification, voice, habitat, distribution, migration, banding status, reproduction, survival, habits, and food.
QL681 P35   BMER: ZOOL

DH102 Jones, John Oliver. 1990. **Where the Birds Are: A Guide to all 50 States and Canada.** New York: Morrow. 400 p.

Compilation of information from national wildlife refuges and other organizations. Lists birding hotlines, bird clubs, descriptions and basic maps of birding areas, and a directory of wildlife refuges for each state/province. Data tables cover phylogenetic orders, and birds' seasonal status.
MTRL SCI/TECH

DH103 Sibley, C.G. and B. Monroe. 1991. **The Distribution and Taxonomy of Birds of the World.** New Haven, CN: Yale University Press. 1111 p.
QL678 S52 ROMU

DH104 Speirs, John Murray. 1985. **Birds of Ontario.** 2 vols. Toronto: Natural Heritage/ Natural History.

Volume 1 contains colour photographs, with short sketches of each species. Volume 2 provides more information and extended species counts. The *Atlas of the Breeding Birds of Ontario* compiled by Michael D. Cadman, Paul F.J. Eagles, and Frederick M. Helleiner, (University of Waterloo Press, 1987) (QL685.5 O6 A75 BMER; ZOOL), is the first Canadian breeding

bird atlas completed and published. Maps almost 300 species of birds nesting in Ontario from 1981 to 1985.
QL685.5 O6S67   BMER

DH105   Terres, John K. 1980. **The Audubon Society Encyclopedia of North American Birds.**   New York: Knopf. 1109 p.

Comprehensive coverage, with 6,000 entries on 847 species of birds in Canada, United States, Baja California, Greenland, and Bermuda. Illustrated. Biographical references, definitions, major articles.
QL681 T43   BMER

DOMESTIC ANIMALS

DH106   Cary, Pam. 1987. **The Horse: A Complete Encyclopedia.** London: Octopus Books. 224 p.

Written for the beginning horse enthusiast with illustrated articles on the history of the horse, descriptions of breeds, horse care, and sports. Another noted source in this area is *International Encyclopedia of Horse Breeds* by Jane Kidd (HP Books, 1986).

DH107   **The Complete Book of the Dog.** 1985. Ed. by Lizzie Boyd. New York: Holt Rinehart and Winston. 224 p.

Encyclopedia of dog breeds, including evolution and domestication, care of dogs as pets, behaviour, anatomy, training, and a description of dog breeds recognized by the American and United Kingdom Kennel Clubs. A pet care book called *Pet Owner's Guide to Dogs* (Howell Book House, 1986) (TPL), written by a noted authority Kay White, also provides advice for new pet owners and information on various breeds.

DH108   Harper, Don. 1987. **The Practical Encyclopedia of Pet Birds for Home and Garden.** New York: Harmon Books/Crown. 208 p.

Guide to care of pet birds, including feeding, handling, basic health care and breeding; cages and flights, and houses or enclosures for birds in the garden. Popular pet birds are described.

DH109   **Harper's Illustrated Handbook of Cats.** 1985. Ed. by Roger Caras. New York: Harper & Row. 191 p.

Provides information on North American cat breeds with colour photographs. Also includes a rating section for each breed for its companionship potential in various situations and a section on cat health and veterinary care. A general work about cats is by Dennis Kelsey-Wood, *The Atlas of Cats of the World: Domesticated and Wild* (TFH Publications, 1989), which describes 31 wild cats of the world and many domestic cats. The evolution of cats, and their domestication is discussed. A section on pet care is also included.

FISH AND MARINE MAMMALS

DH110   Axelrod, Herbert R. 1989. **Dr. Axelrod's Atlas of Freshwater Aquariam Fishes.** 3d ed. Neptune City, NJ: T.F.H. Publications. 797 p.

Arranged by geographic region, with colour photographs of each fish and information as to its feeding habits, reproduction, lighting requirements, temperament, and recommended aquarium. Designed for the advanced systematist. Hobbyists might use *Popular Tropical Fish for Your Aquarium*, (TAB Books, 1982). Marine fish for aquaria are described in *Dr. Burgess's Atlas of Marine Aquarium Fishes* (T.F.H Publications, 1989), and in *Popular Marine Fish for*

Your Aquarium by Martyn Haywood (TAB Books, 1982).
SF437 A93 ROMU (2d ed, 1986)

DH111 **Encyclopedia of Aquatic Life.** 1985. Ed. by Andrew C. Campbell, and Keith E. Banister. New York: Facts on File. 349 p.

Introduction to aquatic zoology with signed articles organized in 3 large sections: aquatic mammals (whales, dolphins and sirenians), fish, and aquatic invertebrates. Illustrated, and includes bibliography.
QL120 E53 ROMU

DH112 **Handbook of Freshwater Fishery Biology.** 1969–1972. 3d ed. 2 vols. Comp. by K.D. Carlander. Ames, IA: Iowa State University Press.

First published in 1953. Cumulation of data on age, growth, length, weight and other life history of the freshwater fishes of Canada and United States. Citations to further literature.
QL625 C373 BMED; ZOOL

DH113 **Handbook of Marine Mammals.** 1981–1989. 4 vols. Ed. by Sam H. Ridgway and Richard Harrison. London, Toronto: Academic Press.

Each volume covers different families, each chapter a different species. Volume 1: *The Walrus, Sea Lions, Fur Seals and Sea Otter*; Volume 2: *Seals*; Volume 3: *The Sirenians and Baleen Whales*; Volume 4: *River Dolphins and the Larger Toothed Whales*. Covers anatomy, physiology, behaviour, distribution, reproduction, the effects of man, and history of the scientific name. Includes bibliographic references, tables, charts, maps. Illustrated.
QL713.2 H35 BMED

DH114 McAllister, Don E. 1990. **A List of the Fishes of Canada.** Ottawa: National Museum of Natural Sciences. *Syllogeus* (series) no. 64. 310 p.

Lists all known species in Canadian marine, brackish, and fresh waters. Arranged by family, order, class, species and sub-species. English and French common and scientific names included. Another guide is *Freshwater Fishes of Canada* (Fisheries Research Board of Canada, 1979) (QL626 S284 SCC (1973)) which provides detailed information and illustrations for over 180 species of fish.
Sy150 no.64 ROMU

DH115 Minasian, Stanley M., Kenneth C. Balcomb and Larry A. Foster. 1984. **The World's Whales: The Complete Illustrated Guide.** Washington: Smithsonian Books. 224 p.

Describes morphology, biology, distribution, and status of living species, with numerous photographs and illustrations, brief glossary, bibliography, name and subject indexes. For information on whales found in Canada, consult *Guide to Watching Whales in Canada* (Dept. of Fisheries and Oceans, 1986) (QL737 C4B58 BMED).
QL737.C4 M664 ROMU

DH116 Nelson, Joseph S. 1984. **Fishes of the World.** 2d ed. New York: Wiley. 523 p.

Intended for fishery biologists and museum systematists for classification purposes. Describes orders, suborders, and families of fishes. Anatomical data and ecological status provided. Includes worldwide distribution maps and drawings.
QL618 N4 BMED

DH117 Robins, Richard. 1980. **List of Common and Scientific Names of Fishes from the United States and Canada.** 4th ed. Bethesda, MD: American Fisheries Society. 174 p.

Guide to the distribution of freshwater fish of the United States and Canada and well as some species found in the continental shelf to a depth of 200 meters. Includes a list of common names that reflect broad current usage.
QL618 A48 BMED

DH118 **Yearbook of Fishery Statistics,** 1947- Rome: Food and Agriculture Organization. annual.

Includes Catches and Landings; Fishery Commodities etc.
SH1 Y4 BMES   or   ZZ EM10 F38 GOVT

ENDANGERED SPECIES

DH119 **The Official World Wildlife Fund Guide to Endangered Species of North America.** 1990. 2 vols. Ed. by David W. Lowe, John R. Mathews, and Charles J. Moseley. Washington: Beacham Publishing.

Describes over 500 plants and animals that have been listed as endangered or threatened. Volume 1 includes plants and mammals, Volume 2 birds, fishes, insects, and other species. Each entry includes a detailed essay, a locater map, black and white photographs, tabular information on food, habits, reproduction and threats to the species, and a short bibliography. Each volume contains geographic indexes, species index, colour photographs, and a glossary. Volume 2 contains directory information.
QL84.24 O34 ROMU Ref

DH120 **On the Brink: Endangered Species in Canada.** 1989. Ed. by James A. Burnett and others. Saskatoon: Western Producer Prairie Books. 192 p.

One of a series of books sponsored by Environment Canada as a means of informing Canadians about the most pressing environmental issues in Canada today. Detailed descriptions are accompanied by photographs or paintings. Also includes range maps indicating distribution of each species.
QL84.24 O57 BMED

DI HEALTH SCIENCES

Consumer Health and Nutrition, Drug Information, and Occupational Health and Safety begin at entry numbers DI58, DI72, and DI86 respectively.

Guides to the Literature

DI1 Basler, B.K. and T.G. Basler. 1977. **Health Science Librarianship: A Guide to Information Sources.** Detroit: Gale Research. 200 p.

Annotated bibliography for librarianship in all of the health sciences: medicine, nursing, allied health, etc. in Canada and United States. History of medicine as a subject is excluded. Divided by subject areas based on collection and maintenance of health sciences library collection. Contains comprehensive annotations and short introductory paragraphs in each section, with an author and title index.

Collection development aids can also be found in "Core Lists", which are periodically published in health sciences journals. An example are the "Brandon Lists", by A.N. Brandon, published in the *Bulletin of the Medical Library Association* as an article "Selected List of Books and Journals for the Small Medical Library".
R026.61 AB15H

DI2 Chen, Ching-Chih. 1981. **Health Sciences Information Sources.** Cambridge, MA: MIT Press. 767 p.

Annotated reference guide to health sciences literature in all forms including periodicals, monographs, technical reports, government documents, etc. as well as selection tools, guides, handbooks for use by health sciences librarians. Materials are grouped in each section by subject, arranged by title. Primary as well as secondary sources are included. Review sources, when available, are provided. Reference lists specify important titles in each subject. Detailed table of contents, author and title indexes.
R610 A518H

DI3 Crawford, D.S. and M.A. Flower. 1985. **CANHEALTH: A Guide for Canadian Health Sciences Libraries.** Ottawa: Canadian Health Libraries Association. 97 p.

A guide to "Canadian information resources for the use of health sciences librarians working in Canada". Outlines the structure of the health sciences library community in Canada, and lists Canadian publications and services, including royal commissions, legislation, government documents, statistics, etc. of interest to health sciences librarians.
026.61097 C222C

DI4 Encyclopedia of Health Information Sources. 1987. Ed. by Paul Wasserman and Suzanne Grefsheim. Detroit: Gale Research. 483 p.

A bibliographic guide to approximately 13,000 citations for publications, organizations and other sources of information on more than 450 health related subjects. Broad scope covering more than 14 kinds of sources. Material prior to 1980 is excluded.
Z66658 E57 BMER

DI5 Haselbauer, Kathleen J. 1987. **A Research Guide to the Health Sciences: Medical, Nutritional and Environmental.** New York: Greenwood. 655 p.

A discussion of major reference sources in the fields of health, nutrition and environmental sciences. Approximately 2,000 critically evaluated titles are included.
Z6658 H35 BMER

DI6 Information Sources in the Medical Sciences. 1984. 3d ed. Ed. by L.T. Morton and S. Godbolt. London: Butterworths. 534 p.

Revised edition of Morton's *Use of Medical Literature* (2d ed., 1977). Comprehensive listing of information sources in the field of medicine and related sciences. Outline of general works is followed by a listing of works according to specialty. Historical, biographical and bibliographical sources in medicine covered briefly.
R118 M67 BMER

DI7 Roper, F. and J. Boorkman. 1984. **An Introduction to Reference Sources in the Health Sciences.** Chicago: Medical Library Association. 302 p.

Various types of reference and information sources and their use in reference work in the health sciences are covered. Emphasis is on U.S. publications, with some Canadian works included. Scope is broad rather than specific.
Z6658 R66 BMER

Bibliographies and Catalogues

DI8 Bibliography of the History of Medicine, 1985- . Bethesda, MD: U.S. National Library of Medicine. annual with quinquennial cumulation.

Citations taken mainly from *HISTLINE*, the history of medicine database supported by NLM. Individual and collective biographies are included.
Z6658 U54 O2 BMER

DI9 Bibliography of the History of Medicine of the United States and Canada, 1939–1960. 1964. 2d ed. Ed. by Genevieve Miller. Baltimore, MD: Johns Hopkins Press. 428 p.

This work is a reissue in consolidated form of the "Bibliography of the History of Medicine of the United States and Canada" which has been published annually since 1940 in the *Bulletin of the History of Medicine*. Divided into 16 subject areas, with an author index included.
Z6661 U5M5 BMER

DI10 Blake, J.B. and C. Roos. 1967. **Medical Reference Works, 1679-1966: A Selected Bibliography.** Chicago: Medical Library Association. 343 p. *Supplements*: 1970, 1973, 1975.

An annotated list of reference tools accessing medical, bioscientific and allied health literature held in the U.S. National Library of Medicine. Arrangement is by broad subject area with

international coverage. History of medicine is excluded.
Z6658 B632 BMER

DI11 Core Collection in Nursing and the Allied Health Sciences: Books, Journals, Media. 1990. Ed. by Annette Peretz. Phoenix, AZ: Oryx Press. 236 p.

A fully annotated guide to nearly 1,000 current books and non-print materials in 67 nursing and allied health subjects.
Z6675 N7 P46 BMER

DI12 Current Bibliographies in Medicine, 1988- . Bethesda MD: National Library of Medicine.

Continues the National Library of Medicine's *Literature Search Series*, which ceased publication in 1987 and the *Specialized Bibliography Series* which ceased in 1988. Each year approximately twenty bibliographies are published on current biomedical topics. The National Library of Medicine's computer databases are used to compile the citations; therefore the format of *CBM* is similar to other print sources published by National Library of Medicine such as *Index Medicus* (DI23).
Z6660 C787 BMER

DI13 Flemming, Tom and Diana Kent. 1990. **Sourcebook of Canadian Health Statistics.** Toronto: Canadian Health Libraries Association. 100 p.

Annotated bibliography of published sources of Canadian statistical information on health and health care. Covers vital and morbidity statistics, health care expenditures and utilization, personnel, education, chronic care, etc. Search strategies are discussed.
362.10971 AF599S

DI14 Medical and Health Care Books and Serials in Print, 1985- . 2 vols. New York: R.R. Bowker. annual.

Continues *Medical Books and Serials in Print* (1978–1984). Authors, title and subject indexes to in-print titles. Lists approximately 62,000 books and 11,000 serials from U.S., Canadian, and foreign publishers. Includes vendor listing of serials available online. Covers all fields of medicine, the behavioural sciences, health care, nutrition, etc., including veterinary medicine.
Z6658 M422 BMER

DI15 Morton, L.T. 1983. **A Medical Bibliography. An Annotated Check-list of Texts Illustrating the History of Medicine.** 4th ed. Aldershot, U.K.: Gower. 1000 p.

An updated version of Garrison and Morton's *Medical Bibliography* (1st ed, 1943). Annotated list of important contributions to medical literature with personal name and subject indexes.
R610 AG242 M3

DI16 NLM Current Catalog, 1966- . Bethesda, MD: National Library of Medicine. quarterly with annual, quinquennial cumulation.

Supersedes *NLM Catalog, 1960-1965* (6 volumes, 1966). Lists all items acquired by the NLM including all current monographs, serials, audiovisuals and microcomputer software distributed by the Medical Library Association. Subject as well as name and title sections are provided for both monographs and serials, with a separate section for medical reference books. Arranged by subject, according to MeSH.

Available online as *CATLINE* on *MEDLINE*.
Z6676 U486 BMER

DI17   Cumulative Index to Nursing & Allied Health Literature (CINAHL), 1983- . Glendale, CA: CINAHL. bimonthly, annual cumulation.

Indexes periodical literature in English for nurses, allied health professionals, medical librarians and others interested in health care issues. Covers over 300 international journals from 13 allied health fields and health sciences librarianship. Also included are biomedical, behavioural sciences, business, educational and popular literature articles. Separate indexes provide references to pamphlets, books and dissertations. Available online as *Nursing and Allied Health* and on CD-ROM.
Z6675 N7C83 BMER

Abstracts, Indexes and Databases

DI18   Current Contents: Clinical Medicine, 1973- . Philadelphia: Institute for Scientific Information. weekly.

Provides table of contents pages for 850 journals. (See DA15 for more information.) Also useful for Health Sciences are *Current Contents* in the following areas: *Agriculture, Biology and Environmental Sciences*; *Life Sciences*; and *Social and Behavioral Sciences*.
QD1 BMER

DI19   Excerpta Medica, 1947- . Amsterdam: Elsevier Science. 44 sections in numerous volumes. monthly with annual cumulation.

International abstracting service for medical related literature with particular emphasis on English-language European and Japanese sources. Complements *Index Medicus*. Excellent source for drug and pharmacological information. Available online and on CD-ROM as *EMBASE*.
R100 E895 BMER

DI20   FAMLI (Family Medicine Literature Index), 1980- . Willowdale, ON: College of Family Physicians of Canada. annual.

Comprehensive annual index to the literature of family medicine. Available online.
Z6660 F35 BMER

DI21   Health Periodicals Database, 1988- . Foster City, CA: Information Access Co. Updated weekly.

Covers health, medicine and nutrition topics for laypersons and professionals taken from 600 health and medical periodicals. When available, author's abstracts from technical journals supplemented by "consumer summaries". Some full text coverage. Reference guide available. No print version is available. In addition, Information Access Co. produces *Health Index*, which also provides consumer health information, such as fitness, nutrition, alcohol and drug abuse, healthy lifestyles, pregnancy, etc, taken from popular, business and academic journals and newspapers. Available online (1977-, updated monthly), and on CD-ROM.

DI22   Hospital Literature Index, 1945- . Chicago: American Hospital Association. quarterly with annual cumulation.

Guide to English language literature on hospitals and health care facility administration,

including organization, administration, economics, policy and planning, and theory of health care systems, taken from a variety of health care and non-health care journals. Available online.
Z6675 H75A52 BMER

DI23   Index Medicus: Including Bibliography of Medical Reviews, 1960- . Bethesda, MD: U.S. National Library of Medicine. monthly.

Index to over 3,500 biomedical journals in all languages (70% English). Access by author or subject headings based on controlled vocabulary (Medical Subject Headings, MeSH). Journal coverage revised annually. Supporting documentation such as list of MeSH terms, explanation of MeSH hierarchical structure and journals covered, published in January issues of *Index Medicus*. Annotated version of MeSH and Permuted MeSH are published as additional search aids.

A separate section entitled *Bibliography of Medical Reviews* appears in each issue which lists review articles of recent biomedical literature on all topics.

IM is available online or on CD-ROM as *MEDLINE* through *MEDLARS* and other vendors. Available in abridged form, published monthly, as *Abridged Index Medicus* and in annual cumulations as *Cumulated Abridged Index Medicus*.

Two reference manuals useful for online searching of *MEDLINE* are: *The Basics of Searching MEDLINE* (National Library of Medicine, 1989) (025.0661 N277BA), and *Online Services References Manual* (National Library of Medicine, 1988) (R025.524 O58V), which includes *MEDLINE*.

For assistance in locating journal holdings, the union list *Canadian Locations of Journals Indexed for MEDLINE / Dépôts canadiens des revues indexées pour MEDLINE* (1990, 19th ed., CISTI) (Z6660 C52 BMER) should be consulted.
Z6660 I42 BMER

DI24   Index to Dental Literature, 1962- . Chicago: American Dental Association and U.S. National Library of Medicine. quarterly.

Includes citations for journal articles, and for papers published in symposia and proceedings. Articles are indexed using (MeSH), and an alphabetical list of dental descriptors (MeSH terms related to dentistry) is included. Recently published dental books, and dissertations and theses, and a separate "Bibliography of Dental Reviews" is included in each issue. Available online and on CD-ROM on *MEDLINE*.
Z6668 I45 DENT

DI25   Index to Health Information, 1988- . Bethesda, MD: Congressional Information Service. quarterly.

Cumulated annually into Abstracts and Index volumes. Provides in-depth indexing to publications of U.S. federal and state governments, intergovernmental organizations, and other non-governmental institutions and organizations which contain health statistics and policy studies. Indexed materials available on microfiche from CIS.

DI26   International Nursing Index, 1966- . Philadelphia: American Journal of Nursing. quarterly.

Covers worldwide nursing literature. Available online. The Institute of Scientific Information has also created *Nursing Citation Index*, which lists all items cited in the articles indexed in *INI*.
Z6675 N7 I58 BMER

Reviews and Annuals

DI27 Annual Review Series, 1932- . Palo Alto, CA: Annual Reviews.

In-depth reviews with extensive bibliographies, in over 20 subject areas, e.g. *Annual Review of Public Health* (1981- RA421 A66 BMES), and *Annual Review of Medicine* (1950- R101 A5 BMES).

DI28 Index to Scientific Reviews. 1974- See DA22n for full entry information.

DI29 The World Book Health and Medical Annual, 1987- . Chicago: World Book. annual.

Supplement to the *World Book Encyclopedia* (AI15), this annual covers medical topics of popular interest, and is not a systematic overview of all medical developments of the year of publication.

DI30 Year Book Series, 1901- . Chicago: Year Book Medical Publishers. annual.

Comprised of 36 different yearbooks, each devoted to one medical area of specialization. Abstracts the year's best articles from more than 700 US and foreign medical and allied health journals. Each entry includes bibliographic information, as well as signed critical evaluations. Author and Drug/Subject index is included. Examples include *Year Book of Otolaryngology - Head and Neck Surgery* (1985), *Year Book of Geriatrics and Gerontology* (1988).

Encyclopedias and Dictionaries

DI31 The American Medical Association Encyclopedia of Medicine. 1989. Ed. by Charles B. Clayman. New York: Random House. 1184 p.

Includes more than 5,000 medical terms with 2,200 illustrations and photographs. Written for the lay person, defines common and rare disorders, symptoms, drugs with their generic, brand-name and major pharmaceutical groupings, and tests, procedures, and surgical operations. Indexed and cross-referenced.
R610.3 A512

DI32 Dictionnaire anglais français des sciences medicales / English French Dictionary of Medical and Paramedical Sciences. 1984. Comp. by W.J. Gladstone. St. Hyacinthe, PQ: Edisem. 1081 p.

Another multilingual dictionary is the classic *Elsevier's Medical Dictionary in Five Languages: English, French, Italian, Spanish and German* (2d rev. ed, 1975) (R121 E45 BMER).
R121 G52 BMER

DI33 Dorland's Illustrated Medical Dictionary. 1988. 27th ed. Philadelphia: W.B. Saunders. 1888 p.

A standard dictionary of medical terminology aimed to meet the needs of students and practitioners of medicine and related fields. Includes a section on pronunciation, transliteration, word formation, and various useful appendices such as lists of syndromes, medical tests, etc. Used by NLM for preparation of *Index Medicus* and various *MEDLARS* databases.
R121 D73 BMER

DI34 **Encyclopedia and Dictionary of Medicine, Nursing, and Allied Health.** 1987. 4th ed. Philadelphia: W.B. Saunders. 1427 p.

Encyclopedic dictionary containing current terms used in health sciences. Short cross-referenced encyclopedic articles for organs, systems, diseases, concepts in health care, and patient care are included. Numerous appendices are included.
R121 M65 BMER

DI35 Hamilton, Betty and Barbara Guidos. 1988. **MASA: Medical Acronyms, Symbols, and Abbreviations.** 2d ed. New York: Neal Schumann. 278 p.

Quick reference to over 32,000 abbreviations and acronyms arranged alphabetically. Followed by brief symbols section.
R123 M236 BMER

DI36 **International Dictionary of Medicine and Biology.** 1986. 3 vols. New York: John Wiley.

Comprehensive unabridged interdisciplinary medical dictionary with concise definitions and etymologies in biology and medicine as well as anthropology, biomedical engineering, environmental health, and veterinary medicine. Contains more than 151,000 terms with cross-references. Entries for the individuals for whom syndromes are named are included, along with biographical data.
R121 I58 BMER

DI37 Magalini, Sergio. 1990. **Dictionary of Medical Syndromes.** 3d ed. Philadelphia: Lippincott. 1042 p.

Provides information about individual syndromes or "symptom complexes" from every branch of medicine. For most syndromes, includes name, synonyms, symptoms, signs, etiology, pathology, diagnostic procedures, therapy, prognosis, and a bibliography which contains citations to the original description of the syndrome and to current studies on the condition. Includes combined subject/eponym index.
RC69 M35 BMER

DI38 **Mosby's Medical, Nursing and Allied Health Dictionary.** 1990. 3d ed. St. Louis, MO: C.V. Mosby. 1608 p.

A comprehensive dictionary which provides current definitions for nursing and allied health, as well as medical terminology. Definitions are written in encyclopedic style with illustrations, charts, and tables. Includes a colour atlas of human anatomy, detailed appendices, anatomy tables, drug names and drug interactions, and other information.
R121 M69 BMER

DI39 **Stedman's Medical Dictionary.** 1990. 25th ed. Baltimore, MD: Williams and Wilkins. 1784 p.

The first edition of this classic work appeared in 1911. Includes "Medical Etymology" section and "Subentry Index", a valuable master cross-reference in locating elusive subentry terms within the vocabulary. 518 in-text illustrations include 24 colour anatomical plates. Also included are pharmacological, and dental terms. Provides technical medical vocabulary, with definitions requiring little knowledge of medical terminology.
R121 S8 BMER

DI40 **Taber's Cyclopedic Medical Dictionary.** 1989. 16th ed. Ed. by Clayton Thomas. Philadelphia: F.A. Davis Company. 2401 p.

Provides coverage of the basic medical terminology plus material specific to nursing and many allied health disciplines. Standard abbreviations and synonyms, illustrations and tables are included. Detailed information on measurement systems, conversion rules, nutritive value of food, symptoms and signs of drug abuse. Extensive cross references.
R121 T14 BMER

DI41 Webster, J. 1988. **Encyclopedia of Medical Devices and Instrumentation.** 4 vols. New York: Wiley.

More than 250 articles emphasizing the contributions of engineering, physics, and computers in many areas of medicine. Covers broad topics as well as specific instruments. Historical overviews, illustrations and bibliographies included.
R856 A3E53 BMER

Handbooks

DI42 **The American Medical Association Handbook of First Aid and Emergency Care.** 1990. 2d ed. Ed. by Stanley M. Zydlo and James A. Hill. New York: Random House. 352 p.

Entries are arranged alphabetically and each contains a "what to do" list, symptoms, care, and treatment. Sports injuries are included.

DI43 **Canadian Health Care Management,** 1986- . 2 vols. Toronto: MPL Communications. looseleaf.

Service for senior health care professions, highlighting current trends and activities, reports, legislation, management techniques, in the Canadian health care system. Volume 1 contains core material, which includes articles on managing services, administrative controls, etc. Volume 2 contains topical material on current events. Supplemented by the monthly journal *The Dispatch.*

DI44 **Conn's Current Therapy,** 1949- . Philadelphia: W.B. Saunders. annual.

(43rd ed, 1991). Provides the practicing physician with an up-to-date definitive reference for problems frequently encountered in practice. Many expert contributors recommend drugs and therapeutic methods. Indexed.
RM101 C872 BMES

DI45 **Current Medical Diagnosis and Treatment.** 1974- . Norwalk, CT: Appleton & Lange. annual.

Comprehensive source for information on currently accepted methods of diagnosis and treatment of medical diseases and disorders. Other titles by publisher cover obstetrics, pediatrics and surgery, etc.
RC71 C872 OS BMER

DI46 **Handbook of Medical Library Practice.** 1982. 4th ed. 3 vols. Chicago: Medical Library Association.

A practical set of manuals for health sciences librarians that provides instructional information on collection organization and dissemination of health science library resources, service and management. Scope is U.S. medical and academic health science libraries. Volume 1: *Public Services in Health Science Libraries*; Volume 2: *Technical Services;* Volume 3: *Administration and Health Science Librarianship.*
026.61 M48H4 or Z675 M4H33 BMER

DI47 Merck Manual: A Handbook of Diagnosis and Therapy, 1899- . Ed. by Robert Berkow. Rahway, NJ: Merck. irregular.

(15th ed., 1987). The most widely used medical text in the world, with goal of providing useful information to practicing physicians, medical students, and health care professionals. Discusses diseases and disorders, common clinical procedures and laboratory tests; new technological procedures are described. Current therapy is listed. Detailed index.
RC55 BMES

DI48 Scientific American Medicine, 1986- . New York: Scientific American Inc. looseleaf, updated monthly.

Describes basic principles of diagnosis and therapy and is a guide for physicians in clinical decision making. Includes a section on current topics in medicine, diseases, interdisciplinary medicine, etc., with detailed index.
R11 S3 BMER

Meetings

DI49 Information about health sciences meetings and conferences can be found in *World Meetings: Medicine*, DA73, and *Directory of Published Proceedings: Series SEMT- Science/ Engineering/ Medicine/ Technology*, DA25. *Medical Meetings*, (Laux Company, bimonthly), contains international listings of meetings and and meeting facilities, and the *Journal of the American Medical Association, (JAMA)*, publishes "Reference Directories" twice yearly which lists international meetings by date.

Statistics

DI50 Health Reports, 1989- . Ottawa: Statistics Canada, Ministry of Supply and Services. quarterly.

Statistical data on many topical areas in the health field in Canada. Includes highlights of recently released data and analytical articles supporting the statistical information. Graphs and charts complement the text.
RA407 A1H43 PRRS

DI51 Hospital Statistics Preliminary Annual Report, 1970- . Ottawa: Statistics Canada, Ministry of Supply and Services. annual.

Bilingual report containing statistics on hospital utilization and expenditures across Canada. There is a similar publication entitled *Hospital Statistics*, published by the Ontario Ministry of Health (RA983 A4 O5853 BMER). American hospital statistics can be found in the similarly titled *Hospital Statistics* (1946-, American Hospital Association, annual) (RA981 A2A6234 BMER), which provides data on U.S. hospital usage, personnel, facilities and services, finances, revenue, and hospital approval and affiliations.
RA983 A1A262 BMES

DI52 World Health Statistics Annual / Annuaire de statistiques sanitaires mondiales, 1962- . Geneva: World Health Organization. annual.

Complete source of vital statistics, lifetables, morbidity rates, etc. for every country in the world. Published quarterly and cumulated in this annual publication.
RA407 W6O2 BMER

Directories

DI53 Canadian Handbook of Medical and Surgical Specialists, 1988- . Don Mills, ON: Southam Business Information and Communications Group. annual.

Directory of medical specialists listed alphabetically by specialty. Includes school/date of graduation and a geographical alphabetical list by province and by city. Information about medical societies, including dates and locations of conventions and meetings is provided. Compiled in cooperation with the Royal College of Physicians and Surgeons, and La Corporation Professionelle des Médécins du Québec. A similar work for the U.S. is *Directory of Medical Specialists* (Chicago: Marquis Who's Who, 1990, 3 vols.) (R712 A1D5 BMER)
R729.5 S6 C35 BMER

DI54 Canadian Hospital Directory, 1953- . Toronto: Canadian Hospital Association. annual.

Contains extensive information about hospitals in Canada. Arrangement by province, with address, phone number, departments, administrators, number of beds, outpatient health service centres, nursing stations. National and provincial departments of Health and Welfare, a buyer's guide, and educational programs in various health fields also included. A statistical compendium includes health and hospital expenditures, measures of patient utilization and personnel paid hours. The Canadian Hospital Association also publishes separate directories for long-term care hospitals, nursing homes, centres for mentally/physically handicapped and special care centres. As well, Statistics Canada publishes *List of Canadian Hospitals* (1988- annual) (RA983 A1A285 BMER), containing similar information.

Hospitals in the United States are listed in *American Hospital Association Guide to the Health Care Field* (Chicago, AHA, annual).
RA977 C33 BMER

DI55 Canadian Medical Directory, 1955- . Don Mills, ON: Southam Business Information and Communications Group Inc. annual.

An alphabetical and geographic listing of Canadian physicians and surgeons, hospitals and medical facilities and recent graduates, schools, associations and societies including addresses and phone numbers and brief biographical information. Provincial lists such as *Ontario Medical Directory* (1878- . Toronto: College of Physicians and Surgeons, annual) are also available.

A similar work for the U.S. is *American Medical Directory* (Chicago: AMA, 1906- biennial) (R712 A1A6 BMER).
R713.01 C3 BMER

DI56 Health Sciences Information in Canada: Associations. 1984. Ottawa: Canada Institute for Scientific and Technical Information.

Lists all groups whose goals relate to the physical and emotional health of Canadians, including nearly 500 associations in all areas of health sciences. Contact person, address and phone numbers, date of establishment, statement of purpose, membership, etc. are provided. Arranged geographically by province with a federal chapter. A related title is *Health Sciences Information in Canada: Libraries* (CISTI, 1986, Z675 M4H43 BMER), a directory of libraries which contain over 500 titles in a health sciences collection.
R118.4 C2H42 BMER

DI57 **Medical and Health Information Directory**, 1978- . 3 vols. Detroit: Gale Research. triennial.

(5th ed, 1989-90). "Comprehensive source of information on medical and health related organizations and programs, publications and libraries in the United States". Master name and keyword indexes included.
R118.4 U6M4 BMER

Consumer Health Information

Additional information on nutrition, food, and cookery is available in *Agriculture*, Section DJ, under "Food and Food Production".

Guides, Bibliographies and Indexes

DI58 **Consumer Health and Nutrition Index**, 1985- . Ed. by A.M. Rees. Phoenix, AZ: Oryx Press. quarterly.

Provides access to information covered in 80 specialized and general interest periodicals written for health-conscious laypersons, particularly in areas of nutrition, diseases, drugs, exercise, etc. See also *Health Periodicals Database* and *Health Index* (DI21), two databases which also contain information of interest to consumers.

DI59 **Consumer Health Information Source Book.** 1990. 3d ed. Ed. by Alan M. Rees and Catherine Hoffman. Phoenix, AZ: Oryx Press. 210 p.

An annotated bibliography and directory to over 1,700 sources for consumer/patient health information. Part 1 is an introductory chapter on health information and medical consumerism. Parts 2 and 3 list sources of information, including clearinghouses and information centres, hotlines, and services available to the public. Catalogs, pathfinders and other publications for the consumer health library collections are included.
Z6673 R43 BMER

DI60 Szilard, Paula. 1987. **Food and Nutrition Information Guide.** Englewood, CO: Libraries Unlimited. 358 p.

Guide to "standard reference sources, diet manuals, nutrition and food consumption surveys, government publications and other specialized nutrition sources." Covers food standards, regulations, analysis, etc.
Z5776 N8594 BMER

Encyclopedias and Handbooks

DI61 **The American Medical Association Family Medical Guide.** 1987. Rev. ed. Ed. by Jeffrey R.M. Kunz and Asher J. Finkel. New York: Random House. 832 p.

Intended for use in the home. Sections deal with healthy lifestyles, symptoms and self-diagnosis, simple explanations of diseases, and caring for the sick. Includes charts, illustrations, index. Another work of the American Medical Association for home use is *Home Medical Advisor: The New Self Help Guide to Symptoms, Diseases and Medical Emergencies* (1988).
RC81 A543 BMER

DI62 **Canada's Food Guide Handbook.** 1982. Rev. ed. Ottawa: Health and Welfare Canada. 56 p.

Written for nutritionists, dietitians, and the lay person, includes information on Canada's Food Guide, use of the Food Guide in various settings,

explanations of nutritional concepts, and a resource list to further reading. Related publications also from Health and Welfare Canada include *Recommended Nutrient Intakes for Canadians* (1983) (TX353 R49 BMER), which replaces the *Dietary Standard for Canada*, and *Nutrient Value of Some Common Foods* (1988) (TX 551 C23 BMER), which lists the nutrient values and content of over 700 commonly used foods in Canada.
TX360 C3C365 BMER

DI63   The Columbia Encyclopedia of Nutrition. 1988. Ed. by Myron Winick. New York: Putnam. 349 p.

Written for the lay reader, provides current and authoritative information about nutrition, including vitamins, caffeine, salt, cancer prevention. Indexed.
QP141 C58 BMER

DI64   Complete Book of Vitamins and Minerals. 1988. Ed. by *Consumer Guide*. Lincolnwood, IL: Publications International. 320 p.

Written for the consumer, provides information on the function of nutrients, their value, dangers of deficiency and overdose. Includes "Supplement Product Profiles" which lists product names, manufacturer, dosage, nutrients included, and comments. Other similar works are H. Winter Griffith's *Complete Guide to Vitamins, Minerals and Supplements* (Fisher Books, 1988) which includes a section on medicinal herbs, and Sheldon Saul Hendler's *Vitamin and Mineral Encyclopedia* (Simon & Schuster, 1990), which describes and evaluates acids, lipids and their derivatives.

DI65 Dunne, Lavon J. 1990. **Nutrition Almanac.** 3d ed. New York: McGraw Hill. 313 p.

The value of nutrients, their role and the benefits from particular vitamin and mineral supplements are discussed. Includes a "Table of Food Composition" which presents a nutrient analysis of over 600 foods, and a "Nutrient Allowance Chart", which provides a breakdown of individual nutrients needs based on body size, metabolism, and caloric requirements.

A useful handbook for consumers is Brice Kratzer's *Nutrition: Where Have All These Labels Been?* (Dallas Sandt), which describes the kinds of information found on food labels with respect to nutrition, calories, recommended daily allowances, etc. Examples of labels from 1,200 foods in "generic" rather than "brand" name categories are provided in a consistent format for easy comparison.
RA784 N86 SIGR

DI66 Garrison, Robert H. Jr. and Elizabeth Somer. 1985. **The Nutrition Desk Reference.** New Canaan, CT: Keats Publishing. 274 p.

Covers nutrition basics and research for laypersons and professionals.

DI67   The Healthsharing Book: Resources for Canadian Women. 1985. Ed. by K. McDonnell and M. Valverde. Toronto: The Women's Press. 199 p.

Written by members of Women Healthsharing, the work is a resource manual on issues related to women's health, of interest to Canadian women. *Healthsharing Magazine*, published nationally by Women Healthsharing (Toronto, 1979- quarterly), provides current information on this topic.
RA778 H43 BMER

DI68 The Marshall Cavendish Illustrated Encyclopedia of Family Health: Doctor's Answers. 1984. 24 vols. Freeport, NY: Marshall Cavendish.

More than 900 individual articles, arranged alphabetically, give factual information about each topic for the layperson. Topics include pregnancy and childbirth, aging, health problems of men and women, keeping fit, medicines and drugs, and emergencies and first aid, alternative medicine, mental health, dental health, etc. Each article features a special section giving the "Doctor's" straightforward answers to the most relevant questions.
R121 M69 BMER

DI69 Mayo Clinic Family Health Book. 1990. Ed. by David E. Larson and others. New York: Morrow. 1378 p.

Home health care guide, covering such areas as life cycles, keeping fit, diseases and disorders, and modern medical care, diagnosis, and therapy. Indexed.

DI70 The New A to Z of Women's Health. 1989. Ed. by Christine Ammer. New York: Facts on File. 496 p.

Comprehensive guide to over 900 medical terms for women, covering birth to old age. Topics include diet, health, exercise, weight control, infertility, pregnancy. Useful as a layperson's guide to obstetrics and gynecology. Cross referenced with subject index.

DI71 Understanding Canada's Prescription Drugs: A Consumer's Guide, see DI85 for full entry information.

Drug Information

DI72 Snow, Bonnie. 1989. **Drug Information: A Guide to Current Resources.** Chicago: Medical Library Association. 243 p.

An extensive bibliographic guide to drug information designed for use as a "self-study text". Covers such topics as sources of information, terminology, issues of concern, and problems in drug information provision.
615.1 AS674D or RS91 S66 BMER

DI73 Canadian Drug Identification Code / Code canadien d'identification des drogues, 1972- . Vanier, ON: Drug Information Division, Health and Welfare Canada. annual.

Supersedes the *Canadian Formulary*. The *Code* lists over 18,000 drug products offered for sale in Canada, with an alphabetical listing by product trade name and product identification numbers, drug identification numbers, manufacturer, and active ingredient code. The *Code* represents the closest equivalent to an official national compendium available in Canada. Useful companions to the Canadian *Code* would be the *United States pharmacopeia XXII - National formulary XVII* (1989), and the *British pharmacopeia and National formulary*, as well as the *Cumulative list of proposed international nonproprietary names for pharmaceutical substances* (1962-) published by the World Health Organization.
RS6 C35 BMER

DI74 Canadian Medical Association. 1990. **Guide to Prescription and Over-the-Counter Drugs.** Ed. by M.S. Berner and G.N. Rotenberg. Montreal: Reader's Digest Association (Canada). 592 p.

Includes information about brand name and generic drugs, vitamins, minerals and food additives. Published in the United States under the same name, but by the American Medical Association.
RM301.12 C36 BMER

DI75 Compendium of Pharmaceuticals and Specialties (Canada), 1960- . Toronto: Canadian Pharmaceutical Association. annual.

(CPS, 25th ed. 1990). Standard work used by pharmacies and doctor's offices for information on drug products available in Canada, with indications, contra-indications, precautions, adverse effects, overdose symptoms, treatments, dosage and suppliers. Includes colour product recognition charts. Information is provided by pharmaceutical manufacturers. CPA also publishes *Self-Medication: A Reference for Health Professionals* (1988, 3d ed) (RM671 A1C35 BMER).
RS141.23 C62 BMER

DI76 Drug Evaluations, 1986- . Milwaukee, WI: American Medical Association. quarterly.

Formerly called *AMA Drug Evaluations* (RM300 A5462 BMER), the last edition published in 1986. Contains information for physicians and health care professionals on the clinical use of drugs, including comparative evaluations, adverse reactions, precautions and drug interactions. Organized into sections and chapters based on therapeutic classification (e.g. neurologic drug, respiratory drugs) with three introductory chapters. An annual bound version is available.
RM300 A5462 BMER

DI77 Drug Facts and Comparisons. 1987. Philadelphia: J.B. Lippincott. 2200 p.

Bound version of monthly looseleaf edition called *Facts and Comparisons*. Provides easy comparison of therapeutic aspects of similar products, and through a cost index figure, a comparison of prices of similar products.
RM300 D743 BMER

DI78 Handbook of Non-Prescription Drugs, 1967- . Ed. by E. Feldman. Washington: American Pharmaceutical Association. irregular.

(8th ed, 1986). Written and reviewed by pharmaceutical authorities, this book is designed for pharmacists providing customer counselling in the choice of over-the-counter (OTC) drugs. Includes only American OTC products.
RM671 A1H35 BMER

DI79 Jacobs, M. and K. O'Brien Fehr. 1987. **Drugs and Drug Abuse: A Reference Text.** 2d. ed. Toronto: Addiction Research Foundation. 640 p.

Designed for general public and "special public" such as hospital emergency departments, police, judges, lawyers, social workers and teachers.
RC564 D784 BMED (1983)

DI80 Martindale: The Extra Pharmacopoeia, 1883- . London: The Pharmaceutical Press. quinquennial.

(1989, 29th ed.) Comprehensive source of drug information for the practicing physician. Entries on some 4,000 substances arranged in 72 chapters. Abstracts of important papers and publications are included. Developments in

therapeutics, and drugs to treat infections are given high priority. Also includes a directory of manufacturers; an index to clinical uses, as well as a general index. Available online.
RS141.3 U3 BMER

DI81 **Merck Index: An Encyclopedia of Chemicals, Drugs, and Biologicals,** 1889- . Rahway, NJ: Merck & Co. irregular.

(11th ed, 1989). An index to more than 10,000 organic chemicals, mostly of medicinal significance, "serving chemists, pharmacists, physicians and others in allied professions". Includes therapeutic category and biological activity index, formula index, cross-index of names. International in scope. Literature references provided. Available online.
RS356 M524 BMER

DI82 **Meyler's Side Effects of Drugs: An Encyclopedia of Adverse Reactions and Interactions.** 1987. 11th ed. Ed. by M.N. Dukes. Amsterdam: Elsevier. 960 p.

Covers the adverse reactions to and interactions of medicinal substances. Contains reviews of more than 9,000 articles published annually on clinically relevant side effects and interactions of all drugs currently in use. Includes index of drugs and index of side effects. Available online and on CD-ROM as *SEDBASE*.
RM301 S532 BMER

DI83 **PDR: Physician's Desk Reference: Drug Interactions and Side Effects Index,** 1947- . Oradell, NJ: Medical Economics Books. annual; updated by supplements.

(44th ed, 1990). This U.S. equivalent of *CPS* (DI75) is an annual compilation of drug information provided by American drug manufacturers. Includes drug manufacturers' index, product category index, generic and chemical name index, conversion tables, discontinued products list. Another *PDR* book available from the same publisher is *Physician's Desk Reference Consumer's Guide to Nonprescription Drugs* (1990, 11th ed.) The former is available online and on CD-ROM.
RS75 P5 BMER

DI84 Sittig, Marshall. 1988. **Drug Companies and Products Worldwide Guide.** Kingston, NY: Sittig & Noyes. 596 p.

A list of international pharmaceutical companies, providing address, telephone numbers, a list of manufactured products (with generic and trade names), and product information (date of introduction, and purpose). Used as a companion volume to *Pharmaceutical Manufacturing Encyclopedia* (Noyes, 1988, 2 vols), (RS51 S56 BMER), which describes the manufacturing process, raw materials used, and product separation techniques, of almost 1,300 pharmaceuticals available worldwide. A related publication is *World Pharmaceuticals Directory* (Unlisted Drugs, 1980- published triennially) (RS74 W67 BMER), which lists over 200,000 drugs and 8,200 pharmaceutical research and marketing organizations worldwide.
RS356 S58 BMER

DI85 Smith D. 1989. **Understanding Canadian Prescription Drugs: A Consumer's Guide to Correct Use.** Toronto: Key Porter Books. 389 p.

Endorsed by the Canadian Pharmaceutical Association and directed to the Canadian health care consumer. Provides general instructions on administering medication, an index of Canadian trade versus generic drug names, and specific drug instructions arranged alphabetically by generic drug name. Instructions include purpose, interactions, precautions, possible reactions, refill information, and storage information.

Appendices give information on foods high in potassium for those taking diurectics, information for diabetics, and tips for detecting drug tampering.
RS51 S65 BMER

Occupational Safety and Health

DI86 CCINFO databases. 1986- . Hamilton, ON: Canadian Centre for Occupational Health and Safety.

The Canadian Centre for Occupational Health and Safety (CCOHS) provides a computerized information service called *CCINFO* to government, management and labour for occupational health and safety concerns. The service is available online as *CCINFOline* and on CD-ROM as *CCINFOdisc*. There are over 45 databases available on *CCINFOline*. Access to *CCINFOdisc* is available through four series: Series A1 *MSDS* (Material Safety Data Sheets); Series A2 *CHEM Data*; Series B1 *OHS Source*; and Series B2 *OHS Data*; each series containing a selection of databases.

DI87 Encyclopaedia of Occupational Health and Safety. 1983. 3d rev. ed. 2 vols. Ed. by Luigi Parmeggiani. Geneva: International Labour Office.

Intended for use by those who are concerned with or responsible for workers' health and safety. Covers fields of toxicology and occupational hygiene, occupational cancer, diseases of agricultural workers, occupational safety, and psycho-social problems. Bibliographic references are included with each entry. Arranged in alphabetical order with an analytical index.
HD7261 I44 BMER

DI88 Handbook of Occupational Safety and Health. 1989. 4th ed. Ottawa: Communications Division, Treasury Board of Canada. 459 p.

Contains main directives and standards of health and safety in the workplace within the federal public service. Includes policies dealing with smoking, protective clothing, employee assistance; legislation; standards; procedures; advisory notes; guides and fire protection services.
KE4979 A72 T74 ENGR

DI89 Occupational Health & Safety Management Handbook. 1989. 1 vol. Ed. by Frances Makdessian and Scott Williams. Toronto: Corpus Information Services.

Contains current information on federal and provincial government legislation, services and contacts; critical statutes for areas of accident writing, employer duties, labelling requirements, etc; WHMIS; workers' compensation appeals. Also lists organizations, information sources, professional development and education resources, software, and consultants.
HD7658 C6 BMER

DJ AGRICULTURE

This section includes agriculture, food and food production, wines, veterinary science, and forestry. For gardening and horticulture see the section on Botany in *Biological Sciences*, DH.

Agriculture

Bibliographies and Guides

DJ1 Agricultural and Animal Sciences Journals and Serials: An Analytical Guide. 1986. Comp. by Richard Jensen and Connie Lamb. Westport, CT: Greenwood Press. 211 p.

A bibliography with short, nonevaluative entries describing some 370 research-oriented serials in the fields of agricultural economics, agronomy, animal science, fisheries, forestry, horticulture, and veterinary science. Appendices list online databases and microform and reprint companies. Includes geographical, publisher, subject and title indexes.

DJ2 The Green Revolution: An International Bibliography. 1986. Comp. by M. Bazlul Karim. Westport, CT: Greenwood Press. 288 p.

Includes annotated entries to over 2,000 monographs, reports, articles published in scholarly and popular journals, papers presented at conferences on the agricultural developments and economic aspects in developing countries. Organized by geographical region with several subject chapters.
Z5075 D44 K37

DJ3 Guide to Sources for Agricultural and Biological Research. 1981. 2d ed. Ed. by J.R. Blanchard and L. Farrell. Berkeley, CA: University of California Press. 735 p.

Contains 5,779 annotated, evaluative entries taken from the agricultural literature published between 1958–1979 in the areas of food and food production, wildlife management, agricultural implications of pollution control, and maintenance of the environment. Organized by subject. Updates *Literature of Agricultural Research* (1958).
Z5071 G83 BMER

DJ4 **Information Sources in Agriculture and Food Science.** 1981. Ed. by G.P. Lilley. London: Butterworths. 618 p.

A basic guide to agricultural research for undergraduate students. Includes mainly British resources, arranged in 2 parts: General Areas and Specialized Areas. Part one lists databases, maps as sources, statistics, libraries, and their uses. Specialized areas include agricultural engineering, herbicides, husbandry, agrarian history, forestry, etc.

Abstracts, Indexes and Databases

DJ5 **AGRICOLA,** 1976- . Beltsville, MD: U.S. Dept. of Agriculture, National Agricultural Library. database

Database contains over 2.5 million citations to worldwide literature, including books, journal articles, book chapters and government reports, in the National Agricultural Library and other cooperating institutions. Coverage includes all areas of general agriculture, including animal and plant science, agricultural pests and diseases, veterinary medicine, aquaculture, animal and human nutiriton, rural sociology, agricultural economics, soil science, forestry, pollution as related to agricultural processes, energy in agriculture, and agricultural information systems. Available online and on CD-ROM. Print versions include *National Agricultural Library Catalog* (DJ12), *Bibliography of Agriculture* (DJ7), and *Food and Nutrition Quarterly Index* (DJ38).

Agricultural Terms, As Used in the Bibliography of Agriculture, (2d ed. Oryx Press, 1978) (Z695.1 A4T54 ROBA; BMER) contains over 37,000 terms used in the National Agricultural Library database, with cross references. North American emphasis.

DJ6 **AGRINDEX,** 1975- . Rome: Food and Agriculture Organization, United Nations. monthly.

Produced from *AGRIS*, the international information system for the agricultural sciences and technology, with references to current international research and development literature relevant to food, agriculture and allied fields. Classified subject order; indexes for personal and corporate authors, commodities, report and patent numbers. Especially useful for information published in or about developing countries. Available online and on CD-ROM.
Z5073 A456 BMER

DJ7 **Bibliography of Agriculture,** 1942- . Phoenix, AZ: Oryx Press. monthly.

Citations to over 100,000 journal articles, pamphlets, government documents, special reports and proceedings each year. Arranged within 96 broad subject categories such as plant science, food science, human nutrition, etc. Based on the data from the National Agricultural Library (NAL). Available online and on CD-ROM as *AGRICOLA* (DJ5).
Z5071 U52 BMER

DJ8 **Biological and Agricultural Index,** 1964- . New York: H.W. Wilson. monthly.

Continues *Agricultural Index* (1916-1964). Subject index to approximately 200 general American, Canadian and other Commonwealth scientific journals. Covers areas of agriculture, agricultural chemicals, economics, engineering, animal husbandry, biochemistry, food science, forestry, genetics, horticulture, plant pathology, etc. Available online and on CD-ROM.
Z5073 A452 BMER

DJ9 CAB Abstracts, 1973- . Wallingford, Oxon, U.K: Commonwealth Agricultural Bureaux (CAB) International. monthly.

CAB Abstracts in print form comprises a series of some 50 abstract journals each covering an aspect of agricultural research, including *Review of Pathology, Veterinary Bulletin, Dairy Science Abstracts, Nutrition Abstracts, Agriculture Engineering Abstracts, Soils and Fertilizers.* Each journal abstracts international literature, and approximately 130,000 items from some 8,500 journals are abstracted annually. The database contains over 2.3 million citations to articles and other literature covering topics in agriculture, applied biology, sociology and economics, animal science, dairy science, agricultural technology, engineering, forestry, veterinary medicine, etc. Available online and on CD-ROM.

DJ10 CCINFO databases, 1986- . Hamilton, ON: Canadian Center for Occupational Health and Safety.

The Canadian Centre for Occupational Health and Safety (CCOHS) provides a computerized information service called *CCINFO* to government, management and labour for occupational health and safety concerns. The service is available online as *CCINFOline* and on CD-ROM as *CCINFOdisc*. Series A1 *MSDS* (Material Safety Data Sheets) contains several databases of interest to agriculturalists, including *Regulatory Information on Pesticide Products (RIPP)*, which provides ready to use information on products under Agriculture Canada's *Pest Control Products Act*; *Pest Management Research Information System*; *Maximum Residue Limits in Foods*, etc.

DJ11 Current Contents: Agriculture, Biology and Environmental Sciences, 1970- weekly.

Includes animal sciences, veterinary medicine and animal health, as well as agricultural topics. See DA15 for full entry information.

DJ12 U.S. National Agricultural Library. National Agricultural Library Catalog, 1966- . Totawa, NJ: Rowman & Littlefield. monthly; semi-annual, and annual cumulation.

Supplement to *Dictionary Catalog of the National Agricultural Library* (1862-1965, 73 vols). The *Catalog* provides a list of new additions to the NAL. Entries arranged by broad subjects; indexes for specific subjects, personal and corporate authors, titles.
Z5076 U5 BMER

DJ13 World Agricultural Economics and Rural Sociology Abstracts, 1958- . Wallingford, Oxon, U.K: CAB International. monthly.

Provides abstracts to articles on agricultural economics, supply/demand and prices, marketing and distribution, international trade, fram economics, and rural sociology, among other topics. Includes an annual geographic index. Available online and on CD-ROM through *CAB Abstracts* (DJ9).
HD1401 W6

Reviews, Annuals and Statistical Sources

DJ14 FAO Yearbook, 1976- . Rome: Food and Agriculture Organization. annual.

In two parts: *Production*, and *Trade*. The *FAO Production Yearbook*, formerly *Production Yearbook* (1958-75), provides statistical data on food and agriculture, such as land population, agricultural production, food supplies, wages, freight rates, etc. Tables are included. The *FAO*

Trade Yearbook, formerly *Trade Yearbook* (1958-75), provides statistics on trade in agricultural products, and the value of agricultural trade by country. Both are updated by *FAO Monthly Bulletin of Statistics* (1978-).

FAO also publishes *FAO Fertilizer Yearbook* (1952-, annual), (UN9 FA F21 EFS GOVT) which discusses world production, consumption, and prices of fertilizer, with tables of import/export figures.
UN9 FA Y22 EFS GOVT

DJ15 The State of Food and Agriculture, 1947- . Rome: Food and Agriculture Organization. annual.

Title varies. Each issue focuses on a particular topic or topics in agriculture (e.g. Women in Developing Agriculture). All issues also include tables for agricultural, fishery, and forest products statistics, as well as the amount of production, the volume of exports and imports, and country data indicating the importance of agriculture in the country's economy.
S401 U6A317 BMES

DJ16 World Agricultural Statistics: FAO Statistical Pocketbook, 1983- . Rome: Food and Agriculture Organization. annual with quarterly updates.

Provides concise data on important indicators (land use, population, production of crops, fish and forest products, food supply, means of production, and external trade), relating to agriculture, fishery, forestry and food for a 25 year period. Covers all countries and continents. More detailed information can be found in *FAO Yearbooks* (DJ14).
UN9 FA W53 EFS GOVT

DJ17 World Crop and Livestock Statistics, 1948-1985: Area, Yield and Production of Crops. 1987. Rome: Food and Agriculture Organization. 760 p.

Updates the 1966 FAO *World Crop Statistics*. Includes statistics on 237 crops and major livestock products from 170 countries. Similar tables are found in the FAO *Production Yearbook*.
UN9 FA3 1987 F01 GOVT

DJ18 The Yearbook of Agriculture, 1894- . Washington: Government Printing Office. annual.

Prepared by the U.S. Department of Agriculture. Each volume discusses specific topics in agriculture, for example, *Animal Health* (1984), *Farm Management* (1989), and *Using Our Natural Resources* (1983). A more specialized publication is *Yearbook of Agricultural Co-operation* published annually by the Agricultural and Food Research Council since 1927, which provides international data on co-operative farming developments, research, and concerns.
S21 A35 ESCS

Dictionaries

DJ19 Dalal-Clayton, D.B. 1985. **Black's Agricultural Dictionary.** 2d ed. London: A.C. Black. 432 p.

Contains entries to over 4,000 terms used primarily in British agriculture.
S411 D35 BMER (1981)

DJ20 Haensch, G. 1986. **Dictionary of Agriculture in Six Languages: German, English, French, Spanish, Italian, Russian.** 5th rev. ed. Amsterdam: Elsevier. 1264 p.

Lists of equivalent words of some 11,000 terms in food and agriculture, economic and sociological agriculture, animal production, plant

cultivation, farm buildings and machinery, etc. In German followed by five other languages. Regional differences are noted, e.g. American and British variations. Indexed.
S411 H34 BMER (4th, 1975)

DJ21 Schlebecker, John T. 1989. **The Many Names of Country People: An Historical Dictionary from the Twelfth Century Onward.** Westport, CT: Greenwood Press. 325 p.

A unique dictionary describing the meaning and history of names of people involved in agriculture since 1100 AD to present day from North America, Great Britain, Canada, Australia, New Zealand, South Africa, and the West Indies. Useful for agricultural historians. Includes terms such as "bumpkin", "stablehand", "capelclawer".
S411 S34 BMED

Handbooks and Manuals

DJ22 Briggs, H.M. 1980. **Modern Breeds of Livestock.** 4th ed. New York: Macmillan. 802 p.

Handbook describing the various breeds of cattle, swine, sheep, goats, and horses mainly found in North America.
MTRL SCI/TECH

DJ23 **Canadian Farm Buildings Handbook.** 1988. Ottawa: Agriculture Canada. 155 p.

Lists guidelines for design and evaluation of farm buildings, complementing the *Canadian Farm Building Code*. Useful for planning, layout and construction of farm buildings.

DJ24 Clayton, J.S. 1977. **Soils of Canada.** 2 vols. Ottawa: Research Branch, Department of Agriculture.

Comprehensive description and analysis of Canadian soil, discussing formation, distribution and utlization of soil in Canada. Volume 1 *Soil Report*, written at both general and technical levels, includes colour plates; Volume 2 *Soil Inventory* includes distribution, temperature, and moisture in areas across Canada. A 44 page glossary of terms is included. An international source is the *Handbook of Soils and Climate in Agriculture* (CRC Press, 1982), which lists data on soils and soil conservation.
S599.1 A1S6 BMED

DJ25 **CRC Handbook of Plant Science in Agriculture.** 1987. 2 vols. Boca Raton, FL: CRC Press.

Selection of papers which act as a guide to current information on economically important crops. Some topics include genetics, environmental factors and plant growth, production and utilization.
SB91 C775 ESCI

DJ26 Culpin, C. 1986. **Farm Machinery.** 11th ed. London: Collins. 450 p.

A handbook of farm machinery, including tractors, ploughs, pumps, root-harvesting machinery, equipment for livestock husbandry and milk production, environment control aspects. Many illustrations.
MTRL SCI/TECH

DJ27 Grigg, D.B. 1974. **The Agricultural Systems of the World: An Evolutionary Approach.** Cambridge: Cambridge University Press. 358 p.

A useful reference work for students of agriculture describing the history and evolution of modern agriculture, with an analysis of various systems used around the world. Extensive bibliographies are included. Another work by

A.N. Duckham, *Farming Systems of the World* (Chatto & Windus, 1970) (S493 D79 BMED), provides a chapter on farming systems used in Canada.
S439 G788 BMED

DJ28   Manual of Pest Control. 1984. 5th ed. Ed. by A.S. West. Ottawa: National Defence. 40 p.

An extensive, well-illustrated manual for information on the life cycles and habits of pests (insect, animal and plant), and methods, equipment and materials needs for their control. For users of pesticide, for both domestic and commercial purposes, there is the *Pesticide Handling: A Safety Manual* (4th ed, Health and Welfare Canada, 1986) (SB952.5 S67 BMER).
SB950 M3 BMER

DJ29   Nyvall, Robert F.   1989.   **Field Crop Diseases Handbook.** 2d ed. New York: Van Nostrand Reinhold. 817 p.

Provides information on 1,200 diseases affecting 25 field crops, from alfalfa to wild rice. Entries include bacteria, fungi, nematodes, etc. Bibliographies and a glossary are included. Indexed.
MTRL SCI/TECH

DJ30   Pest Control Canada: A Pesticide Reference Manual. 1990. 6th ed. Burlington, ON: PACS. 234 p.

Directory of 2,400 pesticides and herbicides, listing producers, laboratories, and poison control centers, as well as general information about the pesticides.
HD9660 P33C36 FORE

DJ31   The Pesticide Manual: A World Compendium. 1987. 8th ed. Croydon, U.K.: British Crop Protection Council. 1081 p.

List of pesticides and compounds in use, compounds no longer in use, list of further references, a directory of companies, and indexes listing Chemical Abstracts Registry Numbers, and common and trade names of pesticides used.
SB951 M48 FORE (1968)

DJ32 Watterson, Andrew. 1988. **Pesticide Users' Health and Safety Handbook: An International Guide.** New York: Van Nostrand Reinhold. 504 p.

Discussion of over 200 pesticides, discussing usage and hazards. Includes detailed appendices listing agencies, U.S. legislation, etc, and helpful fact sheets.
SB951 W36 Ref ERIN

Directories

DJ33   ACCIS Guide to United Nations Information Sources on Food and Agriculture. 1987. Comp. by the Advisory Committee for the Coordination of Information Systems. Rome: Food and Agriculture Organization. 124 p.

Listing of libraries, documentation centers, specialized centers involved with food or agriculture, databases, and other publications, mostly within the United Nations system, are included in this guide. Arranged by subject, it includes the technical, social and economical aspects of feed and agriculture, fisheries, but excludes forestry. Entries describe the source, size of collection, databases available, and contact names. Complements, but does not overlap *Agricultural Research Centres* (DJ35).
S494.5 I47A22 BMER

DJ34 **Agricultural & Veterinary Sciences International Who's Who.** 1987. 3d ed. 2 vols. Harlow, U.K: Longman.

Entries include short biographical information on 7,500 internationally renowned agricultural and veterinary scientists in disciplines of agricultural economics, agricultural engineering, botany, aquaculture, food science and technology, horticulture, soil science, forestry, plant production, veterinary medicine and zoology.

DJ35 **Agricultural Research Centres: A World Directory of Organizations and Programmes.** 1988. 9th ed. 2 vols. Harlow, U.K: Longman.

Directory listing over 8,000 international public and private organizations and laboratories active in agricultural and veterinary science. Profiles list official title, address, telephone numbers, products, affiliations, activities and publications. Organized by country. Detailed subject index.

Atlases

DJ36 **Atlas of Canadian Agriculture.** 1979. Comp. by M.J. Toughton. London, ON: Department of Geography, University of Western Ontario. 104 p.

A portfolio of maps based on the 1971 Census of Agriculture.
G1116 J1T74 MAPL fo

Food and Food Production

This section includes information on the commercial production of food, nutritive values of food, and cookery. For sources related to food production for the home gardener, see the Botany and Horticulture section in Biological Sciences, DH38-DH65. Nutrition from a medical perspective is found in the Consumer Health and Nutrition section in Health Sciences, DI58-DI71.

Guides, Bibliographies and Indexes

DJ37 **Food and Nutrition Information Guide,** 1987. See DI60 for full entry information.

DJ38 **Food and Nutrition Quarterly Index,** 1985- . Phoenix, AZ: Oryx Press. quarterly.

The most complete and current source of information on nutrition. Index of the cataloguing records in the U.S. Department of Agriculture Food and Information Center. Organized into main subject sections: agriculture; geography, climate and history; education, extension and advisory work; administration and legislation; economics, development and rural sociology; food science and food products; human nutrition; home economics; and auxiliary disciplines. Includes indexes for author, title, subject, and intellectual level.

DJ39 Green, Syd. 1985. **Keyguide to Information Sources in Food Science and Technology.** New York: H.W. Wilson. 231 p.

Annotated guide to sources in food technology and food science on topics such as beverages, dairy products, food additives, etc. Also includes a directory of selected international organizations, and indexes for names, subjects, organizations, and geographic areas.
TP370.5 G76 BMER

Encyclopedias, Dictionaries, Handbooks and Annuals

DJ40 Adrian, J. 1988. **Dictionary of Food and Nutrition.** New York: VCH. 233 p.

Dictionary-type handbook with data relating to the chemistry, physiology, biochemistry, nutrition, and processing of foods. Includes tables and appendices on the composition of foods. A related publication is the *Dictionary of Food Ingredients* by Robert Igoe (Van Nostrand Reinhold, 1989) (TX551 I26 BMER), which describes ingredients in foods, use of food additives, both natural and preservatives, functions of ingredients, and other topics.
QP141 A37813 BMED

DJ41 **Advances in Food and Nutrition Research**, 1948- . New York: Academic Press. irregular.

Critical review with bibliographies, at the professional level. Formerly *Advances in Food Research* (1948-1988).
TX537 BMES

DJ42 Catsberg, C.M.E. 1990. **Food Handbook.** Chichester, U.K: Ellis Horwood. 382 p.

Information on food production, technologies, consumption, nutrition, with chapters on various types of foods, or topics relating to foods.

DJ43 Coyle, L. Patrick. 1982. **The World Encyclopedia of Food.** New York: Facts on File. 790 p.

Contains over 4,000 entries of varying length on international food and beverages, including the history of the food, method of consumption, description, geographic locations found, etc. Photographs and drawings included as well as charts on nutritive values, and a section on wine are included.
R641.0321 C881 EDUC

DJ44 **Foods and Food Production Encyclopedia.** 1982. Ed. by Douglas M. Considine. New York: Van Nostrand Reinhold. 2305 p.

Contains over 1,200 entries, with tables and illustrations, on food production, including the initiation of the natural food-growth cycle (seed, roots); nurturing of plants and animals to harvest time; and the food processing and production phase. Methods and practices from around the world are discussed.
TX349 F67 BMER

DJ45 **Knott's Handbook for Vegetable Growers.** 1988. 3d ed. Ed. by Oscar A. Lorenz. New York: Wiley. 456 p.

Compendium on commercial vegetable production, with information on soils, planting times, fertilizers, watering, pests and diseases, seed production, storage, harvesting, and greenhouse vegetable production. Technological advances are discussed. Tables, charts, diagrams, and illustrations are provided. A similar publication is Walter Splittstoesser's *Vegetable Growing Handbook: Organic and Traditional Methods* (3d ed, Van Nostrand Reinhold, 1990), which contains information on vegetable culture, including descriptions of the plant, culture, harvesting, and common agriculture problems associated with vegetable production.
SB321 K49 ERI

DJ46 Lewis, Richard J. 1989. **Food Additives Handbook.** New York: Van Nostrand Reinhold. 592 p.

Information on the food industry, listing over 1,300 food additives, with each entry listing identifiers, properties, food-related uses, occu-

pational restrictions, and toxicological data. U.S. regulations for shipping, handling, and use of substances are outlined, as well as a safety profile summarizing major products for toxicity, reactivity, and other dangerous properties. In Canada, consult Linda Pim's *Additive Alert: A Guide to Food Additives for the Canadian Consumer* (Rev. ed., Doubleday, 1990) (TX553 A3P5 SIGS 1983), or *Legislative Review and Encyclopedia of Food Chemicals* (Food in Canada, 1983-) (TX553 A3L4), which lists laws and legislation in Canada pertaining to food additives.
TX553 A3L49 BMER

DJ47 Newcombe, Duane. 1989. **The Complete Vegetable Gardener's Sourcebook.** Rev. ed. New York: Prentice Hall. 408 p.

Information on vegetable gardening, soils, nutrients, organic gardening, greenhouse gardening, seed types, and general information about varieties, days of growth, size of yield and plant descriptions. Indexed, with tables, illustrations and lists of suppliers.
MTRL SCI/TECH

DJ48 Tanaka, Tyozaburo. 1976. **Tanaka's Cyclopedia of Edible Plants of the World.** Tokyo: Yugaku-sha Publishing Co. 924 p.

An international handbook describing edible plants, their distribution, common and Latin names, recipes, and references to further information. Fodder and plants used for drugs are not included. Another work which lists edible and inedible plants that are used for food or economic value is George Usher's *Dictionary of Plants Used by Man* (Hafner, 1974) (QK9 U82 BMER).
QK98.5 A1T36 BMER

Wine

DJ49 Johnson, Hugh. 1985. **The World Atlas of Wine: A Complete Guide to the Wines and Spirits of the World.** 3d ed. New York: Simon & Schuster. 320 p.

A standard reference work for information about wine. Chapters include an introduction to wine and wine making; choosing and caring for wine; wine growing regions in France, West German, Southern and Eastern Europe, the Mediterranean, and North America; and the production of spirits and liqueurs. Wine growing districts, with descriptions of prominent wines and vintners, and maps of the various regions are also included. Bibliographies are provided at the end of chapters.

Other standards include *Alexis Lichine's New Encyclopedia of Wines and Spirits* (5th ed, Knopf/Random House, 1987) (MTRL SCI/TECH), which describes the history of wine and wine making, with an emphasis on European wines, and Tom Stevenson's *Sotheby's World Wine Encyclopedia: A Comprehensive Guide to the Wines of The World* (Little, Brown, 1988) (MTRL) which describes wines from all over the world.
TP548 J66 MAPL (1978)

DJ50 Robinson, Jancis. 1986. **Vines, Grapes and Wines.** New York: Knopf/Random House. 280 p.

A basic reference guide to information about the nine "classic" grape varieties used for wines, (including Cabernet, Sauvignon, Merlot, Pinot Noir, Syrah, Riesling, Chardonnary, Sauvignon Blanc, Sémillon, and Chenin Blanc). In addition to maps of where the variety grows, and illustrations of leaf and grape clusters, information on how it grows, how it is tended, the microclimates

and soils used is also provided. The wine production in the five largest world vineyards is analyzed, and there is a country-by-country survey of grape growing.
MTRL SCI/TECH

Veterinary Science

DJ51 **Animal Health Yearbook,** 1958- . Rome: Food and Agriculture Organization, World Health Organization, and International Office of Epizootics. annual.

Provides information on animal diseases, data on international trade in livestock and livestock products, worldwide disease occurences (e.g. rabies) and controls for mammals and birds, bees and fish. Arranged geographically. Indexed.
SF600 A55 BMES (1965-1988)

DJ52 Blood, D.C. 1989. **Veterinary Medicine: A Textbook of the Diseases of Cattle, Sheep, Pigs, Goats, and Horses.** 7th ed. London: Baillière Tindall. 1502 p.

Handbook of general and special medicine for livestock animals. *Zoo and Wild Animal Medicine* edited by M.E. Fowler. (W.B. Saunders Co., 1986) is a handbook to general and special medicine for amphibians and reptiles, birds, mammals, invertebrates.
SF745 B65 BMED (1963)

DJ53 **Black's Veterinary Dictionary.** 1988. 16th ed. Ed. by Geoffrey West. Totowa, NJ: Barnes & Noble. 703 p.

A standard reference work for veterinary medicine, covering the anatomy, physiology, diseases, diagnosis and treatment, and first aid of large and small animals. A similar work is *Concise Veterinary Dictionary* (Oxford University Press, 1988), which covers anatomy, husbandry, endocrinology, immunology, surgical operations, toxicology, diseases, physiology and biochemistry.
SF609 M5 BMER

DJ54 **The Merck Veterinary Manual: A Handbook of Diagnosis and Therapy for Veterinarians.** 1986. 6th ed. Rahway, NJ: Merck & Co. 1677 p.

Manual for treatment of North American animals. Sections include anatomy and physiology, behaviour, clinical procedures, fur, laboratory and zoo animals, husbandry and nutrition, poutlry, toxicology, and pharmacology. Indexed.
SF745 M4 PHAR

DJ55 **The Veterinary Annual,** 1957- . Bristol, U.K: Scientechnica. annual.

Extensive articles, with bibliographies, on current topics in veterinary science, as well as general articles on livestock, domestic, and wild animals. A similar work published in North America is *Advances in Veterinary Science and Comparative Medicine* (Vol. 13, 1969-, Academic Press, annual) (FS745 A282 BMES 1969-1989).
SF601 V48 BMES (1959-1986)

Forestry

DJ56 **Canada's Forest Inventory.** 1986. Ottawa: Supply and Services. 60 p.

Published at approximately five year intervals. Summarizes data on "the extent, ownership, productivity, species composition, maturity and volume of the forest resource" in all regions of Canada.
SD145 B65 ESCI

DJ57   Databook on Endangered Tree and Shrub Species and Provenances. 1986. Rome: Food and Agriculture Organization. 524 p.

Guide to 81 international tree and shrub species which the FAO has determined to have an international socioeconomic importance, and which are considered to be threatened with extinction. Entries include a botanical description, distribution, ecology, uses, conservation measures recommended or currently in place.
QK86 A1D37 ESCI

DJ58   The Encyclopedia of Wood: A Tree-by-Tree Guide to the World's Most Versatile Resource. 1989. Ed. by Aidan Walker. New York: Facts on File. 192 p.

Information on the appearance, properties, and uses of 150 types of timber from around the world. Also is an overview of the world wood industry. Information on tree anatomy, growth patterns for grain and texture, deforestation and conservation, and aspects of the wood industry from logging and milling to finishing. Includes distribution maps and charts summarizing wood characteristics, as well as colour photographs, and a glossary.

There are several classic works in this area, others including *Wood Structure and Identification* by H.A. Core (Syracuse University Press, 1979) (SD536 C67 FORE) which focuses on wood properties; and *Commercial Timbers of the World* by Douglas Patterson (5th ed, Gower Publishing, 1988) (TS804 T57 FORE), which emphasizes the architectural and engineering requirements of timber, its properties, and general information on timbers.
TA419 E53 ESCR

DJ59   Forestry Abstracts, 1939- . Oxon, U.K: CAB International. monthly.

Provides over 6,000 abstracts each year on forestry, silviculture, forest management, mycology and pathology, catchment management, conservation, arboriculture, and other subjects. CAB International also publishes *Forest Products Abstracts*, which deals with the forest products industry, the use of wood, types of timber, surface finishes, pulp industries, and marketing and trade (monthly, 1978-) (SD430 F64 BMER; ESCR). Both are available online through *CAB Abstracts* (DJ9).
SD1 F66 FORE

DJ60   Forestry Handbook. 1984. 2d ed. Ed. for the Society of American Foresters. New York: Wiley. 1335 p.

A handbook for the practicing forester, with information on forest ecology, geology, soils, climatology, insect and disease management, timber measurements, logging, and other areas. Includes bibliographies.
SD373 F58 FORE

DJ61   Forest Inventory Terms in Canada / Terminologie de l'inventaire des forêts du Canada. 1989. 3d ed. Ed. by B.D. Haddon. Chalk River, ON: Forestry Canada. 109 p.

Describes the terminology of Canadian forest and land classifications, mapping, field sampling, remote sensing, and other information of interest to foresters. International forestry terminology is found in *Forestry and Forest Products Vocabulary* by M. Ruokonen (Commonwealth Agricultural Bureaux, 1984) (SD126 R8 FORE), which defines over 14,000 terms. Corresponds to terms used in *Forestry Abstracts* and *Forestry Products Abstracts* (DJ59).
SD126 C36 ESCR

DJ62 Johnson, H. 1984. **Hugh Johnson's Encyclopedia of Trees.** Rev. ed. Ed. by D. Taylor. London: Mitchell Beazley. 336 p.

First edition published as *The International Book of Trees* (1973). This work is a guide to the trees of the world, with over 1,000 illustrations, providing information on rates of growth, botanical names, etc. A reference section on how to select trees for gardens is included. A similar work is *The Oxford Encyclopedia of Trees of the World* (Oxford University Press, 1981) (QK475 O93 BMER). For trees of North America, a comprehensive 2 volume work is *The Audubon Society Field Guide to North American Trees* (Knopf, 1980) (QK481 L49 SCC), with over 650 species, most with illustrations, and Alan Mitchell's *The Trees of North America* (Facts on File, 1987), covering over 500 species and 320 varietes of trees growing in North America, are frequenty used for tree identification.
QK475 I56 ESCI (1973)

DJ63 Lauriault, Jean. 1989. **Identification Guide to the Trees of Canada.** Markham, ON: Fitzhenry & Whiteside. 479 p.

Covers 149 tree species growing in Canada. Includes English, French, and Latin names of species, the family, distribution, description, history, uses, etc. Also provided are range maps, a bibliography, lists of trees by province and by family.
QK201 L38 ESCI

DJ64 **Successful Forestry: A Guide to Private Forestry Management.** 1989. Ottawa: Canadian Forestry Service. 133 p.

Guide for woodlot owners to basic forestry and silvicultural techniques and forestry management principles. Illustrated.
DS387 W65 S942 ESCI

DJ65 **Taylor's Guide to Trees**, 1988.

Guide to 200 popular trees especially suited to home gardens. See DH45n for full entry information.

DJ66 **Yearbook of Forest Products,** 1967- . Rome: Food and Agriculture Organization. annual.

A cumulative volume 1974-1985 (1986) provides statistics on the production, trade values and consumption of forest products internationally.
HD9750.4 Y42 ESCS

DK ENVIRONMENT AND ENERGY

This section is divided into two sections. References to Environmental literature are numbered DK1 to DK56. References to literature for Energy are numbered DK57 to DK81.

Environment

Bibliographies and Guides to the Literature

DK1 Clark, B.D. 1980. **Environmental Impact Assessment: A Bibliography with Abstracts.** New York: Mansell/R.R. Bowker. 516 p.
Contains almost 1,000 entries with information of an international nature for private developers, public agencies and professionals.
Z5853 I57C47 BMER; ENGR

DK2 **Directory of Published Proceedings: PCE: Pollution Control/Ecology,** 1974- . Harrison, NY: InterDok. annual.
List of published international conference proceedings on pollution control and ecology arranged chronologically by conference date, with editor/location/subject and sponsor indexes.
Z5862 D56 BMER

DK3 **ELIAS,** 1972- . Ottawa: Environment Canada Library. Database.
The *ELIAS Database* indexes the collections of more than 20 libraries participating in the Environment Canada Departmental Library. Available online.

DK4 **Environmental Bibliography,** 1973- . Santa Barbara, CA: Environmental Studies Institute. database. updated bimonthly.
Contains citations to articles in over 360 international periodicals in the areas of general human ecology, atmospheric studies, energy, land resources, water resources, and nutrition and health. Available online and on CD-ROM as *NISC Disc*, and in print as *Environmental*

Periodicals Bibliography - EPB (bimonthly with annual cumulation), which reproduces the tables of contents of 350 periodicals.

DK5   Environmental Resource Directory. 1989. Toronto: Public Focus. 183 p. biennial. looseleaf with updates.

Identifies pamphlets, booklets, fact sheets, books, kits, audio visuals, periodicals and some performances and presentations. Includes material according to six educational levels ranging from kindergarten to adult.
Z5863 E55 E58 ENGR

DK6   Handbook on Climate Data Sources of the Atmospheric Environment Service. 1989. Ottawa: Canadian Climate Program, Environment Canada. 206 p.

Lists data sources available from the Atmospheric Environment Service, including data kept, record period, and Canadian coverage. Includes tables and charts.
QC981 H25 PASR

DK7   Miller, E. Willard and Ruby M. Miller. 1989. **Environmental Hazards: Air Pollution.** Santa Barbara, CA: ABC-Clio. 250 p.

Bibliography providing an introduction to the subject of air pollution, biographies of key activists and scientists, a chronology of air pollution events, and texts of important speeches and reports. Annotated entries for the major works in the field are included, ranging from acid rain to ozone layer depletion and destruction of the rain forest. Another work relating specifically to the greenhouse effect is John Nordquist's *The Greenhouse Effect: A Bibliography*, (Reference and Research Services, 1990) (Z6683 A8N67) which cites literature published between 1980 and 1989.
HC110 A8M55 ROBA

DK8   Toxic and Hazardous Materials: A Sourcebook and Guide to Information Sources. 1987. Ed. by James Webster. New Haven, CT: Greenwood Press. 431 p.

Comprehensive bibliography of over 1,600 information sources (periodicals, newsletters, indexes, databases, government documents, books) relating to toxic and hazardous materials. Air, land and water pollution, acid rain, waste disposal, radioactive materials, testing and analysis, transportation, spills, and cleanups are some of the subjects covered.
Z7914 S17769 ENGR

Abstracts, Indexes and Databases

DK9   Abstracts on Health Effects of Environmental Pollutants, 1972– . Philadelphia: Biosciences Information Service of Biological Abstracts. monthly.

Material of interest to health related environmental pollution research. Includes concept, author, biosystematic, generic and subject indexes.
RA565 A126 BMER

DK10   Aqualine Abstracts, 1985– . Oxford, UK: Pergamon Press. biweekly.

"Provides comprehensive coverage of world's

scientific and technical literature on water, wastewater, associated engineering services and the aquatic environment." Includes some 8,000 abstracts annually. Available online as *AQUALINE*.
TD201 A7 ENGR

DK11 AQUAREF, 1970- . Ottawa: Environment Canada Inland Waters Directorate (WATDOC). Database.

AQUAREF contains references on the subject of Canadian water resources, air pollution, and other environmental topics taken from over 200 Canadian and foreign journals, government reports and documents. WATDOC also produces *CENV* (Canadian Environment), (1970-) which "includes bibliographical records and abstracts of science and technology literature relevant to the Canadian environment", and *ENV*, a database containing citations to French language literature.

DK12 Current Contents: Agriculture, Biology and Environmental Sciences, 1961– . weekly. See DA15 for full entry information.

DK13 Ecological Abstracts, 1974- . Norwich: Geo Abstracts. 6 issues per year.

Each issue contains over 1,500 abstracts in areas of general ecology, marine ecology, freshwater ecology, applied ecology, evolution and historical ecology, etc. Available online on *GEOBASE* (CK10).
QH540 E27 BMER

DK14 Ecology Abstracts, 1975- . Bethesda, MD: Cambridge Science Abstracts (CSA). monthly with annual index.

Contains citations and abstracts to world literature in the area of ecology, including ecosystems, soil studies, pollution of the environment, urban environments, etc. Available online and on CD-ROM.

DK15 Enviro/Energyline Abstracts Plus, 1971- database. See DK70 for full entry information.

DK16 Environment Abstracts, 1971- . New York: R.R. Bowker. monthly with annual cumulation.

Monthly issues contain abstracts and indexes to worldwide environmental literature in areas of hazardous waste, acid rain, etc. Also included are rulings from the *Federal Register* and patents from the U.S. Patent and Trademark Office *Official Gazette* (DA33n). Bowker also publishes *Environment Abstracts Annual*, which provides a listing of the abstracts published in the monthly issues, but with additional sections, such as a chronology of the key environmental events of the year and a review of legislative changes. The organization is by subject keyterms, geographical keyterms and index, industry keyterms for products and services. Available online and on CD-ROM as part of *Enviro/Energyline Abstracts Plus*, DK70.
Z5862 E59

DK17 Pollution Abstracts, 1970- . Bethesda, MD: Cambridge Scientific Abstracts. bimonthly.

Contains references to environment-related literature on pollution, its sources and its controls. Subjects covered include air pollution, environmental quality, noise pollution, pesticides, radiation, solid wastes, and water pollution. Available online and on CD-ROM as part of *Pollution/Toxicology CD-ROM* (DK18).

DK18 Pollution/Toxicology CD-ROM (PolTox), 1981- . Bethesda, MD: Cambridge Scientific Abstracts. Database. updated quarterly.

Citations and abstracts to international literature covering pollution and toxicology. Includes seven databases: *Aquatic Sciences and Fisheries Abstracts, Part 3; Aquatic Pollution and Environmental Quality; Ecology Abstracts; Food and Science Technology Abstracts; Health and Science Safety Abstracts; Pollution Abstracts; Toxicology Abstracts; and TOXLINE*.

DK19 RTECS (Registry of Toxic Effects of Chemical Substances) Database, 1975- . Bethesda, MD: U.S. National Library of Medicine.

Provides data on chemical toxicity measurements on over 100,000 substances and their effects on man and the environment. Information includes CAS Registry Numbers, toxicity/biomedical effects, U.S. exposure standards and regulations. Available online on *CCINFOline* or on CD-ROM on *CCINFOdisc* (DI86). As of 1988, Health and Welfare Canada has produced *IRPTC/Legal* (*RSCPT/Legal* for French database) (International Register of Potentially Toxic Chemicals), a database "containing the full text of Canadian federal laws and regulations governing the use of toxic chemicals." Also covers legal information from 22 other countries and several international organizations.

DK20 TOXLINE, 1965- database.

Covers the adverse effects of chemicals, drugs, and physical agents on living systems. See DF15 for full entry information.

Reviews and Annuals

DK21 Advances in Environmental Science and Engineering, 1979- . New York: Gordon and Breach Science Publishers. annual.

Articles dealing with current analysis of air, water, and land processes and health effects, as well as the legal aspects, safety standards, alternative energy sources, environmental protection, and administration of resources.
TA170 A37 (1979-1986) ENGS

DK22 Advances in Environmental Science and Technology, 1968– . New York: Wiley-Interscience. irregular.

Beginning with Volume 7, each volume is devoted to a specific topic within the field. For example, Volume 22 (1989) is entitled *Aquatic Toxicology and Water Quality Management*.
TD172 A38 ENGS

Encyclopedias and Dictionaries

DK23 Ashworth, William. 1990. **The Environmental Encyclopedia.** New York: Facts on File. 424 p.

Includes articles in earth science, chemistry and forestry as they relate to environmental sciences. Includes a list of associations for environmental issues.

DK24 Coleman, Ronny and Kara Hewson Williams. 1988. **Hazardous Materials Dictionary.** Lancaster, PA: Technomic Publishing. 176 p.

Dictionary of terms that apply to the handling of hazardous materials and emergency management used by the trucking, railway and environmental protection industries.
T55.3 H3C54 ENGR

DK25 Cross-Reference Index of Hazardous Chemicals, Synonyms, and CAS Registry Numbers. 1990. Philadelphia: J.B. Lippincott. 576 p.

Dictionary which "provides a means for identifying hazardous chemical substances based on the substance name commonly used in chemistry and by industry." Designed to allow individuals to identify and locate information in the CAS registry on hazardous substances in their workplace. Organized in two parts: name section and CAS number section.
T55.3 H3 C76 ENGR

DK26 A Dictionary of the Environment. 1989. 3d ed. Comp. by M. Allaby. New York: Van Nostrand Reinhold. 423 p.

Explains 6,000 words, phrases from all environmental disciplines. Covers international environmental events such as Chernobyl and Three Mile Island. Other dictionaries include: *Dictionary of Environmental Protection: In Four Languages: English, German, French, Russian*, (Elsevier, 1988) (TD169.3 D53 ENGR), which is a comprehensive list of technical terms used in contemporary environmental literature; and *Environmental Engineering Dictionary* (Government Institutes, 1990), which provides definitions of various environmental engineering terms.
QH540.4 A44 BMER

DK27 The Earth Report 2: Monitoring the Battle for Our Environment. 1990. London: Mitchell Beazley. 176 p.

Two part report; Part 1 contains essays on major environmental issues written by noted scholars in their fields; Part 2 consists of shorter articles listing major environmental concerns. Cross referenced and indexed. Updates *Earth Report: The Essential Guide to Global Ecological Issues* (Price, Stern, Sloan, 1988)
GF75 E27 SCAR; ROBA (1988)

DK28 Encyclopedia of Environmental Control Technology. 1989- in progress. 4 vols. Ed. by Paul Cheremisinoff. Houston, TX: Gulf Publishing Company.

Volumes 1-4 now available in this projected 8 volume set. Discusses basic and high technology/specialized topics related to environmental and industrial pollution control problems and solutions, including new technology used, research activities, future trends. Volume 1: *Thermal Treatment of Hazardous Wastes*; Volume 2: *Air Pollution Technology*; Volume 3: *Wastewater - Sludge Treatment and Groundwater Effects*; Volume 4: *Containment of Hazardous Wastes*.
TD191.5 E5 ENGR

DK29 Encyclopedia of Environmental Science and Engineering. 1983. 3 vols. Ed. by J.R. Pfafflin and E.N. Ziegler. New York: Gordon and Breach.

Overview of environmental areas and related engineering practice.
TD9 E5 ENGR

Handbooks

DK30 The Canadian Green Consumer Guide. 1989. Toronto: Pollution Probe. 164 p.

DK - Environment and Energy

"An activity guide for all ages, designed to produce a healthier, greener, environment" (subtitle).
TX337 C2C35 SIGS

DK31 Canada Water Year Book, 1975– . Ottawa: Dept. of the Environment. irregular.
A series on the fresh water resources in Canada.
GB707 C354 PASR

DK32 Canadian Water Quality Guidelines. 1987- . Ottawa: Environment Canada, Water Quality Branch, Inland Waters Directorate. looseleaf.
Comprehensive document detailing all current water quality guidelines for a wide variety of contaminants.
TD226 A1C35 ENGR

DK33 Cheremisinoff, Paul N. 1989. **Hazardous Materials Emergency Response: Pocket Handbook.** Lancaster, PA: Technomic Publishing. 161 p.
Handbook for personnel involved with hazardous waste cleanup work in managing wastes operations. Lists U.S. federal regulations, properties of hazardous materials, equipment, emergency planning, containment, cleanup techniques and decontamination, and safety issues. Detailed appendices and bibliography included. A similar work is Travis P. Wagner's *Hazardous Waste Q & A* (Van Nostrand Reinhold, 1990) (KF3946 W34 ENGR), which is a guide for personnel involved with hazardous wastes, explaining U.S. regulations in Resource Conservation and Recovery and Hazardous Materials Transportation. Organized by subjects, e.g. transportation provisions, groundwater monitoring, and written in a question and answer format.
T55.3 H3 C487 ENGR

DK34 Complete Guide to Environmental Careers. 1989. Washington: Island Press. 328 p.
Job outlook, salaries, requirements, nature of careers in hazardous waste management, environmental education, air quality, and other areas as described by professionals in the field.
TD170.2 C66 ENGR

DK35 CRC Handbook of Environmental Control. 1972. 6 vols. Cleveland, OH: CRC Press.
Provides information in tabular form which is useful in the evaluation of the environment. Six volumes cover: 1) Air Pollution, 2) Solid Waste, 3) Water Supply and Treatment, 4) Wastewater Treatment and Disposal, 5) Hospital and Health Care Facilities, 6) Index.
TD145 C2 ENGR

DK36 Dangerous Goods Regulations, 26th ed, 1983- . Montreal: International Air Transport Association. biennial.
(32nd ed., 1991). Provides advice on national and international safety rules and laws for air transportation of dangerous goods. Published in several languages: English, French, Spanish and German.
T55.3 H3 I64 ENGR

DK37 Dangerous Properties of Industrial Materials. 1989. 7th ed. 3 vols. See DL112 for full entry information.

DK38 De Zuane, John. 1990. **Handbook of Drinking Water Quality: Standards and Controls.** New York: Van Nostrand Reinhold. 523 p.

Intended as a ready-reference work for professionals involved with drinking water and regulatory issues.

DK39 EnviroTIPS, 1984-85. 49 vols. Ottawa: Environment Canada.

Series of manuals called *The Environmental and Technical Information for Problem Spills (EnviroTIPS)*. Provides comprehensive information on chemicals that are frequently spilled in Canada, for use by environmentalists to assess their effects on the environment.
TP149 E58 ENGI

DK40 Handbook of Environmental Data on Organic Chemicals. 1983. See DF51 for full entry information.

DK41 Hazardous Chemicals Desk Reference. 1987. See DF48 for full entry information.

DK42 Hazardous Materials Transport Guide. 1984. Washington: Bureau of National Affairs. 366 p.

Organized in two parts: Part one discusses U.S. federal requirements in transportation of hazardous materials, wastes, and chemicals. Part two highlights responses required for transportation emergencies such as accidents and spills.
KF3945 H383 ENGR

DK43 Instrumentation for Environmental Monitoring. 1983–1986. 2d ed. 2 vols. New York: Wiley.

Results of a survey of the National Science Foundation and the U.S. Department of Energy for the measurement of quality of the environment in 3 areas: Volume 1: *Radiation*; Volume 2: *Water*; Volume 3: *Air*. Each volume identifies contaminants, lists instruments used to detect contaminants and makes recommendations for the development of new techniques.
TD193 I56 ENGR

DK44 Jeffrey, Michael I. 1989- . **Environmental Approvals in Canada.** Toronto: Butterworths. looseleaf.

Updated several times a year, this loose-leaf document provides backgound and overview information on the environmental assessment process in Canada. It also contains selected cases and commentary about environmental management principles. A discussion of future directions is included, as are appendices of current legislation, an index of public hearings before the Environmental Assessment Board, referrals and notices and Environmental Assessment Board and Joint Board Rules of Practice and Procedure and Scoping Procedures.
KF3775 J44 LAW

DK45 Methods of Air Sampling and Analysis. 1989. 3d ed. Ed. by James P. Lodge, Jr. New York: Lewis Publishers. 763 p.

Describes and evaluates methods used in sampling and analyzing air quality.
TD890 I53 ENGR

DK46 Miller, E. W. 1990. **Environmental Hazards: Radioactive Materials and Wastes: A Reference Handbook.** Santa Barbara, CA: ABC-Clio. 298 p.

Includes articles on all aspects of radioactive waste, from the nature of radiation to emergency planning and preparedness. Includes a directory of private, U.S. government, and international organizations. Extensive bibliography listing multi-media sources is provided.

DK47 NIOSH Manual of Analytical Methods. 1984. 3d ed. Ed. by Peter M. Eller. Cincinnati, OH: U.S. National Institute for Occupational Safety and Health.

Contains over 100 NIOSH-approved sampling and measurement methods for over 200 toxic substances. Indexes of names and synonyms are included, as are chapters on Quality Assurance, Air Sampling, Development and Evaluation of Methods, and Biological Samples.
RC967 N34 BMED

DK48 Patty's Industrial Hygiene and Toxicology. 1978–1982. 2 vols. Ed. by George D. Clayton and Florence Clayton. Cincinnati, OH: American Conference of Governmental Industrial Hygienists.

Volume 1: *General Principals* provides historical background and toxicological effects of metals, sulphur and phosphor compounds, epoxies, nitro- and amino- compounds, esters, ethers, phenols, and aldehydes. Volume 2A: *Toxicology* provides a review of carcinogenesis and a toxicological review of halogens, alkaline materials, nitrosamines, amines, and hydrocarbons. Volume 2B: *Toxicology* provides a review of toxicological data regarding glycols, inorganic compounds, alcohols, ketones, polymers, phosphates, acids and a cumulative index for all three volumes.
HD7263 P32 ENGR

DK49 Statistical Record of the Environment Worldwide. 1991. Ed. by Arsen Darnay. Detroit: Gale Research. 950 p.

Provides statistical data, arranged by subject, extracted from United Nations Environment Programme and U.S. government information, on environmental issues. Includes charts, tables, and graphs.

Atlases

DK50 Climatic Atlas Canada / Climatique Canada: A Series of Maps Portraying Canada's Climate. 1984-1988. 4 series, 5 vols. Ottawa: Atmospheric Environment Service, Environment Canada.

Depicts climate of Canada using maps. Series includes *Temperature and Degree Days; Precipitation; Pressure, Humidity, Cloud, Visibility...;* and *Bright Sunshine and Solar Radiation*. Updated by monthly and weekly journal *Climatic Perspectives* (1979-) (QC985 A1C55 PRRS).
G1116 C8C55 MAPL fo

DK51 Middleton, Nick. 1989. **Atlas of Environmental Issues.** New York: Facts on File. 63 p.

Colour illustrations and maps with essays explaining environmental concepts such as acid rain, alternative energy, deforestation, oil pollution, endangered species and wildlife. Of interest to young readers but useful for a wide audience.
912 M629At CR OISE

Directories

DK52 Canadian Sources of Environmental Information. 1989. Prepared by Environment Canada. Ottawa: Supply and Service. 457 p.

Provides a national inventory of specialists in various fields of the environmental sciences and related disciplines. Includes alphabetical lists of specialists and index to subject expertise. Supersedes *Directory of Canadian Environmental Experts*. *Canadian Environmental Directory*

(Gale Research, 1991) (TD171.5 C3C3 SMCR) lists individuals, agencies, firms and associations active in Canada in environmental issues. Also includes a list of resource centers and databases available online and on CD-ROM.
TD178.7 C2 N322 ENGR

DK53 Directory of Environmental Information Services. 1990. 3d ed. Ed. by Thomas F.P. Sullivan. Rockville, MD: Government Institutes, Inc.

Thorough listing of all U.S. federal and state government resources, international professional, scientific and trade organizations, international newsletters, magazines and periodicals, and international databases and data services. *Environmental Information Directory* (Gale Research, 1991), lists over 4,000 U.S. federal and state organizations, private sector facilities and services, and publications and information services available in environmental issues.

DK54 Directory of Hazardous Waste Services. 1989–90. 3d ed. Don Mills, ON: Corpus Information Services. 330 p.

An alphabetical listing of more than 700 Canadian companies indexed first by province and secondly by specialty. *Hazardous Waste Management Facilities Directory: Treatment, Storage, Disposal and Recycling* (Noyes Publications, 1990) (TD1040 H375 ENGR) is a listing of American commercial hazardous waste management facilities, their services, indicating type of waste managed.
TD811.5 D47 ENGR

DK55 World Directory of Environmental Organizations. 1989. 3d ed. Ed. by Thaddeus Trzyna. Sacramento, CA: California Institute of Public Affairs. 176 p.

International listing of global organizations, government and nongovernment agencies, and databases involved with environmental concerns. Includes highlights of the United Nations Environmental Programme (1990–1995) and landmark events or conferences held from 1945 to date of publication.
S920 W57 Ref ROMU

DK56 World Guide to Environmental Issues and Organizations. 1990. Ed. by Peter Brackley. Harlow, U.K: Longman Current Affairs. 386 p.

In addition to an extensive essay discussing major environmental issues, also includes a directory of 250 international, regional and national organizations and government departments involved with environmental issues. There is also a section describing "green" parties, international and regional treaties, conventions, agreements, etc., and a bibliography of sources. Sponsored by United Nations Environment Programme.
TD170 W67 ENGR

Energy

The following are reference materials for the area of Energy.

Bibliographies and Guides to the Literature

DK57 Balachandran, S. 1980 . **Energy Statistics: A Guide to Information Sources.** Detroit: Gale Research. 272 p.

Detailed analyses of recurring statistical data sources in 40 serials with other sources noted.
Z5853 P83 B25 ENGR

DK58 Darrow, Ken and Mike Saxenian. 1986. **Appropriate Technology Sourcebook: A Guide to Practical Books for Village and Small Community Technology.** Rev. ed. Stanford, CA: Appropriate Technology Project, Volunteers in Asia. 800 p.

Brief reviews of 1,150 international and U.S. publications with prices and ordering information.
T47 D37 ENGR

DK59 Guide to the Energy Industries. 1983. Cambridge, MA: Harfax: Ballinger Pub. 328 p.

2,930 entries include "market research reports, investment banking reports, sources of industry statistics, financial and economic studies, forecasts, directories, journal articles, numeric databases, monographs, handbooks, conference reports and newsletters." International coverage.
Z5853 P83 G85 ENGR

DK60 Information Sources in Energy Technology. 1988. Ed. by L.J. Anthony. London: Butterworths. 324 p.

The guide consists of 16 bibliographic essays on energy in general (fuel technology, combustion, steam and boiler plants, electrical energy, energy conservation, etc) as well as specific sources of energy (solid fuels, liquid fuels, nuclear energy, solar energy, etc). Includes a list of international energy agencies.
TJ163.17 I54 ENGR

DK61 Pearson, Barbara C. and Katherine B. Ellwood. 1987. **Guide to the Petroleum Reference Literature.** Littleton, CO: Libraries Unlimited. 193 p.

Arranged by type of reference work, contains 420 descriptive entries on periodicals, databases, statistical sources, and indexing and abstracting services available to the petroleum industry.
Z6972 P38 ENGR

DK62 Weber, R. David. 1982. **Energy Information Guide.** 3 vols. Santa Barbara, CA: ABC-Clio Information Services.

More than 12,000 reference works, including databases, on energy and energy related topics. Material arranged under topics with cumulative author, title, subject and document number indexes.
Z5853 P83 W38

Abstracts, Indexes and Databases

DK63 DOE Energy Data Base (EDB), 1974- . Oak Ridge, TN: U.S. Department of Energy. database. updated biweekly.

Contains citations and abstracts on all aspects of energy (nuclear energy, fossil and synthetic fuels, renewable energy resources, conservation, storage, environmental concerns, etc., taken from U.S. Department of Energy literature, U.S. government departments, and other selected sources. Available online. Some of this information is available through *Energy Abstracts for Policy Analysis*, DK67.

DK64 DRI Canadian Energy, 1989- . Toronto: Data Resources of Canada. database. updated irregularly.

Database of information about major fuels produced and used by Canadian provinces taken from Statistics Canada, Canadian Petroleum Association and other agencies.

DK65 Energy, 1960- . Bala Cynwyd, PA: The WEFA Group. database. updated daily.

Provides daily, weekly, monthly, quarterly, and annual statistics on the supply and demand of major forms of energy for the U.S. and internationally. Available online only.

DK66 Energy Abstracts, 1974– . New York: Engineering Information. monthly.

Abstracts of the world's literature in the field of energy. Part of a multidisciplinary service which includes records from *Engineering Index* and other databases. Available online through *COMPENDEX* and on CD-ROM through *COMPENDEX Plus*, (DL14).
TJ163.2 E54 ENGR

DK67 Energy Abstracts for Policy Analysis, 1974–1989. Washington: Superintendent of Documents, Department of Energy, GPO. monthly.

Covered nontechnical literature related to policy, legislative and regulatory aspects of energy issues. Also available online.
TJ163.2 E456 ENGR

DK68 Energy Information Abstracts, 1976 -. New York: R.R. Bowker. monthly with annual cumulation.

Indexes and abstracts worldwide energy literature. Includes latest developments in energy resources, production, consumption, etc. Also published is the annual volume, *Energy Information Abstracts Annual*, which provides selected abstracts on energy research and developments taken from the monthly publications, as well as yearly review of trends in the energy field, and energy statistics for the year. Available online and on CD-ROM as part of *Enviro/Energyline Abstracts Plus*, DK70.
HD9502 A1E6 ENGR

DK69 Energy Research Abstracts, 1976– . Washington: Superintendent of Documents, Department of Energy, GPO. monthly.

Covers all aspects of energy including environmental aspects, energy policy and conservation. Beginning with 1991, includes only report literature of federal, state and foreign governments research organizations and universities. Canadian material included. Patent applications, theses, conference papers of U.S. Dept. of Energy and its contractors also included. Available online as *Energy Science and Technology*, and through *DOE Energy Data Base* DK63.
Z5853 P83 E65 ENGR

DK70 Enviro/Energyline Abstracts Plus, 1971- . New York: R.R. Bowker. CD-ROM database. monthly.

A CD-ROM product which provides citations and abstracts dealing with environmental and energy-related topics. A compilation of data contained in 3 separate databases: 1) *Energyline* (1976- monthly), listing citations and abstracts included in over 3,500 international periodicals plus other literature dealing with the technical and policy-oriented aspects of energy; 2) *Enviroline* (1970- monthly), listing citations and abstracts to 5,000 periodicals and literature covering all environmental topics; and 3) *Acid Rain* (1984- bimonthly), which includes information on acid rain research, development, policy, causes and effects, taken from worldwide literature.

DK71 Fuel and Energy Abstracts, 1960- . London: Institute of Fuel. bimonthly.

Contains over 1,500 abstracts in each issue from over 800 international journals, reports, surveys, conference proceedings, and statistical analyses on all scientific, technical, commercial and environmental aspects of fuel and energy.
TP316 F42 ENGR

DK72 P/E News, 1975- . New York: Central Abstracting and Indexing Service, American Petroleum Institute. database. updated weekly.

Indexes publications which contain current political, social, and economic information related to the petroleum energy industry. Available in print as *Petroleum/Energy Business News Index* (monthly with annual cumulation).

Reviews and Annuals

DK73 Annual Review of Energy, 1976– . Palo Alto, CA: Annual Reviews Inc. annual.

"Continuing review and discussion of the significant issues related to energy: the technologies of energy generation and end use; regional and global energy systems; environmental and societal impacts of energy systems; the economics and politics of energy; and scientific and research frontiers in energy."
TJ163.2 A55 ENGS

DK74 Financial Times Oil and Gas International Year Book, 1978 -. Harlow, U.K: Longman. annual.

Contains financial, property and exploration, operations, production and reserves information on worldwide oil and gas companies.

Handbooks and Dictionaries

DK75 Energy Analysis of 108 Industrial Processes. 1984. Ed. by Harry L. Brown. Atlanta, GA: Fairmont Press. 314 p.

Covers processes ranging from bread baking to iron and steel forging. See also Peter Osborn's *Handbook of Energy Data and Calculations including Directory of Products and Services* (Butterworths, 1985) (TJ163.3 O86 ENGR)
TJ163.2 E458 ENGR

DK76 Energy and Environmental Terms: A Glossary. 1988. Ed. by Peter Brackley. Brookfield, VT: Gower. 189 p.

Offers easily understood definitions to many of the technical terms used by environmentalists and energy professionals. Includes tables for symbols, chemical elements, names and formulae, geological time scale, and conversion factors. Abbreviations and acronyms are also included.
TJ163.16 B73 ENGI

DK77 Energy Statistics Sourcebook, 1986 -. Tulsa, OK: PennWell Books. annual.

Provides basic statistics for the oil and gas industry compiled from the *Oil and Gas Journal* energy database. Major segments of the industry, such as exploration and drilling, refining, imports and exports, offshore activities are included as separate chapters, with monthly and annual statistical data provided. International statistics can be found in *Energy Statistics* (Paris, OECD, 1988-) (ZZ ED 110 E57 GOVT) which includes international supply and demand; and *Energy Statistics Yearbook* (1982- United Nations) (UN2 S10 W52 GOVT) which provides energy data (energy production, imports and exports, stock changes, consumption, electricity) for countries, geographical areas, and the world, in a manner which allows for comparison of energy trends.which includes global data on trends and developments of all forms of energy. Available online and on diskette.

DK78 Energy Terminology: A Multi-Lingual Glossary 1986. 2d ed. Oxford: Pergamon Press. 539 p.

Defines approximately 1,500 terms in English, French, German and Spanish. Arranged in 19 broad subject areas. Another dictionary is *Dictionary of Energy* (Nichols/GP Publishing, 1983) (TJ163.16 D5 SMCR 1983).
TJ163.16 E54 ENGR

DK79 Handbook of Energy Systems Engineering: Production and Utlization. 1985. Ed. by Leslie C. Wilbur. New York: Wiley. 1775 p.

Written for the practicing mechanical engineer.
TJ163.9 H35 ENGR

DK80 Solar Energy Dictionary. 1982. Comp. by D.V. Hunt. New York: Industrial Press. 411 p.

Broad scope covers biomass, ocean energy, hydro-electric power in addition to solar energy.
TJ810 H86 ENGR

Directories

DK81 The World Energy Directory: Organizations and Research Activities in Non-Atomic Energy. 1988. 3d ed. Harlow, U.K: Longman. 431 p.

Profiles over 2,000 research laboratories and institutions in 94 countries, primarily United States and European countries, with Third World and Communist countries covered in less detail, which carry out, promote or fund research on coal conversion technology, solar energy, wind power, electrical engineering, energy conversion, etc. English translations are provided for company names, company affiliations, operations, financial situation, and other useful information.
TJ163.165 W6 ENGR (1985)

DL ENGINEERING

Additional information on Chemical Engineering can be found in Section DF, *Chemistry and Chemical Engineering*.

Bibliographies and Guides to the Literature

DL1   Encyclopedia of Physical Sciences and Engineering Information Sources. 1989. New York: Gale Research. 736 p.

A bibliographic guide to approximately 16,000 citations. Organized into 425 subject fields ranging from "abrasives" to "zinc".
Q145 E56 ENGR

DL2   Engineering Societies. 1963. **Classed Subject Catalog. Engineering Societies Library [New York].** 12 vols. Boston: G.K. Hall. *Ten Supplement(s)* 1964–1973 (10 vols, 1965–1974).

Additional supplements appear as *Bibliographic Guide to Technology* (1975- Z7913 B5 ENGR). The Engineering Societies Library is the largest engineering library in the U.S. It is an historic archive for engineering material as well as a current resource. The catalogues include monographs, pamphlets, serials, reports, films, government publications, etc. The main set of this catalogue lists about 185,000 items with separate index volume. A second revised edition, 1982, is available from G.K. Hall on 22 microfilm reels. This is a cumulative edition, in one alphabet, with revisions to reflect current terminology (e.g. energy, bioengineering, lasers, computer technology) (mfm ZE564 ENGR).
Z5854 N47 ENGR

DL3   Information Sources in Engineering. 1985. 2d ed. Ed. by L.J. Anthony. London: Butterworths. 579 p.

A guide to the structure and organization of engineering literature as a whole and to a wide range of specialized subject fields within the discipline.
T10.7 I54 ENGR

DL4   Information Sources in Science and Technology, 1988. See DA3 for full entry information.

DL5   Pure and Applied Science Books 1876–1982. See DA5 for complete entry.

DL6 Schenk, Margaret T. and Webster, James K. 1984. **What Every Engineer Should Know About Engineering Information Resources.** New York: Marcel Dekker. 216 p.

Aimed at practicing engineers. Describes structure and organization of literature and gives a small number of key sources.
T10.7 S34 ENGR

DL7 Scientific and Technical Books and Serials in Print, 1978- annual. See DA8 for full entry information.

DL8 Scientific and Technical Information Sources, 1977. See DA9 for full entry information.

Abstracts, Indexes and Databases

DL9 Aeronautical Engineering: A Special Bibliography with Indexes, 1970- . Washington: Scientific and Technical Information Office, NASA. monthly.

Provides citations and abstracts of reports and journal articles on aerodynamics and aeronautics taken from *Scientific and Technical Aerospace Reports (STAR)* DL32, and *International Aerospace Abstracts* (DL26).
Z5063 A2A4 ENGR

DL10 Applied Mechanics Reviews, 1948- . New York: American Society of Mechanical Engineers. monthly with annual cumulated index.

Covers approximately 400 periodicals in applied mechanics and related mechanical engineering subjects. Includes book reviews and review articles. Available online.
TA1 A63953 ENGR

DL11 Applied Science and Technology Index, 1913-. monthly, annual cumulation.

Contains citations to articles in engineering and related subject fields. See DA13 for full entry information.

DL12 Chemical Abstracts, 1907- . weekly.

Includes chemical technology as well as pure chemistry. See DF7 for full entry information.

DL13 Chemical Engineering Abstracts, 1982- . Nottingham, U.K: Royal Society of Chemistry. monthly with annual cumulation.

Abstracts for over 4,500 entries each year, organized in 22 sections, including heat transfer, diffusional operations, reactors, plant equipment. Available online and on CD-ROM as *CEBA* (Chemical Engineering and Biotechnical Abstracts) (1989-).
TP155 C36 ENGR

DL14 COMPENDEX, 1969- . New York: Engineering Information Inc. database. updated monthly.

Encompasses all fields of engineering, related fields in applied science and energy. Includes English-language citations and abstracts to more than 4,500 journals, reports, monographs and conference proceedings worldwide in more than 20 languages. Cumulation of *Engineering Index, Bioengineering Abstracts* and *Energy Abstracts*. Available on CD-ROM as *Compendex Plus*.

DL15 Computer and Control Abstracts, 1966- . monthly; semi-annual cumulative indexes.

The foremost index in the field of computers and control engineering. Covers journals, conference publications, reports, books, dissertations. Available as Series "C" of *Science Abstracts*. See DC4 for full entry information.

DL16 Current Contents: Engineering, Technology & Applied Sciences, 1961- weekly.

See DA15 for full entry information.

DL17 Current Technology Index, CTI, 1981- . London: Library Association, 1962- monthly, annual cumulation.

Supersedes *British Technology Index*, 1962—1980. British equivalent of *Engineering Index* (DL21). A subject index to approximately 300 British periodicals covering all aspects of engineering and technology. Includes a *Catchword and Trade Name Index*, a separate monthly publication which lists catchwords, product names, names of firms and organizations mentioned in *CTI*. Available online.
Z7913 C87 ENGR

DL18 Electronics and Communications Abstracts, 1961- . Brentwood, U.K: Multi-Science Pub. Co. bimonthly with annual cumulation.

Citations and abstracts of journal articles, books, reports, government documents in fields of electrical engineering, electronics and communications. Subject covered include electronic systems, electronic physics. Available online.
TK5101 A1E48 ENGR

DL19 Electrical and Electronics Abstracts, 1966- . London / Piscataway, NJ: IEEE. monthly with semi-annual cumulative indexes.

"Forms the world's major English language abstracting service (for) electrotechnology." Covers all aspects of the area; entries in a classified order with author, subject index. Available as "Series B" of *Science Abstracts* (DA21); and available online as part of *INSPEC* (DA19). References to electrical and electronic-related abstracts, book reviews, articles and conference publications published in other IEEE publications can found using the annual *Index to IEEE Publications* (1971-) (Z5833 I6 ENGR).
TK1 E35 ENGR

DL20 Energy Research Abstracts, 1976- monthly.

Contains abstracts of reports, journal articles, books, conference papers, of interest to engineers. See DK69 for full entry information.

DL21 Engineering Index, 1884- . New York: Engineering Index. monthly.

EI is a compilation of abstracts and items from over 4,500 international professional and trade journals, conference proceedings, technical reports and books, encompassing all engineering disciples worldwide. Subject arrangement with subdivisions; author, keyword indexes. Available online and on CD-ROM as *COMPENDEX* (DL14).
Z5851 E62 ENGR

DL22 Ergonomics Abstracts, 1969- . Birmingham, U.K: Ergonomics Information Center. quarterly.

Covers literature in area of human engineering, drawing from psychology, physiology, biomechanics, and work design literature. Includes citations and abstracts as well as book reviews.
TA166 E73 ENGR

DL23 Geotechnical Abstracts, 1970- . Essen, Germany: German National Society of Soil Mechanics and Foundation Engineering. monthly.

Contains over 1,500 abstracts in 500 international journals and other literature in the subject of structural engineering, including geological aspects, site investigation, rock-engineering problems, and construction methods.
TA630 G4 ENGR

DL24 Government Reports Announcements and Index, 1975- biweekly.

Indexes government sponsored technical reports. See DA32 for full entry information.

DL25 Index to Scientific and Technical Proceedings, 1978- monthly with semi-annual cumulation. See DA26 for full entry information.

DL26 International Aerospace Abstracts, 1961- . Washington: NASA. semi-monthly.

Covers the world's literature in aeronautics and space science and technology as published in periodicals, books, meeting papers, conference proceedings, translations of journals and journal articles. Companion publication, *STAR* (DL32)- covers technical report literature in the field. Available online as *Aerospace Database*.
TL787.7 I67 ENGR

DL27 International Civil Engineering Abstracts, 1982- . Dublin: Construction Industry Translations and Information Services (CITIS). 10 issues / year.

Continues *I.C.E. Abstracts* (1974-81). Contains abstracts to more than 400 international books, journal articles and reports in the field of civil engineering. Available on CD-ROM as *CITIS CD-ROM*.
TA1 I4752 ENGR

DL28 ISMEC: Mechanical Engineering Abstracts, 1988- . Bethesda, MD: Cambridge Scientific Abstracts. bimonthly.

Continues *ISMEC Bulletin* (1973-1987). "Indexes international literature dealing with mechanical engineering and related fields." Available online.
TJ1 I72 ENGR

DL29 Metals Abstracts, 1968- . monthly.

Abstracts for metals and metallurgy of interest to mining engineers. See DG21 for full entry information.

DL30 Referativnyi Zhurnal, 1953- irregular annual.

Contains over 30 sections each month on engineering topics. See DA20 for full entry information.

DL31 Science Citation Index, 1945- bimonthly with annual cumulation. See DA22 for full entry information.

DL32 **Scientific and Technical Aerospace Reports (STAR),** 1963- . Washington: NASA. semi-monthly.

STAR covers the literature of space and aeronautics contained in technical reports commissioned by the U.S. and other national governments. Subject arrangement. Subject, corporate and personal authors, contract and report numbers indexes are included. Companion publication *International Aerospace Abstracts* (DL26). Available online as *Aerospace Database*.
TL501 S3 PASR

Reviews and Annuals

DL33 **Advances in Applied Mechanics,** 1948- . San Diego, CA: Academic Press. irregular annual.

Each volume contains articles of current developments in applied mechanics.
TA350 A4 ENGS

DL34 **Advances in Astronautical Sciences,** 1957- . San Diego, CA: American Astronautical Society. annual.

English language articles dealing with astronautics and outer space exploration presented at international American Astronautical Society (AAS) proceedings and meetings. Supplemented by *Science and Technology Series* (1964-); *AAS History Series* (1977-) which includes selected works in aerospace history; and *AAS Microfiche Series* (1968-) which consists of technical papers not published in the *AAS* hard cover copy.
TL787 A35 ENGS

DL35 **Advances in Biochemical Engineering / Biotechnology,** 1983- . New York: Springer-Verlag. irregular. 2/3 issues per year.

Formerly called *Advances in Biochemical Engineering*. (1971-1982). Each volume contains articles on topics in biochemical engineering and biotechnology, for example, Volume 25 *Chromatography*; Volume 33 *Bioproducts*; Volume 43 *Applied Molecular Genetics*. Cumulative author index in each volume.
TP248.3 A382 ENGS

DL36 **Advances in Biotechnological Processes,** 1983- . New York: Wiley-Liss. annual.

Presents "comprehensive reviews of current developments and applications in biotechnology" (bioengineering) written by leaders in their fields. Each volume focuses on a theme: Volume 12 *Biological Waste Treatment*; Volume 14 *Viral Vaccines*.
TA164 A47 ENGS

DL37 **Advances in Chemical Engineering,** 1956- . Orlando, FL: Academic Press. irregular annual.

Each volume contains articles containing a review and evaluation of work being done in various fields in chemical engineering with emphasis on high technology and environmental protection and health. Cumulative table of contents for previous volumes is included in each volume available up to Volume 11 (1981).

DL38 **Advances in Electronics and Electron Physics,** 1954- . London: Academic Press. irregular, 2-3 issues per year, with supplements.

Provides comprehensive reviews of advances in electronics and electron physics in each issue. *Supplements* cover a single theme with lengthier reviews.
TK7800 A37 ENGS

DL39 **Advances in Engineering Software,** 1978- . Southampton, U.K: Computational Mechanics Publications. quarterly.

Articles focus on "new ideas and research development which will have a significant practical application of computers in engineering."
TA345 A48 ENGS

DL40 **Advances in Environmental Science and Engineering,** 1979- annual. See DK21 for full entry information.

DL41 **Advances in Heat Transfer,** 1964- . Orlando, FL: Academic Press. irregular annual.

Volumes published contain lengthy articles with detailed references. Designed to fill information gap between regularly published journals and university-level textbooks.
QC320 A1A3 ENGS

DL42 **Advances in Nuclear Science and Technology,** 1962- . New York: Plenum. annual.

Articles on current developments and advances in nuclear engineering and nuclear physics.
TK9001 A3 ENGS

DL43 **Annual Review of Fluid Mechanics,** 1969- . Palo Alto, CA: Annual Reviews. annual.

Comprehensive coverage of current trends and advances in fluid mechanics written by noted authorities. Includes bibliographies.
QC145 A57 ENGS

* * * *

DL44 **Annual Review of Materials Science,** 1971- . Palo Alto, CA: Annual Reviews. annual.

Comprehensive articles with bibliographies written by experts in the field outlining advances in materials science.
TA401 A73 ENGS

DL45 **Developments in Food Preservation,** 1981- . London: Elsevier Applied Science Publishers. irregular.

Part of the *Development* series published by Elsevier containing articles on various subjects. Other titles in the series include: *Developments In... Hydraulic Engineering; Soil Mechanics; Water Treatment; Geophysical Exploration; Fracture Mechanics; Lighting*, etc.
TP368 D47 ENGS

DL46 **Kempe's Engineers Yearbook,** 1894- . 2 vols. London: Morgan-Grampian. annual.

Classic engineering reference manual, covering all types of engineering, and including topics such as legal aspects, patents, industrial safety.
TA151 A1K4 ENGR

DL47 **Progress in Astronautics and Aeronautics,** 1960- . New York: Academic Press. 2-3 issues per year.

Several volumes containing papers and monographs published each year, each devoted to a specific topic in astronautical and aeronautical science. Formerly called *Progress in Astronautics and Rocketry* (Vols. 1-8). A similar reviewing service is *Progress in Aerospace Sciences* (1961-, Pergamon, quarterly) (TL500 P72 ENGS).
TL507 P75 ENGS

General Encyclopedias and Dictionaries

General encyclopedias and dictionaries in the major engineering disciplines are listed first, followed by general handbooks. Encyclopedias, dictionaries and handbooks in specialized areas in engineering, such as construction, fluid mechanics, and robotics follow the general handbooks.

DL48   ABBR: Abbreviations for Scientific and Engineering Terms. 1983. Montreal: Canadian Standards Association. 280 p.

In two separate sections: one for 7,000 terms and word combinations; and one for 6,800 abbreviations. Includes terms and abbreviations frequently used in drawings and in engineering and scientific writing.
Q179 A22 ENGR

DL49   Encyclopedia of Environmental Science and Engineering, 1983. 3 vols. See DK29 for full entry information.

DL50   Encyclopedia of Physical Science and Technology, 1987- 15 vols. See DA41 for full entry information.

DL51   Encyclopedia of Polymer Science and Engineering. 1985-1990. 2d ed. 17 vols plus supplement and index. New York: Wiley.

Contains lengthy signed articles written at a general level on topics in polymer science and related engineering processes. The supplement updates information found in the 17 volume set, and the index also contains additional articles.

The index provides the only access to the work.
TP1087 E46 ENGR

DL52   Industrial Engineering Terminology. 1990. Rev. ed. Norcross, GA: Industrial Engineering and Management Press. var. pg.

Contains definitions of terms used in industrial engineering, based on the American National Standards Institute (ANSI) standard Z94.0. Organized in 17 sections, including biomechanics, cost engineering, materials processing, and manufacturing systems.
T55.5 I5 ENGR

DL53   Kirk-Othmer Encyclopedia of Chemical Technology, 1978-1984, 3d ed. See DF32 for full entry information.

DL54   McGraw-Hill Encyclopedia of Electronics and Computers. 1988. 2d ed. Ed. by Sybil Parker. New York: McGraw Hill. 1047 p.

A compilation of articles drawn from the *McGraw Hill Encyclopedia of Science and Technology* (6th ed, 1987) (DA43). Covers computers from the engineering and electronics perspective.
TK7804 M48 ENGR

DL55   McGraw-Hill Encyclopedia of Science and Technology. 1987, 6th ed. See DA43 for full entry information.

DL56   Ullmann's Encyclopedia of Industrial Chemistry, 1985- in progress. See DF34 for full entry information.

General Handbooks

DL57 American Society for Metals. 1978–1989. **Metals Handbook.** 9th ed. 15 vols. Metals Park, OH: ASM International.

Covers properties of irons and steels and nonferrous metals and alloys; processing and fabrication.
TA459 A53 ENGR

DL58 Bradley, Howard B. 1987. **Petroleum Engineering Handbook.** Richardson, TX: Society of Petroleum Engineers. var. pg.

Major reference work with 59 chapters in three sections: 1) Mathematics (1 chapter); 2) Production Engineering (18 chapters); 3) Reservoir Engineering (40 chapters). Articles are written by experts in their fields. Chapters 58 and 59 contain units and standards.
TN870 P493 ENGR

DL59 **Chemist's Ready Reference Handbook,** 1990.

Compendium of data, laboratory techniques and procedures of interest to chemists and chemical engineers. See DF49 for full entry information.

DL60 **Civil Engineer's Reference Book.** 1989. 4th ed. Ed. by L.S. Blake. London: Butterworths. 960 p.

Written for engineers and civil engineering students. Arranged in 42 sections including: strength of materials; reinforced and prestressed concrete design; underwater work; demolition, etc. Includes line drawings, references, U.K. standards, and appendices.
TA151 P95 ENGR

DL61 **Composite Index for CRC Handbooks.** 1977. 2d ed. See DA14 for full entry information.

DL62 **Electronics Engineers' Handbook.** 1989. 3d ed. Ed. by D.G. Fink. New York: McGraw Hill. var. pg.

Handbook on electronic concepts, principles, materials, devices, systems, and integrated circuits.
TK7825 E34 ENGR

DL63 **Engineering Formulas.** 1986. 5th ed. McGraw Hill. var. pg.

Technical and mathematical formulas listed in a brief guide.
TA151 G4713 ENGR

DL64 **Fundamentals Handbook of Electrical and Computer Engineering.** 1982-83. 3 vols. Ed. by Sheldon Chang. New York: Wiley.

Information on core areas of electrical computer engineering systems, circuit design, devices, etc.
TK151 F86 ENGI

DL65 **Gas Tables.** 1983. 2d ed. Ed. by Joseph Keenan. New York: Wiley. 211 p.

Consists of tables of thermodynamic properties of air products, combustion, component gases, and compressible flow functions. Available in two versions, one in English units and the other in SI unit notation.
QC161.5 K43 PASR

DL66 Handbook of Human Factors. 1986. Ed. by G. Salvendy. New York: Wiley. 1874 p.

"This handbook provides vital information about the effective design and use of systems requiring the interaction among human, machine (computer), and environment." Chapter 1 describes the relationship between "human factors" and industrial engineering and gives a brief guide to the literature.
TA166 H275 ENGR

DL67 Handbook of Industrial Engineering. 1982. Ed. by G. Salvendy. New York: Wiley. var. pg.

Contains 107 chapters organized into 14 main areas, some of which include quality assurance, ergonomics, computers, industrial engineering. Written for a varied audience, and covers techniques, total system approaches, manufacturing and services applications. Many charts, tables and graphs. Indexed.
T57.23 H36 ENGR

DL68 Handbooks and Tables in Science and Technology, 1983. 2d ed. See DA2 for full entry information.

DL69 Index of Polymer Trade Names. 1987. See DF45n for full entry information.

DL70 Jones' Instrument Technology. 1987. 5 vols. 4th ed. Ed. by B.E. Noltingk. London: Butterworths.

Reflects developments in electronics, gas analysis and other subjects. Volumes include: 1) *Mechanical Measurements* 2) *Measurement of Temperature and Chemical Composition* 3) *Electrical and Radiation Measurement* 4) *Instrumentation Systems* and 5) *Automatic Instruments and Measuring Systems*.
TA165 J6 ENGR

DL71 Juran's Quality Control Handbook. 1988. 4th ed. Ed. by J.M. Juran. New York: McGraw-Hill. 1872 p.

All aspects of quality control, including economics, specifications, statistical control methods, organizations problems, and other related topics.
TS156 Q3J83 ENGR

DL72 Marks' Standard Handbook for Mechanical Engineers. 1987. 9th ed. Ed. by Eugene A. Avallone. New York: McGraw-Hill. 1867 p.

Covers conventional physical science and engineering topics, transportation, electrical and electronic engineering, and building construction and equipment. Indexed, with illustrations and tables. Formerly *Mechanical Engineers Handbook*.
TJ151 M37 ENGR

DL73 Perry's Chemical Engineer's Handbook. 1984. 6th ed. See DF47 for full entry information.

DL74 Standard Handbook for Civil Engineers. 1983. 3d ed. Ed. by F.S. Merrit. New York: McGraw Hill. var pg.

Information on construction management, materials, structural theory and design, and other areas of civil engineering, with section on environmental controls.
TA151 S8 ENGI

DL75 Standard Handbook for Electrical Engineers. 1987. 12th ed. Ed. by D.G. Fink. New York: McGraw-Hill. 2248 p.

Major electrical engineering handbook, published since 1907. Covers topics in generation transmission, distribution and control of electric power, nuclear power, energy conservation, alternative energy sources, computer technology, high voltage transmissions, etc. Companion volume to *Electronic Engineer's Handbook* (McGraw Hill, 1982). Also useful is Charles Belove's *Handbook of Modern Electronics and Electrical Engineering* (Wiley, 1986) (TK7825 H38 ENGR).
TK151 S83 ENGR

DL76 Tuma, Jan J. 1989. **Handbook of Numerical Calculations in Engineering.** New York: McGraw-Hill. 406 p.

"Definitions, theorems, computer models, numerical examples, tables of formulas, tables of functions." The *Standard Handbook of Engineering Calculations*, edited by Tyler Hicks (McGraw Hill, 1985) (TA151 H52 ENGR), covers specific engineering calculations used in solving problems in the fields of civil, architectural, mechanical, electrical, electronics, chemical and process plant, control, aeronautical and astronautical, marine, nuclear and sanitary engineering and engineering economics.
TA335 T85 ENGR

Specialized Encyclopedias, Dictionaries and Handbooks

Aerospace/Aviation

DL77 Aviation/Space Dictionary. 1990. 7th ed. Fallbrook, CA: Aero Publisher. 461 p.

Defines technical terms used in aviation and space flight activities, aerodynamics, and air traffic control. Also includes appendices which complement the definitions and supply additional information on larger concepts (aeronautical charts, airport lighting).
TL600 A85 ENGR

Automotive

DL78 Automotive Electric / Electronic Systems. 1988. Ed. by U. Adler. Stuttgart: Robert Bosch GmbH. 347 p.

Articles taken from *Bosch Technical Instruction* series. Topics includes types of engines, alternators, generators, ignition, fuel supply, and other automotive systems. Includes illustrations and diagrams.
TL272 A76 ENGR

DL79 Chilton's Automotive Service Manuals. Radnor, PA: Chilton.

One of several annual repair manuals, for use by professional mechanics and "do-it-yourselfers". Contains repair outlines and illustrations. Chilton's *Labour Guide and Parts Manual* provides prices for services and parts in yearly cumulations, for example, *Chilton's Automotive Service Manual 1987-91*; *Chilton's Labour Guide and Part Manual 1982-89*; *Chilton's Import Automotive Service Manual 1982-89*; *Chilton's Import Labour Guide and Price Manual 1986-90*; *Chilton's Motor/Age Truct and Van Service Manual 1986-90*.
MTRL SCI/TECH

DL80 Glossary of Automotive Terms. 1988. Warrendale, PA: Society of Automotive Engineers. 609 p.

A compendium of terms taken from SAE Standards, Recommended Practices and Information Reports. Covers land and sea vehicles.
TL9 G563 ENGR

Biotechnology

DL81 *Comprehensive Biotechnology.* 1985. 4 vols. with *Supplement.* Ed. by Murray Moo-Young. Oxford: Pergamon Press.

"The principles, applications and regulations of biotechnology in industry, agriculture and medicine." The first supplement covers animal biotechnology.
TP248.2 C66 ENGR

Ceramics

DL82 O'Bannon, Loran S. 1984. *Dictionary of Ceramic Science and Engineering.* New York: Plenum Press, 302 p.

Approximately 8,000 brief descriptions of terms used in ceramic sciences and engineering, many not found in any other reference source.
TP788 O2 ENGR

Circuitry

DL83 Bushsbaum, W. 1981. *Encyclopedia of Integrated Circuits: A Practical Handbook of Essential Reference Data.* 2d ed. Englewood Cliffs, NJ: Prentice-Hall. 420 p.

Describes, from a user's perspective, what integrated circuits do and their performance in equipment. Contains over 200 brief descriptions, functional blocks, logic diagrams, and applications of over 200 integrated circuits. Appendices with glossary and technical information and a list of IC catalogues included. Another handbook, *Designer's Handbook of Integrated Circuits* (McGraw Hill, 1984) (TK7874 D476 ENGI), includes charts of IC devices arranged according to family of IC.
TK7874 B77 ENGR

DL84 *International Encyclopedia of Integrated Circuits.* 1989. Blue Ridge Summit, PA: TAB Professional and Reference Books. 1063 p.

"Overview of currently available integrated circuit technology" with diagrams, text and charts. Cross-referenced with index and a list of circuits.
TK7874 I5623 ENGR

Construction

DL85 *Handbook of Steel Construction.* 1989. 4th ed. Willowdale, ON: Canadian Institute of Steel Construction. var. pg.

Current practical information on the use of steel and construction. Divided into nine sections including standards, commentary on standards, connections and tension, compression, etc. In the U.S. the major reference in this area is *Manual of Steel Construction* (1986, American Institute of Steel Construction) (TA684 A3585 ENGR).
TA684 C25 ENGR

DL86 *Lansdowne's Construction Cost Handbook,* 1990- . London, ON: David K. Lansdowne and Partners. annual.

Handbook "utilized extensively by all disciplines of the construction industry" on construction costs and related matters. Updated by

Lansdowne Letter, published quarterly. Lists detailed unit rates in all areas of construction (concrete, metals, doors, mechanical), costs of labour, materials, and total in-place costs including overhead and profit, for areas across Canada. Part 4 lists associations, Part 5 tables and appendices. Another handbook is Hanscomb's *Yardsticks for Costing: Cost Data for the Canadian Construction Industry* (Southam, 1968- annual) (TH435 Y27); similar U.S. data in *Building Construction Cost Data* (Means Company, 1942- annual) (TH435 B84) and *Means Estimating Handbook* (1990) (TH435 M463).
TH435 L27 ENGR

DL87 Means Illustrated Construction Dictionary. 1985. Ed. by Kornelis Smit. Kingston, MA: R.S. Means Company. 577 p.

Defines over 12,000 commonly used terms presently used in the construction trades. Definitions are nontechnical, and illustrations are used for clarification. Includes slang, regional and colloquial terms.
TH9 M4 ENGR

DL88 Metric Design Manual: Precast and Prestressed Concrete. 1982. Ottawa: Canadian Prestressed Concrete Institute. 383 p.

Design manual for precast prestressed concrete using metric units in the SI system of weights and measures. The Canadian Portland Cement Association has published a looseleaf publication *Metric Design Handbook for Reinforced Concrete Elements* (1980-) which has up-to-date information on design information and aids along with guidelines to CSA Standards and in a wide range of engineering subjects (TA683.22 M5 ENGR).
TA683.7 M47 ENGR

DL89 National Building Code of Canada, 1985. Ottawa: National Research Council. 454 p.

Basis for building laws for Canada and the provinces. Includes standards, requirements for safety, ventilation, access, structural design. Updated by pocket supplements. Another related standard is the *National Fire Code of Canada 1990* (6th ed, National Research Council, 1990) (TH9506 A47 ARCH), which covers fire prevention, laws and legislation in Canada. For additional information on standards, consult the Standards subsection in section DA *General Reference in Science and Technology*.
TH226 N28 ENGR

DL90 Sweet's Canadian Construction Catalogue File, 1966- . 4 vols. Scarborough, ON: McGraw Hill Information Systems Company of Canada. annual.

Used by design and construction professionals for current product information. Contains indexed information from catalogues of product manufacturers in 16 sections from sitework to electrical products. Formerly *Canadian Construction Catalog File*.
TH455 C3 ENGR

DL91 Timber Design Manual. 1980. Ottawa: Laminated Timber Institute of Canada. 512 p.

Practical guide for timber industry professionals in the use of glued-laminated and sawn timber in construction. Based on Canadian standards and codes. Information on stresses, designs, timber technology.
TA666 L3 ARCH

Electronics

DL92 Langley, Graham. 1986. **Telephony's Dictionary.** 2d ed. Chicago: Telephony Publishing Corp. 402 p.

"Defining 16,000 telecommunication works and terms." A more comprehensive work is the International Electro-Technical Commission (IEC)'s *International Electrotechnical Vocabulary* (3d ed, 1973- in progress) (TK9 I48 ENGR) which is a standard dictionary in 22 parts listing terms in several languages.
TK5102 L36 ENGR

Fluid Mechanics

DL93 **Encyclopedia of Fluid Mechanics.** 1986- in progress. Ed. by Nicholas P. Cheremisinoff. Houston, TX: Gulf Publishing Company.

Volume 8 is the latest volume published in this set, expected to be 12 volumes. Long articles, written by specialists on topics such as aerodynamics and compression flows, polymer flow engineering, gas dynamics, plasma flows, rheology, and non-Newtonian flows, etc. Supplemented by *International Journal of Engineering Fluid Mechanics* (1988-).
TA357 E53 ENGR

Gases

DL94 American Gas Association. 1985. **AGA Gas Handbook.** Ed. by Kersti Ahlberg. Lidingo, Sweden: AGA AB. 582 p.

Describes 67 industrial gases including physical and chemical property data. Also available is *Handbook of Compressed Gases* (Reinhold, 1990, 3d ed) (TP761 C65C6 ENGI) which lists basic information on compressed gases, uses, transportation, safety and rules and regulations.
TP242 A6 ENGR

DL95 **Nondestructive Testing Handbook.** 1982- in progress. 2d ed. Columbus, OH: American Society for Nondestructive Testing.

Handbook for information relating to gas leakage and leak detectors. Estimated 9 volume series. Completed to volume 4 (1986). Volumes published include: Volume 1: *Leak Testing*; Volume 2: *Liquid Penetrant Tests*; Volume 3: *Radioactive and Radiation Testing*; and Volume 4: *Electromagnetic Testing*.
TA410 M32 ENGR

Heating/Cooling

DL96 **ASHRAE Handbook & Product Directory,** 1972- . 4 vols. New York: American Society of Heating, Refrigerating and Air Conditioning Engineers. annual.

Four volumes (*Applications; Equipment; Systems; Fundamentals*) revised individually on a 4 year cycle. Each volume has a handbook section and a product section which is updated annually.
TH7011 A4 ENGR

Lighting

DL97 **IES Lighting Handbook.** 1981-. 5th ed. 2 vols. Volume 1 (1984, revised); Volume 2 (1981). Ed. by John Kaufman. New York: Illuminating Engineering Society of North America.

With the 1981 edition, the *Handbook* has been split in two volumes: *Reference Volume* and *Application Volume*, for updating purposes. Contains information on lighting for educational, residential, industrial, and transportation, as well as other information on colour, measurements, vision.
TK4161 I45 ENGR

Machinery

DL98   Tool and Manufacturing Engineers Handbook. 1983. 4th ed. 5 vols. Ed. by Thomas J. Drozda. Dearborn, MI: Society of Manufacturing Engineers.
"A reference book for manufacturing engineers, managers, and technicians." Volumes are titled: Volume 1 *Machinery;* Volume 2 *Forming;* Volume 3 *Materials, Finishing and Costing;* Volume 4 *Qaulity Control and Assembly;* and Volume 5 *Manufacturing Management.*
TS176 T63 ENGR

DL99   Weck, Manfred. 1984. **Handbook of Machine Tools.** 4 vols. New York: Wiley.
Translated from German. Contains information on all types of machine tools and processes, including developments in automation and control technology. Volume 1: *Types of Machines, Forms of Construction and Applications;* Volume 2: *Construction and Mathematical Analysis;* Volume 3: *Automation and Controls;* Volume 4 *Metrological Analysis and Performance Tests.*
TJ1185 W38213 ENGR

*   *   *   *

Marine Technology

DL100   Glossary of Marine Technology Terms. 1980. London: Heinemann. 177 p.
Some 1,400 terms defined which pertain to marine technology, science, and engineering. While British, the terms used are those used in the international shipping industry.
V23 G56 ENGR

Materials

DL101   Encyclopedia of Materials Science and Engineering. 1986. 7 vols. plus *Supplements* to Volumes 1, 2, 3 . Ed. by Michael B. Bever. Oxford: Pergamon Press.
Covers all aspects of materials science and engineering. Material is arranged alphabetically; list of contributors, author citation index, subject index. Volume 1 includes a bibliographic essay on materials information sources.
TA402 E53 ENGR

DL102   Encyclopedia of Polymer Science and Engineering. 1985-1990. 2d ed. 17 vols. *Index* and *Supplement* to Vol. 17B. New York: Wiley.
First published 1964–1977 as *Encyclopedia of Polymer Science*. Individual volumes contain lengthy, signed articles with bibliographic references on topics in polymer science and related engineering processes, written for the lay person but also of use to scientists and engineers. Emphasis expanded to include biomedical sciences and technological developments such as CAD. Includes conversion factors and SI units. Available on CD-ROM.
TP1087 E46 ENGR

DL103 Modern Plastics Encyclopedia.
1941- . New York: McGraw-Hill. annual.

An annual review organized in four sections: 1) Textbook, covering topics in materials, chemicals, primary processing, fabricating and finishing, 2) design guide, 3) databank, 4) suppliers. Issued as part of the periodical *Modern Plastics*.
TP986 A1M62 ENGR

DL104   Polymer Science Dictionary. 1989.
See DF19   for full entry information.

DL105 Reference Book for Composites Technology. 1989. 2 vols. Ed. by Stuart M. Lee. Lancaster, PA: Technomic Publishing Co. Inc.

Covers polymeric matrix composites, metal matrix composites and ceramic matrix composites.
TA418.9 C6R35 ENGR

Metallurgy

DL106   Dictionary of Mining, Mineral and Related Terms, 1968.

The standard dictionary in the field, of interest to engineers.   See   DG45 for   full entry information.

DL107 SME Mineral Processing Handbook. 1985. Ed. by Norman L. Weiss. New York: Society of Mining Engineers of the American Institute of Mining, Metallurgical and Petroleum Engineers. var. pg.

Intended for engineers as a "compilation of the operations that convert ores and mineral concentrates into useful products." Contains sections on the history of mining, unit operations and processes, process plants and general information. Indexed.
TN502 S64 ENGR

Production

DL108   Production Handbook. 1987. 4th ed. Ed. by John A. White.   New York: Wiley. 1100 p.

Production management concepts are discussed including   manpower,   methods,   machines, material, money, space and system.
T56 P76 ENGR

Robotics

DL109 International Encyclopedia of Robotics: Applications and Automation. 1988. 3 vols. Ed. by Richard C. Dorf. New York: Wiley.

Includes articles which discuss the theory and applications of robots written by robotics experts around the world, many from Japan and Europe. Cross referenced and indexed. In 1990, the same editors and publishers produced the single volume *Concise International Encyclopedia of Robotics: Applications and Automation* (TJ210.4 I572 ENGR)
TJ210.4 I57 ENGR

Rubber

DL110 Rubber Technology Handbook. 1989. Ed. by Werner Hofmann. Munich / New York: Hanser Publishers. 611 p.

Handbook covering all aspects of rubber technology with comprehensive bibliographies to

further information. Sections on natural rubber, synthetic rubber, rubber chemicals and additives, processing, testing and analysis, and trade names and manufacturers. Indexed; includes appendices.
TS1890 H69313 ENGR

Soil Mechanics

DL111 Barker, John. 1981. **Dictionary of Soil Mechanics and Foundation Engineering.** London: Construction Press. 210 p.

Over 2,500 entries cover definitions used in "civil engineering design and construction, design of structures, foundation engineering, geology, geotechnics, ground engineering, ground exploration, mineral prospecting, mining, offshore engineering and surveying."
TA710 B37 ENGR

Toxic Substances

DL112 Sax, Irving N. 1989. **Dangerous Properties of Industrial Materials.** 7th ed. 3 vols. New York: Van Nostrand Reinhold.

Volume 1 contains brief essays on toxicology, carcinogenesis, and genetic toxicology, and index for names and CAS (Chemical Astracts Services) registry numbers. Volumes 2 and 3 contain 20,000 entries listing systematic names arranged alphabetically, with physical and chemical data, toxicological information, and bibliographic information. Entries also cite CAS Registry Numbers, NIOSH RTECS (Registry of Toxic Effects of Chemical Substances), DOT (U.S. Dept. of Transportation) Guide Numbers, and EPA (Environment Protection Agency) numbers. International coverage with some foreign terms.
T55 S37 ENGR

Water Treatment

DL113 Scott, John S. 1981. **Dictionary of Waste and Water Treatment.** Woburn, MA: Butterworths. 359 p.

Some 6,000 brief definitions of U.K. and U.S. terminology associated with water treatment and supply, sewerage, sewage treatment and disposal, and many other aspects of public health engineering.
TD791 S35 ENGR

INDEXES

AUTHOR INDEX

References are to entry number.

Abbott, Tucker, DH82
Abler, Thomas, CF31
Abraham, Gerald, BF53
Aby, Stephen H., CG1
Adrian, J., DJ40
Adshead, Gordon, AF8
Advisory Committee for the Co-ordination of Information Systems, AN8-AN9;
Aiken, Barbara B., CJ62
Ainslie, Patricia, BE99
Alain, J.M., CD7
Alderton, David, DH88
Alexander, Anne, AD40
Alger, Mark S.M., DF19
Allen, C.W., DD21
Allibone, Samuel, AD59
Allodi, Mary, BE46; BE100
Alston, Sandra, AD22
Altick, Richard, BD1; BD4
Altman, P.L., DH31
American Gas Association, DL94
American Geographical Society, CK1
American Historical Association, CJ1
American Society for Metals, DL57
American Society for Testing and Materials, DA37
Ames, John G., AM120
Ammer, C., CC34
Amos, William, BD48

Amtmann, Bernard, AD24; AD28
Anderson, G.L., BD2
Andriot, John L., AM103
Anger, William, CE48
Anthony, A, DF1
Anthony, L.J., DK60; DL3
Archambault, Ariane, AJ28; AJ78
Arem, Joel E., DG29
Armour, Robert A., BG44
Armstrong, G.H., AK52
Arnason, H.H., BE52
Arnold, E.N., DH8
Arnold, Janet, BE77
Arnstein, Joel, AJ58
Arntzen, E., BE1
Arora, Ved P., AD52
Aros, Andrew A., BG61
Art Institute of Chicago Ryerson Library, BE10
Artibise, Alan F.J., AD53; CA68; CJ73
Ash, Lee, AA53
Ashley, Thomas, CI29
Ashworth, William, DK23
Assn of Canadian Television and Radio Artists, BG3
Atkins, Robert, BE13
Atkins, Stephen E., CD53
Aubin, Paul, CJ63
Aubrey, Irene, AC43
Audouze, Jean, DD38

525

Auster, Ethel, CI1
Aversa, Elizabeth S., BA1
Avis, Walter S., AJ22-23
Axelrod, Herbert R., DH110

Bailey, William G., AM104
Baker, Blanche M., BG26
Baker Library [Harvard University], CC2
Baker, Nancy L., BD4
Balachandran, M., CC3
Balachandran, S., DK57
Balakrishnan, T.R., CA47
Balanchine, George, BG17
Baldick, Chris, BD20
Bales, Eugene F., BB20
Ball, John, BG27
Ballou, Patricia K., CG46
Banfield, W.F., DH91
Banks, Margaret A., CE1
Bannister, David, CA69
Bardis, P.D., CG10
Barker, John, DL111
Barker, Robert L., CG43
Barlow, Harold, BF28
Barnes, Eleanor, AM55
Barnhart, Clarence L.
Barrett, Jane R., CD6
Bartlett, John, AH60
Barzun, Jacques, CJ10
Basler, B.K., DI1
Basler, T.G., DI1
Bateson, Frederick W., BD4
Baugh, Albert C., BD92
Baxter, Angus, AL40
Beaulieu, André, AD45; AM45
Beaudette, L. A., DG20
Beaumont, Cyril William, BG18
Beaumont, Jane, CD6
Becker, Felix, BE27
Beckett, Kenneth A., DH44
Beckwith, John, BF36
Bédé, Jean Albert, BD27
Beeching, Cyril L., AJ37
Beers, Henry P., CJ95
Bejermi, John, AM11
Bélisle, Louis-Alexandre, AJ84
Bell, David J., BC26

Bell, Eric Temple, DB27
Bell, George G, AM20
Belove, Charles, DL75
Bendrick, Jeanne, DB15
Bénézit, Emmanuel, BE22
Benjamin, Jules, CJ1
Benson, Eugene, BG40
Bercuson, David J., CJ79
Bergeron, Claude, BE69
Bergeron, Léandre, AJ85
Berkowitz, Freda P., BF9
Berner, M.S., DI74
Berring, Robert C.
Besancon, Robert M., DE22
Besterman, Theodore, AD1
Biagini, Mary K., BD100
Bingham, J., BD161; BD163
Binstock, R.G., CG21
Birrell, Andrew, BE110
Bishop, Olga B., AM-25; AM34-36; AM51; CJ64
Black, Henry Campbell, CE33
Blackburn, Rae, CE2
Blair, Edward P., BC74
Blake, J.B., DI10
Blanck, Jacob N., BD80
Blazek, Ron, BA1
Bleckman, Isaac A., CG25
Bliss, Alan J., AJ42
Bliss, J.M., CJ65
Block, Walter, CB11
Blood, D.C., DJ52
Blumhofer, Edith L., BC40
Bodian, Nat G., AB15
Boivin, B., DH62
Boivin, Henri-Bernard, AD41
Bond, Mary E., AH2
Bonnenfant, Jean-Charles, AM45
Boorkman, J., DI7
Bottle, R.T., DH2
Boucher, François, BE78
Boudon, Raymond, CG11
Boult, Reynauld, CE16
Boussinot, Roger, BG54
Bowles, S.E., BG74
Boyce, Gray C., CJ35
Boyle, G.M., AD22
Bracken, James K., BD5

Bradley, Howard B., DL58
Bray, W., CF50
Brazil, Mary Jo, CG16
Bregman, Alvan, AC10
Brehier, Emile, BB21
Brewer, Annie M., AJ2
Brewer, James Gordon, CK3
Bridson, Gavin D.R., BE94
Briggs, Geoffrey, AH40
Briggs, H.M., DJ22
Brisman, Shimeon, BC33
British Library, AD9-11
British Library. Dept of Manuscripts, AD98
British Library. Dept of Printed Books, AD7-8; BF21
Brockman, William S., BF1
Bronshtein, I.N., DB7
Brosseau, Mathilde, BE70
Brown, Barbara E., CC6
Brown, Craig, CJ88
Brown, Samuel R., CF2
Browne, Turner, BE102
Bruhn, Wolfgang, BE79
Bruno, Frank, CH14
Bull, Storm, BF25
Buono, Yolande, AD46; AD48
Burington, Richard S., DB8
Burkert, W., BC78
Burnett, David, BE45; BE50
Burnett, James A., DH120
Burrows, Sandra, AF25
Bushsbaum, W., DL83
Butcher, David, AM82
Butler, Alban, BC54
Butler, David, CD49
Butterworth, Rod R., AJ49
Buttlar, Lois J., CI2
Byerly, Greg, AB38
Bynagle, Hans E., BB1
Cadman, Michael, DH104
Campbell, Colin, CD40
Campbell, H.C., AB37
Campbell, Robert Jean, CH15
Canada Institute for Scientific and Technical Information, AB41
Canada. House of Commons, AM6; AM66-67
Canada. Senate, AM68-AM69
Canadian Film Institute, AG8

Canadian Institute for Historical Microreproductions, AD23
Canadian Law Information Council, CE3
Canadian Medical Association, DI74
Canadian Music Centre, BF22
Cannons, Harry G.T, AA5
Caponigi, A. Robert, BB23
Cariou, Mavis, AC10
Carlyon, Richard, BC86
Carpenter, C.H., BC81
Carpenter, Charles A., BD142
Carroll, Charles R., CG24
Carson, R.A.G., BE75
Carter, Sarah, CG48
Cary, Pam, DH106
Catsberg, C.M.E., DJ42
Chafetz, Morris, CG31
Chaffers, William, BE84
Chaliand, Gerard, AK20
Chamberlain, Ken, BE87
Chandler, Ralph C., CD21
Chandler, Tertius, CA70
Chandna, K., AA42
Chen, Ching-Chih, DA9; DI2
Cheremisinoff, Paul N., DK33
Cherns, J.J., AM1
Cheveldayoff, Wayne, CC28
Christie, Innis M., CE12
Clapham, Christopher, DB16
Clapp, Jane, BE54
Clark, Audrey N., CK12
Clark, B.D., DK1
Clayton, J.S., DJ24
Clement, Wallace, CD10
Clerk, Nathalie, BE70
Clifton, Daniel, CJ49
Cline, Ruth K., CG33
Cloutier, André, AK36
Coe, Michael, CF57
Cohen, Aaron I., BF35
Cohen, Morris L., CE4
Cohen-Stratyner, Barbara, BG19
Colbeck, M., AD22
Coleman, Ronny, DK24
Collard, Eileen, BE80
Collard, Elizabeth, BE88
Collier, Clifford, BG13

Collinge, N. E., BD178
Colombo, John Robert, AH61; CJ84
Columbia University, BE62
Columbia University. School of Library Service, AA6
Commager, Henry S., CJ96
Conference on British Studies, CJ120
Congressional Information Service, AM115
Connolly, L.W., BG40
Conron, Brandon, AL47
Cook, Chris, CJ12; CJ44-45; CJ126
Cook, Francis R., DH88
Cooke, O.A., CJ68
Cooper, Andrew F., DG7
Coppleston, Frederick, BB22
Corbeil, Jean-Claude, AJ28; AJ74; AJ78; AJ91
Cordingley, Audrey, AD31
Core, H.A., DJ58
Corley, Nora T., CF32
Cortada, James W., DC3; DC16
Coulombe, Michel, BG56
Council of Planning Librarians, CA72
Cox, Nancy, BD56
Cox, Sandra J., AC10
Coyle, L. Patrick, DJ43
Crampton, William, AH41
Crane, David, CB12
Crawford, D.S., DI3
Crellin, Ian, BG45
Crosby, Everett, CJ37
Crystal, David, BD179-180
Cuddon, J.A., AH70; BD28; CL3
Cullinan, B., BD171
Culpin, C., DJ26
D'Aleo, Richard, AM105
Dahmus, Joseph, CJ41
Dalal-Clayton, D.B., DJ19
Dane, Jean, CE5
Danton, J. Periam, AA13
Darrow, Ken, DK58
Davenport, Millia, BE81
Davis, Barbara Kerr., BD101
Davis, Brian, DH45
Davis, Elisabeth B., DH1; DH39
Davis, Louis B.Z., CE30
de Brie, G.A., BB12
de Bruyn, J., AJ64

de Ford, Miriam Allen, CJ50
de Mowbray, Stephen, CJ128
de Stricker, Ulla, CC29
De Charms, Desirée, BF10
De George, Richard T., BB2
De Sola, Ralph, AJ35
De Zuane, John, DK38
Delaney, John, BC54
DeLong, Linwood, CD46
Desbarats, Aileen, AK1
Deschenes, Gaston, AM49
DesRuisseaux, Pierre, AJ86
Deutsch, Babette, BD130
DeVorkin, David H., DD1
Diagram Group, BC11
DiCanio, Margaret, CG34
Dickinson, Terence, DD18
Diehl, Katherine S., BF46
Dimitrov, Theodore D., AN2; AN7
Dionne, Narcisse-Eutrope, AD44
Ditmars, R.L., DH88
Dixon, Dougal, DG33
Donnelly, Jack, CD61
Dorman, Phae H., DF2
Dossick, Jesse J., AF43
Doughty, Arthur G., CJ91
Drache, Daniel, CD10
Drew, Bernard A., BD114
Dreyer, J.L.E., DD30
Dreyfuss, Henry, AJ59
Dubé, Audrey, AM33
Dubois, Diane, AC38
Dubreuil, Lorraine, AK17
Duckham, A.N., DJ27
Duckles, Vincent, BF2
Dulong, Gaston, AJ89
Dun & Bradstreet, CC53
Dun & Bradstreet of Canada, CC72
Dunbar, Gary S., CK4
Dunham, William, DB18
Dunne, Lavon J., DI65
Dunning, John, BG81
Dupré, Paul, AJ79
Dyment, Alan R., BG46
Dysart, Jane I., CC29
Eagles, Paul F.J., DH104
Edmunds, Robert A., DC20

Edwards, Margaret H., AD54
Egoff, Sheila, BD165
Ehresmann, Donald, BE1; BE65
Eldin, Herbert, DH46
Eliade, Mircea, BC15
Elliot, Jeffrey, CD55
Ellis, Linda, CF47
Ellwood, Katherine B., DK61
Engineering Societies, DL2
England, Claire, AC6
Enser, A.G.S., BG62
Erickson, Millard J., BC47
European Communities. Commission, AN30-31
European Communities. Statistical Office, AN32
Evans, Charles, AD70
Evans, Graham, CD22
Evans, Karen, AD22
Everett, T.H., DH48
Evinger, William, AM100
Farmer, D.H., BC54
Farr, Dorothy, BE26
Farrell, Barbara, AK1
Fay, John J., CG30
Feather, Leonard, BF38
Fee, Margery, BD102; BD133
Feigert, Frank, CD47
Fenster, Valmai Kirkham, BD85
Ferguson, Bob, CL9
Fetzer, Mary K., AN10
Filby, P. William, AL43
Findlay, P., CG41
Fink, D.G., DL62; DL75
Finlay, James C., DH98
Finley, E.G., CI3
Fisher, Kim N., BG48
Fitch, Thomas P., CC36
Fleming, Patricia, AD39; AD50
Flemming, Tom, DI13
Fletcher, Banister, BE66
Fletcher, John, CB6
Flexner, Stuart B., AJ57
Flick, Ernest W., DF42
Flodin, Mickey, AJ49
Flower, M.A., DI3
Follett, Wilson, AJ67
Ford, Percy, AM83
Forman, Robert J., BD143

Forsey, Eugene, AM13
Forsyth, Adrian, DH93
Forsyth, Joseph, AM59
Fortin, Marcel, BD68
Foss, Charles, BE92
Fowke, E., BC81
Fowler, H.W., AJ68
Fox-Davies, Arthur Charles, AH42
Franck, Irene, CK22
Frank, R.S., BC35
Fraser, Janet, BD56
Frayser, Suzanne G., CG39
Frazer, J.G., BC82
Freeman-Grenville, G.S.P., CJ18
Freitag, Wolfgang, BE4
Frey, Albert, BE75
Frick Art Reference Library, New York, BE12
Frick, Elizabeth, CJ6
Frohne, Dietrich, DH55
Frum, Linda, CI33
Fuld, James J., BF11
Fuld, Leonard, CC13
Gacs, Ute, CF24
Gagnon, André, AC37
Gagnon, Ann, AC37
Gagnon, Philéas, AD20
Gall, Gerald L., CE46
Gallagher, Diane, AA50
Gallichan, Gilles, AD45
Galloway, Strome, AH38
Gamlin, Linda, DH72
Gardner, Frank M., BD103
Garrison, Robert H. Jr., DI66
Gassner, John, BD147
Gaudet, Franceen, AF25
Geahigan, Priscilla C., CC10
Geddes, C.L., BC29
Gentilcore, R. Louis, AK37; CJ85
Geological Survey of Canada, DG27; DG52
Germain, Julien, CD7
Gernsheim, Helmut, BE103
Gibbons, S.R., CJ46
Gibson, Dyanne, CI33
Gilchrist, Brian, AE17
Gilpin, Alan, CB15
Gladstone, W.J., DI32
Glasse, Cyril, BC30

Glazer, J., BD171
Gledhill, D., DH49
Gnarowski, Michael, BD58
Godfrey, W. Earl, DH100
Gombrich, E.H.J., BE51
Good, Carter, V., CI18
Goodall, Brian, CK14
Gorman, G.E., BC42
Goss, John, AK23
Gould J., CA18
Goulet, Cyrille, CE38
Gourman, Jack, CI35
Gowans, Alan, BE71
Grabois, Aryeh, CJ41
Graff, Henry F., CJ10
Granatstein, J.L., CJ79
Grandpré, Pierre de, BD69
Grant, Gail, BG23
Grant, Michael, AL64; CJ32
Grant, Neil, AK24
Grasham, W.E., CD7
Gravel, Pierre Bettez, CF3
Gray, Martin, BD95
Great Britain. Central Statistical Office, CA63
Great Britain. HMSO, AM96
Green, Debbie, AG8
Green, Jonathon, AJ51
Green, Stanley, BF39
Green, Syd, DJ39
Greenhill, Ralph, BE110
Gregory, Ruth W., AH53
Grenville, J.A.S., CD31
Grice, Joel D., DG53
Grieb, Kenneth J., CJ112
Griffith, H. Winter, DI64
Grigg, D.B., DJ27
Grimal, Pierre, BC83-84;
Gross, Charles, CJ122
Gross, Ernie, BC19
Grout, Donald J., BF51
Grun, Bernard, CJ19
Guerry, Herbert, BB6
Guilbeault, Claude, AM40
Guilmette, Pierre, BG13
Guinagh, Kevin, AJ43
Haas, M.L., CF35
Haensch, G., DJ20

Haight, Willet Ricketson, AD29
Hajnal, Peter I., AN3; AN11-12
Hale, Elizabeth, AK9
Halkett, Samuel, BD46
Hall, James, BE15
Halliwell, Leslie, BG64; BG82
Halpenny, Francess, AL32
Hamel, Reginald, AL49
Hamelin, Jean, AD45; AL32; AM45
Hamilton, Betty, DI35
Hamilton, David A., BG16
Hamilton, R.M., AH62
Hamilton, William B., AK52
Hancock, Ian, AJ72
Hanson, Richard, BD56
Harder, Kelsie B., AK53
Hare J., AD46
Hare, John, AL49
Harner, James L., BD7
Harper, Don, DH108
Harper, J. Russell, BE36
Harris, Chauncy Dennison, CK6
Harris, Cole, CJ87
Harris, Diana K., CG19-20
Harris, Ernest E., BF3
Harris, Robin S., CI4
Hartt, Frederick, BE51
Hartzler, Judith, BD100
Harvard University. Peabody Museum of Archaeology and Ethnology Library, CF4
Harvey, Paul, BD160
Haselbauer, Kathleen J., DI5
Hastings, James, BC64
Haviland, Virginia, BD169
Havlice, Patricia, BE24; BE55; BF12; CJ2
Hawkes, Jacquetta Hopkins, CF19
Hawkins, Donald T., AB39
Hayes, Greg, CK23
Head, C. Grant, AK37; CJ85
Hecker, Helen, CK24
Hefele, Bernhard, BF4
Heggie, Grace, AF8; CD9
Heilbron, J.L., DE1
Heizer, Robert Fleming, CF48
Helleiner, Frederick M., DH104
Henderson, George Fletcher, AM28
Hendler, Sheldon Saul, DI64

Hesslein, Shirley, CG16
Heyer, Anna H., BF13
Higgins, Marion V., AM30
Hill, A. David, CK7
Hinckley, Karen, BD104
Hinson, Maurice, BF14
Hirschfelder, Arlene, CF33
Hodges, John C., AJ69
Hodgkiss, A.G., AK2
Hodgson, Terry, BG38
Hoffleit, Dorrit, DD24
Hoffman, Frank W., BF5
Hoffman, Herbert, BD132
Holler, Frederick L., CD2
Holmes, George, CJ42
Holmes, Marjorie C., AM60
Home, R.W., DE2
Hordeski, Michael F., DC23
Horecky, Paul, CJ127
Horst, R. Kenneth, DH50
Houghton, Walter E., AF24
Howard, Rhoda E., CD61
Howes, F., DH52
Howland, M.S., CJ6
Hoy, Helen, BD106
Huber, Thomas P., CK15
Hubin, Allen J., BD115
Huchtmeier, W.K., DD25
Hudon, Michelle, CI8
Humphreys, Christmas, BC24
Hunter, Sam, BE52
Hurt, Charlie D., DA3
Husén, Torsten, CI19
Illingworth, Valerie, DC17; DD12
Immelmann, Klaus, DH74
International Commission on Zoological Nomenclature, DH75
International ISBN Agency, AB4
International Union of Pure and Applied Chemistry, DF31
Iosipescu, Michael, CE12
Ireland, Norma Olin, BD153; CG54
Irwin, Barbara, CJ64
Isaacson, Richard T., DH42
Jackson, Byron M., CD34
Jackson, Joan S., CJ50
Jackson, Roland, BF6

Jacobs, M., DI79
Jacobstein, J. Myron, CE9
Janson, H.W., BE51
Jean, Marcel, BG56
Jeffrey Michael I., DK44
Jeffries, John, AN28; CE5
Jenner, Catherine, CE18
Jenness, Diamond, CF44
Jennisen, T., CG41
Johansson, Eve, AM5
Johnson, Hugh, DJ49; DJ62
Johnson, J.K., CD43
Johnson, William, BE106
Jones, John Oliver, DH102
Jones, Lois Swan, BE5
Jones, Peter, CD57
Jones, R.E., AL67
Julian, John, BF47
Kallman, Helmut, BF29
Kalnay, Alanna, AC6
Kaplan, Jonathan, BC36
Kassis, Hanna, BC31
Katz, Bill, AE7
Katz, Ephraim, BG58
Keller, Dean H., BD154
Kelly, J.N.D., BC56
Kelsey-Wood, Dennis, DH109
Kemper, Robert V., CF7
Kennedy, James R., BC5; CG3
Kent, Diana, DI13
Kidd, Jane, DH106
Kiehl, Erich H., BC1
King, Robert C., DH21
King, Thomas B., BE89
Kinkle, Roger D., BF40
Kirby, David K., BD105
Kirwin, W.J., AJ7
Kister, Kenneth F., AI4; AJ4; AK4
Kittel, Gerhard, BC70
Klein, Barry T., CF45
Klein, Ernest., AJ40
Klinck, Carl F., AL47; BD70
Kline, Morris, DB29
Koeppe, Richard P., CI26
Kohlenberger, John R., BC60
Konigsberg, Ira, BG59
Koster, Donald N., BD81

Kostof, Spiro, BE67
Kowaliczko, Beatrice, CJ89
Kronick, David A., DH3
Kruschke, Earl R., CD34
Kurian, George Thomas, CA40; CJ55
Lacey, A.R., BB16
Laferriere, C., AM28
Lagacé, Robert, CF5
Lakos, Amos A., DG7
Lambert, David, DG55
Lamonde, Yvan, BD68
Land, Brian, AH6; AM8; AM25; CC12
Lang, Kenneth, DD21
Langdon, John E., BE90
Langer, William L., CJ14
Langley, Graham, DL92
Lapidus, Dorothy Farris, DG37
Laplante, Louise, BF36
Larkin, Robert, CK14
Lass, A., AJ47
Lauriault, Jean, DJ63
Lavin, Michael R., CC13
Leacy, F.H., CA50
Leary, Lewis Gaston, BD82
Lecker, Robert, BD59
Ledoux, Denise, AM28
Lee, Mein-ven, AJ91
Leftwich, A.W.A., DH77
Leonard, William T., BG39
Lerner, Loren R., BE6
Lessard, Michel, BE91
Levine, M.L., BC23
Lewanski, Richard, AA53
Lewin, Albert, AJ53
Lewin, Esther, AJ53
Lewine, Richard, BF15
Lewis, Richard J., DJ46
Li, Tz-chung, CA3
Library of Congress, AD13-AD 19; AD93; AE8; AG13; AK10-AK11
Library of Congress. Manuscripts Section, AD100
Library of Congress. National Union Catalog, BF23
Light, Beth, CG49
Line, Les, DH85
Linteau, Paul-André, CJ63
Litchfield, Jack, BF57
Little, R. John, DH54

Littlefield, David, CJ134
Lochhead, Douglas, AD4
Loeb, Catherine, CG48
Loewenberg, Alfred, BF44
Logasa, Hanna, BD155
Longman, Larry, AG32
Lort, John C., AD54
Lowndes, William Thomas, AD58
Lowther, Barbara, AD54; AM61
Luckyj, Natalie, BE26
Luginbuhl, Christian B., DD26
Lusis, Andy, DD1
MacDonald, Christine, AM63
MacDonald, Colin S., BE37
MacEllven, Douglas, CE10
MacLean, Norman, DH21
Macmillan, Keith, BF36
MacTaggart, Hazel I., AM52-53
Maddox, G.L., CG21
Magalini, Sergio, DI37
Magel, Charles R., CG22
Magill, Frank N., AL54; BD113; DE31
Magriel, Paul David, BG14
Mahler, Gregory, CD8
Maillet, Lise, AM38
Maitland, Leslie, BE70
Maizell, Robert E., DF3
Makdessian, Frances, DI89
Makkai, Adam, AJ54
Malin, David, DD27
Mangone, Gerard J., DG56
Manthorne, Jacquie, CG52
Marquis, Hugette, BE91
Marsden, Brian G., DD28
Marsh, James H., AI18; CJ82
Marshall, A.R., CI24
Marshallsay, Diana, AM91
Martin, Daniel W., CD5
Martin, Marlene M., CF36
Marulli-Koenig, Luciana, AN2
Marx, Siegfried, DD44
Mason, Lauris, BE96
Matheson, E., AB2
Mathien, Thomas, BB3
Matlins, Antoinette Leonard, DG57
Matthews, Geoffrey J., AK38; AK40; CJ87
Maurice, E. Grace, AD96-97

Mawson, C.D.S., AJ44
May K.O., DB1
Mayer, Ralph, BE16
Mazur, C., 49
McAllister, Don E., DH114
McCage, James P., BC43
McCann, Richard Dyer, BG52
McDonnell, K., DI67
McDonough, Don, BG25
McDonough, Irma, AC37
McDowell, Patricia, CF40
McEvedy, Colin, CJ16
McGee, Timothy J., BF52
McInerny, Ralph M.
McInnis, Raymond G., CH2
McKay, W.A., AL33
McKenzie, Karen, BE7
McLeish, Kenneth, BC23; BD101
McMann, Evelyn de R., BE38
McMenemy, John, CD24
McMillan, Patricia, CG3
McQuarrie, Jane, AC38; BD133
Meacham, Mary, BD169
Meadows, A.J., DC25
Means, Spencer, BD15
Mehrtens, John M., DH90
Meikeljohn, Christopher, CF37
Melton, J.G., BC38
Menditto, Joseph, CG29
Mennie-de Varennes, Kathleen, AL44
Mercer, Anne, AL51; BD76; BD133
Mersky, Roy M., CE9
Messenger, William E., AJ64
Metford, J.C.J., BC48
Middleton, Nick, DK51
Miller, Clara G., CJ64
Miller, E. Willard, DK7; DK46
Miller, Melanie Ann, DH70
Miller, P.M., CA20
Minasian, Stanley M., DH115
Miska, John, BD61
Mitchell, Alan, DJ62
Mitchell, Mary E., CE22
Mitchell, Richard Scott, DG41
Molnar, John E., AD68
Monro, Isabel S., BE57
Montgomery, A.C., AA38

Monty, Vivienne, CC33
Moody, Marilyn K., AM111
Moore, Geoffrey H., CB20
Moore, Melita H., CB20
Moore, Patrick, DD11; DD39
Morehead, Joe, AM108
Morgan, Henry J., AD27; AL30
Morin, Cimon, BE74
Morisset, Micheline, AG6
Moritz, Albert, BD71
Moritz, Theresa, BD71
Morley, Marjorie, AD55
Morley, William F.E., AD25
Morris, Peter, BG68
Morris, William, AJ70
Morrison, Paul G., AD60, AD61
Morrow, Robert Jr., AK38
Morton, L.T., DI6; DI15
Moscovitch, A., CG41
Moss, John. BD107
Moss, Martha, BE107
Moure, Nancy, BE57
Moyles, R.G., BD62
Muirden, James, DD20
Mulhall, Michael George, CA41
Mulligan, Gerald A., DH55
Munro, Derek B., DH55
Munsterberg, Hugo, BE18
Murdock, George, CF5; CF20
Murray, James A.H., AJ8
Myers, Bernard S., BE17
Myers, Jay, CJ90
Myers, Kurtz, BF58
National Archives of Canada,
 see Public Archives of Canada
National Film Board of Canada, AG15; AG16
National Gallery of Canada, BE8; BE48-49
National Information Center for Educational Media,
 AG17
National Library of Canada, AE17; AF45
Nebenzahl, Kenneth, AK28
Nelson, Joseph S., DH116
New, W.H., BD72
New York Public Library. Reference Dept, BF24
New York Public Library. Research Libraries, AM3;
 BD144; BG29

New York Public Library. Research Libraries. Performing Arts Research Center, BG15
Newberry Library Center for the History of the American Indian, CF39
Newberry Library. Edward E. Ayer Collection, CF38
Newcombe, Duane, DJ47
Newhall, Beaumont, BE108
Newman, Dorothy, AH50
Newnham, Jeffrey, CD22
Nicholson, N.L., AK5
Nilon, Charles H., BD84
Nilsen, Kirsti, AC6
Norman, Jean, AH50
Normandin, Pierre, AM11
Northwest Territories, AM64
Nowlan, Robert A., BG69
Nyberg, Cheryl, CE51
Nyvall, Robert F., DJ29
O'Bannon, Loran S., DL82
O'Brien Fehr, K., DI79
O'Brien, Robert, CG31
O'Day, Danton, CI33
O'Dea, Agnes C., AD40
O'Reilly. W., DG62
Ollé, James G.H., AM84
Olson, Kent C., CE4
Olton, Roy, CD26
Ontario. Legislative Assembly, AM77; AM78
Ontario. Management Board of Cabinet, AM22
Ontario. Ministry of Government Services, AM23
Organisation for Economic Co-operation and Development, AN33-35;
Osier, Donald V., CH3
Osmanczyk, Edmund Jan, AN23
Overmeier, Judith A. 1989. , DH4
Paetow, Louis, CJ35
Page, Donald M., CD6
Page, G.T., CI24
Paikeday, Thomas M., AJ25
Pain, Howard, BE92
Pal, Gabriel, DH5
Palardy, Jean, BE92
Palgrave, R.H.I., CB18
Palmer, James C., CI25
Parker, James, AH43
Parker, Mary Ann, BF7
Parry, Caroline, AH55

Parry, Pamela J., BE56
Parry, R.B., AK6
Partnow, Elaine, AH66
Partridge, Eric H., AJ55
Pasachoff, Jay, DD19
Patterson, Douglas, DJ58
Patterson, Margaret, BD7
Pearson, Barbara C., DK61
Pearson, Roger, CF17
Peel, Bruce B., AD56
Pellant, Chris, DG60
Pemberton, John E., AM85
Pepermans, Raymond, CD25
Pepper, M., BC22
Pepper, S., CG49
Petteys, Chris, BE26
Pevsner, N., BE64
Pickup, Laurie, CA69
Pim, Linda, DJ46
Pipics, Z, AA40
Plano, Jack C., CD21; CD26
Plant, Richard, BG27
Platt, Colin, CJ43
Polking, Kirk, BD51
Pollard, A.W., AD60
Poore, Benjamin Perley, AM118
Popplestone, John A., CH23
Postlethwaite, T. Neville, CI19
Potvin, Gilles, BF29
Pough, F.H., DG48
Poulton, H.J., CJ6
Powell, James M., CJ38
Pratt, T.K., AJ7
Price, David H., CF20
Pritchard, James, BC76
Pross, Catherine, AM37
Prucha, Francis P., CJ100
Pryce, David, CJ131
Prytherch, Roy, AA1
Public Archives of Canada, AD96; AD97; AK14; BE11
Purcell, Gary, AA2
Rai, Priya Muhar, BC28
Rainwater, R., BE1
Raistick, D., CE11
Rand, Benjamin, BB10
Ray, Martyn S., DF4

Read, P.G., DG43
Reading, Hugo F., CA21
Redgrave, G.R., AD60
Reed, Jeffrey G., CH5
Reese, William L., BB17
Reginald, Robert, CD55
Rehrauer, G., BG49
Reichler, Joseph, CL12
Reid, Darrel R., CD41
Reid, Dennis, BE53
Reid, J.H.S., CJ65
Reynolds, F.E., BC25
Ricard, François, BD68
Richard, Stephen, AM86; AM88
Ridpath, Ian, DD12
Riggs, Timothy A., BE97
Rinfret, Edouard G., BD151
Ripley, Gordon, AL51; BD76; BD133
Ritchie, Maureen, CG46; CG48
Robert, Paul, AJ82
Roberts, Charles G.D.
Roberts, Willard Lincoln, DG44
Robichaud, Michele, AM33
Robins, Richard, DH117
Robinson, Jancis, DJ50
Robinson, Judith Schiek, AM109-110;
Rodgers, Frank, AM87; AM89
Rogers, Helen, AA57; AB31
Roget, Peter M., AJ61
Rohn, Peter H., CD17
Room, Adrian, BE75; DD17
Roos, C., DI10
Roper, F., DI7
Rosenberg, Betty, BD108
Rotenberg, G.N., DI74
Rothwell, Helene, AG24
Rown, S.R., CG1
Royal Astronomical Society of Canada, DD32
Royal Historical Society, CJ123
Ruokenen, M., DJ61
Ryder, Dorothy E., AC2
Ryom, Peter, BF18
Sabin, Joseph, AD68
Sabina, Ann, DG48
Sadler, Judith DeBoard, CG37
Sainsbury, Diana, DH23
Salem, James M., BD152; BG43

Saltman, Judith, BD165
Sample, Gordon, BD158
Sarjeant, William A.S., DG8
Sattler, Helen Roney, DG33
Sax, N. Irving, DF48; DL112
Saxenian, Mike, DK58
Sayegh, Kamal, CA78
Schaaf, William L., DB2
Schenk, Margaret T., DL6
Scheven, Yvette, CJ143
Schiff, Marilyn, BE50
Schlachter, Gail A, AA2; AA10
Schlebecker, John T., DJ21
Schlesinger, Benjamin, CG23; CG37
Schultz, Jon S., CE52
Schuster, Mel, BG53
Schwarzkopf, LeRoy, AM107
Scoggan, H.J., DH58
Scott, James A., DH86
Scott, John S., DL113
Seal, Robert, DD1
Sealock, R.B., AK54
Searing, Susan, CG48
Sears, Jean L., AM111
Sears, Minnie E., BF19
Sebert, L.M., AK5
Segsworth, V., CD7
Seymour-Smith, Charlotte, CF17
Seymour-Smith, Martin, BD28
Shafritz, Jay H., CD27; CI26
Shapiro, Nat, BF20
Shaw, H., BD28
Shaw, Ralph R., AD71
Shaw, Warren, CJ131
Sheehy, Eugene P., AC4
Shepherd, William R., CJ26
Shiel, Suzanne, CA47
Shields, D., AH62
Shipley, Joseph T., BD152
Shoemaker, Richard H., AD71-72
Shortt, Adam, CJ91
Showers, Victor, CA45
Shugar, Gershon J., DF49
Sibley, C.G., DH103
Sidgwick, John Benson, DD20
Simpson, J.A., AJ8
Sinclair, Mary Jane T., CE53

Singleton, Paul, DH23
Sinnott, Roger, DD30
Sippl, Charles, DC18
Sirois, Antoine, BD63
Sittig, Marshall, DI84
Sive, Mary R., AG27
Slavens, Thomas P., BB4; BC5
Smallwood, Carol, AM112
Smith D., DI85
Smith, Lillian B., BD171
Smith, Lyn Wall, BE57
Smith, Miranda, DH59
Smith, R., BC88
Smith, R.C., DH6
Smith, Stuart, CH24
Snow, Bonnie, DI72
Somer, Elizabeth, DI66
Soper, Elizabeth W., CI26
Soper, Mary Ellen, AA41
South, M., BC88
Speake, J., BC23
Speirs, John Murray, DH104
Spencer, Michael, AM104
Spiegel, Murray R., DB13
Sports Federation of Canada, CL10
Stacey, Robert, BE101
Stambler, Irwin, BF41-42
Stanford, Geoffrey H., AH58
Stansfield, Wiliam D., DH21
Stark, Richard, CL1
Statistics Canada, CA51-CA61; CC23; CI44
Staton, Frances, AD22
Steele, Apollonia, BD64
Steinberg, S.H., CJ18; CJ22
Steinsaltz, Adin, BC37
Stelter, Gilbert A., CA68
Sternberg, Martin L.A., AJ49
Stevens, Gerald, BE89
Stevenson, Burton, AH68
Stevenson, John, CF44-45; CJ126
Stevenson, Tom, DJ49
Stockholm Int'l Peace Research Institute, CD59
Stoddard, Richard, BG26
Stokes, Donald W., DH79
Story, G.M., AJ7
Story, Norah, CJ92
Stott, J.C., AL67

Strathern, Gloria M., AD51; AD54
Stratton, P., CH24
Strauss, Diane Wheeler, CC14
Strong, James, BC60
Struik, D.J., DB30
Strunk, W. Oliver, BF55
Studwell, William E., BG16
Sundquist, Kenneth E., AM53
Sutherland, Z., BD171
Sutton, Roberta Briggs, AH69
Swan, Conrad, AH44
Sylvestre, Guy, AL47
Szilard, Paula, DI60
Tanaka, Tyozaburo, DJ48
Tatham, A.F., AK2
Tayyeb, R., AA42
Terres, John K., DH105
Theriault, Yvon, AM50
Thewlis, James, DE21
Thibault, Claude, CJ77
Thibault, Danielle, AJ63
Thieme, Ulrich, BE27
Thomas, Clara, AL50
Thomas J.B., CI24
Thomison, Dennis, AA10
Thompson, George A., BD11
Thompson, Lawrence S., AD69
Thomson, Ian, AN29
Thorndike, E.L., AJ31
Thrush, Paul W., DG45
Tice, Terrence N., BB4
Tod, Dorothea D., AD31
Todd, Loreto, AJ72
Toronto Public Library, AD22
Tozzer Library, CF4
Tremaine, Marie, AD22; AD26
Troy, Leo, CC37
Trudel, Marcel, CJ93
Truett, Carol, AB29
Truitt, Evelyn M., BG71
Tully, R. Brent, DD41
Tuma, Jan J., DB14; DL76
Tunnell, Arthur L., AL34
Turner, D.J., AG6
U.S. Bureau of the Census, CA67
U.S. Bureau of Mines, DG28
U.S. Central Intelligence Agency, AH30

Author Index 537

U.S. National Agricultural Library, DJ12
U.S. National Technical Information Service, AM117
Unesco, AN15
Unesco. Computerized Documentation System, AN16
Unesco. Division of the Unesco Library, Archives and Documentation Services, AN17
Unger, Merrill F., BC72
Union des Écrivains Québécois, BD75
United Nations, AN13
United Nations. Dag Hammarskjold Library, AN18-19; AN24
United Nations. Dept of International Economic and Social Affairs, AN25
United Nations. Dept of Public Information, AN20
United Nations. Library, AN21
United Nations. Sales Section, AN22
United Nations. Statistical Office, CA43-44;
United States, see U.S.
Usher, George, DJ48
Valverde, M., DI67
van Caenegem, R.C., CJ36
van der Leeden, Frits, DG46
Varet, Gilbert, BB12
Vehrenberg, Hans, DD42
Ver Nooy, Winifred, BD155
Verrall, Catherine, CF40
Verschueren, Karel, DF51
Villeneuve, Michel, AK36
Vinay, J-P., AJ87
Vine, W.E., BC72
Vlach, Milada, AD46; AD48
Vollmer, Hans, BE28
Wagner, Anton, BD141
Wai, Lokky, CA47; CF41
Wakeman, Geoffrey, BE94
Waldman, Carl, CF46
Waldon, Freda Farrell, AD25
Walford, A.J., AC5
Walker, Michael, CB11
Wallechinsky, David, AH74; CL7
Waller, Adrian, AB11
Wallot, P., AD46
Ward, D.C., DG9
Wass, Hannelore, CG27
Wasserman, Paul, CE6
Wasserstein, Bernard, CD31
Waterston, Elizabeth, CJ78

Watson-Jones, Virginia, BE29
Watt, Robert, AD59
Watters, Reginald E., BD65
Watterson, Andrew, DJ32
Webb, William, CA6
Weber, R. David, DK62
Webster, Donald D., BE93
Webster, J., DI41
Webster, James K., DL6
Weck, Manfred, DL99
Wehr, Hans, AJ90
Weiner, Alan R., BD15
Weiner, E.S.C., AJ8
Weinrich, Peter, CD9
Weir, Alison, AL46
Weiss, Allan, BD125
Wells, Dorothy P., CG24
Wentworth, Harold, AJ57
Wepsiec, Jan, CG4
Wertsman, Vladimir F, AA31
Westfall, Gloria, AM2; CA36
Whalon, Marion K., BG2
Wheaton, B.R., DE1
Wheeler, G.O., DG35
Whitaker, Joseph, AH27
Whitby, Thomas J., CG39
White, Carl M., CA6
White, Jess, CL6
White, William, BC72
Whitehouse, David, CF60
Whiteside, Don, CF42
Whiteson, Leon, BE72
Widdowson, J.D.A., AJ7
Wilke, Max, BE79
Williams, Miller, BD137
Williams, Scott, DI89
Williamson, Mary F., BE6-7
Wilson, John F., BC5
Winearls, Joan, AK16; CJ85
Wing, Donald, AD61
Winter, Ruth, DF36
Winters, Kenneth, BF29
Winters, Wendell D., DH3
Wolfe, Gary K., BD124
Wolfheim, Jaclyn H., DH97
Wolman, Benjamin, CA23
Wood, Christopher, BE33

Woodbury, Marda, CI5
Woodhead, Peter, CF49
Woodhouse, S.C., AJ93
Woodress, James Leslie, BD105
World Council of Churches, BC57
Wray, James D., DD43
Wright, Janet, BE70
Wyczynski, Paul, AL49
Wyman, Donald, DH61
Wynar, B., AC1
Yawching, Donna, AH1

Yogis, John A., CE12
York, Henry E., CD2
Yurkiw, Peter, AD97
Zilkha, A., AJ97
Zink, Steven, AM112
Zombeck, Martin, DD37
Zusne, Leonard, CH25
Zwicker, Barrie, AH11
Zwirn, Jerrold, AM113

TITLE INDEX

References provided are to entry number.

A to Zoo: Subject Access to Children's Picture Books, BD172
A-V Online, AG17
ABBR: Abbreviations for Scientific and Engineering Terms, DL48
Abbreviations Dictionary, AJ35
ABC POL SCI: Advanced Bibliography of Contents: Political Science and Government, CD12
ABHB: Annual Bibliography of the History of the Printed Book and Libraries, AA3
Abingdon Bible Handbook, BC74
Abingdon Dictionary of Living Religions, BC10
Aboriginal People: A Selected Bibliography Concerning Canada's First People, CF42
ABPR, AD75
Abracadabra: Sélection de livres québécois pour enfants, AC44
Abridged Biography and Genealogy Master Index, AL6
Abridged Index Medicus, DI123
Abridged Readers' Guide, AF17
Abstract Journal Informatics 1963–1976, AA14
Abstracts and Indexes in Science and Technology, DA1
Abstracts for Social Workers, 1965-1977, CG42
Abstracts in Anthropology, CF8
Abstracts in Social Gerontology, CG18
Abstracts of English Studies, BD12
Abstracts of Music Literature, BF27

Abstracts on Health Effects of Environmental Pollutants, DK9
Academic American Encyclopedia, AI12
Access Canada: Micromedia's Directory of Canadian Information Resources, AH1
Access Register, AM17
Access to Standards Information, DA36
Access to U.S. Government Information, AM113
ACCIS Guide to United Nations Information Sources on Food and Agriculture, DJ33
Acid Rain, DK70
ACM Guide to Computing Literature, DC2
Acquisitions, BF22
Acronyms and Abbreviations in Library and Information Work: A Reference Handbook of British Usage, AA38
Acronyms, Initialisms and Abbreviations Dictionary, AJ34
Actor Guide to the Talkies, BG61
Additive Alert: a Guide to Food Additives, DJ47
Administration publique canadienne: bibliographie, CD7
Advances in Applied Mechanics, DL33
Advances in Astronautical Sciences, DL34
Advances in Biochemical Engineering / Biotechnology, DL35
Advances in Biotechnological Processes, DL36
Advances in Chemical Engineering, DL37
Advances in Computers, DC10

Advances in Education (series), CI19
Advances in Electronics and Electron Physics, DL38
Advances in Engineering Software, DL39
Advances in Environmental Science and Engineering,, DK21
Advances in Environmental Science and Technology,, DK22
Advances in Food and Nutrition Research, DJ41
Advances in Geophysics, DG24
Advances in Heat Transfer, DL41
Advances in Librarianship, AA20
Advances in Library Administration and Organization, AA20
Advances in Library Automation and Networking, AA20
Advances in Nuclear Science and Technology, DL42
Advances in Serials Management, AA20
Advances in Veterinary Science and Comparative Medicine, DJ55
Aeronautical Engineering: A Special Bibliography with Indexes, DL9
Aerospace Database, DL26
Africa Bibliography, CJ142
Africa, CJ144
Africa Since 1914: A Historical Bibliography, CJ140
Africa South of the Sahara,, CJ145
African Book Publishing Record, CJ141
AFVA Evaluations, BG73
AGA Gas Handbook, DL94
AGI Data Sheets: for Geology, DG47
AGRICOLA, DJ5
Agricultural & Veterinary Sciences International Who's Who, DJ34
Agricultural and Animal Sciences Journals and Serials: An Analytical Guide, DJ1
Agricultural Research Centres: A World Directory, DJ35
Agricultural Systems of the World: An Evolutionary Approach, DJ27
Agricultural Terms, DJ5
AGRINDEX, DJ6
ALA Glossary of Library and Information Science, AA32
ALA/GODORT Guide to Official Publications of Foreign Countries, AM2
ALA Handbook of Organization and Membership Directory, AA55

ALA Membership Directory, AA55
ALA World Encyclopedia of Library and Information Services, AA28
ALA Yearbook of Library and Information Services: A Review of Library Events, AA21
Alberta Bibliography 1954–1979: A Provincial Bibliography, AD51
Alberta Government Publications, AM58
Album of American History, CJ103
Alcohol/Drug Abuse Dictionary and Encyclopedia, CG30
Alexis Lichine's New Encyclopedia of Wines and Spirits, DJ49
Allgemeines Kunstler-Lexikon, BE27
Allgemeines Lexikon der Bildenden Kunstler, BE27
Allgemeines Lexikon der Bildenden Kunstler des XX Jahrhunderts, BE28
Allusions: Cultural, Literary, Biblical and Historical: A Thematic Dictionary, AJ50
Almanac of American History, CJ104
Almanac of American Politics 1990, CD50
Almanac of British Politics, CD49
Almanac of Famous People, AL5
Alternative Library Literature: A Biennial Anthology, AA22
Alternative Press Index, AF3
Alternatives to Laboratory Animals, DH81
Amateur Astronomer's Handbook, DD20
America: History and Life,, CJ7
American and British Genealogy and Heraldry: A Selected List of Books, AL43
American Art Directory, BE39
American Authors, 1600–1900, AL60
American Bibliography: A Chronological Dictionary..., AD70
American Bibliography: A Preliminary Checklist for 1801–1819, AD71
American Book Publishing Record, AD75
American Book Trade Directory, AB1
American Book-Prices Current, AD89
American BPR Annual, AD75
American Catalogue of Books, 1876–1910, AD73
American Doctoral Dissertations, AF39
American Drama Criticism, BD140
American Fiction 1900-1950, BD105
American Fiction to 1900: A Guide to Information Sources, BD105

American Film Institute Catalog of Motion Pictures, AG1
American Heritage Children's Dictionary, AJ27
American Heritage Dictionary of Science, DA54
American Heritage Dictionary of the English Language, AJ9
American Heritage Larousse Spanish Dictionary: Spanish/English, English/Spanish, AJ101
American Historical Review, CJ9
American Horticultural Society Encyclopedia of Garden Plants, DH44
American Hospital Association Guide to the Health Care Field, DI54
American Humanities Index, BA2
American Institute of Physics Handbook, DE25
American Library Directory, AA44
American Literary Scholarship, BD78
American Literature and Language, BD81
American Literature, English Literature and World Literatures in English Series, BD2
American Medical Association Encyclopedia of Medicine, DI31
American Medical Association Family Medical Guide, DI61
American Medical Association Handbook of First Aid and Emergency Care, DI42
American Medical Directory, DI55
American Men & Women of Science, DA62
American Men and Women of Science: Social and Behavioral Sciences, CA24
American Poetry Index, BD138
American Political Dictionary, CD26
American Prose and Criticism, BD79
American Reference Books Annual, AC1
American Sign Language: A Comprehensive Dictionary, AJ49
American Statistics Index, CA64
American Studies: An Annotated Bibliography, CJ94
American Universities and Colleges, CI28
American Writers: A Collection of Literary Biographies, BD86
Americana Annual, AI6
Amphibian Species of the World, DH87
Amy Vanderbilt Complete Book of Etiquette, AH45
An de nouveautés (France), AD83
Analytical Abstracts, DF5

Analytical Concordance to the Revised Standard Version of the New Testament, BC60
Anatomy of Wonder: A Critical Guide to Science Fiction, BD117
Ancient History Atlas 1700BC to 565AD, CJ29
Anger's Digest of Canadian Law, CE48
Animal Behavior Abstracts, DH66
Animal Health Yearbook, DJ51
Animal Identification: A Reference Guide, DH67
Annals of American Literature 1602-1983, BD87
Annals of Opera, 1597–1940, Compiled From the Original Sources, BF44
Année psychologique, CH10
Anniversaries and Holidays, AH53
Annotated Bibliography of Canada's Major Authors, BD59
Annotated Bibliography of Canadian Demography 1966–1982, CA47
Annotated Bibliography of Genealogical Works in Canada, AL44
Annotated Bibliography of Selected Chinese Reference Works, CJ149
Annotated Standing Orders of the House of Commons 1989, AM6
Annotated World List of Selected Current Geographical Serials, CK8
Annuaire de statistiques sanitaires mondiales,, DI52
Annuaire démographique, CA43
Annuaire des bibliothèques canadiennes, AA45
Annuaire des dépôts d'archives canadiens, AD94
Annuaire des femmes du Canada, CG52
Annuaire du Canada, AH15
Annuaire du Québec, AH13
Annuaire statistique, CA42; CA44
Annuaires canadiens 1790–1987: une bibliographie, AH2
Annual Abstract of Statistics, CA63
Annual American Catalog, AD73
Annual Bibliography of British and Irish History, CJ123
Annual Bibliography of English Language and Literature, BD3
Annual Bibliography of Ontario History 1980-1985, CJ64
Annual Book of ASTM Standards, DA37
Annual Departmental Reports of the Dominion of Canada, 1925-1930, AM71

Annual Index to Poetry in Periodicals, BD138
Annual Obituary, AL8
Annual Register of Grant Support, AH4
Annual Register: A Record of World Events, AH21
Annual Reports on the Progress of Chemistry, DF17
Annual Review of Anthropology, CF9
Annual Review of Astronomy and Astrophysics, DD6
Annual Review of Computer Science, DC11
Annual Review of Energy, DK73
Annual Review of Fluid Mechanics, DL43
Annual Review of Information Science and Technology, AA23
Annual Review of Materials Science, DL44
Annual Review of Medicine, DI27
Annual Review of Nuclear and Particle Science, DE13
Annual Review of Psychology, CH11
Annual Review of Public Health, DI127
Annual Review of Sociology, CG5
Annual Review Series, DI27
Annual Reviews in Fluid Mechanics, DL93
Annual Survey of American Poetry, BD138
Anthropological Fieldwork: An Annotated Bibliography, CF3
Annotated Bibliography of Genealogical Works in Canada, AL44
Anthropological Glossary, CF17
Anthropological Index, CF10
Anthropological Literature, CF11
Anthropology Journals and Serials: An Analytical Guide, CF1
Apparent Places of Fundamental Stars, DD22
Applied Mechanics Reviews, DL10
Applied Science and Technology Index, DA13
Applied Social Science Index and Abstracts, CA7
Appraisal: Science Books for Young People, AC47
Appropriate Technology Sourcebook, DK58
Aqualine Abstracts, DK10
AQUAREF, DK11
Aquatic Sciences and Fisheries Abstracts, DH68
ARBA Guide to Biographical Dictionaries, AL1
ARBA Guide to Library Science Literature, 1970–83, AA4
ARBA Guide to Subject Encyclopedias and Dictionaries, AI2
Archaeological Atlas of the World, CF60
Archaeologists' Year Book, CF21

Archaeology: A Bibliographical Guide to the Basic Literature, CF48
Architectural Periodicals Index, BE60
Architecture of the Picturesque in Canada, BE70
Architecture Series: Bibliography, BE61
Architecture: A Bibliographic Guide, BE65
Arctic Bibliography, CJ162
Armoiries drapeaux et emblemes floraux du Canada, AH37
Arms Control and Disarmament, Defense and Military, International Security and Peace: A n Annotated Guide to Sources, 1980-1986, CD53
Arms Control, Disarmament, and Military Security Dictionary, CD55
Arms, Flags and Emblems of Canada, AH37
Art and Architecture in Canada: A Bibliography and Guide to the Literature to 1981, BE6
Art and Pictorial Press in Canada: Two Centuries of Art Magazines, BE7
Art Books: A Basic Bibliography of Monographs on Artists, BE4
Art et architecture au Canada: bibliographie ... à 1981, BE6
Art Gallery of Ontario: Selected Works, BE44
Art Index, BE9
Art Information: Research Methods and Resources, BE5
Art of Literary Research, BD1
Art Sales Index, BE58
Art: A History of Painting, Sculpture, Architecture, BE51
Artbibliographies modern, BE11
Articles on American Literature, 1900-1950, BD82
Artist Biographies Master Index, BE21
Artist's Handbook of Materials and Techniques
Artistes au Canada, BE34
Artists in Canada, BE34
ArtQuest, BE58
Arts and Humanities Citation Index, BA310
Arts in America: A Bibliography, BE2
Artspeak: A Guide to Contemporary Ideas, Movements, and Buzzwords, BE13
ASHRAE Handbook & Product Directory, DL96
Asia and the Pacific, CJ151
Asian Literature in English: A Guide to Information Sources, BD2

Asimov's Biographical Encyclopedia of Science and Technology, DA63
Asimov's Chronology of Science & Discovery, DA59
Aslib Index to Theses Accepted for Higher Degrees.. (Great Britain), AF44
ASLIB Directory, AA47
ASSIA: Applied Social Science Index and Abstracts, CA7
Associations Canada 1991: An Encyclopedic Directory, AH5
ASTIS Current Awareness Bulletin, DG10
Astronomischer Jahresbericht, DD2
Astronomical Almanac, DD23
Astronomy and Astronautics: An Enthusiast's Guide to Books and Periodicals, DD1
Astronomy and Astrophysics Abstracts, DD2
Astronomy Handbook, DD20
Astrophysical Formulae, DD21
Astrophysical Quantities, DD21
Atlantic Canadian Imprints, 1801–1820: A Bibliography, AD39
Atlantic Provinces Book Reviews, AC26
Atlantic Provinces Checklist, AD38
Atlas de la Nouvelle France, CJ93
Atlas linguistique de l'Est du Canada, AJ89
Atlas national du Canada, AK41
Atlas of African History, CJ147
Atlas of American History, CJ105
Atlas of Ancient America, CF57
Atlas of Archaeology, CF56
Atlas of Canadian Agriculture, DJ36
Atlas of Cats of the World, DH109
Atlas of Central America and the Caribbean, CJ114
Atlas of Classical Archaeology, CF58
Atlas of Classical History, CJ28
Atlas of Columbus and the Great Discoveries, AK28
Atlas of Deep-Sky Splendors, DD42
Atlas of Early Man, CF19
Atlas of Environmental Issues, DK51
Atlas of Mankind, CF18
Atlas of Medieval Europe, CJ43
Atlas of Medieval Man, CJ43
Atlas of New France, CJ93
Atlas of North American Indians, CF46
Atlas of Plant Life, DH46
Atlas of the Breeding Birds of Ontario, DH104
Atlas of the Greek and Roman World in Antiquity, CJ29
Atlas of the Middle East, CJ135
Atlas of the Planets, DD39
Atlas of the Solar System, DD39
Atlas of the World Today, AK24
Atlas of World Cultures, CF20
Atlas of World Cultures: A Geographical Guide to Ethnographic Literature, CF20
Atlas thématique du Canada et du monde, AK36
Atlases Available in North America, AK4
Audiocassette Finder, AG17
Audiovisual Review Digest, AG17
Audubon Society Book of Insects, DH85
Audubon Society Encyclopedia of North American Birds, DH105
Audubon Society Field Guide to North American Rocks and Minerals, DG48
Audubon Society Field Guide to North American Wildflowers: Eastern Region, DH43
Audubon Society Field Guide to North American Trees, DJ62
Australian Literature to 1900, BD2
Australian National Dictionary, AJ6
Australians: A Historical Library, CJ160
Author and Subject Catalogues of the Library of the Peabody Museum, CF4
Author Biographies Master Index, AL52
Author Catalogues (Library of Congress), AD14
Author Index with Citations, AA5
Authors and Artists for Young Adults
Automotive Electric/Electronic Systems, DL78
AV Market Place: A Multimedia Guide, AG2
Avery Index to Architectural Periodicals, BE62
Aviation/Space Dictionary, DL77
Awards, Honors and Prizes: An International Directory, AH31
Ayer Directory of Publications, AE6

Baker's Biographical Dictionary of Musicians, BF34
Ballet Plot Index, BG16
Barnhart Dictionary Companion, AJ15
Barnhart Dictionary of Etymology, AJ39
Baseball America's Almanac / Directory, CL12
Baseball Encyclopedia: The Complete and Official Record of Major League Baseball, CL12

BASELINE, BG4
Bases de données canadiennes lisibles par machine, AB31
BBC Pronouncing Dictionary of British Names, AJ46
BCLA Reporter, AC26
Beddoe's Canadian Heraldry, AH38
Behind the Scenes, BG33
Benét's Reader's Encyclopedia, BA11
Best Books for Children: Preschool Through Grade Six, AC36
Best Books for Junior High Readers, AC36
Best Detective Fiction, BD116
Best Encyclopedias: A Guide to General and Specialized Encyclopedias, AI4
Best in Children's Books, AC48
Best Plays of [year], BG34
Beyond Picture Books, AC36
BGMI, AL6
B.H.A.: Bibliography of the History of Art, BE3
Bible Almanac, BC73
Biblical Quotations, BC23
Biblio, Catalogue (France), AD83
Bibliographer's Manual of English Literature, AD58
Bibliographia Canadiana, CJ77
Bibliographia Cartographica, AK7
Bibliographia Philosophia, 1934-1945, BB12
Bibliographic Guide to Anthropology and Archaeology, CF4
Bibliographic Guide to Conference Publications, DA23
Bibliographic Guide to Dance, BG15
Bibliographic Guide to Government Publications, AM3
Bibliographic Guide to Maps and Atlases, AK8
Bibliographic Guide to Music, BF24
Bibliographic Guide to North American History, CJ58
Bibliographic Guide to Psychology, CH1
Bibliographic Guide to Technology, DL2
Bibliographic Guide to the History of Computing, Computers, and the Information Processing Industry, DC3
Bibliographic Guide to Theatre Arts, BG29
Bibliographic Index, AD2
Bibliographic Style Manual, AJ63
Bibliographical Handbooks, CJ120
Bibliographical Services Throughout the World, AD3

Bibliographie annotée d'ouvrages généalogiques au Canada, AL44
Bibliographie d'histoire de l'art, BE3
Bibliographie de bibliographies québécoises, AD41
Bibliographie de l'enseignement supérieur au Canada, CI4
Bibliographie de l'histoire du Québec et du Canada, CJ63
Bibliographie de la France: Bibliographie officielle, AD83
Bibliographie de la philosophie, BB5
Bibliographie de la philosophie au Canada: une guide à recherche, BB3
Bibliographie des bibliographies canadiennes, AD4
Bibliographie du droit canadien, CE16
Bibliographie du Québec 1821–1967, BNQ, AD42
Bibliographie du Québec: une mensuelle des publications québécoises, AD43
Bibliographie géographique internationale, CK9
Bibliographie internationale d'anthropologie sociale et culturelle, CF6
Bibliographie internationale de science économique, CB7
Bibliographie internationale de science politique, CD4
Bibliographie internationale de sociologie, CG2
Bibliographie nationale du Canada, AD35
Bibliographie nationale française depuis 1975, AD83
Bibliographies d'études de littérature canadienne comparée, 1930-1987, BD63
Bibliographies for African Studies 1970–1986, CJ143
Bibliographies in American History, 1942–1978: Guide to Materials for Research, CJ95
Bibliography and Index of Geology, DG2
Bibliography and Index of Geology Exclusive of North America, DG2
Bibliography and Research Manual of the History of Mathematics, DB1
Bibliography of Agriculture, DJ7
Bibliography of American Literature, BD80
Bibliography of Asian Studies, CJ150
Bibliography of Astronomy, 1970–1979, DD1
Bibliography of Bibliographies in American Literature, BD84
Bibliography of Bibliographies of Legal Materials, CE13
Bibliography of British Columbia, AD54; AM61

Bibliography of Canadian and Comparative Federalism, CD41
Bibliography of Canadian Bibliographies, AD4
Bibliography of Canadian Children's Books and Books for Young People 1841–1867, AD28
Bibliography of Canadian Folklore in English, BC81
Bibliography of Canadian Imprints, 1751–1800, AD26
Bibliography of Canadian Law, CE16
Bibliography of Canadian Theatre History, BG27
Bibliography of Canadiana: Being Items in the Public Library ..., AD22
Bibliography of Canadiana Published in Great Britain, 1519–1763, AD25
Bibliography of Commonwealth Law Reports, CE14
Bibliography of Dancing, BG14
Bibliography of Dental Reviews, DI24
Bibliography of Discographies, BF56
Bibliography of Economic Geology, DG3
Bibliography of English Language Theatre and Drama in Canada 1800-1914, BD141
Bibliography of Federal Data Sources Excluding Statistics Canada, CA51
Bibliography of Geographic Thought, CK2
Bibliography of Geography, CK6
Bibliography of Higher Education in Canada, CI4
Bibliography of Latin American Bibliographies, CJ111
Bibliography of Latin American Bibliographies Published in Periodicals, CJ111
Bibliography of Legal Materials for Non-Law Librarians, CE18
Bibliography of Library Economy, AA5
Bibliography of Manitoba from Holdings in the Legislative Library of Manitoba, AD55
Bibliography of Medical Reviews, DI123
Bibliography of Newfoundland, 1611–1975, AD40
Bibliography of North American Geology, DG2
Bibliography of Official Statistical Yearbooks and Bulletins, CA36
Bibliography of Ontario History, 1867-1976; 1976-1986, CJ64
Bibliography of Philosophical Bibliographies, BB6
Bibliography of Philosophy in Canada: A Research Guide, BB3
Bibliography of Philosophy, Psychology and Cognate Subjects, BB10
Bibliography of Place–Name Literature: United States and Canada, AK54
Bibliography of Publications Issued by Unesco ...1946 to 1971, AN15
Bibliography of Publications on Unesco, AN17
Bibliography of Reference Works for Cinema Studies, BG45
Bibliography of Studies in Comparative Canadian Literature, 1930–1987, BD63
Bibliography of the History of Art, BE3
Bibliography of the History of Medicine, DI8
Bibliography of the History of Medicine of the United States and Canada, 1939–1960, DI9
Bibliography of the Prairie Provinces to 1953, AD56
Bibliography of Works on Canadian Foreign Relations, 1945–1970, CD6
Bibliotheca Americana, AD68
Bibliotheca Britannica, AD59
Bibliotheca Canadensis, AD27
Bibliothèque nationale, AD5-AD6
Bibliothèques et musées des arts du spectacle dans le monde, BG11
Bibliothèques specialisées au Canada, AA50
BIO-BASE, AL6
Biographical Books, 1876–1949; 1950-1980, AL2
Biographical Dictionaries and Related Works: An International Bibliography.., AL3
Biographical Dictionaries Master Index, AL6
Biographical Dictionary of American Science: 17th Through 19th Centuries, DA62
Biographical Dictionary of Dance, BG19
Biographical Dictionary of Psychology, CH25
Biographical Dictionary of Scientists, DA64
Biographical Dictionary of Scientists: Astronomers, DD9
Biographical Dictionary of Scientists: Mathematicians, DB28
Biographical Dictionary of Scientists: Physicists, DE30
Biographical Directory of Anthropologists Born Before 1920, CF22
Biographical Directory of National Librarians, AA56
Biographies canadiennes - françaises, AL29
Biographies of Inuit Artists, BE35
Biography Almanac, AL5
Biography and Genealogy Master Index, AL6

Biography Index, AL7
Biological Abstracts, DH7
Biological Abstracts / RRM, DH8
Biological and Agricultural Index, DH9; DJ8
Biological Reviews, DH16
Biology Data Book, DH31
BIOSIS, DH7
BIOSIS Previews, DH10
Biotechnology Bibliographies, DG20
Bird-finding Guide to Canada, DH98
Birds of Canada, DH100
Birds of Ontario, DH104
Birds: A Guide to the Literature, DH70
Black's Agricultural Dictionary, DJ19
Black's Law Dictionary, CE33
Black's Veterinary Dictionary, DJ53
Blackwell Dictionary of Historians, CJ11
Blackwell Encyclopedia of Political Thought, CD20
Bloomsbury Good Reading Guide, BD101
Blue Book [of Community Services, CG44
BNBMARC, AD64
Bodian's Publishing Desk Reference, AB15
Bolshoi Anglo Russkii Slovar, AJ100
Book of Canadian Antiques, BE93
Book of Costume, BE81
Book of Jewish Books, BC35
Book of Popular Science, DA47
Book of the States, AM123
Book of World Famous Music: Classical, Popular and Folk, BF11
Book Publishers in Canada, AB2
Book Publishing Record, AD75
Book Review Digest, AC31
Book Review Index, AC32
Book Review Index: Periodical Reviews 1976-1984, AC32
Book Review Index: Reference Books 1965–1984, AC32
Book Trade in Canada: With Who's Where, AB2
BOOKBANK (Whitaker's), AD65; AD66
Booklist, AC15
Bookman's Annual, AC14
Bookman's Glossary, AB16
Books and Periodicals Online, AB30
Books for Children to Read Alone, AC36
Books for College Libraries: ... 50,000 Titles, AC8
Books in Canada, AC26

Books in English, AD64
Books in Print, AD76
Books in Print Plus, AD76
Books in Series, AD74
Books of the Month & Books to Come, AD65
Books on Demand 1980, AD90
Books Out of Print, AD76
Bookseller, AD65-66
BOSS Directory of Computer Software and Services, DC28
Botanical Reviews, DH38
Bourinot's Rules of Order, AH58
Boutell's Heraldry, AH39
Bowker Annual of Library and Book Trade Information, AA25; AB12
Bowker International Serials Database Update, AE13
Bowker's Complete Video Directory, AG3
"Brandon Lists" (Health Sciences), DI1
Breakthroughs: A Chronology of Great Achievements in Science and Mathematics 1200–1930, DA59
Breviate of Parliamentary Papers, AM91
Brewer's Dictionary of Phrase and Fable, BA12
BRI Master Cumulation, 1965–1984, AC32
Bright Star Catalogue, DD24
Britain: An Official Handbook, AH22
Britain's Royal Families: The Complete Genealogy, AL46
Britannica Book of the Year, AI8
Britannica Junior Encyclopedia, AI16
Britannica World Data Annual, AI8
British Archives: A Guide to Archive Resources, AD99
British Authors Before 1800, AL61
British Authors of the Nineteenth Century, AL62
British Book News, AC16
British Books in Print, AD66
British Columbia Government Publications Monthly Checklist, AM62
British Education Index, CI6
British Film Catalogue, 1895-1985, AG4
British Government Publications: An Index, AM88
British Historical Facts, 1688-1760, CJ126
British Historical Statistics, CA62
British Humanities Index, AF6
British Librarianship and Information Work 1981–1985, AA24
British Library Catalogue on CD-ROM, AD9

British Library General Catalogue of Printed Books, AD9; AD10
British Library General Subject Catalogue, AD11
British Library Guide to the Catalogues and Indexes of the Dept. of Manuscripts, AD98
British Museum General Catalogue of Printed Books to 1955, AD7
British National Bibliography, AD64
British National Film & Video Catalogue, AG5
British News Index, AF30
British Official Publications, AM85
British Political Facts 1900-1985, CD49
British Technology Index, DL17
British Union Catalogue of Periodicals, AE19
British Writers, BD93
Brochures québécoises, 1764–1972, AD45
Brock Bibliography of Published Canadian Plays in English, 1766–1978, BD141
Brockhaus Enzyklopadie, AI22
BRS / Search System Users' Manual, AB40
Building Canada: An Architectural History of Canadian Life, BE71
Building Construction Cost Data, DL86
Building Library Collections on Aging: ... Core List, CG16
Building Women's Studies Collections: A Resource Guide, CG47
Building Your Biblical Studies Library, BC1
Bulletin of the Center for Children's Books, AC48
Bulletin signalétique: philosophie, BB9
Bulletin signalétique: histoire et sciences des religions, BC6
Bureau of the Census Catalog, CA67
Burke's Landed Gentry, AL41
Burke's Peerage and Baronetage, AL41
Burke's Presidential Families of the United States, AL41
Burke's Royal Families of the World, AL41
Burns Mantle Theatre Yearbook, BG34
Business Index, AF11
Butler's Lives of the Saints, BC54
Butterflies of North America, DH86
Butterflies: A Colour Field Guide, DH86

CA (online databases), DF7
CAB Abstracts, DJ9
Cabinet Makers of the Eastern Seaboard, BE92
CACTUS, AE15
Cambridge Ancient History Series, CJ30
Cambridge Atlas of Astronomy, DD38
Cambridge Bibliography of English Literature, BD91
Cambridge Dictionary of Biology, DH18
Cambridge Encyclopedia, AI9
Cambridge Encyclopedia of Africa, CJ146
Cambridge Encyclopedia of Archaeology, CF12
Cambridge Encyclopedia of Archaeology, CF51
Cambridge Encyclopedia of Astronomy, DD10
Cambridge Encyclopedia of China, CJ157
Cambridge Encyclopedia of Earth Sciences, DG30
Cambridge Encyclopedia of India, Pakistan, Bangladesh, ..., CJ152
Cambridge Encyclopedia of Language, BD179
Cambridge Encyclopedia of Latin American and the Caribbean, CJ115
Cambridge Encyclopedia of Life Sciences, DH24
Cambridge Encyclopedia of Space, DD10
Cambridge Encyclopedia of the Middle East and North Africa, CJ136
Cambridge Guide to English Literature, BD22
Cambridge Guide to Literature in English, BD22
Cambridge Guide to the Material World, DA40
Cambridge Guide to World Theatre, BG35
Cambridge Handbook of American Literature, BD89
Cambridge Historical Encyclopedia of Great Britain and Ireland, CJ125
Cambridge History of American Literature, BD87
Cambridge History of English Literature, BD94
Cambridge Illustrated Thesaurus of Physics, DE16
Cambridge Italian Dictionary, AJ98
Cambridge Medieval History, CJ39
Cambridge Signorelli Dizionario, AJ98
CAN/OLE II System Guide, AB41
Canada and International Peace and Security: A Bibliography, CD54
Canada and its Provinces: A History ..., CJ91
Canada and the World: An Atlas Resource, AK38
Canada atlas toponymique, AK35
Canada Gazette, AM74
Canada Gazetteer Atlas, AK35
Canada Handbook, AH14

Canada, la paix et la securité internationales: une bibliographie, CD54
Canada on Stage: Canadian Theatre Review Yearbook, BG30
Canada Since 1867: A Bibliographical Guide, CJ74
Canada, the State of the Federation, CD41
Canada Votes 1935–1988, CD47
Canada Water Year Book, DK31
Canada Year Book, AH15; AM7
Canada: A Portrait: The Official Handbook of Present Conditions and Recent Progress, AH14
Canada: Symbols of Sovereignty, AH44
Canada's Food Guide Handbook, DI62
Canada's Forest Inventory, DJ56
Canada's North: The Reference Manual, CJ80
Canada's Playwrights: A Biographical Guide, BD145
Canada's Printed Record: A Bibliographic Register, AD23
Canada's Urban Past: A Bibliography to 1980 and Guide to Canadian Urban Studies, CA68
Canadian Abridgement, CE2
Canadian Advertising Rates and Data, AE3
Canadian Almanac and Directory, AH16
Canadian Annual Review of Politics and Public Affairs, CD42
Canadian Annual Review of Public Affairs, 1901-38, CD42
Canadian Architectural Periodicals Index: 1940–1980, BE69
Canadian Art, BE48
Canadian Art Sales Index, BE59
Canadian Book Review Annual, AC9
Canadian Books for Children: A Guide to Authors and Illustrators, AL67
Canadian Books for Young People, AC37
Canadian Books in Print: Subject Index, AD34
Canadian Books In Print: Author and Title Index, AD33
Canadian Catalogue of Books, 1791–1895, AD29
Canadian Catalogue of Books, AD32
Canadian Centenary Series: A History of Canada, CJ81
Canadian Chamber Music, BF22
Canadian Chemical Register, DF38
Canadian Children's Literature, AC50
Canadian Constitutional Law Handbook, CE30
Canadian Consumer, AH35

Canadian Dictionary for Children, AJ29
Canadian Dictionary: French English, English French, AJ87
Canadian Directories, 1790–1987: A Bibliography and Place-Name Index, AH2
Canadian Directory of Parliament, 1867–1967, CD43
Canadian Drug Identification Code, DI73
Canadian Economic Observer, CA53
Canadian Education Index, CI8
Canadian Education Thesaurus, CI8
Canadian Encyclopedia, CJ82
Canadian Encyclopedic Digest, CE48
Canadian Environmental Directory, DK52
Canadian Ethnic Groups Bibliography, CF25
Canadian Farm Building Code, DJ23
Canadian Farm Buildings Handbook, DJ23
Canadian Feature Film Index, 1913-1985, AG6
Canadian Feminist Thesaurus, CG50
Canadian Fiction: An Annotated Bibliography, BD102
Canadian Film Digest Yearbook, BG63
Canadian Films for Children and Young Adults, AG26
Canadian Fitness Sourcebook, CL10
Canadian Football League Facts, Figures and Records, CL13
Canadian Foreign Relations, CD6
Canadian Formulary, DI73
Canadian French Books in Print, AD36
Canadian Glass, BE89
Canadian Government Programmes and Services, AM9
Canadian Government Publications Catalogue, AM29
Canadian Government Publications: A Manual For Librarians, AM30
Canadian Green Consumer Guide, DK30
Canadian Handbook of Medical and Surgical Specialists, DI53
Canadian Health Care Management, DI43
Canadian Historical Documents Series, CJ66
Canadian History in Documents, 1763–1966, CJ65
Canadian Hospital Directory, DI54
Canadian Index of Scientific Translations, DA27
Canadian Indian Bibliography, 1969-1970, CF31
Canadian ISBN Publishers Directory, AB3
Canadian Jazz Discography, 1916–1980, BF57
Canadian Law List, CE42
Canadian Legal Directory, CE43

Canadian Legal System, CE46
Canadian Legislatures: The [year] Comparative Study, AM10
Canadian Library Handbook, AA45
Canadian Library Yearbook, AA45
Canadian Library-Related Expertise, AA57
Canadian Literature Index, BD56
Canadian Literature/Littérature canadienne, AC17
Canadian Local Histories to 1950, CJ67
Canadian Locations of Journals Indexed for MEDLINE, DI123
Canadian Machine-Readable Databases, AB31
Canadian Magazine Index, AF7
Canadian Medical Directory, DI55
Canadian Men and Women of the Time, AL30
Canadian Men and Women of the Time: A Biographical Dictionary, AL31
Canadian Military Experience 1867-1983: A Bibliography, CJ68
Canadian Minerals Yearbook, DG25
Canadian News Facts, AF31
Canadian News Index, AF26
Canadian Newspaper Index, AF26
Canadian Newspapers on Microfilm, AE1
Canadian Novelists, 1920–1945, AL50
Canadian Official Publications, AM25
Canadian Parliamentary Guide, AM11
Canadian Parliamentary Handbook, AM11
Canadian Patent Office Record, DA33
Canadian Peace Directory, CD56
Canadian Periodical Index, AF8
Canadian Philately: Bibliography and Index, 1864–1973, BE74
Canadian Photography, 1839–1920, BE110
Canadian Picture Books, AC38
Canadian Plays: A Supplementary Checklist to 1945, BD141
Canadian Poetry in Selected English-Language Anthologies, BD133
Canadian Political Facts, 1945–1976, CD40
Canadian Political Parties, 1867–1968: A Historical Bibliography, CD9
Canadian Poster Book: 100 Years of the Poster in Canada, BE101
Canadian Press Newsfile, AF26
Canadian Public Administration: Bibliography, CD7
Canadian Publishers Directory, AB14

Canadian Reference Sources: A Selective Guide, AC2
Canadian Register of Research and Researchers in the Social Sciences, CA25
Canadian Representatives Abroad, CD45
Canadian Selection: Books and Periodicals for Libraries, AC10
Canadian Selection: Filmstrips, AG24
Canadian Serials Directory, AE2
Canadian Silversmiths, 1700–1900, BE90
Canadian Social Science Data Archive, CA26
Canadian Social Trends, CA54
Canadian Socio-Economic Information Management System, CA55
Canadian Sources of Environmental Information, DK52
Canadian Statistical Review, CA53
Canadian Statistics Index, AM26; CA48
Canadian Studies Data, CJ89
Canadian Studies: Foreign Publications and Theses, CJ69
Canadian Style: A Guide to Writing and Editing, AJ63
Canadian Theatre Review Yearbook, BG30
Canadian Theses (Microfiche), AF45
Canadian Theses, AD45
Canadian Trade Marks, DA34
Canadian Translations, AF46
Canadian Water Quality Guidelines, DK32
Canadian Watercolours and Drawings in the Royal Ontario Museum, BE46
Canadian Who's Who, AL31
Canadian Women's Directory, CG52
Canadian Word Book, AJ24
Canadian World Almanac and Book of Facts, AH18
Canadian Writer's Handbook, AJ64
Canadian Writer's Market, AB11
Canadian Writers, AL47
Canadian Writers and Their Works: Poetry and Fiction Series, BD66
Canadian Writers Series, AL48
Canadiana, 1867–1900, Monographs, AD30
Canadiana: Canada's National Bibliography, AD35
CANHEALTH: A Guide for Canadian Health Sciences Libraries, DI3
CANMET, DG20
CANREG, CA25
CANSIM, CA55

CARD: Canadian Advertising: Rates & Data, AE3
Carswell's Directory of Canadian Lawyers, CE42
Cassell's Latin-English, English-Latin Dictionary, AJ94
Catalog of Books Represented by Library of Congress Printed Cards, AD14
Catalog of Cometary Orbits, DD28
Catalog of Government Publications in the Research Libraries, AM3
Catalog of the Public Documents of Congress ... , 1893-1940, AM121
Catalog of the Theatre and Drama Collections, BD144; BG29
Catalogue (Quebec), AM47
Catalogue collectif des impressions québécoises, 1764–1820, AD48
Catalogue collectif des manuscrits conservés dans les dépôts d'archives canadiens, AD97
Catalogue d'imprimés canadiens, AD23
Catalogue de journaux canadiens sur microfilm, AE1
Catalogue de l'éditeur officiel, AM47
Catalogue de l'édition au Canada français, AD36
Catalogue de la bibliothèque de la galerie nationale du Canada, BE8
Catalogue de la bibliothèque des archives publiques, (Canada), AD96
Catalogue de la bibliothèque nationale du Québec, AD43
Catalogue de la collection nationale de cartes et plans, AK14
Catalogue des livres canadiens en librairie, AD33
Catalogue des publications en française du gouvernement de l'Ontario, AM54
Catalogue général des livres imprimés, (France), AD6
Catalogue général des livres imprimés de la bibliothèque nationale: auteurs, (France), AD5
Catalogue numérique des cartes, AK13
Catalogue of British Official Publications Not Published by HMSO, AM97
Catalogue of Canadian Choral Music, BF22
Catalogue of Canadian Minerals, DG50
Catalogue of Microfiches of English Monographs Available in the Micro-Library of OECD, AN33; AN34
Catalogue of National Map Collection, AK14
Catalogue of Printed Music in the British Library to 1980, BF21

Catalogue of Publications on Sale, AN35
Catalogue of the Library of the Arctic Institute of North America, (Montreal), CJ163
Catalogue of the Library of The National Gallery of Canada, BE8
Catalogue of the Public Archives Library of Canada, AD96
Catalogue of the Universe, DD27
Catalogues and Directories, AG13
Catalogues and Indexes of British Government Publications, AM96
Catholic Bible Study, BC74
Catholic Encyclopedia, BC52
CATLINE, DI16
CCINFO databases, DF6; DI86; DJ10
CD:Education, CI7
CD-ROM Directory 1990, AB19
CD-ROM Yearbook, AB20
CD-ROMS In Print, AB21
CEA Handbook, CI30
CEBA, DF9; DL13
Census Catalog and Guide, CA67
Census Dictionary (Canada), CA56
Census Handbook, CA56
Census of Canada, CA57
Central America in the Nineteenth and Twentieth Centuries: An Annotated Bibliography, CJ112
Century of Serial Publications in Psychology 1850–1950: An International Bibliography, CH3
CENV, DK11
Challinor's Dictionary of Geology, DG31
Chambers Biology Dictionary, DH18
Chambers 20th Century Thesaurus, AJ60
Chambers Biographical Dictionary, AL11
Chambers Dictionary of Science and Technology, DA50
Chambers English Dictionary, AJ17
Chambers Thesaurus, AJ60
Chambers Twentieth Century Dictionary, AJ17
Chambers World Gazetteer, AK43
Charlton Standard Catalogue of Canadian Coins, BE73
Check List of Canadian Imprints, 1900–1925, AD31
Check List of United Nations Documents, AN21
Checklist 76, AM119
Checklist of American Copies (STC), AD60
Checklist of American Imprints, AD72

Checklist of British Official Serial Publications, AM89
Checklist of Canadian Literature and Background Materials, 1628–1960, BD65
Checklist of Indexed Canadian Newspapers, AF25
Checklist of Indexes to Canadian Newspapers, AF25
Checklist of Law Reports and Statutes in Canadian Law Libraries, CE17
Checklist of Saskatchewan Government Publications, AM57
Checklist of United States Public Documents, 1789-1909, AM119
CHEM Sources - USA, DF52
Chemical Abstracts, DF7
Chemical Abstracts Service Source Index (CASSI), DF8
Chemical Engineering Abstracts, DF9; DL13
Chemical Engineering Bibliography, (1967-1988), DF4
Chemical Formulary, DF39
Chemical Industries: An Information Sourcebook, DF2
Chemical Industry Directory, DF53
Chemical Patents Index, DA35
Chemical Research Faculties: An International Directory, DF54
Chemical Reviews, DF18
Chemical Technician's Ready Reference Handbook, DF49
Chemical Titles, DF10
CHEMINFO, DF11
Chemist's Ready Reference Handbook, DF49
Chicago Manual of Style, AJ65
Child Abuse: An Annotated Bibliography, CG24
Child Care: An Annotated Bibliography, CG37
Child Development Abstracts and Bibliography, CH6
Childcraft Dictionary, AJ33
Children and Books, BD171
Children's Authors and Illustrators, AL52; AL67
Children's Book Review Index, AC32
Children's Books in Print, (Whitaker's), AD66
Children's Books in Print, (Bowker), BD162
Children's Britannica, AI16
Children's Catalog, AC39
Children's Choices of Canadian Books, AC40
Children's Literature: A Guide to Reference Sources, BD169
Children's Literature: A Guide to the Criticism, BD163
Children's Media Market Place, AB22
Chilton's Automotive Service Manuals, DL79
China Facts and Figures, CJ153
Choice: Current Reviews for College Libraries, AC18
Choix de livres canadiens pour la jeunesse, AC43
Choix de publications gouvernementales, AM47
Christian Periodical Index, BC41
Chronicle of Canada, CJ83
Chronicle of the 20th Century, CJ49
Chronology of English Literature, BD95
Chronology of the Ancient World, CJ31
Chronology of the Medieval World 800–1491, CJ40
Chronology of World History, CJ18
CINDA 86 (1982–1986), DE4
Cinema Booklist, BG49
Cinema: A Critical Dictionary: The Major Film-Makers, BG55
CIS Index, AM115
CIS US Serial Set Index, AM115
Cities of the United States, CA71
CITIS, DL27
Civil Engineer's Reference Book, DL60
CLA Directory of Members, AA58
Classed Subject Catalog. Engineering Societies Library [New York], DL2
Classical and Medieval Literature Criticism, BD159
Classical Greek and Roman Drama: An Annotated Bibliography, BD143
Classical Music Discographies, BF56
CLIC Guide to Computer Assisted Legal Research, CE3
Climatic Atlas Canada, DK50
Climatic Perspectives, DK50
Climatique Canada: A Series of Maps Portraying Canada's Climate, DK50
Clothing in English Canada Circa 1867 to 1907, BE80
CM: A Reviewing Journal of Canadian Materials for Young People, AC49
CNI Clips, AF26
Code canadien d'identification des drogues, DI73
Code international de nomenclature zoologique, DH75
Coins: Ancient, Mediaeval & Modern, BE75
Collection of Definitions in Federal Statutes, CE38
College & Research Libraries, AC24
College Blue Book, CI39

College DBase, CI39
Collier's Encyclopedia, AI5
Collier's Year Book, AI5
Collins Dictionary of Canadian History: 1867 to the Present, CJ79
Collins French-English/English French Dictionary, AJ77
Collins Italian-English/English-Italian Dictionary, AJ98
Collins-Klett German-English/English-German Dictionary, AJ96
Collins-Robert French-English/English-French Dictionary, AJ77
Collins-Sansoni Italian-English/English-Italian Dictionary, AJ98
Color Atlas of Galaxies, DD43
Color Encyclopedia of Gemstones, DG29
Colour Atlas of Poisonous Plants, DH55
Columbia Dictionary of Modern European Literature, BD27
Columbia Encyclopedia of Nutrition, DI63
Columbia Granger's Index to Poetry, BD128
Columbia Lippincott Gazetteer of the World, AK44
Columbo's Canadian Quotations, AH61
Combined Retrospective Index to Book Reviews in History 1838–1974, AC35
Combined Retrospective Index to Book Reviews in Humanities Journals, BA10
Combined Retrospective Index to Book Reviews In Scholarly Journals, 1886-1974, AC35
Combined Retrospective Index to Journals in Political Science, 1886–1974, CD13
Commercial Timbers of the World
Commissions of Inquiry, (Canada), AM28
Committee Reports Published by HMSO, AM88
Commonwealth Universities Yearbook, CI31
Compact Dictionary of Canadian English, AJ26
Companion to the Medieval Theatre, BG36
Comparative Statutory Sources: U.S, Canadian, Multinational, CE52
COMPENDEX, DL14
Compendium of Chemical Terminology, DF31
Compendium of Pharmaceuticals and Specialties (Canada), DI75
Compendium of Seashells, DH82
Compendium of University Statistics, CI45
Complete Book of Ballets, BG18

Complete Book of Bible Quotations, BC23
Complete Book of the Dog, DH107
Complete Book of the Olympics, AH74, CL7
Complete Book of Vitamins and Minerals, DI64
Complete Concordance to the Bible, BC60
Complete Dictionary of Television and Film, BG59
Complete Encyclopedia of Popular Music and Jazz, 1900–1950, BF40
Complete Film Dictionary, BG59
Complete Guide to Buying Gems, DG57
Complete Guide to Environmental Careers, DK34
Complete Guide to Flags, AH41
Complete Guide to French Canadian Antiques, BE91
Complete Guide to Heraldry, AH42
Complete Guide to Modern Dance, BG25
Complete Guide to Vitamins, Minerals and Supplements, DI64
Complete Hebrew English Dictionary, AJ97
Complete Reference Guide to United Nations Sales Publications, 1946–1978, AN14
Complete Stories of the Great Ballets, BG17
Composer Resource Manuals, BF7
Composite Index for CRC Handbooks, DA14
Compositeurs canadiens contemporains, BF36
Comprehensive Bibliography of English-Canadian Short Stories, 1950–1983, BD125
Comprehensive Biotechnology, DL81
Comprehensive Dissertations Index, AF42
Comprehensive Etymological Dictionary of the English Language, AJ40
Comprehensive Grammar of the English Language, AJ66
Comprehensive Index to the Publications of the United States Government, 1881-1893, AM120
Comprehensive Insect Physiology, Biochemistry, and Pharmacology, DH83
Compton's Encyclopedia and Fact Index, AI13
Compton's Multi-Media Encyclopedia
Compton's Precyclopedia, AI17
Compton's Yearbook, AI13
CompuMath Citation Index, (CMCI), DB3
Computer & Control Abstracts, DC4
Computer and Mathematics Search, DB3
Computer Book Review, DC2
Computer Database, DC5
Computer Index of Neutron Data, DE4

Computer Industry Almanac, DC26
Computer Library, DC6
Computer Literature Index, DC8
Computer Publishers and Publications, AB23
Computer Readable Data Bases, AB32
Computer Science Source Book, DC15
Computing in Musicology, BF48
Computing Information Directory, DC1
Computing Reviews, DB6
Computing Reviews, DC2
Concise American Heritage Dictionary, AJ9
Concise Bibliography of English Canadian Literature, BD58
Concise Cambridge History of English Literature, BD94
Concise Chemical and Technical Dictionary, DF20
Concise Chronology of English Literature, BD95
Concise Columbia Encyclopedia, AI10
Concise Dictionary of American Biography, AL36
Concise Dictionary of American Literary Biography, AL55
Concise Dictionary of Biology, DH22
Concise Dictionary of British Literary Biography, AL55
Concise Dictionary of Canadianisms, AJ6
Concise Dictionary of Chemistry, DF26
Concise Dictionary of Christian Theology, BC47
Concise Dictionary of Classical Mythology, BC83
Concise Dictionary of Law, CE34
Concise Dictionary of Mathematics, DB16
Concise Dictionary of National Biography, AL13
Concise Dictionary of Physics and Related Subjects, DE21
Concise Earth Book World Atlas, AK21
Concise Encyclopedia of Archaeology, CF52
Concise Encyclopedia of Australia, CJ160
Concise Encyclopedia of Biochemistry, DF21
Concise Encyclopedia of Islam, BC30
Concise Encyclopedia of Mineral Resources, DG32
Concise Encyclopedia of Psychology, CH19
Concise Encyclopedia of Western Philosophy and Philosophers, BB13
Concise History of Canadian Painting, BE53
Concise International Encyclopedia of Robotics, DL109
Concise Marine Almanac, DG56

Concise Oxford Companion to American Literature, BD89
Concise Oxford Dictionary of Ballet, BG20
Concise Oxford Dictionary of Current English, AJ19
Concise Oxford Dictionary of English Etymology, AJ41
Concise Oxford Dictionary of English Literature, BD97
Concise Oxford Dictionary of Literary Terms, BD20
Concise Oxford Dictionary of Zoology, DH22
Concise Oxford English Arabic Dictionary, AJ90
Concise Oxford History of Music, BF53
Concise Science Dictionary, DA51
Concise Theological Dictionary, BC49
Concordance of the Qur'an, BC31
Conference Papers Index, DA24
Congressional Masterfile, AM115
Congressional Publications and Proceedings, AM113
Congressional Quarterly Almanac, AM98
Conn's Current Therapy, DI44
CONSER (Cooperative ONline SERials), AE4
Consolidated Index of Statutory Instruments, AM73
Consolidated Regulations of Canada, 1978, AM73
Consommateur canadien, AH35
Consumer Health and Nutrition Index, DI58
Consumer Health Information Source Book, DI59
Consumer Reports, AH36
Consumer's Dictionary of Cosmetic Ingredients, DF36
Contemporary American Women Sculptors, BE29
Contemporary Architects, BE63
Contemporary Art and Artists, BE56
Contemporary Artists, BE23
Contemporary Atlas of China, CJ154
Contemporary Authors, AL53
Contemporary Canadian Art, BE50
Contemporary Canadian Composers, BF36
Contemporary Canadian Photography, BE109
Contemporary Canadian Politics: ...Bibliography, 1970–1987, CD8
Contemporary Designers, BE83
Contemporary Foreign Language Writers, AL57
Contemporary Graphic Artists, BE95
Contemporary Literary Criticism: Yearbook, BD29
Contemporary Newsmakers, AL19
Contemporary Photographers, BE103
Contemporary Psychology, CH12

Contemporary Sociology, CG6
Contemporary Theatre, Film, and Television, BG5
Contents Pages in Education, CI9
Contributions to a Short-title Catalogue of Canadiana, AD24
Cooperative ONline SERials, AE4
Cooperative Union Serials System List, AE15
Core Collection in Nursing and the Allied Health Sciences: Books, Journals, Media, DI11
Corpus Administrative Index, AM15
Corpus Almanac and Canadian Sourcebook, AH19
Corpus Directory and Almanac of Canada, AH19
Corpus Juris Secundum, CE49
Cosmetic and Toiletry Formulations, DF42
County and City Data Book (U.S.), CA65
CPL Bibliographies, CA72
CPS (Pharmaceuticals), DI75
CRC Handbook of Chemistry and Physics, DA42
CRC Handbook of Environmental Control, DK35
CRC Handbook of Mathematical Sciences, DB9
CRC Handbook of Microbiology, DH32
CRC Handbook of Physical Properties of Rocks, DG51
CRC Handbook of Plant Science in Agriculture, DJ25
CRC Handbook of Tables for Probability and Statistics, DB10
CRC Standard Mathematical Tables, DB11
Creative Canada, BG6
Crime Fiction 1749–1980, BD115
Critical Dictionary of English Literature..., AD59
Critical Dictionary of Sociology, CG11
Critical Guide to Catholic Reference Books, BC43
Critical Index: A Bibliography of Articles on Film, BG52
Critical Survey of Drama, BD146
Critical Survey of Literary Theory, BD30
Critical Survey of Long Fiction, BD111
Critical Survey of Mystery and Detective Fiction, BD113
Critical Survey of Poetry Series, BD129
Critical Survey of Short Fiction, BD111
Critical Temper: A Survey of Modern Criticism, BD31
Critical Terms for Science Fiction and Fantasy, BD124
Criticial Survey of Poetry, BD129

Cross-Reference Index of Hazardous Chemicals, Synonyms, and CAS Registry Numbers, DK25
Crowell's Handbook of Classical Mythology, BC79
Crown Guide to the World's Great Plays, BD152
Cuadra Directory, AB33
Cumulated Fiction Index, 1945–1960, BD109
Cumulated Magazine Subject Index, 1907–1949, AF21
Cumulative Author Index for Poole's Index, AF23
Cumulative Book Index, AD77
Cumulative Book List, AD65
Cumulative Index of Sociology Journals 1971–1985, CG7
Cumulative Index to Nursing & Allied Health Literature (CINAHL), DI17
Cumulative Index to Revised Statutes of Ontario, AM75
Cumulative Index to the Annual Catalogues of HMSO 1922–1972, AM96
Cumulative Index to the Monthly Catalog, AM122
Cumulative Title Index to U.S. Public Documents, AM119
Current Abstracts of Chemistry and Index Chemicus, DF12
Current Advances in Microbiology, DH17
Current Awareness in Biological Sciences, DH12
Current Bibliographies in Medicine, DI12
Current Biography, AL12
Current Cataloging Database, AD18
Current Chemical Reactions (CCR), DF13
Current Contents, DA15
Current Contents: Arts and Humanities, BA5
Current Contents: Clinical Medicine, DI18
Current Contents: Social and Behavioural Sciences, CA8
Current Geographical Publications, CK1
Current Index to Journals in Education, AA11
Current Index to Journals in Education, CI10
Current Inquiries of the Government of Canada, AM12
Current Law Index, CE23
Current Literature on Aging, CG17
Current Mathematical Publications, DB4
Current Medical Diagnosis and Treatment, DI45
Current Papers in Physics, DE6
Current Physics Index, DE7

Current Publications Index (Statistics Canada), CA61
Current Research, DG27
Current Research in Britain, AF40
Current Research in Library and Information Science, AA12
Current Research in the Geological Sciences in Canada, DG27
Current Technology Index, CTI, DL17
CUSS List (Coop. Union Serials System), AE15
Cyclopedia of Literary Characters II, BD49
Cyclopedia of World Authors II, AL54; BD32

Dance Encyclopedia, BG21
Dance Handbook, BG22
Dance Resources in Canadian Libraries, BG13
Dangerous Goods Regulations, DK36
Dangerous Properties of Industrial Materials, DL112
Database of Databases, AB32
Database of Wildlife Research, DH69
Databook on Endangered Tree and Shrub Species, DJ57
DataMap: Index of Published Tables of Statistical Data, CA31
DAVID, AG21
Days to Remember: Observances of Significance, AH52
Deadline Data on World Affairs, AF33
Death and Dying A to Z, CG25
Death Education II: An Annotated Resource Guide, CG27
Debates, (Canada. Senate), AM68
Debates, (Ontario), AM77
Debates: Official Report, (Canada. House of Commons), AM66
Debrett's Correct Form, AH46
Debrett's Etiquette and Modern Manners, AH47
Debrett's Guide to Tracing your Ancestry, AL42
Debrett's Kings and Queens of Europe, AL42
Debrett's Peerage and Baronetage 1990, AL42
Debrett's Presidents of the U.S.A, AL42
Débuts de l'estampe imprimé au Canada: vues et portraits, BE100
Demographic Yearbook, CA43
Dépôts canadiens des revues indexés pour MEDLINE, DI123

Descriptive Catalogue of the Government Publications of the United States, 1774–1881, AM118
Design in Canada: 1940–1987, BE87
Designer's Handbook of Integrated Circuits, DL83
Deutsche Bibliographie, AD86
Deutsche Nationalbibliographie, AD87
Developments in Food Preservation, DL45
Diagnostic and Statistical Manual of Mental Disorders: DSM-III-R, CH16
DIALOG (Manuals), AB43
Diccionario de la Lengua Española, AJ101
Dictionaries, Encyclopedias and Other Word-Related Books, AJ2
Dictionary Buying Guide, AJ4
Dictionary Catalog, AA6
Dictionary Catalog of the Dance Collection, BG15
Dictionary Catalog of the Edward E. Ayer Collection of Americana and American Indians ..., CF38
Dictionary Catalog of the Music Collection, BF24
Dictionary Companion, (Library Science), AJ15
Dictionary of Acronyms and Abbreviations in Library and Information Science, AA42
Dictionary of Agriculture in Six Languages, DJ20
Dictionary of American Biography, AL36
Dictionary of American English on Historical Principles, AJ5
Dictionary of American History, CJ105
Dictionary of American Idioms, AJ54
Dictionary of American Library Biography, AA59
Dictionary of American Slang, AJ57
Dictionary of Anonymous and Pseudonymous English Literature, BD46
Dictionary of Anthropology, CF17
Dictionary of Architecture, BE64
Dictionary of Art Terms and Techniques, BE16
Dictionary of Astronomical Names, DD17
Dictionary of Ballet, BG20
Dictionary of Ballet Terms, BG20
Dictionary of Behavioral Science, CA23
Dictionary of Bible and Religion, BC45
Dictionary of Biblical Interpretation, BC61
Dictionary of Biochemistry and Molecular Biology, DH23
Dictionary of Birds, DH99
Dictionary of Books Relating to America, AD68
Dictionary of Botany, DH54

Dictionary of British Watercolour Artists up to 1920, BE33
Dictionary of Canadian Artists, BE37
Dictionary of Canadian Biography, AL32
Dictionary of Canadian Economics, CB12
Dictionary of Canadian English, AJ23
Dictionary of Canadian Law, CE35
Dictionary of Canadian Quotations and Phrases, AH62
Dictionary of Canadianisms on Historical Principles: Dictionary of Canadian English, AJ6
Dictionary of Catch Phrases, AJ55
Dictionary of Ceramic Science and Engineering, DL82
Dictionary of Chinese and Japanese Art, BE18
Dictionary of Christian Ethics, BC50
Dictionary of Christian Lore and Legend, BC48
Dictionary of Christian Spirituality, BC46
Dictionary of Classical Mythology, BC83
Dictionary of Clichés, AJ55
Dictionary of Coin Names, BE75
Dictionary of Comparative Religion, BC12
Dictionary of Computing and Information Technology, DC25
Dictionary of Computing, DC17
Dictionary of Concepts in General Psychology, CH23
Dictionary of Concepts in Human Geography, CK14
Dictionary of Concepts in Physical Geography, CK15
Dictionary of Concepts in the Philosophy of Science, DA60
Dictionary of Contemporary Slang, AJ51
Dictionary of Contemporary Usage, AJ70
Dictionary of Costume, BE82
Dictionary of Data Communications, DC18
Dictionary of Data Processing, DC19
Dictionary of Economics and Financial Markets, CB15
Dictionary of Education, CI18
Dictionary of Educational Acronyms, Abbreviations, and Initialisms, CI25
Dictionary of English Law, CE36
Dictionary of Environmental Protection, DK26
Dictionary of Eponyms, AJ37
Dictionary of Ethology, DH74
Dictionary of Food and Nutrition, DJ40
Dictionary of Food Ingredients, DJ40

Dictionary of Foreign Phrases and Abbreviations, AJ43
Dictionary of Foreign Terms Found in English and American Writings, AJ44
Dictionary of Foreign Words and Phrases in Current English, AJ42
Dictionary of Gemmology, DG43
Dictionary of Genetics and Cell Biology, DH21
Dictionary of Genetics, DH21
Dictionary of Gerontology, CG20
Dictionary of Historical Terms, CJ12
Dictionary of Human Geography, CK14
Dictionary of Hymnology, BF47
Dictionary of Jargon, AJ51
Dictionary of Key Words in Psychology, CH14
Dictionary of Library and Educational Technology, AA33
Dictionary of Linguistics and Phonetics, BD180
Dictionary of Literary Biography, AL55
Dictionary of Literary Pseudonyms, BD45
Dictionary of Literary Terms, BD28
Dictionary of Literary Themes and Motifs, BD23
Dictionary of Medical Syndromes, DI37
Dictionary of Medieval Civilization, CJ41
Dictionary of Microbiology and Molecular Biology, DH23
Dictionary of Mining, Mineral and Related Terms, DG45
Dictionary of Modern Critical Terms, BD33
Dictionary of Modern English Usage, AJ68
Dictionary of Modern Written Arabic, AJ90
Dictionary of Musical Themes, BF28
Dictionary of Named Effects and Laws in Chemistry, Physics and Mathematics, DA52
Dictionary of National Biography, AL13
Dictionary of Newfoundland English, AJ7
Dictionary of Numismatic Names, BE75
Dictionary of Opera and Song Themes, BF28
Dictionary of Organic Compounds, DF23
Dictionary of Oriental Literatures, BD24
Dictionary of Personality and Social Psychology, CH20
Dictionary of Philosophy and Psychology, BB15
Dictionary of Philosophy and Religion, BB17
Dictionary of Philosophy, BB16, BB17
Dictionary of Plants Used by Man, DJ48

Dictionary of Political Analysis, CD26
Dictionary of Political Economy
Dictionary of Prince Edward Island English, AJ7
Dictionary of Pronunciation, AJ47
Dictionary of Quotations in Sociology, CG10
Dictionary of Religious and Spiritual Quotations, BC22
Dictionary of Religious Quotations, BC22
Dictionary of Rocks, DG41
Dictionary of Saints, BC54
Dictionary of Science & Technology: English-French/French-English, DA56
Dictionary of Scientific Biography, DA65
Dictionary of Scientific Units Including Dimensionless Numbers and Scales, DA53
Dictionary of Slang and Unconventional English, AJ55
Dictionary of Social Sciences Methods, CA20
Dictionary of Soil Mechanics and Foundation Engineering, DL111
Dictionary of Statistics, CA41
Dictionary of Subjects and Symbols in Art, BE15
Dictionary of Technology: English-German/German-English, DA57
Dictionary of the Bible, BC64
Dictionary of the Environment, DK26
Dictionary of the Flowering Plants and Ferns, DH52
Dictionary of the History of Ideas, BB14
Dictionary of the History of Science, DA60
Dictionary of the Middle Ages, CJ41
Dictionary of the Physical Sciences, DE18
Dictionary of the Social Sciences, CA18
Dictionary of the Social Sciences, CA21
Dictionary of the Underworld, AJ55
Dictionary of Useful and Everyday Plants and Their Common Names, DH52
Dictionary of Victorian Painters, BE33
Dictionary of Waste and Water Treatment, DL113
Dictionary of Women Artists, BE26
Dictionary of World Literary Terms, BD25
Dictionary of World Politics, CD22
Dictionary of Zoology, DH77
Dictionnaire actif Nathan, AJ77
Dictionnaire anglais français des sciences medicales, DI32
Dictionnaire biographique du Canada

Dictionnaire canadien: français-anglais, anglais-français, AJ87
Dictionnaire critique et documentaire des peintres, sculpteurs, dessinateurs et graveurs, BE22
Dictionnaire de la langue québécoise, AJ85
Dictionnaire des canadianismes, AJ89
Dictionnaire des écrivains québecois contemporains, BD75
Dictionnaire des expressions québécoises, AJ86
Dictionnaire des oeuvres littéraires du Québec, BD67
Dictionnaire du cinéma québécois, BG56
Dictionnaire du français plus: À l'usage francophone amérique, AJ88
Dictionnaire général de la langue française au Canada, AJ84
Dictionnaire nord-américain de la langue française au Canada, AJ84
Dictionnaire pratique des auteurs québécois, AL49
Dictionnaire thématique visuel français-anglais, AJ78
Dietary Standard for Canada, DI62
Dietrich, AF14
Digest of Education Statistics, CI42
Directories in Print, AH3
Directories of Canadian Libraries, AA46
Directory and Index of Standards, DA38
Directory: Historical Agencies in North America, CJ59
Directory of Alcohol and Drug Treatment Resources of Ontario, CG28
Directory of American Philosophers, BB18
Directory of Archives and Manuscript Repositories in the United States, AD94
Directory of Associate Composers, BF36
Directory of Associations in Canada, AH6
Directory of British Official Publications, AM86
Directory of Canadian Archives, AD94
Directory of Canadian Environmental Experts, DK52
Directory of Canadian French-language Audiovisual Materials, AG21
Directory of Canadian Map Collections, AK17
Directory of Canadian Private Residential Schools, CI29
Directory of Canadian, Québec and Regional Studies in Canada, CJ89
Directory of Canadian Records and Manuscripts, AD94

Directory of Canadian Universities, CI33
Directory of Community Services in Metropolitan Toronto, CG44
Directory of Computer Assisted Research in Musicology, BF48
Directory of Computer Software and Services, DC28
Directory of Directories, AH3
Directory of Education (Ontario), CI30
Directory of Environmental Information Services, DK53
Directory of Federal Government Programs and Services for Women, CG53
Directory of Federally Supported Research in Universities, DA68
Directory of Funding Sources for Canadian Studies, CJ89
Directory of General Records (Ontario), AM22
Directory of Grants in the Humanities, BA13
Directory of Hazardous Waste Services, DK54
Directory of Information Sources in the United Kingdom, AA47
Directory of International Migration Study Centers, Research Programs and Library Resources, CF26
Directory of International Statistics, CA32
Directory of Library and Information Professionals, AA60
Directory of Library and Information Retrieval Software for Microcomputers, AB24
Directory of Medical Specialists, DI53
Directory of Museums and Living Displays, BE40
Directory of Online Databases, AB33
Directory of Periodicals Online, AE5
Directory of Personal Information Banks, (Ontario), AM22
Directory of Portable Databases, AB35
Directory of Published Proceedings. Series: SEMT: Science, Engineering, Medicine, Technology, DA25
Directory of Published Proceedings. SSH: Social Sciences, Humanities, CA1
Directory of Published Proceedings: PCE: Pollution Control/Ecology, DK2
Directory of Records, Provincial Ministries and Agencies, (Ontario), AM22
Directory of Social Science Information Cources, CA29

Directory of Social Science Research Centres and Institutes at Canadian Universities, CA27
Directory of Special Libraries (Toronto), AA50
Directory of Special Libraries and Information Centers, AA48
Directory of the American Psychological Association, CH29
Directory of the Canadian Psychological Association, CH30
Directory of United Nations Databases and Information Services, AN8
Directory of United Nations Serial Publications, AN9
Directory: Historical Agencies in North America, CJ59
Discoverers: An Encyclopedia of Explorers and Exploration, CK19
Discovery of the World: Maps of the Earth and the Cosmos, AK9
Dissertation Abstracts International, AF42
Distribution and Taxonomy of Birds of the World, DH103
Dizionario delle lingue - italiana e inglese, AJ98
DLB Documentary Series, AL55
DLB Yearbook, AL55
Doctoral Research on Canada and Canadians, 1889-1983, AF43
Documentation Abstracts, AA15
Documentation of the European Communities: A Guide, AN29
Documentation politique internationale, CD14
Documentation sur la recherche féministe, CG50
Documents, (European Communities), AN30
Documents of American History, CJ96
Documents of International Organizations, AN4
DOE Energy Data Base (EDB), DK63
Dorland's Illustrated Medical Dictionary, DI33
Dorsey Dictionary of American Government and Politics, CD27
Dr. Axelrod's Atlas of Freshwater Aquariam Fishes, DH110
Dr. Burgess's Atlas of Marine Aquarium Fishes, DH110
Drama Dictionary, BG38
Drama Scholars' Index to Plays and Filmscripts, BD158
Dramatist's Bible, BG31

DRI Canadian Energy, DK64
Drug Abuse Bibliography, CG29
Drug Evaluations, DI76
Drug Facts and Comparisons, DI77
Drug Information: A Guide to Current Resources, DI72
Drugs and Drug Abuse: A Reference Text, DI79
Drugs of Addiction and Non-Addiction, CG29
Drury's Guide to Best Plays, BD152
Duden Das grosse Wörterbuch der deutschen Sprache, AJ95

Early Canadian Children's Books, 1763–1840, AD28
Early Painters and Engravers in Canada, BE36
Earth and Astronomical Sciences Research Centres: A World Directory, DG61
Earth Book World Atlas, AK21
Earth Report 2: Monitoring the Battle for Our Environment, DK27
Earth Science Reviews, DG26
Ecce Homo: An Annotated Bibliographic History of Physical Anthropology, CF7
Ecological Abstracts, DK13
Ecology Abstracts, DK14
Economic Books Current Selections, CB3
Economic Selections, CB4
Economics and Business: ... Bibliography, CB4
Economics Working Papers: A Bibliography, CB5
Écrivains canadiens, AL47
Education au Canada: une bibliographie, CI3
Education Authorities Directory and Annual, CI34
Education in Canada: A Bibliography, CI3
Education in Canada: A Statistical Review, CI44
Education Index, CI11
Education Statistics Bulletin, CI44
Education: A Guide to Reference and Information Sources, CI2
Educational Film & Video Locator, AG10
Educational Media and Technology Yearbook, CI14
Eerdmans Bible Dictionary, BC62
Eerdmans' Handbook to the Bible, BC74
EFLA Evaluations, BG73
Eighteenth Century Short Title Catalogue, AD62
Electrical and Electronics Abstracts, DL19
Electrical Patents Index, DA35
Electronic Encyclopedia, AI12

Electronic Engineer's Handbook, DL75
Electronics and Communications Abstracts, DL18
Electronics Engineers' Handbook, DL62
Elementary School Library Collection, AC41
ELIAS, DK3
Elsevier's Dictionary of Library Science, Information and Documentation in Six Languages, AA34
Elsevier's Dictionary of Nuclear Science and Technology in Six Languages, DE20
Elsevier's Medical Dictionary in Five Languages, DI32
Elsevier's Russian-English Dictionary, AJ100
EMBASE, DI19
Emergency Librarian, AC51
Emily Post's Etiquette, AH48
Enciclopedia dello spettacolo, BG37
Enciclopedia Europea Garzanti, AI23
Enciclopedia Italiana de Scienze, Lettere ed Arti, AI23
Enciclopedia Universal Illustrada Europeo-Americana, AI24
Encyclopedia Britannica, AI8
Encyclopaedia of Occupational Health and Safety, DI87
Encyclopaedia of Psychic Science, CH18
Encyclopaedia of the Social Sciences, CA17
Encyclopaedia Universalis, AI20
Encyclopaedic Dictionary of Physical Geography, CK13
Encyclopaedic Dictionary of Physics, DE21
Encyclopedia Americana, AI6
Encyclopedia and Dictionary of Medicine, Nursing, and Allied Health, DI34
Encyclopedia Barsa, AI24
Encyclopedia Buying Guide, AI4
Encyclopedia Judaica, BC34
Encyclopedia of Aging, CG21
Encyclopedia of Alcoholism, CG31
Encyclopedia of American Facts and Dates, CJ106
Encyclopedia of American History, CJ107
Encyclopedia of American Political History, CD51
Encyclopedia of American Religions: Religious Creeds, BC13
Encyclopedia of Anthropology, CF13
Encyclopedia of Aquatic Life, DH111
Encyclopedia of Archaeological Excavations in the Holy Land, BC68

Encyclopedia of Asian History, CJ155
Encyclopedia of Associations, AH7
Encyclopedia of Astronomy and Astrophysics, DD11
Encyclopedia of Biblical and Christian Ethics, BC51
Encyclopedia of Bioethics, BC14
Encyclopedia of Birds, DH99
Encyclopedia of Chemical Processing and Design, DF24
Encyclopedia of Computer Science and Technology, DC21
Encyclopedia of Dance and Ballet, BG21
Encyclopedia of Death, CG26
Encyclopedia of Drug Abuse, CG31
Encyclopedia of Earth Sciences, DG34
Encyclopedia of Economics, CB14
Encyclopedia of Education, CI15
Encyclopedia of Educational Research, CI16
Encyclopedia of Environmental Control Technology, DK28
Encyclopedia of Environmental Science and Engineering, DK29
Encyclopedia of Evolution, DH73
Encyclopedia of Fluid Mechanics, DL93
Encyclopedia of Folk, Country, and Western Music, BF41
Encyclopedia of Governmental Advisory Organizations, AM99
Encyclopedia of Health Information Sources, DI4
Encyclopedia of Historic Places, CJ13
Encyclopedia of Homosexuality, CG38
Encyclopedia of Human Biology, DH27
Encyclopedia of Human Evolution and Prehistory, CF14
Encyclopedia of Integrated Circuits, DL83
Encyclopedia of Islam, BC30
Encyclopedia of Jazz in the Seventies, BF38
Encyclopedia of Judaism, BC34
Encyclopedia of Language, BD178
Encyclopedia of Legal Information Sources, CE6
Encyclopedia of Library and Information Science, AA29
Encyclopedia of Mammals, DH92
Encyclopedia of Marriage, Divorce and the Family, CG34
Encyclopedia of Materials Science and Engineering, DL101

Encyclopedia of Mathematics and Its Applications, DB20
Encyclopedia of Mathematics, DB19
Encyclopedia of Medical Devices and Instrumentation, DI41
Encyclopedia of Microcomputers, DC22
Encyclopedia of Minerals, DG44
Encyclopedia of Music In Canada, BF29
Encyclopedia of Native American Tribes, CF46
Encyclopedia of Natural Insect and Disease Control, DH47
Encyclopedia of Occultism and Parapsychology, CH18
Encyclopedia of Occultism, CH18
Encyclopedia of Philosophy, BB15
Encyclopedia of Photography, BE104
Encyclopedia of Physical Science and Technology, DA41
Encyclopedia of Physical Sciences and Engineering Information Sources, DL1
Encyclopedia of Physics, DE22
Encyclopedia of Polymer Science and Engineering, DL51; DL102
Encyclopedia of Pop, Rock, and Soul, BF42
Encyclopedia of Psychology, CH19
Encyclopedia of Religion and Ethics, BC14
Encyclopedia of Religion, BC15
Encyclopedia of Reptiles and Amphibians, DH89
Encyclopedia of Social Work, CG45
Encyclopedia of Sociology, CG12
Encyclopedia of Special Education, CI17
Encyclopedia of Statistical Sciences, DB21
Encyclopedia of the Biological Sciences, DH28
Encyclopedia of the First World, CJ55
Encyclopedia of the Musical Theatre, BF39
Encyclopedia of the Second World, CJ55
Encyclopedia of the Third World, CJ55
Encyclopedia of the United Nations and International Relations, AN23
Encyclopedia of the USSR 1905 to the Present: Lenin to Gorbachev, CJ131
Encyclopedia of Ukraine, CJ129
Encyclopedia of Unbelief, BC16
Encyclopedia of Wood, DJ58
Encyclopedia of Words and Phrases, Legal Maxims: Canada 1825–1985, CE37

Encyclopedia of World Art, BE14
Encyclopedia of World Faiths: An Illustrated Survey of the World's Living Religions, BC17
Encyclopedia of World History, CJ14
Encyclopedia of World Literature in the 20th Century, BD26
Encyclopedia USA, CJ108
Encyclopedias and Dictionaries of the World, AI3
Encyclopedic Dictionary of Mathematics, DB22
Encyclopedic Dictionary of Psychology, CH20
Encyclopedic Handbook of Cults in America, BC38
Encyclopédie du bon français dans l'usage contemporain, AJ79
Encyclopédie du cinéma, BG54
Energy Abstracts, DK66
Energy Abstracts for Policy Analysis, DK67
Energy Analysis of 108 Industrial Processes, DK75
Energy and Environmental Terms: A Glossary, DK76
Energy, DK65
Energy Information Abstracts, DK68
Energy Information Guide, DK62
Energy Research Abstracts, DK69
Energy Science and Technology, DK69
Energy Statistics Sourcebook, DK77
Energy Statistics Yearbook, DK77
Energy Statistics: A Guide to Information Sources, DK57
Energy Terminology: A Multi-Lingual Glossary, DK78
Energyline, DK70
Engineering Formulas, DL63
Engineering Index, DL21
Engineering Mathematics Handbook, DB14
English Canadian Literature to 1900, BD62
English Catalogue of Books, 1901-1968, AD63
English French Dictionary of Medical and Paramedical Sciences, DI32
English Historical Documents, CJ121
English Language Films, BG67
English Poetry 1660-1800: A Guide to Information Sources, BD2
English-Greek Dictionary, AJ93
English-Russian/Russian-English Dictionary, AJ100
Enviro/Energyline Abstracts Plus, DK70
Enviroline, DK70
Environment Abstracts, DK16
Environmental Approvals in Canada, DK44

Environmental Bibliography, DK4
Environmental Encyclopedia, DK23
Environmental Engineering Dictionary, DK26
Environmental Hazards: Air Pollution, DK7
Environmental Hazards: Radioactive Materials and Wastes: A Reference Handbook, DK46
Environmental Impact Assessment: A Bibliography, DK1
Environmental Information Directory, DK53
Environmental Periodicals Bibliography, DK4
Environmental Resource Directory, DK5
EnviroTIPS, DK39
Eponyms Dictionaries Index, AJ38
Ergonomics Abstracts, DL22
ERIC, AA19; CJ13
ESPIAL Canadian Database Directory, AB37
Essai de bibliographie canadienne, AD20
Essay and General Literature Index, AF37
ESTC, AD62
Ethnic and Native Canadian Literature: A Bibliography, BD61
Ethnographic Atlas, CF20
Ethnographic Bibliography of North America, CF36
Études canadiennes: publications et thèses étrangères, CJ69
Europa World Year Book, AH23; CJ53
Europa Year Book: A World Survey, AH23
European and American Painting, Sculpture, and Decorative Art, BE49
European Authors, 1000-1900, AL63
European Historical Statistics, 1750-1975, CA37
European Political Dictionary, CD26
European Research Centres, AH10
European Writers, AL56
European Writers, BD34
Eurostat Catalogue, AN32
Everyman's Dictionary of Abbreviations, AJ36
Everyman's Dictionary of Dates, CJ17
Everyone's United Nations, CD29
Evolution of Life, DH72
Excerpta Botanica, DH40
Excerpta Medica, DI19
Exhaustive Concordance of the Bible, BC60
Exploring the Arts: Film and Video Programs for Young Viewers, AG26
Exploring the Night Sky, DD18
Expository Dictionary of Biblical Words, BC72

Faber Dictionary of Euphemisms, AJ52
Face of the Nation 1987, CG45
Face to Face with Talent, BG3
Fact Book on Higher Education, CI43
Facts on File Dictionary of Archaeology, CF53
Facts on File Dictionary of Astronomy, DD12
Facts on File Dictionary of Biology, DH19
Facts on File Dictionary of Chemistry, DF26
Facts on File Dictionary of Education, CI26
Facts on File Dictionary of Geology and Geophysics, DG37
Facts on File Dictionary of Human Geography, CK14
Facts on File Dictionary of Marine Science, DG37
Facts on File Dictionary of Physics, DE23
Facts on File Dictionary of Religions, BC18
Facts on File Encyclopedia of World Mythology and Legend, BC80
Facts on File English/Chinese Visual Dictionary, AJ91
Facts on File English/French Visual Dictionary, AJ78
Facts on File Junior Visual Dictionary, AJ28
Facts on File Visual Dictionary, AJ74
Facts on File World Political Almanac, CD30
Facts on File: A Weekly World News Digest, AF32
Familiar Quotations, AH60
Families in Transition, CG37
FAMLI (Family Medicine Literature Index), DI20
Famous Mineral Localities of Canada, DG53
Famous Names in Engineering, DA65
Fantasy for Children, BD166
Fantasy Literature for Children and Young Adults, BD166
Fantasy Literature: A Reader's Guide, BD118
FAO Fertilizer Yearbook, DJ14
FAO Production Yearbook, DJ14
FAO Trade Yearbook, DJ14
FAO Yearbook, DJ14
Far East and Australasia, CJ148
Farm Machinery, DJ26
Farming Systems of the World, DJ27
Feature Films: A Directory, AG11
Federal Data Base Finder, AM106
Federal Royal Commissions, 1867-1966, AM28
Federal Statistical Data Bases, AM100
Federal Statistical Directory, AM100
Federal Year in Review, CD41

FEDFIND: Your Key to Finding Federal Government Information, AM105
Fiction Catalog, AC11
Fiction, Folklore, Fantasy & Poetry for Children, 1876–1985, BD167
Field Crop Diseases Handbook, DJ29
Field Guide to Geology, DG55
Field Guide to Rocks and Minerals, DG48
Field Guide to the Reptiles and Amphibians of Britain and Europe
Field Guide to the Stars and Planets, DD19
Fifteen Centuries of Children's Literature, BD161
Film: A Reference Guide, BG44
Film & Video Finder, AG17
Film and Video Catalogue, AG15
Film Book Bibliography, BG46
Film Canada Yearbook, BG63
Film Companion, BG68
Film Directors, BG72
Film Encyclopedia, BG58
Film Index: A Bibliography, BG47
Film Literature Index, BG50
Film Review Annual, BG79
Film Review Index, BG75
Film/Video Canadiana, AG12
Filmed Books and Plays, BG62
Financial Statistics of Education, CI44
Financial Times Oil and Gas International Year Book, DK74
Finding List of British Royal Commission Reports, 1860–1935, AM90
Finding the Source in Sociology and Anthropology, CF2
Fine Arts: A Bibliographic Guide to Basic Reference Works, Histories and Handbooks, BE1
First Stop: The Master Index to Subject Encyclopedias, AI1
Fishes of the World, DH116
Fitzhenry & Whiteside Book of Canadian Facts and Dates, CJ90
Five Year's Work in Librarianship, AA24
Flags of All Nations, AH41
Flora of Canada, DH58
Focus on Canada, CA58
Focus on Families: A Reference Handbook, CG33
Food Additives Handbook, DJ46

Food and Nutrition Information Guide, DI60
Food and Nutrition Quarterly Index, DJ38
Food Handbook, DJ42
Foods and Food Production Encyclopedia, DJ44
Football Register, CL14
Ford Lists of British Parliamentary Papers, AM91
Foreign Affairs Bibliography, CD1
Foreign Gazetteers of the U.S. Board on Geographic Names, AK45
Foreign Language Films, BG67
Forest Inventory Terms in Canada, DJ61
Forest Products Abstracts, DJ59
Forestry Abstracts, DJ59
Forestry and Forest Products Vocabulary, DJ61
Forestry Handbook, DJ60
Forms of Address, AH50
Forthcoming Books, AB14; AD78
Forthcoming International Scientific and Technical Conferences, DA69
Foundation Directory, AH8
Four Thousand Years of Urban Growth, CA70
Fowler's Modern English Usage, AJ68
Free Publications from U.S. Government Agencies, AM104
French-English Visual Dictionary, AJ78
French Books in Print, AD84
French Periodical Index, AF10
Freshwater Fishes of Canada, DH114
From Women's Eyes: Women Painters in Canada, BE26
Fuel and Energy Abstracts, DK71
Fundamentals Handbook of Electrical and Computer Engineering, DL64
Fundamentals of Legal Research, CE9
Funding for Anthropological Research, CF23
Funk & Wagnalls Canadian College Dictionary, AJ22
Funk & Wagnalls New Comprehensive International Dictionary of the English Language, AJ10
Funk & Wagnalls New Encyclopedia, AI7
Furniture of French Canada, BE92

G.F. Handel: A Guide to Research, BF7
Gage Canadian Dictionary, AJ23
Gale Directory of Publications and Broadcast Media, AE6
Gallery of Ghosts, AD61
Gardener's Illustrated Encyclopedia of Trees & Shrubs, DH45
Gardening: A Guide to the Literature, DH42
Gardner's Art Through the Ages, BE51
Gardner's Chemical Synonyms and Trade Names, DF27
Gas Tables, DL65
Gazette du bureau des brevets, DA33
Gazetteer of Canada, AK46
General Catalog of HI Observations of Galaxies, DD25
General Inventory: Manuscripts, (Canada), AD96
General Periodical Index, AF11
General Physics Advance Abstracts, DE7
General Reference Books for Adults, AC3
General Science Index, DA18
Genetic Engineering and Biotechnology Related Firms Worldwide Directory, DH33
Genreflecting: A Guide to Reading Interests in Genre Fiction, BD108
Geo Abstracts, CK11
Geo-Archive, DG17
GEOBASE, CK10
Geocom Bulletin, DG3
Geographers: Biobibliographical Studies, CK20
Geographical Abstracts, CK11
Geographical Bibliography for American Libraries, CK5
Geographical Review, CK8
Geography: A Resource Book for Secondary Schools, CK7
Geoline, DG12
Geologic Reference Sources, DG9
Geological Abstracts, DG13
Geological Reference File, DG2
Geological Survey of Canada, DG19
Geologists and the History of Geology: ... Bibliography, DG8
Geology and Economic Minerals of Canada, DG52
Geology of Canada, DG35
Geomechanics Abstracts, DG14
Geophysics and Tectonics Abstracts, DG13
GeoRef, DG2
GeoRef Thesaurus and Guide to Indexing, DG2
GEOS, DG12
Geoscan, DG15
Geotechnical Abstracts, DL23

Geotitles Weekly, DG17
German Books in Print, AD88
Gerontological Abstracts, CG18
Gesamtverzeichnis des Deutschsprachigen Schriftums, 1700–1910; 1911–1965, AD85
GIP UNISIST Newsletter, AD3
Glass in Canada, BE89
Glossary of Astronomy and Astrophysics, DD13
Glossary of Automotive Terms, DL80
Glossary of Basic Archival & Library Conservation Terms, AA35
Glossary of Geology, DG36
Glossary of Marine Technology Terms, DL100
Glossary of Terms Used in Heraldry, AH43
Glossary of the Third World, CJ55
Going Places: The Guide to Travel Guides, CK23
Golden Bough: A Study in Magic and Religion, BC82
Goode's World Atlas, AK22
Gordon's Print Price Annual, BE58
Gothic Revival in Canadian Architecture, BE70
Gourman Report: [2 items] ...Rating of Undergraduate Programs; Graduate & Professional Programs, CI35, CI139
Gouvernement du Canada annuaire téléphonique, AM14
Government of Canada Publications, AM29
Government of Canada Telephone Directory, AM14
Government of Ontario Telephone Directory, AM21
Government of Canada Style Manual for Writers and Editors
Government Publications (Great Britain), AM96
Government Publications Relating to Alberta: ... 1905-1968, AM59
Government Reference Books, (U.S.), AM107
Government Reference Serials, (U.S.), AM107
Government Relations Handbook, AM15
Government Reports Announcements and Index, AM117; DA32
Government Research Directory, AH10
GPO Monthly Catalog, AM122
Gradline, CI39
Gran Enciclopedia Rialp, AI24
Grand larousse de la langue français, AJ80
Grand Larousse encyclopédique en dix volumes, AI21

Grand Robert de la langue française: dictionnaire alphabétique et analogique de la langue française, AJ82
Grande encyclopédie, AI21
Granger's Index to Poetry, BD128
Grant & Hackh's Chemical Dictionary, DF28
Grants Register, AH9
Great Foreign Language Writers, AL57
Great Soviet Encyclopedia, AI25
Great World Atlas, AK25
Great Writers of the English Language, BD35
Greek and Latin Authors 800 B.C. - A.D. 1000, AL64
Greek English Lexicon, AJ93
Greek Religion in the Archaic and Classical Periods, BC78
Green Papers, (Canada), AM33
Green Revolution: ...Bibliography, DJ2
Greenhouse Effect: A Bibliography, DK7
Grolier Academic Encyclopedia, AI12
Grosse Brockhaus, AI22
Grove's Dictionary, BF31
Grzimek's Animal Life Encyclopedia, DH94
Grzimek's Encyclopedia of Evolution, DH73
Grzimek's Encyclopedia of Mammals, DH94
Guide de la littérature québécoise, BD68
Guide des archives littéraires, BD60
Guide des archives photographiques Canadiennes, BE111
Guide des sources généalogiques au Canada, AL45
Guide du chercheur en histoire canadienne, CJ71
Guide for a Small Map Collection, AK1
Guide to American Literature, BD85
Guide to American Poetry Explication, BD131
Guide to Animal Tracking and Behavior, DH79
Guide to Basic Information Sources in Chemistry, DF1
Guide to British Government Publications, AM87
Guide to British Poetry Explication, BD131
Guide to Buddhist Religion, BC25
Guide to Canadian Diplomatic Relations 1925–1983, CD46
Guide to Canadian Ministries Since Confederation, July 1, 1867–February 1, 1982, CD48
Guide to Canadian Photographic Archives, BE111
Guide to Canadian Reference Sources, AC2

Guide to Critical Reviews, BG43
Guide to Departments of Anthropology, CF23
Guide to Departments of Geography in the United States and Canada, CK21
Guide to Departments of Sociology, Anthropology and Archaeology, CF23
Guide to Eastern Literatures, BD6
Guide to English and American Literature, BD4
Guide to Federal Programs and Services, AM16
Guide to Hindu Religion, BC26
Guide to Historical Literature, CJ1

Guide to Identification and Acquisitions of Canadian Government Publications: Provinces and Territories, AM37
Guide to Information Sources in Geographical Sciences, CK3
Guide to Information Sources in the Botanical Sciences, DH39
Guide to International Legal Research, CE7
Guide to Legislative Libraries and Public and School Agencies in Canada, AA46
Guide to Managing Statistics Canada Publications in Libraries, AM32
Guide to Microforms in Print, AD92
Guide to Multicultural Resources, CF27
Guide to Official Publications of Foreign Countries, AM2
Guide to Official Publications of New Brunswick 1952-1970, AM40
Guide to Oriental Classics, BD6
Guide to Parliamentary Papers, (Gt Britain), AM83
Guide to Periodicals and Newspapers in the Public Libraries of Metropolitan Toronto, AE16
Guide to Places of the World, AK47
Guide to Popular U.S. Government Publications, AM104
Guide to Prescription and Over-the-Counter Drugs, DI74
Guide to Provincial Library Agencies in Canada, AA46
Guide to Reference Books, AC4
Guide to Reference Books for Islamic Studies, BC29
Guide to Reference Material, AC5
Guide to Reference Materials for Canadian Libraries, AC6
Guide to Reprints, AD91

Guide to Research on North American Indians, CF33
Guide to Research Using *The Canadian Abridgement*, CE2
Guide to Selected Federal Agency Programs and Publications for Librarians and Teachers, AM112
Guide to Sources for Agricultural and Biological Research, DJ3
Guide to Sources of Educational Information, CI5
Guide to the Ancient World: A Dictionary of Classical Place Names, CJ32
Guide to the Collection of the Film Library of the Canadian Film Institute, AG8
Guide to the Energy Industries, DK59
Guide to the Foundations of Public Administration, CD5
Guide to the Gods, BC86
Guide to the Literature of Art History, BE1
Guide to the Literature of Astronomy, DD1
Guide to the Official Publications of the European Communities, AN28
Guide to the Petroleum Reference Literature, DK61
Guide to the Pianist's Repertoire, BF14
Guide to the Principal Parliamentary Papers Relating to the Dominions, AM93
Guide to the Sources of Medieval History, CJ36
Guide to the Study of Medieval History, CJ35
Guide to the Study of the United States of America, CJ97
Guide to the Study of United States History Outside the U.S, 1945–1980, CJ98
Guide to U.S. Government Publications, AM103
Guide to U.S. Government Serials and Periodicals, AM103
Guide to U.S. Government Statistics, AM103
Guide to Unesco, AN11
Guide to United Nations Organization, Documentation and Publishing for Students, Researchers, Librarians, AN12
Guide to Watching Whales in Canada, DH115
Guinness Book of Records, AH71
Guinness Book of World Records, AH71
Guinness Sports Record Book, AH72; CL4

* * * *

Halliwell's Film Guide, BG64
Halliwell's Filmgoer's Companion, BG64
Halliwell's Television Companion, BG82
Halsbury's Laws of England, CE50
Hammond Large Type World Atlas, AK26
Hammond Past Worlds: The Times Atlas of Archaeology, CF59
Hammond-Barnhart Dictionary of Science, DA54
Han ying tz'u tien, AJ92
Handbook for Research in American History, CJ100
Handbook: Member Churches, BC57
Handbook of Aging and the Social Sciences, CG21
Handbook of Applicable Mathematics, DB12
Handbook of Applied Chemistry, DF43
Handbook of Applied Meteorology, DG54
Handbook of Artificial Intelligence, DC13
Handbook of Biochemistry and Molecular Biology, DH36
Handbook of Chemistry and Physics, DA42; DE27; DF44
Handbook of Christian Theologians, BC55
Handbook of Compressed Gases, DL94
Handbook of Computers and Computing, DC14
Handbook of Contemporary Fiction for Public Libraries and School Libraries, BD100
Handbook of Costume, BE77
Handbook of Drinking Water Quality: Standards and Controls, DK38
Handbook of Energy Data and Calculations, DK75
Handbook of Energy Systems Engineering, DK79
Handbook of Environmental Data on Organic Chemicals, DF51
Handbook of Freshwater Fishery Biology, DH112
Handbook of Grants and Subsidies of the Federal and Provincial Governments, CC31
Handbook of Human Factors, DL66
Handbook of Industrial Engineering, DL67
Handbook of Latin American Studies, CJ116
Handbook of Living Religions, BC18
Handbook of Machine Tools, DL99
Handbook of Marine Mammals, DH113
Handbook of Mathematical Tables and Formulas, DB8
Handbook of Mathematics, DB7
Handbook of Medical Library Practice, DI46
Handbook of Middle American Indians, CF43

Handbook of Modern Electronics and Electrical Engineering, DL75
Handbook of Modern History: World History Since 1870, CJ46
Handbook of Modern Sociology, CG13
Handbook of Non-Prescription Drugs, DI78
Handbook of North American Birds, DH101
Handbook of North American Indians, CF43
Handbook of Numerical Calculations in Engineering, DL76
Handbook of Occupational Safety and Health, DI88
Handbook of Physical Calculations, DE28
Handbook of Polymer Science and Technology, DF45
Handbook of Sociology, CG13
Handbook of Soils and Climate in Agriculture, DJ24
Handbook of South American Indians, CF43
Handbook of Space Astronomy and Astrophysics, DD37
Handbook of Steel Construction, DL85
Handbook on Climate Data Sources, DK6
Handbook on the Care and Management of Laboratory Animals, DH81
Handbook to Literature, BD28
Handbook: Member Churches, BC57
Handbooks and Tables in Science and Technology, DA2
Handbooks to the Modern World, CJ54
Hansard, AM66
Hansard's Catalogue and Breviate of Parliamentary Papers 1696–1834, AM92
Hanscomb's Yardsticks for Costing, DL86
Harbrace College Workbook for Canadian Writers, AJ69
Harper Atlas of the Bible, BC76
Harper Atlas of World History, CJ24
Harper Dictionary of Contemporary Usage, AJ70
Harper Dictionary of Foreign Terms, AJ44
Harper Dictionary of Science, DA54
Harper's Bible Commentary, BC63
Harper's Bible Dictionary, BC63
Harper's Illustrated Handbook of Cats, DH109
Harrap's English French Dictionary of Slang and Colloquialisms, AJ81
Harrap's French and English Science Dictionary, DA58
Harrap's New Standard French-English Dictionary, AJ81

Harrod's Librarians' Glossary of Terms Used in Librarianship, AA36
Harvard Guide to American History, CJ99
Hawley's Condensed Chemical Dictionary, DF29
Hazardous Chemicals Desk Reference, DF48
Hazardous Chemicals on File, DF48
Hazardous Materials Dictionary, DK24
Hazardous Materials Emergency Response: Pocket Handbook, DK33
Hazardous Materials Transport Guide, DK42
Hazardous Waste Management Facilities Directory (U.S.), DK54
Hazardous Waste Q & A, DK33
Health Index, AF11; DI21
Health Periodicals Database, DI21
Health Reports, DI50
Health Science Librarianship: A Guide to Information Sources, DI1
Health Sciences Information in Canada, DI56
Health Sciences Information in Canada, DI56
Health Sciences Information Sources, DI2
Healthsharing Book: Resources for Canadian Women, DI67
Henderson's Dictionary of Biological Terms, DH20
Heritage of Upper Canadian Furniture, BE92
High School Mathematics Library, DB2
Hinduism: A Select Bibliography, BC27
HISTLINE, DI8
Histoire de la littérature française du Québec, BD69
Historian's Handbook, CJ6
Historical Abstracts, CJ8
Historical Atlas of Africa, CJ147
Historical Atlas of Canada, CJ87
Historical Atlas of South Asia, CJ156
Historical Atlas of the United States, CJ109
Historical Catalogue of Statistics Canada Publications, 1918–1980, CA59
Historical Dictionary of Data Processing, DC16
Historical Dictionary of North American Archaeology, CF54
Historical Periodicals Directory, CJ3
Historical Sets, Collected Editions, & Monuments of Music, BF13
Historical Statistical Supplement (Canadian Economic Observer), CA53
Historical Statistics of Canada, CA50
Historical Statistics of the United States, CA65

Historical Tables 58 BC- AD 1985, CJ22
Historiography: An Annotated Bibliography, CJ4
History & Guide to Judaic Encyclopedias & Lexicons, BC33
History of Anthropology: A Research Bibliography, CF7
History of Architecture on the Comparative Method, BE66
History of Architecture: Settings & Rituals, BE67
History of Art, BE51
History of Biology, DH4
History of Canada: An Annotated Bibliography, CJ72
History of Canadian Literature, BD72
History of Children's Literature, BD168
History of Classical Physics, DE2
History of Modern Art: Painting, Sculpture, Architecture, Photography, BE52
History of Modern Astronomy & Astrophysics, DD1
History of Modern Geography: An Annotated Bibliography of Selected Works, CK4
History of Modern Physics, DE1
History of Philosophy, BB21-BB22
History of Photography from 1839 to the Present, BE108
History of Western Music, BF51
History of Western Philosophy, BB23
HMSO Annual Catalogue, AM96
HMSO Publications in Print on Microfiche, AM96
Hockey Encyclopedia, CL15
Hoffman's Index to Poetry, BD132
Holy Qur'an, BC31
Home Medical Advisor, DI61
Homosexuality: A Research Guide, CG38
Horn Book Guide, AC52
Horn Book Magazine, AC53
Horror Literature: A Reader's Guide, BD118
Horse: A Complete Encyclopedia, DH106
HORTI, DH51
Horticultural Abstracts, DH41
Horticultural Research International, DH63
Hortus Third: A Concise Dictionary, DH54
Hospital Literature Index, DI22
Hospital Statistics Preliminary Annual Report, DI51
Houghton Mifflin Canadian Dictionary, AJ24
Housing: A Multi-Disciplinary Dictionary, CA78
How Canadians Govern Themselves, AM13
How to Find Chemical Information, DF3

How to Find Information on Canadian Natural Resources, DH5
How to Find the Law, CE4
How to Succeed at University, CI33
How to Use a Law Library, CE5
HRAF Source Bibliography, CF5
Hsin han ying tz'u tien, AJ92
Hugh Johnson's Encyclopedia of Trees, DJ62
Human Relations Area Files, CF5
Human Resources Abstracts, CG40
Humanities Index, BA9
Humanities: A Selective Guide to Information Sources, BA1
Hutchinson Encyclopedia, AI9
Hydro-Abstracts, DG18
Hymns & Tunes: An Index, BF46

IBZ, AF14
Identification Guide to the Trees of Canada, DJ63
Idioms & Phrases Index, AJ56
IES Lighting Handbook, DL97
Illustrated Bible Handbook, BC74
Illustrated Dictionary & Concordance of the Bible, BC65
Illustrated Dictionary of Microcomputers, DC23
Illustrated Dictionary of Place Names: United States & Canada, AK53
Illustrated Dinosaur Dictionary. DG33
Illustrated Encyclopedia of Mankind, CF16
Illustrated Encyclopedia of Medieval Civilization, CJ41
Illustrated Encyclopedia of New Zealand, CJ161
Illustrated Encyclopedia of Space Technology, DD14
Illustrated Encyclopedia of Wildlife, DH95
Illustrated Encyclopedia of World Geography, CK16
Illustrated History of Canada, CJ88
Illustrated Natural History of Canada, DH29
Images of the Land: Canadian Block Prints 1919–1945, BE99
Imprimés dans le bas-Canada, AD46
IMS Directory of Publications, AE6
In Search of Your British & Irish Roots
In Search of Your Canadian Roots: Tracing Your Family Tree in Canada, AL40
In Search of Your European Roots, AL40
Index analytique, AF16

Index de l'actualité, AF27
Index des films canadiens de long métrage, AG6
Index des périodiques d'architecture Canadiens: 1940–1980, BE69
Index Herbariorum, DH64
Index Islamicus, BC32
Index Medicus, DI23
Index of Economic Articles in Journals & Collective Volumes, CB10
Index of Manuscripts in the British Library, AD98
Index of Mathematical Papers, DB5
Index of Paintings Sold in the British Isles During the Nineteenth Century, BE58
Index of Polymer Trade Names, DF45
Index of Printers, Publishers & Booksellers (Wing), AD61
Index of Printers, Publishers & Booksellers (STC), AD60
Index to Afro-American Reference Resources, CF28
Index to American Photographic Collections, BE105
Index to Art Periodicals, BE10
Index to Artistic Biography, BE24
Index to AV Producers & Distributors, AG17
Index to Biographies of Contemporary Composers, BF25
Index to Book Reviews in the Humanities, BA10
Index to British Literary Bibliography, BD90
Index to British Parliamentary Papers on Canada & Canadian Boundary, 1800-1899, AM93
Index to Canadian Legal Literature, CE24
Index to Canadian Legal Periodical Literature, CE25
Index to Canadian Poetry in English, BD133
Index to Characters in the Performing Arts, BG7
Index to Children's Poetry, BD173
Index to Critical Film Reviews in British & American Film Periodicals, BG74
Index to Current Urban Documents, CA73
Index to Dental Literature, DI24
Index to Education Journals, AA11
Index to Fairy Tales, Myths & Legends, BD174
Index to Federal Programs & Services, AM16
Index to Festschriften in Librarianship, AA13
Index to Foreign Legal Periodicals, CE26
Index to Full Length Plays, 1944 to 1964, BD153
Index to Health Information, DI25
Index to IEEE Publications, DL19
Index to International Statistics, CA33

Index to Legal Periodicals, CE27
Index to Literature on the American Indian, CF34
Index to Municipal Data, CA74
Index to One Act Plays, 1900–1964, BD155
Index to Periodical Articles Related to Law, CE28
Index to Personal Information, AM17
Index to Plays in Periodicals, BD154
Index to Poetry for Children & Young People, BD175
Index to Publications of the Geological Survey of Canada, DG19
Index to Publications of the U.S. Congress, AM115
Index to Record Reviews, BF58
Index to Religious Periodical Literature, BC8
Index to Reproductions of American Paintings, BE57
Index to Saturday Night, AF8
Index to Scientific & Technical Proceedings, DA26
Index to Scientific Book Contents, DA26
Index to Scientific Reviews, DA22
Index to Social Sciences & Humanities Proceedings, CA11
Index to the Financial Post, AF8
Index to the Wilson Author Series, AL59
Index to Theses with Abstracts Accepted for Higher Degrees by the Universities of Great Britain ..., AF44
Index to U.S. Government Periodicals, AM116
Index to Women of the World from Ancient to Modern Times, CG54
Index Translationum, AF47
India Who's Who, CJ159
Indian Bibliographical Series, CF39
Indian Literature in English, 1827-1979, BD2
Indians of Canada, CF44
Indians of North America, CF35
Industrial Engineering Terminology, DL52
Informatics Abstracts, AA14
Informatika, AA14
Information China, CJ157
Information Industry Directory, AB25
Information Industry Factbook, AB26
Information Please Almanac: The New Universe of Information, AH24
Information Please Sports Almanac, AH73; CL5
Information Reports & Bibliographies, AA7
Information Science Abstracts, AA15
Information Sources in Agriculture & Food Science, DJ4

Information Sources in Cartography, AK3
Information Sources in Children's Literature, BD169
Information Sources in Economics, CB6
Information Sources in Energy Technology, DK60
Information Sources in Engineering, DL3
Information Sources in Physics, DE3
Information Sources in Politics & Political Science, CD3
Information Sources in Science & Technology, DA3
Information Sources in the Earth Sciences, DG6
Information Sources in the Life Sciences, DH2
Information Sources in the Medical Sciences, DI6
Information Sources of Law, CE8
Information Sources of Political Science, CD2
InfoSource: Sources of Federal Government Information, AM17
InfoTrac, AF11
InfoWorld Consumer Product Review, DC29
INIS Atomindex: An International Abstracting Service, DE8
INPADOC Patent Gazette, DA33
Insects & Arachnids of Canada, DH84
INSPEC, DA19
Instrumentation for Environmental Monitoring, DK43
Interdisciplinary Approaches to Canadian Society, CJ73
Intergovernmental Relations in Canada, CD41
International Abstracts of Biological Sciences, DH12
International Acronyms, Initialisms & Abbreviations Dictionary, AJ34
International Aerospace Abstracts, DL26
International African Bibliography 1973-1978, CJ142
International Bibliography, Information, Documentation, AN6
International Bibliography of Biography, AL4
International Bibliography of Economics, CB7
International Bibliography of Historical Sciences, CJ5
International Bibliography of Jewish History & Thought, BC36
International Bibliography of Periodical Literature Covering All Fields of Knowledge, AF14
International Bibliography of Political Science, CD4
International Bibliography of Research in Marriage & the Family, CG35
International Bibliography of Social & Cultural Anthropology, CF6
International Bibliography of Sociology, CG2

International Bibliography of the History of Religions, BC6
International Bibliography of the Social Sciences, CA2
International Bibliography of Theatre, BG28
International Bibliography of Translations, AF47
International Bibliography: Publications of Intergovernmental Organizations, AN6
International Book Trade Directory, AB1
International Books in Print, AD82
International Civil Engineering Abstracts, DL27
International Code of Botanical Nomenclature, DH49
International Code of Zoological Nomenclature, DH75
International Dictionary of Ballet, BG24
International Dictionary of Education, CI24
International Dictionary of Films & Filmmakers, BG57
International Dictionary of Graphic Symbols, AJ58
International Dictionary of Medicine & Biology, DI36
International Dictionary of Psychology, CH24
International Dictionary of Sports & Games, AH70; CL3
International Dictionary of Women's Biography, AL14
International Directory of Anthropologists, CF24
International Directory of Arts, BE41
International Directory of Government, CD28
International Directory of Little Magazines & Small Presses, BD136
International Directory of Non-Official Statistics Sources, CA36
International Directory of Philosophy & Philosophers, BB19
International Directory of Psychologists Exclusive of the U.S.A, CH31
International Directory to Geophysical Research, DG62
International Documents for the 80s, AN2
International Economic Indicators, CB20
International Electrotechnical Vocabulary, DL92
International Encyclopedia of Astronomy, DD12
International Encyclopedia of Comparative Law, CE47
International Encyclopedia of Education: Research & Studies, CI19
International Encyclopedia of Higher Education, CI20
International Encyclopedia of Horse Breeds, DH106
International Encyclopedia of Integrated Circuits, DL84
International Encyclopedia of Physical Chemistry & Chemical Physics, DF30
International Encyclopedia of Population, CG14
International Encyclopedia of Psychiatry, Psychology, Psychoanalysis & Neurology, CH21
International Encyclopedia of Robotics, DL109
International Encyclopedia of Sociology, CG15
International Encyclopedia of the Social Sciences, CA19
International Encyclopedia of Women Composers, BF35
International English Usage, AJ72
International Film Guide, BG65
International Foundation Directory, AH9
International Guide to Library & Information Science Education, AA49
International Handbook of Bilingualism & Bilingual Education, BD181
International Handbook of Human Rights, CD61
International Handbook of National Parks & Nature Reserves, CK25
International Handbook of Women's Education, CI21
International Handbook on Race & Race Relations, CF29
International Higher Education, CI22
International Historical Statistics, CA38
International Index to Film Periodicals, BG51
International Information, AN3
International ISBN Directory, AB4
International Legal Books in Print, CE19
International List of Geographical Serials, CK8
International Literary Market Place, AB5
International Medieval Bibliography, CJ35
International Motion Picture Almanac, BG66
International Nursing Index, DI26
International Peace Directory, CD56
International Political Science Abstracts, CD14
International Relations Dictionary, CD26
International Research Centres Directory, AH10
International Standard Bible Encyclopedia, BC66
International Television Almanac, BG84
International Television & Video Almanac, BG84
International Who's Who, AL15
International Who's Who in Music, BF37
International Zoo Yearbook, DH76

Internationale Bibliographie der Zeitschriftenliteratur, AF14
Interpreter's Dictionary of the Bible, BC67
Introduction to British Government Publications, AM84
Introduction to Canadian Amphibians & Reptiles, DH88
Introduction to Children's Literature, BD171
Introduction to Library Research in Women's Studies, CG48
Introduction to Reference Sources in the Health Sciences, DI7
Introduction to United States Public Documents, AM108
Inventaire chronologique (Québec), AD44
Inventaire général: manuscrits (Canada), AD96
Inventory of Marriage & Family Literature, CG35
Inventory of Ontario Newspapers, 1703–1986, AE17
IRPTC/Legal, DK19
Irregular Serials & Annual, AE13
Islamic Near East & North Africa, CJ134
ISMEC: Mechanical Engineering Abstracts, DL28
IT Focus, DA21

Jackson's Silver & Gold Marks of England, Scotland & Ireland, BE84
Japan Foundation Basic Japanese English Dictionary, AJ99
Jazz-Bibliography, BF4
Jazz (Discographies), BF56
Jewish Encyclopedia, BC34
Jones' Instrument Technology, DL70
Journal Citation Reports, DA22
Journal des marques de commerce, DA34
Journal of Economic Literature, CB8
Journals / Journaux (Canada, House of Commons), AM67
Journals of the Legislative Assembly of Ontario, AM78
Journals of the Senate of Canada / Journaux du Sénat du Canada, AM69
Journey Through Genius, DB18
Junior Authors & Illustrators Series, AL68
Junior Book of Authors, AL68
Junior Encyclopedia of Canada, AI18
Junior High School Library Catalog, AC42
Juran's Quality Control Handbook, DL71

Kaleidoscope: Current World Data, AF33
Keesing's Contemporary Archives, AF34
Keesing's Record of World Events, AF34
Kempe's Engineers Yearbook, DL46
Key Facts in Soviet History, CJ128
Key Government Documents Database (Canadian), AM29
Key Sources in Comparative & World Literature, BD11
Key Thinkers Past & Present, CA22
Keyguide to Information Sources in Animal Rights, CG22
Keyguide to Information Sources in Archaeology, CF49
Keyguide to Information Sources in Cartography, AK2
Keyguide to Information Sources in Food Science & Technology, DJ39
Ki-es-ki, CI30
Kirk Othmer Encyclopedia of Chemical Technology, DF32
Kirk-Othmer Concise Encyclopedia of Chemical Technology, DF32
Kirkus Reviews, AC19
Kister's Atlas Buying Guide, AK4
Kister's Concise Guide to Best Encyclopedias, AI4
Klett Pons Grosswörterbuch, AJ96
Knott's Handbook for Vegetable Growers, DJ45
Kobbe's Complete Opera Book, BF43
Kodansha Encyclopedia of Japan, CJ158
Koran, BC31
KWIC Index of International Standards, DA39
KWIC Index to Services, AM23
KWIC Index to Your Ontario Government Services, AM23

Laboratory Techniques in Archaeology: A Guide to the Literature, 1920-1980, CF47
Lambert's Worldwide Government Directory, CD38
Lange's Handbook of Chemistry, DF46
Langenscheidt's Condensed Muret Sanders German Dictionary, AJ96
Langenscheidt's Encyclopedic Dictionary of the English & German Languages, AJ96
Language of Canadian Politics: A Guide to Important Terms & Concepts, CD24

Language of the Foreign Book Trade, AB17
Lansdowne's Construction Cost Handbook, DL86
Larousse Dictionary of Painters, BE25
Larousse dictionnaire des canadianismes, AJ89
Larousse Encyclopedia of Archaeology, CF55
Larousse Encyclopedia of Modern History, CJ47
Larousse Gardening & Gardens, DH53
Larousse World Mythology, BC84
Latin America & the Caribbean: A Directory of Resources, CJ113
Latin American Studies, CJ113
Laurentiana parus avant 1821, AD46
Law & Legal Information Directory, CE44
Law Books in Print, CE19
Law Books in Review, CE20
Law Books Published, CE19
Lawrence Lande Collection of Canadiana, AD21
Lawyer's Desk Book, CE31
Lawyers' Law Books, CE11
Laying the Foundations, 1849–1899, AD54
LCMARC: Books All, AD12
LCMARC: Books Canada, AD12
Legal Bibliography of the British Commonwealth of Nations, CE21
Legal Desk Book, CE31
Legal Journals Index, CE29
Legal Research Handbook, CE10
Legal Research in England & Wales, CE5
Legal Writing & Research Manual, CE12
Let's Celebrate, AH55
Letitia Baldrige's Complete Guide to Executive Manners, AH49
Letitia Baldrige's Complete Guide to the New Manners for the 90's, AH49
Letters in Canada, AC20
Lexicon of Economic Thought, CB11
Lexicon Universal Encyclopedia, AI12
Librarian's Companion: A Handbook of Thousands of Facts, AA31
Librarian's Practical Dictionary in 22 Languages, AA40
Librarian's Thesaurus, AA41
Librarians' Glossary of Terms Used in Librarianship, AA36
Libraries in the United Kingdom & the Republic of Ireland, AA47
Library & Book Trade Almanac, AA25; AB12

Library & Information Science Abstracts, AA16
Library & Information Science Annual, AA26
Library & Information Science Journals & Serials: An Analytical Guide, AA8
Library & Information Sciences: An Abstract Newsletter, AA17
Library Association Year Book, AA24
Library Hi Tech Bibliography, AA9
Library Journal, AC21
Library Lit. - the Best of, AA27
Library Literature, AA18
Library of Congress Catalog - Books, AD17
Library of Congress Catalogs: Music, Books on Music & Sound Recordings, BF23
Library Reference Plus, AB6
Library Research Guide to History, CJ6
Library Research Guide to Religion & Theology, BC5
Library Research Guide to Sociology, CG3
Library Science Abstracts, AA16
Library Science Annual, AA26
Library Science Dissertations, AA10
Library Technology Reports, AA30
Library Use: A Handbook for Psychology, CH5
Life Sciences Organizations & Agencies Directory, DH34
Linda Frum's Guide to Canadian Universities, CI33
List of Alberta Publications & Legislation, AM58
List of Common & Scientific Names of Fishes from the United States & Canada, DH117
List of Geographical Atlases in the Library of Congress, AK10
List of Publications of the Government of Newfoundland & Labrador, 1974-1979, AM42
List of the Fishes of Canada, DH114
List of Unesco Documents & Publications, AN16
Liste bimestrille/annuelle des périodiques du gouvernement du Québec, AM48
Liste collective des journaux canadiens, AE17
Liste des livres disponibles de langue française, AD36
Liste mondiale des périodiques specialisés dans les sciences sociales, CA16
Listes de contrôle des recueils de jurisprudence et des statuts dans les bibliothèques de droit du Canada, CE17
Literary Archives Guide, BD60
Literary Criticism Index, BD15

Literary History of Canada: Canadian Literature in English, BD70
Literary History of England, BD92
Literary History of the United States, BD87
Literary Manuscripts at the National Library of Canada, BD60
Literary Market Place, AB7
Literary Research Guide, BD7
Literary Writings in America: A Bibliography, BD83
Literature & the Child, BD171
Literature Criticism from 1400 to 1800, BD37
Literature of Geography, CK3
Literature of Medieval History, 1930–1975, CJ35
Literature of Rock, 1954–1978, BF5
Literature of the Film, BG46
Literature of the Life Sciences, DH3
Literature on Modern Art, BE11
Literature on the History of Physics in the 20th Century, DE1
Littérature canadienne, AC17
Littérature canadienne pour la jeunesse, AC50
Lively Arts Information Directory, BG8
Living Snakes of the World in Color, DH90
Livres blancs et livres verts au Québec, AM49
Livres canadiens pour la jeunesse, AC37
Livres d'images canadiens, AC38
Livres de l'enfance et livres de la jeunesse au Canada, AD28
Livres disponibles (France), AD84
Livres du mois (France), AD83
Livres verts (Canada), AM33
Livres-hebdo (France), AD83
Loanwords Dictionary, AJ45
Loanwords Index, AJ45
Local Histories of Ontario Municipalities, 1951–1977: A Bibliography, CJ62
LOMA: Literature on Modern Art, BE11
London Bibliography of the Social Sciences, CA4
London Review of Books, AC27
Longman Dictionary of Contemporary English, AJ20
Longman Dictionary of English Idioms, AJ20
Longman Dictionary of Geography: Human & Physical, CK12
Longman Dictionary of Psychology & Psychiatry, CH22
Longman Dictionary of the English Language, AJ20

Longman Dictionary of 20th Century Biography, AL16
Longman Guardian New Words, AJ21
Longman Guide to Bible Quotations, BC23
Longman Handbook of Modern European History 1763 to 1985, CJ44
Longman Handbook of World History Since 1914, CJ45
Longman Illustrated Dictionary of Astronomy & Astronautics: The Terminology of Space, DD12
Longman Pronunciation Dictionary, AJ48
Longman Register of New Words, AJ21
Looking At Architecture in Canada, BE71
Lovejoy's College Guide, CI39

Macmillan Bible Atlas, BC75
Macmillan Biographical Encyclopedia of Photographic Artists & Innovators, BE102
Macmillan Book of Canadian Place Names, AK52
Macmillan Book of Proverbs, Maxims & Famous Phrases, AH68
Macmillan Concise Dictionary of World History, CJ15
Macmillan Dictionary for Children, AJ29
Macmillan Dictionary of Anthropology, CF17
Macmillan Dictionary of Biography, AL17
Macmillan Dictionary of Canadian Biography, AL33
Macmillan Dictionary of Information Technology, AA37
Macmillan Dictionary of Psychology, CH24
Macmillan Dictionary of Quotations, AH63
Macmillan Encyclopedia of Architects, BE68
Macmillan Encyclopedic Dictionary of Numismatics, BE75
Macmillan Family Encyclopedia, AI12
Macmillan Film Bibliography, BG49
Macmillan Guide to Modern World Literature, BD27
Macmillan Illustrated Encyclopedia of Dinosaurs & Prehistoric Animals, DG33
Macmillan Student Encyclopedia of Sociology, CG15
Macmillan World History Factfinder, CJ16
Macrothesaurus for Information Processing in the Field of Economic & Social Development, AN25
Magazine Index, AF11
Magazines for Libraries, AC12

Magazines for Libraries, AE7
Magazines for Young People, AE7
Magic World of Words, AJ29
Magill's Bibliographies, BD8
Magill's Cinema Annual, BG67
Magill's Literary Annual, BD16
Magill's Survey of Cinema, BG67
Magill's Survey of Science: Earth Science Series, DG38
Magill's Survey of Science: Life Science Series, DH30
Magill's Survey of Science: Space Exploration Series, DD15
Main Catalog of the Library of Congress 1898–1980, AD13
Major International Treaties since 1945, CD31
Major Modern Dramatists, BD148
Major Twentieth Century Writers, AL58
Making a World of Difference: A Directory of Women in Canada, CG52
Mammal Species of the World: Taxonomic & Geographic References, DH96
Mammals of Canada, DH91
Mammals of the American North, DH93
Mammals of the Canadian Wild, DH93
Man, Myth & Magic: The Illustrated Encyclopedia of Mythology, BC85
Manitoba Government Publications, AM56
Manual of Patent Office Practice, DA33
Manual of Pest Control, DJ28
Manual of Steel Construction (U.S.), DL85
Manuel de bibliographie philosophique, BB12
Many Names of Country People: An Historical Dictionary, DJ21
Map Catalog: Every Kind of Map & Chart on Earth, AK12
Map Collections in the United States & Canada, AK18
Mapping of North America, AK23
Mapping Upper Canada, 1780-1867, AK16
Maps of Canada, AK5
Marks & Monograms on European & Oriental Pottery & Porcelain, BE84
Marks' Standard Handbook for Mechanical Engineers, DL72
Marshall Cavendish Illustrated Encyclopedia of Family Health: Doctor's Answers, DI68

Martindale - Hubbell Law Directory, CE45
Martindale: The Extra Pharmacopoeia, DI80
Martindale-Hubbell Law Digest, CE45
Martindale-Hubbell Bar Register, CE45
MASA: Medical Acronyms, Symbols, & Abbreviations, DI35
Master Index to Poetry: An Index to Poetry in Anthologies & Collections, BD134
Master List of Nonstellar Optical Astronomical Objects, DD29
Masterpieces of Canadian Art From the National Gallery of Canada, BE45
Masterplots II, BD112
Masters Abstracts International, AF42
Mathematical Handbook of Formulas & Tables, DB13
Mathematical Reviews, DB5
Mathematical Thought from Ancient to Modern Times, DB29
Mathematics Dictionary, DB23
Mathematics Illustrated Dictionary, DB15
MATHSCI, DB6
Mayo Clinic Family Health Book, DI69
McGraw-Hill Concise Encyclopedia of Science & Technology, DA43
McGraw-Hill Dictionary of Art, BE17
McGraw-Hill Dictionary of Chemical Terms, DF33
McGraw-Hill Dictionary of Earth Sciences, DG39
McGraw-Hill Dictionary of Modern Economics, CB16
McGraw-Hill Dictionary of Physics & Mathematics, DB24
McGraw-Hill Dictionary of Scientific & Technical Terms, DA55
McGraw-Hill Encyclopedia of Astronomy, DD16
McGraw-Hill Encyclopedia of Electronics & Computers, DL54
McGraw-Hill Encyclopedia of Physics, DE24
McGraw-Hill Encyclopedia of Ocean & Atmospheric Sciences, DG40
McGraw-Hill Encyclopedia of Science & Technology, DA43
McGraw-Hill Encyclopedia of the Geological Sciences, DG40
McGraw-Hill Encyclopedia of World Drama, BD150
McMichael Canadian Art Collection, BE47
Means Estimating Handbook, DL86
Means Illustrated Construction Dictionary, DL87
Mechanical Engineers Handbook, DL72

Media Review Digest, BG77
Medical Acronyms, Symbols, & Abbreviations, DI35
Medical & Health Care Books & Serials in Print, DI14
Medical & Health Information Directory, DI57
Medical Bibliography, DI15
Medical Bibliography: An Annotated Check-list of Texts Illustrating the History of Medicine, DI15
Medical Books & Serials in Print, DI14
Medical Meetings, DI49
Medical Reference Works, 1679-1966: A Selected Bibliography, DI10
Medical Research Centres, AH10
Medieval Studies: A Bibliographical Guide, CJ37
Medieval Studies: An Introduction, CJ38
MEDLARS, DI23
MEDLINE, DI123
Men of Mathematics, DB27
Mental Measurements Yearbook, CH26
Merck Index: An Encyclopedia of Chemicals, Drugs, & Biologicals, DI81
Merck Manual: A Handbook of Diagnosis & Therapy, DI47
Merck Veterinary Manual, DJ54
Merit Students Encyclopedia, AI14
Merit Students Yearbook, AI14
MeSH, DI123
Metadex, DG21
Metals Abstracts, DG21
Metals Handbook, DL57
Methods of Air Sampling & Analysis, DK45
Metric Design Manual: Precast & Prestressed Concrete, DL88
Meyler's Side Effects of Drugs, DI82
Microbiology Abstracts, DH15
Microcomputer Index, DC9
Microcomputer Software Guide Online, DC31
Microcomputer Software Sources, AB29
Microform Market Place, AB8
Microform Review, AC23
Microform Review, AD92
Microlog: Canadian Research Index, AM31
Middle East & North Africa, CJ138
Middle East, CJ137
Middle East Studies Handbook, CJ139
Milestones in Science & Technology, DA61
Mineral Commodity Summaries, DG59

Mineral Facts & Problems, DG59
Mineral Processing Handbook, DL107
Mineralogical Abstracts, DG22
Minerals Handbook, DG59
Minerals Yearbook, DG28
Minutes of Proceedings, AM69
MIT Dictionary of Modern Economics, CB17
MLA Handbook for Writers of Research Papers, Theses & Dissertations, AJ69
MLA International Bibliography of Books & Articles, BD14
MNT (Mining Technology), DG20
Modern American Literature, BD88
Modern American Usage: A Guide, AJ67
Modern Art: Painting / Sculpture / Architecture, BE52
Modern Australian Prose, 1901-1975, BD2
Modern Breeds of Livestock, DJ22
Modern British Literature, BD96
Modern Canadian Architecture, BE72
Modern Canadian Children's Books, BD165
Modern Drama Scholarship & Criticism 1966–1980, BD142
Modern English Canadian Prose, BD2
Modern English Usage, AJ68
Modern Geography: An Encyclopedic Survey, CK17
Modern Hebrew-English Dictionary, AJ97
Modern Plastics Encyclopedia, DL103
Modern Researcher, CJ10
Modern Scientists & Engineers, DA66
Monthly Bulletin of Statistics (United Nations), CA44
Monthly Catalog of United States Government Publications, AM122
Monthly Checklist of State Publications, AM124
Monthly Products Announcements (U.S. Census), CA65
Montreal Museum of Fine Arts Spring Exhibition, BE38
More Junior Authors
Mosby's Medical, Nursing & Allied Health Dictionary, DI38
Motion Picture Directors: A Bibliography of Articles, BG53
Motion Picture Guide Annual, BG78
Motion Picture Guide, BG78
Motion Picture Performers: A Bibliography of Magazine & Periodical Articles, 1900–1969, BG53
Mottoes, AH64

Movie Characters of Leading Performers of the Sound Era, BG69
Mozley & Whiteley's Law Dictionary, CE39
Multicultural Information Resources: A Guide to Metropolitan Toronto, CF27
Multicultural Information: Selected Bibliography (Canada), CF25
Multilingual Thesaurus of Geosciences, DG42
Municipal Year Book & Public Service Directory (U.K.), CA76
Municipal Year Book (U.S.), CA76
Murder in Print: A Guide to Two Centuries of Crime Fiction, BD116
Museums Directory of the United States & Canada, BE43
Music Directory Canada, BF49
Music Education: A Guide to Information Sources, BF3
Music in Print Series, BF16
Music Index: The Key to Current Music Periodical Literature, BF26
Music of Canada, BF52
Music Reference & Research Materials, BF2
Music: A Guide to the Reference Literature, BF1
Musical America International Directory of the Performing Arts, BF50
Musik in Geschichte und Gegenwart, BF30
Mythical & Fabulous Creatures, BC88
Mythologies of the World, BC88
Mythology of All Races, BC87
Mythology: An Illustrated Encyclopedia, BC86

Names in the History of Psychology, CH25
Names of Plants, DH49
National Agricultural Library Catalog, DJ12
National Atlas of Canada, AK41
National Atlas of the United States of America, AK42
National Building Code of Canada, DL89
National Cyclopedia of American Biography, AL37
National Directory of Newsletters & Reporting Services, AE9
National Fire Code of Canada, DL89
National Geographic Atlas of North America, AK27
National Geographic Atlas of the World, AK27
National Heraldry of the World, AH40

National Index of American Imprints Through 1800, AD70
National Inventory of Documentary Sources in the United States, AD101
National Inventory of Documentary Sources of the United Kingdom & Ireland, AD99
National Newspaper Index, AF28
National Register of Microform Masters, AD93
National Union Catalog of Manuscript Collections, AD100
National Union Catalog Pre-1956 Imprints: A Cumulative Author List, AD14
National Union Catalog. Audiovisual Materials, AG13
National Union Catalog. Books, AD18
National Union Catalog. Cartographic Materials, AK11
National Union Catalog. U.S. Books, AD19
National Union Catalog: 1956 Through 1967, AD15
Native Peoples of Canada, CF37
Native Peoples of Canada in Contemporary Society, CF41
Naturalists Directory International, DH35
Naturalists' Directory & Almanac International, DH35
Nature & Use of the HRAF Files, CF5
Navigations, Traffiques & Discoveries, 1774–1848, AD54
Nearby Galaxies Atlas, DD41
Nelson Canadian Atlas, AK40
Nelson's Complete Concordance of the New American Bible, BC60
Neoclassical Architecture in Canada, BE70
New A to Z of Women's Health, DI70
New Acronyms, Initialisms & Abbreviations, AJ34
New Age Encyclopedia, BC39
New & Forthcoming Canadian Books, AD37
New Book of Knowledge, AI19
New Book of Popular Science, DA47
New Book of World Rankings, CA40
New Books (U.S. Government), AM122
New Brunswick Government Documents, AM41
New Cambridge Bibliography of English Literature, BD91
New Cambridge Modern History, CJ48
New Canadian Quotations, AH61
New Catholic Encyclopedia, BC52
New Century Classical Handbook, CJ33

New Chinese English Dictionary, AJ92
New Columbia Encyclopedia, AI10
New Dictionary of American Slang, AJ57
New Dictionary of Birds, DH99
New Dictionary of Heraldry, AH43
New Dictionary of Theology, BC49
New Encyclopaedia Britannica, AI8
New English Dictionary on Historical Principles, AJ8
New English Russian Dictionary, AJ100
New Film Index: A Bibliography of Magazine Articles in English 1930–1970, BG52
New Governmental Advisory Organizations, AM99
New Grove Dictionary of American Music, BF31
New Grove Dictionary of Jazz, BF31
New Grove Dictionary of Music & Musicians, BF31
New Grove Dictionary of Musical Instruments, BF32
New Grove Dictionary of Opera, BF31
New Guide to Modern World Literature, BD27
New Harvard Dictionary of Music, BF33
New Illustrated Encyclopedia of World History, CJ14
New International Atlas, AK29
New International Dictionary of Acronyms in Library & Information Science, AA39
New International Dictionary of Biblical Archaeology, BC68
New New Words Dictionary, AJ13
New Oxford Annotated Bible, BC59
New Oxford Atlas, AK30
New Oxford Guide to Writing, AJ69
New Oxford History of Music, BF53
New Palgrave: A Dictionary of Economics, CB18
New Penguin Guide to Compact Discs & Cassettes, BF59
New Practical Guide to Canadian Political Economy, CD10
New Reader's Guide To African Literature, BD9
New Republic of Childhood, BD165
New Research Centers, AH10
New Sabin, AD69
New Serial Titles: A Union List of Serials, AE18
New Strong's Exhaustive Concordance of the Bible, BC60
New Technical Books, AC22
New Testament Abstracts, BC7
New Video Encyclopedia, AG32
New York Botanical Garden Illustrated Encyclopedia of Horticulture, DH48
New York Review of Books, AC28
New York Theatre Critics Reviews, BG42
New York Times Biographical Service, AL18
New York Times Book Review, AC29
New York Times Encyclopedia of Film, BG60
New York Times Encyclopedia of Television, BG85
New York Times Film Reviews, BG79
New York Times Index, AF29
New York Times Obituaries Index, 1858–1968, AL9
New York Times Theatre Reviews, BG42
Newcomer's Guide to Services in Ontario, AM23
Newnes Dictionary of Dates, AH54
NEWSEARCH, AF28
Newsletters Directory, AE9
Newsletters in Print, AE9
Newsmakers, AL19
Newspaper Hansard (Ontario), AM77
Newspapers in Microform, 1948–1983, AE8
Newspeak, AJ51
NEWSTEX, AF26
NFB Film Guide: The Productions of the National Film Board of Canada from 1939 to 1989, AG16
NGC 2000.0, DD30
NICEM Index, AG17
Nightwatch: An Equinox Guide to Viewing the Universe, DD18
999 Questions About Canada, CJ84
Nineteenth Century Readers' Guide to Periodical Literature, 1890–1899, AF22
Nineteenth Century Short Title Catalogue, AD63
Nineteenth-Century Literature Criticism, BD38
Nineteenth-Century Photography, BE106
Nineteenth-Century Pottery & Porcelain in Canada, BE88
NIOSH Manual of Analytical Methods, DK47
NIV Exhaustive Concordance, BC60
NLM Catalog, DI16
NLM Current Catalog, DI16
Nobel Prize Winners: Chemistry, DF55
Nobel Prize Winners: Literature, BD39
Nobel Prize Winners: Physics, DE31
Nondestructive Testing Handbook, DL95
North American Horticulture: A Reference Guide, DH65
Norton/Grove Concise Encyclopedia of Music, BF31
Norton's 2000.0 Star Atlas & Reference Handbook, DD31

Notable Canadian Children's Books, AC43
Notable Names in American History, AL37
Notices en langue française du Canadian Catalogue of Books 1921–1949, AD32
NRCPUBS, DA4
NRSV Concordance Unabridged, BC60
NSTC, AD63
NUC Books, AD18
NUC Register of Additional Locations, AD12
Nuclear Science Abstracts, DE8
Numeric Map Catalogue, AK13
Numerical Finding List of British Command Papers Published 1933-1961/62, AM94
Nursing & Allied Health, DI17
Nursing Citation Index, DI26
Nutrient Value of Some Common Foods, DI62
Nutrition Almanac, DI65
Nutrition Desk Reference, DI66
Nutrition: Where Have All These Labels Been?, DI65

Obituaries on File, AL10
Observateur économique canadienne, CA53
Observatories of the World, DD44
Observer's Handbook, DD32
Observing Handbook & Catalogue of Deep Sky Objects, DD26
Occupational Health & Safety Management Handbook, DI89
Oceanic Abstracts, DG23
Official Congressional Directory, AM101
Official Directory of Canadian Museums & Related Institutions, BE42
Official Gazette of the United States Patent Office, DA33
Official Journal (Patents) (U.K.), DA33
Official Museum Directory, BE43
Official NFL Encyclopedia, CL14
Official Publications in Britain, AM82
Official Publications of the Soviet Union & Eastern Europe, 1945–1980, AM4
Official Publications of Western Europe, AM5
Official Publishing: An Overview, AM1
Official World Wildlife Fund Guide to Endangered Species of North America, DH119
Old Master Print References: A Selected Bibliography, BE96

Old Testament Abstracts, BC7
Ologies & -Isms: A Thematic Dictionary, AJ76
On Cassette: A Comprehensive Bibliography, AG18
On the Brink: Endangered Species in Canada, DH120
On the Screen: A Film Television & Video Research Guide, BG48
On-line Searching: A Dictionary & Bibliographic Guide, AB38
One-Parent Family in the 1980s: Perspective & Annotated Bibliography 1978–1984, CG37
Online Information Retrieval: Bibliography 1964–1982, AB39
Ontario Architecture, BE71
Ontario Gazette, AM79
Ontario Government Information, AM23
Ontario Government Publications, AM54
Ontario Government: Structure & Functions, AM20
Ontario Medical Directory, DI55
Ontario Public Sector: The Periodical of Official Personnel, AM24
Ontario Sessional Papers, 1868–1948, AM80
Ontario Since 1867: A Bibliography, CJ64
Ontario's Heritage: A Guide to Archival Resources, AD95
Ontario's History in Maps, AK37
Ontario's History in Maps, CJ85
Optical Publishing Directory, AB27
OPUS, BF60
Oral History: A Reference Guide & Annotated Bibliography, CJ2
Orbis Geographicus: World Directory of Geography, CK21
Organization of the Government of Canada, AM18
Origin & Meaning of Place Names in Canada, AK52
Original Index to Art Periodicals, BE12
Originals: Who's Really Who in Fiction, BD48
Origins of Photography, BE108
Osborn's Concise Law Dictionary, CE40
Ottawa's Senior Executives Guide, AM19
Ottemiller's Index to Plays in Collections, BD157
Our Choice / Your Choice: Canadian Children's Books, AC44
Outline of Cultural Materials, CF5
Outline of World Cultures, CF5
Overview of Canadian Education, CI23
Oxford American Dictionary, AJ14
Oxford Bible Atlas, BC76

Oxford Children's Thesaurus, AJ61
Oxford Childrens Dictionaries, AJ30
Oxford Classical Dictionary, CJ33
Oxford Companion to American Literature, BD89
Oxford Companion to American Theatre, BG40
Oxford Companion to Canadian History & Literature, CJ92
Oxford Companion to Canadian Literature, BD73
Oxford Companion to Canadian Theatre, BG40
Oxford Companion to Children's Literature, BD170
Oxford Companion to Classical Literature, BD160
Oxford Companion to English Literature, BD97
Oxford Companion to Gardens, DH56
Oxford Companion to Law, CE32
Oxford Companion to the Decorative Arts, BE85
Oxford Companion to the Theatre, BG41
Oxford Companion to Twentieth Century Art, BE19
Oxford Dictionary of Art, BE16
Oxford Dictionary of English Etymology, AJ41
Oxford Dictionary of Natural History, DH22
Oxford Dictionary of Popes, BC56
Oxford Dictionary of Quotations, AH65
Oxford Dictionary of Saints, BC54
Oxford Encyclopedia of Trees of the World, DJ62
Oxford English Dictionary, AJ8
Oxford English-Italian/Italian-English Dictionary, AJ98
Oxford Guide to English Usage, AJ71
Oxford Guide to Heraldry, AH42
Oxford Guide to the English Language, AJ71
Oxford History of English Literature, BD98
Oxford Illustrated Encyclopedia of the Arts, BA14
Oxford Illustrated History of Medieval Europe, CJ42
Oxford Illustrated Literary Guide to Canada, BD71
Oxford Latin Dictionary, AJ94
Oxford Minidictionary, AJ71
Oxford Senior Dictionary, AJ30
Oxford Students Dictionary, AJ30
Oxford-Duden German Dictionary, AJ96
Oxford-Duden Pictiorial English Japanese Dictionary, AJ99
Oxford-Duden Pictorial Dictionary, AJ74
Oxford-Duden Pictorial English-Chinese Dictionary, AJ91
Oxford-Duden Pictorial French-English Dictionary, AJ78
Oxford-Duden Pictorial German English Dictionary, AJ96
Oxford-Duden Pictorial Spanish-English Dictionary, AJ101

P/E News, DK72
Painting in Canada, BE53
PAIS Foreign Language Index, AF15
PAIS International in Print, AF15
Palladian Style in Canadian Architecture, BE70
Palomar Observatory Sky Survey, DD40
Papal Encyclicals, 1740–1981, BC44
Papal Pronouncements, 1740–1978, BC44
Paperbound Books in Print, AD79
Parliamentary Publications Past & Present (Quebec), AM50
Parliaments of the World: A Comparative Reference Compendium, CD32
Patent Office Record, DA33
Patterns of Poetry: An Encyclopedia of Forms, BD137
Patty's Industrial Hygiene & Toxicology, DK48
PDR: Physician's Desk Reference, DI84
Peace Movements of the World, CD56
Peace Research Abstracts Journal, CD58
Peace Resource Book, CD56
Peacekeeping: An Annotated Bibliography, CD57
Penguin Canadian Dictionary, AJ25
Penguin Dictionary of Archaeology, CF50
Penguin Dictionary of Decorative Arts, BE86
Penguin Dictionary of Religions, BC18
People's Chronology, CJ18
People's Chronology: A Year by Year Record, AH56; CJ21
Performance Practice, Medieval to Contemporary: A Bibliographic Guide, BF6
Performing Arts Biography Master Index, BG9
Performing Arts Books, 1876–1981, BG1
Performing Arts Libraries & Museums of the World, BG11
Performing Arts Research, BG2
Performing Arts Resources, BG10
Perigree Visual Dictionary of Signing, AJ49
Periodex, AF16
Periodical Title Abbreviations, AE10

Periodicals in Canadian Law Libraries: A Union List, CE22
Permanent & Provisional Standing Orders of the House of Commons, AM6
Perry's Chemical Engineer's Handbook, DF47
Pest Control Canada: A Pesticide Reference Manual, DJ30
Pesticide Handling: A Safety Manual, DJ28
Pesticide Manual: A World Compendium, DJ31
Pesticide Users' Health & Safety Handbook, DJ32
Peters Atlas of the World, AK31
Peterson Field Guide Series, DH78
Peterson First Guide to the Solar System, DD19
Petit Robert, AJ82
Petroleum/Energy Business News Index, DK72
Petroleum Engineering Handbook, DL58
Pharmaceutical Manufacturing Encyclopedia, DI84
Philatélie canadienne, BE74
Philosopher's Guide, BB2
Philosopher's Index, BB8-BB9
Philosophy: A Guide to the Reference Literature, BB1
Phonolog Reporter, BF61
Photography Books Index: A Subject Guide to Photo Anthologies, BE107
Physical Review Abstracts, DE7
Physics Abstracts, DE9
Physics Briefs, DE10
Pictorial History of Costume, BE79
Picturesque Expressions, AJ56
Pinyin Chinese English Dictionary, AJ92
Play Index, BD156
Plays: A Classified Guide to Play Selection, BD156
Playwright's Guide to Canadian Non-Profit Professional Theatre, BG33
Pocket Dictionary of Signing, AJ49
Pocket Oxford Dictionary, AJ19
Poet's Market, BD136
Poetry Explication: A Checklist of Interpretation Since 1925
Poetry Handbook: A Dictionary of Terms, BD130
Poetry Index Annual, BD135
Poetry Markets for Canadians, BD136
Point de repère: Index analytique (Québec), AF16
Poisonous Plants of Canada, DH55
Political Handbook of the World, CD33
Political Parties & Elections in the United States: An Encyclopedia, CD51

Political Parties of the World, CD34
Political Science Abstracts, CD15
Political Science: A Guide to Reference & Information Sources, CD2
Pollack's Fundamentals of Legal Research, CE9
Pollution Abstracts, DK17
Pollution/Toxicology CD-ROM (PolTox), DK18
Polymer Handbook, DF45
Polymer Science Dictionary, DF19
Poole's Index to Periodical Literature, AF23
Popular Dictionary of Buddhism, BC24
Popular Marine Fish for Your Aquarium, DH110
Popular Music (Discographies), BF56
Popular Music, 1920–1979, BF20
Popular Song Index, BF12
Popular Titles & Subtitles of Musical Compositions, BF9
Popular Tropical Fish for Your Aquarium, DH110
Poverty & Human Resources Abstracts, CG40
Practical Encyclopedia of Pet Birds for Home & Garden, DH108
Practical Handbook of Biochemistry & Molecular Biology, DH36
Practical Handbook of Microbiology, DH32
Praeger Encyclopedia of Art, BE17
Prefixes & Other Word-Initial Elements of English, AJ75
Prentice-Hall Encyclopedia of Information Technology, DC20
Prentice-Hall History of Music Series, BF54
Primates of the World: Distribution, Abundance, & Conservation, DH97
Prince Edward Island Provincial Government Publications Checklist, AM45
Princeton Encyclopedia of Classical Sites, CJ32
Princeton Handbook of Poetic Terms, BD137
Princteon Encyclopedia of Poetry & Poetics, BD137
Print Council Index to Oeuvre-Catalogues of Prints by European & American Artists, BE97
Print Reference Sources, BE96
Printmaking & Picture Printing, BE94
Printmaking in Canada: The Earliest Views & Portraits, BE100
Pro Football Guide, CL14
Production Handbook, DL108
Products & Services (Canada Census), CA56
Profile Index, AM31

Profiles in Canadian Literature, BD74
Progress in Astronautics & Aeronautics, DL47
Pronouncing Dictionary of American English, AJ47
Provincial Royal Commissions & Commissions of Inquiry, 1867-1982: A Selective Bibliography, AM38
Pseudonyms & Nicknames Dictionary, AL20
PsycBOOKS, CH4
Psychiatric Dictionary, CH15
Psychological Abstracts, CH8
Psychological Bulletin, CH13
Psychware Sourcebook, CH32
PsycINFO, CH9
PsycSCAN, CH9
Public Administration: A Bibliographic Guide, CD5
Public Administration & Management Vocabulary, CD25
Public Administration Dictionary, CD21
Public Affairs Information Service Bulletin, AF15
Public Library Catalog, AC13
Public Policy Dictionary, CD34
Publicat Index, AM31
Publications Catalogue [British Columbia], AM62
Publications Catalogue [Northwest Territories], AM64
Publications of the European Communities, AN31
Publications of the Government of British Columbia, 1871-1947, AM60
Publications of the Government of Ontario, AM51-AM53
Publications of the Government of the North-West Territories, 1867-1905 & of the Province of Saskatchewan, 1905-1952, AM63
Publications of the Government of the Province of Canada, 1841-1867, AM35
Publications of the Governments of Nova Scotia, Prince Edward Island, New Brunswick, 1758-1952, AM34
Publications of the National Research Council of Canada, 1916–1981, DA4
Publications of the Province of Nova Scotia, AM43
Publications of the Province of Upper Canada & of Great Britain Relating to Upper Canada, 1791-1840, AM36
Publications officielles (France), AD83
Publications parlementaires hier et d'aujourd'hui (Québec), AM50
Publications Reference File (U.S. Govt), AM122

Publisher's Practical Dictionary in 20 Languages, AB18
Publishers, Distributors, & Wholesalers of the United States, AB10
Publishers International Directory, AB4
Publishers Weekly, AB13
Publishers' Directory, AB9
Publishers' International ISBN Directory, AB4
Publishers' Trade List Annual, AD80
Pure & Applied Science Books 1876–1982, DA5
Purnell's History of the 20th Century, CJ51

QL/SEARCH: User's Manual & Database Description Manual, AB42
Quality Control Handbook, DL71
Quarterly Bibliography of Computers & Data Processing, DC8
Quarterly Index Islamicus, BC32
Québec: Trois siècles d'architecture, BE71
Québécois Dictionary, AJ85
Queen Anne Revival Style in Canadian Architecture, BE70
Queen's Printer Publications Catalogue (British Columbia), AM62
Quick Canadian Facts: The Canadian Pocket Encyclopedia, AH20
Quill & Quire, AB14
Quotable Woman, 1800–1981, AH66
Quotable Woman From Eve to 1799, AH66
Quotation Location: A Quotation Seeker's Source Guide, AH67
Quotations Database, AH65

R & D Projects in Documentation & Librarianship, AA12
RADAR, AF16
Radials Bulletin, AA12
Radio & Television: A Selected, Annotated Bibliography, BG86
Radio Soundtracks: A Reference Guide, BG81
Rand McNally Atlas of World History, CJ25
Random House College Dictionary, AJ11
Random House Dictionary of the English Language, AJ11
Random House Encyclopedia, AI11

Random House Handbook, AJ69
Read All Your Life: A Subject Guide to Fiction, BD101
Reader's Adviser, AC14
Reader's Digest Encyclopedia of Garden Plants & Flowers, DH44
Reader's Encyclopedia, BA11
Reader's Encyclopedia of World Drama, BD147
Readers' Guide Abstracts, AF17
Reader's Guide to Canadian History, CJ74
Readers' Guide to Periodical Literature, AF17
Reader's Guide to the Canadian Novel, BD107
Reader's Guide to the Great Religions, BC20
Reader's Guide to Twentieth-Century Science Fiction, BD123
Ready Reference to Philosophy East & West, BB20
Recensement Canada, CA56
Recently Published Articles, CJ9
Recommended Nutrient Intakes for Canadians, DI62
Recommended Reference Books for Small & Medium-Sized Libraries, AC1
Recueil des définitions des lois fédérales, CE38
Referativnyi Zhurnal, DA20
Reference & Subscription Books Reviews, AC23
Reference Book for Composites Technology, DL105
Reference Books Bulletin, AC15
Reference Books Bulletin, AC23
Reference Books for Young Readers, AC45
Reference Encyclopedia of the American Indian, CF45
Reference Guide to American Literature, BD85
Reference Services Review, AC24
Reference Sources in Library & Information Services, AA2
Reference Sources on Canadian Education, CI1
Reference Works in British & American Literature, BD5
Register of Canadian Honours, AH32
Registre des distinctions honorifiques canadiennes, AH32
Règlement annoté de la Chambre des communes (Canada), AM6
Religion & Society in North America: An Annotated Bibliography, BC2
Religion Index One: Periodicals, BC8
Religion Index Two: Multi-Author Works, BC8
Religions on File, BC11

Religious & Inspirational Books & Serials in Print, BC3
Religious & Theological Abstracts, BC9
Religious Books, 1876–1982, BC3
Religious Studies Review, BC4
REPÈRE, AF16
Répertoire bibliographique de la philosophie, BB11
Répertoire canadien sur l'education, CI8
Répertoire d'art et d'archéologie, BE3
Répertoire de l'édition au Québec, AD36
Répertoire des associations du Canada, AH6
Répertoire des centres et instituts de recherche en science sociale dans les universités canadiennes, CA27
Répertoire des films de l'ONF: la production de l'Office National du Film du Canada de 1939 à 1989, AG16
Répertoire des normes, DA38
Répertoire des oeuvres d'Antonio Vivaldi, BF18
Répertoire des publications gouvernementales du Québec de 1867 à 1964, AM45
Répertoire des publications seriées canadiennes, AE2
Répertoire des universités canadiennes, CI33
Répertoire géographique du Canada, AK46
Répertoire international des sources musicales, BF17
Répertoire mondial des institutions de sciences sociales, CA29
Répertoire officiel des musées canadiens et institutions connexes, BE42
Répertoire récréation, CL10
Répertoire toponymique du Québec, AK48
Répertoires des bibliothèques canadiennes, AA46
Reports on Progress in Physics, DE14
Reprint Bulletin Book Review, AC23; AD91
Reptiles of the World, DH88
Republic of Childhood, BD165
Research Abstracts, AF42
Research Catalogue (American Geographical Society), CK1
Research Centers Directory, AH10
Research Guide for Psychology, CH2
Research Guide for Undergraduate Students: English & American Literature, BD4
Research Guide to Biography & Criticism, BD41
Research Guide to Philosophy, BB4
Research Guide to Religious Studies, BC5

Research Guide to the Health Sciences: Medical, Nutritional & Environmental, DI5
Research in British Universities, Polytechnics & Colleges, AF40
Research in Education, AA19; CI13
Resource Reading List 1990: Annotated Bibliography of Resources by & about Native People, CF40
Resources for Feminist Research, CG50
Resources for Native Peoples Studies, CF32
Resources in Education, AA19; CI13
Retrospective Index to Film Periodicals, 1930-1971, BG52
Retrospective Index to Theses of Great Britain & Ireland, AF44
Revell Bible Dictionary, BC69
Reverse Acronyms, Initialisms & Abbreviations Dictionary, AJ34
Review of Historical Publications Relating to Canada, CJ76
Reviewing Librarian, AC54
Reviews in Anthropology, CF9
Reviews of Modern Physics, DE15
Revised Regulations of Ontario 1980, AM76
Revised Statutes of Canada, 1985, AM72
Revised Statutes of Ontario, 1980, AM75
RHS Encyclopedia of House Plants Including Greenhouse Plants, DH44
RIBA Annual Review, BE60
Right College, CI39
RILA, BE3
RILM: Abstracts of Music Literature, BF27
Robert's Rules of Order, AH59
Robert-Collins Dictionnaire français-anglais/anglais-français, AJ77
Rocks & Minerals for the Collector, DG48
Rocks, Minerals & Fossils of the World, DG60
Rodale's Encyclopedia of Indoor Gardening, DH57
Rodale's Garden Insect, Disease & Weed Identification Guide, DH59
Rodale's Illustrated Encyclopedia of Herbs, DH60
Roget's Junior Thesaurus, AJ61
Romans, Their Gods & Their Beliefs, BC78
Roth's American Poetry Annual, BD138
Royal Canadian Academy of the Arts / Academie royale des arts du Canada: Exhibitions & Members 1880–1979, BE38
Royal Commissions (Great Britain), AM90

RQ (Reference Quarterly), AC24
RSCPT/Legal, DK19
RTECS (Registry of Toxic Effects of Chemical Substances) Database, DK19
Rubber Technology Handbook, DL110
Rule Book, CL6
Russia & the Soviet Union: A Bibliographic Guide to Western-Language Publications, CJ127
Russia, the USSR, & Eastern Europe: A Bibliographic Guide, CJ127

Safire's Political Dictionary, CD27
Sage Family Studies Abstracts, CG36
Sage Public Administration Abstracts, CD18
Sage Urban Studies Abstracts, CA77
St. James Reference Guide to English Literature, BD99
Saskatchewan Bibliography, AD52
Saskatchewan Government Publications, AM57
School Library Journal, AC55
Schwann-1 Record & Tape Guide, AG19; BF60
Science & Technology Illustrated, DA48
Science Abstracts, DA21
Science & Technology Annual Reference Review, AC7
Science Books & Films, AC25
Science Citation Index, DA22
Science Fiction & Fantasy Book Review Annual, BD119
Science Fiction & Fantasy Book Review Index, BD121
Science Fiction & Fantasy Reference Index, 1878-1985, BD120
Science Fiction & Fantasy Research Index, BD120
Science Fiction Book Review Index 1923-1973, BD121
Science Fiction, Fantasy, & Horror, BD122
Science Fiction, Horror & Fantasy Film & Television Credits, BG70
Science Fiction in Print, BD122
Science Year (World Book Annual), DA44
Scientific American Medicine, DI48
Scientific & Technical Aerospace Reports (STAR), DL32
Scientific & Technical Books & Serials in Print, DA8
Scientific & Technical Information Sources, DA9

Scientific & Technical Organizations & Agencies Directory, DA71
Scientific & Technical Societies of Canada, DA70
Scientific Research in British Universities and Colleges, AF40
SciSearch, DA22
Scott's Standard Post Stamp Catalogue, BE76
Scrapbook Debates (Ontario), AM77
Scribner Desk Dictionary of American History, CJ105
Sculpture Index, BE54
Searchable Physics Information Notices, DE7
Searching DIALOG: The Complete Guide, AB43
Sectional Lists (HMSO), AM96
SEDBASE, DI82
Select Bibliography of the Sikhs & Sikhism
Select Committees of the Legislative Assembly of Ontario: 1867-1978, AM55
Select List of British Parliamentary Papers, AM91
Selected Theatre Criticism, BG43
Selected Videos & Films for Young Adults, AG26
Selecting Instructional Media: A Guide, AG27
Selective Bibliography for the Study of English & American Literature, BD4
Selective Inventory of Social Science Information & Documentation Services, CA29
Self-Medication: A Reference for Health Professionals, DI75
Senior High School Library Catalog, AC46
Sequels, BD103
Serial Publications in Anthropology, CF1
Serial Publications in the British Parliamentary Papers, AM89
Serial Sources for the BIOSIS Database, DH7
Serials Directory, AE11
Serials in the British Library, AE19
Serials on Aging, CG16
Sessional Papers of the Dominion of Canada, 1867-1925, AM70
Sexual Abuse of Children in the 1980's: Ten Essays & an Annotated Bibliography, CG23
Sexual Abuse of Children: A Resource Guide & Annotated Bibliography, CG23
Shakespearean Criticism, BD159
Shepherd's Historical Atlas, CJ26
Short Story Criticism, BD126
Short Story Index, BD127

Short-title Catalogue of Books Printed in England, Scotland, ... 1641–1700, AD61
Short-Title Catalogue of Books Printed in England, Scotland, ... 1475–1640, AD60
Shorter New Cambridge Bibliography of English Literature, BD91
Shorter Oxford Dictionary on Historical Principles, AJ18
Sikh Studies, BC28
Sikhism & the Sikhs: An Annotated Bibliography, BC28
Silent Films, BG67
Similes Dictionary, AJ56
SIPRI Yearbook: World Armaments & Disarmament, CD59
16MM Films Available From the Public Libraries of Metropolitan Toronto, AG20
Sketches of Celebrated Canadians, AL30
Small Basic Music Library: Essential Scores & Books, BF8
SME Mineral Processing Handbook, DL107
Smith's Guide to the Literature of the Life Sciences, DH6
Social Protest from the Left in Canada, 1870–1970, CD9
Social Science Encyclopedia, CA22
Social Science Reference Sources: A Practical Guide, CA3
Social Sciences Citation Index, CA13
Social Sciences Index, CA14
Social Sciences: Cross Disciplinary Guide to Selected Sources, CA5
Social SciSearch, CA13
Social Work Dictionary, CG43
Social Work Research & Abstracts, CG42
SocioFile, CG9
Sociological Abstracts, CG9
Sociology of Aging: An Annotated Bibliography & Sourcebook, CG19
Sociology: A Guide to Reference & Information Sources, CG1
Sociology: An International Bibliography of Serial Publications, 1880–1980, CG4
Software Catalog: Microcomputers, DC30
Software Encyclopedia, DC31
Software Publishers' Catalogs Annual, DC30

Title Index 585

Software Reviews on File, DC32
Soils of Canada, DJ24
Solar Energy Dictionary, DK80
Something About the Author, AL69
Song Index, BF19
Songs in Collections: An Index, BF10
Songs of the Theatre, BF15
Sotheby's World Wine Encyclopedia, DJ49
Source Book of Mathematics, 1200–1800, DB30
Source Readings in Music History From Classical Antiquity through the Romantic Era, BF55
Source-book of Canadian History: Selected Documents, CJ65
Sourcebook for the Performing Arts, BG11
Sourcebook of Canadian Health Statistics, DI13
Sourcebook of Library Technology, AA30
Sources & Literature of English History from the Earliest Times to about 1485, CJ122
Sources of Information in Librarianship & Information Science, AA1
Sources of Information in the Social Sciences, CA6
Sources: The Directory of Contacts for Editors, Reporters & Researchers, AH11
South America, Central America & the Caribbean, CJ117
Sovetskaia Entsiklopediia, AI25
Soviet & East European Political Dictionary, CD26
Soviet Mathematical Encyclopedia, DB19
Soviet Union & Eastern Europe, CJ133
Soviet Union, CJ132
Special Collections in College & University Libraries, AA54
Special Libraries Association Directory, AA61
Special Libraries in Canada, AA50
Special List of Canadian Government Publications, AM29
Speech Index, AH69
SPIN (Searchable Physics Information Notices), DE7
Sport & Recreation for the Disabled, CL1
Sport & Recreation Index, CL2
SPORT Database, CL2
SPORT Discus, CL2
SPORT Thesaurus, CL2
SportBiblio, CL1
Sports Directory, CL10
Sports Market Place, CL11
Sports Rules Encyclopedia, CL6

SportSearch, CL2
Stage, Scenery, Machinery & Lighting, BG26
Standard Dictionary of Canadian Biography, AL34
Standard Handbook for Civil Engineers, DL74
Standard Handbook for Electrical Engineers, DL75
Standard Handbook of Engineering Calculations, DL76
Standard Periodical Directory, AE12
Standard Postage Stamp Catalogue, BE76
Standing Orders of the House of Commons, AM6
STAR, DL32
Star Catalog, DD33
Stars & Stellar Systems: Compendium of Astronomy & Astrophysics Series, DD34
Stars, Galaxies, Cosmos: A Catalog of Astronomical Anomalies, DD35
StatCan Reference, CA61
State & Metropolitan Area Data Book, CA65
State Legislative Sourcebook, AM125
State of Food & Agriculture, DJ15
Statesman's Year Book Historical Companion, AH25
Statesman's Year-Book World Gazetteer, AK49
Statesman's Year-Book: Statistical & Historical Annual of the States of the World, AH25
Statistical Abstract of the United States, CA65
Statistical Record of the Environment Worldwide, DK49
Statistical Reference Index, CA66
Statistical Tables for Biological, Agricultural & Medical Research, DH37
Statistical Yearbook (United States), CA44
Statistics Africa, CA34
Statistics America, CA34
Statistics Asia & Australasia, CA34
Statistics Canada Catalogue, CA61
Statistics Canada Publications List, CA61
Statistics Europe: Sources for Social, Economic & Market Research, CA34
Statistics on Alcohol & Drug Use in Canada & Other Countries, CG32
Statistics Sources: A Subject Guide, CA35
STATPACK (United States statistics), CA66
Statutes of Canada, AM72
Statutes of the Province of Ontario, AM75
Statutory Orders & Regulations (Canada), AM73
Stedman's Medical Dictionary, DI39
Steinberg's Dictionary of British History, CJ125

Stoddart English/Chinese Visual Dictionary, AJ91
Stoddart Visual Dictionary, AJ74
Story of Art, BE51
Strategic Atlas: Comparative Geopolitics of the World's Powers, AK20
Strategic Minerals: A Bibliography, DG7
Stroud's Judicial Dictionary of Words & Phrases, CE41
Student's Dictionary of Psychology, CH24
Student's Guide to History, CJ1
Student's Guide to Ontario Universities, CI33
Studies in Human Sexuality: A Selected Guide, CG39
Studies on Women Abstracts, CG51
Study Abroad, CI40
Subject Catalog, AD16
Subject Catalogue of the House of Commons Parliamentary Papers, 1801-1900, AM95
Subject Catalogues of Printed Books, 1975–1985 (Great Britain), AD11
Subject Collections in European Libraries, AA53
Subject Collections: A Guide to Special Book Collections, AA53
Subject Compilations of State Laws 1988–1990: An Annotated Bibliography, CE51
Subject Guide to Books in Print, AD76
Subject Guide to Forthcoming Books, AD78
Subject Guide to Major United States Government Publications, AM109
Subject Guide to U.S. Government Reference Sources, AM109
Subject Index of Modern Books, AD8
Subject Index to Canadian Poetry in English for Children & Young People, BD176
Subject Index to Poetry for Children & Young People, BD177
Subscription Books Bulletin, AC23
Successful Forestry: A Guide to Private Forestry Management, DJ64
Suffixes & Other Word-Final Elements of English, AJ76
Survey of Canadian Herbaria, DH62
Sweet's Canadian Construction Catalogue File, DL90
Symbol Sourcebook: An Authoritative Guide to International Graphic Symbols, AJ59
Synopsis & Classification of Living Organisms, DH80

Taber's Cyclopedic Medical Dictionary, DI40
Tables of Physical & Chemical Constants & Some Mathematical Functions, DE29
Talmud: The Steinsaltz Edition, BC37
Tanaka's Cyclopedia of Edible Plants of the World, DJ48
Tapping the Government Grapevine, AM110
Taschenbuch der Mathematik, DB7
Taylor's Guide to Trees, DH45
Technical Book Review Index, AC31
Technical Manual & Dictionary of Classical Ballet, BG23
Telephony's Dictionary, DL92
Ten Years of United Nations Publications, AN20
Tenth Mental Measurements Yearbook, CH26
Terminologie de l'inventaire des forêts du Canada, DJ61
Terminology Bulletins, CD25
Tessier 86: répertoire 83-86 des documents audiovisuel canadiens, AG21
Test Critiques, CH27
Tests in Print III, CH28
Thames & Hudson Dictionary of Art & Artists, BE20
Theatre & Allied Arts, BG26
Theatre & Cinema Architecture, BG26
Theatre canadien d'expression française, BD151
Theatre Companies of the World, BG32
Theatre Listing: A Directory of English Language Canadian Theatres from Coast to Coast, BG33
Theatre World, BG34
Theatre: Stage to Screen to Television, BG39
Thematic List of Descriptors (Social Sciences), CA2
Theological & Religious Reference Materials, BC42
Theological Dictionary of the New Testament, BC70
Theological Dictionary of the Old Testament, BC71
Thesaurus of English Words & Phrases, AJ61
Thesaurus of ERIC Descriptors, AA43
Thesaurus of Psychological Index Terms, CH9
Thesaurus of Slang, AJ53
Theses in Canadian Political Studies, CD11
Theses on English-Canadian Literature, BD64
Thèses canadiennes, AF45
Thèses canadiennes en science politique, CD11
Third Barnhart Dictionary of New English, AJ15
Third World Guide 89/90, AF35
This Day in Religion, BC19

Thorndike-Barnhart Dictionaries, AJ23
Timber Design Manual, DL91
Times Atlas & Encyclopaedia of the Sea, AK32
Times Atlas of the World, AK33
Times Atlas of World History, CJ27
Times Concise Atlas of the World, AK33
Times Index, AF30
Times Index–Gazetteer of the World, AK50
Times Literary Supplement, AC30
Times of India Directory & Yearbook, Including Who's Who, CJ159
Timetables of History, CJ19
Title Guide to the Talkies, BG61
Titles & Forms of Address: A Guide to Correct Use, AH51
To the Ends of the Earth: The Great Travel & Trade Routes of Human History, CK22
Tool & Manufacturing Engineers Handbook, DL98
Topical Reference Books, AC3
Toronto Immigrant Services Directory, CF27
Toxic & Hazardous Materials: A Sourcebook, DK8
TOXLINE, DF15
Tracing Your Ancestors in Canada, AL45
Trade Marks Journal, DA34
Traductions canadiennes, AF46
Transdex, AF48
Translations Register Index, DA29
Travel for the Disabled: A Handbook, CK24
Travellers: Canada to 1900, CJ78
Treaties & Alliances of the World, CD17
Trees of North America, DJ62
Trends: The Canadian University in Profile, CI45
Trésor de la langue française XIXe - XXe siècle (1789-1960), AJ83
True Daughters of the North: Canadian Women's History, An Annotated Bibliography, CG49
Tune in Yesterday: The Ultimate Encyclopedia of Old-Time Radio, 1925–1976, BG81
Turtles & Tortoises of the World, DH88
12,000 Words: A Supplement to Webster's Third, AJ12
20th Century, CJ51
Twentieth Century Author Biographies Master Index, AL52
Twentieth Century Authors, AL65
Twentieth Century Children's Writers, AL70
Twentieth Century Literary Criticism, BD42
Twentieth Century Romance & Gothic Writers, BD43
Twentieth-Century Evangelicalism, BC40
Twenty Thousand Years of Fashion, BE78

UFAW Handbook on the Care & Management of Laboratory Animals, DH81
UKMARC, AD64
Ullmann's Encyclopedia of Industrial Chemistry, DF34
Ulrich's International Periodicals Directory, AE13
Ulrich's Update, AE13
Understanding Canadian Prescription Drugs: A Consumer's Guide, DI85
UNDEX, AN18
UNDOC: Current Index (United Nations), AN18
Unesco List of Documents & Publications, AN16
Unesco Statistical Digest, CA42
Unesco Statistical Yearbook, CA42
Union List of Canadian Newspapers, AE17
Union List of Foreign Topographic Map Series Available in Canadian Map Collections, AK15
Union List of Manuscripts in Canadian Repositories, AD97
Union List of Scientific Serials in Canadian Libraries, AE20
Union List of Serials in the Libraries of the United States & Canada, AE22
Union List of Serials in the Social Sciences & Humanities: CANUC:S, AE21
United Nations Disarmament Yearbook, CD59
United Nations Document Series Symbols, 1945–1977; Cumulative List with Indexes, AN24
United Nations Documentation: A Brief Guide, AN13
United Nations Documents & Publications: A Research Guide, AN10
United Nations Documents Index, AN18
United Nations Handbook, AN26
United Nations Publications Catalogue, 1990–1991, AN22
United Nations Sales Publications, 1972–1977: Cumulative List with Indexes, AN19
United States Catalog: Books in Print, AD77
United States Dictionary of Places, AK55
United States Government Manual, AM102
United States Government Publications Catalogs, AM112

United States Political Science Documents, CD19
UNITT's Canadian Price Guide to Antiques & Collectables, BE59
Universal Reference System: Political Science, CD15
Universalia, AI20
Universities, Enrolment & Degrees, CI44
Universities Telephone Directory, CI33
University of Chicago Spanish Dictionary, AJ101
University of Toronto Quarterly, AC20
Unreluctant Years, BD171
Updating Statutes & Regulations for all Canadian Jurisdictions, CE53
Upper Canadian Imprints, 1801–1841: A Bibliography, AD50
Urban Affairs Annual Reviews, CA77
Urban & Regional References, 1945-1969, CA79
Urban Documents Microfiche Collection, CA73
Urban Transport & Planning, CA69
U.S. Books, AD19
U.S. Government Books, AM122
USA & Canada, CJ60
Use of Biological Literature, DH2
Use of Medical Literature, DI6
User's Guide to 1986 Census Data (Canada), CA56
Using a Law Library, CE1
Using Government Publications (U.S.), AM111
Using the Biological Literature, DH1

Van Nostrand Reinhold Encyclopedia of Chemistry, DF35
Van Nostrand's Scientific Encyclopedia, DA45
Variety Film Reviews, 1907–1989, BG80
Variety's Complete Home Video Directory, AG3
Vegetable Growing Handbook, DJ45
Vertical File Index, AF38
Verzeichnis Lieferbarer Bücher, AD88
Veterinary Annual, DJ55
Veterinary Medicine, DJ52
Video Movies: A Core Collection for Libraries, AG28
Video Rating Guide for Libraries, AG29
Video Source Book, AG22
Vines, Grapes & Wines, DJ50
Vistas in Astronomy, DD8
Vital Speeches of the Day, AH69
Vitamin & Mineral Encyclopedia, DI64
VNR Concise Encyclopedia of Mathematics, DB25

Vocabulaire de l'administration publique et de la gestion, CD25
Votes & Proceedings (Canada), AM67
Votes & Proceedings (Ontario), AM78

Walford's Concise Guide to Reference Material, AC5
Walker's Mammals of the World, DH92
Water Encyclopedia, DG46
Water Resources Abstracts, DG18
Webb Society Deep-Sky Observer's Handbook, DD36
Webster's Biographical Dictionary, AL21
Webster's Dictionary of English Usage, AJ73
Webster's New Dictionary of Synonyms, AJ62
Webster's New Geographical Dictionary, AK51
Webster's New World Childrens Dictionary, AJ27
Webster's New World Dictionary of American English, AJ16
Webster's Ninth New Collegiate Dictionary, AJ12
Webster's Standard American Style Manual, AJ65
Webster's Third New International Dictionary, Unabridged, AJ12
Weekly Checklist (Canadian Government Publications), AM29
Weekly Record, AD81
Welfare State in Canada, CG41
Wellesley Index to Victorian Periodicals, AF24
Westcott's Plant Disease Handbook, DH50
Western Canada Since 1870, AD53
Western Europe, CJ118
Western Europe: A Political & Economic Survey, CJ119
Western Series & Sequels, BD114
Westminster Dictionary of Christian Ethics, BC50
Westminster Historical Atlas to the Bible, BC77
What Every Chemical Technologist Wants to Know About.., DF47
What Every Engineer Should Know About Engineering Information Resources, DL6
Where the Birds Are: A Guide to all 50 States & Canada, DH102
Whitaker's Almanack, AH27
Whitaker's Book List, AD65
Whitaker's Books in Print, AD66
Whitaker's Children's Books in Print, AD66
Whitaker's Classified Monthly Book List, AD67

Whitaker's Publishers in the United Kingdom & Their Addresses, Whitaker's Weekly List on Microfiche, AD66
White Papers / Livres blancs, 1939-1987, AM33
Who Was Who, AL26
Who Was Who in America, AL39
Who Was Who in American Art, BE32
Who Was When? A Dictionary of Contemporaries, CJ50
Who Was Who in the Greek World 776 BC - 30 BC, CJ34
Who Was Who in the Roman World 753 BC– AD 476, CJ34
Who Was Who in the Theatre, BG5
Who Was Who on Screen, BG71
Who's Who, AL22
Who's Who in America: A Biographical Dictionary of Notable Living Men & Women, AL38
Who's Who in American Art, BE30
Who's Who in Art 1898–1947, BE32
Who's Who in Art: Biographies of Leading Men & Women in the World of Art Today, BE31
Who's Who in Canada, AL35
Who's Who in Canadian Literature, AL51; BD76
Who's Who in Canadian Sports, CL9
Who's Who in Classical Mythology, BC79
Who's Who in Economics, CB19
Who's Who in Entertainment, 1989/90, BG12
Who's Who in European Institutions, Organizations, & Enterprises, AL24
Who's Who in European Politics, CD52
Who's Who in Graphic Art, BE98
Who's Who in International Organizations, AL24
Who's Who in Japan 1987–88, AL24
Who's Who in Library & Information Services, AA60
Who's Who in Quebec, AL29
Who's Who in Religion, BC21
Who's Who in Science in Europe, DA66
Who's Who in South African Politics, CD52
Who's Who in Special Libraries, AA61
Who's Who in Technology, DA67
Who's Who in the Ancient World, CJ33
Who's Who in the Arab World 1990–91, AL24
Who's Who in the League of Canadian Poets, BD139
Who's Who in the Socialist Countries of Europe, AL24
Who's Who in the Theatre, BG5

Who's Who in the U.K. Information World 1990, AA62
Who's Who in the World, AL25
Who's Who of American Women, AL14
Who's Who of American Women & Women of Canada, AL14
Who's Who of Canadian Women, AL14
Who's Who. International Red Series, AL23
Who's Who in American Politics, CD52
Wildlife Database, DH69
Willing's Press Guide, AE14
Wilson Library Bulletin, AC24
Wilson Standard Catalogs, AC11
Winston Dictionary of Canadian English, AJ26
Women Anthropologists, CF24
Women in American History: A Bibliography, CJ102
Women in Canada: A Bibliography 1965–1982
Women in the Third World, CG55
Women: A Bibliography of Bibliographies, CG46
Women's Movements of the World: An International Directory & Reference Guide, CG55
Women's Studies Abstracts, CG51
Women's Studies: A Checklist of Bibliographies, CG46
Women's Studies: A Guide to Information Sources, CG48
Women's Studies: A Recommended Core Bibliography 1980–1985, CG48
Wood Structure & Identification, DJ58
Words on Tape: An International Guide to the Audio Cassette Market, AG23
World Agricultural Economics & Rural Sociology Abstracts, DJ13
World Agricultural Statistics: FAO Statistical Pocketbook, DJ16
World Almanac & Book of Facts, AH28
World Almanac Dictionary of Dates, AH57; CJ23
World Armaments & Disarmement: The SIPRI Yearbook, CD59
World Atlas of Archaeology, CF61
World Atlas of Wine, DJ49
World Authors, 1950–1970, AL66
World Bibliographical Series, CJ57
World Bibliography of Bibliographies, AD1
World Bibliography of International Documentation, AN7
World Bibliography of Oriental Bibliographies, AD1

World Book Dictionary, 1990, AJ33
World Book Encyclopedia, AI15
World Book Health & Medical Annual, DI29
World Christian Encyclopedia, BC53
World Crop & Livestock Statistics, 1948-1985, DJ17
World Development Report, CA46
World Dictionary of Awards & Prizes, AH33
World Directory of Environmental Organizations, DK55
World Directory of Map Collections, AK19
World Directory of Mathematicians, DB31
World Directory of Minorities, CF30
World Directory of Peace Research & Training Institutions, CD56
World Directory of Social Science Institutions, CA29
World Economic Data, CB21
World Economic Survey, CB22
World Education Encyclopedia, CI27
World Encyclopedia of Food, DJ43
World Encyclopedia of Peace, CD60
World Encyclopedia of Political Systems & Parties, CD34
World Energy Directory, DK81
World Fact File, AH29-AH30
World Facts & Figures, CA45
World Film Directors, BG72
World Guide to Abbreviations of Organizations, AJ34
World Guide to Environmental Issues & Organizations, DK56
World Guide to Libraries, AA51
World Guide to Library, Archive, & Information Science Associations, AA63
World Guide to Scientific Associations & Learned Societies, DA71
World Guide to Special Libraries, AA52
World Health Statistics Annual, DI52
World in Figures, CA45
World Index of Economic Forecasts, CB23
World List of Scientific Periodicals, DA12
World List of Scientific Periodicals Published in the Years 1900–1960, DA12
World List of Social Science Periodicals, CA16
World Mapping Today, AK6
World Meetings, DA72
World Meetings: Medicine, DA72
World Meetings: Social & Behavioral Sciences, Human Services, & Management, CA30

World Nuclear Directory, DE32
World of Games: Their Origins & History, CL8
World of Learning, CI41
World of Mathematics, DB26
World of Science Encyclopedia, DA48
World of Winners, AH34
World Painting Index, BE55
World Patents Index, DA35
World Pharmaceuticals Directory, DI84
World Philosophy: Essay-Reviews of 225 Major Works, BB24
World Statistics in Brief, CA44
World Tables, CA46
World Translations Index, DA29
World Treaty Index, CD17
World Who's Who of Women, AL14
World Who's Who of Women, CG56
World's Major Languages, BD182
World's Whales, DH115
Worldmark Encyclopedia of the Nations, CJ56
Worldwide Government Directory, CD38
Worldwide Travel Information Contact Book, CK26
Writer's Directory, BD44
Writer's Handbook, BD51
Writer's Market, BD136
Writer's Resource Guide, BD52
Writers for Children: Critical Studies of Major Authors, BD163
Writers for Young Adults: Biographies Master Index, AL72
Writing A to Z, BD51
Writings on American History, CJ101
Writings on British History, CJ124
Wyman's Gardening Encyclopedia, DH61

Year Book Series (Medicine), DI30
Year in Review: Intergovernmental Relations in Canada, CD41
Year's Work in English Studies, BD18
Year's Work in Librarianship, AA24
Year's Work in Modern Language Studies, BD19
Yearbook of Agricultural Co-operation, DJ18
Yearbook of Agriculture, DJ18
Yearbook of American & Canadian Churches, BC58
Yearbook of Comparative & General Literature, BD17

Yearbook of Fishery Statistics, DH118
Yearbook of Forest Products, DJ66
Yearbook of International Organizations, AH12
Yearbook of Science & Technology, DA43
Yearbook of Science & the Future, DA46
Yearbook of the United Nations, CD39

Yearbook on Human Rights, CD62
Yesterday's Authors of Books for Children, AL71
Yukon Bibliography: 1897–1963, AD57
Zoo & Wild Animal Medicine, DJ52
Zoological Record, DH71

SUBJECT INDEX

References provided are to entry number.
Please note that no attempt has been made to provide
subject indexing in depth. The following entries serve
as a general guide. See also the Table of Contents.

Abbreviations, AJ134-AJ136
Aerospace, DL1-DL77
Africa, CJ140-CJ147
Aging, CG16-CG21
Agriculture, DJ1-DJ66
Alberta, AD51; AM58
Alcoholism, CG28-CG32
Almanacs, AH13-AH30
Alternative Movements, BC38-BC39
American Literature *see* Literature, American
Amphibians, DH87-DH90
Ancient History, CJ28-CJ34
Animal Rights, CG22
Animals, Livestock, DJ1-DJ66
Animals *see* Zoology
Anthropology, CF1-CF61
Antiques, BE84-BE93
Arabic Dictionaries, AJ90
Archaeology, BC68; CF47-CF61
Architecture, BE60-BE72
Archives, AD91; AD94
Arctic, CJ162-CJ163
Area Studies, CJ52-CJ163

Art, BE1-BE59
Art Galleries, BE39-BE49
Art History, BE50-BE53
Artists, BE21-BE38
Asia, CJ149-CJ159
Associations, AH5-AH7
Astronautics, DL1-DL77
Astronomy, DD1-DD4
Atlantic Provinces, AD38-AD40; AM39-AM44
Atlas, DK50-DK51
Atlases, AK1-AK55; BC75-BC88; CF18-CF20; CF56-CF61; CJ24-CJ29; CJ85; CJ87; CJ93; CJ114; CJ147; CJ154; CJ156; DJ35
Atlases, Bible, BC75-BC77
Auction Records, BE58-BE59
Audio-Visual Materials, AG1-AG32
Australasia, CJ148-CJ161
Australia, CJ160
Authors, AL47-AL72; BD29-BD44; BD54; BD66; BD75-BD76; BD86; BD93
Automotive, DL78-DL80
Aviation, DL77
Awards and Prizes, AH31-AH34

Subject Index

Ballet, BG13-BG25
Banking, CC1-CC78
Bible, BC59-BC77
Bible Concordances, BC60
Bibliographies of Bibliographies, AD1-AD4
Biographical Dictionaries, AL11-AL39
Biography, AL1-AL72
Biology, DH1-DH120
Biotechnology, DL35-DL36; DL81
Birds, DH70; DH98-DH105; DH108
Book Reviews, AC26-AC35
Book Trade, AB1-AB18
Botany, DH38-DH65
British Columbia, AD54; AM60-AM62
British Literature *see* Literature, British
Buddhism, BC24-BC25
Business, CC1-CC78
Business Services, CC70-CC74
Canada, Bibliography. AD20-AD57
Canada, History, CJ61-CJ93
Canadian English Dictionaries, AJ22-AJ26
Canadian French Dictionaries, AJ84-AJ89
Canadian Literature *see* Literature, Canadian
Caribbean, CJ111-CJ117
Cassettes, AG18; AG23; BF59-BF61
Central America, CJ111-CJ117
Ceramics, DL82
Characters, Film, BG69
Characters, Literary, BD48-BD49
Chemical Engineering, DF1-DF55
Chemistry, DF1-DF55
Child Abuse, CG23-CG24
Children's Authors, AL67-AL72
Children's Books, AC36-AC55
Children's Dictionaries, AJ27-AJ33
Children's Literature, BD161-BD177
China, CJ149-CJ157
Chinese Dictionaries, AJ91-AJ92
Christianity, BC40-BC77
Chronologies, CJ17-CJ23; CJ31; CJ49-CJ51; DA59
Cinema, BG44-BG80
Circuitry, DL83-DL84
Classical Dictionaries, AJ193-AJ94
Classical Literature *see* Literature, Classical
Climate, DK50

Coins, BE73; BE75
Computer Science, DC1-??
Computers, AB19-AB43
Concordances, Bible *see* Bible Concordances
Conference Papers, DA23-DA26
Conferences, DA69; DA72
Construction, DL85-DL91
Consumer Health, DI58-DI71
Consumer Information, AH35-36; CC75-78
Costume, BE77-BE82
Criticism, Literary, BD29-BD44
Dance, BG13-BG25
Database Directories, AB30-AB37
Database Searching, AB38-AB43, CC29
Dates, AH52-AH57
Death, CG25-CG27
Decorative Arts, BE83-BE93
Dictionaries, AJ1-AJ101
Dinosaurs, DG33
Disarmament, CD53-CD60
Discographies, BF56-BF61
Dissertations Indexes, AF39-AF45
Domestic Animals, DH106-DH109
Drama, BD140-BD158
Drug Information, DI72-DI85
Drugs, CG28-CG32
Earth Sciences, DG1-DG62
Eastern Europe, CJ127-CJ130
Economics, CB1-CB24
Education, CI1-CI45
Electronics, DL1-75; DL83-DL84; DL92
Emblems, AH37-AH44
Encyclopedias, AI1-AI25
Encyclopedias, Science, DA40-DA48
Endangered Species, DH119-DH120
Energy, DK57-DK81
Engineering, DL1-DL113
Environment, DK1-DK56
Eponyms, AJ37-AJ38
Ethnic Studies, CF25-CF46
Ethnology, CF1-CF61
Etiquette, AH45-AH51
Europe CJ118-CJ133
European Communities, AN28-AN32
Events, AH52-AH57

Family, CG33-CG37
Fantasy Literature, BD117-BD124
Far East, CJ148-CJ159
Fiction, BD100-BD127
Film, BG44-BG80
Film Catalogues, AG1-AG23
Finance, CC1-CC78
Fish, DH110-DH118
Flags, AH41
Fluid Mechanics, DL43, DL93
Folklore, BC81; BD167
Food, DJ37-DJ50
Food Production see Food
Foreign Words and Phrases, AJ42-AJ45
Forestry, DJ56-DJ66
Forms of Address, AH45-AH51
Foundations, AH4; AH8-9
France, Bibliography, AD5-AD6; AD83-AD84
French Dictionaries, AJ77-AJ89
Games, CL1-CL15
Gardening see Horticulture
Gases, DL94-DL95
Gazetteers, AK43-AK51
Gemstones, DG29; DG43; DG57
Genealogy, AL40-AL46
Genetics, DH1-DH37
Geography, CK1-CK26
Geology, DG1-DG62
German Dictionaries, AJ96
Germany - Bibliography, AD85-AD88
Gerontology, CC16-CC21
Government, CD1-CD52; AM1-AM125
Government Publications, AM1-AM125
Government Publications - Pre-Confederation, AM34-AM36
Government Publications, Provincial, AM37-AM65
Grammars, AJ63-AJ73
Grants, BA12; CC31
Graphic Arts, BE94-BE101
Great Britain, Bibliography, AD7-AD11; AD58-AD67
Great Britain, Government Publications, AM82-AM97
Great Britain, History, CJ120-CJ126
Greek Dictionaries, AJ93
Health Science, DI1-DI189
Heating/Cooling, DL96
Hebrew Dictionaries, AJ97
Heraldry, AH37-AH44; AL40-AL46

Hinduism, BC26-BC28
History, Art see Art History
History, CJ1-CJ163
History, Music, see Music History
Holidays, AH52-AH57
Horror Fiction, BD117-BD124
Horticulture, DH38-DH65
Human Rights, CD61-CD62
Humanities, General, BA1-BA13
Hymnology, BF46-BF47
India, CJ159
Information Industry, AB19-AB43
Information Science, AA1-AA63
Intergovernmental Publications, AN1-AN35
International Organizations, AN1-AN35
International Relations, CD1-CD62
Invertebrates, HH82-DH86
Islam, BC29-BC32
Italian Dictionaries, AJ98
Japan, CJ158
Japanese Dictionaries, AJ99
Judaism, BC33-BC37
Labour, CC44
Language, BD178-BD182
Latin America, CJ111-CJ117
Latin Dictionaries, AJ94
Law, CE1-CE53
Legal Materials, CE1-CE53
Legislative Publications (Ontario), AM75-AM80
Librarians, AA55-AA63
Libraries, AA44-AA52
Library Science, AA1-AA63
Life Sciences, DH1-DH120; DI1-DI189
Lighting, DL97
Literary Criticism, BD29-BD44
Literary Genres, BD100-BD158
Literature, BD1-BD177
Literature, American BD77-BD89
Literature, British, BD90-BD99
Literature, Canadian, BD53- BD76
Literature, Children's see Children's Literature
Literature, Classical, BD161-BD177
Machinery, DL98-DL99
Mammals, DH91-DH97
Manitoba, AD55; AM56
Manuscripts, AD91; AD94
Marine Mammals, DH110-AH118

Marine Technology, DL100
Marriage, CG33-CG37
Materials, DL 44; DL101-DL105
Mathematics, BD1-BD31
Mediaeval History, CJ35-CJ43
Medicine, DI1-DI189
Meetings *see* Conferences
Metallurgy, DL106-107
Metals, DG1-DG62
Microbiology, DH1-DH37
Microforms, AB8, AD92-AD93
Middle East, CJ134-CJ139
Military, CD53-CD60; CJ68
Minerals, DG1-DG52
Minerals, DL106-107
Mining, DG1-DG62
Modern History, CJ44-CJ51
Mottoes, AH64
Museums, BE39-BE49
Music, BF1-BF61
Music History, BF51-BF55
Musicians, BF34-BF37
Mysteries, Fiction, BD113-BD116
Mythology, BC78-BC88; BD174
National Bibliography, AD1-AD101
National Library Catalogues, AD5-AD19
Native Peoples, CF25-CF46
Natural History, DH1-DH120
New Brunswick, AM40-AM41
New Zealand, CJ161
Newfoundland, AM42, AJ7
News Services, AF31-AF35
Newspaper Directories, AE1-AE14
Newspaper Indexes, AF25-AF30
North Africa, CJ134-CJ139
Northwest Territories, AM63; AM64; CJ80
Nova Scotia, AM43
Nuclear Science, DE1-DE32
Nutrition, DI5; DI58-71; DJ37-DJ48
Obituaries, AL8-AL10
Occupational Safety and Health, DI86-DI89
Occupations, CC27
Ontario, Bibliography, AD49-AD50; CJ64-CJ65
Ontario, Government Publications, AM51-AM55
Ontario Legislative Publications *see* Legislative Publications (Ontario)
Opera, BF43-BF45

Organization for Economic Cooperation and Development, AN33-AN35
Out-of-Print Materials, AD89-AD91
Parliamentary Procedure, AH58-AH59
Parliamentary Publications (Canada), AM66-AM74
Patents, DA33-DA35
Peace, CD53-CD60
Performing Arts, BG1-BG86
Periodical Directories, AE1-AE14
Periodical Indexes, AF1-AF24
Pesticides, DJ1-DJ66
Pets, DH106-DH109
Pharmaceutical, DI72-DI85
Philosophy, BB1-BB24
Phonograph Records, AG19; BF23; BF56-60
Photography, BE102-BE111
Physics, DE1-DE32
Place Names, AK52-AK55
Play Indexes, BD153-BD158
Poetry, BD128-BD139; BD173; BD175-BD177
Political Science, CD1-CD62
Pollution, DK1-DK56
Popular Music, BF38-BF42
Prince Edward Island, AJ7; AM44
Prints, BE94-BE101
Proceedings *see* Conference Papers
Pronunciation, AJ46-AJ48
Provincial Government Publications *see* Government Publications, Provincial
Pseudonyms, AL20; BD45-BD46
Psychology, CH1-CH32
Public Administration, CD1-CD62
Publishers, AB2-AB29
Quebec, Bibliography, AD41-48
Quebec, Government Publications, AM45-AM50
Quotations, AH60-AH69; CG10; BC22-23
Radio, BG81-BG86
Rare Books, AD89
Record Books, AH70-AH74
Reference Books, Guides to, AC1-AC15
Religion, BC1-BC88
Reprints, AD90-91
Reproductions, Art, BE54-BE57
Reptiles, DH87-DH90
Research Centres, AH10
Reviews, Book, AC26-AC35
Reviews, Film, BG73-BG80

Reviews, Theatre, BG42-BG43
Robotics, DL109
Rubber, DL110
Russia, CJ127-CJ130
Russian Dictionaries, AJ100
Saskatchewan, AD52; AM57
Science, DA1-DA72
Science Fiction, BD117-BD124
Scientists, DA62-DA67
Selection Aids, AC1-??
Serials Directories, AE??
Sex and Sex Roles, CG38-CG39
Short Stories, BD125-BD127
Sign Language, AJ49
Slang Dictionaries, AJ50-AJ57
Social Sciences, CA1-CA79
Social Work, CG40-CG45
Sociology, CG1-CG56
Soil Mechanics, DL111
Song Indexes, BF10; BF12; BF19
Soviet Union, CJ127-CJ130
Space, DD1-DD4
Spanish Dictionaries, AJ101
Speeches, AH69
Sports, CL1-CL15
Sports Records, AH70-AH74
Stamps, BE74; BE76
Standards, DA36-DA39
Star Atlases, DD38-DD43
State Government Publications, AM123-125
Statistical Information, CA31-CA67; CB20-CB23; CC3; CC22-CC24; CCl42-Cl45
Statistics, Environment, DK49
Statistics, Health, DI51-DI52
Statutory Materials, CE48-CE53
Style Manuals, AJ63-AJ73
Symbols, AJ58-AJ59
Synonyms, AJ60-AJ62
Technical Reports, AM31; DA32
Television, BG81-BG86
Tests and Measurement, CH26-CH28
Theatre, BG26-BG43
Theses Indexes, AF39-AF45
Toxic Substances, DL112
Trade Bibliography, AD20-AD88
Trade Directories, CC38-CC58
Trademarks, DA34

Translation Indexes, AF46-AF48
Translations, AF46-AF47; DA29
Travel Guides, CK22-CK26
Treaties, CD17, CD31
Union Lists (Periodicals), AE15-AE22
United Nations, AN1-AN27; CD39
United States, Bibliography, AD12-AD19; AD68-AD81
United States, Government Publications, AM98-AM125
United States, History, CJ94-CJ110
Urban Materials, CA68-CA79
Usage Manuals, AJ63-AJ73
Veterinary Science, DJ51-DJ55
Visual Dictionaries, AJ28; AJ91; AJ99; AJ101; AJ174, AJ173
Water, DG18; DK10-DK11; DK31-32; DK38; DL113
Western Canada, Bibliography, AD51-AD57
Western Europe, CJ118-CJ126
Westerns, Fiction, BD114
Wine, DJ49-DJ50
Women and Women's Studies, AL14; CG46-CG56; CJ102; DI67
Word Elements, AJ75-AJ76
Writers Guides, BD50-BD52
Young Adult Books, AC36-AC55
Yukon, AD57; CJ80
Zoology, DH64-DH120